Germany and the Confessional Divide

GERMANY AND THE CONFESSIONAL DIVIDE

Religious Tensions and Political Culture, 1871–1989

Edited by

Mark Edward Ruff and Thomas Großbölting

berghahn
NEW YORK · OXFORD
www.berghahnbooks.com

First published in 2022 by
Berghahn Books
www.berghahnbooks.com

© 2022 Mark Edward Ruff and Thomas Großbölting

All rights reserved. Except for the quotation of short passages
for the purposes of criticism and review, no part of this book
may be reproduced in any form or by any means, electronic or
mechanical, including photocopying, recording, or any information
storage and retrieval system now known or to be invented,
without written permission of the publisher.

Library of Congress Cataloging-in-Publication Data

Names: Ruff, Mark Edward, editor. | Großbölting, Thomas, editor.
Title: Germany and the Confessional Divide: Religious Tensions and Political
　　Culture, 1871–1989 / [edited by] Mark Edward Ruff and Thomas Großbölting.
Description: New York: Berghahn Books, 2022. | Includes bibliographical
　　references and index.
Identifiers: LCCN 2021039740 (print) | LCCN 2021039741 (ebook) |
　　ISBN 9781800730878 (hardback) | ISBN 9781800730885 (ebook)
Subjects: LCSH: Germany—Church history—19th century. | Germany—Church
　　history—20th century. | Catholic Church—Relations—Protestant churches—
　　History. | Protestant churches—Relations—History. | Christianity and politics—
　　Germany—History. | Church and state—Germany—History.
Classification: LCC BR853 .G47 2021 (print) | LCC BR853 (ebook) |
　　DDC 274.3—dc23/eng/20211015
LC record available at https://lccn.loc.gov/2021039740
LC ebook record available at https://lccn.loc.gov/2021039741

British Library Cataloguing in Publication Data

A catalogue record for this book is available from the British Library

ISBN 978-1-80073-087-8 hardback
ISBN 978-1-80073-088-5 ebook

Contents

List of Figures and Tables		vii
Acknowledgments		viii
Introduction		1
	Mark Edward Ruff and Thomas Großbölting	
Chapter 1	The *Kulturkampf* and Catholic Identity	26
	Jeffrey T. Zalar	
Chapter 2	"Time to Close Ranks": The Catholic *Kulturfront* during the Weimar Republic	51
	Klaus Große Kracht	
Chapter 3	The Revolution of 1918/19: A Traumatic Experience for German Protestantism	75
	Benedikt Brunner	
Chapter 4	The Confessional Divide in Voting Behavior	101
	Jürgen Falter	
Chapter 5	The Fascist Origins of German Ecumenism	125
	James Chappel	
Chapter 6	Conversion as a Confessional Irritant: Examples from the Third Reich	145
	Benjamin Ziemann	

Chapter 7	Imperfect Interconfessionalism: Women, Gender, and Sexuality in Early Christian Democracy *Maria Mitchell*	170
Chapter 8	Importing Controversy: The Martin Luther Film of 1953 and Confessional Tensions *Mark Edward Ruff*	194
Chapter 9	In the Presence of Absence: Transformations of the Confessional Divide in West Germany after the Holocaust *Brandon Bloch*	216
Chapter 10	A Tense Triangle: The Protestant Church, the Catholic Church, and the SED State *Claudia Lepp*	242
Chapter 11	A Minority between Confession and Politics: Catholicism in the Soviet Zone of Occupation and the GDR (1945–90) *Christoph Kösters*	271
Chapter 12	The Churches and Changes in Missionary Work: Biconfessionalism and Developmental Aid to the "Third World" since the 1960s *Florian Bock*	300
Chapter 13	Deconfessionalization after 1945: Protestants and Catholics, Jews and Muslims as Actors within the Religious Sphere of the Federal Republic of Germany *Thomas Großbölting*	324
Conclusion	Closing Reflections *Mark Edward Ruff and Thomas Großbölting*	347
Index		357

Figures and Tables

Figures

4.1. Nazi Party members by their municipalities' political traditions. Created by the author.   110

4.2. New Nazi Party members in the Old Reich by size of place of residence, date of entry, and confessional character of place of residence. Created by the author.   116

4.3. Departures from the Nazi Party by size of place of residence, date of entry, and confessional context. Created by the author.   119

Tables

4.1. New members of the Nazi Party from 1925 to 1945 by the confessional character of their municipality of residence. Created by the author.   111

4.2. Average share of Catholics in the various confessional categories (municipalities with Nazi Party members only).   112

4.3. Entry to the Nazi Party by size of municipality, confession, and period of joining. Created by the author.   114

4.4. Departures from the Nazi Party by confessional milieu and time period (Old Reich only). Created by the author.   118

Acknowledgments

The idea for this volume was born in 2016. We would like to thank the members of a reading group in gender and German history—Rebecca Bennette, Martina Cucchiara, Maria Mitchell, Michael O'Sullivan, Aeleah Soine, and Lisa Zwicker—who offered invaluable insights on individual chapters, including the introduction. We are most grateful to Jeffrey Verhey and Alex Skinner for their work on the translations. Eric Sears, a recent PhD from Saint Louis University, graciously helped us with our edits on short notice. Finally, we would like to thank the staff and editors at Berghahn Books, including Chris Chappel, Sulaiman Ahmad, Elizabeth Martinez, and Mykelin Higham, who have shepherded this book from its moment of inception to its completion.

Mark Edward Ruff, Saint Louis University
Thomas Großbölting, Forschungsstelle für Zeitgeschichte in Hamburg

Introduction

Mark Edward Ruff and Thomas Großbölting

A widely heralded study appearing in 2017, just months before the 500th anniversary of Luther's posting the 95 Theses in Wittenberg, announced that the Catholic-Protestant divide both in Germany and Western Europe was mostly a relic of the past.[1] According to the study, not only were 98 percent of German Protestants and 97 percent of Catholics willing to accept each other as family members: many had found common ground over once irreconcilable points of dogma. Sixty-one percent of German Protestants and 58 percent of Catholics had come to believe that both good works and faith were necessary for salvation. These were percentages that would have been anathema to church leaders of the 1950s, to say nothing of the great Protestant and Catholic reformers of the sixteenth century. The sense of confessional distinctiveness had dwindled to such an extent—62 percent of Germans saw Catholics and Protestants as more similar than different—that scandals in one church no longer led to outpourings of triumphalism in the other: they adversely affected morale and membership in both.[2] When Franz-Peter Tebartz-van Elst, the Catholic Bishop of Limburg, gained notoriety for his first-class travel and lavish spending on luxuries such as a gold bathtub in his own opulently renovated quarters, it was not only infuriated Catholics who left their church. Protestants too dropped their membership in their churches, even though no Protestant leaders had been implicated in this series of scandals that culminated in Tebartz-van Elst's resignation as bishop of Limburg in 2014 and transfer to Rome, where he serves as a papal delegate for catechesis.

Such attitudes and behaviors would have been unthinkable in earlier eras and even as late as the 1960s.[3] Though Catholics and Protestants had lived and worked next to each other in many regions, mutual suspicion tended to remain the rule. Parish administrators had long dutifully recorded the numbers of "mixed marriages," one of the biggest sources of confessional acrimony in the nineteenth century.[4] That mistrust towards intermarriage remained pervasive in the early Federal Republic and was the premise of a bestselling novel from 1963, Heinrich Böll's *Clown*. The main character, a young underemployed Protestant clown and convert to agnosticism, found himself abandoned by his Catholic girlfriend, Marie, with whom he had lived together out of wedlock for six years. His refusal to allow any future children to be baptized and raised Catholic prompted her to leave him for a progressive Catholic with powerful connections to the German Catholic establishment, including politicians in the Christian-Democratic Union (CDU). "Catholics make me nervous, because they are unfair," the major character opined in a reflection on both his miserably impoverished state and the seeming political and cultural dominance of Catholics in the early Federal Republic.[5]

But the confessional animosities of earlier generations amounted to far more than a wariness of mixed marriages. From the Weimar through the National Socialist era and even well into the first decades of the German Democratic Republic and the Federal Republic, they were fueled by memories of the *Kulturkampf*. This notoriously violent struggle between 1871 and 1887 between a repressive Protestant-dominated state and the Catholic Church had led to the imprisonment of nearly nineteen thousand priests, police sweeps, and unprecedented fines levied against laity and clergy. But it was not only the mass disruption to the church's sacramental functions that Catholics remembered. They smarted under the anti-Catholic invective pouring out of the pens of politicians, churchmen, academics, journalists, and polemicists that raised menacing allegations of superstition, cultural backwardness, and even of treason for their having allegedly placed their loyalties to Rome and not to the German nation.[6] Catholics drew an obvious lesson: Germany was a Protestant-dominated nation and Catholics were a minority subject to persecution seemingly on a whim.

Protestants, in contrast, justified their contempt towards the less educated minority through fears that Catholics might someday wield substantial political power and in turn despoil German culture and national identity. Trepidation about the loss of a privileged theological, political, and cultural status aggrieved many politically active Protestants, particularly those of a conservative and nationalist bent. Frequently caught in the middle through the Weimar era were Jews, who were often forced to triangulate between the culturally dominant confessional majority and a beleaguered minority that was also the target of disdain and prejudice.

These observations bring us to this volume's leading questions. First, why did confessional tensions inflamed in the nineteenth century persist so long into the twentieth century? As obvious as this question may seem, it resists easy answers. Complicating our understanding is the fact that confessional acrimony often seemed insignificant in comparison with the socioeconomic and class-based ideological hatreds that brought Germany to the brink of civil war at various points in the first half of the twentieth century and proved to be crucial ingredients in the coming to power of both the Nazis and the Communists. Equally challenging is that confessional tensions tended to ebb and flow. They typically became most pronounced directly after tumultuous political transitions in 1870–71, 1918–19, and 1945–49 in which political power appeared to be up for grabs. And hence our second question: how, why, and under what circumstances did smoldering tensions reignite during subsequent eras of political turmoil and uncertainty?

That religious tensions would ease was anything but self-evident. Germany was the birthplace of confessional division, the home of Martin Luther and the first wave of Protestant reformers. The massive social, economic, and political transformations of the nineteenth and twentieth centuries notwithstanding, the modern German confessional map remained the legacy of the Reformation era with its mantra, *cuius regio, eius religio*. Through the early 1960s, this landscape was dominated by Catholics and Protestants, free churches, small Jewish communities and a smattering of freethinkers notwithstanding. The confessional divide was a permanent and powerful driving force in German history and in its political culture.[7] And yet confessional tensions did wane. This simple statement of fact leads us to our third *Leitfrage*: How did a divide long deemed unbridgeable ultimately close, so that by the 2010s most Germans outside of shrinking ecclesiastical circles were utterly ignorant of basic theological doctrines that had ushered in centuries of confessional strife? Did tensions subside because of initiatives to promote tolerance and ecumenism? Or did they ease because of the erosion of religious communities, dechristianization, and secularization, changes unfolding over decades that affected all faiths and confessions?

And finally: what were the consequences, short-term and long-term alike, of the confessional strife of the late nineteenth and early twentieth centuries? The former are easy to identify: renewed prejudice, an integralist retreat behind confessional walls, and political acrimony. But for often conflicting personal and ideological reasons, many churchmen, theologians, and statesmen also became convinced that it was necessary for Germany to shed its confessional animosities. In the service of secularism, the higher good of the nation, ecumenism or simply maintaining what became known as the confessional peace, troubled confessional histories needed to be turned into relics, divisive theologies superseded, and new interdenominational political alliances forged. Was it indeed these conscious and deliberate attempts to brook the confessional divides in Germany that caused tensions to wane? And did these attempts to overcome confessional division open the door to something worse, notably an embrace of extreme ideologies on the left and right, both of which promised to put an end to confessional strife by force if necessary?

These leading questions are all interrelated. They rest on the premise that the strife of the *Kulturkampf* era left behind a legacy in Germany more toxic than in other Western nations also beset by religious tensions and prejudice like Switzerland, the Netherlands, and the United States. The lone exception was the struggle over Ireland within the United Kingdom, but this conflict was anomalous since it not only brought together confessional, ethnic, linguistic, political, and historical tensions but was also rooted in what was tantamount to colonial conquest and exploitation. German unification, in contrast, had proceeded almost entirely on a voluntary basis, even if had been facilitated by military conquest and the annexation of Danish and French territory. Unification nonetheless led to political upheaval, as the creation of a new state altered the balance of power between Catholics and Protestants politically and culturally. As German liberals and conservatives ruthlessly and pitilessly waged their *Kulturkampf* against Catholics, they ensured that the confessional divide remained hardwired into the structure of political parties through the 1960s. Apprehensive of renewed victimization, practicing Catholics were far more likely to vote for parties that were officially Catholic, like the Center Party, and the CDU/CSU, which though interconfessional was perceived as a Catholic party. Protestants were understandably reluctant to cast their votes for parties that were de jure or de facto Catholic. They dispersed their votes instead across the political spectrum, from Communists and socialists on the one end to liberals, conservatives, and eventually National Socialists. The range of parties available for Jews was even smaller. They were usually prohibited from joining conservative or nationalist parties, and few were going to vote for avowedly Catholic parties.

Three Instances of Confessional Trauma

This volume accordingly puts at center stage the traumatic legacy of three episodes of upheaval from the late nineteenth and early twentieth centuries in which each confession felt singled out. For Catholics, it was the *Kulturkampf* of the 1870s during which the bigotry, brutality, and disruptions to church ritual and life so scarred the laity and clergy that they were constantly on the look-out for fresh rounds of persecution and confessional prejudice. For Protestants, it was the collapse of the Hohenzollern monarchy, the creation of a secular republic in 1918, and the loss of their privileged status as an established state church that left behind wounds.

For decades, officials in the twenty-eight Protestant state churches—Lutheran, Reformed, and United alike—were left adrift, largely unable to come to terms with their changed status. Such fears informed their responses to Nazi attempts to launch a united *Reichskirche* in 1933 and 1934 and establish "Positive Christianity" as a religious foundation for the Reich. Protestants were unable to forge unity until after the war. But even in the new German Protestant church, the *Evangelische Kirche Deutschland* (EKD), resentments, internal rivalries, and fissures arising between 1933 and 1945, and a nostalgia for the pre-1918 past, left their mark, particularly during its tumultuous founding in 1945.[8]

For both Catholics and Protestants, it was the Nazi war against each of their churches, the so-called Catholic and Protestant *Kirchenkampf*, that prompted anguished soul-searching. As a third instance of ecclesiastical trauma, these "church struggles" entailed direct confrontation between the Nazi state and the churches over such flashpoints as the presence of crucifixes in schools, and the right to maintain youth organizations, religious festivals, and processions outside of church walls. But they were far more complicated than later narratives of ecclesiastical resistance to state oppression would have it. The majority of Christians in Germany, and indeed many churchmen themselves, came to support the Nazi dictatorship. The Protestant church struggle broke out over not just whether but how to implement the National Socialist ideology and agenda for national renewal within the church. Even within the more unified Catholic Church, internal tensions flared over whether and how to support the Nazi program for national renewal. In both churches, these struggles were accompanied by enormous hopes of a religious renaissance that might renew the German nation as a whole.

On the heels of exhausting internal struggles and demoralizing defeat after defeat in the struggle against the National Socialist state, a tiny but powerful elite of laity and clergy could look only outside their confessional home for support. It embraced interconfessional cooperation. It did so first in the resistance against Hitler, which brought together Catholics and Protestants. Its survivors opted to forgo the comforts and purity of a restored confessional Center Party in favor of interconfessionalism. But as Catholic laity secured the most important seats of power in the new CDU, Protestant leaders in the new party, to say nothing of those in the SPD and FDP, feared being overrun by what they perceived to be a Roman Catholic political steamroller. Well into the 1960s, confessional animosities again bedeviled those politicians and churchmen who had believed that these were a relic of the past.

In sum, many Catholics and Protestants at times of political uncertainty dwelled on what confessional rivals had done to them in the past and what they might do to them again. Church leaders were haunted by the damage inflicted on their institutions during these eras of upheaval. Viewing the SED's campaign against the churches in the GDR, they feared its recurrence in the west. The past could not easily be filed away.

Confessional trauma played itself out on multiple fronts. On the national level, it shaped how Catholics, Protestants, and Jews responded to constitutions, political parties, political ideologies, and nationalist platforms.[9] On the ecclesiological level, it informed how church leaders understood and interacted with those of different confessions and religions theologically.[10] How Catholics and Protestants had interacted with Jews had a bearing on how they responded to Muslim immigration starting in the late 1950s. Within each religious body, finally, these traumas opened up divisions over how to respond to confessional "others," long erroneously but understandably perceived as monolithic. On one extreme stood confessional militants, usually religious integralists, seeking confrontation and/or a full retreat behind ghetto walls. Moderates urged cooperation with representatives from other denominations at the highest level of politics while keeping the rank and file isolated and protected. Some went a step further, adapting to the *Leitkultur* selectively, while striving to remain faithful to traditions, rituals, and beliefs. They could be both Catholics and Germans, even if their vision of the German nation fundamentally differed from that of Protestants.[11] On the other extreme were bridge-builders who adapted to the "other side." Accused by confessional integralists of selling out and overcompensating, they were willing to risk traditional identities and beliefs in a bid to refute prejudicial stereotypes. They, in turn, accused their intraconfessional integralist opponents of clinging to retrograde "ghetto" identities and siege mentalities.

On all of these levels, intraconfessional fissures opened up over whether it was legitimate to have multiple identities. Could one simultaneously have allegiance to a particular confession and to something else, be it a social class, a potentially rival political party, or the German nation? This question had no easy answer, and the messiness and incoherence of confessional responses to it serve as a central theme of this volume.

The Historiography of Confessional Identity

These questions about the complexity of confessional identity emerge out of a historiography taking root from the 1980s through the early 2000s that sought to place religion, piety, and above all religious and confessional conflict back at the center of nineteenth-century German social and political life. At the same time, the answers proposed in this volume are informed by the critical rejoinders since the early 2000s to this "rediscovery" of religion and religious conflict.

How did this historiography of what might be called nineteenth-century confessionalization emerge? In Germany until at the least the mid-1980s, writing about religious history had long been the province of church historians, or *Kirchenhistoriker*, who belonged to theology and not history departments or *Fakultäten*. It was almost unheard of for a Catholic to research a Protestant topic or vice versa, let alone for a person with no faith commitments to write nonpolemical "objective" scholarship about religion. Because of centuries-old turf battles and the fact that *Kirchenhistoriker* in Germany to this day are required to be formal members of their churches, most German church historians had confessional commitments to uphold that were particularly pronounced during the ideological battles of the 1970s at German universities. In addition, these church historians tended to be specialists in political, diplomatic, and on occasion intellectual history. By the same token, it was rare for profane historians to venture into religious history.[12] Those who did so, like the Bonn historian Konrad Repgen, were historians of politics and diplomacy.[13] The result, to put it polemically, was pictures of old men in musty church towers.

At the same time, for the pioneers of social history, such as Hans-Ulrich Wehler, who were gaining currency in both the United States and Germany from the 1960s through the 1980s, religion played little to no role.[14] This meant that some of the earliest studies of how confessional differences shaped German political culture and religious institutions were carried out by sociologists like Gerhard Schmidtchen.[15] Their findings naturally sought to shed light on the complicated politics of the 1970s and 1980s, but the confessional differences and prejudices described clearly had roots in the second half of the nineteenth century. For the focus of inquiry to shift to this foundational period, historians in both the United States and Germany had to make a break with how social history was being carried out. The social history of the era was heavily indebted to modernization theories, which placed secularization as one of the chief outcomes of modern society. Religion was destined to wane because of industrialization, urbanization, and the rise of modern society. Noting the unexpected vibrancy of American evangelicalism in the late 1970s and 1980s, historians like Jonathan Sperber and Thomas Nipperdey laid the contours for a social history of religion for the long nineteenth century by turning secularization theories on their head.[16] They postulated a Catholic religious revival in the nineteenth century that they argued was the result of Catholics both resisting but more importantly adapting to modernity. For Sperber, this religious revival which predated the *Kulturkampf* provided a foundation for subsequent resistance against the Protestant-dominated state during the struggle of the 1870s. This revival had been made possible by a period of chastening in which untampered and unruly Catholic popular piety had been gradually disciplined by ecclesiastical authorities. Organizations long led by laity came under clerical control; pilgrimages, processions, and *Vereine* were transformed with relatively little opposition.

These ideas found much fuller expression in the models of "social-moral milieux," which by the 1990s emerged as the most viable alternative to traditional forms of confessional history.[17] This concept was the brainchild of the sociologist M. Rainer Lepsius, who in turn had borrowed the term "Catholic milieu" from the left-wing Catholic and institutional church critic Carl Amery.[18] Lepsius argued that German politics in the *Kaiserreich* and Weimar Republic had been shaped and destabilized by the rivalries between Catholic, socialist, and liberal worlds. Appealing to constituencies fearful that rivals would inflict harm, each milieu was characterized by a degree of cultural and social separation. The developers of milieu theory saw the formation of a milieu as a phenomenon of modern society and a negative self-definition as a hallmark of milieu identity.[19] Socialists defined themselves in opposition to liberals while Catholics did in opposition to socialists, liberals, and conservatives, whose leadership and base was largely Protestant. Symbols and rituals thus assumed an undeniable potency. In putting special emphasis on Marian forms of piety, for instance, Catholics could easily anticipate angered reactions in Protestant circles.

The milieu paradigms were derived from the politics of the *Kaiserreich*. Indeed, there was universal consensus that the Catholic milieu experienced its highwater mark in the 1870s and 1880s, when anti-Catholic fervor was at its peak. But what about the eras thereafter? When and why did the milieus erode? Was it in 1933, during the Nazi era, during the wave of expulsions and resettlement from 1944 through 1949, or only in the 1960s? One solution to this problem was advanced by the German historian Olaf Blaschke, who labeled the entire era from 1815 through 1960 a "second confessional era," fully cognizant that the notion of a nineteenth-century confessionalism might seem "exotic" to sober, secular-minded social historians steeped in Enlightenment ideals of rationality.[20] For Blaschke, religion had persisted—and its renewal in the nineteenth century brought with it a resumption of tribal identities. Like the "first confessional era," of the notoriously violent sixteenth and seventeenth centuries, the second saw a surge of polemics, divisive politics, and above all an extension of confessional identities to once unrelated areas of everyday life: confessional partisans overvalued and exaggerated confessional differences.

In light of the expansive claims of the milieu model and the paradigm of a second confessional era, it is hardly surprising that both were met with criticism.²¹ The Catholic world, many pointed out, was as heterogenous as it was homogeneous: it was socially, economically, and culturally diverse. Critics noted that even the most violent excesses of the *Kulturkampf* era described by historians like David Blackbourn in his classic study, *Marpingen*, never came close to the devastating, religiously-rooted violence of the sixteenth and seventeenth centuries.²² As traumatic as this era proved to be for Catholics, it lacked the equivalent to the wars of religion or the Thirty Years War to propel death tolls into the hundreds of thousands and even millions.

Nor were the confessional conflicts of the nineteenth and twentieth century life or death matters theologically. Confessional stereotyping only rarely drew from the theological categories and metaphors of the Reformation era. To be sure, some confessional warriors of the 1870s, 1920s, and 1950s saw themselves as carrying on the legacy of their forefathers from the sixteenth and seventeenth centuries. They held on to dismissive stereotypes of the Catholic rank and file as prone to superstition and uncritical obedience to clerical leaders. But even here, the theological landscape of the nineteenth and twentieth century would have been largely unrecognizable to those from centuries earlier. In this earlier era, cultural and religious values focused on man's place in the universe and in a sinful world. These values accordingly gave greater urgency to structures of authority, the hierarchical nature of things, the necessity for salvation, church-state relations and martyrdom. By the nineteenth century, however, religion no longer occupied the same place in politics, the economy, and science. As governments and organizational forms became increasingly complex and specialized, religion became detached, both abruptly and gradually, from domains of life increasingly identified as secular. In the wake of the Enlightenment, educated German Protestants were using categories of reason now deemed "scientific" (*wissenschaftlich*) as a tool to assess faith claims. Such use of "reason" would have been anathema to reformers like Martin Luther and Huldrych Zwingli. In contrast to the early modern era, it was possible for Germans, particularly Protestants, to escape their religious confines altogether. Though small in number, these free-thinkers, atheists, agnostics, or secularists, what Todd Weir has called the fourth confession, exerted a disproportionate influence on politics and culture.²³ Those less willing to take such a fateful leap remained formal members of their church or synagogue but rarely practiced, ignoring the dictates, teachings, and prohibitions of their pastors, priests, or rabbis. Some found greater meaning in socialist gymnastics clubs or nationalist associations like the Pan-German Leagues and cast their votes accordingly. Even the Catholic world was less unified than church leaders had made it appear. Not all Catholics followed the dictates of clerical leaders. Many disregarded church exhortations on basic questions of what to read, which clubs to join, and even which political party to vote for.[24]

As a result, confessional divisions were never as pronounced as those of the sixteenth and seventeenth centuries. One could certainly speak of a "Protestant milieu" and of confessional Lutheran and Reform enclaves in regions like Pomerania and universities like Tübingen. But at the same time, Catholics and Protestants came into contact with each other more frequently than models of confessionalism would have assumed. Both at the grassroots and at the highest levels of politics, those of different confessions could cooperate, if only temporarily.[25]

Beginning in the early 2000s, a wave of historians like Helmut Walser Smith, Michael Gross, Róisín Healey, Till van Rahden, and Lisa Zwicker accordingly began to focus on not just points of conflict but of intersection between Germany's confessional communities. But they expanded their lens to include not only Catholics and Protestants but Jews.[26] Though frequently driven by conflict, these triangular interactions proved more complex than had been anticipated. All three groups triangulated against one another. Cooperation could give way to conflict—and vice versa. Confessional identity thus proved complex and prone to change. Crucially, these historians integrated gender into their analyses. In hindsight, it is astonishing that gender remained so conspicuously absent from earlier analyses. By the nineteenth century, women increasingly made up the majority of those regularly in the church pews, forms of piety were identified as feminine, and women often used the safe spaces offered by the church as tools of emancipation.[27] To be sure, paradigms of the "feminization" of religion have not remained uncontested, but this wave of research made it abundantly clear that perceptions of masculinity and femininity strongly shaped confessional perceptions and relations. In bullying confessional adversaries, gendered language became the norm. Jesuit priests were dismissed as feminine and weak, while Protestant politicians and theologians were exalted as masculine and heroic. It will take an analysis drawn from the history of emotions to analyze why these terms designed to hurt and extol resonated emotionally for so long.

This Volume's Task: Analyzing Religious Identities and Confessional Relations in the Twentieth Century

This volume's task is to pursue these lines of inquiry much further into the twentieth century than has so far been the case. Many analyses of confessional relations come to a close in the year 1914, an obvious caesura in light of the upheaval to come. While edited volumes from Olaf Blaschke and others did include chapters on the Nazi and postwar eras, historians writing on the German churches have nonetheless generally focused on questions for which confessional relations were peripheral. How did the churches respond to dictatorships and persecution under National Socialism and Communism?[28] How did they deal with membership declines, the erosion of once vibrant subcultures and "secularization"? There have been notable exceptions to the scholarly neglect of confessional tension in the twentieth century. These are the vivid descriptions of the politics of the early Federal Republic provided by Frank Bösch, Maria Mitchell, and Kristian Buchna that underscore how confessional conflict pervaded the CDU, its interconfessional mantra notwithstanding.[29] At the core of their analyses was a simple reality: the altered demographics of the Federal Republic lent Catholics a political power that they had not enjoyed before, which rekindled Protestant fears.

With this observation in mind, this volume seeks to explore how political upheaval and demographic changes shaped and altered confessional relations. It starts from the premise that confessional tensions in Germany from the turn of the century through the early 1960s were not driven primarily by processes of confessionalization redolent of the Reformation era. Contrary to Blaschke's claims, they originated instead in cultural, religious, and political developments of the nineteenth and early twentieth century that threatened to undermine confessional identities and self-understandings. They were the product of political upheaval that threatened to alter the political, societal, and cultural balance of power between Catholics and Protestants and that left behind a bitterly enduring sense of victimization. Such resentments were, in fact, a sign of the interdependence between the confessions, even where the cooperation between them was limited.

This volume thus specifically focuses on how confessional relations were altered by changes both abrupt and long-term. The abrupt changes included revolution in 1918, genocide under the Nazis, and the wave of expulsions and resettlements in 1918–19 and again in 1945–46, which destroyed the homogeneity of regions that for centuries had been neatly Catholic or Protestant. In the long term, both churches struggled with challenges posed by the Nazi and Communist dictatorship. During the postwar era and particularly by the late 1950s, moreover, they were forced to confront additional challenges. In the wake of the Holocaust, both churches were held to account for the tragic consequences of Christian antisemitism. Interest in dialogue with Jewish partners grew, perhaps not coincidentally, when membership in Jewish communities had dwindled in the wake of genocide and emigration. The gradual arrival of millions of Muslim immigrants over many decades also altered confessional relations. Jews and Muslims both were given an importance that extended far beyond their proportionately small numbers: antisemitism, philosemitism, Islamophilia, and Islamophobia were likewise out of proportion to the size of Jewish and Islamic communities. Not least, both major confessions were forced to confront the loss of their own—or what was variously referred to as religious erosion, secularization, materialism, the loss of God, the loss of faith, the loss of values, dechristianization or an exodus from the churches (Entkirchlichung).

Tellingly, the churches tended to address these challenges separately, even though both were profoundly affected. Different institutional structures and a legacy of mistrust certainly helps explain why they tended to "go it alone." But another reason is arguably just as decisive: different theological understandings of the ecclesia. Few Catholic and Protestant conservatives shared understandings of what had caused "secularization." For such Catholics, it was the spirit of Protestant individualism and the destruction of sacramental authority which had undermined religious authority. For Protestant conservatives (as well as liberal *Kulturprotestanten*), it was the remains of medieval superstition. Both positions were convenient rationalizations. Protestants knew that Catholics were more "intact" and less divided, while Catholics envied Protestant academic, cultural, and scientific achievement.

Though the churches continued to move on separate paths more often than not, members of both churches on occasion sought to overcome or at the least temper confessional strife. Their attempts, successful or not, are a focus of many of this volume's chapters. Under what circumstances did Catholics, Protestants, and Jews seek to bridge the confessional divide? Did their efforts dilute confessional identities? Above all, how did changing confessional relations alter religious identities, allegiances, and practices?

Methodologically, the volume will draw on the insights and methodologies emerging out of the social, cultural, political, gender, and intellectual history of the last several decades. But it also weaves the findings of theologians into our picture of German church history. Many accounts of confessional conflict did not always show a full awareness of the theological; few historians are trained theologians. And yet without an understanding of theology, the confessional tensions of the nineteenth and twentieth century will make little sense, for theology was infused into how the churches approached those of other confessions and faiths. In such a context, churchmen naturally looked back to the Reformation era for guidance—but only selectively. They picked and chose. Truth claims from the Reformation era persisted but only partially, depending on confession. Which claims fell by the wayside, which were retained, which were altered? Understanding the confessional conflicts of the nineteenth and twentieth century—as well as the attempts to overcome them—thus also requires an understanding of these truth claims and the modifications to which they were subjected in the wake of the Enlightenment. In most instances, it was the modification of earlier truth claims that inflamed confessional tensions. And yet by the last third of the twentieth century, it was these alterations that helped defuse them. Catholics and Lutherans could even come together on Reformation Day, 31 October 1999, to sign a highly lauded joint statement on justification and grace.[30]

The specific chapters in this volume come from both senior and younger scholars. The products of recent research, they offer fresh interpretations. But all are shaped by the reality noted by virtually every observer of the German religious landscape: Germany was historically a biconfessional land in which confessional identity, even for the less devout and nonpracticing, continued to play a significant role in shaping social interactions, the choice of a spouse, levels of education, and career prospects. But as much as the Peace of Westphalia had sought to maintain the confessional peace by keeping the confessions apart as much as possible, doing so was increasingly difficult because of social, economic, and political changes following the defeat of Napoleon. These brought Germans of different faith backgrounds closer together, certainly at the highest level of politics but often locally as well. The Prussian state expanded, annexing predominantly Catholic states in the west of Germany. As Germany unified, newly created political parties had to identify their voter base and craft identities and platforms out of them. This was not hard to do. The dislocations brought on by rapid economic growth and industrialization led to massive internal migrations of both Catholics and Protestants into new regions during the course of the nineteenth century. The potential for conflict between a Protestant-dominated national state with a Protestant monarchy and Catholic and Jewish minorities was thus massive. Protestants, differences between Lutheran, Reformed, United, *Kulturprotestanten* notwithstanding, saw themselves as the *Leitkultur* and Catholics as a cultural threat.

Jeffrey T. Zalar's chapter accordingly explains how Catholics and Protestants clashed over the idea of culture. To Protestant charges that Catholics were dividing the nation, Catholics argued that Catholicism historically had provided the unity of Christendom: it was Protestantism that had destroyed this and continued to do so through its many fissures. As much as they refuted these allegations, Catholics could not overcome the specter of the *Kulturkampf*. Catholics responded by compensating—and overcompensating. They proclaimed themselves to be Germans as good as their Protestant cousins and strove to be their intellectual and political equals. Yet all of their striving paid few dividends. Protestants continued to perceive Catholics as a threat. They did so because Catholics neither folded nor converted. They continuously found ways to respond in ways that Protestants could never equal. They mobilized; they created their own political party. They experienced a religious revival, one with no real equivalent in Protestantism. Jealous Protestants, and especially half-secularized *Kulturprotestanten*, were frightened because Catholics had withstood the onslaught. Protestants continued to see Catholics as cultural inferiors; all of the Catholic intellectual toiling merely diluted their confessional identity. According to Zalar, Catholics found themselves in a highly unstable place that he labels "Zwischenkatholizismus."

Such fears were magnified by the Revolution of 1918, even though one of the bastions of a Protestant state—the Hohenzollern monarchy—had been toppled, the Catholic Center Party was a full-fledged partner in numerous coalition governments during Weimar, and four Catholics served as chancellor. Many Catholics of the day saw the 1920s and 1930s as a second *Kulturkampf*, as does Klaus Große Kracht. He points to the renewed ideological offensive against the church through the so-called Evangelical League (*Evangelischer Bund*). At the local level, violence frequently broke out between Catholics and Protestants during processions and pilgrimages in confessionally mixed regions. In response, Catholics took an approach that might seem schizophrenic. On the one hand, they assumed a defensive crouch, seeing themselves besieged by Protestants, liberals, socialists, and Communists, which they saw as part of the same larger materialist enemy. On the other hand, they went on the offensive, mobilizing laity under the aegis of the hierarchy through initiatives like Catholic Action and triumphantly proclaiming their hostility towards modernism in all of its forms. The result, Große Kracht argues, was a susceptibility to authoritarianism, particularly when it promised to sweep away common ideological and political enemies. The efforts of Catholic intellectuals to combat modernism through a religiously-centered quasi-authoritarianism thus proved illusory. Their initiatives were not strong enough to withstand the Nazi onslaught. Trauma ironically paved the way for its recurrence.

For Protestants, however, the trauma from the Revolution of 1918 was arguably even greater. The Hohenzollern monarchy was gone. The Weimar constitution brought about a much stricter separation of church and state than had hitherto been the case. Socialists and liberals clamored for further restrictions on the role of the churches in education and politics. Benedikt Brunner in turn focuses on how the revolution represented a fundamental rupture in Protestant self-understanding. It emerged fearful of an even more thorough separation of church and state than proved to be the case. Ironically, Protestants found succor through the efforts of Catholics, their confessional rivals, whose resistance to a more complete breach between church and state helped preserve the integrity of the Protestant state churches.

Yet even these joint efforts against the secularizing forces in the Weimar Republic did not bring about a rapprochement between Protestants and Catholics. The divisions between the two remained deep and seemingly unbridgeable. They were powerfully represented in the election results of 1932 and 1933. Jürgen Falter provides an incisive analysis of what is now commonplace: Catholics voted for the Nazis at far lower percentages than did Protestants, regardless of whether they lived in rural, semirural or highly industrialized regions. In the semifree elections of March 1933, only one-third of Catholics supported the Nazis in contrast to half of non-Catholics, whose ranks included Protestants, Jews, members of free churches as well as the religiously unaffiliated. Falter argues that confessional identities and political structures account for this gulf in support. Some Catholic bishops had threatened their flock with excommunication were they to join the Nazi party, the SA, or SS. Many Protestant clergy and theology students, often those chafing because of nationalist grievances, were attracted to the Nazi party because of its promises to resurrect Germany's national destiny. But social pressures arguably played an even greater role. The Catholic world, like the socialist world, had its own network of institutions and structures that made it more resistant to Nazi siren calls. Some, if not most, of this was the result of gender. Long a pillar of the Catholic milieu, Catholic women were far less likely to join and vote for the Nazis than men. Those openly supporting the Nazis were thus apt to be stigmatized, particularly in tight-knit communities, rural or urban. The confessional divide remained.

James Chappel argues that confessional tensions thus became a source of concern for a number of Catholic intellectuals, who in turn began calling for ecumenism. But this proto-ecumenical movement scarcely resembled the progressive ecumenical movement of the postwar era. In fact, its origins were Fascist—to use Chappel's term—in inspiration. They sought to build bridges not just to Protestants but above all to National Socialists, whom they saw as the only force capable of healing Germany's confessional divisions. Chappel thus suggests that the Nazis—and not the CDU—represented the first truly interconfessional German political party. Scholars like the *Kirchenhistoriker* Joseph Lortz accordingly argued that Luther was not as demonic as the forces of the Counter-Reformation had made him out to be. In fact, doctrinaire Catholicism bore some of the blame for the tragedy of the Reformation, which had divided Christendom and Germany. The true foils, instead, were the Jews.

But as was also the case with the German Christians, these bridge-builders rarely found their efforts welcomed by the Nazis. Both churches found themselves subjected to waves of persecution between 1933 and 1945. During these tumultuous years, the two major confessions painstakingly observed each other and their responses to National Socialism. But even at the highest institutional levels, they rarely cooperated with each other to fend off persecution. It was not only lingering confessional animosities that were responsible: it was the reality that Protestants in particular were so caught up in internal schisms over theology and over how to position themselves vis-à-vis National Socialism that a united front with Catholics was impossible. Yet the multiple schisms within German Protestantism during the so-called *Kirchenkampf* did bring some Protestants closer to Catholicism. They prompted a not insignificant number of high-ranking Protestants to convert or consider converting to Catholicism during the 1930s. Benjamin Ziemann shows how their interest was not driven by ecumenism but by the fact that Catholicism appeared to them to be a bastion of Christian unity: it was a welcome contrast from seemingly ceaseless theological and political infighting. Conversion was, to be sure, the most radical of steps. Along with mixed marriages, it ranked as one of the greatest confessional irritants, particularly for Catholics. Since the days of the German Empire, the number of Catholics converting to Protestantism had consistently been higher than that of Protestants formally adopting Catholicism.

But in the years following the Nazi seizure of power, it was the prospect of Protestant conversions like that of the Confessing Church leader and Dahlem minister, Martin Niemöller, that sent shock waves through Protestant communities around the world. While interned in the Sachsenhausen concentration camp, Niemöller seriously entertained the idea of conversion, a consideration driven at least partially by frustration and despair at the state of the Prussian state church, the Old Prussian Union (APU). The international press picked up the story, even if it did not always relay it accurately. So too did the Gestapo, which sent him to Dachau along with two and then three Catholic priests, whom they hoped would provide the finishing touches for his conversion. But Niemöller stopped short. It was the entreaties of his wife, Else, as mediated by the Lutheran theologian Hans Asmussen, who persuaded him to put the brakes on any jump to Rome. This wave of conversions, both consummated and aborted, proved in hindsight to have been a dead end, Ziemann concludes. The end of the Nazi era spelled the death knell for the divisive German Christian movement, while the creation of the Protestant Church of Germany (EKD), an umbrella for the twenty-eight state churches, provided a unity of sorts for Protestants. Instead of pursuing ecumenical initiatives with Catholic brethren, Niemöller himself returned to the knee-jerk anti-Catholicism redolent of the old Evangelical League (*Evangelischer Bund*), which his father had enthusiastically supported.

It was thus only in resistance circles that Catholics and Protestants began working together in an ecumenical spirit, one born out of necessity.

Out of resistance, they forged the interconfessional CDU in 1945. The bridge-builders of the 1930s were thus not the political pathbreakers of the 1940s. But as Maria Mitchell argues the hallmark of the new party was not only its interconfessionalism, one that unlike that of the Nazis was now anchored in a commitment to democratic values. It was its commitment to traditionalist positions on culture and gender. The CDU, like the Center Party of the 1920s, was thus shaped by a paradox: it strove to legislate public morality in the hopes of rebuilding a Christian West and implement family values. It did so knowing full well that this might restrict the careers of women who had suddenly gained new employment opportunities in the aftermath of the war and also drive Protestant women over to other parties. And yet the CDU-CSU's electoral base was disproportionately female. How then did the CDU's interconfessionalism and its commitment to traditional gender roles coexist? Mitchell argues that confessional tensions rose in the CDU as its commitment to conservative gender norms increased.

It is those confessional tensions that are the focus of Mark Edward Ruff's chapter on the controversies in 1953 and 1954 over an American film, *Martin Luther*. Conceived in the late 1940s and early 1950s to combat "Catholic totalitarianism," this film was produced by an ecumenical consortium of rival American Lutheran synods for whom anti-Catholicism served as a rallying and unifying cry. Shot in Germany, *Martin Luther* was the equivalent of throwing gasoline on the fire, since relations between Catholics and Protestants had been deteriorating since the late 1940s. Several of its scenes ran afoul of the German film commission and had to be cut. Its release caused consternation within Catholic circles in the CDU, who saw it as endangering the "confessional peace." No less than Chancellor Konrad Adenauer had to intervene, but it was ultimately Protestants who succeeded in finding a solution. The German parliamentary president Hermann Ehlers, a devout Protestant, downplayed tensions by finding a common enemy—the superficiality of an American import. Also playing a crucial role in these discussions was Joseph Lortz, the one-time Catholic bridge-builder to National Socialism. He had objected to historically and theologically inaccurate scenes, but it was Lortz's monumental history of the Reformation that had informed the script. Lortz was quoted months after the release as being satisfied with the film.

It would be a mistake, however, to reduce German confessional tensions to a simple Catholic-Protestant divide even in the post-1945 era, where once vibrant Jewish communities had been greatly diminished because of emigration between 1933 and 1939 and genocide. Brandon Bloch argues that the absence of Jews shaped Catholic-Protestant relations in West Germany "like a spectral presence." Former religious dissidents, some persecuted by the Nazi regime, urged their churches to renounce anti-Jewish prejudice and build ties to the few remaining Jewish communities. It was paradoxically, Bloch concludes, only the destruction of Jewish communities that allowed Christian-Jewish dialogue to emerge. Auschwitz became the pivotal and defining event for Christian reflection. Ecumenical activists could engage in theological dialogue without having to grapple with the practical challenges of a multireligious society. The same could not be said for Christian relations with Muslims, who today constitute a highly visible, vocal, and growing six percent of the population. Whether Muslims can be integrated into German society has remained one of the *Leitmotifs* of German politics—and these questions have spilled over to Germany's now growing Jewish communities. The arrival of Muslims has clearly complicated Jewish-Christian dialogue. Some immigrants brought with them anti-Jewish prejudice; the German left became increasingly critical of Israel following its conquests in the 1967 war. Complicating Christian-Jewish relations yet further was the fact that the two major confessions tended to pursue dialogue separately. This too should not surprise. Because of differing ecclesiastical structures, theologies, and institutional histories, Catholics could not speak for Protestants and vice versa.

Such dialogue was not present in East Germany. Claudia Lepp argues, moreover, that ecumenism was in short supply in the German Democratic Republic. Cooperation between Catholics and Protestants under the Communist dictatorship was scattered at best. In the 1950s, the relationship between both churches and the state became increasingly confrontational as the state began to assert its ideological agenda with greater severity. Consistent with its Marxist-Leninist ideology, it saw both churches as a threat, especially the majority Protestant church. The state strove to break up the coherent front that the Protestant churches had forced by measures such as making all *Jugendweihe*, a secular equivalent of confirmation, all but mandatory. It rewarded those Protestant clergy and seminarians who sought to build a "church within socialism." The state also pursued a strategy of divide and conquer to ensure that cooperation between Catholics and Protestants would not materialize. To a significant extent, the churches played into its hands. Starting with the Berlin Bishop Alfred Bengsch, whose diocese straddled both sides of Berlin, Catholics opted for "political abstinence," rarely speaking out publicly even on questions of growing importance in the late 1970s and 1980s such as the environmental and peace movements. Protestants, in contrast, played a much more substantial role in the revolution of 1989, helping steer it in a more peaceful direction. But even here, Lepp urges caution. The revolution of 1989 was not a Protestant revolution: it was a societal revolution, the product of happenstance and not design, for which the Protestant church had provided assistance.

Christoph Kösters elaborates on observations made by Lepp. He explains why Catholics proved less courageous than Protestants in standing up to the SED, particularly during the revolution of 1989. Catholics were not only a minority in East Germany: they were situated within the heartland of Lutheranism and historically had to rely on financial and administrative sustenance from the West and South. But this diaspora was subjected not only to the whims of a majority Protestant church but also to the ideological and political dictates of a revolutionary Communist state formally committed to atheism. Fears of state repression led the Catholic church to adopt a position of "political abstinence." This de facto retreat from the public sphere was no doubt intended as a repudiation of Protestant attempts to build a "church within socialism." But in practice, Catholic political abstinence turned this "double diaspora" into a ghetto, one impervious to the spirit of "aggiornamento" or openness coming from the Second Vatican Council in the 1960s. The church lost influence and proved unable to stem the tide of state-driven secularization sweeping across the East by the 1960s and 1970s. Recognizing that their church was now operating within a "secular, materialist environment," Catholic leaders were reduced to attempts to assert a relevant "Christian" presence. They did so by attempting to mobilize the laity, but their role had been consciously minimized by earlier church strategies of letting only priests and bishops speak politically for the church. The theological and structural deficits of this strategy, Kösters argues, became apparent in the 1980s as the church was unable to act with coherence, unity, and force. The church had indeed rejected Communist materialism but at the price of its larger societal relevance.

What then caused the decline in confessional tensions? Udi Greenberg has argued elsewhere that decolonization provided a decisive push.[31] Catholics and Protestants had competed vigorously against each other in the mission field abroad. With the break-up of colonial empires, such competition ceased and cooperation could ensue. But this argument works far better for Great Britain and France, whose vast empires persisted into the 1950s and 1960s, than for Germany, whose colonial holdings were wrested from it during the World War I. Florian Bock argues that it was the need to assuage a guilty conscience following the crimes committed between 1933 and 1945 that led Catholics and Protestants to reengage with the "Third World," this time in the form of vast development aid. By the late 1960s and with the end of decolonization, Florian Bock shows, church officials were pioneering new approaches for development aid that eschewed imposing religious beliefs and values in favor of cultural dialogue. The latter was far more in keeping with the ecumenical spirit gaining strength in some part of the Protestant and Catholic worlds by the late 1950s and especially the 1960s in the wake of the Second Vatican Council. But as James Chappel's contribution also makes clear, even in the 1930s, the push towards ecumenism was a movement of well-educated religious elites. And the ecumenical movement was not present to any extent in the GDR. For Bock, ultimately, the impulse was one that transcended confessional boundaries—and ultimately brought Catholics and Protestants together, even if they retained their own organizations for administering developmental aid.

Thomas Großbölting argues that confessional tensions diminished because of changing patterns of religiosity. Catholics and Protestants alike distanced themselves from religious institutions; as they did so, earlier animosities waned. But what was cause and what was effect? Did German religious practices diminish because the old confessional identities handed down over generations no longer held the power they once did? Or did a decline in attendance at worship and in ancillary organizations allow Germans to let go of confessional stereotypes? If one were unsure about one's own religious identity, how could one condemn those of others? How could one object to marrying a Protestant if one didn't know what it meant to be a Catholic? Not least, the arrival of millions of Muslims, the majority of whom were Turkish, altered Germany's confessional landscape. No longer did Catholics and Protestant use a new religious minority to "triangulate" against each other. Instead, they saw themselves as sailing in the same beleaguered sea of religious indifference and religious pluralism in which church institutions continued to exist, but they were shorn of their cultural and spiritual power.

Reflecting on centuries of religious strife in Germany, Tilman Benedikowski observed that "a proper war of faith runs through our past and has changed human beings."[32] But it is clear today that this "war of faith" has finally run its course. This volume's task is to ponder why.

Mark Edward Ruff is Professor of History at Saint Louis University. He is the coeditor of three volumes on Christianity and Catholicism in the nineteenth and twentieth centuries and the author of two monographs, including *The Battle for the Catholic Past in Germany, 1945–1980* (Cambridge University Press, 2017). He has received research fellowships from the American Council of Learned Societies (ACLS), the National Endowment of the Humanities (NEH), and the Alexander-von-Humboldt Stiftung.

Thomas Großbölting is Director of the Forschungsstelle für Zeitgeschichte in Hamburg and Professor of Contemporary History at the University of Hamburg. From 2009 to 2020 he was Principal Investigator at the Cluster of Excellence "Religion and Politics," University of Münster. His recent books include *Wiedervereinigungsgesellschaft. Aufbruch und Entgrenzung in Germany since 1989/90* (2020), *Was glaubten die Deutschen 1933–1945?* (coedited with Olaf Blaschke, 2020), and *Losing Heaven: Religion in Germany since 1945* (2016).

Notes

1. Pew Research Center, "Five Centuries after Reformation, Catholic–Protestant Divide in Western Europe has Faded," 31 August 2017. Retrieved 16 March 2021 from https://www.pewforum.org/2017/08/31/five-centuries-after-reformation-catholic-protestant-divide-in-western-europe-has-faded/.
2. Ibid.
3. Michael Maurer, *Konfessionskulturen. Die Europäer als Protestanten und Katholiken* (Leiden: Brill, 2019), 7.
4. Tillmann Bendikowski, *Der deutsche Glaubenskrieg. Martin Luther, der Papst und die Folgen* (Munich: Bertelsmann, 2016), 154–55.
5. Heinrich Böll, *Ansichten eines Clowns* (Munich: DTW, 1963), 95.
6. Helmut Walser Smith, *German Nationalism and Religious Conflict: Culture, Ideology, Politics, 1870–1914* (Princeton: Princeton University Press, 1995), 72. See also Manuel Borutta, *Antikatholizismus: Deutschland und Italien im Zeitalter der europäischen Kulturkämpfe* (Göttingen: Vandenhoeck & Ruprecht, 2010).
7. See Bendikowski, *Der deutsche Glaubenskrieg*. This book presents an overview both extensive and superficial (especially for the twentieth century) of the confessional tensions at the heart of German religious life.
8. Martin Greschat, *Die evangelische Christenheit und die deutsche Geschichte nach 1945: Weichenstellungen in der Nachkriegszeit* (Stuttgart: Kohlhammer, 2002).
9. See for instance, Derek Hastings, *Catholicism and the Roots of Nazism: Religious Identity and National Socialism* (Oxford, UK: Oxford University Press, 2010).
10. John Connelly, *From Enemy to Brother: The Revolution in Catholic Teaching on the Jews, 1933–1965* (Cambridge, MA: Harvard University Press, 2012).
11. For this position, see Rebecca Ayako Bennette, *Fighting for the Soul of Germany: The Catholic Struggle for Inclusion after Unification* (Cambridge, MA: Harvard University Press, 2012).
12. For two notable exceptions, see Wolfgang Schieder, "Kirche und Revolution: Sozialgeschichtliche Aspekte der Trierer Wallfahrt von 1844," *Archiv für Sozialgeschichte* 14 (1974): 419–54; and Ronald J. Ross, *Beleaguered Tower: The Dilemma of Political Catholicism in Wilhelmine Germany* (South Bend: University of Notre Dame Press, 1976).
13. Mark Edward Ruff, *The Battle for the Catholic Past in Germany, 1945–1980* (Cambridge, UK: Cambridge University Press, 2017), 227–31.
14. See Georg Iggers, *The Social History of Politics: Critical Perspectives in West German Historical Writing since 1945* (New York: St. Martin's Press, 1985); Philipp Stelzel, *History after Hitler: A Transatlantic Enterprise* (Philadelphia: University of Pennsylvania Press, 2018).
15. Gerhard Schmidtchen, *Protestanten und Katholiken. Soziologische Analyse konfessioneller Kultur* (Bern: Francke, 1973); Gerhard Schmidtchen, ed., *Konfession—eine Nebensache? Politische, soziale und kulturelle Ausprägungen religiöser Unterschiede in Deutschland* (Stuttgart: Kohlhammer, 1984).
16. Margaret Lavinia Anderson, *Windhorst: A Political Biography* (Oxford, UK: Clarendon Press, 1981); Richard Evans, "Religion and Society in Modern Germany," *European Studies*

Review 12 (1982): 249–88; Jonathan Sperber, *Popular Catholicism in Nineteenth-Century Germany* (Princeton: Princeton University Press, 1984); Thomas Nipperdey, *Religion im Umbruch: Deutschland, 1870–1918* (Munich: Beck, 1988).

17. Arbeitskreis für kirchliche Zeitgeschichte, "Das katholische Milieu als Forschungsaufgabe," *Westfälische Forschungen* 43 (1993): 588–654; Michael Klöcker, "Das katholische Milieu als historische Forschungsperspektive—mit besonderer Berücksichtigung der Rheinlande (Fazit 2010)," in *Religionen und Katholizismus, Bildung und Geschichtsdidaktik, Arbeiterbewegung— Ausgewählte Aufsätze*, ed. Michael Klöcker (Frankfurt am Main: Peter Lang, 2011), 477–95.

18. Carl Amery, *Kapitulation oder Katholizismus Heute* (Reinbek: Rowohlt, 1963); M. Rainer Lepsius, "Parteiensystem und Sozialstruktur: Zum Problem der Demokratisierung der Deutschen Gesellschaft," in *Die deutschen Parteien vor 1918*, ed. Gerhard A. Ritter (Cologne: Kiepenheuer and Witsch, 1973), 56–80.

19. According to the Arbeitskreis für kirchliche Zeitgeschichte, "Die Formierung von Mílieus ist ein Phenomen der modernen Gesellschaft. Ein Milieu ist als eine sozial abgrenzbare Personengruppe Träger kollektiver Sinndeutung von Wirklichkeit. Es prägt reale Verhahensmuster a.us, die sich an einem Werte und Normenkomplex orientieren, hier als Milieustandard bezeichnet. Institutionen führen in den Milieustandard ein und stützen ihn." Arbeitskreis für kirchliche Zeitgeschichte, "Das katholische Milieu," 588–654.

20. Olaf Blaschke, "Ein Zweites Konfessionelles Zeitalter?," *Geschichte und Gesellschaft* 26 (2000): 38–75; Olaf Blaschke, "Der 'Dämon des Konfessionalismus.' Einführende Überlegungen," in *Konfessionen im Konflikt: Deutschland zwischen 1800 und 1970: Ein zweites konfessionelles Zeitalter*, ed. Olaf Blaschke (Göttingen: Vandenhoeck & Ruprecht, 2002), 13–70.

21. For critiques, see: Carsten Kretschmann and Henning Pahl, "'Ein zweites konfessionelles Zeitalter?' Vom Nutzen und Nachteil einer neuen Epochensignatur," *Historische Zeitschrift* (2003): 369–92; Anthony Steinhoff, "'Ein zweites konfessionelles Zeitalter?' Nachdenken über die Religion im langen 19. Jahrhundert," *Geschichte und Gesellschaft* 30 (2004): 549–70; Benjamin Ziemann, "Säkularisierung, Konfessionalisierung, Organisationsbildung. Dimensionen der Sozialgeschichte der Religion im langen 19. Jahrhundert," *Archiv für Sozialgeschichte* 47 (2007): 484–507; Christopher Clark and Wolfram Kaiser, *Culture Wars: Secular-Catholic Conflict in Nineteenth Century Europe* (Cambridge, UK: Cambridge University Press, 2009); and Benjamin Ziemann, "Kirchen als Organisationsform der Religion. Zeithistorische Perspektiven," *Zeithistorische Forschungen/Studies in Contemporary History*, Online-Ausgabe, 7 (2010): 440–46.

22. David Blackbourn, *Marpingen: Apparations of the Virgin Mary in a Nineteenth-Century German Village* (Oxford, UK: Clarendon Press, 1993).

23. Todd Weir, *Secularism and Religion in Nineteenth-Century Germany: The Rise of the Fourth Confession* (Cambridge, UK: Cambridge University Press, 2014); Rebekka Habermas, ed., *Negotiating the Secular and the Religious in the German Empire: Transnational Approaches* (New York: Berghahn Books, 2019).

24. On Catholic reading habits, see Jeff Zalar, *Reading and Rebellion in Catholic Germany, 1770–1914* (Cambridge, UK: Cambridge University Press, 2019).

25. Lucian Hölscher, *Geschichte der protestantischen Frömmigkeit in Deutschland* (Munich: Beck Verlag, 2005), 331–41; Derek Hastings, "Fears of a Feminized Church: Catholicism, Clerical Celibacy, and the Crisis of Masculinity in Wilhelmine Germany," *European History Quarterly* 38, no. 1 (2008): 34–65.

26. Wolfgang Altgeld, *Katholizismus, Protestantismus, Judentum: Über religiös begründete Gegensätze und nationalreligiöse Ideen in der Geschichte des deutschen Nationalismus* (Mainz: Matthias-Grünewald-Verlag, 1992); and Dagmar Herzog, *Intimacy and Exclusion: Religious Politics in Pre-Revolutionary Baden* (Princeton: Princeton University Press, 1996); Till van Rahden, *Juden und andere Breslauer: Die Beziehungen zwischen Juden, Protestanten und Katholiken in einer deutschen Großstadt von 1860 bis 1925* (Göttingen: Vandenhoeck & Ruprecht, 2000); Helmut Walser Smith, *Catholics, Protestants and Jews in Germany, 1800–1914* (New York: Berg, 2001);

Róisín Healy, *The Jesuit Specter in Imperial Germany* (Boston: Brill, 2003); Michael B. Gross, *The War against Catholicism: Liberalism and the Anti-Catholic Imagination in Nineteenth-Century Germany* (Ann Arbor: University of Michigan, 2004); Uffa Jensen, *Gebildete Doppelgänger: Bürgerliche Juden und Protestanten im 19. Jahrhundert* (Göttingen: Vandenhoeck & Ruprecht, 2005); Lisa Zwicker, *Dueling Students: Masculinity, Conflict, and Politics in German Universities, 1890 to 1914* (Ann Arbor: University of Michigan Press, 2011).

27. Irmtraud Götz von Olenhusen, "Die Feminisierung von Religion und Kirche im 19. und 20. Jahrhundert: Forschungsstand und Forschungsperspektiven," in *Frauen unter dem Patriarchat der Kirche: Katholikinnen und Protestantinnen im 19. und 20. Jahrhundert*, ed. Imtraud Götz von Olenhusen (Stuttgart: Kohlhammer, 1995), 8–21; Norbert Busch, "Die Feminisierung der Frömmigkeit," in *Wunderbare Erscheinungen: Frauen und katholische Frömmigkeit im 19. und 20. Jahrhundert*, ed. Irmtraud Götz von Olenhusen (Paderborn: Schöningh, 1995), 203–19; Patrick Pasture and Jan Art, *Beyond the Feminization Thesis: Gender and Christianity in Modern Europe* (Leuven: Leuven University Press, 2012); Michael O'Sullivan, *Disruptive Power: Catholic Women, Miracles, and Politics in Modern Germany, 1918–1965* (Toronto: University of Toronto Press, 2018), 12–15.

28. Mark Edward Ruff, *The Battle for the Catholic Past in Germany, 1945—1980*.

29. Martin Greschat, "Konfessionelle Spannungen in der Ära Adenauer," in *Adenauer und die Kirchen*, ed. Ulrich von Hehl (Bonn: Bouvier Verlag, 1999), 195–216; Frank Bösch, *Die Adenauer CDU: Gründung, Aufstieg und Erfolg einer Erfolgspartei, 1945–1970* (Munich: DVA Verlag, 2001); Maria Mitchell, *The Origins of Christian Democracy: Politics and Confession in Modern Germany* (Ann Arbor: University of Michigan Press, 2012); Kristian Buchna, *Ein klerikales Jahrzehnt? Kirche, Konfession und Politik in der Bundesrepublik während der 1950er Jahre* (Baden-Baden: Nomos, 2014).

30. For the full text, see: https://www.lutheranworld.org/sites/default/files/Joint%20Declaration%20on%20the%20Doctrine%20of%20Justification.pdf. Retrieved 16 March 2021.

31. Udi Greenberg, "Protestants, Decolonization, and European Integration, 1885–1961," *Journal of Modern History* 89, no. 2 (2017): 314–54.

32. Bendikowski, *Der deutsche Glaubenskrieg*, 9.

Bibliography

Altgeld, Wolfgang. *Katholizismus, Protestantismus, Judentum: Über religiös begründete Gegensätze und nationalreligiöse Ideen in der Geschichte des deutschen Nationalismus*. Mainz: Matthias-Grünewald-Verlag, 1992.

Amery, Carl. *Kapitulation oder Katholizismus Heute*. Reinbek: Rowohlt, 1963.

Anderson, Margaret Lavinia. *Windhorst: A Political Biography*. Oxford, UK: Clarendon Press, 1981.

Arbeitskreis für kirchliche Zeitgeschichte. "Das katholische Milieu als Forschungsaufgabe." *Westfälische Forschungen* 43 (1993): 588–654.

Bendikowski, Tillmann. *Der deutsche Glaubenskrieg. Martin Luther, der Papst und die Folgen*. Munich: Bertelsmann, 2016.

Bennette, Rebecca Ayako. *Fighting for the Soul of Germany: The Catholic Struggle for Inclusion after Unification*. Cambridge, MA: Harvard University Press, 2012.

Blackbourn, David. *Marpingen: Apparitions of the Virgin Mary in a Nineteenth-Century German Village*. Oxford, UK: Clarendon Press, 1993.

Blaschke, Olaf. "Der 'Dämon des Konfessionalismus.' Einführende Überlegungen." In *Konfessionen im Konflikt: Deutschland zwischen 1800 und 1970: Ein zweites konfessionelles Zeitalter*, edited by Olaf Blaschke, 13–70. Göttingen: Vandenhoeck & Ruprecht, 2002.

———. "Ein Zweites Konfessionelles Zeitalter?" *Geschichte und Gesellschaft* 26 (2000): 38–75.

Böll, Heinrich. *Ansichten eines Clowns*. Munich: DTW, 1963.
Borutta, Manuel. *Antikatholizismus: Deutschland und Italien im Zeitalter der europäischen Kulturkämpfe*. Göttingen: Vandenhoeck & Ruprecht, 2010.
Bösch, Frank. *Die Adenauer CDU: Gründung, Aufstieg und Erfolg einer Erfolgspartei, 1945–1970*. Munich: DVA Verlag, 2001.
Buchna, Kristian. *Ein klerikales Jahrzehnt? Kirche, Konfession und Politik in der Bundesrepublik während der 1950er Jahre*. Baden-Baden: Nomos, 2014.
Busch, Norbert. "Die Feminisierung der Frömmigkeit." In *Wunderbare Erscheinungen: Frauen und katholische Frömmigkeit im 19. und 20. Jahrhundert*, edited by Irmtraud Götz von Olenhusen, 203–19. Paderborn: Schöningh, 1995.
Clark, Christopher, and Wolfram Kaiser. *Culture Wars: Secular-Catholic Conflict in Nineteenth Century Europe*. Cambridge, UK: Cambridge University Press, 2009.
Connelly, John. *From Enemy to Brother: The Revolution in Catholic Teaching on the Jews, 1933–1965*. Cambridge, MA: Harvard University Press, 2012.
Evans, Richard. "Religion and Society in Modern Germany." *European Studies Review* 12 (1982): 249–88.
Götz von Olenhusen, Irmtraud. "Die Feminisierung von Religion und Kirche im 19. und 20. Jahrhundert: Forschungsstand und Forschungsperspektiven." In *Frauen unter dem Patriarchat der Kirche: Katholikinnen und Protestantinnen im 19. und 20. Jahrhundert*, edited by Imtraud Götz von Olenhusen, 8–21. Stuttgart: Kohlhammer, 1995.
Greenberg, Udi. "Protestants, Decolonization, and European Integration, 1885–1961." *Journal of Modern History* 89, no. 2 (2017): 314–54.
Greschat, Martin. *Die evangelische Christenheit und die deutsche Geschichte nach 1945: Weichenstellungen in der Nachkriegszeit*. Stuttgart: Kohlhammer, 2002.
———. "Konfessionelle Spannungen in der Ära Adenauer." In *Adenauer und die Kirchen*, edited by Ulrich von Hehl, 195–216. Bonn: Bouvier Verlag, 1999.
Gross, Michael B. *The War against Catholicism: Liberalism and the Anti-Catholic Imagination in Nineteenth-Century Germany*. Ann Arbor: University of Michigan Press, 2004.
Habermas, Rebekka, ed. *Negotiating the Secular and the Religious in the German Empire: Transnational Approaches*. New York: Berghahn Books, 2019.
Hastings, Derek. *Catholicism and the Roots of Nazism: Religious Identity and National Socialism*. Oxford, UK: Oxford University Press, 2010.
———. "Fears of a Feminized Church: Catholicism, Clerical Celibacy, and the Crisis of Masculinity in Wilhelmine Germany." *European History Quarterly* 38, no. 1 (2008): 34–65.
Healy, Róisín. *The Jesuit Specter in Imperial Germany*. Boston: Brill, 2003.
Herzog, Dagmar. *Intimacy and Exclusion: Religious Politics in Pre-Revolutionary Baden*. Princeton: Princeton University Press, 1996.
Hölscher, Lucian. *Geschichte der protestantischen Frömmigkeit in Deutschland*. Munich: Beck Verlag, 2005.
Iggers, Georg. *The Social History of Politics: Critical Perspectives in West German Historical Writing since 1945*. New York: St. Martin's Press, 1985.
Jensen, Uffa. *Gebildete Doppelgänger: Bürgerliche Juden und Protestanten im 19. Jahrhundert*. Göttingen: Vandenhoeck & Ruprecht, 2005.
Klöcker, Michael. "Das katholische Milieu als historische Forschungsperspektive—mit besonderer Berücksichtigung der Rheinlande (Fazit 2010)." In *Religionen und Katholizismus, Bildung und Geschichtsdidaktik, Arbeiterbewegung—Ausgewählte Aufsätze*, edited by Michael Klöcker, 477–95. Frankfurt am Main: Peter Lang, 2011.
Kretschmann, Carsten, and Henning Pahl. "'Ein zweites konfessionelles Zeitalter?' Vom Nutzen und Nachteil einer neuen Epochensignatur." *Historische Zeitschrift* (2003): 369–92.
Lepsius, M. Rainer. "Parteiensystem und Sozialstruktur: Zum Problem der Demokratisierung der Deutschen Gesellschaft." In *Die deutschen Parteien vor 1918*, edited by Gerhard A. Ritter, 56–80. Cologne: Kiepenheuer and Witsch, 1973.

Maurer, Michael. *Konfessionskulturen. Die Europäer als Protestanten und Katholiken*. Leiden: Brill, 2019.

Mitchell, Maria. *The Origins of Christian Democracy: Politics and Confession in Modern Germany*. Ann Arbor: University of Michigan Press, 2012.

Nipperdey, Thomas. *Religion im Umbruch: Deutschland, 1870–1918*. Munich: Beck, 1988.

O'Sullivan, Michael. *Disruptive Power: Catholic Women, Miracles, and Politics in Modern Germany, 1918–1965*. Toronto: University of Toronto Press, 2018.

Pasture, Patrick, and Jan Art. *Beyond the Feminization Thesis: Gender and Christianity in Modern Europe*. Leuven: Leuven University Press, 2012.

Pew Research Center, "Five Centuries after Reformation, Catholic–Protestant Divide in Western Europe has Faded," 31 August 2017. Retrieved 16 March 2021 from https://www.pewforum.org/2017/08/31/five-centuries-after-reformation-catholic-protestant-divide-in-western-europe-has-faded/.

Ross, Ronald J. *Beleaguered Tower: The Dilemma of Political Catholicism in Wilhelmine Germany*. South Bend: University of Notre Dame Press, 1976.

Ruff, Mark Edward. *The Battle for the Catholic Past in Germany, 1945—1980*. Cambridge, UK: Cambridge University Press, 2017.

Schieder, Wolfgang. "Kirche und Revolution: Sozialgeschichtliche Aspekte der Trierer Wallfahrt von 1844." *Archiv für Sozialgeschichte* 14 (1974): 419–54.

Schmidtchen, Gerhard, ed. *Konfession—eine Nebensache? Politische, soziale und kulturelle Ausprägungen religiöser Unterschiede in Deutschland*. Stuttgart: Kohlhammer, 1984.

———. *Protestanten und Katholiken. Soziologische Analyse konfessioneller Kultur*. Bern: Francke, 1973.

Smith, Helmut Walser. *Catholics, Protestants and Jews in Germany, 1800–1914*. New York: Berg, 2001.

———. *German Nationalism and Religious Conflict: Culture, Ideology, Politics, 1870–1914*. Princeton: Princeton University Press, 1995.

Sperber, Jonathan. *Popular Catholicism in Nineteenth-Century Germany*. Princeton: Princeton University Press, 1984.

Steinhoff, Anthony. "'Ein zweites konfessionelles Zeitalter?' Nachdenken über die Religion im langen 19. Jahrhundert." *Geschichte und Gesellschaft* 30 (2004): 549–70.

Stelzel, Philipp. *History after Hitler: A Transatlantic Enterprise*. Philadelphia: University of Pennsylvania Press, 2018.

Van Rahden, Till. *Juden und andere Breslauer: Die Beziehungen zwischen Juden, Protestanten und Katholiken in einer deutschen Großstadt von 1860 bis 1925*. Göttingen: Vandenhoeck & Ruprecht, 2000.

Weir, Todd. *Secularism and Religion in Nineteenth-Century Germany: The Rise of the Fourth Confession*. Cambridge, UK: Cambridge University Press, 2014.

Zalar, Jeff. *Reading and Rebellion in Catholic Germany, 1770–1914*. Cambridge, UK: Cambridge University Press, 2019.

Ziemann, Benjamin. "Kirchen als Organisationsform der Religion. Zeithistorische Perspektiven." *Zeithistorische Forschungen/Studies in Contemporary History, Online-Ausgabe* 7 (2010): 440–46.

———. "Säkularisierung, Konfessionalisierung, Organisationsbildung. Dimensionen der Sozialgeschichte der Religion im langen 19. Jahrhundert." *Archiv für Sozialgeschichte* 47 (2007): 484–507.

Zwicker, Lisa. *Dueling Students: Masculinity, Conflict, and Politics in German Universities, 1890 to 1914*. Ann Arbor: University of Michigan Press, 2011.

Chapter One

THE KULTURKAMPF AND CATHOLIC IDENTITY

Jeffrey T. Zalar

Introduction: "They Are No Good Patriots"

The stirrings of organized nationalism in Germany early in the nineteenth century provoked Catholic unease about a reckless *Germanomanie* (German mania) that impiously threatened the divine order of Europe.[1] Already by mid-century, however, Catholics warmed to the prospect of integrating into a unified national state. To the Protestant-liberal argument that this integration demanded they surrender their spiritual loyalty to Rome as proof of their legitimacy, they responded with scoffing disbelief. The missionaries to the ancient pagans who imparted the Christian substance of the nation, they observed, were Catholics, not Protestants. Pride of place was theirs, therefore, on the grounds of both heroism and ancestral lineage. And as the more authentic exemplars of deep German meanings, the new nation needed Catholics. Their moral sense and long custodianship of civilized life would redound to the common good now just as it had throughout the impressive epoch of medieval Christendom. They argued further that while Catholicism at the core of Christendom had been a source of unity, Protestantism, with its rebellious origins and fragmentation, had been a source of division.[2] The anchorage and élan of a unified national community could be only the historic faith, not any of its newer, fissiparous alternatives. Surrender their spiritual loyalty to Rome as an intolerable confessional particularism? The "international" character of this particularism was a basic feature of the German essence, they concluded, and they saw no reason to abandon it.

Meanwhile, their loyal service during the 1866 war against Austria and their hatred of revolutionary France placed them on a common footing with Protestant Germans in the frenetic final drive toward national unification.³ Protestants might sneer that they were "no good patriots," but in fact, their patriotism was on their sleeves, if one only troubled to look.⁴ No: as selfsame members of the national community, they believed they deserved the esteem of their neighbors, and they insisted with offended justice that Protestant-liberal slurs against them were not only insulting, but inconsistent with a right understanding of Germany's true identity. "We hope with confidence," the venerable *Der Katholik* opined in fall 1870 in the aftermath of the Franco-Prussian War, "that the Germany that emerges from the conflicts of today will have room for both [the German and the Catholic] ideas, and that the Catholic Church will not be consumed by the liberal rhetoric that has hijacked the German name."⁵

Catholics pleaded for inclusion in the new Empire on the basis of arguments like these. Within eight months of its founding, they realized that their arguments had fallen on deaf ears. "That in the late war our Catholic soldiers shed their blood," the *Bote für Stadt und Land* in Xanten (northwest of Essen) editorialized bitterly in August 1871, "that almost all of our religious orders were involved so remarkably in nursing care, that we made sacrifices like all other Germans, which we did out of love of country and neighbor, this our thankless Liberalism forgot long ago."⁶ This bitterness and the grave disappointment in which it was planted only intensified. Protestant liberals and their secularist allies, those "martinets of modernity" who so decisively sealed the public culture of Imperial Germany with their own stamp, wanted nothing to do with solemn reflections on ancient missions, on the dubious marvels of medieval Christendom, or on the alleged civilizational triumphs of a benighted and bygone age.⁷ They wanted nothing to do with a Catholicism whose international schemes, so they said, were behind the Franco-Prussian War in the first place, and whose superstitions, ignorance, and effeminacy had laid a degenerate Catholic France low before its pious, rational, and more manly Protestant victors.⁸ The creation of the German nation was their accomplishment, they made clear, the culmination of Protestant feats in history that since the sixteenth century had unfolded teleologically by God's design. They intended now to secure and defend it. They, not Catholics, would set the criteria of national belonging; they, not Catholics, rightly enjoyed all of the preferments and perquisites that holy power bestowed.⁹

The tempestuous civil conflict that developed in the fledgling Empire from these very different apprehensions of national history and identity was the *Kulturkampf*, or "struggle for culture." Pitting the Protestant-liberal establishment against Roman Catholics, who constituted thirty-six percent of the total population, it ran from 1871–78, although it was not formally concluded until 1887. It was characterized by a farrago of swinging legal assaults by the national state on the Roman Catholic Church and its influence in every relevant sphere of public life. These assaults included interference in marriage and education, intrusions on the independence of seminaries and religious orders, abrogation of the rights of clergy, and the dissolution and expulsion of the Jesuit Order. Hundreds of priests went to jail or had their citizenship cancelled for violating the law against anti-government sermonizing or for refusing to pay fines slapped on them by state authorities. Bishops went into exile for opposing restrictions on their prerogative to appoint priests to parish assignments. Monks and nuns saw their houses shuttered before the state expelled them, too, from the country.

Complementing and supplying the terms of this legal pressure was an aggressive public rhetoric that reviled Catholic culture as such as an unsuitable medium for transmitting approved national values. This rhetoric came through in overlapping streams of criticism from government pronouncements, an antagonistic newspaper press, and a wave of pamphleteering, whose calls to arms against everything Catholic functioned for liberal elites as "a rich and elaborate ritual of identity."[10] The lamentation of Catholic faults played upon a set of implacable binary oppositions. Drawing upon Enlightenment pretensions about public rectitude, these oppositions were coded positive and negative: modern vs. medieval; national vs. international; freedom vs. fetters; reason vs. prejudice; urbanity vs. rusticity; male vs. female. In radically simplifying complicated matters of confessional history, these oppositions charged the everyday experience of the *Kulturkampf* with powerful emotions grounded in defensive outrage, wounded pride, visceral communal allegiance, and mobilized confrontation. They also made the *Kulturkampf* not only a legal but a symbolic conflict affecting nearly every dimension of German affairs.[11]

The symbolic insults directed at Catholics fused Protestant spiritual traditions with the guiding ideas of liberal statecraft. They centered on perceptions of faith, knowledge, and respectability.[12] Catholic faith, Protestant liberals charged, was inimical to German nationhood. Its appeals to organic relationships in a unified European Christendom affronted German pride and special purpose, while its doctrinal expectation of obedience to a foreign pope raised the specter of fifth-column political treachery that might strangle the nation in its cradle. "Die römische Frömmigkeit ist undeutsch"—Roman piety is un-German—liberals declared flatly, an intolerable fact that rendered Catholics unreliable, even dangerous. Catholic intellectual traditions, meanwhile, failed epistemic tests in an age of rational progress that liberal anti-clericals were determined to lead. Imposed by an odious clergy bent on controlling the laity, these traditions threatened "popular stultification" (*Volksverdummung*) that would leave Germany vulnerable in the highly competitive conditions of industrial capitalism and imperial contest.[13] Catholics themselves, who derived overwhelmingly from agricultural, proletarian, and other *déclassé* sectors of the economy, posed a critical threat to middle-class *Kultur*, that proud set of literary and aesthetic appreciations that liberals took for granted as the animating spirit of national freedom, personal autonomy, and communal self-government. With their mawkish pious texts, poor diction, and embarrassing folk customs, "trivial" and "half-educated" Catholics from the vulgar throng would surely overwhelm truly cultured life, undermining self-mastery at the center of the liberal project in personal ethics with all of its implications for civilizational weakness and decay. Because "weakness" implied femininity in the bourgeois imagination, Catholics deserved to be treated as subordinate "women" who were physically, mentally, and emotionally incompetent to exercise public authority.[14]

The legal persecution and rhetorical harassment by which Protestant liberals asserted their hegemony sparked among Catholics the indignation of an aggrieved minority. Losing their ability to shape the conditions in which they existed and inflamed by a sense of pervasive injustice, many became involved in the Center Party, the Catholic political party founded in 1870 to fight for their interests. Others appealed to the spiritual, vocational, and literary associations of their subculture. Here they found comfort and mutual support under the leadership of priests, who helped them comprehend their exclusion and articulate faith-based responses to it. Subscriptions to Catholic newspapers and other vehicles of loyalist cultural commentary increased; attitudes toward Protestants, which had rarely been warm, became hostile; hatred of liberals and secularists became vigorous.

As real as these temptations toward obdurate closure were, however, the *Kulturkampf* as a decisive event in their consciousness also opened Catholics to fresh possibilities. Already in the 1870s and at the height of the civil conflict, tendencies just as strong encouraged negotiations that might win for them a fully integrated position in the new Reich. Oppressed by attacks from so many directions at once that made serious claims on their religious, intellectual, and social behavior, many Catholics undertook an evaluation of the principles on which this behavior rested to see how far they could be stretched in meeting the demands set upon them by their opponents. What would it take to defeat the charge that they were disloyal to the nation? How might they establish bona fides as "good Germans"? What was the scope for rethinking or even revising their intellectual traditions, so that laming accusations of their "stupidity" and "deficit in education" (*Bildungsdefizit*) could be overturned, the penalties these accusations imposed relaxed? And what about their social "inferiority"? Wasn't it true that Catholics were indeed behind—far behind—Protestant

Germans by nearly every index of economic and occupational attainment? That their relationship to High German arts and letters in the tradition of *Kultur* was negligible, at least among the great mass of Catholics, who were more likely to read an almanac or a rowdy tale of brigandage than Goethe's *Faust* or a sophisticated canonical play by Friedrich Schiller? Wasn't there something in the Protestant smart set's charge that Catholics lacked respectability with good reason? As difficult as it was for them to abide these snubs, there was a sense of growing urgency among Catholics that while their subordinate position was hardly all their own doing, as a community there was work to be done in catching up with the times. The remainder of this chapter explores how they got busy adapting to the world in which they had no choice but to live, so that the estranging torments of another *Kulturkampf* would never be suffered again.

Faith: "In the Joyful Fulfillment of Their Duties to the Fatherland"

The question of whether Catholics could be reliable Germans had a long history. It flared whenever Protestant states with Catholic minorities underwent trial, such as in Prussia during the Seven Years' War from 1756–63 or in 1813 in the drive to expel Napoleon from German lands. Among the wide spectrum of abuses hurled at them by Protestants, the charge that Catholics were disloyal to the nation was the most embittering. Most Catholics simply could not fathom why their loyalty was called into question, especially given their service in military formations for the national cause. And despite themes in their idea of the nation that drew from uniquely Catholic sensibilities, their support for the nation as conceived by Protestants was very strong. It never failed even under the duress of the *Kulturkampf*. They welcomed the nation on the *Kleindeutsch* ("small Germany," excluding Austria) model, they heralded unification as a triumph of "Germanness," and they pledged their aid in achieving the nation's "place in the sun" by supporting, for example, the creation of a colonial empire and opposing the widely perceived national threat of "barbarous" Russia.[15] Believers at all levels, in fact, including the bishops, only matured in their national devotion. Impelling them were the icy isolation of the *Kulturkampf* and the duty the regime imposed to demonstrate nationalist credentials as a requirement of participation in public life.

Attempts to establish these credentials could be seen everywhere. Catholics brought national symbols like flags and coats of arms into their homes, proudly declaring that they were both "good Catholics" and "true Germans." Children began repeating the lessons of their history schoolbooks. These lessons rejected the prevalent Catholic view that modernity was a tale of decline beginning with the Protestant Reformation in favor of the official line that all of German history led up to the creation of the Second Empire. University students experienced a great upsurge in nationalist feeling, which they expressed by downplaying confessional differences and taking part in nationalist cults.[16] Entire families joined in national festivals and competitions, while Catholic societies, even the most pious among them, recognized national events during their meetings. The nineteenth century's "nationalization of the masses" embraced Catholics, too.[17]

The clergy, for their part, supported this popular nationalism with gusto. In the Westphalian diocese of Paderborn, the vicar general routinely gave priests permission to bless the flags of local shooting clubs, a practice that had been forbidden in the past for its nationalist overtones.[18] Priests added nationalist tropes to the spiritual discourse of the Sacred Heart of Jesus cult, acknowledging thereby the "newly awoken desire" for integration in the national community.[19] The confessional press emphasized patriotic as well as Christian duties in a "spirit of sacrifice out of love for the Fatherland."[20] And in every diocese of the Reich, the clergy expressed nationalist sentiments during the Mass, a surprising turn of events given that Roman centralism was even then demanding the standardization of local liturgical traditions. For example, in 1896, a prayer mandated for inclusion in all High Masses solemnized national unification on its twenty-fifth anniversary.[21] Prayers were also said for the health, wisdom, and happy marriages of members of the royal family, while hymns extolled the emperor's virtues. Catholics, it turned out, had a special affection for Kaiser Wilhelm II. He had come to power after the *Kulturkampf* and was therefore unmarred by its events. He retired Chancellor Otto von Bismarck, their archenemy during the 1870s. His social policies aligned with those of the Center Party and he placed himself, rhetorically at least, above the din of divisive politics. The adulation inspired by these facts accorded with symbolic gestures. Although the emperor worried with embarrassment that giddy celebrations of his birthday were becoming unseemly, Catholic Church bells pealed annually in support of them. If his birthday fell on a Friday, Catholics everywhere received a dispensation from dietary regulations, so that their participation in festive meals would not be diminished.[22] After the emperor survived an assassination attempt in March 1901, the bishop of Paderborn ordered every church in his diocese to pray three Our Fathers after the homily and to sing the *Te Deum* (traditional hymn of praise to God) following the High Mass "in gratitude for merciful protection."[23] Later that year, upon the death of the emperor's mother, the cardinal archbishop of Cologne ordered that priests read the death notice in its entirety from the pulpit the following Sunday and, in order to salve the painful "wound" to the "noble heart of our beloved Kaiser," ring the funeral bells for the next two weeks between the hours of noon and 1:00 pm. "Our sympathy on the occasion of this grief," the Cardinal expressed in his instruction, "is just as deep and sincere as the admiration and love that we bear for our Emperor and our King."[24] The dichotomy between priests and laity, so frequently noted in studies of Catholic integration into modern communities, shrinks in light of what might be termed the "nationalization of the Mass."

Similar enthusiasms framed assessments of military culture. In 1886, the cardinal archbishop of Cologne added a general intercession to the Mass for the "royal commanders and all German forces on the seas and land."[25] Church hymns employed the rhythms of Prussian military marches. The Catholic press urged communities to welcome home veterans, who themselves could hardly filter out the nationalist rhetoric that permeated their service, as "true sons of the fatherland and of their church."[26] In addition to finding them jobs, communities should enlist veterans in the struggle against "unpatriotic" Social Democrats, an ominous suggestion of militarized measures against left-wing political opponents. Members of veterans' organizations, such as the *Kriegerverein*, the *Militär-Begräbniß-Verein*, and the *Schützengilden* had their flags, which they carried with them as they processed into Mass, blessed by parish priests.[27] The practice was a violation of Church law, but also of Prussian civil decree, which came down in a rescript of the cultural ministry in 1869 that limited consecrations to official army flags only. Priests blessed the veterans' flags anyway in positive response to their parishioners' demands that the Church endorse their patriotic exuberance. When German troops deployed to southwest Africa in 1904 for what resulted in the decimation of tens of thousands of tribesmen, women, and children, Antonius Fischer, the cardinal archbishop of Cologne, gave this instruction to his priests:

> With respect to the events in German Southwest Africa, which has made necessary the dispatch of German troop formations, I decree that in the general prayer after the words "in all the Fatherland belief and fear of the Lord, loyalty and unity always grow and increase," the following intercession be incorporated: "bless also, O Lord, the weapons of our troops, which fight in Southwest Africa for the cause of our beloved Fatherland. Grant them triumphant success, so that after the restoration of order they return home crowned with glory."[28]

In 1913, upon the centenary of the Battle of the Nations against Napoleon, which had brought about the "glorious rise of the nation," Fischer's successor, Felix von Hartmann, ordered all churches in his diocese to sing the *Te Deum* for the foundation of the Iron Cross, the Prussian military decoration which Emperor Wilhelm I re-commissioned at the commencement of the Franco-Prussian War.[29] Enthusiasm for the war in 1914 was avid, at least among those who did not have to fight it. "The warlike sons of our fatherland have gone into the field with joyful courage," wrote a seminary professor in Trier, who was also a member of the diocesan Spiritual Council.[30] "It is a sublime sight to see such noble enthusiasm flare up in so many hearts. A people that falls in with such determination behind its national ideals must add victory colors to their flag." The bishops blessed the Army's cannon as their church's sons rolled them into Belgium.

These several examples, along with the strong endorsement among most Catholics—clerical and lay—for such policies as Germanization and the Navy legislation, indicated broad acceptance of even chauvinistic and aggressive German nationalism. They may have insisted that their feelings be understood in the context of commitments to their faith, but all the same their community was an important site of nation-building, regardless of Protestant assertions otherwise. Threaded into these feelings were powerful desires for acceptance on the basis of emotive credentials that proved they were capable of bearing responsibility for the country's destiny. And in meeting this responsibility, the argument ran, they merited full equality. In late 1903, and in the atmosphere of gathering international crisis on the road to World War I, Archbishop Cardinal Fischer from Cologne offered his thoughts on those who tried to divide Catholics from the national community: "I protest in the name and in accordance with the wishes of twenty million Catholic German subjects, who hold true to Rome and the popes but who also stand true to Emperor and Empire, and who in their Roman Catholic faith, handed down to them by their parents over centuries of time, feel no restrictions whatsoever in fulfilling their duties to the fatherland with loyalty and comprehensive joy."[31] The hour and doom of fulfillment approached.

Knowledge: "*Deus scientiarum!* God Is also the God of the Sciences"

The roots of Catholics' "deficit in education" reached to the seventeenth century, when upon the conclusion of the religious wars the distribution of armies placed Catholics disproportionately in the impecunious rural areas of the Old Reich. To the *Kulturkämpfer* of the 1870s, however, there was only one way to account for their poor academic performance in relation to that of Protestants: clerical interference in learning. Insisting upon reason's duty to square with faith, limiting reading by the exclusions of the Index of Forbidden Books, and issuing warnings against empiricism, Darwinism, and the material reduction of nature were nothing more and nothing less, Protestants maintained, than strategies of clerical mind control that incarcerated people in a kind of Platonic intellectual bondage. It was absolutely imperative for the survival of the nation that this bondage be broken. The

German people could then step forward in a competitive age with the intellectual freedom necessary for scientific advance, industrial growth, and military innovation.

Catholics did not agree that their church was hostile to the life of the mind. Still less did they agree that their intellectual traditions were foolish or that they themselves were inherently "*dumm*" (stupid), a charge they heard repeatedly throughout the nineteenth century. And yet, their intellectual "backwardness," easily documented by school enrollments and their underrepresentation in learned professions, contributed powerfully to their biting sense of inferiority. Their worries only grew when the new state immediately raised popular education to the national agenda, drawing an iron linkage among academic attainment, occupational ascent, and social acceptance. In 1883, Carl Ludwig von Bar, a Prussian jurist and professor at the University of Göttingen, laid down the state's expectations with all clarity and concreteness: "The church must seek to achieve a certain connection with the highest intellectual life of the nation, if she does not want to be permanently alienated."[32]

The Catholic laity got this message loud and clear. Although they contended fiercely for the maintenance of their confessional schools, already in the 1870s they agreed that German education and scientific scholarship (*Wissenschaft*) were worthy of pride and that their promotion was essential to Germany's national flourishing.[33] The Catholic press covered scientific developments generously, while their advertisements drew readers to medicaments and other household items developed from "the latest research" and bearing the endorsements of laboratory "experts."[34] Priest-naturalists who maintained specimen collections in their rectory parlors were not unheard of, and clerical reading in science increased, if only to send the signal that priests remained men of communal significance whose point of view mattered.[35] "There is no division between faith and reason, no antagonism between the church and science," wrote a priest in 1899 in the very first article published in *Pastor Bonus*, the clerical journal of the diocese of Trier. "On the contrary, never has a child been more cared for and loved by a mother than *Wissenschaft* by the church. *Deus scientiarum!* Through His church God is also the God of the sciences."[36]

While there were theological authorizations within their tradition for reconciling with science, this reconciliation is best understood in the context of cultural conflict we have been discussing. A case in point for demonstrating the adjustment was the journal *Natur und Offenbarung* (*Nature and Revelation*), the most popular middle-class Catholic vehicle for communicating scientific learning. When it began its run in 1855, it championed traditional, largely metaphysical claims about the phenomenal world. By the time it ceased publication in 1910, it championed a perspective of predominantly materialist naturalism that was all but indistinguishable in intellectual principle from the secular journals on which the popularization of science in Germany turned.

One of the primary concerns of *Natur und Offenbarung*'s editors was to establish Catholic intellectual credibility by pursuing two interrelated strategies. The first was to read Catholics into the history of science in order to share in its prestige. Contributors reminded their audience of pertinent facts: the practical empiricism inherent in modern science developed in medieval monasteries; the beginnings of mathematical astronomy were Catholic; the Dominican Albert the Great (d. 1280) was the first western scholar known to have employed the scientific method; Copernicus (d. 1543) was a Polish cleric; and Galileo (d. 1642) died a faithful son of the Church.[37] These and other reminders were meant to build Catholics' confidence in their own history while binding them to *Wissenschaft*, a union required for inclusion in the nation.

The second strategy was to demonstrate that Catholics as Catholics were more adept at the discipline of *Wissenschaft*, because they more carefully policed the boundary between method and passion. The journal heaped enormous praise on the exacting methods of science and reveled in the facts these methods produced. But if these facts were to enjoy the authority they deserved, contributors urged, their evaluation must not be distorted. Sources of distortion included dogmatic secularism, which exaggerated science's explanatory competence, the unscientific immanence of the monists, and the charlatanry of so many popular science readers. For example, one of the most widespread hoaxes of scientific biology in the nineteenth century, to which even Darwin succumbed, was the alleged existence of human beings with tails. Journal contributors rejected it by referring to the Book of Genesis, which for them and in this case supplied self-evident proof of their view.[38] When it came to Darwin, the balance of the journal's commentary on his core conclusions was positive, even if this commentary joined international concern that many of these conclusions lacked experimental evidence, a point Darwin himself conceded.[39] Journal contributors were more likely to criticize not Darwin, but the traction that atheists derived from his ideas and the application of these ideas to objectionable fields like racial anthropology and phrenology. It was simply untrue, contributors insisted, that "accidental" variations in appearance expressed species-differences among human types: the global history of encounter between Indigenous peoples and Catholic missionaries alone demonstrated that all human beings, regardless of appearance, were endowed with intellectual souls and the capacity for civilization.[40] Those who disagreed, remarked one contributor in 1883, allowed their "subjective opinions" to pollute their research. In consideration of such opinions, he continued in a savage turn of phrase, "We are of the view that many researchers in natural science today believe more than they know."[41]

The journal asserted Catholic credibility in the natural-scientific project, then, on both historical and procedural grounds. Its objective in doing so was not so much to defeat science as to enter into it, reimagine and redeem it in a way that was neither mechanistic, which was an affront to providence, nor party to claims of cosmic competence, which was an affront to virtue. Skeptical Protestants, liberals, and secularists accorded this effort no merit. But their derision does not diminish the significance of the journal's attempt to include Catholics in the natural scientific field or to expand the map of Catholic knowledge about nature. How this map expanded ultimately had to do with a reorientation of intellectual appetite, a move of tremendous epistemic importance that played out on the journal's pages. Understanding this move requires a brief word of background.

Since late antiquity, *studiositas* had been the preferred Catholic way of knowing about the natural world. It denoted a specific ordering of the affections with regard to nature whose object was to participate lovingly in it, to approach nature knowingly as a gift given by God to everyone in common.[42] As a general axiom of intellectual engagement, then, it comported with tendencies in Catholicism that favored the unseen over the seen, the spiritual over the temporal, providence over chance, eternity over novelty, sanctity over practicality, union over use, and community over individuality. When it came to the force of desire impelling the study of nature, *studiositas* counseled a hermeneutic of discretion. This discretion appeared variously across the tradition: in Augustine's (d. 430) admonition against amusement spectacle; in Hugh of St. Victor's (d. 1141) warnings against "an empty desire for knowledge . . . in which the mind is busied rather than edified"; in Thomas Aquinas's (d. 1274) dictum that a person's "natural urge to find out" had to be guided by the good.[43] *Studiositas*, in fact, was structured to prevent the abuse of natural desire, as well as reason, should they slip the bonds of piety in pursuit of "hidden" or "excessive" knowledge.

The sinful opposite of *studiositas* was *curiositas*. Associated already by Tertullian (d. 220) with pagan ways of knowing, *curiositas* denoted a crass and vulgar appetite for knowledge about nature whose object was not intimate communion with gift and Giver, but novelty of discovery, magisterial control, and selfish manipulation of natural goods as private possessions. It hampered legitimate industry. Its emphasis on control insulted divine intentions. And any private utilitarian use sequestered nature against the satisfaction of communal needs. Moreover, the intense hunger to know that *curiositas* excited inevitably led to a corruption of the good, as the noble aims of knowledge surrendered either to a domineering will to power or the seduction of pointless experiment. When it came to the force of desire impelling the study of nature, *curiositas* promoted not a hermeneutic of discretion, but a hermeneutic of license, voracity, and depth akin to Foucault's medical gaze.[44]

Now Protestant liberals, as well as individuals who were in a position to bestow the intellectual credibility that Catholics wanted, such as the custodians of scientific learning in the universities, state bureaucracies, and popular education movement, laughed off *Natur und Offenbarung* as just another obscurantist Catholic journal. If this were true, we might expect the journal to defend *studiositas* as the intellectual appetite appropriate to nature. The truth was the opposite. Despite occasional appeals to pious edification, it endorsed *curiositas* in all its particulars, including in the critical area of novelty of discovery.

At bottom, *Natur und Offenbarung* was a clearinghouse of information on new developments in the natural sciences. Addressing every conceivable field and the topics within them, it provided laymen's reports on the cascade of learning published in academic journals: movements of planets, fish that build nests, thermodynamics, the biology of worms, glycerin compounds found in beer, the geophysics of global volcanic activity, color photography—everything. Written by specialists and stressing the "newest discoveries," the journal's massive section entitled "*Wissenschaftliche Rundschau*" ("Scientific Review") dominated the content of every volume.[45] In this section, praise for *curiositas* was often explicit, for example, in the field of medicine. "To no type of operation is curiosity more suitable," one contributor remarked, "than [in blood] transfusion."[46]

The journal expressed the discourse of discovery in other ways as well. In 1889, a letters-to-the-editor section appeared with the title, "*Fragen und Antworten*" ("Questions and Answers"). Readers' questions were a riot of *curiositas*: Can animals commit suicide? How do I know if this snake is poisonous? Can coal and iron make a new alloy? Does the red light emanating from the back of this star make it the Winnecke Comet? Can songbirds hold their breath? Will the world ever run out of coal? "Can you tell me the zoological name of a small threadlike worm that I frequently find under the wings of *Bostrychus typographus* [engraving beetle]?" (A parish priest-naturalist submitted this last question.) What kind of gas can I use to exterminate moths in my closet? Have experiments been conducted to determine the cold-tolerance of plants and animals? Is there a temperature beneath which all life dies?[47] Questions like these presupposed the eclipse of *studiositas* in favor of the novelty, utility, and, in some cases, unethical triviality of *curiositas*.

This analysis is rendered more precise by considering a remark delivered by a contributor in 1892. "In every thinking man's heart," he began, "lies a quiet yearning to gaze over the boundaries" of established knowledge.[48]

"Thinking man's heart" is a classic Catholic turn of phrase. In the ensemble of meanings associated with Catholic learning, "heart" always implied the condition of receptive love characteristic of all authorized knowledge under God. Catholic thought was acquisitive, yes, but it was also gracious, meditative, ruminative. And yet here "heart" figures not as a receptive love of a gift given within the limits of divine dispensation but as the seat of an exclusively rational and anxious "yearning" to transcend the limits of knowledge through successive acts of intellectual aggrandizement. "Gazing" also appears in Catholic tradition, but always in connection with ecstatic experience and the beatific vision. It is a purified type of sight engraced to the blessed, whose merits are rewarded through joyful contemplation of the mystical Subjects of the Holy Trinity. Indeed, "gaze" is often rendered in monastic Latin as *contemplare*. "This is a vision," declared Bernard of Clairvaux (d. 1153), "that charms rather than terrifies; that does not arouse an inquisitive restlessness, but restrains it; that calms rather than wearies the senses. Here one may indeed be at rest. The God of peace pacifies all things, and to gaze on this stillness is to find repose."[49] Notice the poetic emphases on loving participation rather than driving purpose, on reception rather than sensory interference, on the hermeneutic of discretion rather than license, voracity, and depth.

In *Natur und Offenbarung*, however, gazing was secularized as it trained the sense of sight not on the Subjects of Divinity, but on the objects of matter, which became thereby one's private possessions. For an example, let us consider microscopes. Catholics were agog for microscopes—no less enthusiastic, it seems, than the practitioners of Free Religious monism, who studied the natural world at home with microscopes in a domestic rite of the "atheist sacred."[50] In 1900, a journal contributor reflected on science experiments undertaken in Catholic homes: "Neither natural science as such nor practical living in our times can do without the microscope. Whoever possesses the means and comprehension should not refrain from becoming aware of the smallest worlds through one's own personal gaze. [One must] penetrate as deeply as possible."[51] License ("should not refrain"), voracity ("the smallest worlds"), and depth ("as deeply as possible"). According to Philip Ball, the use of microscopes marked the decisive turn to the scientific mindset, for with them no object was too small or too trivial, however well hidden by God, to study. Microscopes drew people, he says, from edification into the hunger of curiosity.[52] They drew in hungry Catholics as well. Their effort to overturn the charge of *Bildungsdefizit* as a strategy of their inclusion was this comprehensive; their willingness to rework the most foundational elements of their intellectual tradition was this accommodating.

Respectability: "The Best Possible Sounding Title"

In 1891, a million Catholics proud of their zeal in relation to what they viewed as lax Protestant piety went on pilgrimage to Trier in the southern Rhineland. Here they venerated the Holy Coat of Jesus, the alleged tunic worn by Christ until his crucifixion. As in 1844, the last time the Holy Coat had been made available, Protestant liberals howled with acidic mockery not only against devotions to objects whose validity could not be established by historical research and whose "magical" properties were cancelled by materialism, but against the lower-class fanatics and dupes who believed in them. This kind of embarrassing spectacle, they held, only confirmed that Catholics were reptiles who did not deserve their respect or their support in easing the limits of the strict social hierarchy they superintended.

Catholics' inability to garner this respect and support injured them sharply. They were all too aware of where they stood as a confessional community compared to the sophistication and refinement of their self-declared social betters. But to be so bullied about, to have their faces rubbed in their second-rate status in the press, in the workplace, and in school settings was an everyday humiliation. This humiliation corresponded with a palpable fear that if they did not find a way to rise in society, the desperate conditions in which most Catholics already lived would worsen as Germany industrialized and they would find themselves permanently in thrall to a Protestant middle class that would do nothing to relieve their economic insecurity.[53] The *Münchner Neuesten Nachrichten* put the matter plainly in 1896:

> Despite all the declamations, with mathematical certainty Catholics will be gradually driven out of the more important and influential positions in the nation's intellectual and occupational life. In the first instance, they will be impoverished, and as a result of this impoverishment, they will be increasingly unable to send their children to higher schools. The already existing imbalance [between the confessions] will increase, and in the end no exhortation will make any difference, because the resources for responding to it will be absent.[54]

Darkening this gloomy scenario further was the intolerable probability that as Catholics sank, they would become susceptible to the appeals of hateful Social Democrats and Communists, who were already campaigning in Catholic communities to turn out adherents to their causes. And if pauperized Catholics fled to the religiously indifferent or atheistic Left, the entire enterprise in Catholic Christianity in Germany would be mortally imperiled.

It was with this alarming prospect in view that the bishops, the Center Party leadership, the Catholic workers and trade movements, the library and press organizations, and other groups concerned with popular uplift, including the women's initiatives, bound themselves to reformist educational and cultural programs in a pressing strategy of social leveling.[55] Getting underway in earnest at the *fin-de-siècle*, this drive for "parity" with Protestants at all levels of education, occupation, and government service intended to spark ambitions among the lower-class laity to go after better schooling and jobs. In accumulating the assets that such schooling and jobs conferred, the social gap would close, and in prospering, Catholics might lay a claim to the respectability they so badly desired. "We Catholics must pay greater attention to vocational training, so that we can work at all levels," declared Heinrich Falkenberg, a close observer of everyday Catholic life.

> We no longer live in old agrarian states with limited possibilities for progress, but in a modern economic order . . . Instead of always calling on state aid, working people should do everything they can to increase their personal professional competence and that of their cooperative organizations. Above all, we Catholics must force our way into leading positions in big business and industry, and therefore we must pursue humanistic higher learning and secondary schooling with equal zeal.[56]

Lower-class Catholics, among whom "the word 'education' [achieved] a ring of magic," responded eagerly to these programs.[57] Awakened to the idea that their lives could gather speed through learning, they took advantage of education where they found it: "folk evenings" in their parishes that alerted them to higher possibilities in the diversifying industrial workplace; extension courses in such areas as geography, history, technology, and art; zoo and aquarium trips; attendance at public lectures; reading about science and studying for promotional exams in their confessional libraries. Workers looked up to autodidact role models who had made it out of the sweating underclass through learning. Parents chased shoddy teachers from local schools, including in rural areas. They also pushed their sons toward the humanistic secondary schools or *Gymnasien*, gateways to the middle class, even if a professional career came at the expense of a vocation to the priesthood.

Enkindled by their training, ever more men pursued "the best possible sounding title," which in technical industry meant a skilled job or a foremanship, not standing the line.[58] They embraced military service as noncommissioned officers, which later on opened up for them positions in the railways, postal administration, and office employment in all areas of the economy, where they earned better pay and qualified for pensions. They also took white-collar jobs as clerks, small business assistants, and other positions involving some authority in the fast-growing tertiary sector of the economy. Women, meanwhile, entered the petty professional workforce as secretaries, typists, telegraphists, department store sales representatives, rail delivery personnel, schoolteachers, and librarians. Maria Schmitz, the leader of the Catholic female teacher movement, captured women's sentiments well when she wrote in 1907, "in the other academic professions we are also interested in not lagging behind. For starters, education as such is a tremendous good . . . Knowledge of all kinds confers influence and helps in the great struggle over worldviews. Nor is the economic side of the question to be overlooked. We are of course concerned that the money that circulates in our country not flow past our pockets."[59]

Similar aspirations were even more insistent among middle-class Catholics, who stood nearer to the boundary line with Protestant Germans and so felt the tug of crossing it more keenly. While individual members of this class could be loyal to their faith and its pieties, as a whole they wanted a smoother synthesis of Catholicism and bourgeois culture to escape the "ghetto" in which they found themselves so disagreeably situated.[60] This desire led to compromises of faith, about which they were generally unconcerned, if only they might satisfy the indices of status and project a model of "decent" thinking and behavior. In May 1907, the *Ulmer Volksbote* in Württemberg published a sarcastic account of such compromises, which is worth quoting in full:

> There are Catholics who fulfill their Christian duty at home and in the church. But when it comes to professing their faith freely and before the world, they fearfully refrain from every act of public worship. By themselves they may very well engage in Christian thinking, but they do not participate, for example, in the Corpus Christi procession—with this they do not trouble themselves. "I could be seen," is an often-heard excuse, "perhaps even by a higher civil servant or manager," who is so "cultivated" [*gebildet*] and so "high ranking" [*vornehm*], that he might laugh at such "medieval," perhaps even "common," religious ceremonies. Yes, they see themselves being made a laughing stock and exposed to the reproach of "backwardness"! This is why so many Christians, especially those who count themselves among the "educated," hold back from the public expression of their Catholic faith: the cowardly fear of man![61]

By cowardice or by conviction, bourgeois Catholics would not be denied the standing they desired, if they had anything to say about it. They reacted fiercely to the restrictions they faced in higher education and government service. They complained about lower-class co-religionists, whose poverty and customary ways retarded the upward mobility of them all. They distanced themselves from priests they deemed insufficiently educated and therefore a millstone around their necks. They read what they wished, openly reviling the Index of Forbidden Books and demanding its cancellation. They threw themselves into *Kultur* and the cult of *Bildung* (cultivation), filling their private libraries with all the iconic volumes from the canon of national literature. Tired of being ridiculed as "women" unequal to public leadership, in Bavaria middle-class men demanded a "manlier" brand of Catholicism, whose racialist and eugenic overtones betrayed an all-too-easy alignment with incipient *völkisch* thought.[62] The vanguard of this movement was the group of radicals associated with the journal *Das Neue Jahrhundert*, which began publication in 1901 and took as its motto "*Religion, Deutschtum, Kultur*." In their craving to be recognized by others on the forward edge of cultural development, they declared the fundamental compatibility between Catholicism and a racially centered nationalism.[63] On 8 November 1904, a priest gave a speech on contemporary cultural trends to the Harmonia Catholic Businessman's Association in Trier. He worried that tendencies in this direction would result in something like a "new religion": "And as one once looked insanely toward the fourth dimension, so today people expect the birth of a third Reich in which heathenism and Christianity will unite in a higher synthesis."[64] He did not have long to wait.

Conclusion: The Problem of Being "*Zwischen*"

For their impassioned statements of national loyalty, for their straining to prove their intellectual fitness by embracing secular science, for all their climbing and social truckling, Catholics received little benefit. The Protestant-liberal establishment lampooned their efforts at integration, denouncing them as forever-false brothers, hopelessly ignorant puppets of clerical manipulation, and *arriviste poseurs*. There is something sad in Catholics' dogged commitment to carry on. "Fighting for equality . . . requires greater self-confidence," a concerned politician remarked in 1918 upon the conclusion of the Great War. "With fresh and open courage we must get rid of false modesty and restraint. We must free ourselves from false fears of others caused by systematic oppression. We have to do away with any remaining backwardness."[65] While Catholics did increase their presence in higher occupations and schooling, their *Bildungsdefizit* and all that it entailed endured well into the 1960s, above all due to historic Protestant advantages that were hard to overcome without state intervention in their favor. The legacy of the *Kulturkampf* lived on.

And it lived on, perhaps most fundamentally, because the majority of Catholics would not let go of the idea that God intended them to be active participants in the world they inhabited. In this, they only showed their proper formation in faith. As a matter of theological foundations and historical development, Catholicism eschewed withdrawal. It was a culture-forming religion and had been so in Germany since Saint Boniface (d. 754) evangelized the Frisian pagans with books under his arm. This culture-forming capacity rested upon a set of key thematic couplets, whose subtle presence can be felt across the history we have just reviewed: church and state, which must coexist in harmony in service to the common good; faith and reason, which have their proper objects and ends but which are responsible to one another; the *vita contemplativa* of ardent devotion to the unseen God and the *vita activa* of comprehensive involvement in the secular order. Building upon Enlightenment traditions, the *Kulturkämpfer* tried to break these couplets apart and reverse the order of their elements, superordinating state over church, reason over faith, and the secular *vita activa* over the pious *vita contemplativa*. These disruptions to relationships at the deepest level of Catholics' self-understanding severely rattled their sensibilities. These disruptions led, on the one hand, to shock, confusion, emotional outburst, and intellectual and moral panic as Catholics reacted negatively to the forcible reordering of their world. They also led, on the other hand, to reconsideration, modification, negotiation, and compromise as Catholics positively tried to put a synthetic world back together. Ultimately, these maneuvers left them somewhere in the middle between the secular German culture that was rapidly coming into being and their faith tradition as it had been historically constituted. They were "*zwischen*"—between—a turn of phrase that began to appear prominently in German Catholic discourse by 1900.[66] It described a faith community that in the maelstrom of competing centripetal and centrifugal forces groped at best toward a firm existence in the prolonged political and religious struggles of modern Germany.

After World War I, the instability of *Zwischenkatholizismus* only deepened. New political alternatives expanded the range of possible affiliations, some of which were ferociously anti-Catholic. Materialism, scientism, and atheism grew in confidence, while the academic establishment became all but completely secular, further challenging the foundations of Catholic learning. The technologies of leisure, meanwhile—gramophone, radio, cinema, television—created new social behaviors in a new regime of respectability centered on imaginative stimulation over which Church authorities had little or no control. Values and vocabularies drawn from these developments facilitated political, intellectual, and personal exchanges of all kinds. Informed by these exchanges, Catholics adopted a diversity of overlapping identities across a wide spectrum of alliances with secular culture, some of which overshadowed religion as such and nearly all of which encouraged a transgressive attitude toward religious community, doctrine, and clerical authority. In such conditions, *Zwischenkatholizismus* played out with decidedly uneven results, as Catholics tried to articulate an effective response to a relentlessly secular modernity while trying to decide concurrently what it meant to be a Catholic in the first place. About the only thing on which nearly all of them agreed was that no effort at confessional integrity was worth enticing another *Kulturkampf*, even if that meant genuflections before monstrous political and moral evil, insouciance toward their intellectual traditions in pursuit of positions, and a collapse into secular lifestyles to fit in. These and other preferences did nothing to forestall one of the most dramatic contractions of any national church in the history of Catholicism after the 1960s: mass rejection of basic doctrines, abandonment of the sacraments, unrenewed church affiliations, precipitous decline in vocations to the ministerial priesthood and consecrated life, and prodigious reductions in the number of active parishes.[67] In June 1872, at the commencement of the *Kulturkampf*, the satirical journal *Kladderadatsch* published a poem entitled "To War with Rome."[68] It assured its readers that "teutonic" victory over the Roman Church, in which all Germans had a role to play, was simply a matter of time. So it would seem.

Jeffrey T. Zalar is Associate Professor of History and the inaugural holder of the Ruth J. and Robert A. Conway Endowed Chair in Catholic Studies at the University of Cincinnati. His 2019 book, *Reading and Rebellion in Catholic Germany, 1770–1914*, published by Cambridge University Press, received the 2020 George A. and Jean S. DeLong Book History Book Prize from The Society for the History of Authorship, Reading, and Publishing (SHARP).

Notes

1. Quoted in Joseph Hansen, *Preußen und Rheinland von 1815 bis 1915. Hundert Jahre politischen Lebens am Rhein* (Cologne: Rheinland-Verlag, [1918] 1990), 51.

2. Rebecca Ayako Bennette, *Fighting for the Soul of Germany: The Catholic Struggle for Inclusion after Unification* (Cambridge, MA: Harvard University Press, 2012), 39, 119–20, 163, and 192; and Frank Becker, "Konfessionelle Nationsbilder im Deutschen Kaiserreich," in *Nation und Religion in der deutschen Geschichte*, ed. Heinz-Gerhard Haupt and Dieter Langewiesche (Frankfurt: Campus, 2001), 406–7.

3. Siegfried Weichlein, "Nationsbilder und Staatskritik im deutschen Katholizismus des 19. und 20. Jahrhunderts," in *Religion und Nation. Katholizismen im Europa des 19. und 20. Jahrhunderts*, ed. Urs Altermatt and Franziska Metzger (Stuttgart: Kohlhammer, 2007), 137–51.

4. "Können 'Ultramontane' Patrioten sein?" *Eucharius. Sonntagsblatt für die Diöcese Trier* 6, 24 (1866): 219–21.

5. "Der große Krieg," *Der Katholik* 50 (1870): 269.

6. Quoted in Holger Schmenk, *Xanten im 19. Jahrhundert. Eine rheinische Kleinstadt zwischen Tradition und Moderne* (Köln: Böhlau, 2008), 266.

7. David Blackbourn, *Marpingen: Apparitions of the Virgin Mary in Nineteenth-Century Germany* (New York: Alfred A. Knopf, 1994), xxxiv.

8. Friedhelm Jürgensmeier, *Die katholische Kirche im Spiegel der Karikatur: Der deutschen satirischen Tendenzzeitschriften von 1848 bis 1900* (Trier: Neu & Co., 1969), 137–38; and A. J. Hoover, "God and German Unification: Protestant Patriotic Preaching during the Franco-Prussian War, 1870–71," *Fides et Historia* 18, no. 2 (1986): 24–26.

9. Helmut Walser Smith, *German Nationalism and Religious Conflict: Culture, Ideology, Politics, 1870–1914* (Princeton: Princeton University Press, 1995), 17–49.

10. Michael B. Gross, *The War against Catholicism: Liberalism and the Anti-Catholic Imagination in Nineteenth-Century Germany* (Ann Arbor: The University of Michigan Press, 2004), 26; and Róisín Healy, *The Jesuit Specter in Imperial Germany* (Boston: Brill, 2003).

11. Smith, *German Nationalism and Religious Conflict*, 64–65.

12. Frank-Michael Kuhlemann, "Erinnerung und Erinnerungskultur im deutschen Protestantismus," *Zeitschrift für Kirchengeschichte* 119, no. 1 (2008): 37–38.

13. Gross, *The War against Catholicism*, 74–127.

14. Ibid., 185–239; and Manuel Borutta, "Das Andere der Moderne. Geschlecht, Sexualität und Krankheit in antikatholischen Diskursen Deutschlands und Italiens (1850–1900)," in *Kollektive Identitäten und kulturelle Innovationen. Ethnologische, soziologische und historische Studien,* ed. Werner Rammert et al. (Leipzig: Leipziger Universitätsverlag, 2001), 62ff.

15. Bennette, *Fighting for the Soul of Germany*, 187–88.

16. Lisa Fetheringill Zwicker, *Dueling Students: Conflict, Masculinity, and Politics in German Universities, 1890–1914* (Ann Arbor: University of Michigan Press, 2011), 165–96.

17. George L. Mosse, *The Nationalization of the Masses: Political Symbolism and Mass Movements in Germany from the Napoleonic Wars through the Third Reich* (New York: Meridian, 1975). See also Barbara Stambolis, "Nationalisierung trotz Ultramontanisierung oder: 'Alles für Deutschland. Deutschland aber für Christus.' Mentalitätsleitende Wertorientierung deutsche Katholiken im 19. und 20. Jahrhundert," *Historische Zeitschrift* 269, no. 1 (1999): 57–97; and Barbara Stambolis, "Nation und Konfession im Spannungsfeld: Aspekte historischer Vereinsforschung am Beispiel des Schützenwesens," *Historisches Jahrbuch* 120 (2000): 199–226.

18. Stambolis, "Nation und Konfession," 203–4 n25.

19. Norbert Busch, "Frömmigkeit als Faktor des katholischen Milieus: Der Kult zum Herzen Jesu," in *Religion im Kaiserreich: Milieus—Mentalitäten—Krisen,* ed. Olaf Blaschke and Frank-Michael Kuhlemann (Gütersloh: Chr. Kaiser/Gütersloher Verlagshaus, 1996), 160–65.

20. For example, *Charitas. Zeitschrift für die Werke der Nächstenliebe im katholischen Deutschland* 1, no. 2 (1896): 32–33; and A. Camerlander [Anton Huonder], *Sind die Jesuiten Deutschfeindlich? Ein Beitrag zur Geschichte des Deutschtums im Ausland,* 2nd. ed. (Freiburg: Caritas-Verlag, 1913), v.

21. Dieter Langewiesche, "Reich, Nation und Staat in der jüngeren deutschen Geschichte," *Historische Zeitschrift* 254 (1992): 341–81.

22. For example, "Feier des Geburtstags Seiner Majestät," *Kirchlicher Amtsanzeiger für das Bisthum Trier* 37, no. 1 (1893): 2.

23. "Gebete zum Dank für die Errettung Sr. Majestät des Kaisers," *Amtliches Kirchenblatt für die Diöcese Paderborn* 44, no. 5 (1901): 37.

24. *Kirchlicher Anzeiger für die Erzdiözese Köln* 41, no. 15 (1901): 86–87.

25. *Kirchlicher Anzeiger für die Erzdiözese Köln* 26, no. 5 (1886): 51.

26. "Aus der kaserne ins Privatleben zurück!" *Extrabeilage zum Paulinus-Blatt* no. 40 (3 October 1909): 1.

27. "Die Einweihung von Fahnen nichtkirchlicher Vereine betr," *Kirchlicher Amtsanzeiger für das Bisthum Trier* 34, no. 13 (1890): 120.

28. *Kirchlicher Anzeiger für die Erzdiözese Köln* 44, no. 17 (1904): 98.

29. "Kirchliche Gedenkfeier am 10. März 1913," *Kirchlicher Anzeiger für die Erzdiözese Köln* 53, no. 4 (1913): 20–21.

30. "Zum Weltkrieg," *Pastor Bonus. Zeitschrift für kirchliche Wissenschaft und Praxis* 26 (1913–14): 705.

31. "Katholisch und National," *Paulinus-Blatt. Sonntagsblatt für die christliche Familie* 29, no. 30 (1903): 235.

32. Carl Ludwig von Bar, *Staat und katholische Kirche in Preußen* (Berlin: Verlag von Julius Springer, 1883), 55.

33. Bennette, *Fighting for the Soul of Germany*, 122–56.

34. For example, Barbara Wieland, "Der katholische Hausstand und das Sonntagsblatt. Belehrung—Werbung—Lebensgestaltung," in *Das katholische Sonntagsblatt (1850–2000). Württembergischer Katholizismus im Spiegel der Bistumspresse*, ed. Hubert Wolf and Jörg Seiler (Ostfildern: Schwabenverlag, 2001), 91; and "Welche Rolle spielt die Biene bei der Obstgewinnung?" *Extrabeilage zum Paulinus-Blatt* no. 3 (18 January 1903): 2.

35. Many sources describe the activities of priest-naturalists, including obituaries published in *Natur und Offenbarung. Organ zur Vermittlung zwischen Naturforschung und Glauben für Gebildete aller Stände* (henceforth NuO): "Heinrich Rodenstein," *NuO* 25 (1879): 768; "Nekrolog," *NuO* 26 (1880): 448; and "Todes-Anzeige," *NuO* 28 (1882): 640. See also Jeffrey T. Zalar, *Reading and Rebellion in Catholic Germany, 1770–1914* (Cambridge, UK: Cambridge University Press, 2019), 202–7.

36. Peter Einig, "Die Vorgeblichen Widersprüche zwischen Glaube und Wissen," *Pastor Bonus. Zeitschrift für kirchliche Wissenschaft und Praxis* 1 (1889): 16.

37. Examples include: Friedrich Michelis, review of "Die gesammten Naturwissenschaften populär dargestellt," *NuO* 8 (1862): 278–80; Schanz, "Nicolaus Copernicus," *NuO* 22 (1876): 741–55; and an unsigned review of "Galileistudien. Historisch-theologische Untersuchungen über die Urtheile der römischen Congregation im Galileiprocesse," *NuO* 29 (1883): 369–73.

38. Mohnike, "Geschänzte Menschen," *NuO* 23 (1877): 610–20; and Janet Browne, *Darwin's Origin of Species: A Biography* (New York: Grove Press, 2006), 114–15.

39. D.v.S., "Carl Darwin," *NuO* 28 (1882): 375–81; and unsigned review of "Charles Darwin und sein Verhältnis zu Deutschland," *NuO* 33 (1887): 108–11.

40. Carl Berthold, "Die neuere ungläubige und die christliche Naturauffassung," *NuO* 23 (1877): 92–106; Martin Gander, "Gehirn und Verstand," *NuO* 34 (1888): 619–27; Erich Wasmann, "Zur neueren Geschichte der Entwicklungslehre in Deutschland," *NuO* 42 (1896): 193–215; and Gustav Brühl, "Die Herkunft der amerikanischen Urbevölkerung und ihrer Kultur," *NuO* 49 (1903): 641–53.

41. Unsigned review of "Glaube und Aberglaube in der neueren Naturwissenschaft," *NuO* 29 (1883): 444.

42. Paul J. Griffiths, *Intellectual Appetite: A Theological Grammar* (Washington, DC: Catholic University of America Press, 2009), 20–22.

43. Augustine, *De Vera Religione*, chapters 95 and 100 in *Augustine: Earlier Writings*, ed. J.H.S. Burleigh (Philadelphia: The Westminster Press, 1953), 274 and 276; Hugh of St. Victor, *Didascalicon*, trans. Jerome Taylor (New York: Columbia University Press, 1961), 128–29; and Thomas Aquinas, *Summa Theologica* 2a2ae, question 166a.2.

44. Michel Foucault, *The Birth of the Clinic: An Archaeology of Medical Perception*, trans. A. M. Sheridan Smith (New York: Vintage, 1994), ix–xix and 107–73.

45. For example: "Neueste Entdeckungen aus dem Gebiete der Naturwissenschafte," *NuO* 16 (1870): 49 and Otto Feeg, "Die letzten Errungenschaften auf dem Gebiete der Chemie," *NuO* 42 (1896): 633–34.

46. Landois, "Die Transfusion des Blutes," *NuO* 13 (1867): 535–36.

47. For this section, see "Fragen und Antworten," *NuO* 35 (1889): 192 and 512; 37 (1891): 382; 38 (1892): 64 and 576; 42 (1896): 384; and 44 (1898): 128.

48. Max Maier, "Größe und Bau des Weltalls," *NuO* 38 (1892): 65.

49. Quoted in Bernard McGinn, ed., *The Essential Writings of Christian Mysticism* (New York: Random House, 2006), 33.

50. Todd H. Weir, *Secularism and Religion in Nineteenth-Century Germany: The Rise of the Fourth Confession* (New York: Cambridge University Press, 2014), 89 and 104. See also Landois, "Die Mikrophotographie und ihre Bedeutung für den Naturforscher," *NuO* 16 (1870): 219–232; and Handmann, "Das Mikroskop und seine Dienste für das praktische Leben," *NuO* 21 (1875): 26–37.

51. R. H. "Mikroskopische Salonpräparate," *NuO* 46 (1900): 335–36.

52. Philip Ball, *Curiosity: How Science Became Interested in Everything* (Chicago: University of Chicago Press, 2013).

53. Martin Baumeister, *Parität und katholische Inferiorität. Untersuchungen zur Stellung des Katholizismus im Deutschen Kaiserreich* (Paderborn: Ferdinand Schöningh, 1987), 44.

54. Quoted in Wilhelm Spael, *Das katholische Deutschland im 20. Jahrhundert: Seine Pionier- und Krisenzeiten 1890–1945* (Würzburg: Echter-Verlag, 1964), 149–50.

55. Wilfried Loth, "Soziale Bewegungen im Katholizismus des Kaiserreichs," *Geschichte und Gesellschaft* 17, no. 1 (1991): 279–310.

56. Heinrich Falkenberg, *Wir Katholiken und die deutsche Literatur* (Bonn: Carl Georgi, Universitäts-Buchdruckerei und Verlag, 1909), 191.

57. "Lesehallen oder Volksbibliotheken?" *Pastoralblatt* 35 (1901): 42. For this section, see Zalar, *Reading and Rebellion*, 207–17.

58. Quoted in Michael Klöcker, *Katholisch—von der Wiege bis zur Bahre. Ein Lebensmacht im Zerfall?* (Munich: Kösel-Verlag, 1991), 246–47.

59. Quoted in Annette Drees, "Profession, Konfession und Geschlecht. Profilierungsbestrebungen katholischer Lehrerinnen Anfang des 20. Jahrhunderts," in *Beruf und Religion im 19. und 20. Jahrhundert*, ed. Frank-Michael Kuhlemann and Hans-Walter Schmuhl (Stuttgart: W. Kohlhammer, 2003), 123.

60. Antonius Liedhegener, *Christentum und Urbanisierung: Katholiken und Protestanten in Münster und Bochum 1830–1933* (Paderborn: Ferdinand Schöningh, 1997), 211–12.

61. Quoted in Oliver Zimmer, "Nation und Religion. Von der Imagination des Nationalen zur Verarbeitung von Nationalisierungsprozessen," *Historische Zeitschrift* 283, no. 3 (2006): 654–55.

62. Derek Hastings, "Fears of a Feminized Church: Catholicism, Clerical Celibacy, and the Crisis of Masculinity in Wilhelmine Germany," *European History Quarterly* 38, no. 1 (2008): 34–65.

63. Karl Hausberger, *Thaddäus Engert (1875–1945). Leben und Streben eines deutschen "Modernisten"* (Regensburg: Friedrich Pustet, 1996), 70. See also Jörg Haustein, *Liberal-katholische Publizistik im späten Kaiserreich: "Das Neue Jahrhundert" und die Krausgesellschaft* (Göttingen: Vandenhoeck & Ruprecht, 2001).

64. "Ueber das Lesen verbotener Bücher," *Extrabeilage zum Paulinus-Blatt* no. 47 (20 November 1904): 2. For a deeper analysis of this foreboding theme, see Derek Hastings, *Catholicism and the Roots of Nazism: Religious Identity and National Socialism* (Oxford, UK: Oxford University Press, 2010).

65. Andreas Grunenberg, "Die Stellung der Katholiken in Deutschland. Die Paritätsfrage," in *Deutschland und der Katholizismus. Gedanken zur Neugestaltung des deutschen Geistes- und Gesellschaftslebens*, Vol. 2: *Das Gesellschaftsleben*, ed. Max Meinertz and Hermann Sacher (Freiburg: Herder, 1918), 170–71.

66. Historians address the realities of being *"zwischen,"* for the term appears frequently in the titles of their scholarship. Just a few examples include Thomas Mergel, *Zwischen Klasse und Konfession. Katholisches Bürgertum im Rheinland 1794–1914* (Göttingen: Vandenhoeck & Ruprecht, 1994); Arbeitskreis für kirchliche Zeitgeschichte (AKKZG), Münster, "Katholiken zwischen Tradition und Moderne. Das katholische Milieu als Forschungsaufgabe," *Westfälische Forschungen* 43 (1993): 588–654; and Karl Gabriel, "Zwischen Tradition und Modernisierung. Katholizismus und katholisches Milieu in den fünfziger Jahren der Bundesrepublik," in *Kirchliche Zeitgeschichte: Urteilsbildung und Methoden*, ed. Anselm Doering-Manteuffel and Kurt Nowak (Stuttgart: W. Kohlhammer, 1996), 248–62.

67. Mark Edward Ruff, *The Wayward Flock: Catholic Youth in Postwar West Germany, 1945–1965* (Chapel Hill: The University of North Carolina Press, 2005); Thomas Großbölting, *Der verlorene Himmel. Glauben in Deutschland seit 1945* (Göttingen: Vandenhoeck & Ruprecht, 2013); Jack D. Shand, "The Decline of Traditional Christian Beliefs in Germany," *Sociology of Religion* 59, no. 2 (1998): 179–84; and "Pope Francis Laments the 'Erosion' of the Faith in Germany," https://www.catholicnewsagency.com/news/pope-francis-laments-the-erosion-of-the-faith-in-germany-86251, retrieved 15 December 2020.

68. "Zum Krieg mit Rom," *Zentrums-Album des Kladderadatsch 1870–1910* (Berlin: A. Hofmann & Co., 1912), 21.

Bibliography

Arbeitskreis für kirchliche Zeitgeschichte (AKKZG), Münster. "Katholiken zwischen Tradition und Moderne. Das katholische Milieu als Forschungsaufgabe." *Westfälische Forschungen* 43 (1993): 588–654.

Aquinas, Thomas. *Summa Theologica* 2a2ae, question 166a.2.

Augustine. *De Vera Religione*, chapters 95 and 100 in *Augustine: Earlier Writings*, edited by J.H.S. Burleigh. Philadelphia: Westminster Press, 1953.

Ball, Philip. *Curiosity: How Science Became Interested in Everything*. Chicago: University of Chicago Press, 2013.

Baumeister, Martin. *Parität und katholische Inferiorität. Untersuchungen zur Stellung des Katholizismus im Deutschen Kaiserreich*. Paderborn: Ferdinand Schöningh, 1987.

Becker, Frank. "Konfessionelle Nationsbilder im Deutschen Kaiserreich." In *Nation und Religion in der deutschen Geschichte*, edited by Heinz-Gerhard Haupt and Dieter Langewiesche, 389–418. Frankfurt: Campus, 2001.

Bennette, Rebecca Ayako. *Fighting for the Soul of Germany: The Catholic Struggle for Inclusion after Unification*. Cambridge, MA: Harvard University Press, 2012.

Blackbourn, David. *Marpingen: Apparitions of the Virgin Mary in Nineteenth-Century Germany*. New York: Alfred A. Knopf, 1994.

Borutta, Manuel. "Das Andere der Moderne. Geschlecht, Sexualität und Krankheit in antikatholischen Diskursen Deutschlands und Italiens (1850–1900)." In *Kollektive Identitäten und kulturelle Innovationen. Ethnologische, soziologische und historische Studien*, edited by Werner Rammert et al., 59–75. Leipzig: Leipziger Universitätsverlag, 2001.

Browne, Janet. *Darwin's Origin of Species: A Biography*. New York: Grove Press, 2006.

Busch, Norbert. "Frömmigkeit als Faktor des katholischen Milieus: Der Kult zum Herzen Jesu." In *Religion im Kaiserreich: Milieus—Mentalitäten—Krisen*, edited by Olaf Blaschke and Frank-Michael Kuhlemann, 136–65. Gütersloh: Chr. Kaiser/Gütersloher Verlagshaus, 1996.

Camerlander, A. [Anton Huonder]. *Sind die Jesuiten Deutschfeindlich? Ein Beitrag zur Geschichte des Deutschtums im Ausland*. 2nd ed. Freiburg: Caritas-Verlag, 1913.

Drees, Annette. "Profession, Konfession und Geschlecht. Profilierungsbestrebungen katholischer Lehrerinnen Anfang des 20. Jahrhunderts." In *Beruf und Religion im 19. und 20. Jahrhundert*, edited by Frank-Michael Kuhlemann and Hans-Walter Schmuhl, 112–28. Stuttgart: W. Kohlhammer, 2003.

Einig, Peter. "Die Vorgeblichen Widersprüche zwischen Glaube und Wissen." *Pastor Bonus. Zeitschrift für kirchliche Wissenschaft und Praxis* 1 (1889): 16.

Falkenberg, Heinrich. *Wir Katholiken und die deutsche Literatur*. Bonn: Carl Georgi, Universitäts-Buchdruckerei und Verlag, 1909.

Foucault, Michel. *The Birth of the Clinic: An Archaeology of Medical Perception*. Translated by A. M. Sheridan Smith. New York: Vintage, 1994.

Gabriel, Karl. "Zwischen Tradition und Modernisierung. Katholizismus und katholisches Milieu in den fünfziger Jahren der Bundesrepublik." In *Kirchliche Zeitgeschichte: Urteilsbildung und Methoden*, edited by Anselm Doering-Manteuffel and Kurt Nowak, 248–62. Stuttgart: W. Kohlhammer, 1996.

Griffiths, Paul J. *Intellectual Appetite: A Theological Grammar*. Washington, DC: Catholic University of America Press, 2009.

Gross, Michael B. *The War against Catholicism: Liberalism and the Anti-Catholic Imagination in Nineteenth-Century Germany*. Ann Arbor: University of Michigan Press, 2004.

Großbölting, Thomas. *Der verlorene Himmel. Glauben in Deutschland seit 1945*. Göttingen: Vandenhoeck & Ruprecht, 2013.

Grunenberg, Andreas. "Die Stellung der Katholiken in Deutschland. Die Paritätsfrage." In *Deutschland und der Katholizismus. Gedanken zur Neugestaltung des deutschen Geistes- und Gesellschaftslebens*, Vol. 2: *Das Gesellschaftsleben*, edited by Max Meinertz and Hermann Sacher, 159–74. Freiburg: Herder, 1918.

Hansen, Joseph. *Preußen und Rheinland von 1815 bis 1915. Hundert Jahre politischen Lebens am Rhein*. Cologne: Rheinland-Verlag, (1918) 1990.

Hastings, Derek. *Catholicism and the Roots of Nazism: Religious Identity and National Socialism*. Oxford, UK: Oxford University Press, 2010.

———. "Fears of a Feminized Church: Catholicism, Clerical Celibacy, and the Crisis of Masculinity in Wilhelmine Germany." *European History Quarterly* 38, no. 1 (2008): 34–65.

Hausberger, Karl. *Thaddäus Engert (1875–1945). Leben und Streben eines deutschen "Modernisten."* Regensburg: Friedrich Pustet, 1996.

Haustein, Jörg. *Liberal-katholische Publizistik im späten Kaiserreich: "Das Neue Jahrhundert" und die Krausgesellschaft*. Göttingen: Vandenhoeck & Ruprecht, 2001.

Healy, Róisín. *The Jesuit Specter in Imperial Germany*. Boston: Brill, 2003.

Hoover, A. J. "God and German Unification: Protestant Patriotic Preaching during the Franco-Prussian War, 1870–71." *Fides et Historia* 18, no. 2 (1986): 20–31.

Hugh of St. Victor. *Didascalicon*. Translated by Jerome Taylor. New York: Columbia University Press, 1961.

Jürgensmeier, Friedhelm. *Die katholische Kirche im Spiegel der Karikatur: Der deutschen satirischen Tendenzzeitschriften von 1848 bis 1900*. Trier: Neu & Co., 1969.

Klöcker, Michael. *Katholisch—von der Wiege bis zur Bahre. Ein Lebensmacht im Zerfall?* Munich: Kösel-Verlag, 1991.

Kuhlemann, Frank-Michael. "Erinnerung und Erinnerungskultur im deutschen Protestantismus." *Zeitschrift für Kirchengeschichte* 119, no. 1 (2008): 30–44.

Langewiesche, Dieter. "Reich, Nation und Staat in der jüngeren deutschen Geschichte." *Historische Zeitschrift* 254 (1992): 341–81.

Liedhegener, Antonius. *Christentum und Urbanisierung: Katholiken und Protestanten in Münster und Bochum 1830–1933*. Paderborn: Ferdinand Schöningh, 1997.

Loth, Wilfried. "Soziale Bewegungen im Katholizismus des Kaiserreichs." *Geschichte und Gesellschaft* 17, no. 1 (1991): 279–310.

McGinn, Bernard, ed. *The Essential Writings of Christian Mysticism*. New York: Random House, 2006.

Mergel, Thomas. *Zwischen Klasse und Konfession. Katholisches Bürgertum im Rheinland 1794–1914*. Göttingen: Vandenhoeck & Ruprecht, 1994.

Michelis, Friedrich. Review of "Die gesammten Naturwissenschaften populär dargestellt." *Natur und Offenbarung. Organ zur Vermittlung zwischen Naturforschung und Glauben für Gebildete aller Stände* 8 (1862): 278–80.

Mosse, George L. *The Nationalization of the Masses: Political Symbolism and Mass Movements in Germany from the Napoleonic Wars through the Third Reich*. New York: Meridian, 1975.

"Pope Francis Laments the 'Erosion' of the Faith in Germany." *Catholic News Agency*, 20 November 2015. Retrieved 15 December 2020 from https://www.catholicnewsagency.com/news/pope-francis-laments-the-erosion-of-the-faith-in-germany-86251.

Ruff, Mark Edward. *The Wayward Flock: Catholic Youth in Postwar West Germany, 1945–1965*. Chapel Hill: University of North Carolina Press, 2005.

Schanz. "Nicolaus Copernicus." *Natur und Offenbarung. Organ zur Vermittlung zwischen Naturforschung und Glauben für Gebildete aller Stände* 22 (1876): 741–55.

Schmenk, Holger. *Xanten im 19. Jahrhundert. Eine rheinische Kleinstadt zwischen Tradition und Moderne*. Köln: Böhlau, 2008.

Shand, Jack D. "The Decline of Traditional Christian Beliefs in Germany." *Sociology of Religion* 59, no. 2 (1998): 179–84.

Smith, Helmut Walser. *German Nationalism and Religious Conflict: Culture, Ideology, Politics, 1870–1914*. Princeton: Princeton University Press, 1995.

Spael, Wilhelm. *Das katholische Deutschland im 20. Jahrhundert: Seine Pionier- und Krisenzeiten 1890–1945*. Würzburg: Echter-Verlag, 1964.

Stambolis, Barbara. "Nation und Konfession im Spannungsfeld: Aspekte historischer Vereinsforschung am Beispiel des Schützenwesens." *Historisches Jahrbuch* 120 (2000): 199–226.

———. "Nationalisierung trotz Ultramontanisierung oder: 'Alles für Deutschland. Deutschland aber für Christus.' Mentalitätsleitende Wertorientierung deutsche Katholi-ken im 19. und 20. Jahrhundert." *Historische Zeitschrift* 269, no. 1 (1999): 57–97.

Unsigned review of "Galileistudien. Historisch-theologische Untersuchungen über die Urtheile der römischen Congregation im Galileiprocesse." *Natur und Offenbarung. Organ zur Vermittlung zwischen Naturforschung und Glauben für Gebildete aller Stände* 29 (1883): 369–73.

Weichlein, Siegfried. "Nationsbilder und Staatskritik im deutschen Katholizismus des 19. und 20. Jahrhunderts." In *Religion und Nation. Katholizismen im Europa des 19. und 20. Jahrhunderts*, edited by Urs Altermatt and Franziska Metzger, 137–51. Stuttgart: Kohlhammer, 2007.

Weir, Todd H. *Secularism and Religion in Nineteenth-Century Germany: The Rise of the Fourth Confession*. New York: Cambridge University Press, 2014.

Wieland, Barbara. "Der katholische Hausstand und das Sonntagsblatt. Belehrung—Werbung—Lebensgestaltung." In *Das katholische Sonntagsblatt (1850–2000). Württembergischer Katholizismus im Spiegel der Bistumspresse*, edited by Hubert Wolf and Jörg Seiler, 61–108. Ostfildern: Schwabenverlag, 2001.

Zalar, Jeffrey T. *Reading and Rebellion in Catholic Germany, 1770–1914*. Cambridge, UK: Cambridge University Press, 2019.

Zimmer, Oliver. "Nation und Religion. Von der Imagination des Nationalen zur Verarbeitung von Nationalisierungsprozessen." *Historische Zeitschrift* 283, no. 3 (2006): 617–56.

"Zum Krieg mit Rom." *Zentrums-Album des Kladderadatsch 1870–1910*. Berlin: A. Hofmann & Co., 1912.

Zwicker, Lisa Fetheringill. *Dueling Students: Conflict, Masculinity, and Politics in German Universities, 1890–1914*. Ann Arbor: University of Michigan Press, 2011.

Chapter Two

"TIME TO CLOSE RANKS"

The Catholic *Kulturfront* during the Weimar Republic

Klaus Große Kracht
Translated by Jeffrey Verhey

By the end of the 1880s, the *Kulturkampf* between the Catholic Church and the Prussian government was resolved, at least officially. The so-called Peace Laws (*Friedensgesetze*) of 1886 and 1887 had taken the sting out of the most important points of contention, and the Holy See and the German Empire had returned to an amicable diplomatic relationship. However, among German Catholics the memory of the *Kulturkampf* remained powerful and indeed outlasted the German Empire. When, a few days after 9 November 1918, the new revolutionary Prussian government stated it was going to eliminate any and all Church influence in the schools to draw a line between church and state, the Prussian bishops pointedly warned Christians about the dangers of a new *Kulturkampf*: "What is at stake here is enormous: it concerns the glory of God, the name Jesus Christ, and your Holy Church . . . In the years of the *Kulturkampf* you closed ranks and rallied firmly around your bishops and your priests. And this Catholic unity was victorious. Because in the long run nothing could stand up to this Catholic unity, this Catholic unanimity. Now a new *Kulturkampf* is starting which will be much worse. Therefore it is once again time to close ranks."[1]

This appeal was at least partly successful. Even before the first meeting of the National Assembly, the radically secular Prussian Minister of Education and the Arts Adolph Hoffmann had resigned and the government had switched to a moderate course in regard to the Church. This shift enabled Catholics to participate in government. And their participation was essential, given how difficult it was during the Weimar Republic to find a majority in Parliament. Indeed, through 1932 the Center Party, the political representation of German Catholics, participated in all national governments and furnished the Republic no fewer than four times with its Chancellor.[2] Nevertheless, even in the golden 1920s tensions between Catholics and Protestants remained. Especially in rural areas, Catholics and Protestants continued to live and socialize within separate worlds. They rejected so-called mixed marriages between couples from different denominations. In those regions where Catholics and Protestants lived side by side, Catholic pilgrimages and processions were not infrequently accompanied by violent fights and riots.[3] Unaffected by the new conditions of the Weimar Republic, the *Evangelische Bund*, an association founded in 1886 towards the end of the *Kulturkampf* to promote the interests of German Protestants, continued its notorious attacks against Catholics. Leading the response on the Catholic side was the *Winfriedbund*, founded in 1920. Although it had far fewer members than its Protestant counterpart, the *Winfriedbund* did aim to convert Protestants and to defend the "truth of the Catholic faith in Germany against the attacks of the Protestants."[4]

Accordingly, any interdenominational efforts faced difficulties. The Catholic trade union leader Adam Stegerwald was unable to expand the Center Party into a Christian people's party, and the right-wing Catholics who tried to work together with national-conservative Protestants in the *Deutschnationale Volkspartei* (DNVP) were likewise unsuccessful.[5] Even at the theological level, during the Weimar Republic there was no progress toward any ecumenical understanding, especially after Pope Pius XI in his 1928 encyclical *Mortalium animos* forbade Catholics from participating in ecumenical events and movements.[6]

Thus it makes sense to talk about a "second" *Kulturkampf* during the 1920s and 1930s.[7] However, if we compare this situation to the first wave of conflict between Catholicism and liberal Protestant nationalism in the nineteenth century, this *Kulturkampf* differed, on the one hand, in that it was embedded in broad, transnational conflicts. This *Kulturkampf* was not only about the rights of the Catholic Church in a liberal nation-state, but also—at the latest since the October Revolution of 1917—a struggle between political-religious ideological groups opposed to each other on a global scale.[8] On the other hand, this new *Kulturkampf* differed from the previous one in that Catholics now had far greater self-confidence than they had had half a century before. In the first *Kulturkampf*—especially during the long last phase—German Catholics had focused on overcoming their social "inferiority" in the cultural, scientific, and political life of Germany, in other words, on overcoming discrimination by Protestants.[9] In the second *Kulturkampf*, in contrast, many Catholic intellectuals engaged in debates with other religious and ideological conceptions with the aim of nothing less than to be acknowledged as the sole representative of truth and morality. They thus claimed to be superior to other denominations and worldviews.

This chapter will examine this Catholic *Kulturfront* in detail, concentrating on how the twofold expansion of the original *Kulturkampf* constellation in the 1920s and early 1930s came about. The starting point will be the so-called crisis of modernism with respect to the Papal Magesterium in the first decade of the twentieth century. During these years the course was set which would later lead to an abrupt distancing from and rejection of contemporary efforts to modernize Catholicism. Closely linked to the onset of a Catholic anti-modernism was the formation of Catholic Action as part of a strategy to mobilize Catholic laity; Catholic Action had an authoritarian, intransigent attitude. In the middle of the 1920s intellectual debates, the new militant self-image of German Catholicism ultimately manifested itself in a demonstrative, publicly exhibited *Siegkatholizismus*, a Catholicism with a triumphalist edge. Associated with this was the formulation of a polarized worldview: Catholicism faced an amorphous enemy which combined the characteristics of Protestantism, liberalism, and communism. In 1933, the pitfalls of this hypertrophic form of Catholicism, which claimed that it alone was the true *Weltanschauung*, were revealed when not a few Catholic intellectuals in Germany welcomed the beginning of Hitler's rule as a new authoritarian turn against the ills of modernity. This chapter will conclude with a brief look at the period after 1945.

Anti-modernism

Whereas the *Kulturkampf* was resolved in the course of the 1880s in Germany, in other parts of Europe it was just getting started. Particularly in the French Third Republic in the last decades of the nineteenth century, significant tensions mounted between the Catholic Church and a secular government whose goal was the strict separation of church and state. In 1905, when a law was passed which enacted this strict separation, in essence reducing the French Church to the status of a private law association, the Holy See responded angrily with a declaration of war on all attempts to deny the Church its ancestral rights in state and society. The liberal principle of the separation of church and state was for Pius X—who was very different in this regard from his predecessor Leo XIII, who sought compromise and conciliation—only one element of a larger set of dangerous ideas he subsumed under "modernism."[10] In his encyclical *Pascendi dominici gregis* from 1907, he defined "modernism" curtly as the "synthesis of all heresies."[11] As part of an "unchecked passion for novelty," agnostic and atheistic teachings had spread throughout the modern world and had even penetrated into the writings of Catholic intellectuals.[12] Pius X condemned everything being discussed in the philosophical, intellectual debates of the time—whether it was the historical-critical biblical exegesis, unbiased and confessionally neutral scientific research, or new approaches to comparative religious studies—and he placed these developments in the context of contemporary attacks on the ancestral rights of the Church: "The first step in this direction was taken by Protestantism; the second is made by modernism; the next will plunge headlong into atheism."[13]

With this, Pius X formulated an interpretation of history which shaped and defined right-wing intellectual Catholicism in the first half of the twentieth century. According to him, the falling away from God began with the division of the Christian church during the Reformation. It continued during the modernization brought about by the Enlightenment and by liberalism, and in the near future atheism would emerge victorious over the church of Christ. In order to eliminate this danger, Pius X called for the new, total integration of the state and society under the roof of the Roman Catholic Church. This is precisely what is expressed in the maxim of his pontificate: "*Instaurare omnia in Christo*"—to renew everything in the spirit of Christ.[14] This fundamentalist worldview rejected any differentiation between the profane and the religious, between church and state, and between science and faith. Ultimately, every aspect of society had to submit to the Church's authority.

Pius X's ecclesiastical-theological fellow campaigners against "modernism" were quite correctly characterized by reform-oriented Catholics as "integralists," for they placed great emphasis on a full-fledged, integral Catholicism unwilling to compromise with the profane world.[15] Ultimately, "integralism" was nothing less than the ecclesiastical version of modern totalitarian concepts of order. Accordingly, years later the Jesuit scholar of social ethics Oswald von Nell-Breuning defined "integralism" as the term "for a religious totalitarianism which wants to derive from faith (alone) the answer to all questions of private and public life, which accordingly denies the various cultural fields . . . any relative autonomy a[nd] attempts to place these areas (or at the very least the activities of the believers in these areas) fundamentally under the *potestas directa* of the church."[16]

To fight "modernism" in their own ranks, Pius X and his fellow campaigners began to closely monitor and supervise theological training as well as to spy on those suspected of deviation and, if necessary, to discipline them. From 1910 on, seminarians and priests were also required to take a formal "anti-modernism" oath in which they vowed to stay away from all views and beliefs branded heretical.[17] The new spirit of ecclesiastical integralism also entered the circles of Catholic laity through religious journalism, in Germany and Austria in particular through the works of a handful of conservative Catholic authors such as Richard Kralik and Joseph Eberle.[18] The founding of the Catholic Association of Academics (*Katholischen Akademikerverbandes*) in 1913 took place in the spirit of Catholic anti-modernism as well. The association was launched under the auspices of the General Secretary of the Association, Franz-Xaver Münch, who drew the association closer to the new "Liturgical Movement," which was interested above all in austere and rigorous church rituals.[19] Whereas Catholic intellectuals in Germany at the end of the nineteenth century were concerned above all with emphasizing their contribution to scientific progress and to German national culture, the spokesmen of the Catholic Association of Academics were more concerned with articulating a strict apology for Roman Catholicism and with asserting the position of Catholic intellectuals vis-à-vis other currents of thought.[20] This stance for an integralist Catholicism even found expression in the official name of the association: "Federation of Associations of Catholic Academics for the Care and Upkeep of the Catholic Weltanschauung" (*Verband der Vereine katholischer Akademiker zur Pflege katholischer Weltanschauung*). "Weltanschauung" here meant much more than just a private, religious faith: it was a comprehensive worldview, including politics, society, and culture, all of which now were to be viewed from the standpoint of the Church's doctrine of salvation.[21]

Catholic Action

Anti-modernism was also the intellectual basis for Pius X's attempts to reorganize lay Catholicism under the aegis of "Catholic Action" and to bind lay Catholicism more closely to the guidelines and instructions of the hierarchy. The origins of Catholic Action lie in Italy. According to Pius X, lay Catholicism there had become too involved in political discussions of the Italian nation-state, whose legitimacy had not been recognized by the Vatican. Accordingly, in 1904 the Pope dissolved the traditional Catholic lay associations in his native country and replaced them with new ones. These new associations had a more authoritarian structure, which soon became known as *Azione Cattolica*. The development of this new lay movement, led by the bishops, did not follow a clearly articulated plan, but rather occurred in multiple stages. Only under Pius XI did a sturdy organizational format for Catholic Action emerge, which was then recommended as a model for other countries.[22] The differences in the specific structure of Catholic Action in the individual countries were sometimes considerable, but the objective was always the same: the active commitment of the laity to the "Christianization of society," or—in the words of Pius X: *instaurare omnia in Christo*.[23]

In Germany, the public became aware of the papal guidelines for Catholic Action by the mid-1920s. In 1928, the new mobilization of the laity would become the most widely-discussed topic at the national Catholic Day (*Katholikentag*) in Magdeburg.[24] The *Katholikentag*, also known as the General Assembly of German Catholics, was a major event usually held every two years by Catholic associations in Germany, one intended to highlight the unity and strength of the Catholic part of the nation. Nuntius Eugenio Pacelli (who would become Pope Pius XII) summed up the objectives and goals of Catholic Action on this occasion in these words: Catholic Action "seeks to integrate the activity of the laity with that of the priests to form a powerful phalanx and to turn this phalanx into a *acies bene ordinata* in the hands of the bishops and their representatives on earth."[25] For Pacelli, unity and subordination to the bishops were prerequisites for successful lay activity. Michael Keller, who in 1947 would become the bishop of Münster, even spoke of "a mobilization of Catholic laity" and compared the structure of Catholic Action to that of an army: just as lower staff officers carry out the orders of the Supreme Army Command, so too do the institutions and organization of Catholic Action follow the instructions of the ecclesiastical authority.[26] "Lay Catholics to the front!" was accordingly the motto of a regional Catholic meeting in 1928.[27] What was needed were "radical" Catholic men and women who fought from their place in secular society for the interests of the Church and who followed the Church's instructions.[28]

There was very little room in this sort of thinking for ecumenical endeavors or even for efforts which promoted Catholics living peacefully side-by-side with the faithful of other denominations. Although there were seldom explicit jabs against the Protestants in the programmatic writings of Catholic Action, clearly ecumenical efforts could not thrive in such soil. The Catholic claim that one alone was in possession of the truth was too clearly articulated. One could, for example, read in a programmatic treatise of Catholic Action by the Jesuit Friedrich Muckermann that the Catholic Church was the church of the "absolutely compelling truth," and that the pope was the "Vicar of Christ, the highest authority on earth."[29]

Ultimately, however, the pope's authority was brought into play less against Protestants and more against modern culture itself: according to Muckermann, the "festive masses today no longer gather in just the cathedrals and churches, but rather in the stadiums, the movie theaters, and the enormous spaces which have been opened for an enormous congregation by radio's invisible waves."[30] In the "intoxicating music of these sites of a highly developed civilization," the verses of the psalms were no longer heard.[31] Catholic Action's slogans addressed this "dark something of a terrible revolution," a "revolution of the contemporary age against God's eternal throne"—the separation of church and state, new opportunities and possibilities for consumption and leisure, and the uncontrollable flow of communication in the modern age.[32] Catholic Action's semantic front lines ran less along the old confessional boundaries and more along the challenges raised by secularization. The enemy had changed its shape—it was now bigger, more menacing, but also much more amorphous than it had been fifty years earlier, during the first *Kulturkampf*.

"*Siegkatholizismus*" or Catholic Triumphalism

The debates within the intellectual Catholicism of the Weimar period were influenced above all by perceived conflict with the modern world. This conflict was largely characterized as a struggle against the decline and decay of what had allegedly been an intact Christian culture. Since the Reformation, this culture had been attacked by diverse secularization processes. Karl Adam, a professor of dogmatic theology in Tübingen, published a book in 1924 which would be widely read in the following years, *Das Wesen des Katholizismus* ("The Essence of Catholicism"). In this book, based on lectures he had given to the Catholic Academic Association, he juxtaposed the "bursting vitality" and the "eternal youth" of the "old, venerable church" against the "wasteland of the present."[33] The "hallmark of the modern man" was that modern man had been "uprooted." At the end of a long process of decay and deterioration stood "the autonomous, separated from God . . . man, who only negates." Adam also employed the anti-modernist narrative, which since Pius X had dominated conservative Catholics' understanding of history: "The 'break away from the church' in the sixteenth century led logically to a 'break away from Christ' in the eighteenth century and from there to a 'break away from God' in the nineteenth century. With this, modern spirituality was torn from its most important, deepest place in our lives: from its being rooted in the absolute . . . ."[34]

Already before the publication of the book, Adam had made it clear in a speech to Catholic academics what in his opinion was modern man's only salvation if he or she did not want to perish in the "desert" of the present. "There is only one salvation for the modern age: back to the Catholic Church and back to its faith."[35] Adam was by no means the only artist or writer working in the field of cultural Catholicism during Weimar who claimed that the Catholic *Weltanschauung* was the only true *Weltanschauung*. In the same year that *Das Wesen des Katholizismus* appeared, the Catholic philosopher Peter Wust published a programmatic article with the title *Die Rückkehr des deutschen Katholizismus aus dem Exil* ("The Return of German Catholicism from Exile"). The argument here went far beyond what was suggested by the title, for Wust called less for the integration of Catholic artists and writers into the German majority culture and more for a victory over that majority, the modern and deeply Protestant-influenced *Weltanschauung*. With a great deal of self-confidence Wust wrote that German Catholicism had "finally stepped out of its anxious, nervous, tense defensive posture . . . and has gone over to the intellectual and spiritual offensive."[36] Thus, a new Catholic "cultural front" (*Kulturfront*) of self-assertion was rising up to fight the present trend to degeneration: "German Catholics, your time has come!"[37]

The Jesuit Erich Przywara, editor of the influential Jesuit journal *Stimmen der Zeit* and a regular guest at the meetings of the Catholic Association of Academics, likewise did not think highly of the relativization of confessional identities. He thought the only appropriate response to the present-day crisis was a "Catholicism with the undiminished claim that 'there is no salvation outside the church.'"[38] For after the "collapse of the modern spirit," according to Przywara, "a timid, cleverly rational Catholicism of compromise and of a certain minimizing" could no longer provide the necessary degree of orientation, "only a victorious Catholicism (*Sieg-Katholizismus*), energetically proclaiming that it alone was right" could be the answer to the day's problems.[39] Accordingly, Przywara was unable to see anything of value in interdenominational encounters. True Catholics realized that they had "nothing in common with other religions and denominations."[40]

In the years after World War I, this fighting Catholicism, claiming that it alone was true, cast its spell on quite a number of Catholic intellectuals. The entranced included theologians and members of holy orders, the leading figures of the Catholic Association of Academics and the Liturgical Movement, and polarizing figures such as the constitutional law scholar Carl Schmitt, later to play an infamous role in the Third Reich, or Hugo Ball, a former Expressionist author.[41] During the war, Ball had caught people's attention with Dadaistic parodies of sung Catholic masses, but then he returned to a strict Catholicism.[42] Indeed, the anti-Protestantism in Ball's works was even more crass than that found in the works of many other Catholic *Kulturkämpfer* in the 1920s, even if Ball was most interested in articulating a critique of modernity. In his book, *Die Folgen der Reformation* ("The Consequences of the Reformation"), which also appeared in 1924, Ball sharply criticized the Reformation and Lutheranism:

> the complete reversal of the concepts of morality, which Luther undertook . . . confirms the original sin of our nation: its paradoxical concept of freedom, a sense of complaceny and pleasure in a state of wildness . . . And indeed: the pleasure in a successful destruction—the so-called Schadenfreude—and the

canonization of the profane are the meaning of Lutheranism, whose apogee is the glorification of all attacks on the spirit, the elimination of all morality, the *destruction* of religion and of the human conscience.[43]

Clearly, Hugo Ball and the vehement *Siegkatholiken* of the Weimar Republic did not represent a "Catholicism of compromise," a Catholicism of reconciliation and understanding toward those who thought differently. Their Catholicism asserted that only the Catholic religion was right, and it was exactly this clarity that made it so attractive in the religious market of the Weimar Republic. Compared to this, Protestant intellectuals in the Weimar Republic had little to offer. To be sure, the new dialectical theology, which assumed a crass opposition between divine revelation and the affairs of this world, employed language similar to that of the *Siegkatholiken*.[44] Ultimately, however, Protestantism, in part because of its denominational plurality but also because of the fundamental importance it attached to the individual's direct relationship with God, was unable to offer an equivalent for intellectuals looking for general truth, stability, and authority.[45] Intelligent, perceptive contemporaries such as the Protestant theologian and religious historian Ernst Troeltsch saw this quite clearly. Given the general disorientation in the years after World War I, many people flocked, according to Troeltsch, to a fundamental rejection of modernity and its promises about freedom: "The return to the authority of the church and to a . . . corporative manner of life appear to be the only answer to all the incurable problems of modernity. In this regard, Catholicism naturally has a great advantage . . . German Protestantism, on the other hand, will hardly be of much importance."[46]

Anti-communism

In spite of the friction between the denominations and in spite of occasional jabs by Catholics against Protestants, it had been clear since 1917 at the latest that the actual enemy stood outside Christianity: this was revolutionary communism with its materialistic-atheistic *Weltanschauung*. Already in 1919 one could read in *Stimmen der Zeit* that "Bolshevism" was not just "*a* global issue (*Weltfrage*)" but "*the* global issue."[47] A year later, readers learned that the "Bolshevist storm surge" consisted of nothing less than "denying the divine and hating God."[48]

One of the loudest voices warning about the Bolshevik danger in Germany was the abovementioned Jesuit Friedrich Muckermann, a former army chaplain who had been arrested by Red Army soldiers in 1919 in Vilnius and held captive by the Bolshevists for more than eight months.[49] After his return to Germany, the Jesuit priest published an anti-Communist pamphlet in 1920 in which he painted the Bolsheviks as "devils in human form" and warned his fellow believers to take note: "By God, do not make a pact with the devil! There must be no negotiations and no concessions. Bolshevism is the plague itself."[50]

Muckermann was not only an important anti-Communist Catholic journalist; he was also an important propagandist for Catholic Action, as we have seen: In 1928 he gave the keynote speech on Catholic Action at the Magdeburg Katholikentag.[51] Along with the political activities of the Center Party and the efforts of individual religious associations, Catholic Action was indeed one of the major pillars of the Catholic Church's anti-Communist agitation.[52] Communism was considered as "the embodiment and the compilation of all those pursuits and ambitions . . . against which Catholic Action must fight."[53]

Numerous brochures with titles such as *Nacht über Rußland. Der Kampf der Bolschewisten gegen das Christentum* ("Night over Russia: The Struggle of the Bolsheviks against Christianity") or *Der Bolschewismus droht* ("The Threat from Bolshevism") circulated among politically-engaged Catholics.[54] The Bishops Conference took up the topic and heard speeches on "The Dangers from Bolshevism."[55] The Archbishop of Munich and Freising, Michael Cardinal von Faulhaber, said in a sermon: "Western civilization must not perish in the Bolshevist anti-culture . . . The Catholic Church has given birth to Western civilization, and in the crusades it defended Western civilization against oriental barbarism from the east. Today, too, the Catholic Church will equip crusaders fighting the new spiritual crusade with spiritual weapons."[56]

The motif of a new—even if only a spiritual and intellectual—crusade did not come out of nowhere. At the beginning of February 1930 Pius XI called Catholics around the world to a *crociata di preghiera* (crusade of prayer) against the *fronte antireligioso* (anti-religious front) of Bolshevism.[57] In his encyclical *Divini Redemptoris*, published seven years later, Pius XI once again condemned Bolshevism as a system "full of errors" and "in opposition both to reason and to Divine Revelation." He placed Bolshevism within the familiar anti-modern narrative of his predecessor: ". . . we are now reaping the fruits of the errors so often denounced by Our Predecessors and by Ourselves. It can surprise no one that the Communistic fallacy should be spreading in a world already to a large extent de-Christianized."[58]

Bolshevism appears here basically as the last link of a movement which began at the very latest with the liberal secularism of the nineteenth century, if not indeed many centuries earlier. This "plague of anti-clericalism" had been criticized already in 1925 by Pius XI:

This evil spirit, as you are well aware, Venerable Brethren, has not come into being in one day; it has long lurked beneath the surface. The empire of Christ over all nations was rejected. The right which the Church has from Christ himself, to teach mankind, to make laws, to govern peoples in all that pertains to their eternal salvation, that right was denied. Then gradually the religion of Christ came to be likened to false religions and to be placed ignominiously on the same level with them. . . . There were even some nations who thought they could dispense with God, and that their religion should consist in impiety and the neglect of God.[59]

Communism became an all-purpose enemy that bundled together all the sins of modernity—materialism, liberalism, and secularism. In this scenario, the perceived dangers from communism were not only hypertrophic: they were also so broad that all the dangers the Church faced in the modern age could be perceived as latent Bolshevik tendencies. This was expressed above all in the newly coined term "cultural Bolshevism," which included everything that German Catholics—as well as other culturally-conservative groups—regarded as indecent, areligious, and corrupting. "It is cultural Bolshevism when in German criminal law blasphemy and adultery go unpunished, when divorce is made even easier, when the walls of our moral order are to be torn down even further," as the Archbishop of Munich Michael Cardinal von Faulhaber once again put it in his anti-Communist sermon about the prayer crusade of 1930.[60]

Faced with this enemy, the old opposition to Protestantism finally faded. Even if in the 1920s Catholics and Protestants were not yet able to form a common *Kulturfront* vis-à-vis "godless, wicked Bolshevism," there was, even among the most virulent propagandists of a Catholic *Weltanschauung*, a willingness to open up to interdenominational ideas in the face of the threat from the common enemy. The current "Catholic movement," according to Friedrich Muckermann in 1933, is "in any case not characterized by the opposition to Protestantism or, more generally speaking, by any positive religious attitude, but rather by its opposition to absolute anti-religion."[61] Catholics were indeed looking for "allies" in areas "where souls were still (filled) with the same faith in God and in Christ."[62]

The Authoritarian Temptation

In the late Weimar Republic, many right-wing Catholics were searching for allies in their battle against "godless Bolshevism." These Catholics, however, did not move toward interconfessionalism. Rather, their search for allies moved them into a dangerous proximity to authoritarian designs, including neo-corporatist models for social order and ultimately attempts by those like Karl Adam to build bridges to the Hitler movement.[63] These Catholics had always harbored a great skepticism towards liberal rights and freedoms, championing instead the value of institutionalized authority.

This was already apparent in Carl Schmitt's influential 1923 publication *Römischer Katholizismus und politische Form* ("Roman Catholicism and Political Form").[64] In this slim book, the Catholic hierarchy was presented as an alternative to modern bourgeois society and its two most important institutions—the liberal market economy and formal democracy. Whereas in modern bourgeois society a system of supply and demand governed how private people interact, the Catholic Church alone retained the strength for genuine political representation, for the Church did not symbolize individual interests but rather the "*civitas humana*" as a whole by representing Christ. Herein, according to Schmitt, lay "one of their sociological secrets."[65] For this form of representation is not a representation of lobby groups, where interests are negotiated by parliamentary representatives, but rather a form of representation, according to Schmitt, "from above."[66] The pope does not receive his authority on the basis of his personal qualifications or formal rules, but solely and exclusively through the office conferred: "The pope is not the prophet but the Vicar of Christ," his position dating back "in an unbroken chain to the personal mandate and the concrete person of Christ."[67] The authority associated with this office manifested itself publicly in the dignity of its bearer. The pope differentiated himself from the social sphere in that he expressed himself authoritatively in a speech act characterized by "no discussion and no reasoning."[68]

This "pathos of authority," which Schmitt identified as the essence of Roman Catholicism, can also be found in the writings of other Catholic right-wing intellectuals in German-speaking countries during the late Weimar Republic, especially among representatives of the so-called *Reichstheologie*.[69] *Reichstheologie* refers to a political-theological program that took as its point of reference the hierarchical social structure of the medieval Holy Roman Empire, with its two leaders, the pope and the Kaiser. The authority of these two leaders was bound together in an alliance of throne and altar.[70] The idea of the Holy Roman Empire, according to Friedrich Muckermann, "is as worthwhile today as it was then. It is the salvation of humanity. Certainly it is given unto the church to save the individual soul . . . . But the whole cultural power of Christianity can develop unchecked only in the perfect body of the community of a people . . . "[71] In other words, in order for Christ's seeds to sprout, what was needed was a state that enabled the Church to develop without inhibiting its power to shape lives. Instead of a church-state separation in the liberal sense, there would be a new, integrated unity of secular and spiritual rule.[72] According to an additional *Reichstheologie* theorist, the Cologne priest Robert Grosche, this unity could only be realized if the political order were to embrace authority as the Catholic Church had done decades earlier with its proclamation of papal infallibility at the First Vatican Council. In an unmistakeable reference to current political events in Germany, Grosche wrote in 1933: "When in 1870 papal infallibility was proclaimed, the church anticipated, at a higher level, that historic decision that is presently being made at the political level: for authority and against discussion, for the pope and against the sovereignty of the councils, for a leader and against Parliament."[73] Therefore, according to Grosche, it was the task of Catholics to participate in the political rebuilding of Germany, "without a false fear of the total state." This new political form could become the "nucleus of the Reich," "if it is a state full of genuine authority and real dignity."[74]

In 1933, Grosche and other right-wing Catholic intellectuals joined together under the patronage of Vice-Chancellor Franz von Papen to found the *Kreuz und Adler*, a short-lived association of intellectuals whose goal was to increase the strength of the *Reichsidee* in church and state.[75] The proponents of the *Reichsidee* received assistance and support from Ildefons Herwegen, the abbot of Maria Laach, a Benedictine Abbey rich in tradition. Herwegen was highly respected in the Liturgical Movement as well as in the Catholic Association of Academics. At a conference of the association in July 1933, about 150 important figures from the ecclesiatical and political world came together in order to discuss the idea and shape of the Reich, among them Carl Schmitt, Robert Grosche, and Peter Wust.[76] In his keynote speech, Herwegen stated apodictically: "What the liturgical movement is for the religious realm, fascism is for the political realm . . . Let us say yes without any reservations to the new sociological construct of the total state, which is certainly analogous to the structure of the church. The church occupies the same place in the world as today's Germany in politics."[77] And Franz von Papen, who had just returned from Rome after the signing of the *Reichskonkordat*, made the following appeal to those present: "Let us forget old resentments from the days of the *Kulturkampf*; let us bring German Catholicism out of the defensive position it unfortunately has had into an attack stance to construct the Third Reich."[78]

The pathos formula of an anti-modernist *Siegkatholizismus*, used again and again by right-wing Catholic intellectuals from the middle of the 1920s, culminated at the beginning of the Third Reich in numerous professions of loyalty by Catholics to the Führer and the Fatherland.[79] It now appeared to them as if the principles underlying the structure of the church and the state were remarkably similar. It also seemed that the old rifts between the Protestant majority and the Catholics, who had been fighting for equal opportunities and recognition, had been overcome: the "old resentments" were not going to burden the new German *Volksgemeinschaft* any longer.[80]

In 1933, Catholic right-wing intellectuals like Grosche, Herwegen, and others were of course a minority of German Catholics. German Catholicism was anything but a religion of intellectuals: it was rooted in rural areas and among the working class. The pointed arguments found in the political-theological *Reichsmythos* thus were certainly not representative of German Catholicism in 1933, even though the basic anti-modern and authoritarian foundation was widespread. After the Catholic bishops in Germany at the end of March 1933 had significantly softened their previous warnings and denunciations of the National Socialist movement, they declared in June of the same year that—in spite of their insistence on the rights of the Church—they did not find it difficult "to appreciate and acknowledge the new emphasis placed on authority in the German political system."[81] They insisted that especially in the Church, "the word and meaning of authority are particularly valued and have produced that complete unity and victorious resilience that even our opponents admire."[82]

A Brief Look at the Period after 1945

The bishops' talk of the "victorious resilience" and of Catholic "unity" proved to be a fallacy. Despite the ratification of the *Reichskonkordat*, the Catholic Church in Germany was increasingly on the defensive. Its legal, guaranteed rights were increasingly restricted and curtailed, and the religious policy of the Nazi state pushed it more and more out of the public sphere. Within a few months, initial hopes of a harmonious unity between church and state were dashed.[83] Already in 1933 Grosche lost his lectureship at the Düsseldorf Art Academy and had to cease the publication of his parish's church newspaper; the Gestapo wound up keeping an eye on him, warning him about his involvement in the Church's youth movement.[84] In contrast, Carl Schmitt enjoyed a meteoric rise and a brilliant career in the early Nazi state—and he did not shy away from malicious antisemitic remarks.[85] Nevertheless, by 1936 he fell into disfavor, not least because of his Catholic temperament.[86] Because of the ignoble role he had played in the first years of the Third Reich, Schmitt lost his right to teach after 1945. He remained an outsider within the political and intellectual culture of the Federal Republic until his death in 1985. Isolated, intransigent, unrepentant, and sarcastic, he retreated to his hometown of Plettenberg in Sauerland and pondered his fate. On 16 June 1948, he noted in his diary: "This is the secret to my complete intellectual and journalistic existence: the struggle for genuine Catholic intensification" (*die eigentliche katholische Verschärfung*).[87] At the end of 1949 he noted with a good dose of resignation and self-pity: "What are you actually? I am a Catholic layman who belongs to the German people and the German state! What do you mean by that? What I mean is that it is better for me to be silent. From the right and from the left, from above and from below, by all the objective powers of a spiritual and secular nature, my mouth has been stuffed."[88]

However, Schmitt's intellectual sarcasm was unusual for Catholics in postwar Germany. All in all, after 1945 both Catholicism and the Catholic Church enjoyed broad social recognition and had many opportunites to exert political and cultural influence. Many contemporaries regarded the church as the real "victor amidst the ruins."[89] Politically, thanks to Konrad Adenauer and the new Christian Democratic Party, Catholicism was at the center of (West) German politics and society.[90] Catholics no longer needed a new Catholic *Kulturfront* against people of other Christian denominations. From now on Catholics and conservative Protestants would work together in the Christian Democratic Union (CDU).[91] In spite of renewed interdenominational frictions in West German society in the 1950s, Catholics and Protestants ultimately came together, not least because they had to fight a common enemy at the start of the Cold War: "Bolshevism" indeed survived National Socialism and the Third Reich as the archenemy of Christianity.[92] Given the division of Germany after World War II, the battle against "godless Communism" took on a renewed, mobilizing, and integrative significance.[93] This binds the postwar period of German Catholicism with the time before 1945. The success story of the Federal Republic, in particular its rapid domestic pacification and its integration into the geopolitical "West," owed no small part to this new cooperation between Catholics and Protestants. The confessions now stood together to save the alleged Christian Occident from the attack from the "Communist East."

Klaus Große Kracht is Professor (apl.) of Modern and Contemporary History at the University of Münster. His research areas include European cultural and religious history of the nineteenth and twentieth centuries, especially the history of German Catholicism. He is currently working on a research project on the sexual abuse of minors by Catholic priests in the diocese of Münster. The author of numerous books and articles, his monographs include *Die zankende Zunft: Historische Kontroversen in Deutschland nach 1945* (2005) and *Die Stunde der Laien? Katholische Aktion in Deutschland im europäischen Kontext 1920–1960* (2016).

Notes

1. "Hirtenwort der deutschen Bischöfe, 20 December 1918," in *Akten deutscher Bischöfe über die Lage der Kirche 1918–1933*, Vol. 1: 1918–1925 and Vol. 2: 1926–1933, ed. Heinz Hürten (Paderborn: Schöningh, 2007), 43. On the further development of the memory of the *Kulturkampf*, see Christoph Kösters, "'Kulturkampf' im Dritten Reich—Zur Deutung der Konflikte zwischen NS-Regime und katholischer Kirche im deutschen Episkopat," in *Die Kirche und die Verbrechen im nationalsozialistischen Staat*, ed. Thomas Brechenmacher and Harry Oelke (Göttingen: Wallstein , 2011), 67–112.

2. The most competent overview of the history of German Catholicism in the first half of the twentieth century can still be found in Heinz Hürten, *Deutsche Katholiken 1918 bis 1945* (Paderborn: Schöningh, 1992); on the debate on the direction of the Center Party during the early years of the Weimar Republic, see Stefan Gerber, *Pragmatismus und Kulturkritik. Politikbegründung und politische Kommunikation im Katholizismus der Weimarer Republik (1918–1925)* (Paderborn: Schöningh, 2016).

3. Manfred Kittler, "Konfessioneller Konflikt und politische Kultur in der Weimarer Republik," in *Konfessionen im Konflikt. Deutschland zwischen 1800 und 1970: ein zweites konfessionelles Zeitalter*, ed. Olaf Blaschke (Göttingen: Vandenhoeck & Ruprecht, 2002), 243–96.

4. Walter Fleischmann-Bisten, *Der Evangelische Bund in der Weimarer Republik und im sogenannten Dritten Reich* (Frankfurt am Main: Peter Lang, 1989), 187–210. On the *Winfriedbund*, see the memoir by Gisbert Menge, "Bilder aus dem ersten Jahrzehnt des Winfriedbundes," *Die Friedensstadt* 3 (1930): 1–12; the quote is from the letter from Cardinal Bertram to Nuncio Eugenio Pacelli, 31 January 1923, in Hürten, *Akten*, 484.

5. Bernhard Forster, *Adam Stegerwald (1874–1945). Christlich-nationaler Gewerkschafter, Zentrumspolitiker, Mitbegründer der Unionsparteien* (Düsseldorf: Droste, 2003); Larry Eugene Jones, "Catholics on the Right: The Reich Catholic Committee of the German National People's Party, 1920–33," *Historisches Jahrbuch* 126 (2006): 221–67.

6. Pius XI, *Mortalium animos*, Encyclical Letter, 1 June 1928, retrieved 4 June 2021 from http://w2.vatican.va/content/pius-xi/en/encyclicals/documents/hf_p-xi_enc_19280106_mortalium-animos.html.

7. See the articles in the special issue "Europe's Interwar Kulturkampf," *Journal of Contemporary History* 53, no. 3 (2018): 489–661; and the preliminary considerations in Todd H. Weir, "A European Culture War in the Twentieth Century? Anti-Catholicism and Anti-Bolshevism between Moscow, Berlin and the Vatican 1922 to 1933," *Journal of Religious History* 39 (2015): 280–306.

8. Todd H. Weir, "Introduction: Comparing Nineteenth- and Twentieth-Century Culture Wars," *Journal of Contemporary History* 53, no. 3 (2018): 489–502.

9. Martin Baumeister, *Parität und katholische Inferiorität. Untersuchungen zur Stellung des Katholizismus im Deutschen Kaiserreich* (Paderborn: Schöningh, 1987).

10. Michael Burleigh, *Earthly Powers. The Clash of Religion and Politics in Europe from the French Revolution to the Great War* (London: Harper Collins, 2005), 311–64.

11. Pius X, *Pascendi dominici gregis*, Encyclical Letter, 9 August 1908, retrieved 4 June 2021 from http://www.vatican.va/content/pius-x/en/encyclicals/documents/hf_p-x_enc_19070908_pascendi-dominici-gregis.html, § 39.

12. Ibid., § 13.

13. Ibid., § 39. On the conflict between "modernists" and "anti-modernists" in transnational Catholicism at the turn of the century, see Claus Arnold, *Kleine Geschichte des Modernismus* (Freiburg: Herder, 2007).

14. See in this context the inaugural encyclical of Pius X, *E supremi apostolatus cathedra*, Encyclical Letter, retrieved 4 June 2021 from http://www.vatican.va/content/pius-x/en/encyclicals/documents/hf_p-x_enc_04101903_e-supremi.html.

15. See Émile Poulat, *Intégrisme et catholicisme intégral* (Paris: Casterman, 1969).

16. Oswald von Nell-Breuning, "Integralismus," in *Lexikon für Theologie und Kirche*, Second Edition, Vol. 5 (Freiburg: Herder, 1957–68): 717–19.

17. In Germany, however, bishops were able to tone down the anti-modernist measures and to have the requirement to take the oath suspended (*Suspens*) for professors of theology at German universities. See Arnold, *Modernismus*, 125.

18. See Otto Weiß, *Kulturkatholizismus. Katholiken auf dem Weg in die deutsche Kultur 1900–1933* (Regensburg: Friedrich Pustet, 2014), 34–36, 51–56, 115–18.

19. On the "Liturgical Movement" in Germany, see Hürten, *Katholiken*, 41–48.

20. Weiß, *Kulturkatholizismus*, 81–85; Marcel Albert, "Zwecks wirksamer Verteidigung und Vertretung der katholischen Weltanschauung." *Der Katholische Akademikerverband 1913–1938/39* (Cologne: Erzbischöfliche Diözesan- und Dombibliothek, 2010).

21. See, too, Siegfried Weichlein, "Zwischenkriegszeit bis 1933," in *Handbuch der Religionsgeschichte im deutschsprachigen Raum, Bd. 6/1: 20. Jahrhundert—Epochen und Themen*, ed. Volkhard Krech and Lucian Hölscher (Paderborn: Schöningh, 2015), 101.

22. John Pollard, "Pius XI's Promotion of the Italian Model for Catholic Action in the World Wide Church," *Journal of Ecclesiastical History* 63 (2012): 758–84.

23. Klaus Große Kracht, *Die Stunde der Laien? Katholische Aktion in Deutschland im europäischen Kontext* (Paderborn: Schöningh, 2016).

24. Generalsekretariat des Zentralkomitees der deutschen Katholiken, ed. *Bericht über den Katholikentag in Magdeburg, 5. bis 9. September 1928* (Paderborn: Bonifacius, 1928).

25. Ibid., 21.

26. Michael Keller, *Katholische Aktion. Eine systematische Darstellung ihrer Idee* (Osnabrück: Jonscher, 1933), 12, 46.

27. *Laien an die Front! Praktische Gedanken zur Katholischen Aktion. Referate gehalten auf dem Oberhessischen Katholikentag in Ilbenstadt 1928* (Dülmen: Laumann, 1928).

28. See, too, Wilhelm Damberg, "'Radikal katholische Laien an die Front.' Beobachtungen zur Idee und Wirkungsgeschichte der Katholischen Aktion," in *Siegerin in Trümmern. Die Rolle der katholischen Kirche in der deutschen Nachkriegsgesellschaft*, ed. Joachim Köhler and Damian van Melis (Stuttgart: Kohlhammer, 1998), 142–60.

29. Friedrich Muckermann, *Katholische Aktion* (Munich: Ars Sacra, 1929), 20, 29.

30. Ibid., 11.

31. Ibid.

32. Ibid., 12–13.

33. Karl Adam, *Das Wesen des Katholizismus* (Augsburg: Haas & Grabherr, 1924), 6. On Adam, see Robert Anthony Krieg, *Karl Adam. Catholicism in German Culture* (South Bend: University of Notre Dame Press, 1992).

34. Adam, *Wesen des Katholizismus*, 6–8.

35. Karl Adam, "Der moderne Mensch und der katholische Glaube," in *Glaube und Glaubenswissenschaft im Katholizismus. Vorträge und Abhandlungen*, ed. Karl Adam (Rottenburg: Bader, 1923), 164. The rhetoric the Tübinger professor of theology employed—"Am katholischen Wesen wird die Welt genesen" ("the Catholic spirit shall heal the world") reminded one of the Pan German slogan before 1918: "Am deutschen Wesen wird die Welt genesen" ("the German spirit shall heal the world").

36. Peter Wust, "Die Rückkehr des deutschen Katholizismus aus dem Exil," in *Die Rückkehr aus dem Exil. Dokumente der Beurteilung des deutschen Katholizismus der Gegenwart*, ed. Karl Hoeber (Düsseldorf: Schwann, 1926), 26.

37. Ibid., 25, 35.

38. Erich Przywara, "Integraler Katholizismus," in *Ringen der Gegenwart. Gesammelte Aufsätze 1922–1927*, ed. Erich Przywara (Augsburg: Filser, 1929), 141.

39. Ibid., 140.

40. Erich Przywara, "Wohin?" in Ibid., 129.

41. See Albrecht Langner, "Weimarer Kulturkatholizismus und interkonfessionelle Probleme," in *Probleme des Konfessionalismus in Deutschland seit 1800*, ed. Anton Rauscher (Paderborn: Schöningh, 1984), 71–115; Thomas Ruster, *Die verlorene Nützlichkeit der Religion. Katholizismus und Moderne in der Weimarer Republik*, 2nd ed. (Paderborn: Schöningh, 1997); Weiß, *Kulturkatholizismus*, 95–173; James Chappel, *Catholic Modern: The Challenge of Totalitarianism and the Remaking of the Church* (Cambridge, MA: Harvard University Press, 2018), 22–58.

42. On Ball, see Wiebke-Marie Stock, *Denkumsturz. Hugo Ball. Eine intellektuelle Biographie* (Göttingen: Wallstein, 2012); on Schmitt, see Reinhard Mehring, *Carl Schmitt, Aufstieg und Fall. Eine Biographie* (Munich: Beck, 2009); and Manfred Dahlmeier, *Carl Schmitt und der deutsche Katholizismus 1888–1936* (Paderborn: Schöningh, 1998). Dahlmeier also discusses Ball, who was friends with Schmitt for a while, 553–59.

43. Hugo Ball, "Die Folgen der Reformation," in *Hugo Ball, Die Folgen der Reformation / Zur Kritik der deutschen Intelligenz (= Sämtliche Werke und Briefe, Bd. 5)*, ed. Hans Dieter Zimmermann (Göttingen: Wallstein, 2005), 107.

44. Thus Karl Adam saw in the dialectical theology elements which were quite similar in a way to those of the theological renewal in Catholicism: Karl Adam, "Die Theologie der Krisis," *Hochland* 23, no. 2 (1926): 271–86.

45. On the new approaches in the German-speaking Protestant theology of the 1920s, see Jan Rohls, *Protestantische Theologie der Neuzeit*, Vol. 2: *Das 20. Jahrhundert* (Tübingen: Mohr Siebeck, 1997), 244–60.

46. Ernst Troeltsch, "Die Krisis des Historismus," in *Ernst Troeltsch, Schriften zur Politik und Kulturphilosophie (1918–1923), Ernst Troeltsch Kritische Gesamtausgabe*, Vol. 15, ed. Gangolf Hübinger and Johannes Mikuteit (Berlin: De Gruyter, 2002), 453.

47. Bernhard Duhr, "Der Bolschewismus. Übersicht," *Stimmen der Zeit* 97 (1919): 133.

48. Bernhard Duhr, "Die Wurzeln des Bolschewismus. Eine ernste Mahnung auch für uns," *Stimmen der Zeit* 99 (1920): 402.

49. Herbert Gruber, *Friedrich Muckermann S.J. 1883–1946* (Mainz: Grünewald, 1993); see also Muckermann's memoirs: Friedrich Muckermann, *Im Kampf zwischen zwei Epochen. Lebenserinnerungen* (Mainz: Grünewald, 1973), 166–82.

50. Friedrich Muckermann, *Wollt ihr das auch? Wie ich den Bolschewismus in Rußland erlebte* (Düsseldorf: Verband der katholischen Jünglings-Vereinigungen Deutschlands, 1920), 3–4.

51. *Bericht über den Katholikentag 1928*, 191–208; the speech was also later published separately in Muckermann, *Katholische Aktion*.

52. See Ulrich Kaiser, *Realpolitik oder antibolschewistischer Kreuzzug? Zum Zusammenhang von Rußlandbild und Rußlandpolitik der deutschen Zentrumspartei 1917–1933* (Frankfurt am Main: Peter Lang, 2005). See also Horst W. Heitzer, "Deutscher Katholizismus und 'Bolschewismusgefahr' bis 1933," *Historisches Jahrbuch* 113 (1993): 355–87. Klaus Große Kracht, "Campaigning Against Bolshevism: Catholic Action in Late Weimar Germany," *Journal of Contemporary History* 53, no. 3 (2018): 550–73.

53. Johannes Straubinger, *Christentum der Tat* (Stuttgart: Kepplerhaus, 1932), 103.

54. Josef Froberger and Stephan Berghoff, *Nacht über Russland. Der Kampf der Bolschewisten gegen das Christentum* (Cologne: Gilde, 1930); Friedrich Muckermann, *Der Bolschewismus droht* (Cologne: Katholische Tat, 1931).

55. "Referat über die Bolschewismusgefahr, Fulda [6.8.1930]," in Hürten, *Akten*, 1067–74.

56. Kardinal Faulhaber, "Der Religionskrieg in Rußland eine Zeit- und Weltfrage," in *Rufende Stimmen in der Wüste der Gegenwart. Gesammelte Reden, Predigten, Hirtenbriefe*, ed. Kardinal Faulhaber (Freiburg: Herder, 1931), 22.

57. "Lettre Pius' XI to Cardinal Basilius Pompili," *Acta Apostolicae Sedis* 22 (1930), 80–93, retrieved 4 June 2021 from http://www.vatican.va/archive/aas/documents/AAS-22-1930-ocr.

pdf; Philippe Chenaux, *L'Église catholique et le communisme en Europe 1917–1989: de Lénine à Jean-Paul II* (Paris: Cerf, 2009), 86–88.

58. Pius XI, *Divini Redemptoris*, Encyclical Letter, 19 March 1937, retrieved 4 June 2021 from http://www.vatican.va/content/pius-xi/en/encyclicals/documents/hf_p-xi_enc_19370319_divini-redemptoris.html, § 14, §16.

59. Pius XI, *Quas Primas*, Encyclical Letter, 12 November 1925, retrieved 4 June 2021 from http://www.vatican.va/content/pius-xi/en/encyclicals/documents/hf_p-xi_enc_11121925_quas-primas.html, § 24.

60. Faulhaber, "Religionskrieg," 22.

61. Friedrich Muckermann, "Die katholische Bewegung im Deutschland der Gegenwart," in *Deutscher Geist. Kulturdokumente der Gegenwart*, ed. Carl Langer and Ernst Adolf Dreyer (Leipzig: Voigtländer, 1933), 68.

62. Ibid., 66. As a matter of fact, there was occasional cooperation between Catholics and Protestants in the field of anti-Communist propaganda, for example, in the *Bund zum Schutz der abendländischen Kultur* (League for the Protection of Occidental Culture), founded in 1930. On this and on the broader context, see Stéphanie Roulin, *Un credo anticommuniste. La Commisson Pro Deo de l'Entente internationale anticommuniste ou la dimension religieuse d'un combat politique (1924–1945)* (Lausanne: Antipodes, 2010), 175–96.

63. Lucia Scherzberg, *Kirchenreform mit Hilfe des Nationalsozialismus. Karl Adam als kontextueller Theologe* (Darmstadt: Wissenschaftliche Buchgesellschaft, 2001); an overview of the political options in German right-wing Catholicism in the Weimar period can be found in Reinhard Richter, *Nationales Denken im Katholizismus der Weimarer Republik* (Münster: Lit, 2000).

64. The work was published in 1925 in a second edition of the Catholic Academic Association's series of publications (*Schriftenreihe des katholischen Akademikerverbandes*). All of the following citations are taken from the second edition of the reprint from 1954: Carl Schmitt, *Römischer Katholizismus und politische Form*, 2nd ed. (Stuttgart: Klett-Cotta, 2002).

65. Ibid., 31–32.

66. Ibid., 43.

67. Ibid., 23–24.

68. Ibid., 39.

69. Ibid., 31.

70. Klaus Breuning, *Die Vision des Reiches. Deutscher Katholizismus zwischen Demokratie und Diktatur (1929–1934)* (Munich: Kösel, 1969); Weiß, *Kulturkatholizismus*, 232–43.

71. Friedrich Muckermann, *Der Mönch tritt über die Schwelle. Betrachtungen über die Zeit* (Berlin: Etthofen, 1932), 140; see also Weiß, *Kulturkatholizismus*, 232.

72. It is clear that there was no space for Protestantism in such a state; nevertheless, even for the proponents of the *Reichstheologie* the anti-Protestant outcome was less important than the anti-modern one. On the relationship between the Catholic *Reichstheologie* and conservative movements within Protestant theology, see Breuning, *Vision*, 131–50.

73. Robert Grosche, "Die Grundlagen einer christlichen Politik der deutschen Katholiken," *Die Schildgenossen. Katholische Zweimonatsschrift* 13 (1933–34): 48.

74. Ibid., 52; on Grosche see: Richard Goritzka, *Der Seelsorger Robert Grosche (1888–1967). Dialogische Pastoral zwischen Erstem Weltkrieg und Zweitem Vatikanischen Konzil* (Würzburg: Seelsorge Echter, 1999).

75. Breuning, *Vision*, 225–35.

76. On this meeting, the so-called third *Soziologische Sondertagung des Katholischen Akademikerverbandes*, see Ibid., 207–11; Weiß, *Kulturkatholizismus*, 234–36; Marcel Albert, *Die Benediktinerabtei Maria Laach und der Nationalsozialismus* (Paderborn: Schöningh, 2004), 71–91.

77. Quoted in Wilhelm Spael, *Das katholische Deutschland im 20. Jahrhundert. Seine Pionier- und Krisenzeiten 1890–1945* (Würzburg: Echter, 1964), 309.

78. Franz von Papen, "Zum Reichskonkordat," *Der katholische Gedanke* 6 (1933): 335; see Breuning, *Vision*, 211.

79. See the classic work, unsurpassed to this day, by Ernst-Wolfgang Böckenförde, "Der deutsche Katholizismus im Jahre 1933. Eine kritische Betrachtung," in *Kirche und christlicher Glaube in den Herausforderungen der Zeit. Beiträge zur politisch-theologischen Verfassungsgeschichte 1957–2002*, ed. Ernst-Wolfgang Böckenförde (Münster: Lit, 2004), 115–42.

80. Kösters, *Kulturkampf*, 75; Manfred Gailus and Armin Nolzen, eds., *Zerstrittene 'Volksgemeinschaft.' Glaube, Konfession und Religion im Nationalsozialismus* (Göttingen: Vandenhoeck & Ruprecht, 2011).

81. "Hirtenbrief des deutschen Episkopats, 3. Juni 1933," in *Akten deutscher Bischöfe über die Lage der Kirche 1933–1945*, Vol. 1, ed. Bernhard Stasiewski (Mainz: Matthias Grünewald, 1968), 241.

82. Ibid.

83. Hürten, *Katholiken*, 272–98; Christoph Kösters and Mark Edward Ruff, eds., *Die katholische Kirche im Dritten Reich. Eine Einführung* (Freiburg: Herder, 2011).

84. On the biographical details, see: Marcel Albert, "Robert Grosche. Stadtdechant von Köln (1888–1967)," in *Portal Reihnische Geschichte*, retrieved 4 June 2021 from http://www.rheinische-geschichte.lvr.de/Persoenlichkeiten/robert-grosche/DE-2086/lido/57c6d803506a94.74616954.

85. Raphael Gross, *Carl Schmitt und die Juden. Eine deutsche Rechtslehre* (Frankfurt am Main: Suhrkamp, 2000).

86. Mehring, *Schmitt*, 378–80.

87. Carl Schmitt, *Glossarium. Aufzeichnungen der Jahre 1947–1951*, ed. Eberhard von Medem (Berlin: Duncker & Humblot, 1991), 165; see Bernd Wacker, ed., *Die eigentlich katholische Verschärfung . . . Konfession, Theologie und Politik im Werk Carl Schmitts* (Munich: Wilhelm Fink, 1994).

88. Schmitt, *Glossarium*, 283.

89. See Joachim Köhler and Damian van Melis, eds., *Siegerin in Trümmern. Die Rolle der katholischen Kirche in der deutschen Nachkriegsgesellschaft* (Stuttgart: Kohlhammer, 1998).

90. Frank Bösch, *Die Adenauer-CDU. Gründung, Aufstieg und Krise einer Erfolgspartei 1945–1969* (Stuttgart: DVA, 2001); Maria Mitchell, *The Origins of Christian Democracy: Politics and Confession in Modern Germany* (Ann Arbor: University of Michigan Press, 2012).

91. In the postwar era Robert Grosche, too, strongly supported the new Catholic-Lutheran understanding and strongly opposed a purely Catholic Party—such as the Center Party had been. See Robert Grosche, *Kölner Tagebuch 1944–46*, ed. Maria Steinhoff, 2nd. ed. (Cologne: Bachem, 1992), 123.

92. Kristian Buchna, *Ein klerikales Jahrzehnt? Kirche, Konfession und Politik in der Bundesrepublik während der 1950er Jahre* (Baden-Baden: Nomos, 2014).

93. Stefan Creuzberger and Dierk Hoffmann, eds., *"Geistige Gefahr" und "Immunisierung der Gesellschaft." Antikommunismus und politische Kultur in der frühen Bundesrepublik* (Munich: Oldenbourg, 2014).

Bibliography

Adam, Karl. *Das Wesen des Katholizismus*. Augsburg: Haas & Grabherr, 1924.

———. "Der moderne Mensch und der katholische Glaube." In *Glaube und Glaubenswissenschaft im Katholizismus. Vorträge und Abhandlungen*, edited by Karl Adam, 143–65. Rottenburg: Bader, 1923.

———. "Die Theologie der Krisis." *Hochland* 23, no. 2 (1926): 271–86.

Albert, Marcel. *Die Benediktinerabtei Maria Laach und der Nationalsozialismus.* Paderborn: Schöningh, 2004.

———. "Robert Grosche. Stadtdechant von Köln (1888–1967)." In *Portal Reihnische Geschichte.* Retrieved 4 June 2021 from http://www.rheinische-geschichte.lvr.de/Persoenlichkeiten/robert-grosche/DE-2086/lido/57c6d803506a94.74616954.

———. *"Zwecks wirksamer Verteidigung und Vertretung der katholischen Weltanschauung." Der Katholische Akademikerverband 1913–1938/39.* Cologne: Erzbischöfliche Diözesan- und Dombibliothek, 2010.

Arnold, Claus. *Kleine Geschichte des Modernismus.* Freiburg: Herder, 2007.

Ball, Hugo. "Die Folgen der Reformation." In *Hugo Ball. Die Folgen der Reformation / Zur Kritik der deutschen Intelligenz (= Sämtliche Werke und Briefe, Bd. 5),* edited by Hans Dieter Zimmermann, 7–134. Göttingen: Wallstein, 2005.

Baumeister, Martin. *Parität und katholische Inferiorität. Untersuchungen zur Stellung des Katholizismus im Deutschen Kaiserreich.* Paderborn: Schöningh, 1987.

Böckenförde, Ernst-Wolfgang. "Der deutsche Katholizismus im Jahre 1933. Eine kritische Betrachtung." In *Kirche und christlicher Glaube in den Herausforderungen der Zeit. Beiträge zur politisch-theologischen Verfassungsgeschichte 1957–2002,* by Ernst-Wolfgang Böckenförde, 115–42. Münster: Lit, 2004.

Bösch, Frank. *Die Adenauer-CDU. Gründung, Aufstieg und Krise einer Erfolgspartei 1945–1969.* Stuttgart: DVA, 2001.

Breuning, Klaus. *Die Vision des Reiches. Deutscher Katholizismus zwischen Demokratie und Diktatur (1929–1934).* Munich: Kösel, 1969.

Buchna, Kristian. *Ein klerikales Jahrzehnt? Kirche, Konfession und Politik in der Bundesrepublik während der 1950er Jahre.* Baden-Baden: Nomos, 2014.

Burleigh, Michael. *Earthly Powers. The Clash of Religion and Politics in Europe from the French Revolution to the Great War.* London: Harper Collins, 2005.

Chappel, James. *Catholic Modern. The Challenge of Totalitarianism and the Remaking of the Church.* Cambridge, MA: Harvard University Press, 2018.

Chenaux, Philippe. *L'Église catholique et le communisme en Europe 1917–1989: de Lénine à Jean-Paul II.* Paris: Cerf, 2009.

Creuzberger, Stefan, and Dierk Hoffmann, eds. *"Geistige Gefahr" und "Immunisierung der Gesellschaft." Antikommunismus und politische Kultur in der frühen Bundesrepublik.* Munich: Oldenbourg, 2014.

Dahlmeier, Manfred. *Carl Schmitt und der deutsche Katholizismus 1888–1936.* Paderborn: Schöningh, 1998.

Damberg, Wilhelm. "'Radikal katholische Laien an die Front.' Beobachtungen zur Idee und Wirkungsgeschichte der Katholischen Aktion." In *Siegerin in Trümmern. Die Rolle der katholischen Kirche in der deutschen Nachkriegsgesellschaft,* edited by Joachim Köhler and Damian van Melis, 142–60. Stuttgart: Kohlhammer, 1998.

Duhr, Bernhard. "Der Bolschewismus. Übersicht." *Stimmen der Zeit* 97 (1919): 133–48.

———. "Die Wurzeln des Bolschewismus. Eine ernste Mahnung auch für uns." *Stimmen der Zeit* 99 (1920): 402–13.

Faulhaber, Michael von. "Der Religionskrieg in Rußland eine Zeit- und Weltfrage." In *Rufende Stimmen in der Wüste der Gegenwart. Gesammelte Reden, Predigten, Hirtenbriefe,* edited by Michael von Faulhaber, 14–25. Freiburg: Herder, 1931.

Fleischmann-Bisten, Walter. *Der Evangelische Bund in der Weimarer Republik und im sogenannten Dritten Reich.* Frankfurt am Main: Peter Lang, 1989.

Forster, Bernhard. *Adam Stegerwald (1874–1945). Christlich-nationaler Gewerkschafter, Zentrumspolitiker, Mitbegründer der Unionsparteien.* Düsseldorf: Droste, 2003.

Froberger, Josef, and Stephan Berghoff. *Nacht über Russland. Der Kampf der Bolschewisten gegen das Christentum.* Cologne: Gilde, 1930.

Gailus, Manfred, and Armin Nolzen, eds. *Zerstrittene 'Volksgemeinschaft.' Glaube, Konfession und Religion im Nationalsozialismus*. Göttingen: Vandenhoeck & Ruprecht, 2011.
Generalsekretariat des Zentralkomitees der deutschen Katholiken, ed. *Bericht über den Katholikentag in Magdeburg, 5. bis 9. September 1928*. Paderborn: Bonifacius, 1928.
Gerber, Stefan. *Pragmatismus und Kulturkritik. Politikbegründung und politische Kommunikation im Katholizismus der Weimarer Republik (1918–1925)*. Paderborn: Schöningh, 2016.
Goritzka, Richard. *Der Seelsorger Robert Grosche (1888–1967). Dialogische Pastoral zwischen Erstem Weltkrieg und Zweitem Vatikanischen Konzil*. Würzburg: Seelsorge Echter, 1999.
Grosche, Robert. "Die Grundlagen einer christlichen Politik der deutschen Katholiken." *Die Schildgenossen. Katholische Zweimonatsschrift* 13 (1933–34): 47–52.
———. *Kölner Tagebuch 1944–46*. Edited by Maria Steinhoff. 2nd ed. Cologne: Bachem, 1992.
Gross, Raphael. *Carl Schmitt und die Juden. Eine deutsche Rechtslehre*. Frankfurt am Main: Suhrkamp, 2000.
Große Kracht, Klaus. "Campaigning Against Bolshevism: Catholic Action in Late Weimar Germany." *Journal of Contemporary History* 53, no 3 (2018): 550–73.
———. *Die Stunde der Laien? Katholische Aktion in Deutschland im europäischen Kontext*. Paderborn: Schöningh, 2016.
Gruber, Herbert. *Friedrich Muckermann, S.J. 1883–1946*. Mainz: Grünewald, 1993.
Heitzer, Horst W[alter]. "Deutscher Katholizismus und 'Bolschewismusgefahr' bis 1933." *Historisches Jahrbuch* 113 (1993): 355–87.
Hürten, Heinz, ed. *Akten deutscher Bischöfe über die Lage der Kirche 1918–1933*, Vol. 1: 1918–1925 and Vol. 2: 1926–1933. Paderborn: Schöningh, 2007.
———. *Deutsche Katholiken 1918 bis 1945*. Paderborn: Schöningh, 1992.
Jones, Larry Eugene. "Catholics on the Right: The Reich Catholic Committee of the German National People's Party, 1920–33." *Historisches Jahrbuch* 126 (2006): 221–67.
Kaiser, Ulrich. *Realpolitik oder antibolschewistischer Kreuzzug? Zum Zusammenhang von Rußlandbild und Rußlandpolitik der deutschen Zentrumspartei 1917–1933*. Frankfurt am Main: Peter Lang, 2005.
Keller, Michael. *Katholische Aktion. Eine systematische Darstellung ihrer Idee*. Osnabrück: Jonscher, 1933.
Kittler, Manfred. "Konfessioneller Konflikt und politische Kultur in der Weimarer Republik." In *Konfessionen im Konflikt. Deutschland zwischen 1800 und 1970: ein zweites konfessionelles Zeitalter*, edited by Olaf Blaschke, 243–96. Göttingen: Vandenhoeck & Ruprecht, 2002.
Köhler, Joachim, and Damian van Melis, eds. *Siegerin in Trümmern. Die Rolle der katholischen Kirche in der deutschen Nachkriegsgesellschaft*. Stuttgart: Kohlhammer, 1998.
Kösters, Christoph. "'Kulturkampf' im Dritten Reich—Zur Deutung der Konflikte zwischen NS-Regime und katholischer Kirche im deutschen Episkopat." In *Die Kirche und die Verbrechen im nationalsozialistischen Staat*, edited by Thomas Brechenmacher and Harry Oelke, 67–112. Göttingen: Wallstein, 2011.
Kösters, Christoph, and Mark Edward Ruff, eds. *Die katholische Kirche im Dritten Reich. Eine Einführung*. Freiburg: Herder, 2011.
Krieg, Robert Anthony. *Karl Adam. Catholicism in German Culture*. South Bend: University of Notre Dame Press, 1992.
Laien an die Front! Praktische Gedanken zur Katholischen Aktion. Referate gehalten auf dem Oberhessischen Katholikentag in Ilbenstadt 1928. Dülmen: Laumann, 1928.
Langner, Albrecht. "Weimarer Kulturkatholizismus und interkonfessionelle Probleme." In *Probleme des Konfessionalismus in Deutschland seit 1800*, edited by Anton Rauscher, 71–115. Paderborn: Schöningh, 1984.
"Lettre Pius' XI to Cardinal Basilius Pompili." *Acta Apostolicae Sedis* 22 (1930): 80–93. Retrieved 4 June 2021 from http://www.vatican.va/archive/aas/documents/AAS-22-1930-ocr.pdf.

Lexikon für Theologie und Kirche. 2nd ed. Vol. 5. Freiburg: Herder, 1957–1968.
Mehring, Reinhard. *Carl Schmitt, Aufstieg und Fall. Eine Biographie.* Munich: Beck, 2009.
Menge, Gisbert. "Bilder aus dem ersten Jahrzehnt des Winfriedbundes." *Die Friedensstadt* 3 (1930): 1–12.
Mitchell, Maria. *The Origins of Christian Democracy: Politics and Confession in Modern Germany.* Ann Arbor: University of Michigan Press, 2012.
Muckermann, Friedrich. *Der Bolschewismus droht.* Cologne: Katholische Tat, 1931.
———. *Der Mönch tritt über die Schwelle. Betrachtungen über die Zeit.* Berlin: Etthofen, 1932.
———. "Die katholische Bewegung im Deutschland der Gegenwart." In *Deutscher Geist. Kulturdokumente der Gegenwart,* edited by Carl Langer and Ernst Adolf Dreyer, 63–68. Leipzig: Voigtländer, 1933.
———. *Im Kampf zwischen zwei Epochen. Lebenserinnerungen.* Mainz: Grünewald, 1973.
———. *Katholische Aktion.* Munich: Ars Sacra, 1929.
———. *Wollt ihr das auch? Wie ich den Bolschewismus in Rußland erlebte.* Düsseldorf: Verband der katholischen Jünglings-Vereinigungen Deutschlands, 1920.
Nell-Breuning, Oswald von. "Integralismus." In *Lexikon für Theologie und Kirche,* 2nd ed., Vol. 5, 717–19. Freiburg: Herder, 1957–68.
Papen, Franz von. "Zum Reichskonkordat." *Der katholische Gedanke* 6 (1933): 331–36.
Pollard, John. "Pius XI's Promotion of the Italian Model for Catholic Action in the World Wide Church." *Journal of Ecclesiastical History* 63 (2012): 758–84.
Pope Pius X. *E supremi apostolatus cathedra.* Encyclical Letter. Retrieved 4 June 2021 from http://www.vatican.va/content/pius-x/en/encyclicals/documents/hf_p-x_enc_04101903_e-supremi.html.
———. *Pascendi dominici gregis.* Encyclical Letter, 9 August 1907. Retrieved 4 June 2021 from http://www.vatican.va/content/pius-x/en/encyclicals/documents/hf_p-x_enc_19070908_pascendi-dominici-gregis.html.
Pope Pius XI. *Divini Redemptoris.* Encyclical Letter, 19 March 1937. Retrieved 4 June 2021 from http://www.vatican.va/content/pius-xi/en/encyclicals/documents/hf_p-xi_enc_19370319_divini-redemptoris.html.
———. *Mortalium animos.* Encyclical Letter, 1 June 1928. Retrieved 4 June 2021 from http://w2.vatican.va/content/pius-xi/en/encyclicals/documents/hf_p-xi_enc_19280106_mortalium-animos.html.
———. *Quas Primas.* Encyclical Letter, 12 November 1925. Retrieved 4 June 2021 from http://www.vatican.va/content/pius-xi/en/encyclicals/documents/hf_p-xi_enc_11121925_quas-primas.html.
Poulat, Émile. *Intégrisme et catholicisme integral.* Paris: Casterman, 1969.
Przywara, Erich, ed. *Ringen der Gegenwart. Gesammelte Aufsätze 1922–1927.* Augsburg: Filser, 1929.
Richter, Reinhard. *Nationales Denken im Katholizismus der Weimarer Republik.* Münster: Lit, 2000.
Rohls, Jan. *Protestantische Theologie der Neuzeit,* Vol. 2: *Das 20. Jahrhundert.* Tübingen: Mohr Siebeck, 1997.
Roulin, Stéphanie. *Un credo anticommuniste. La Commisson Pro Deo de l'Entente internationale anticommuniste ou la dimension religieuse d'un combat politique (1924–1945).* Lausanne: Antipodes, 2010.
Ruster, Thomas. *Die verlorene Nützlichkeit der Religion. Katholizismus und Moderne in der Weimarer Republik,* 2nd ed. Paderborn: Schöningh, 1997.
Scherzberg, Lucia. *Kirchenreform mit Hilfe des Nationalsozialismus. Karl Adam als kontextueller Theologe.* Darmstadt: Wissenschaftliche Buchgesellschaft, 2001.
Schmitt, Carl. *Glossarium. Aufzeichnungen der Jahre 1947–1951,* edited by Eberhard von Medem. Berlin: Duncker & Humblot, 1991.
———. *Römischer Katholizismus und politische Form,* 2nd ed. Stuttgart: Klett-Cotta, 2002.

Spael, Wilhelm. *Das katholische Deutschland im 20. Jahrhundert. Seine Pionier- und Krisenzeiten 1890–1945*. Würzburg: Echter, 1964.

Stasiewski, Bernhard, ed. *Akten deutscher Bischöfe über die Lage der Kirche 1933–1945*, Vol. 1: 1933–1934. Mainz: Matthias Grünewald, 1968.

Stock, Wiebke-Marie. *Denkumsturz. Hugo Ball. Eine intellektuelle Biographie*. Göttingen: Wallstein, 2012.

Straubinger, Johannes. *Christentum der Tat*. Stuttgart: Kepplerhaus, 1932.

Troeltsch, Ernst. "Die Krisis des Historismus." In *Ernst Troeltsch: Schriften zur Politik und Kulturphilosophie (1918–1923)*, *Ernst Troeltsch Kritische Gesamtausgabe*, Vol. 15, edited by Gangolf Hübinger and Johannes Mikuteit, 437–55. Berlin: De Gruyter, 2002.

Wacker, Bernd, ed. *Die eigentlich katholische Verschärfung . . . Konfession, Theologie und Politik im Werk Carl Schmitts*. Munich: Wilhelm Fink, 1994.

Weichlein, Siegfried. "Zwischenkriegszeit bis 1933." In *Handbuch der Religionsgeschichte im deutschsprachigen Raum, Bd. 6/1: 20. Jahrhundert—Epochen und Themen*, edited by Volkhard Krech and Lucian Hölscher, 61–112. Paderborn: Schöningh, 2015.

Weir, Todd H. "A European Culture War in the Twentieth Century? Anti-Catholicism and Anti-Bolshevism between Moscow, Berlin and the Vatican, 1922 to 1933." *Journal of Religious History* 39 (2015): 280–306.

———. ed. "Europe's Interwar Kulturkampf." Special issue, *Journal of Contemporary History* 53, no. 3 (2018): 489–661.

———. "Introduction: Comparing Nineteenth- and Twentieth-Century Culture Wars." *Journal of Contemporary History* 53, no. 3 (2018): 489–502.

Weiß, Otto. *Kulturkatholizismus. Katholiken auf dem Weg in die deutsche Kultur 1900–1933*. Regensburg: Friedrich Pustet, 2014.

Wust, Peter. "Die Rückkehr des deutschen Katholizismus aus dem Exil." In *Die Rückkehr aus dem Exil. Dokumente der Beurteilung des deutschen Katholizismus der Gegenwart*, edited by Karl Hoeber, 16–35. Düsseldorf: Schwann, 1926.

Chapter Three

THE REVOLUTION OF 1918/19

A Traumatic Experience for German Protestantism

Benedikt Brunner
Translated by Jeffrey Verhey

Understanding how crises alter attitudes, goals, and, ultimately, perceptions of reality is essential to making sense of the conflicted self-understandings of German Protestantism in the Weimar Republic.[1] The Revolution of 1918–19, coming on the heels of war and national defeat, had a traumatic impact on German Protestant leadership. To explain why this was the case, I begin by focusing on the Protestant Church and the relationship between church and state in the German Empire. This background is necessary in order to show why the German Revolution of 1918–19 and the end of the governance of the regional churches by its territorial rulers (*landesherrliches Kirchenregiment*) proved so traumatic. I then examine immediate reactions to the Revolution and highlight the centrality of the concept of the *Volkskirche*, the people's church, to which all—at least in theory—belonged and which sought to exert influence on state and society. I intend to provide an *intellectual history* of Protestant self-understandings. As Protestants could not agree on how to properly define the role of the Church in the Weimar Republic, I accordingly concentrate on the battles over how to interpret the concept of the *Volkskirche*. I close with a brief reflection on the consequences of these experiences.[2]

The Protestant Church in the "Holy Protestant Empire of the German Nation" through the End of World War I

An understanding of the position the Protestant churches occupied in the German Empire is necessary to understand why the experience of the Revolution proved traumatic to so many Protestant church officials. First, however, it needs to be pointed out that much previous research on the relationship between Protestantism and the German state, meaning primarily the Prussian state, is not free of certain clichés, which can be subsumed primarily under the heading of the coalition of the "throne and altar."[3] Furthermore, historians have all too often accepted the statements of church leaders and leading religious personalities as reflecting the views of all of Protestantism.

Second, the roots of the relationship between the Protestant Church and the state lie in the Reformation. The transfer of the Church governance to the Protestant princes as "emergency bishops" laid the foundation for a development in which the princes took on the role of a *summus episcopus*, that is, the principal bishop or archbishop in a diocese.[4] The course of events in the nineteenth century weakened the role of the princes—and thus also of the consistories.[5] The founding of the German Empire in 1870–71 thus represented a historic break. The Prussian king, who was at the same time the ruler of the large Prussian Regional Church, became the German Kaiser. Thus, he became an important figure of identification and veneration for Protestants throughout all of Germany.

In the following, I would like to briefly discuss some of the catchwords, the key concepts that can be considered to have shaped "Wilhelmine" Protestantism. To begin with, the nation-state, the state in which one lived after the foundation of the German Empire, was welcomed by many Protestants with great enthusiasm.[6] "New Lutheranism" (*Neuluthertum*) developed the idea of a "Christian state." For "New Lutheran" Protestant theorists—Theodor Kliefoth, Otto Karsten Krabbe—the unity of the church and the state was both highly desirable and an ideal which guided their actions.[7] Conservative Christianity gradually became and indeed "so successfully" nationalist that in the words of Kurt Nowak, "it is today no longer natural to remember the historical difficulties in bringing together conservative Protestantism and the nation."[8]

Characteristic of the Protestantism of that time was multiple internal conflicts that made it extremely difficult for one branch to assert its dominance over another.[9] A prime example of this was disputes over the Apostles' Creed, its historical authenticity, and its place in the liturgy that became so charged in the nineteenth and early twentieth centuries that the Prussian Church leadership carried out disciplinary measures against liberal clergy.[10] Another core problem was the handling of the social question. More and more workers were leaving the Church, a reality that belied the Church's self-understanding as a *Volkskirche* that aimed to integrate all social classes in society.

The significance of the term *Volkskirche* for modern Protestant self-understanding cannot be overestimated. Friedrich Mahling (1865–1933), who published systematic reflections on the concept right before the outbreak of World War I, made a distinction between *Volkskirche* in the empirical sense, that is, the church which actually existed, and a *Volkskirche* in the ideal and aspirational sense.[11] He believed that the key to the *Volkskirche* lay in the structure of the Church. Unlike a sect or even a missionary church, one becomes a member by being baptized as an infant. Because of this, the *Volkskirche* according to Mahling took on the enormously important task of education. Religious education conducted by the state was thus an important characteristic of its identity.[12] Closely linked to this was the state support given to the *Volkskirche*. Such assistance, however, did not mean that the Protestant Church was to become a state church. But it was indispensable if one wanted to speak of a *Volkskirche* at all.[13]

Of particular significance after World War I was another feature cited by Mahling:

> The *Volkskirche* provides the state with the highest moral ideas, which the state can use as the basis for its legislation, with the highest moral standards, which the state can use to improve the moral inventory of the people, and with the highest moral goals, which the state as a cultural body can use to guide the people.[14]

He continued:

> Here is where the work of the *Volkskirche* must begin: its members must be so imbued with the spirit of Christ that they bring to expression the moral effects of this spirit in the life of the people, and in so doing help the state to codify its laws to an ever finer and more progressive moral spirit. *Thus the Volkskirche is the authority which, by living in the spirit of God, influences the state when the state undertakes the standardization of its moral and ethical principles and develops these into codified laws.*[15]

After the war and during the revolutionary turmoil of 1918 and 1919, this argument was eagerly taken up by many Protestants and modified to meet the circumstances. If we probe analytically the history of the *Volkskirche* during the Revolution, we will be better able to understand what many Protestants found so traumatic about the experiences of the German Revolution.

Revolution and Trauma:
The Conflict of Opinions over the Revolution

> The curtain has fallen. The game is over, the long cruel game of the World War. A semi-civilized people played the overture, in which there was an assassination. A highly civilized people, where money rules more than in any other

civilization on earth, organized the final act. The weapons are now silent, but the cruelty continues. The bells signaling peace are beginning to ring softly throughout Germany, the long-awaited bells. And yet they are not the ones we longed for. Those had a bright sound. The bells we hear today sound muffled, almost like death knells.[16]

These sentences came from the pen of the retired General Superintendent of Schleswig, Theodor Kaftan (1847–1932). They express the decidedly negative attitude of broad sections of Protestantism to the Revolution and the Versailles peace treaty.[17] However, one should not over-interpret the alarmism in such statements. In a letter from 17 November 1918 to his brother Theodor, Julius Kaftan (1848–1926) expressed himself rather differently. He was unaffected by the Revolution itself. As the university had been closed for three days, he had not been in Berlin during the "period of the shooting."[18] To be sure, there were meetings of the High Consistory, and here the members were concerned above all about the "uncertainty of their financial condition."[19] Even if the letter as a whole was most concerned with pragmatic considerations on how the Church should respond to the new situation, he acknowledged that:

> Now we are living in a time of chaos, and in vain one racks one's brain to imagine where possibly a *power* could be found to challenge the revolutionaries effectively. Who would have thought fourteen days ago that it would have been possible for us to be worried about very different things than about the terrible defeat our enemies have inflicted upon us! And yet so it is today—the inner distress is as great as the outer—and the outer distress is immediate and all-consuming.[20]

Kaftan's letter shows that there was no one single revolutionary experience in the late autumn of 1918, but that there were many individual and regional experiences and perspectives.[21] The timing of the events was also important. This becomes clear from another letter from Kaftan to his brother Theodor, this time from the middle of December 1918. In this letter, Kaftan expressed himself in far more drastic terms. One already has enough burdens—he found it difficult to find his way amidst all the "shame and disgrace," which, indeed, made it hard for him to work in peace or to even breathe.[22] He accused his brother of conflating and condemning militarism and bureaucracy; he himself rejected this idea:

> I have always believed and I still believe that that what our enemies rebuked as militarism was in fact the glory of our crown, the discipline and order of our people, the very foundation of our economic growth—it was a spirit that extended into our science and scholarship, it was the backbone of the new German Empire. . . . If there had been only one man who would have intervened with a firm hand, the revolution would not have taken place in Berlin. The fail-

ure took place at the top. There was no one there who could appeal successfully to the Kaiser's honor as an officer, as for example Bismarck was able to do in his day with the old Kaiser, when the Kaiser wanted to abdicate.[23]

Kaftan claimed that it was the Kaiser's "Easter Message" and his declaration from 7 April 1917, proclaiming he was going to reform the system of Prussian suffrage which had led to national ruin. He also made it clear that as a reaction to the present situation he had become even more Prussian and, indeed, was becoming more Prussian every day.[24] In a further letter, written during the Spartacus uprising in Berlin, Kaftan noted that even if one could hear the rattle and the noise of the machine guns in Steglitz, he personally had not yet experienced anything bad: "In contrast to Berlin it is wonderfully quiet out here."[25] He returned once again to the topic of the defeat and asked his brother whether it did not also leave him speechless that "with the destruction of Prussia the backbone of Germany and of the Protestant German Empire has been broken."[26]

An analysis of the correspondence between the two Kaftan brothers would certainly be a worthy task in its own right, especially given the significance of the two theologians for the Church of their time.[27] While Theodor Kaftan certainly sought pragmatic solutions and tried to adapt to the new conditions, strong backward-looking if not reactionary nostalgia prevailed within Julius, and these emotions were shaped and strengthened by his experiences of the Revolution in Prussia. He clearly rejected the new political system and remained attached to the "Protestant German Empire."[28] His sentiments reflect the huge difficulty so many conservative Protestants had in finding sympathy for the new democracy and in developing new confessional identities and self-understandings.[29] Discussions on these topics, which at times got out of control, often centered on the term *Volkskirche* in an illustration of how difficult it was at this time for Christians in the regional churches to take on the challenges of developing new identities.[30]

At different levels, church officials began to fight over how to interpret and react to the new circumstances. It was, for instance, no coincidence that the rapid rise of Otto Dibelius (1880–1967) in the Church hierarchy began at this time. Not only was he involved institutionally in key decisions, but he articulated these positions in numerous publications; the impact of which was by no means limited to Prussia.[31] For him, too, the primary impulse behind the debates on the Church's self-understanding was the Revolution:

> Then came 9 November 1918. The storm signal of the revolution rang out through the German states, through the German countryside. The Protestant churches of Germany, too, shook as a result of the shocks of those fateful days.

And in the hearts of those who cared deeply for their church the conviction flared up: now is also the beginning of a new era for the church! Now, finally, out of the elitist structures of earlier times a true, free, powerful and vigorous national *Volkskirche* must arise![32]

Dibelius was convinced that both the supporters and the opponents of the Revolution contributed to the spread of this demand for Church renewal. Supporters of the Revolution saw a chance—as with the institutions of the state—to build up the Church from the bottom up and thus to have the Church be a participant in accepting "the gift of a new spirit."[33] Opponents of the Revolution made the demand for a *Volkskirche* in order to save the Church "from destruction by the new spirit (*Geist*)."[34] Only "if the people find their church and the church their people," as Dibelius would characterize opponents' motivations, would it be possible to preserve the Church's heritage.[35] In this line of thought, organic ideas (along with the idea of the *Gemeinschaft*) played a prominent role, as churchmen like Dibelius underscored that they believed there to be a close connection between the church and its people.

Ironically, it was the anti-religious direction of the revolutionary government that ultimately helped along the development of a certain solidarity and unity among church circles, since for the Church it was now a "life and death" struggle.[36] As Dibelius noted:

> It is not surprising that they are preparing to fight! It is not surprising that the great minds from groups with quite different interests have shaken each other's hands and offered to work together! It is not surprising that a movement for a national, people's church has been formed, in all sorts of different places at the same time, with the same intentions, and filled with the same spirit![37]

In these sentences, Dibelius admittedly overstated the unity and the solidarity of the groups he described. Nevertheless, there was a broad consensus with regard to the *Volkskirche*, although definitions of it, inasmuch as one even tried to define it, could diverge considerably.[38] At any rate, the numbers Dibelius cited as evidence for his claims were impressive. According to Dibelius, in a short period over half a million Christians in Prussia had joined together and become members of a "*Volkskirche* association."[39]

The concept of the *Volkskirche*—in one form or another—was at the center of all discussions about the future, regardless of the direction and camp within the church to which one belonged.[40] Among liberal theologians, the term had a special prominence. Martin Rade (1857–1940) used his journal, *Christliche Welt. Evangelisches Gemeindeblatt für Gebildete aller Stände*, to popularize his idea of a *Volkskirche*.[41] In the December 1918 issue of the *Christlichen Welt*, Rade formulated his journal's position and the meaning and purpose of the *Volkskirche* Councils (*Volkskirchenräte*). He rejected a return to the system of state and regional churches (*Landeskirchen*) and argued instead that the time was ripe for a "free Protestant *Volkskirche*, in which Christian piety and Christian communal life would be better off than ever before."⁴² The *Volkskirche* Councils would be a focal point around which all the supporters could gather. The "minister's church" (*Pastorenkirche*) was to give way to the "lay church, [and] the consistory church was to give way to the congregational church."⁴³ When pursuing this goal at a church conference, Rade emphasized that it was important to present a united front. Following up on this article, he also published "Recommendations for the *Volkskirche*-Councils."⁴⁴ In listing his "final goals," he insisted that the *Volkskirche* was to retain a prominent position:

> 1. We want a "free Protestant *Volkskirche*," that is to say, a church which serves the whole of the German people, and which retains its autonomy vis-à-vis the state and enjoys the greatest possible independence from the state's laws and from the government.
>
> . . .
>
> 3. Whatever form the unity of the free Protestant people's church should take, this needs to be the result of discussions among all those called to participate. Furthermore, within the structure of the church there should be the widest possible scope for confessional, historical and *völkisch* diversity.⁴⁵

The strong emphasis on the separation of church and state became weaker in later years, especially among liberal intellectuals. But this openness for even the widest variety of intellectual trends and currents which could come together under the roof of the *Volkskirche* remained an integral part of theological discourse. Employing the terminology of Jörn Retterath, one can say that the discourse was moving in the direction of a pluralistic *Volkskirche*.⁴⁶

In 1919, the liberal Frankfurt theologian Erich Foerster (1865–1945) published an article, "Programmatic Sentences," in the *Christlichen Welt*, in which the concept of the *Volkskirche* diminished in importance. He was more concerned instead with practical matters—restructuring congregations, parish offices, church offices, and thus the Church itself.⁴⁷ An additional example of an early liberal analysis of the concept of the *Volkskirche* can be found in an essay by the Marburg systematic theologian Horst Stephan (1873–1954), in which he identified the *Volkskirche* and the *Sonderkirche* (a term often synonymous for him with the free churches, or *Freikirchen*) as the two possible forms of organization for Protestantism.⁴⁸ In the *Volkskirche*, he argued, "the religious organization is natural, it blends into the community and into the ethnicity and into the state . . . and somehow within this framework it [gives] personal or group peculiarities their space."⁴⁹ In contrast, the *Sonderkirche* was marked by structural peculiarities—what he called the "law of the structure of the organization"—that ultimately led to a multitude of *Sonderkirchen*.[50] In his opinion, Lutheran theology was closer to the *Volkskirche*, whereas the concept of the separate church came out of Calvinism and the Reformed tradition. Stephan argued in favor of an integrative approach toward the Church, an approach which was closest to the conceptual world of the *Volkskirche* since the present state of Protestantism made it necessary to have such a church structure:

> Before the war it seemed that the religious, clerical, and theological differences were enormous; they threatened to tear apart the regional churches (*Landeskirche*), which would have been a mistake similar to the path taken in America. If today in the hour of a general breakdown we go down this path, then the *Volkskirche* will be torn apart—indeed the very nature of German Protestantism as a *Volkskirche* will cease.[51]

In order to avoid this "mistake," everything had "to move in the direction of the *Volkskirche*."[52] One had to strive at the very least for "a structure with the character of a *Volkskirche*" as long as one could somehow hope for its continued existence, even if it was somewhat unclear what concretely was meant by the concept.[53] The confessional and national bias that constituted the concept of the *Volkskirche* thus became clear from such explanations.

When thinking about the structure of the Protestant Church, Theodor Kaftan, a Lutheran who firmly rejected such liberal positions, especially democratization efforts within the Church, also developed concepts along the lines of a *Volkskirche*. Kaftan was of the opinion that the structure of the Church up to the Revolution, whereby the Church was a state church, had outlived its usefulness. What should be pursued now was not the free church but a *Volkskirche* independent from the state (*staatsfreie Volkskirche*):

> Lutheranism and the *Volkskirche* are fundamentally kindred spirits. We, who love our people, naturally do not want the church to move away from them. For us Protestants, the love of the state is in our blood . . . and the state needs the *Volkskirche*. But not only the state needs the *Volkskirche*, so, too—and this is more important—does the church of Jesus Christ need the *Volkskirche*. The *Volkskirche* opens up new paths for the work of the church which no *Freikirche* can offer.[54]

Nevertheless, the state's support was not required in order to "preserve the structure of the church as a *Volkskirche*" because the "backbone of a *Volkskirche* [is] religious customs and traditions."[55] In his view, the cause of disintegration and decay was the growth of an "individual, personal Christianity" that had broken down the very foundations of the *Volkskirche*.[56] As the era of the state church had passed and the free church could only be the last option, the *Volkskirche*, now independent of the state (*staatsfrei*), remained the most desirable of all of options. What did he mean by that?

First of all, Kaftan emphasized that independent of the state did not mean stateless (*staatslos*). Instead, the Church had to have orderly legal relations with the state. The church tax was a central issue, for without it there could be no *Volkskirche*.[57] In other words, Kaftan assumed that the *Volkskirche* always had to have a positive relationship to the state. He concluded by calling for the Church to prepare for the future in three ways. First, the Church was to hold on carefully to the self-government it already possessed.[58] There was no talk of a democratization of the Church by Kaftan. Second, the Church was to become financially independent, even if only gradually. Third, congregations were to become the pillars of the Church by "enlightening through wisdom and power."[59]

In his afterword, published in the middle of December 1918, Kaftan made it clear what he thought of the "dictatorship imposed upon us by the socialist masses."[60] Because of this "unusual situation," the Church was called upon to exercise restraint, and it needed to support the "moderate Social Democrats" in their struggle against the radical groups within the party.[61] At present it was not clear if a state-free church was possible:

> We should hold on to the *Volkskirche* for as long as we can, for the good of the people as well as for the possibilities it offers for us to do our work. The necessary precondition for this, of course, is that the *Volkskirche* remains a church and is not transformed into a religious mishmash, as a result of devastating agitation in imitation of the political agitation.[62]

Kaftan believed that it would be simply wrong "to pass on to the next generation" that which they had inherited—to do so would be to go "from the frying pan into the fire."[63] His reorganization proposals, however, remained quite abstract. In later articles he often emphasized the dangers from any new organization of the Church.[64] He considered the adoption of proportional representation particularly dangerous, since this would further promote the formation of fractions within the Church. The "anticlerical Social Democrats" were another danger, as they had taken on governmental responsibility and would no longer have to grapple with an independent church organization.[65] What he was expressing here was his interest in influencing the state and society in the usual way as a *Volkskirche*, without having to be an advocate *per se* for the new state.

The traumatic experiences of the Revolution, vividly portrayed by Kaftan, brought about a need for orientation. As we have seen, he often couched the debate on the future direction of the Church as a dispute over the correct understanding of the *Volkskirche*. Having a close relationship to the state could, albeit under very different circumstances, still be seen as positive. Liberal forces believed that the time had come for the Church to assume democratic structures and organizations; in church reform they saw parallels to the wave of democratization at the state level. For conservative church officials, freedom from the state meant that control and authority over the Church, and as a result the Church's ability to shape its own affairs, had to be transferred completely to the Church itself—above all to the consistories. While doing this, conservatives wanted to maintain a clear distance from the "revolutionary" forces, however, without giving up their hopes of wielding influence on state and society.

The Question of the Separation of Church and State: How Political Catholicism Saved the Protestant Volkskirche

That the Revolution was perceived by the Church as a traumatic experience was in no small part because the revolutionary government had announced its intention of separating church and state. What had been feared appeared to have become bitter reality with the appointment of the new Prussian Minister for Culture and Education, Adolph Hoffmann (1858–1930). Hoffmann, a member of the USPD, shared this post with his more moderate colleague Konrad Haenisch (1876–1925) from the mainstream SPD (MSPD).[66] Hoffmann aimed to bring about the complete separation of church and state, a fundamental tenet of most Social Democrats.[67] Three of Hoffmann's decisions in particular provoked the church's indignation. On 16 November 1918, he decreed, without the consent of Haenisch, that all state funding previously given to the churches was to be cut off as of 1 April 1919. This state funding made up no less than half of the budget of the Protestant Regional Churches.[68] The effect of this declaration was, as will be shown below, devastating. A second decree would have made it easier for people to leave the Church, and a third decree would have eliminated "the teaching of religion as a proper subject in all of the Prussian schools" and do away with "the Christian character of the schools."[69]

Even though the socialist government's radical policy of drawing a line between the church and the state in Prussia was ultimately not carried out and the much more moderate Haenisch soon took control of the ministry, one should not underestimate the traumatic implications of these early conflicts. Most contemporaries, especially in the more conservative Church leadership in Prussia and elsewhere, remained skeptical of the new state. This attitude was not changed much by the new Weimar constitution, in which the separation of church and state was carried out "in a very moderate fashion."[70]

Wilhelm Kahl (1849–1932), who was elected to the Weimar National Assembly for the German People's Party (*Deutsche Volkspartei*) and who became involved quite early in the Berlin *Volkskirchendienst*, attempted in the last months of 1918 to calm tempers. He pointed out that it was not at all the case that the Church was defenseless against the threatened separation of church and state.[71] Those in political power "will take care not to take on in addition to the social struggle, a fight against religion and the churches they have little chance of winning."[72] The issue of how to deal with the Church (*Kirchenfrage*) could be solved only through a completely new structure for the Church, which had to be based "much more strongly than ever before on the principle of the congregation and the synod."[73] Until this was possible, in order to prepare the necessary measures he called on Protestants to trustingly place the work in the hands of the Protestant High Consistory (*Oberkirchenrat*) and the leadership of the general synod, especially as these had been shorn up by "trusted representatives of all ecclesiastical directions."[74] At stake was the "preservation" of the *Volkskirche*:

> Even after the separation of church and state the *Volkskirche* can not only continue to exist: it can also—if held together by the right spirit—unfold the full riches of its spiritual power more than would be possible under some other constitutional structure. The disintegration of Protestantism into numerous small free churches must be avoided.[75]

Kahl believed that the separation of church and the state was a test out of which blessings could arise.[76] Fellow liberal Heinrich Weinel (1874–1936) in his "Guiding Principles" also emphasized the potential for a positive restructuring of the Church. He rejected explicitly the French and the American model. The former would bring the Church to the brink of collapse and complete fragmentation, while the latter would sever the bond between the churches and national cultural and spiritual development.[77] According to Weinel, the model to be strived for was to be found in Switzerland, where a *Volkskirche* had replaced the old state church. He also provided guidance as to how this was to be implemented:

> The state, respecting the assets of the church, will gradually stop making payments to the church; the state will also give the church time to get its house in order by continuing to collect church taxes. The church remains as large as it was and continues to have the facilities it had. The state guarantees only the freedom of religious belief and the rights of minorities. Anyone who does not actively leave the church remains a member of the church. Of course, the terms for leaving the church are kept as simple as possible: one simply has to

notify the local civil registry office. All orientations and faiths are represented in the church and have equal rights.[78]

Such a turn could only be a blessing for the Church.[79] Admittedly, in such a model the Church would suffer very small losses, and even Weinel saw internal reforms as necessary so that a *Volkskirche* could emerge.

For a third example in this row of liberal voices, let us turn to Leopold Zscharnack (1877–1955), a Professor of Church History in Breslau. In his writing, Zscharnack called on the state not only to safeguard but also to promote the activities of the Church in the interests of its people, "whose future is intertwined with the future of religion and of morality and of the two caring communities."[80] He continued:

> We call for this as a moral obligation and the moral responsibility of the state. We believe this on the basis of that which the church has accomplished for the state up till now—which simply makes it impossible for the state to rape (*Vergewaltigung*) the church, and which instead requires that the church be upheld as a *Volkskirche*. As a *Volkskirche*, even if the church has been shattered by current events and has now taken on the organizational form of a free church, free from the state (*staatsfrei*)! This must remain the goal! Not a "*Vereinskirche*," with its special conditions for joining such as a public profession of faith or confirmation instead of the previously customary baptism as a child![81]

Zscharnack emphasized here the special value of the Church for the community, regardless of the form of government. Rejecting alternative forms of church organization, he emphasized that a *Volkskirche* was a church to which one belonged as a result of being baptized as a child. This suggests that the *Volkskirche* was a popular term in the early phase of the Weimar Republic because by using it one could claim as before that the Church was to exert influence on all of society without, however, having to take a position for or against the democratic state.

In 1919, Otto Dibelius joined this discussion with an essay on the separation of church and state which tellingly appeared in a series dedicated to the "Christian-Moral Reconstruction of the German Fatherland."[82] In this essay, he discussed relatively freely the close connection that had long existed between the church and state. He noted that some Protestants had called for the separation of these two spheres, the most prominent being Adolf Stöcker. But even this "combative . . . personality" was not successful in getting the idea accepted because "others were too concerned that a church that had separated itself from the state would soon cease to be a church comprised of all the people. Instead, the *Volkskirche* might become a shabby free church."[83] All the same, he noted, the revolutionary government had adopted this solution and it was to be expected that the separation of church and state was only a matter of time. After discussing the services that the Church carried out for the state, Dibelius proceeded to formulate his thoughts about the consequences that separating church and state would have for the Church. He stated programmatically that "the path to a new church . . . [had to] start by going down the old path" and that it did not make any sense to want something completely new to emerge.[84] It was important to preserve the legal continuity of the Church before and after the revolutionary period, so that the state did not imagine that the old Church simply no longer existed. Thus, attempts "with 'church councils' in the congregations to build a church 'from below'" were to be rejected.[85]

His essay closed with a call to rally around the Church "more fervently, more deliberately than before," for the Church was "the only power" able to "oppose effectively" the comprehensive secularization of society.[86] This is also the context in which Karl Holl (1866–1926) asked about the extent of the Protestant Church's duty to fight the separation of church and state. Whereas the Catholic bishops had declared they would do everything they could to fight the imminent separation, for the Protestants things were more complicated. First of all, the Protestant Church was still closely allied with the state, because the state, or rather the head of the state, was still the head of the Church, the supreme ecclesiastical authority. In Holl's opinion, it was quite clear that this relationship had to end, if for no other reason than to ensure that the state could not intervene in church life, as the sovereign had once been able to do.

The position of the Protestant Church was also fundamentally different from that of the Catholic Church. For the Protestant Church, the visible church was "not an end in itself; the church did not have to assert itself in all situations and to work continuously to strengthen its external power."[87] The only reason for the church's existence was to win souls for the kingdom of God. For this reason, it was not enough to just be a church joined voluntarily (*Freiwilligkeitskirche*) and whose members were only "a small group of the chosen."[88] One should welcome, therefore, a development similar to that in North America, because there the separation of church and state had not led to a separation of the church and the people.[89]

Arnold Hein, a member of the *Volkskirchlichen Evangelischen Vereinigung*, that is, the Prussian *Kirchenpolitische Mittelpartei*, expressed himself even more forcefully.[90] In his opinion, the decision that Protestants had to make for either the state church or the free church depended on the nature of the state:

> If the state is a cultural nation, a state representing the kingdom of God, then Protestants will choose the state church solution. If the state is a power state (*Machtstaat*), a constitutional state (*Rechtsstaat*), or a welfare state then Prot-

estants will choose the free church solution. The Christian idea of the state naturally leads to the state church; the atheistic idea of the state naturally leads to the free church.[91]

In this essay, Hein confessed frankly that 9 November 1918, had destroyed his "life's ideal," the Prussian state church in which the Church had been the soul of the state. In the new state, which he rejected as atheistic and hostile to the Church, there was nothing left to do but to demand the separation of church and state, albeit with the restriction "that we are sad about the state, for the state is losing its soul."[92] Hein's firm demand for a free church remained, however, an unusual one; indeed, he remained on the periphery of German Protestantism. In all the political and theological currents in the Church, there nonetheless remained a tendency to reject the new form of the state. With Hein, this willingness to reject the new state was combined with a rejection of the state church, which he viewed as the counterpart to the *Volkskirche*.

These few examples show how powerfully this process of negative self-definition proceeded. It was confessional differences—with the free churches, along with and in particular Catholicism—that helped shape new self-understandings. The Westphalian *Konsistorialrat* Friedrich Koch argued for striking a balance "between the rigid monarchical-hierarchical system of the Catholic Church and the political-democratic system of government by the people."[93] This was the path a modern Protestant church constitution had to take: "We believe in the religious and moral and national rebirth of our German people and empire after its external and internal collapse. The German Protestant church, the *Volkskirche* free from the state, will play an essential role in this internal recovery process."[94]

Koch's pointed remarks show that among Church leadership the view was widely shared that an energetic *Volkskirche* would contribute to strengthening Germany again, and, that the correct design and structure of the Church was of great importance in this process. The design and structure of the Catholic Church served here as a counterexample, as we will see when we look at the role of religion during the writing of Weimar-era church constitutions.[95] Of course, distinguishing oneself from the Catholic Church played a much less important role at this level. It was much more important to the protagonists who engaged in this debate to differentiate themselves clearly and unambiguously from any concepts redolent of the free churches.[96] Conceding to becoming a free church, regardless of the theological arguments one could have made for it, would have meant the loss of numerous privileges such as the Church's legal status as a "public body (*Körperschaft des öffentlichen Rechts*)."[97] Nevertheless, denominational prejudices persisted, as can easily be demonstrated by a look at the renowned encyclopedia, *Die Religion in Geschichte und Gegenwart*. According to it, the essence of Catholicism for Catholics lay in "the divine universality of that visible-invisible, natural-supernatural organism, which Christ as the Son of God incarnate had created, and in which he lives on in his mystical body. Catholicism means for Catholics abundance, wholeness, versatility, harmony, balance."[98] Admittedly, the tension between the Roman and the Catholic created a permanent crisis for the Catholic Church. Its future depended "on whether or not—and to what degree—it would be able to develop the Catholic ideal in a freer and purer form—be it inside or outside this circle—than has been possible up till now under papal jurisdiction."[99]

This resentment against Catholicism is quite remarkable, given that the Protestant regional churches were only able to continue to exist as institutions due to political Catholicism, that is, to the Center Party. Although Protestant church leaders believed the newly formed conservative party, the DNVP, represented their interests, this party was never going to be able to be part of a majority coalition in the Weimar National Assembly.[100] In fact, the work of the "Weimar Coalition" turned out, according to Jochen Jacke, to be overwhelmingly positive for the churches "because all of the concessions that the Center Party was able to wring out of its partners to safeguard the interests of the Catholic Church, for reasons of parity also had to be given automatically to the Protestant side."[101] The adoption of the Weimar constitution and its provisions concerning religion was not detrimental to the churches.[102] However, this did not in any way bring about a rapprochement with the Weimar state, with democracy, or even with confessional adversaries. And it did not lead to a rapprochement between Protestants and Catholics, either. The Protestant view of Catholicism was characterized not by gratitude but by continued resentments and prejudices dating back to the *Kulturkampf*. It was only after World War II that a rapprochement would take shape both culturally and politically.[103]

Conclusion: The Lingering Effects of Trauma

The road on which the Church was traveling toward adopting democracy was indeed long and progress towards it slow.[104] Because of the Church's reserve towards the Weimar state, *Volk* and *Volkstum* became in some ways a substitute for democracy. Among the consequences of the trauma must certainly be included the "poor performance" of Protestantism in 1933 and throughout the period of National Socialism.[105] Here, too, the Church's self-understanding as a *Volkskirche*—again with all the different connotations—played a central role. The "German Christians" (*Deutsche Christen*) saw in the *Volkskirche* an apt description of themselves as *völkisch*, racist, exclusive, jingoistic, and as a rule National Socialist. The German Christians were active in missionary work within Germany, and in this way they were active in the *Volkwerdung* of the churchgoers. The representatives of the German Christians wanted to participate in the National Socialist social transformations taking place, thereby taking on an important role both for themselves and for their church in shaping values and morals. One could show that there was widespread agreement between German Christians, the Pastors' Emergency League (*Pfarrernotbund*), and the Confessing Church (*Bekennende Kirche*) over their efforts and aspirations to redesign the imperfect structure of the Church of the interwar years according to the principles of the *Volkskirche*. They sought to bring about a closer union between the Church and the people in order for the Church to have a broader and more effective influence. The Confessing Church became for some of its representatives synonymous with the *Volkskirche*—as a way of differentiating themselves from the *völkisch* attitudes of the German Christians and their commitment to national cultural traditions. A free church solution was something that a majority of the members of the Confessing Church refused to consider.[106]

Only in the 1960s and the 1970s did the Protestant Church fully accept that it was a *Volkskirche* with a pluralistic self-understanding and a democratic foundation—and of course, one has to differentiate here between the East and West German experiences.[107] The church now adroitly started to define the *Volkskirche* as an "institution for freedom." This shift was nudged along by the broader intellectual developments of these years in which the Church aimed to be seen on par with the other institutions of German society, such as the political parties, the business associations, and the trade unions. In other words, in terms of its own self-understanding, the Church had developed into an intermediary between its members and the state. For a long time, the Catholic Church served primarily as a negative foil for the Protestants' own ecclesiastical identity. A productive ecumenism did not occur until the 1960s, at a time when the concept of the *Volkskirche* not only had changed fundamentally but began to lose its significance.

A *Volkskirche*, however, also suggests impartiality. One way to be impartial is to fight for things that are so abstract—such as for example, justice or peace—that they do not necessarily lead to a preordained political position. And that was what exactly made the concept of the *Volkskirche* so successful during the twentieth century: it was malleable. Protestant experiences during and after the Revolution of 1918–19, however traumatic, ensured that it remained so.

Benedikt Brunner is a Research Associate at the Leibniz-Institute for European History in Mainz. He is the author of *Volkskirche. Zur Geschichte eines evangelischen Grundbegriffs (1918–1960)* (2020) and "Von der Staats- zur Volkskirche. Reorganisation des kirchlichen Protestantismus in Weimar, 1918–1925," which appeared in *Zeitschrift für evangelisches Kirchenrecht*.

Notes

1. See Rüdiger Graf, *Die Zukunft der Weimarer Republik. Krisen und Zukunftsaneignungen in Deutschland, 1918–1933* (Munich: Oldenbourg, 2008); Moritz Föllmer, Rüdiger Graf, and Per Leo, "Einleitung: Die Kultur der Krise in der Weimarer Republik," in *Die "Krise" der Weimarer Republik. Zur Kritik eines Deutungsmusters*, ed. Moritz Föllmer and Rüdiger Graf (Frankfurt am Main: Campus-Verlag, 2005), 9–41, 9.
2. Hans Michael Heinig, "Deutungsmachtkonflikte als Deutungs- und Machtkonflikte im Religionsrecht," in *Deutungsmacht. Religion und belief systems in Deutungsmachtkonflikten*, ed. Philipp Stoellger (Tübingen: Mohr Siebeck, 2014), 411–27.
3. See Arnulf von Scheliha, *Protestantische Ethik des Politischen* (Tübingen: Mohr Siebeck, 2013), 124–32.
4. The roots of the close relationship between the state and the church are, of course, to be found in the so-called Constantinian turn. There is a good overview in Reinhold Zippelius, *Staat und Kirche. Eine Geschichte von der Antike bis zur Gegenwart* (Tübingen: Mohr Siebeck, 2009). On the Church regime, see Hans Walter Krumwiede, "Kirchenregiment, Landesherrliches," *Theologische Realenzyklopädie* 19 (1990): 59–68.
5. See Joachim Rogge, "Die außerordentliche Generalsynode von 1875 und die Generalsynodalordnung von 1876. Fortschritt und Grenzen kirchlicher Selbstregierung," in *Die Geschichte der Evangelischen Kirche der Union, Bd. 2: Die Verselbständigung der Kirche unter dem königlichen Summepiskopat (1850–1918)*, ed. Joachim Rogge and Gerhard Ruhbach (Leipzig: Evangelische Verlagsanstalt, 1994), 225–33. The role of the consistories in the history of the Protestant Church, especially in the modern era, has not received enough attention.
6. See Frank Becker, "Protestantische Euphorien. 1870/71, 1914 und 1933," in *Nationalprotestantische Mentalitäten. Konturen, Entwicklungslinien und Umbrüche eines Weltbildes*, ed. Manfred Galius and Hartmut Lehmann. (Göttingen: Vandenhoeck & Ruprecht, 2005), 19–44.
7. See Martin H. Jung, *Der Protestantismus in Deutschland von 1870 bis 1945* (Leipzig: Evangelische Verlagsanstalt, 2002), 46.
8. Kurt Nowak, *Geschichte des Christentums in Deutschland. Religion, Politik und Gesellschaft vom Ende der Aufklärung bis zur Mitte des 20. Jahrhunderts* (Munich: Beck, 1995), 160.
9. Nowak, *Geschichte*, 162.
10. See Julia Winnebeck, *Apostolikumsstreitigkeiten. Diskussionen um Liturgie, Lehre und Kirchenverfassung in der preußischen Landeskirche 1871–1914* (Leipzig: Evangelische Verlagsanstalt, 2016).
11. On further development of the concept of *Volkskirche* in the nineteenth century, see Tobias Sarx, "Zu den Ursprüngen des Begriffs 'Volkskirche' um 1800," *Archiv für Kulturgeschichte* 94 (2012): 113–45. Friedrich Mahling, "Volkskirche, Volksseele, Volksseelsorge, Volksmission," *Neue Kirchliche Zeitschrift* 25 (1914): 85–129, 85.
12. See Mahling, "Volkskirche," 91–95.
13. See Ibid., 96.
14. Ibid., 97.
15. Ibid., 98 (italics in the original).
16. Theodor Kaftan, *Was nun? Eine christlich-deutsche Zeitbetrachtung* (Leipzig: Dörffling & Franke, 1919), 5. See the review of this book by Wilhelm Schubring, [Untitled], *Protes-

tantenblatt 52 (1919): 309–10. See as well Martin Schian, "Was ist jetzt zu tun?" *Preußische Kirchenzeitung* 14 (1918): 388–89.

17. See Boris Barth, *Dolchstoßlegende und politische Desintegration. Das Trauma der deutschen Niederlage im Ersten Weltkrieg, 1914–1933* (Düsseldorf: Droste, 2003), 150–72.

18. Walter Göbell, ed., *Kirche, Recht und Theologie in vier Jahrzehnten. Der Briefwechsel der Brüder Theodor und Julius Kaftan, Vol. 2: 1910–1926* (Munich: Christian Kaiser Verlag, 1967), 674.

19. Göbell, *Kirche*, 674.

20. Ibid., 674.

21. See my forthcoming article: Benedikt Brunner, "An Unsettled Church: Experiences of the Revolution and Planning for the future in German Protestantism, 1918–20," in *Living the German Revolution of 1918–19: Expectations, Experiences, Responses*, ed. Christopher Dillon, Steven Schouten, and Kim Wünschmann.

22. Göbell, *Kirche*, 676.

23. Ibid.

24. On the significance of 1917, see Karl Kupisch, "Der Protestantismus im Epochenjahr 1917," in *Zeitgeist im Wandel, Vol. II: Zeitgeist der Weimarer Republik*, ed. Hans Joachim Schoeps (Stuttgart: Klett, 1968), 33–51.

25. Göbell, *Kirche*, 679.

26. Ibid.

27. Walter Göbell, "Der Kaftan-Briefwechsel. Ein Beitrag zur Geschichte von Theologie und Kirche," *Theologische Literaturzeitung* 81 (1956): 357–60; Hans-Peter Muus, "Zum Briefwechsel der Brüder Kaftan," *Zeitschrift für evangelisches Kirchenrecht* 15 (1970): 401–6.

28. See Günter Brakelmann, "Das 'Heilige evangelische Reich deutscher Nation,'" *Evangelische Kommentare* 4 (1971): 11–15.

29. See the chapters in Richard Ziegert, ed., *Die Kirchen und die Weimarer Republik*. Neukirchen-Vluyn: Neukirchener Verlag, 1994.

30. See the detailed and extensive work by Benedikt Brunner, *Volkskirche. Zur Geschichte eines evangelischen Grundbegriffs, 1918–1960* (Göttingen: Vandenhoeck & Ruprecht, 2020); among the older works, see especially Kurt Meier, "Die zeitgeschichtliche Bedeutung volkskirchlicher Konzeptionen im deutschen Protestantismus zwischen 1918 und 1945," in *Evangelische Kirche in Gesellschaft, Staat und Politik 1918–1945. Aufsätze zur kirchlichen Zeitgeschichte*, ed. Kurt Nowak (Berlin: Evangelische Verlagsanstalt, 1987), 16–39.

31. On Dibelius, see Hartmut Fritz, *Otto Dibelius. Ein Kirchenmann zwischen Monarchie und Diktatur. Mit einer Bibliographie der Veröffentlichungen von Otto Dibelius* (Göttingen: Vandenhoeck & Ruprecht, 1998); and Albrecht Beutel, "Otto Dibelius. Ein Promemoria zum 40. Todestag des preußischen Kirchenfürsten," in *Spurensicherung. Studien zur Identitätsgeschichte des Protestantismus*, ed. Albrecht Beutel (Tübingen: Mohr Siebeck, 2013), 226–44.

32. Otto Dibelius, "Volkskirchenräte, Volkskirchenbund, Volkskirchendienst," in *Revolution und Kirche. Zur Neuordnung des Kirchenwesens im deutschen Volksstaat*, ed. Friedrich Thimme and Ernst Rolffs (Berlin: Verlag von Georg Reimer, 1919), 201–13, 203. For some theoretical background regarding the historical relevance of trauma, see Dominick LaCapra, *History in Transit: Experience, Identity, Critical Theory* (Ithaca: Cornell University Press, 2004), 106–43.

33. Dibelius, "Volkskirchenräte," 203.

34. Ibid.

35. Ibid.

36. Ibid., 204. On the significance of the government's policy measures in regard to the church—above all in Prussia, see the next section.

37. Ibid.

38. There were thus extensive references to the concept of the *Volkskirche*, although there could be considerable differences among those using this term concerning the details and the particulars of the idea.

39. Dibelius, "Volkskirchenräte," 208.
40. On the various schools of thought within the Protestant Church in regard to church policy and politics, see Karl Kupisch, "Strömungen der Evangelischen Kirche in der Weimarer Republik," *Archiv für Sozialgeschichte* 11 (1971): 373–415.
41. On the *Christlichen Welt*, see Reinhard Schmidt-Rost, "Die Christliche Welt. Eine publizistische Gestalt des Kulturprotestantismus," in *Kulturprotestantismus. Beiträge zu einer Gestalt des modernen Christentums*, ed. Hans Martin Müller (Gütersloh: Mohn, 1992), 245–57.
42. [Martin] R[ade], "Was sollen, was wollen wir in der Christlichen Welt? Was soll, was will der Volkskirchen-Rat?" *Christliche Welt* 32 (1918): 498–501, here especially 499. See also the conservative interpretation, which refers explicitly to Adolf Stoecker, in Reinhard Mumm, "Die freie evangelische Volkskirche," *Die Reformation* 18 (1919): 250.
43. R[ade], "Was sollen, was wollen wir in der Christlichen Welt?" 499. On the theme of the minister's church ("Pastorenkirche") see Karl-Wilhelm Dahm, *Pfarrer und Politik. Soziale Position und politische Mentalität des deutschen evangelischen Pfarrerstandes zwischen 1918 und 1933* (Cologne: Westdeutscher Verlag, 1965), 57–60; see as well the thoughts from 1920 of Friedrich Paarmann, "Der Weg zur Volkskirche geht durch die Pastorenkirche," *Protestantenblatt* 53 (1920): 32–38.
44. See R[ade], "Was sollen, was wollen wir in der Christlichen Welt?" 500–1.
45. Ibid., 501. Rade notes here that these sentences have not been adopted by any organization; he is putting them forth as a basis for discussion.
46. See Jörn Retterath, *"Was ist das Volk?" Volks- und Gemeinschaftskonzepte der politischen Mitte in Deutschland 1917–1924* (Berlin: De Gruyter Oldenbourg, 2016).
47. See Erich Foerster, "Programmsätze über die neue Kirche," *Christliche Welt* 33 (1919): 349–52, 349: "The church is a *Volkskirche* in as much as its goal is to imbue all the people with the power of the Christian gospel. The church is a voluntary church inasmuch as it only names as members those who explicitly want to belong to it."
48. In a footnote, Stephan explained that he preferred this concept (*Sonderkirche*) to denomination or sect.
49. Horst Stephan, "Der kirchliche Neubau," *Christliche Welt* 32 (1918): 482.
50. Ibid., 482.
51. Ibid.
52. Ibid., 483.
53. Ibid.: "Thus a national, popular (*volkskirchlich*) church structure with a rich culture of different groups, for ritualistic, dogmatic, charitable or similar purposes. There are examples of this among our Danish neighbors. We must keep our ears open so we can hear all directions, in order to finally learn how we can combine unity with freedom, how we can create a truly great Protestant Church without a papacy of individual groups or a bureaucracy too devoted to schematic thinking."
54. Theodor Kaftan, *Die staatsfreie Volkskirche. Mit einem Nachwort aus der Mitte des Dezembers* (Leipzig: Dörffling & Franke, 1918), 17.
55. Kaftan, *Volkskirche*, 18.
56. Ibid.
57. Ibid., 19: "In a *Volkskirche* the church tax is essential. No *Volkskirche* can live on free contributions."
58. Ibid., 28.
59. Ibid., 29.
60. Ibid., 31.
61. Ibid.
62. Ibid., 32.
63. Ibid., 37.
64. See Theodor Kaftan, "Gefahren der kirchlichen Neubildung," *Allgemeine Evangelisch-Lutherische Kirchenzeitung* 52 (1919): 259–61; and also his article published earlier: Theodor

Kaftan, "Grundsätzliches zum Umbau der Kirche." *Allgemeine Evangelisch-Lutherische Kirchenzeitung* 52 (1919): 117–23.

65. Kaftan, "Gefahren," 260.

66. All ministries during this period were led by two ministers, one from the MSPD and one from the USPD. See Detlev J. K. Peukert, *Die Weimarer Republik. Krisenjahre der Klassischen Moderne* (Frankfurt am Main: Suhrkamp, 1987), 39–44.

67. See Ursula Büttner, *Weimar. Die überforderte Republik 1918–1933. Leistung und Versagen in Staat, Gesellschaft, Wirtschaft und Kultur* (Bonn: Bundeszentrale für politische Bildung, 2010), 270; Klaus Scholder, *Die Kirchen und das Dritte Reich, Vol. I: Vorgeschichte und Zeit der Illusionen 1918–1934* (Berlin: Siedler, 1977), 19–22; Jochen Jacke, *Kirche zwischen Monarchie. Der preußische Protestantismus nach dem Zusammenbruch von 1918* (Hamburg: Christians, 1976), 44–47; Heinz Hürten, *Die Kirchen in der Novemberrevolution. Eine Untersuchung zur Geschichte der Deutschen Revolution 1918/19* (Regensburg: Pustet, 1984), 40–73; as well as the two older studies by Günter Köhler, *Die Auswirkungen der Novemberrevolution von 1918 auf die altpreußische evangelische Landeskirche* (Berlin: Diss. Kirchliche Hochschule 1967), 17–37; and Claus Motschmann, *Evangelische Kirche und preußischer Staat in den Anfängen der Weimarer Republik. Möglichkeiten und Grenzen ihrer Zusammenarbeit* (Lübeck: Matthiesen, 1969), 27–32.

68. See Scholder, *Kirchen*, 20; for the statistics concerning the budget, see Paul Troschke, *Kirchliche Statistik I. Die kirchliche Organisation der Evangelischen, die materiellen Mittel des kirchlichen Lebens* (Berlin: Deutsches Evangelisches Kirchenbundamt, 1930), 94–95.

69. Scholder, *Kirchen*, 20. See also Adolph Hoffmann, "Neue Bahnen im preußischen Ministerium für Wissenschaft, Kunst und Volksbildung," *Pädagogische Zeitung* 47, no. 48 (1918): unpaginated.

70. Büttner, *Weimar*, 270. See Christoph Link, "Das Staatskirchenrecht im Geltungszeitraum der Weimarer Verfassung," in *Staat und Kirche in der neueren deutschen Geschichte. Fünf Abhandlungen*, ed. Christoph Link (Frankfurt am Main: Lang, 2000), 99–133. See also the case study by Karl-Heinrich Lütcke, "'Trennung von Staat und Kirche.' Konflikte und Entwicklungen in Berlin seit 1918." *Jahrbuch für Berlin-Brandenburgische Kirchengeschichte* 66 (2007): 129–56; and Benedikt Brunner, "Von der Staats- zur Volkskirche. Reorganisation des kirchlichen Protestantismus in Weimar, 1918–1925," *Zeitschrift für evangelisches Kirchenrecht* 65 (2020): 249–73.

71. [Wilhelm] Kahl, "Zur Trennung von Staat und Kirche," *Protestantenblatt* 51 (1918): 568–70, here especially 568; Wilhelm Kahl, "Trennung von Staat und Kirche," *Deutsche Juristen-Zeitung* 24 (1919): 124–25; Wilhelm Kahl, "Auf dem Weg zur Volkskirche," *Vossische Zeitung*, 7 August 1921.

72. Kahl, "Trennung," 568. Kahl was, of course, only half right here, as Adolph Hoffmann from the USPD as the Prussian Minister of Culture and Education certainly did seek a confrontation with the churches. See Jacke, *Kirche*, 45–47; Motschmann, *Kirche*, 27–62.

73. Kahl, "Trennung," 569.

74. Ibid., 570. The members of these organizations included, among others, Julius Kaftan, Hermann Kapler, Wilhelm Kahl, E. Evers, Otto Everling, W. Kraemer, H. Lisco, Friedrich Mahling, Wilhelm Philipps, G. Streiter, R. von Sydow, and Gottfried Traub.

75. Ibid., 570.

76. Thus he wrote a little bit later in Wilhelm Kahl, *Die deutsche Kirche im deutschen Staat* (Berlin: Weidmann, 1919), 16: "Here, too, we close our accounts with a good deal of hope. Strengthened and comforted with these wishes at Easter for the German church in the German state we step over the threshold into a new dark period!"

77. See Heinrich Weinel, "Die Volkskirche. Leitsätze für unsere Arbeit," *Christliche Freiheit für Thüringen und Sachsen*, 8 December 1918.

78. Ibid.

79. August Pfannkuche also came out in favor of the Swiss model in August Pfannkuche, *Die Baseler Kirchenverfassung als Vorbild für die Neuverfassung der deutsch-evangelischen Landeskirchen mit Einleitung und Anmerkungen* (Berlin: Hutten-Verlag, o. J. [1919]).

80. Leopold Zscharnack, *Trennung von Staat und Kirche* (Berlin: Verlag des Evangelischen Bundes, 1919), 46; Leopold Zscharnack, "Die Frage des landesherrlichen Kirchenregiments," *Volkskirche* 1 (1919): 113–17. See as well Th[eodor] Lieschke, *Die Trennung von Staat und Kirche und die evangelische Volkskirche* (Freiberg, 1919).

81. Zscharnack, *Trennung*, 46.

82. Otto Dibelius, *Die Trennung von Kirche und Staat. Eine Darstellung und ein Aufruf* (Berlin: Schriftenvertriebsanstalt, 1919). See Fritz, *Dibelius*, 79–89.

83. Dibelius, *Trennung*, 8.

84. Ibid., 18.

85. Ibid., 19.

86. Ibid., 28.

87. Karl Holl, "Wie weit reicht die Pflicht der evangelischen Kirche, gegen die Trennung von Kirche und Staat zu kämpfen?" *Die Reformation* 18 (1919): 36–37, 36.

88. Both quotes in Holl, "Pflicht," 36. See also [Peter] Meinhold, "Volkskirche oder heiliger Rest," in *Aufgaben und Kräfte der Kirche in der Gegenwart. Abhandlungen, D. Johannes Büchsel zum siebzigsten Geburtstag 19. September 1919 dargebracht* (Berlin: Warneck, 1919), 55–61.

89. Albert Dietrich expressed himself in similarly positive terms in Albert Dietrich, "Kirche und Staat," *Die Reformation* 18 (1919): 42–43; so, too, did—somewhat later—Eberhard Baumann, "Wesen, Wert und Verwirklichung einer wahren Volkskirche," *Deutsches Pfarrerblatt* 29 (1925): 835–37, 855–58.

90. See Eckhard Lessing, *Zwischen Bekenntnis und Volkskirche. Der theologische Weg der Evangelischen Kirche der altpreußischen Union (1922–1953) unter besonderer Berücksichtigung ihrer Synoden, ihrer Gruppen und der theologischen Begründungen* (Bielefeld: Luther-Verlag, 1992), 68–102.

91. Arnold Hein, "Kirche und Staat," *Preußische Kirchenzeitung* 15 (1919): 69–72, 70.

92. Ibid., 70.

93. Friedrich Koch, "Grundlagen und Grundfragen der neuen evangelischen Volkskirche," *Kirchliches Jahrbuch für die evangelischen Landeskirchen Deutschlands* 47 (1920): 47; Friedrich Koch, "Auf dem Weg zur neuen Volkskirche in Preußen (ältere Provinzen)," *Kirchliches Jahrbuch für die evangelischen Landeskirchen Deutschlands* 48 (1921): 1–24.

94. Koch, "Grundlagen," 47.

95. See Hans von Soden, *Das Ende der evangelischen Volkskirche Preußens? Betrachtungen zum Ausschußentwurf der neuen Kirchenverfassung für die altpreußische Landeskirche* (Berlin: Hutten-Verlag, 1922), 40.

96. There is a great deal of evidence for this. See Johannes Herz, "Volkskirche und Freikirche," *Volkskirche* 3 (1921): 255–57, reprinted in *Protestantenblatt* 54 (1921): 271–73; [G] Stokmann, "Der Aufruf für eine freie evangelische Volkskirche, von evangelisch-reformirtem [!] Standpunkt aus betrachtet," *Reformierte Kirchenzeitung* 69 (1919): 62–64; Th[eodor] Haarbeck, "Volkskirche oder Bekenntniskirche?" *Auf der Warte* 13 (1919): 2–3.

97. See Siegfried Weichlein, "Von der Staatskirche zur religiösen Kultur. Die Entstehung des Begriffs der 'Körperschaft des öffentlichen Rechts' mit Blick auf die Kirchenartikel der Weimarer Reichsverfassung," in *Baupläne der sichtbaren Kirche. Sprachliche Konzepte religiöser Vergemeinschaftung in Europa*, ed. Lucian Hölscher (Göttingen: Wallstein-Verlag, 2007), 90–116; Alfred Endrös, "Zur Entwicklung und Geschichte des Begriffs 'Körperschaft des öffentlichen Rechts,'" *Zeitschrift für Rechtsgeschichte*, Kan. Abt. 69 (1983): 292–324.

98. [Friedrich] Heiler, "Katholizismus I. Konfessionskundlich," *Die Religion in Geschichte und Gegenwart*, Vol. 3: I-Me (Tübingen: Mohr, 1929), 679–95, 694. See also Heinrich Her-

melink, *Katholizismus und Protestantismus in der Gegenwart vornehmlich in Deutschland* (Gotha: Perthes, 1924).

99. Heiler, "Katholizismus I," 694.

100. See Jacke, *Kirche*, 80–118. Cf. the early anticipation of common interest between Catholics and Protestants regarding the Weimar state by Martin Rade, "Die gemeinsamen Interessen der katholischen und der evangelischen Kirche angesichts der Trennungsfrage," in *Revolution und Kirche. Zur Neuordnung des Kirchenwesens im deutschen Volksstaat*, ed. Friedrich Thimme and Ernst Rolffs (Berlin: Verlag von Georg Reimer, 1919), 110–21.

101. Jacke, *Kirche*, 128.

102. See Hans Michael Heinig, *Prekäre Ordnungen. Historische Prägungen des Religionsrechts in Deutschland* (Tübingen: Mohr Siebeck, 2018), 34–40.

103. See Maria D. Mitchell, *The Origins of Christian Democracy: Politics and Confession in Modern Germany* (Ann Arbor: University of Michigan Press, 2012), 56–75.

104. See Arnulf von Scheliha, "Der deutsche Protestantismus auf dem Weg zur Demokratie," in *Wechselseitige Erwartungslosigkeit? Die Kirchen und der Staat des Grundgesetzes—gestern, heute, morgen*, ed. Hermann-Josef Große Kracht and Gerhard Schreiber (Berlin: De Gruyter, 2019), 57–78.

105. See Manfred Gailus, "Keine gute Performance. Die deutschen Protestanten im 'Dritten Reich,'" in *Zerstrittene "Volksgemeinschaft." Glaube, Konfession und Religion im Nationalsozialismus*, ed. Manfred Gailus and Armin Nolzen (Göttingen: Vandenhoeck & Ruprecht, 2011), 96–121.

106. For a regional example, see Benedikt Brunner, "Ein Volk, ein Reich, eine Kirche? Die Debatten über die Volkskirche im Kontext des mitteldeutschen 'Kirchenkampfes,'" *Neues Archiv für sächsische Geschichte* 90 (2019): 293–310.

107. See Benedikt Brunner, "Ostdeutsche Avantgarde? Der lange Abschied von der 'Volkskirche' in Ost- und Westdeutschland," *Mitteilungen zur Kirchlichen Zeitgeschichte* 10 (2016): 11–43.

Bibliography

Barth, Boris. *Dolchstoßlegende und politische Desintegration. Das Trauma der deutschen Niederlage im Ersten Weltkrieg, 1914–1933*. Düsseldorf: Droste, 2003.

Baumann, Eberhard. "Wesen, Wert und Verwirklichung einer wahren Volkskirche." *Deutsches Pfarrerblatt* 29 (1925): 835–37, 855–58.

Becker, Frank. "Protestantische Euphorien. 1870/71, 1914 und 1933." In *Nationalprotestantische Mentalitäten. Konturen, Entwicklungslinien und Umbrüche eines Weltbildes*, edited by Manfred Galius and Hartmut Lehmann, 19–44. Göttingen: Vandenhoeck & Ruprecht, 2005.

Beutel, Albrecht. "Otto Dibelius. Ein Promemoria zum 40. Todestag des preußischen Kirchenfürsten." In *Spurensicherung. Studien zur Identitätsgeschichte des Protestantismus*, edited by Albrecht Beutel, 226–44. Tübingen: Mohr Siebeck, 2013.

Brakelmann, Günter. "Das 'Heilige evangelische Reich deutscher Nation.'" *Evangelische Kommentare* 4 (1971): 11–15.

Brunner, Benedikt. "Ein Volk, ein Reich, eine Kirche? Die Debatten über die Volkskirche im Kontext des mitteldeutschen 'Kirchenkampfes.'" *Neues Archiv für sächsische Geschichte* 90 (2019): 293–310.

———. "Ostdeutsche Avantgarde? Der lange Abschied von der 'Volkskirche' in Ost- und Westdeutschland." *Mitteilungen zur Kirchlichen Zeitgeschichte* 10 (2016): 11–43.

———. "An Unsettled Church: Experiences of the Revolution and Planning for the future in German Protestantism, 1918–20." In *Living the German Revolution of 1918–19: Expec-*

tations, Experiences, Responses, edited by Christopher Dillon, Steven Schouten and Kim Wünschmann. Oxford University Press, forthcoming.

———. *Volkskirche. Zur Geschichte eines evangelischen Grundbegriffs, 1918–1960*. Göttingen: Vandenhoeck & Ruprecht, 2020.

———. "Von der Staats- zur Volkskirche. Reorganisation des kirchlichen Protestantismus in Weimar, 1918–1925." *Zeitschrift für evangelisches Kirchenrecht* 65 (2020): 249–73.

Büttner, Ursula. *Weimar. Die überforderte Republik 1918–1933. Leistung und Versagen in Staat, Gesellschaft, Wirtschaft und Kultur*. Bonn: Bundeszentrale für politische Bildung, 2010.

Dahm, Karl-Wilhelm. *Pfarrer und Politik. Soziale Position und politische Mentalität des deutschen evangelischen Pfarrerstandes zwischen 1918 und 1933*. Cologne: Westdeutscher Verlag, 1965.

Dibelius, Otto. *Die Trennung von Kirche und Staat. Eine Darstellung und ein Aufruf*. Berlin: Schriftenvertriebsanstalt, 1919.

———. "Volkskirchenräte, Volkskirchenbund, Volkskirchendienst." In *Revolution und Kirche. Zur Neuordnung des Kirchenwesens im deutschen Volksstaat*, edited by Friedrich Thimme and Ernst Rolffs, 201–13. Berlin: Verlag von Georg Reimer, 1919.

Dietrich, Albert. "Kirche und Staat." *Die Reformation* 18 (1919): 42–43.

Endrös, Alfred. "Zur Entwicklung und Geschichte des Begriffs 'Körperschaft des öffentlichen Rechts.'" *Zeitschrift für Rechtsgeschichte, Kan. Abt.* 69 (1983): 292–324.

Foerster, Erich. "Programmsätze über die neue Kirche." *Christliche Welt* 33 (1919): 349–52.

Föllmer, Moritz, Rüdiger Graf, and Per Leo. "Einleitung: Die Kultur der Krise in der Weimarer Republik." In *Die "Krise" der Weimarer Republik. Zur Kritik eines Deutungsmusters*, edited by Moritz Föllmer and Rüdiger Graf, 9–41. Frankfurt am Main: Campus-Verlag, 2005.

Fritz, Hartmut. *Otto Dibelius. Ein Kirchenmann zwischen Monarchie und Diktatur. Mit einer Bibliographie der Veröffentlichungen von Otto Dibelius*. Göttingen: Vandenhoeck & Ruprecht, 1998.

Gailus, Manfred. "Keine gute Performance. Die deutschen Protestanten im 'Dritten Reich.'" In *Zerstrittene "Volksgemeinschaft." Glaube, Konfession und Religion im Nationalsozialismus*, edited by Manfred Gailus and Armin Nolzen, 96–121. Göttingen: Vandenhoeck & Ruprecht, 2011.

Göbell, Walter. "Der Kaftan-Briefwechsel. Ein Beitrag zur Geschichte von Theologie und Kirche." *Theologische Literaturzeitung* 81 (1956): 357–60.

———, ed. *Kirche, Recht und Theologie in vier Jahrzehnten. Der Briefwechsel der Brüder Theodor und Julius Kaftan, Vol. 2: 1910–1926*. Munich: Christian Kaiser Verlag, 1967.

Graf, Rüdiger. *Die Zukunft der Weimarer Republik. Krisen und Zukunftsaneignungen in Deutschland, 1918–1933*. Munich: Oldenbourg, 2008.

Haarbeck, Th[eodor]. "Volkskirche oder Bekenntniskirche?" *Auf der Warte* 13 (1919): 2–3.

Heiler, [Friedrich]. "Katholizismus I. Konfessionskundlich." *Die Religion in Geschichte und Gegenwart*, Vol. 3: *I-Me*. Tübingen: Mohr, 1929.

Hein, Arnold. "Kirche und Staat." *Preußische Kirchenzeitung* 15 (1919): 69–72.

Heinig, Hans Michael. "Deutungsmachtkonflikte als Deutungs- und Machtkonflikte im Religionsrecht." In *Deutungsmacht. Religion und belief systems in Deutungsmachtkonflikten*, edited by Philipp Stoellger, 411–27. Tübingen: Mohr Siebeck, 2014.

———. *Prekäre Ordnungen. Historische Prägungen des Religionsrechts in Deutschland*. Tübingen: Mohr Siebeck, 2018.

Hermelink, Heinrich. *Katholizismus und Protestantismus in der Gegenwart vornehmlich in Deutschland*. Gotha: Perthes, 1924.

Herz, Johannes. "Volkskirche und Freikirche." *Protestantenblatt* 54 (1921): 271–72.

———. "Volkskirche und Freikirche." *Volkskirche* 3 (1921): 255–57.

Hoffmann, Adolph. "Neue Bahnen im preußischen Ministerium für Wissenschaft, Kunst und Volksbildung." *Pädagogische Zeitung* 47, no. 48 (1918).

Holl, Karl. "Wie weit reicht die Pflicht der evangelischen Kirche, gegen die Trennung von Kirche und Staat zu kämpfen?" *Die Reformation* 18 (1919): 36–37.

Hürten, Heinz. *Die Kirchen in der Novemberrevolution. Eine Untersuchung zur Geschichte der Deutschen Revolution 1918/19*. Regensburg: Pustet, 1984.
Jacke, Jochen. *Kirche zwischen Monarchie. Der preußische Protestantismus nach dem Zusammenbruch von 1918*. Hamburg: Christians, 1976.
Jung, Martin H. *Der Protestantismus in Deutschland von 1870 bis 1945*. Leipzig: Evangelische Verlagsanstalt, 2002.
Kaftan, Theodor. *Die staatsfreie Volkskirche. Mit einem Nachwort aus der Mitte des Dezembers*. Leipzig: Dörffling & Franke, 1918.
———. "Gefahren der kirchlichen Neubildung." *Allgemeine Evangelisch-Lutherische Kirchenzeitung* 52 (1919): 259–61.
———. "Grundsätzliches zum Umbau der Kirche." *Allgemeine Evangelisch-Lutherische Kirchenzeitung* 52 (1919): 117–23.
———. *Was nun? Eine christlich-deutsche Zeitbetrachtung*. Leipzig: Dörffling & Franke, 1919.
Kahl, [Wilhelm]. "Zur Trennung von Staat und Kirche." *Protestantenblatt* 51 (1918): 568–70.
Kahl, Wilhelm. "Auf dem Weg zur Volkskirche." *Vossische Zeitung*, 7 August 1921.
———. *Die deutsche Kirche im deutschen Staat*. Berlin: Weidmann, 1919.
———. "Trennung von Staat und Kirche." *Deutsche Juristen-Zeitung* 24 (1919): 124–25.
Koch, Friedrich. "Auf dem Weg zur neuen Volkskirche in Preußen (ältere Provinzen)." *Kirchliches Jahrbuch für die evangelischen Landeskirchen Deutschlands* 48 (1921): 1–24.
———. "Grundlagen und Grundfragen der neuen evangelischen Volkskirche." *Kirchliches Jahrbuch für die evangelischen Landeskirchen Deutschlands* 47 (1920): 34–47.
Köhler, Günter. *Die Auswirkungen der Novemberrevolution von 1918 auf die altpreußische evangelische Landeskirche*. Berlin: Diss. Kirchliche Hochschule, 1967.
Krumwiede, Hans Walter. "Kirchenregiment, Landesherrliches." *Theologische Realenzyklopädie* 19 (1990): 59–68.
Kupisch, Karl. "Der Protestantismus im Epochenjahr 1917." In *Zeitgeist im Wandel, Vol. II: Zeitgeist der Weimarer Republik*, edited by Hans Joachim Schoeps, 33–51. Stuttgart: Klett, 1968.
———. "Strömungen der Evangelischen Kirche in der Weimarer Republik." *Archiv für Sozialgeschichte* 11 (1971): 373–415.
LaCapra, Dominick. *History in Transit: Experience, Identity, Critical Theory*. Ithaca: Cornell University Press, 2004.
Lessing, Eckhard. *Zwischen Bekenntnis und Volkskirche. Der theologische Weg der Evangelischen Kirche der altpreußischen Union (1922–1953) unter besonderer Berücksichtigung ihrer Synoden, ihrer Gruppen und der theologischen Begründungen*. Bielefeld: Luther-Verlag, 1992.
Lieschke, Th[eodor]. *Die Trennung von Staat und Kirche und die evangelische Volkskirche*. Freiberg, 1919.
Link, Christoph. "Das Staatskirchenrecht im Geltungszeitraum der Weimarer Verfassung." In *Staat und Kirche in der neueren deutschen Geschichte. Fünf Abhandlungen*, edited by Christoph Link, 99–133. Frankfurt am Main: Lang, 2000.
Lütcke, Karl-Heinrich. "'Trennung von Staat und Kirche.' Konflikte und Entwicklungen in Berlin seit 1918." *Jahrbuch für Berlin-Brandenburgische Kirchengeschichte* 66 (2007): 129–56.
Mahling, Friedrich. "Volkskirche, Volksseele, Volksseelsorge, Volksmission." *Neue Kirchliche Zeitschrift* 25 (1914): 85–129.
Meier, Kurt. "Die zeitgeschichtliche Bedeutung volkskirchlicher Konzeptionen im deutschen Protestantismus zwischen 1918 und 1945." In *Evangelische Kirche in Gesellschaft, Staat und Politik 1918–1945. Aufsätze zur kirchlichen Zeitgeschichte*, edited by Kurt Nowak, 16–39. Berlin: Evangelische Verlagsanstalt, 1987.
Meinhold, [Peter]. "Volkskirche oder heiliger Rest." In *Aufgaben und Kräfte der Kirche in der Gegenwart. Abhandlungen, D. Johannes Büchsel zum siebzigsten Geburtstag 19. September 1919 dargebracht*, 55–61. Berlin: Warneck, 1919.
Mitchell, Maria D. *The Origins of Christian Democracy: Politics and Confession in Modern Germany*. Ann Arbor: University of Michigan Press, 2012.

Motschmann, Claus. *Evangelische Kirche und preußischer Staat in den Anfängen der Weimarer Republik. Möglichkeiten und Grenzen ihrer Zusammenarbeit*. Lübeck: Matthiesen, 1969.
Mumm, Reinhard. "Die freie evangelische Volkskirche." *Die Reformation* 18 (1919): 250.
Muus, Hans-Peter. "Zum Briefwechsel der Brüder Kaftan." *Zeitschrift für evangelisches Kirchenrecht* 15 (1970): 401–6.
Nowak, Kurt. *Geschichte des Christentums in Deutschland. Religion, Politik und Gesellschaft vom Ende der Aufklärung bis zur Mitte des 20. Jahrhunderts*. Munich: Beck, 1995.
Paarmann, Friedrich. "Der Weg zur Volkskirche geht durch die Pastorenkirche." *Protestantenblatt* 53 (1920): 32–38.
Peukert, Detlev J. K. *Die Weimarer Republik. Krisenjahre der Klassischen Moderne*. Frankfurt am Main: Suhrkamp, 1987.
Pfannkuche, August. *Die Baseler Kirchenverfassung als Vorbild für die Neuverfassung der deutsch-evangelischen Landeskirchen mit Einleitung und Anmerkungen*. Berlin: Hutten-Verlag, o. J. [1919].
R[ade], [Martin]. "Was sollen, was wollen wir in der Christlichen Welt? Was soll, was will der Volkskirchen-Rat?" *Christliche Welt* 32 (1918): 498–501.
Rade, Martin. "Die gemeinsamen Interessen der katholischen und der evangelischen Kirche angesichts der Trennungsfrage." In *Revolution und Kirche. Zur Neuordnung des Kirchenwesens im deutschen Volksstaat*, edited by Friedrich Thimme and Ernst Rolffs, 110–21. Berlin: Verlag von Georg Reimer, 1919.
Retterath, Jörn. *"Was ist das Volk?" Volks- und Gemeinschaftskonzepte der politischen Mitte in Deutschland 1917–1924*. Berlin: De Gruyter Oldenbourg, 2016.
Rogge, Joachim. "Die außerordentliche Generalsynode von 1875 und die Generalsynodalordnung von 1876. Fortschritt und Grenzen kirchlicher Selbstregierung." In *Die Geschichte der Evangelischen Kirche der Union, Bd. 2: Die Verselbständigung der Kirche unter dem königlichen Summepiskopat (1850–1918)*, edited by Joachim Rogge and Gerhard Ruhbach, 225–33. Leipzig: Evangelische Verlagsanstalt, 1994.
Sarx, Tobias. "Zu den Ursprüngen des Begriffs 'Volkskirche' um 1800." *Archiv für Kulturgeschichte* 94 (2012): 113–45.
Scheliha, Arnulf von. "Der deutsche Protestantismus auf dem Weg zur Demokratie." In *Wechselseitige Erwartungslosigkeit? Die Kirchen und der Staat des Grundgesetzes—gestern, heute, morgen*, edited by Hermann-Josef Große Kracht and Gerhard Schreiber, 57–78. Berlin: De Gruyter, 2019.
———. *Protestantische Ethik des Politischen*. Tübingen: Mohr Siebeck, 2013.
Schian, Martin. "Was ist jetzt zu tun?" *Preußische Kirchenzeitung* 14 (1918): 388–89.
Schmidt-Rost, Reinhard. "Die Christliche Welt. Eine publizistische Gestalt des Kulturprotestantismus." In *Kulturprotestantismus. Beiträge zu einer Gestalt des modernen Christentums*, edited by Hans Martin Müller, 245–57. Gütersloh: Mohn, 1992.
Scholder, Klaus. *Die Kirchen und das Dritte Reich, Vol. I: Vorgeschichte und Zeit der Illusionen 1918–1934*. Berlin: Siedler, 1977.
Schubring, Wilhelm. [Untitled]. *Protestantenblatt* 52 (1919): 309–10.
Soden, Hans von. *Das Ende der evangelischen Volkskirche Preußens? Betrachtungen zum Ausschußentwurf der neuen Kirchenverfassung für die altpreußische Landeskirche*. Berlin: Hutten-Verlag, 1922.
Stephan, Horst. "Der kirchliche Neubau." *Christliche Welt* 32 (1918): 480–84.
Stokmann, [G]. "Der Aufruf für eine freie evangelische Volkskirche, von evangelisch-reformirtem [!] Standpunkt aus betrachtet." *Reformierte Kirchenzeitung* 69 (1919): 62–64.
Troschke, Paul. *Kirchliche Statistik I. Die kirchliche Organisation der Evangelischen, die materiellen Mittel des kirchlichen Lebens*. Berlin: Deutsches Evangelisches Kirchenbundamt, 1930.
Weichlein, Siegfried. "Von der Staatskirche zur religiösen Kultur. Die Entstehung des Begriffs der 'Körperschaft des öffentlichen Rechts' mit Blick auf die Kirchenartikel der Weimarer Reichsverfassung." In *Baupläne der sichtbaren Kirche. Sprachliche Konzepte religiöser Verge-

meinschaftung in Europa, edited by Lucian Hölscher, 90–116. Göttingen: Wallstein-Verlag, 2007.

Weinel, Heinrich. "Die Volkskirche. Leitsätze für unsere Arbeit." *Christliche Freiheit für Thüringen und Sachsen*, 8 December 1918.

Winnebeck, Julia. *Apostolikumsstreitigkeiten. Diskussionen um Liturgie, Lehre und Kirchenverfassung in der preußischen Landeskirche 1871–1914*. Leipzig: Evangelische Verlagsanstalt, 2016.

Ziegert, Richard, ed. *Die Kirchen und die Weimarer Republik*. Neukirchen-Vluyn: Neukirchener Verlag, 1994.

Zippelius, Reinhold. *Staat und Kirche. Eine Geschichte von der Antike bis zur Gegenwart*. Tübingen: Mohr Siebeck, 2009.

Zscharnack, Leopold. "Die Frage des landesherrlichen Kirchenregiments." *Volkskirche* 1 (1919): 113–17.

———. *Trennung von Staat und Kirche*. Berlin: Verlag des Evangelischen Bundes, 1919.

Chapter Four

THE CONFESSIONAL DIVIDE IN VOTING BEHAVIOR

Jürgen Falter
Translated by Alex Skinner

At the end of the Weimar Republic, about 63 percent of the Reich population was Protestant, just under a third Catholic, and 0.8 percent Jewish, while around 4 percent were members of another religious community or completely unaffiliated religiously. Compared to the German Empire, this represented a modest shift in the ratio between the two major confessions as a result of the loss of predominantly Catholic territories. As late as 1910, with 62 percent Protestants and 37 percent Catholics, this proportion was somewhat more balanced than after the Treaty of Versailles. Catholics were thus in a clear minority. Compared with the Federal Republic of Germany, the Weimar Republic featured highly homogeneous patterns of residence by confession. More than a quarter of districts (*Kreise*) were almost entirely Protestant (with fewer than 3 percent non-Protestants), while in more than 40 percent of them at least nine out of ten residents were Protestant. Fifteen percent of districts were almost exclusively Catholic (fewer than 3 percent non-Catholics). Just one in seven districts, with at least 25 percent and a maximum of 75 percent of Catholics or Protestants, was confessionally mixed.

The areas of Catholic settlement were chiefly in the west and south of the Reich and in Upper Silesia. Smaller areas of Catholic dominance were also to be found in Südoldenburg, parts of Hesse, Baden, and Württemberg, East Prussia (Warmia in the Ermland), and Thuringia (Eichsfeld). Meanwhile, almost all of northern and central Germany, as well as large parts of eastern Germany, was more than 90 percent Protestant. There were also a number of almost entirely Protestant areas in Bavaria (Middle and Upper

Franconia, the Palatinate), Württemberg, Baden, and Hesse. Finally, the larger towns often featured a substantial minority made up of the "other" confession, other faiths and those unaffiliated with any religion.

The confessional division of the Reich took on political importance chiefly during the *Kulturkampf* of the 1870s and 1880s, when the Center Party (*Zentrumspartei*) established itself as the "political action committee" of the Catholic minority, to use a phrase coined by M. Rainer Lepsius. As a purely Catholic party in the German Empire, the Center Party was of virtually no importance outside the areas of Catholic dominance. Within the mainly Catholic electoral constituencies, however, it emerged as a secure majority party whose position, despite unmistakable symptoms of erosion prior to World War I, seemed virtually unassailable. In the Weimar Republic, too, despite the radically changed electoral system and the extension of suffrage to women and younger age groups, the Center Party and the Bavarian People's Party (BVP), founded by Bavarian Center Party deputies in 1918, continued to dominate in the predominantly Catholic areas of the Reich until 1933. While fewer than 1 percent of voters opted for these two parties in the areas of the Catholic diaspora, in July 1932 they attracted an average of 39.5 percent of voters in the largely Catholic regions. Depending on turnout, their share of valid votes cast was sometimes higher than this.

Meanwhile, other parties struggled in the largely Catholic districts, with none of them managing to achieve above-average election results. Confession produced a clear division between the two Catholic parties on the one hand and the rest of the parties on the other, though in the case of the Communist Party of Germany (KPD) the correlation was very weak. Conversely, it was strong in the case of the Social Democratic Party of Germany (SPD), which attracted only around a third as many votes in the Catholic districts as in non-Catholic ones. Despite certain signs of erosion, this confessional dividing line retained its influence for both Catholic parties until the end of the Weimar Republic. In the main, this also applied to the SPD and the KPD as well as the staunchly Protestant-conservative German National People's Party (DNVP). Only in the case of the two liberal parties, the German People's Party (DVP) and German Democratic Party (DDP) abandoned almost entirely by their voters, did the confessional factor largely lose its significance between 1928 and 1932.

Overall, then, the Center Party and the Bavarian People's Party (BVP) proved remarkably stable. No other parties in the Weimar Republic attracted voters with such consistency as the two Catholic sister groupings. This was true not only nationally but regionally and locally. Only in the (almost) purely Catholic districts did political Catholicism suffer a decline between December 1924 and May 1928 that it was subsequently unable to reverse. This was the same group of districts in which the Center Party and the BVP once again lost a disproportionately high number of votes between July 1932 and March 1933, while they managed to maintain their position without major losses in the Catholic diaspora and confessionally mixed districts despite the National Socialist surge.

Historical regional studies have tended to attribute this stability of the two Catholic parties—all the more surprising given the trends affecting most of the other parties—to their strong roots in a specific milieu. Over the course of the nineteenth century, nothing less than a Catholic subculture did in fact become established in the traditionally Catholic areas of Germany. Largely closed off from the outside world, with its own associations for every field of endeavor and its own morality, it also had its own voting norms centered around the Catholic parties. Individuals could violate this convention only at the risk, metaphorically speaking, of excommunication from their milieu. This explicit electoral norm emerged during the *Kulturkampf* and was repeatedly reinforced, at periodic intervals, by the conflict between an initially Protestant and then laical state and the Catholic minority. It was a norm that determined the political behavior of the vast majority of practicing Catholics until well into the Weimar Republic and even after the creation of the Federal Republic. For decades, it was the taken-for-granted duty of every professed Catholic to cast his or her vote in line with confessional affiliation and not in accordance with regional or functional, class- or social stratum-based factors. This could mean voting only for the Center Party or, if you lived in Bavaria, the Bavarian People's Party, regardless of origin, class, or income. Hence, during the final elections held in the Weimar Republic, political Catholicism still managed to mobilize the support of more than 40 percent of Catholic voters (and thus a clear majority of practicing Catholics).[1] Other parties had fairly meager prospects of attracting members of the Catholic social milieu, given its traditional ties to the Center Party. New political movements such as National Socialism struggled from the outset to appeal to practicing Catholics. In the Catholic regions, it was chiefly unchurched Catholics that they had a chance of winning over.

Just how willing many church-loyal Catholics were to vote as recommended by the representatives of political Catholicism is evident in the reversal of the electoral coalition that elected Paul von Hindenburg as Reich president in 1925 and facilitated his re-election in 1932. In the second round of voting in the election of 1925, Hindenburg, victor of the Battle of Tannenberg and national hero to the political right, had been nominated as a rival to Center Party leader Wilhelm Marx, who had been fielded by the parties of the Weimar coalition. Hindenburg won by the relatively narrow margin of nine hundred thousand votes. He won decisively as the candidate of Protestant Germany, where he took more than twice as many votes as in the Catholic areas, while his opponent, the Catholic Marx from the Rhineland, did best in predominantly Catholic districts.[2]

Seven years later, Hindenburg was the candidate of the Weimar coalition parties. By and large, his opponent Adolf Hitler received the support of the same forces that had got behind the veteran field marshal in 1925. Hindenburg won again, but this time he achieved an absolute majority of valid votes cast. This was the last major electoral victory of the Weimar coalition prior to the National Socialist "seizure of power." That this was a pyrrhic victory is evident in Hindenburg's dismissal of Heinrich Brüning immediately after his re-election and the appointment of Adolf Hitler as Reich chancellor in January 1933. It is interesting to note that in a large-scale reversal of the electoral coalitions, Hindenburg now achieved his best results in those places where he had performed worst seven years earlier and his opponent Marx had dominated, namely in the Catholic regions. Tellingly, in the Protestant areas of the Reich, Hindenburg, despite his status as a symbolic figure within conservative Protestantism, performed far worse than his overall result. Hitler, meanwhile, did best in the former (predominantly Protestant) Hindenburg strongholds, while performing worst on average in the (largely Catholic) districts in which Hindenburg had performed most poorly in 1925.[3]

Hitler's Success in Protestant Areas

We focus on the stability of the "Center fortress," which was partially reversed only in late 1932, and on the differing electoral coalitions in the two Reich presidential elections in order to illustrate both the relative immunity of most Catholic regions to National Socialism prior to 1933 and to bring out the remarkable compliance of many practicing Catholics with the voting advice issuing from their social milieu. On average, up to and including 1933, not just Adolf Hitler but the entire Nazi Party (NSDAP) had a harder time breaking through in districts with a low share of Protestants, and thus a high share of Catholics, than in areas with a Protestant majority. Beginning with the Reichstag election of 1930, we can identify a virtually iron rule: the percentage of Nazi Party votes in districts with a Protestant majority was far higher than in those with a Catholic one. To put it differently, at every Reichstag election after 1928 we can discern an unambiguously positive, very strong statistical correlation between the proportion of Protestant voters and the Nazis' electoral successes. This was most pronounced at the July election of 1932, when there was a 25.6 percent difference in the Nazi Party's election result between the quarter of districts with the lowest share of Protestants and the quarter of districts with the highest share. No other social characteristic influenced National Socialist electoral victories as much as confession. Compared with the Reichstag election of 1928, in the (almost) exclusively Protestant districts the Nazi Party managed to increase its share of the votes by around 41 percent in July 1932, while the figure in the predominantly Catholic areas was only around 16 percent. While the Nazi Party then achieved a somewhat more than average increase in its vote share at the Reichstag election of 1933 in the predominantly Catholic areas (while the Center Party and the BVP saw a small decline in their vote), there was still a significant difference between the Protestant strongholds, where the Nazi Party gained more than 50 percent of votes, and the Catholic diaspora areas, with "only" around 30 percent support for the Nazis.

Protestant Voters Were, on Average, Twice as Likely to Vote for the Nazi Party as Catholics

What are the implications of these statistical correlations, measured at area level, for individual voting behavior? Of course, for want of contemporary opinion polls we have no direct insights into the voting behavior of Catholics or Protestants, let alone the political preferences of practicing and nonpracticing Catholics. Nonetheless, the attribute of "confession" is a particularly apt means of attempting to reconstruct individual voting behavior with the help of the statistical method of ecological regression analysis, since we are dealing here with highly homogenous territorial units, particularly with respect to confessional distribution. Moreover, the statistical correlation between the proportion of Catholics or Protestants and the electoral successes of the Nazi Party or the Center Party was sufficiently close to justify the (always risky) practice of making inferences about the local level in light of the national level. As late as 1928, Catholics and non-Catholics were still more or less equally susceptible or resistant to the Nazi Party; by 1930, about twice as many non-Catholics as Catholics were already voting for the Hitler movement. This difference between the confessional groups intensified again in July 1932 when, according to our calculations, 38 percent of non-Catholic voters voted for the Nazi Party as opposed to just 16 percent of Catholic voters. Translated into the confessional composition of Nazi Party voters, this would mean that during this election only around 17 percent of Nazi Party voters were Catholic, while 83 percent of them were non-Catholics. The difference between Catholics and non-Catholics reduced appreciably for the first time only in November 1932, when the Nazi Party vote among non-Catholic voters declined by 5 percent, but only by

2 percent among Catholic voters as compared with the previous election. Finally, in March 1933, the percentage of Nazi Party voters among Catholics increased by 14 percent, that is, it doubled from November 1932, but rose by only 11 percent among non-Catholic voters. The gap between Catholics and non-Catholics, then, narrowed from 22 points in July 1932 to 19 points in November 1932, and to "just" 16 points in March 1933.

Hence, in the last few months of the Weimar Republic, Catholics' originally fairly strong resistance to National Socialism appears to have lessened. Yet even at this point in time it was far stronger than among the non-Catholic population, and particularly Protestants. In 1933, roughly every second non-Catholic voter supported the Nazi Party, whereas only every third Catholic that took part in the election cast their vote for Adolf Hitler and his movement. Even in 1933, then, just under a quarter of Nazi Party voters were Catholic, while the rest were Protestant, of other faiths, or were not members of one of the two official confessions. Had there only been Protestants living in the German Reich at the time, then assuming the same voting behavior, the Nazi Party would already have managed to achieve an absolute (if slender) majority of Reichstag seats in the summer of 1932. Conversely, had there been only Catholics, the National Socialists would likely never have seized power because they would have struggled to rise beyond the status of a minority party. Of course, such extrapolations always entail a highly speculative element because they presuppose continuity of behavior under changed circumstances. Nonetheless, in this context such a procedure can be justified as a means of clarifying the role played by confession, particularly with respect to susceptibility or immunity to National Socialism.

Confession Retains Its Significance Even in Combination with Other Influencing Factors

Before addressing the question of why Catholics as a whole were more immune to National Socialism, we need to consider whether this resistance was in reality caused by factors other than confession. It is theoretically conceivable, for example, that the rural population as a whole was particularly susceptible to National Socialism and that rural areas were overwhelmingly Protestant, whereas the inhabitants of industrial regions (such as Upper Silesia or the Ruhr region), which were perhaps by historical accident predominately Catholic, were on average less prone to National Socialism. On this premise, confession and Nazi Party vote share would correlate as laid out above. But correlation does not mean causality, and it may well have been other unrelated factors that were responsible for this correlation.

One prerequisite for this would be that predominantly Catholic and Protestant areas differed in their social composition in significant ways. This would assume that far more blue- or white-collar workers, for instance, lived in Catholic districts than in Protestant ones, while Protestant regions were, on average, markedly more rural than Catholic ones, and so on. This, however, was not the case. Generally speaking, predominantly Catholic, confessionally mixed, and mainly Protestant districts differed only slightly in terms of their social composition. The deviations from the Reich average were consistently fairly negligible, in fact in some cases insignificant. The statistical correlation between the proportion of Catholics and the presence of the various social attributes is too weak to support the claim that the correlation we have established between the percentage of non-Catholics or Protestants and the electoral successes of the Nazi Party is spurious. Further analysis, not set out here in detail, shows that the immunizing effect of Catholicism vis-à-vis National Socialism persisted under the most diverse range of conditions. In fact, the influence, identifiable at the level of simple correlation, of other factors such as unemployment, agriculture, or class affiliation, on the Nazis' electoral success often tends to disappear if we control for confession.

The only appreciable difference between Catholic and non-Catholic districts exists with respect to the percentage of individuals employed in the agricultural sector and, bound up with this, the greater number of self-employed and family workers as well as the lower percentage of residents in municipalities with more than five thousand inhabitants in the Catholic areas. This points to the value of investigating the joint influence of the attributes of urbanization and confessional characteristics on the National Socialists' electoral success. After 1928, and particularly after 1930, on average the Nazi Party was more successful in elections the smaller the municipality in which voting took place. At the district level there was an analogous negative statistical correlation, which in fact strengthened until 1933, between the degree of urbanization and Nazi electoral success. If we ascertain whether this correlation applies equally to Protestant and Catholic districts by combining districts' degree of urbanization and confessional share in order to identify possible carry-over effects between these two attributes, what we find is that the introduction of the trait of "urbanization" by no means causes the effect of confessional distribution on Nazi Party performance to disappear. Regardless of whether districts were predominantly rural or urban, where the share of Catholics was high the Nazi Party made far less headway than in those places in which it was low (and the percentage of Protestants correspondingly high). In confessionally mixed areas, regardless of the degree of urbanization, the share of Nazi Party votes lay, without exception, between that of the predominantly Catholic and non-Catholic districts. This correlation persists even if we factor into the analysis other dimensions of urbanization, such as population density or average size of municipality within a district. Between 1928 and July 1932, support for the Nazi Party increased most strongly, by 15.8 percent (1930) and 23.1 percent (1932), in rural Protestant areas, while in the Catholic countryside it increased only by 13 and 18.7 percent respectively. On the other hand, the decline in Nazi Party votes at the November election of 1932 was markedly smaller in the rural Catholic areas, at 2.4 percent, than the Reich average (4.7 percent), and this drop was even more precipitous in rural Protestant areas (6 percent). Finally, in March 1933 the Nazi Party vote share increased in rural Catholic areas by 16.3 percent, well above the Reich average of 12.3 percent. This is another indication that from the second half of 1932 on, the party managed to gain a firmer foothold even in some parts of Catholic Germany.

But the rate of urbanization itself also appears to have exercised an influence, independent of confession, on Nazi electoral success. The evidence for this is that at all the elections considered here, with the exception of the Reichstag election of 1928, the difference in Nazi Party support between Protestant and Catholic rural districts was far greater than in the cities. In July 1932, for example, the gap was 23.9 percent in the essentially rural districts, compared with 12 percent in the largely urban areas. However, this combined effect of confession and urbanization (or municipality size) on the level of support for the Nazi Party turns out to be more complex than we might initially be led to expect by a simple analysis that only considers the relationship between two characteristics at a time. This is because the lowest Nazi Party vote share, with the exception of the election of 1933, was in the rural Catholic areas and small Catholic municipalities, while the party's greatest electoral successes were consistently in the rural Protestant areas.[4] The more urbanized Catholic and Protestant districts lay between these two extremes.

If we assess the likelihood of Catholic and Protestant urban and rural dwellers voting for the Nazi Party at the various Reichstag elections from 1928 on, in other words if we seek to determine individual voting behavior, what we find is that until November 1932 the Nazi Party had a very hard time persuading Catholics to vote for it—far harder, at least, than in the case of non-Catholic urban and rural dwellers. Hence, at the two elections held in 1932, only around every seventh Catholic voter living in a rural area voted for the Nazi Party, and according to our findings, even in March 1933 only just under a third of Catholic rural residents, and no more than one in four Catholic urban dwellers, voted for the National Socialists. These findings also reveal that in November 1932 the Nazi Party lost markedly fewer votes among Catholics than among non-Catholics and that between November 1932 and March 1933 the increase in its vote share among Catholic rural dwellers was around twice that achieved among Catholic urban dwellers. But it was among Protestants living in rural areas that the Hitler movement managed to achieve its greatest successes, with close to one in two voters already voting for it in July 1932. Non-Catholic urbanites proved significantly more resistant. Among this group, assuming that our estimates are correct, only one in three voters opted for the Nazi Party in July 1932, and only one in four in November 1932. Despite this relative degree of resistance, however, non-Catholic urbanites still proved significantly more prone to National Socialism than Catholic urban and rural dwellers did.

The results of this ecological regression analysis are largely corroborated if we examine Nazi Party vote share in the small and smallest municipalities in Baden and Hesse with a view to settlement size and confession.[5] At every Reichstag election from 1930 on, in these two states the Nazi Party was on average markedly stronger in the predominantly Protestant localities than in the confessionally mixed municipalities, and in the latter it was in turn stronger than in the predominantly Catholic ones. On average, in July 1932 and March 1933, the party gained more than 70 percent of the votes in the smallest Protestant municipalities with fewer than five hundred inhabitants, while even in 1933 it managed to gain the backing of only around 40 percent of voters in the smallest Catholic municipalities. At the same time, these results show that at Reichstag elections the Nazi Party broke through electorally in the countryside—even the Protestant countryside—only partially at best in 1930, but advanced across a broad front (at least in these two Reich states) only in July 1932. Our datasets provide no or only limited confirmation of other assertions within the literature on electoral history.

It does in fact appear that no other characteristic influenced the tendency to vote for the Nazi Party as much as confession. Whether this also applies to readiness to join the Nazi Party is by no means a foregone conclusion. The act of becoming a member of a political party is, quite simply, subject to different forces than the willingness to check a box for a party in the anonymity of the voting booth. Membership of a party, particularly in the context of a village or small town, may amount to a quasi-public act; voting for a party, by contrast, is in principle carried out in secret, and is not normally associated with social reprisals or professional disadvantages. Meanwhile, reports of such sanctions, up to and including loss of job, are a common feature of accounts of the "time of struggle" (*Kampfzeit*) by early Nazi Party members. In what follows, we seek to determine whether confessional context was an impediment or was conducive to joining the Nazi Party.

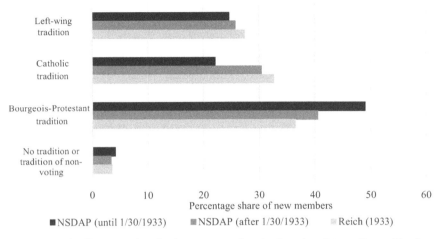

Figure 4.1. Nazi Party members by their municipalities' political traditions. Created by the author.

Confession as a Factor Influencing the Tendency to Join the Nazi Party

Figure 4.1 shows that between 1925 and 1933, measured against population share, those taking up membership in the Nazi Party were in fact greatly overrepresented in municipalities with a bourgeois-Protestant tradition and markedly underrepresented in Catholic municipalities. Prior to the "seizure of power," in Protestant-dominated municipalities Nazi Party membership was almost 15 percent higher than this municipality type's share of the Reich population. In traditionally Catholic municipalities, meanwhile, the level of Nazi Party membership during the same period was around 10 percent lower than this municipality type's share of all the inhabitants of the Reich. In comparison, localities with a strong tradition of support for left-wing parties were relatively weakly underrepresented. Following the "seizure of power," the underrepresentation of the Catholic municipalities and the overrepresentation of the bourgeois-Protestant ones diminished markedly, though the general trend was for the gap to persist in diminished form.[6] If we look at the specific year of entry to the party, a more nuanced picture emerges (see Table 4.1). For example, in the first three years after the party's foundation, a disproportionate number of new members came from confessionally mixed municipalities, while there was below-average growth in membership in predominantly Protestant ones. This changed enduringly from 1928 on. Now there were significantly more new members from predominantly Protestant municipalities than the average for the population as a whole, while the number of those taking up membership from predominantly Catholic municipalities was just as

Table 4.1. New members of the Nazi Party from 1925 to 1945 by the confessional character of their municipality of residence. Legend: row percentage. Reading aid: in 1931, around 68 percent of new members came from predominantly Protestant municipalities (0–24% Catholic), in which around 54 percent of all Reich residents lived at the time. Meanwhile, around only 13 percent of new members that year came from predominantly Catholic (75–100%) municipalities, in which just under 33 percent of the population lived. Created by the author.

Year of entry	0–24 % Catholic	25–49 % Catholic	50–74 % Catholic	75–100 % Catholic
1925	53	21	5	21
1926	47	21	8	23
1927	53	21	7	19
1928	69	12	4	14
1929	67	14	5	14
1930	64	15	6	15
1931	68	13	6	13
1932	66	15	6	13
1933	60	12	7	21
1934	73	12	4	12
1935	37	14	5	45
1936	71	12	2	14
1937	62	12	7	19
1938	49	14	10	27
1939	56	9	6	30
1940	58	14	10	18
1941	58	17	7	18
1942	61	13	6	20
1943	60	12	8	19
1944	59	15	9	17
1945	60	0	20	20
Total	63	15	6	16
Population	54	8	5	33

clearly below the average. While a total of 21.4 percent of the population came from localities with more than 75 percent Catholics, among new Nazi Party members in 1931 the figure was only around 13 percent. This trend continued in 1932. The next year, that of the "seizure of power," the differences between confessional milieus then levelled off to a great extent. That year, and in most of the subsequent years, the tendency to join the Nazi Party was virtually uninfluenced by confession.

Table 4.2. Average share of Catholics in the various confessional categories (municipalities with Nazi Party members only). Created by the author.

Confessional category	0–25 percent	25–50 percent	50–75 percent	75–100 percent
Mean	6 percent	37 percent	63 percent	89 percent
Number of cases	22,274	5,186	2,097	5,633

There are, however, notable deviations from this rule, as in 1935, when around half of all new memberships were taken up in largely Catholic municipalities. This was undoubtedly due to the impact of two drives carried out that year within the framework of two regional campaigns, which saw an increase in those joining the party in the predominantly Catholic Saar region and especially in the mainly Catholic Gau of the Bavarian Eastern March (*Bayerische Ostmark*; later Bayreuth). If this chapter's scope was not restricted to the Old Reich and included consideration of Austria and the Sudetenland, we would again find a disproportionate number of new memberships from predominantly Catholic municipalities in 1938 and 1939 because, of course, Austria and the Sudetenland were predominantly Catholic.

As we have seen, the Nazi Party achieved its best election results in Protestant villages and its worst in the Catholic countryside. The predominantly Protestant and Catholic towns lay between these extremes. In the smallest municipalities with fewer than 250 residents, the differences between confessional areas were far greater still. Thus, in Rhenish Hesse, but also in other areas of the Reich, Protestant villages where more than 90 percent of the votes went to the Nazi Party in 1932 and 1933 were far from a rarity, and the same may be said of Catholic villages in which the Nazi party received almost no votes at all.

If we combine size of municipality and confessional share, we find that the pattern of new Nazi party memberships is very similar to that pertaining to Nazi Party votes. In small, largely Protestant municipalities with fewer than two thousand inhabitants, between 1925 and 1945 the Nazi Party generally achieved above-average recruitment rates at 66 percent of all party memberships within this municipality size category, whereas in predominantly Protestant large towns only around 46 percent of all new party memberships came from this size of municipality (see Table 4.3). If we differentiate according to the period of entry into the party, the correlations are clearer still: prior to the Nazi takeover, in municipalities with fewer than two thousand inhabitants, between 72 percent and 75 percent of all those joining came from predominantly Protestant localities, while between just 10 and 11 percent came from largely Catholic ones. In the case of the small Protestant municipalities, measured against the percentage of voters, this value was far above average, and in the case of small Catholic municipalities far below average. Meanwhile, in predominantly Protestant large towns, the Nazi Party had a far harder time recruiting members both before and after the "seizure of power" than in largely Protestant villages, small towns, and medium-sized towns.

Table 4.3 also reveals that after the appointment of Adolf Hitler as Reich chancellor and the establishment of the Third Reich, the Nazi Party managed to catch up in the Catholic municipalities, though it was unable to achieve quite the same rate of entry as in the predominantly Protestant localities. Along the lines of the elections, prior to the "seizure of power" the Nazi Party strongholds in terms of attracting new members were small Protestant municipalities, while small Catholic municipalities were weak spots or diaspora for the Hitler movement. Following the "seizure of power" the floodgates opened in Catholic areas, with the conclusion in July of 1933 of the *Reichskonkordat* between Nazi Germany and the Vatican no doubt playing a role. However, by then the party was already closed to new members. Even during the Third Reich, when it came to joining the party Catholics in villages were substantially more resistant than those in larger Catholic municipalities and, above all, the residents of small and medium-sized largely Catholic towns.

We are also in a position to ascertain whether, compared with men, women from predominantly Catholic municipalities less frequently joined the Nazi Party than the average for all women or than women from largely Protestant municipalities. This seems plausible given the Catholic Church's reserved stance towards National Socialism and its rejection by many members of the Catholic clergy in predominantly Catholic municipalities, combined with the fact that women's ties to the Church were generally stronger in the Weimar Republic than men's and they were more likely to be influenced by the Church than men. Furthermore, it seems reasonable to assume that the potential effect of Church ties may have been more significant in smaller municipalities than in larger ones due to the greater degree of social control.

Our data does in fact tend to confirm both hypotheses: across all municipality size categories, before the "seizure of power," in municipalities with more than 50 percent Catholics relatively fewer women than men joined the Nazi Party. After 30 January 1933, this correlation persisted, though in somewhat weakened form. Conversely, the assumption that the effect of the confessional context was greater in smaller municipalities than in larger ones finds confirmation only with respect to the smallest and largest of munici-

Table 4.3. Entry to the Nazi Party by size of municipality, confession, and period of joining. Legend: row percentage. Reading aid: of Nazi Party members who had joined by 30 September 1930 in localities with fewer than two thousand inhabitants, around 72 percent were resident in municipalities with fewer than 25 percent Catholics, but in which only around 60 percent of voters lived, and around 11 percent lived in municipalities with more than 75 percent Catholics and home to around 27 percent of voters. Created by the author.

Municipality size category (precise)	Periods of entry	0–24 % Catholic	25–49 % Catholic	50–74 % Catholic	75–100 % Catholic
Up to 2,000 inhabitants	27 February 1925 to 30 September 1930	72	11	6	11
	1 October 1930 to 30 January 1933	75	10	4	10
	31 January 1933 to 31 December 1933	65	7	6	21
	1 January 1 1934 to April 1, 1945	65	10	7	19
	Voters	60	9	5	27
2,000 to 5,000 inhabitants	27 February 1925 to 30 September 1930	69	10	3	18
	1 October 1930 to 30 January 1933	71	10	3	16
	31 January 1933 to 31 December 1933	60	5	2	33
	1 January 1934 to 1 April 1945	65	6	4	24
	Voters	52	6	4	38
5,000 to 20,000 inhabitants	27 February 1925 to 30 September 1930	65	15	5	15
	1 October 1930 to 30 January 1933	70	14	4	13
	31 January 1933 to 31 December 1933	64	11	5	20

	1 January 1934 to 1 April 1945	65	10	4	21
	Voters	58	13	7	22
20,000 to 100,000 inhabitants	27 February 1925 to 30 September 1930	58	21	6	15
	1 October 1930 to 30 January 1933	62	21	7	10
	31 January 1933 to 31 December 1933	58	16	9	17
	1 January 1934 to 1 April 1945	61	16	9	14
	Voters	55	18	11	16
100,000 to 1,000,000 inhabitants	27 February 1925 to 30 September 1930	40	24	7	29
	1 October 1930 to 30 January 1933	49	21	10	20
	31 January 1933 to 31 December 1933	47	18	12	23
	1 January 1934 to 1 April 1945	46	20	14	20
	Voters	43	27	13	17
Total	27 February 1925 to 30 September 1930	62	16	6	16
	1 October 1930 to 30 January 1933	67	14	6	13
	31 January 1933 to 31 December 1933	61	11	7	21
	1 January 1934 to 1 April 1945	61	12	8	18
	Population	54	8	5	33

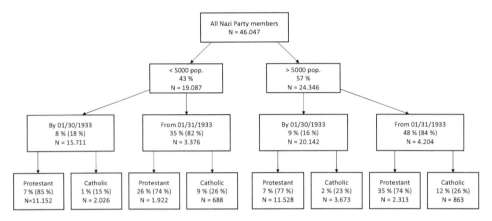

Figure 4.2. New Nazi Party members in the Old Reich by size of place of residence, date of entry, and confessional character of place of residence. Legend: Weighted share. Before the parenthesis: category as a share of all Nazi Party members. Values in parentheses: given subcategory as a share of the relevant supercategory. Reading aid: upon joining the Nazi Party, 1 percent of members from the Old Reich (including the Saar region and Danzig) who had become members prior to the "seizure of power" lived in municipalities with fewer than five thousand inhabitants and a share of Catholics of more than 50 percent. In parentheses: 85 percent of members who had joined prior to 30 January 1933 from municipalities with fewer than five thousand inhabitants lived in localities with a majority Protestant population. Created by the author.

pality size categories. Until the "seizure of power," of new female members 25 percent came from the predominantly Catholic large towns, and just 10 percent from villages. There is no linear relationship with municipality size.[7]

Figure 4.2 once again summarizes the distribution of Nazi Party members across the various confessional contexts with regard to the size of locality and date of joining. A total of around 25 percent of all Nazi Party members in the so-called Old Reich came from predominantly Catholic municipalities and, logically enough, around 75 percent from predominantly Protestant ones. Prior to the "seizure of power," upon joining the party only 3 percent of Nazi Party members lived in municipalities with more than 50 percent Catholics, and around 14 percent in predominantly Protestant localities. Generally speaking, following the Nazis' "seizure of power" Nazi Party members from predominantly Catholic municipalities began to "catch up": now, around 26 percent came from villages and smaller municipalities with more than 50 percent Catholics, whereas "only" 74 percent came from predominantly Protestant areas with fewer than five thousand inhabitants. Previously the figures had been 15 percent and 85 percent. The Nazi Party was similarly successful in predominantly Catholic municipalities with more than five thousand inhabitants. Only 26 percent of the inhabitants of small, medium-sized, and large towns who joined the party after the "seizure of power" came from predominantly Catholic municipalities, while 74 percent came from areas with more than 50 percent Protestants. Overall, prior to the "seizure of power," in Catholic municipalities the Nazi Party had a significantly harder time recruiting members than in predominantly Protestant milieus, a trend that continued, though less dramatically, after January 30, 1933—though the gap was far narrower than in the case of voting.

An Analysis of Those Who Left the Nazi Party

As we have seen, between 1925 and 1933 the Nazi Party had a palpably more difficult time attracting both voters and members in the predominantly Catholic municipalities in our sample than in the largely Protestant areas. Departures from the party exhibit a similar pattern. In all four periods of entry, departure rates among "party comrades" (*Parteigenossen*) from Catholic-dominated municipalities are higher, sometimes significantly, than the rates of entry in this municipality category (see Table 4.4). Thus, prior to the Reichstag election of 1930, only around 11 percent of all new members came from municipalities with more than 75 percent Catholics. The figure for departures from the party was 23 percent. The pattern between 1934 and 1945 was similar, with 19 percent of new party members resident in this municipality category, which saw no less than 33 percent of all departures from the party. Conversely, overall the departure rates in predominantly Protestant municipalities were slightly or significantly below the average for all municipalities.

We can explain the different departure rates with the help of the general incentive model: social pressure, fear of isolation, membership in a political minority, as well as fewer opportunities given the weaker penetration of some Catholic areas by local Nazi Party groups presented obstacles to joining the party while, by the same token, facilitating the decision to leave it.[8] In Catholic areas, the social and personal costs of joining proved disproportionately high, whereas, at least prior to the establishment of the Third Reich, residents in these municipalities, the vast majority of whom were critical of the Nazi Party, typically welcomed a decision to leave it.

Figure 4.3 recapitulates the correlation between confessional context and the probability of leaving the Nazi Party. It emerges that, with just one exception, in every scenario we find more departures in the Catholic than in the Protestant context, regardless of whether those leaving came from localities with fewer or more than five thousand inhabitants and (albeit only in the case of the smaller municipalities) whether they had joined the party prior to or after 30 January 1933. However, among those who had

Table 4.4. Departures from the Nazi Party by confessional milieu and time period (Old Reich only). Legend: around 20 percent of those who had joined the Nazi Party by 14 September 1930 and remained in it were resident in municipalities with 75 percent or more Catholics; of those who left the party again during the same time period, around 23 percent lived in municipalities of this type. During this period of entry, municipalities with fewer than 25 percent Catholics were home to around 61 percent of new party members who stayed in the party, but only 56 percent of those who left it again. Created by the author.

Departure	Periods of entry	0–24 % Catholic	25–49 % Catholic	50–74 % Catholic	75–100 % Catholic
No	by 14 September 1930	65	15	6	14
	by 30 January 1933	67	15	6	12
	by 1 May 1933	62	11	7	20
	by 20 April 1937	61	13	8	18
	Total	62	12	7	18
Yes	by 14 September 1930	59	16	6	19
	by 30 January 1933	66	13	5	16
	by 1 May 1933	55	12	5	27
	by 20 April 1937	80	4	0	16
	Total	61	13	5	20
	Voters	58	14	7	21

joined the party prior to the "seizure of power" the gap is generally greater than among those who joined only after this key date. Overall, the departure rates prior to 1933 were significantly higher than after Hitler's appointment as Reich chancellor. Hence, the confessional character of their areas of residence influenced the likelihood of individuals not just joining but also leaving the Nazi Party, albeit to a much lesser extent than in voting in Reichstag and presidential elections. The fact that the barriers to joining the party were markedly greater prior to the "seizure of power" than after it can also be explained by means of the "General Incentives Theory." Before 1933, particularly during those years when the Nazi Party was still a small seemingly insignificant faction, and especially in the predominantly Catholic municipalities, joining proved to be riskier and associated with higher social costs than after the establishment of the Third Reich. This

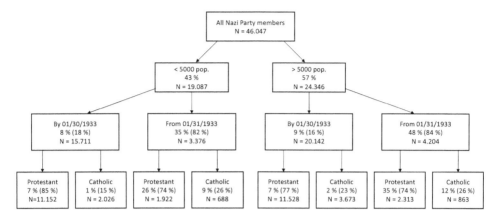

Figure 4.3. Departures from the Nazi Party by size of place of residence, date of entry, and confessional context. Legend: Weighted share. Old Reich (including Saar region and Danzig). Reading aid: 36 percent of Nazi Party members from the Old Reich (including Saar region and Danzig) who had become members prior to the "seizure of power" and who lived in municipalities with fewer than five thousand inhabitants and a share of Catholics of more than 50 percent upon joining the party had left it again by 1945. Created by the author.

also applies, in reverse, to leaving the party. Prior to 1933, above all in the predominantly Catholic localities, this tended to be socially rewarded, but became increasingly risky from 1933 on, though in the Catholic milieu the risk was somewhat moderated by ongoing resistance to National Socialism.

Summary and Synopsis

Studies of voting behavior in the Weimar Republic have revealed confessional affiliation to be the most important determinant of Nazi Party electoral support. From 1930 at the latest there was a very close statistical correlation between the proportion of Protestants and Nazi Party vote share at both municipality and district level: the higher the percentage of Protestant residents, the higher, on average, the share of votes for the Nazi Party. By the same token, the higher the proportion of Catholic inhabitants, the lower on average the percentage of Nazi Party votes. This is one of the closest statistical correlations that can be shown with respect to voting behavior in the Weimar Republic, and it persists even if we factor in the influence of other attributes such as occupational structure, unemployment rate, and size of municipality. Had there only been Catholics in the German Reich in July 1932 and if they had behaved at elections as did the Catholic minority at the time, the Nazi Party would have attracted the votes of no more than 16 percent rather than just under 32 percent of voters; conversely, had the Reich consisted only of Protestants, the Nazi Party would have been chosen by around 38 percent of voters. Translated into valid votes, in this case the Nazi Party would have achieved a vote share of 45 percent rather than "just" 37.4 percent.

Rates of entry into the Nazi Party were also influenced by confessional context, albeit to a far lesser degree than voting behavior. When it comes both to taking up membership as well as departure from the party, there were clear differences between Catholic and Protestant municipalities and districts, though they were less dramatic than in the case of voting behavior. Prior to 1933, far fewer new Nazi Party members came from predominantly Catholic municipalities than from mostly Protestant ones, a gap that narrowed but persisted after 1933. An inverse picture applies to exit from the party: proportionally more of those who left lived in majority Catholic municipalities than in Protestant-dominated ones, though once again the differences were more marked prior to the "seizure of power" than after Hitler's appointment as Reich chancellor.

Why Catholics or Catholic municipalities and regions proved comparatively immune to the Nazi contagion and why, conversely, predominantly Protestant municipalities on average voted so strongly for the Nazi Party, has been the subject of a fair number of "clever" interpretations but few systematic attempts at explanation.[9] Some scholars have identified a certain affinity on the part of many Protestant clergy with "German National" and to some extent antisemitic ideas and ideology, while others have highlighted the existence, since the *Kulturkampf* in the Bismarck era, of a tight-knit Catholic milieu, which was held together not only by a large number of intermediary organizations but also distinguished by clear, immediately recognizable and constantly repeated voting norms. A good Catholic had to vote for the Center Party or the BVP in Bavaria; anything else was long out of the question. Most Catholic clergy and many bishops took a negative view of the Nazi Party, to the point that in a number of dioceses the Church authorities declared active membership in the party incompatible with the Catholic faith and threatened to excommunicate those who held it. This distance from National Socialism, articulated by Church figures and even demanded officially in dioceses such as Mainz, was virtually non-existent in Protestant areas.[10]

We cannot overlook a certain ideological proximity of strong currents within the Protestant church to National Socialism, which a fair number of Protestant theologians extolled as a movement of national renewal. After the Nazi Party's surprise victory at the September elections of 1930, other church dignitaries, who, rather than articulating a deep commitment to Nazism, probably believed themselves to be pursuing a sort of *Realpolitik*, attempted to appropriate the National Socialist movement to advance the Protestant cause. This approach seems to have had unintended consequences. In so doing, they diminished rather than strengthened resistance to National Socialism. Many Protestant clergymen's embrace of the Hitler movement was reinforced not just by their sometimes fanatical antagonism towards Catholicism, but also by German Protestantism's traditional status as a "national church," obedient to the temporal authorities. This tradition seems to have been quite compatible with the National Socialist demand for a German Christianity, in contrast to the "ultramontane" Catholic Church with its unambiguous orientation towards Rome. In light of these realities, it comes as no surprise to read that "a significant number of Protestant theology students show up for classes at university wearing swastika badges, in full view of their professors. The same goes for the seminary students."[11] While Catholic clergy were strictly forbidden to express public support for National Socialism prior to 1933, let alone to apply for membership in the Nazi Party, many Protestant pastors were quite open about their Nazi sympathies. A fair number of them joined the party between 1930 and 1933, probably setting an example for churchgoers, the impact of which should not be underestimated. It seems reasonable to assume that after 1930 a political climate favorable to National Socialism prevailed within broader, mostly rural Protestant circles, which renders comprehensible the mass shift from the Protestant-bourgeois parties to the Nazi Party.

Probably the most important social scientific attempt to explain the phenomena discussed in this article is the theory of political confessionalism put forward by American political scientist Walter Dean Burnham.[12] This theory bears on the relative stability of both the Catholic and socialist parties at Reichstag elections. The idea here is that both types of party turned their voters into loyal supporters by furnishing them with an all-encompassing and comprehensive worldview, a belief system that facilitated a broad-based set of behavioral rules as long as one complied with the "true faith." This received social reinforcement through the integration of voters into a highly developed, tight-knit subculture, that is, a socialist or Catholic social ecosystem with its own associations, newspapers, trade unions and political parties. In addition to the requisite interpretations of political affairs, this supposedly provided ongoing validation and reinforcement of the worldview in question. As a result, on this view, individual voters became enduringly committed to "their" party organization and its objectives, which in turn engendered the high degree of stability that typified the socialist and Catholic camps, even in times of crisis, and the pronounced resistance of these subcultures' members to the National Socialist contagion.

The Protestant-bourgeois camp, by contrast, supposedly consisted essentially of loose associations that could provide neither a comprehensive worldview with associated behavioral expectations and control nor a supportive social milieu through which voters were, so to speak, permanently mobilized and motivated in line with party objectives. The consequences, if this theory is correct, were a lower degree of social cohesion, less pronounced ties to party and thus less behavioral stability as well as weaker immunity to extremist forces. For Burnham, the concept of political confessionalism allows us to explain not just the differences in political behavior between the left-wing and Catholic camps on the one hand and the non-Catholic bourgeois block on the other. It also helps us to explain the extraordinary stability of the voting blocs, which went hand-in-hand with great instability among the political parties, and ultimately the substantial resistance of the left-wing and Catholic electorate to the National Socialist "contagion," as contemporaneous with the extreme "infection" of the "politically unchurched middle classes," as Burnham calls members of the Protestant-bourgeois camp. As far as the influence of confession is concerned, both at the level of voters and—in attenuated form—at the level of party membership, our findings corroborate this explanatory approach.

Jürgen Falter is Senior Research Professor at the University of Mainz. He is the author of fourteen monographs and editor of eighteen volumes, most of which analyze election results and voting patterns in twentieth-century Germany, especially the Nazi era.

Notes

In terms of both findings and wording, the following remarks on voting behavior borrow heavily from the relevant sections in my book: Jürgen W. Falter, *Hitlers Wähler* (Munich: Beck, 1991), 169ff.

1. See Johannes Schauff, *Das Wahlverhalten der deutschen Katholiken im Kaiserreich und in der Weimarer Republik. Untersuchungen aus dem Jahre 1928* (Mainz: Matthias-Grünewald-Verlag, 1975), according to which, even in 1933 "two-thirds of active, practicing Catholics" still voted for the Center Party or BVP. Quoted in Ulrich von Hehl, "Staatsverständnis und Strategie des politischen Katholizismus in der Weimarer Republik," in *Die Weimarer Republik 1928–1933. Politik—Wirtschaft—Gesellschaft*, ed. Karl Dietrich Bracher, Manfred Funke, and Hans-Adolf Jacobsen (Bonn: Bundeszentrale für politische Bildung, 1988), 238–54, 241. Cf. also my essay: Jürgen W. Falter, "Die Wählerpotentiale politischer Teilkulturen 1920–1933," in *Politische Identität und nationale Gedenktag. Zur politischen Kultur in der Weimarer Republik*, ed. Detlef Lehnert and Klaus Megerle (Opladen: Westdeutscher Verlag, 1989), 281–305; and Karl Schmitt, *Konfession und Wahlverhalten in der Bundesrepublik Deutschland* (Berlin: Duncker & Humblot, 1989).

2. Hindenburg narrowly won the second round of the Reich presidential election of 1925 in significant part due to the backing of the BVP, the Center Party's Catholic sister party. The BVP's momentous decision to support Hindenburg most likely made his election possible in

the first place. As a result, Hindenburg gained almost exactly the five hundred thousand votes from the Catholic camp that would otherwise have assured victory for Wilhelm Marx. Cf. my study: Jürgen W. Falter, "The Two Hindenburg Elections of 1925 and 1932: A Statistical Analysis," *Central European History* 23 (1991): 225–41.

3. See my essay: Jürgen W. Falter, "*Die Wahlen des Jahres 1932/33 und der Aufstieg der totalitären Parteien,*" in *Die Weimarer Republik: Das Ende der Demokratie 1929–1933*, ed. Everhart Holtmann (Munich: Bayerische Landeszentrale für Politische Bildungsarbeit, 1995), 271–314.

4. There were, of course, exceptions to this rule here and there, for example within the territory of the former princely abbey of Kempten, where the Catholic peasants voted disproportionately often for the Nazi Party compared to other Catholic agrarian regions. See Dietrich Thränhardt, *Wahlen und politische Strukturen in Bayern 1848–1953. Historisch-soziologische Untersuchungen zum Entstehen und zur Neuerrichtung eines Parteiensystems* (Düsseldorf: Droste, 1973). On certain Catholic municipalities in the southern Black Forest that deviated from the prescribed voting norm and switched to the Nazi Party early on, see Oded Heilbronner, "Der verlassene Stammtisch. Vom Verfall der bürgerlichen Infrastruktur und dem Aufstieg der NSDAP am Beispiel der Region Schwarzwald," *Geschichte und Gesellschaft* 19, no. 2 (1993): 178–201.

5. Ecological regression is a procedure that allows us, under certain conditions, to extrapolate from the relationships between two attributes at area level, such as confessional share and Nazi Party vote share, the individual voting behavior that underpins it. See Falter, *Hitlers Wähler*, 441–43.

6. Figure 4.1 is based on the results of the analysis by Alexander Röckl, "Politische Tradition und NSDAP-Beitritt," in *Junge Kämpfer, alte Opportunisten. Die Mitglieder der NSDAP 1919–1945*, ed. Jürgen W. Falter. (Frankfurt am Main: Campus Verlag, 2016), 217–43.

7. For more detail and evidence as well as more precise counts, see Chapter 3 of Jürgen W. Falter, *Hitlers Parteigenossen. Die Mitglieder der NSDAP 1919–1945* (Frankfurt am Main: Campus Verlag, 2020).

8. On the general incentives model and its application to party-joining and -leaving behavior in the case of the Nazi Party, see Jonas Meßner, "Warum treten Menschen Parteien bei und warum verlassen manche sie wieder? Theoretische Ansätze zur Erklärung von Parteibeitritten und Parteiaustritten am Beispiel der NSDAP," in *Junge Kämpfer, alte Opportunisten. Die Mitglieder der NSDAP 1919–1945*, ed. Jürgen W. Falter (Frankfurt am Main: Campus Verlag: 2016), 41–64; and Jonas Meßner, "Austritte aus der NSDAP 1925–1945," in *Junge Kämpfer, alte Opportunisten. Die Mitglieder der NSDAP 1919–1945*, ed. Jürgen W. Falter (Frankfurt am Main: Campus Verlag, 2016), 271–95.

9. For a theory-guided attempt at explanation, see Walter Dean Burnham, "Political Immunization and Political Confessionalism: The United States and Weimar Germany," *Journal of Interdisciplinary History* 2 (1972): 1–30.

10. See Falter, *Hitlers Wähler*, 169ff. Even here there were exceptions, however, as in Württemberg, where Protestant Bishop Theophil Wurm certainly exercised a degree of influence on his congregation as an avowed opponent of National Socialism. In Württemberg, the Nazi Party had a harder time at elections than in other regions of the German Reich with a similar structure. See Jürgen W. Falter and Hartmut Bömermann, "Die unterschiedlichen Wahlerfolge der NSDAP in Baden und Württemberg: Ergebnis differierender Sozialstruktur oder regionalspezifischer Faktoren?" in *Parteien und regionale politische Traditionen in der Bundesrepublik Deutschland*, ed. Dieter Oberndörfer and Karl Schmitt (Berlin: Duncker & Humblot, 1991), 283–98.

11. Quotation from an article published under the heading "Hakenkreuz und Christentum sind keine Gegensätze" ["There is no Contradiction between the Swastika and Christianity"]. *Sonntagsblatt des arbeitenden Volkes*, 14 December 1930, which was published in Mannheim and aligned with the Protestant and socialist camps. Quoted in Nikolaus Hovorka, ed., *Zwischenspiel Hitler. Ziel und Wirklichkeit des Nationalsozialismus. Sonderabdruck der Berichte zur Kultur-und Zeitgeschichte* (Vienna: Reinhold-Verlag, 1932), 283.

12. Burnham, "Political Immunization," 1–30.

Bibliography

Burnham, Walter Dean. "Political Immunization and Political Confessionalism: The United States and Weimar Germany." *Journal of Interdisciplinary History* 2 (1972): 1–30.

Falter, Jürgen W. "*Die Wahlen des Jahres 1932/33 und der Aufstieg der totalitären Parteien.*" In *Die Weimarer Republik: Das Ende der Demokratie 1929–1933*, edited by Everhart Holtmann, 271–314. Munich: Bayerische Landeszentrale für Politische Bildungsarbeit, 1995.

———. "Die Wählerpotentiale politischer Teilkulturen 1920–1933." In *Politische Identität und nationale Gedenktag. Zur politischen Kultur in der Weimarer Republik*, edited by Detlef Lehnert and Klaus Megerle, 281–305. Opladen: Westdeutscher Verlag, 1989.

———. *Hitlers Parteigenossen. Die Mitglieder der NSDAP 1919–1945*. Frankfurt am Main: Campus Verlag, 2020.

———. *Hitlers Wähler*. Munich: Beck, 1991 (2nd revised and enlarged edition Frankfurt am Main: Campus Verlag, 2020).

———. "The Two Hindenburg Elections of 1925 and 1932: A Statistical Analysis." *Central European History* 23 (1991): 225–41.

Falter, Jürgen W., and Hartmut Bömermann. "Die unterschiedlichen Wahlerfolge der NSDAP in Baden und Württemberg: Ergebnisse differierender Sozialstruktur oder regionalspezifischer Faktoren?" In *Parteien und regionale politische Traditionen in der Bundesrepublik Deutschland*, edited by Dieter Oberndörfer and Karl Schmitt, 283–98. Berlin: Duncker & Humblot, 1991.

"Hakenkreuz und Christentum sind keine Gegensätze." *Sonntagsblatt des arbeitenden Volkes*, 14 December 1930.

Hehl, Ulrich von. "Staatsverständnis und Strategie des politischen Katholizismus in der Weimarer Republik." In *Die Weimarer Republik 1928–1933. Politik—Wirtschaft—Gesellschaft*, edited by Karl Dietrich Bracher, Manfred Funke, and Hans-Adolf Jacobsen, 238–54. Bonn: Bundeszentrale für politische Bildung, 1988.

Heilbronner, Oded. "Der verlassene Stammtisch. Vom Verfall der bürgerlichen Infrastruktur und dem Aufstieg der NSDAP am Beispiel der Region Schwarzwald." *Geschichte und Gesellschaft* 19, no. 2 (1993): 178–201.

Hovorka, Nikolaus, ed. *Zwischenspiel Hitler. Ziel und Wirklichkeit des Nationalsozialismus. Sonderabdruck der Berichte zur Kultur-und Zeitgeschichte*. Vienna: Reinhold-Verlag, 1932.

Meßner, Jonas. "Austritte aus der NSDAP 1925–1945." In *Junge Kämpfer, alte Opportunisten. Die Mitglieder der NSDAP 1919–1945*, edited by Jürgen W. Falter, 271–95. Frankfurt am Main: Campus Verlag, 2016.

———. "Warum treten Menschen Parteien bei und warum verlassen manche sie wieder? Theoretische Ansätze zur Erklärung von Parteibeitritten und Parteiaustritten am Beispiel der NSDAP." In *Junge Kämpfer, alte Opportunisten. Die Mitglieder der NSDAP 1919–1945*, edited by Jürgen W. Falter, 41–64. Frankfurt am Main: Campus Verlag, 2016.

Röckl, Alexander. "Politische Tradition und NSDAP-Beitritt." In *Junge Kämpfer, alte Opportunisten. Die Mitglieder der NSDAP 1919–1945*, edited by Jürgen W. Falter, 217–43. Frankfurt am Main: Campus Verlag, 2016.

Schauff, Johannes. *Das Wahlverhalten der deutschen Katholiken im Kaiserreich und in der Weimarer Republik. Untersuchungen aus dem Jahre 1928*. Mainz: Matthias-Grünewald-Verlag, 1975.

Schmitt, Karl. *Konfession und Wahlverhalten in der Bundesrepublik Deutschland*. Berlin: Duncker & Humblot, 1989.

Thränhardt, Dietrich. *Wahlen und politische Strukturen in Bayern 1848–1953. Historisch-soziologische Untersuchungen zum Entstehen und zur Neuerrichtung eines Parteiensystems*. Düsseldorf: Droste, 1973.

Chapter Five

THE FASCIST ORIGINS OF GERMAN ECUMENISM

James Chappel

Ecumenism and dialogue are normally viewed as "good things." And perhaps they are—but one task of the historian is to find the barbarism in the wake of each document of civilization. Ecumenism takes place not in the heavens, but on earth, and in specific political contexts. Formerly estranged communities can come together in one of two ways. They might join hands on the terms of the more powerful, as for instance when one Protestant denomination swallows another, or when East Germany joined the West. Or they might come together more equitably, in the name of a higher unity. In either case, our political or moral judgment of the case will depend upon the nature of the new community in formation.

In this chapter, I will explore German ecumenism in the early 1930s to show that, in this time and place, interfaith dialogue primarily served the interests of the National Socialists. As such, the most "humanist" and anti-fascist religious thinkers of the period tended to reject ecumenism—not out of religious chauvinism, but because they rejected the new political-theological community that it conjured. Specifically, this chapter will focus on Catholic intellectuals in the 1930s, asking why they did or did not seek dialogue with Protestants. This is a narrow source base, and a narrow temporal framing, but my hope is that it will cast new light on German interconfessionalism in the *longue durée*.[1]

There are two basic hypotheses in play as to how confessional relations improved in Germany. The first is what we might call the "pragmatic" hypothesis, and its defenders focus on social and political history.[2] The idea here is that the attention paid to explosive conflict has obscured the workaday ways in which Catholics and Protestants learned to work together in the late nineteenth century. While it was ever fraught, the tremendous dislocations of World War II completed a long process of *milieu* disintegration at the level of lived reality. The second might be called the "resistance" hypothesis. Drawing more on theological and intellectual history, scholars in this mold argue that it was the experience of the Resistance that riveted Catholics and Protestants together more than ever before, and which gave figures like Yves Congar, Max Metzger, and John Courtney Murray the space to forge the ideas that would eventually filter into more everyday forms of cohabitation.[3]

There is a great deal of truth to both of these accounts, which are after all compatible with one another given that World War II provided the impetus both for the dissolution of the *milieu* and the hegemony of new ideals. And yet something important is missing. To see what it is, we can take political party alignment as a convenient yardstick for interconfessional relations. The "pragmatism" hypothesis helps us to understand, above all, the Center Party. This party was technically interconfessional and open to Protestants. In the Weimar era, despite the almost total lack of theological innovation vis-à-vis Protestants, the Center Party was a bastion of the republic, and thus worked pragmatically with Protestants with great frequency (especially in Prussia).[4] The "resistance" hypothesis, in turn, helps us to understand the Christian Democratic Union, which gathered together both Protestant and Catholic votes into a project that at least claimed to have roots in the anti-fascist resistance.

Both the Center Party and the CDU were institutional mechanisms for interconfessional dialogue, to be sure. But there was another party that came to power between the two, one that was the first party in German history to garner mass support from both Catholics and Protestants. I refer, of course, to the National Socialist Party. Neither story takes the experience of National Socialism seriously (I mean the widespread and emotional experience of being swept into the *Volksgemeinschaft*, not the more sporadic and fraught one of joining the Resistance). My contention in this chapter will be that the National Socialist period provided an important and largely overlooked contribution to the easing of confessional relations in modern Germany.[5] The analysis will largely follow in the footsteps of Ralf Dahrendorf and David Schoenbaum, who decades ago made the controversial claim that the National Socialists had been unwitting modernizers of the German national project, helping to destroy the various subnational identities that had long divided Germans from one another.[6] More directly, it draws on the argument in my book on the Catholic Church, in which I argue that it was in the 1930s, and largely in response to the fascist temptation, that Europe's Catholics abandoned their hopes for confessional statehood and embraced some form of religious freedom.[7]

The Catholic intellectual scene in the early 1930s was vibrant, and could differ dramatically between different regions or different religious orders. To organize the discussion, the bulk of the chapter will be in two parts, each of which will focus on an individual to elucidate the meaning of ecumenism at the time. Both lived in the Rhineland, which was an intellectual center of German-speaking Catholicism. The first will focus on Karl Eschweiler, one of the foremost ecumenical thinkers of the era—and, not coincidentally, an enthusiastic National Socialist. The second section will focus on Waldemar Gurian, a convert to the faith who opposed both ecumenism and Nazism. These two were chosen for three reasons. First, they represented a major constituency of opinion, and each section will root them in a broader constellation of periodicals and politics. Second, they published regularly enough that the evolution of their ideas can be easily tracked. And third, they were for a time rather close friends, who had a falling out once the Nazis came to power. Their personal stories therefore map onto the broader lesson of ecumenical history. The creation of new communities, however welcome it might be, requires the demolition of old ones.

Karl Eschweiler and Ecumenical Nazism

For German Catholics in the wake of World War I, ecumenism did not necessarily mean anything like democracy, human rights, or peace. It meant collaboration with a specific form of Protestantism in pursuit of a specific political project. Given the nature of Weimar Germany, this Protestantism, and this project, was conservative and nationalist. In fact, it was the most revanchist and reactionary of Catholics (Adam Stegerwald, for one) who were arguing for interconfessional collaboration. For what, specifically, would ecumenism have entailed in the 1920s, politically? The Center Party was not, in practice, ecumenical—it was a cross-class alliance of Catholic workers, peasants, and businessmen. Given the state of German Protestantism at the time, ecumenism could only mean a shift to the right—and towards nationalism and against the Jews.[8]

This was the environment in which Karl Eschweiler, a priest born in 1886, began to warm towards Protestantism. Eschweiler is well known, as is his conservative nationalism, but he has been in my view misinterpreted. Vincent Berning and Robert A. Krieg find a sort of medievalism in Eschweiler's approach to politics. This is another version of Ernst-Wolfgang Böckenförde's classic argument, according to which Catholics had never properly made peace with the principles of 1789 and fell back on musty natural law theories to accommodate themselves with reaction and, eventually, with Nazism.⁹

There did exist some Catholic radicals who were so distrustful of modernity, and Jews, that they clung to Nazism as a sort of life raft (Max Buchner might fall into this category). Karl Eschweiler was among them. He was one of the most celebrated and innovative theologians of the era, and his *Die Zwei Wegen der neueren Theologie* (1926) was one of its most-discussed theological tomes. In it, Eschweiler had argued, along the lines of Jacques Maritain, for a thoroughly renovated form of neo-Thomism that might allow Catholicism to grapple intellectually with the modern age.¹⁰

Specifically, Eschweiler was at pains to argue that the Cartesian, rational individual developed organically from scholastic theology and did not represent a subjectivist incursion from the Reformation or the Enlightenment.¹¹ So already in 1926, Eschweiler was evincing skepticism of the standard Catholic attitude towards the Reformation. For centuries, Catholics had viewed Luther as an emissary of Satan, responsible for rupturing the glorious unity of medieval Christendom. In Germany, this view had recently been articulated by two Catholic historians: Hartmann Grisar and Heinrich Denifle. During and after World War I, though, nationalist-minded Catholics began a rehabilitation of Luther. Max Scheler, one of Eschweiler's mentors, had positive things to say about Luther in his enormously popular wartime writings, as did the Church historians Franz Xaver Kiefl and Sebastian Merkle.¹² This discourse was most popular among ultranationalists. Dietrich Eckart, an early bridge-builder between Nazism and Catholicism, lauded Luther for his nationalism and antisemitism in a 1924 volume.¹³ Eschweiler did not write explicitly on Luther in the 1920s, but one clue does help us to see that he was partial to the Luther revival. He translated Maritain's work on aesthetics without qualm, but he refused to do the same for *Three Reformers*—precisely because that book had a long and damning section on Luther.¹⁴

The political turn in his thought first became apparent in his 1930 book, *Johann Adam Möhler's Concept of the Church*—a book that, as was common in the Catholicism of the era, hid explosive claims amidst a dry explication of a venerated intellect of the past. The book used Möhler to authorize a Catholic account of the state that would depart entirely from the one at work in the Wilhelmine and Weimar Church. Eschweiler thought that the Church had grievously erred in trying to retain sovereign power for itself— either through papal politics in Italy or democratic politics in Germany. This inevitably created conflicts between church and state, resolvable only through theology, not treaties. The problem was that the Church was overstepping its bounds: Möhler taught that the Church was an objective reality, like the state, but with utterly different tasks and prerogatives.

To some extent, of course, this had been Catholic dogma since time immemorial. And yet Eschweiler thought that Catholics had not learned the right lessons because they had not kept their conception of the Church in dialogue with changing times and evolving philosophy. The genius of Möhler was that he had confronted German philosophy—his Church concept was, for Eschweiler, "the centerpiece of the Church's confrontation with German idealism." Eschweiler thought that Hegel was right that the nation-state has a key role to play in modern societies, and that it was the primary ethical community to which we belong as social and economic beings. He was wrong, though, to imagine that this would involve the disappearance or subjectivization of the Church itself. Eschweiler's Möhler pointed the way towards a robust ecclesiology that was somehow compatible with an abandonment of the political and economic fields to the state: he envisioned, Eschweiler thought, an alliance between church and state that would mirror the spiritual/corporeal divide in each human person.[15]

In the early 1930s, these abstract considerations were reified in practice by the National Socialists, who promised a strong national state devoted to collaboration with the churches in the name of "positive Christianity." Indeed, a case could be made that the National Socialist party, not the Christian Democratic Union, was the first interconfessional mass party in German history. This should not be taken too far. Catholicism provided a sturdier bulwark against Nazism than Protestantism did (although this was a low bar), and the "brownest" Catholics came from regions where the traditional *milieu* and its institutions were crumbling (as in the Black Forest region).[16] All the same, it can no longer be maintained that Catholicism provided some sort of immunity against Nazism. Stories such as Eschweiler's are crucial because they help us to see that at least some Catholics—modernizing ones, at that—felt that their faith specifically legitimated their collaboration.

In 1930–31, Eschweiler began to turn towards more concrete political issues. He published an article called "Political Theology" in an ecumenical journal called *Religiöse Besinnung* (it was a continuation of *Una Sancta*, the pioneering ecumenical journal of the Weimar era, which had been shut down after the Church ordered Catholics to stop participating). In the article, he rehearsed his critique of the path that Catholic politics and theology had taken since the Middle Ages. Catholics had disavowed state capture while still presenting the state with all manner of political and economic principles, resulting in a complex and regrettable confusion of church-state relations. The central moment in the Scripture, Eschweiler taught, was when Pilate asked Christ, "What is truth?" (John 18:38). With this question, Pilate indicated a division between the spheres of faith and politics while also signaling an alliance between the two (Eschweiler points out that Pilate asks Christ the question rather than presuming to know himself). The medieval Church had neglected this, and in this sense the Reformation can be understood as "fruit from the tree of the Church of Christ."[17] Eschweiler did not mention National Socialism in that essay, but in a contemporaneous one for *Der Ring*, he made it clear that his reasoning led directly to Nazism: the one movement that understood that the salvation of Germany required a genuine alliance between church and state, not a bourgeois demarcation. "The nation is a true and noble public domain," Eschweiler insisted. "The nation naturally fulfills itself in political existence."[18]

Eschweiler was well aware that this sounded suspiciously Protestant, but this was not a problem, in his view. His writings from the period are generous in their interpretation of Luther and the Reformation. The Reformers, he thought, were "not rationalists, but were rather embarked on a religious quest inspired by strong religious feelings." He began to argue that the Reformation was an overreaction to the errors of the medieval Church. He even suggested that the Reformation was not their fault, and that the path had been opened up by the errors of the Baroque Church. "Mere schoolmasters and scribblers," he reasoned, "could not have shattered the unity of the West."[19] Eschweiler was arguing, therefore, that the Protestants had been right about the proper relationship between faith and politics, even if they were wrong about the nature of grace or the necessity of the visible Church. Catholics and Protestants could, therefore, unite politically under the aegis of Hitler because they shared this patrimony. In fact, in Eschweiler's view, they had to. "Only one thing can endanger" the Nazi revolution, he privately despaired: "the incorporation of the confessional opposition into the Nazi fighting front."[20] Once Hitler came to power, he was even more explicit in his belief that Catholics, not Protestants, were the real problem: Luther had pointed the way towards a revived and spiritually united Germany, he argued, but Catholics had been stubbornly attached to political religion and had stood in the way.[21]

The Jews had no place in Eschweiler's imagined political community, and Judaism for Eschweiler, as it had for so many other Christians throughout history, served as a foil to the properly "spiritual" and apolitical faith of the cross. Judaism, he thought, remained beholden to politicized religiosity, and he thought that the tradition of political Catholicism represented a Jewish holdover that needed to be expelled (he called it "Kibitz-diplomacy"). In a letter to Carl Schmitt, he claimed that Leo Strauss's famous critique of Schmitt's work was illegitimate because it was too Jewish, and therefore too beholden to a bankrupt form of theological politics.[22]

By 1933, therefore, Eschweiler was an ecumenical thinker in the name of Nazism: a party member who wrote and lectured to Catholics about how their true fate lay together with Protestants in a new *Volksgemeinschaft*. He was not alone. The majority of Catholic ecumenical discourse in the 1930s was in the service of Nazism. The warming towards Luther in the 1920s already had a nationalist spin. Scheler, Kiefl, Eckart, and Merkle were all pronounced nationalists, and the only one still alive in 1933 (Merkle) supported Hitler.[23]

There were two ecumenical journals at work in Germany in the early 1930s, and a consideration of both shows how entwined Nazism and ecumenism were at the time. The first, already encountered, was called *Religiöse Besinnung*. Edited by a Protestant socialist named Karl Thieme, it was certainly not founded in the name of nationalism. Nonetheless, in the early 1930s there was essentially no other form for ecumenism to take. Its 1932 issue on "political theology" centered around two figures—Eschweiler and the Protestant theologian Friedrich Gogarten—who were both prominent National Socialists. Rather than continue in this line, Thieme shut the journal down in 1933 when he emigrated (we will return to him below).

The second ecumenical journal at the time, *Catholica*, began publishing in 1932 and was a prominent voice for ecumenical Nazism (Eschweiler did write an essay for the journal, but it seems to have never appeared for some reason).[24] The central figure at the journal was Robert Grosche, like Eschweiler a creature of the Rhineland and a forward-thinking Catholic theologian and priest. He came from the same Schmittean circles as Eschweiler and harbored the same resentment of the "political Catholicism" of the Center Party and the concordat. He was well abreast throughout the 1920s of the Catholic grappling with Luther.[25] By 1932, he was going so far as to claim that Catholics should *learn* from Protestants about how to better politicize and nationalize the Church.[26] He became an exponent of *Reichstheologie* which he expressed at a 1933 congress in Maria Laach that brought together the most fascist of Catholic intellectuals and politicians (including Eschweiler).[27] At around the same time, he gave a widely-reprinted lecture on "The Protestants and Us," in which he made, like Eschweiler, an explicit link between this ecclesiology and ecumenism.[28]

Grosche's Eschweiler-esque position is made most clear in a long article for *Catholica* called "The German Catholic and the 'German Christian'" (this latter term referred to the *Deutsche Christen* movement of pro-Nazi Protestants). While both Lutherans and Catholics share in this dispensation, Grosche argued, the concept of the divine *Reich* is only comprehensible from within a Catholic schema in which grace and nature interpenetrate. But he twisted the narrative, as befits a major figure in German ecumenism. Luther, Grosche held, was responding to serious inadequacies in the medieval Church and had not wanted to split Christianity into two warring camps: the Reformation was, rather, a reasonable reform movement that went too far. Luther was rooted in Augustine and the scholastics, and his religious theories offered access to great truths that had been overlooked by the medieval Church. It is thus, for both Protestants and Catholics, "unfinished business."[29]

One of Grosche's primary strategies was to rehabilitate Luther's personality. Since Denifle and Grisar, Catholics had often presumed that Luther was personally depraved, and that his destruction of the Church could be traced to his own wanton habits and lust. Grisar in particular had turned Luther's slogan *Pecca fortiter* ("Sin bravely") from a theological argument about God's mercy into a warrant for licentiousness without responsibility. This particular argument about Luther, it should be noted, was disproven in a separate article in *Catholica* devoted to rehabilitating Luther's image.[30] Grosche clearly argued against this tradition, too. His Luther was not only making reasoned objections against a flaccid Church; he was also a man of personal nobility and profound spirituality.[31]

Grosche filled his journal with similar positions from Catholic luminaries. Franz Taeschner, a well-known Catholic intellectual and defender of Nazism, published a celebration of Luther in which he claimed Luther to be a great national hero on par with Dante (such a claim would have been unthinkable twenty years earlier).[32] Damasus Winzen published "Thoughts on a 'Theology of the Reich'" there, too—an essay that, unlike traditional Catholic exposition of *Reichstheologie* was explicitly ecumenical. He gave an account of the state that was essentially the same as the one given by Eschweiler in his book on Möhler, before drawing once again the ecumenical corollary. "Since Catholics are a minority in Germany," Winzen mused, "preparation for the Reich is unthinkable without the Protestant population." Thankfully, new developments in both Protestant thought and German politics pointed towards a closing of the Catholic–Protestant divide. Protestants, Winzen argued, do Catholics a service by reminding us of the importance of certain forms of piety—specifically baptism—that we have neglected. By strengthening the Christian belief of all Germans, the Protestants are to be thanked. "Truly," he concluded, "the new political situation in Germany necessitates close collaboration between the Churches."[33]

A survey of pro-Nazi ecumenism in the early 1930s is not complete without Joseph Lortz, who would soon become one of the most influential Catholic thinkers in twentieth-century Germany. We will return to his magisterial work on the Reformation in the conclusion, as it did not appear until 1938. Here, the Lortz of the *Machtergreifung* era fits neatly into the *milieu* under analysis here. He was in Bonn at the same time as Eschweiler and Grosche, and he studied with Sebastian Merkle, one of the 1920s trailblazers in the Catholic rehabilitation of Luther. His Church history textbook, prepared in the early 1930s, was nationalist in tone, bemoaning the Reformation as an unnecessary stumbling block to German unity. In the first edition (1932), he included a celebration of *Führerschaft* and dictatorship, which he dreamed was soon to take place in Germany.[34] The next year, he published a long essay on the state of Luther studies—one that found fault with both doctrinaire Catholic (Grisar) and Protestant (Scheel) versions of Luther, neither of which were able to authorize a true dialogue between the confessions. The essay clearly imagined that such a task would be "of great significance for our collective religious and national life."[35] And like so many of these figures, he became an enthusiastic National Socialist. In his 1934 volume defending the Nazis from a Catholic perspective, he made his logic clear: "The confessional split," he declared, "is the deepest wound from which Germany suffers." The Nazis might have the ability to change that. "For the first time in German history," he claimed, "the nation as a whole" could rally behind one leader.[36]

Eschweiler, Grosche, and Lortz were three of the most influential Catholic thinkers of the early 1930s, and they all mobilized ecumenism in the name of National Socialism. It would be naïve to grant too much historical significance to figures like these: Catholic support for Nazism did not depend upon theological gymnastics. All the same, it is at least plausible that German Catholics might have lent temporary support to Nazism in the name of anti-Bolshevism while retaining their same suspicion of Lutherans and other Protestants. It did not happen this way—and it is reasonable to presume that at least one reason for this is that there existed a widespread intellectual movement, extending into schools and pulpits and newspapers, devoted to reinterpreting Luther and to teaching Catholics that Protestants were true partners. It was not the only one in Germany, however. A smaller movement, and one on the losing side of history, insisted that Luther—and Hitler with him—was just as demonic as Catholics had always taught.

Waldemar Gurian and Anti-ecumenical Resistance

Waldemar Gurian was something of a strange figure in Weimar-era Catholicism. As a Russian-Jewish convert, he was certainly set apart. But as a brilliant polemicist and inveterate networker, he found himself at the center of the most vibrant Catholic intellectual culture in Germany. As I have argued elsewhere, he contributed to it, too: his unique position and interests led him to become the originator of totalitarianism theory, which would do so much to reorient Catholic political thought in the middle decades of the twentieth century.[37] He counted Karl Eschweiler among his many friends, and Eschweiler actually baptized his daughter. The two had a great deal in common. They were both in the orbit of the University of Bonn. They were both influenced by Max Scheler and Carl Schmitt, and they were both regular correspondents with the latter. They were both interested in Jacques Maritain (Grosche referred to the three of them as a sort of neo-Thomist triumvirate).[38] And yet, when it came to both ecumenism and Nazism, they could not have been more different. They were on opposing sides of a fault line in Catholic intellectual culture that was not much noticed at the time, but would prove enormously significant in the early 1930s.

Much has been written about Gurian, but one element of his career that has escaped attention is his suspicion of Protestantism. His first book, *The German Youth Movement* (1923), was written when he was under the spell of Max Scheler. And yet, Scheler's warmth towards Protestantism was wholly absent from the text, largely because Gurian, unlike Scheler, had not been concerned to forge an interconfessional unity during the war (he had been very young during the war, and experienced it only insofar as he was regarded as an enemy national). Gurian in this regard followed his other master—Carl Schmitt—to argue that Protestants lacked any appreciation for form, liturgy, or the body, and thus that the Protestant youth movements would prove as uncertain a guide to national renewal as the Protestant churches had.[39]

Throughout the 1920s, Gurian did not change his mind about Protestantism. If anything, he became more convinced as he fell into the orbit of Jacques Maritain and came to believe that the concrete reality of the Church *qua* institution was the indispensable horizon of Catholic life. He was quick to dismiss anyone who felt otherwise or who believed that anything was to be gained by finding common cause with individualist Protestants. He praised Maritain's *Three Reformers*—the book that Eschweiler would not translate because it was too critical of Luther. He condemned Ernst Michel, one of the few left-leaning Catholics who was actually trying to find common cause with Protestants (in this case Eugen Rosenstock-Huessy, with whom Michel founded Frankfurt's Academy of Labor).[40]

This is not necessarily surprising: Catholics in Germany had long made similar claims about Luther. The important factor here is that Gurian did not belong to the circles of traditionalist, medievalist, and often antisemitic Catholics who rehearsed the anti-Protestantism of the past. Those did exist, and they did result in anti-ecumenical anti-Nazism. This was most clearly the case in the circle surrounding Georg Moenius and the *Allgemeine Rundschau*.[41] Moenius and his colleagues—including Friedrich Wilhelm Foerster, a pacifist and among the most controversial and influential Catholic publicists of the period—launched a full-scale critique on Martin Luther in the 1920s and all of the Prussian barbarities with which he was associated. "Modern Protestantism," one of the journal's leaders proclaimed, "sharply rejects humanism. It revives Luther's darkest teachings on the worthlessness of everything human."[42] Moenius and his circle were heroic anti-Nazis in the early 1930s, but for reactionary reasons. This was not Gurian's position, nor was it that of his Rhenish circle. Like Scheler, Schmitt, and Maritain, Gurian sought an updated form of Catholicism that would be in dialogue with modern social science.[43] What is interesting is that Gurian's zeal for a more "modern" Catholicism did not presuppose improved relations with Protestants. Quite the opposite—and he was not alone.

The most progressive and labor-friendly voices of the Catholic 1920s were wary of ecumenism, too. In the battles over the future of the Center Party in the early 1920s, it was the more democratic and laborite wing led by Josef Joos and Josef Wirth who held the line, preferring to focus on courting working-class Catholics rather than reactionary Protestants. Intellectuals gave voice to this sentiment throughout the 1920s. The left-Catholic Walter Dirks worried that "the mysterious 'Christian-German cultural ideal'" was more Romantic than Christian, and that Catholic-Protestant alliances were based on this chimera ("we must be clear," he insisted, "that almost nothing binds us any more to the great majority of Protestants"). Hermann Platz, editor of *Abendland* and one of the few voices for Franco-German peace in the 1920s, agreed with French critics like Henri Massis and Jacques Maritain that Luther, and the Reformation he unleashed, was behind the dissolution of medieval Christendom and all of the woes of modernity.[44]

The reasons for this were twofold: on the one hand, Catholics like Gurian believed that modernity could be salvaged only by nourishing a visible and sacramental Church, which they believed Protestants were out to vanquish. And, more practically, the Protestants that they could have spoken to in the 1920s seldom shared their vision for a more just and egalitarian society (negotiations between the Center and the DNVP, to state the obvious, were not the means to achieve power for labor unions).

This was true in the 1920s, and it was even truer in the early 1930s, when it became clear that ecumenism was gaining momentum—in the name of nationalism and anti-Communism. Anti-fascist intellectuals began, therefore, to critique ecumenism more forcefully. In the *Zeitschrift für Religion und Sozialismus*, for instance, Dirks published an essay in which he complained that Catholics were seeking the wrong allies. They should, he thought, be focusing on the working classes and on the social justice elements of the Catholic tradition—only those social and ideological forces could truly confront fascism. The "dangerous proximity" between the confessions, he pointed out, was coming at the cost of "truth, justice, and love."[45]

Gurian himself was convinced that Catholic-Protestant dialogue could be only in the service of Nazism. His position was not that all of Germany should convert—he was too much a pragmatist for that—but that Germany should return to a more federalist, Wilhelmine system. He explained this most clearly in his 1932 volume, *On the Future of the Reich*. This was his last publication before fleeing to exile, and in it he excoriated Protestants. Since they do not believe in a "visible Church," he taught, they were susceptible to National Socialism. In terms reminiscent of Dirks and clearly directed against Eschweiler, he worried that "Church politics [for Protestants] is no more than national culture-politics." Only an "ecumenical Church," and therefore a false one, was compatible with the "positive Christianity" supposedly defended by the Nazi regime.[46]

The most interesting example of anti-ecumenical Nazism comes in a surprising place: *Religiöse Besinnung,* the aforementioned ecumenical journal run by Karl Thieme, a Protestant socialist and close friend of Gurian's. He shared the irenic, humanist goals that we normally associate with ecumenism, and as such he was strongly opposed to Hitler. And yet, before he left for exile, he determined that the ecumenical project was bankrupt. We have already seen how his journal played host to proto-Nazi arguments from Eschweiler and Gogarten, and Thieme was, like Gurian, horrified to see Protestants aligning themselves institutionally and enthusiastically with the new regime.

In a remarkable series of articles published in 1934 as *Deutsche evangelische Christen auf dem Wege zur katholischen Kirche*, Thieme described how the politicization of the Protestant Church had forced Protestants into the arms of Catholicism. Luther's initial vision, he argued, had been perverted, and Protestantism no longer represented the word of God, "but rather the Nordic-German personality of the Volk." The Protestants had fallen prey to the heretical anthropology of Thomas Hobbes and the corollary heretical politics of Carl Schmitt. Thieme was well aware of Eschweiler, and singled him out as someone who completely misunderstood the nature of ecclesiastical power in the modern age. Eschweiler, though, did not stand in for the Catholic Church, and Thieme was convinced that the Catholics had resisted the fascist temptation better than their Protestant peers. The Protestant Church, Thieme declared, "is no more," having been killed by the same "German Christians" celebrated by Eschweiler. The only remedy, he concluded, was to convert to Catholicism.[47] And convert he did. He hoped to bring entire Protestant communities with him, following the uniate model of some Eastern Christians. This was rebuffed, so Thieme converted himself in 1934—along with about forty other pastors in the so-called "Thieme Circle."[48]

Gurian and Thieme both fled into exile, where they labored to prove to readers that mainstream Catholics and their leaders were making a horrible mistake by choosing to collaborate with totalitarianism and with its Protestant enablers (Gurian founded and edited *Deutsche Briefe*, a periodical single-mindedly devoted to publicizing Hitler's attacks on the Churches). Gurian's relationship with Eschweiler fell apart, as Gurian blamed his former friend for pseudonymous attacks on him.[49] However much they may have had in common personally and even theologically, the two had very different visions for what the role of the Church in modern Germany should be—and very different approaches to ecumenism.

Anti-Communism and the Future of Ecumenism

The main purpose of this chapter has been a simple one: to show that, in the Weimar era and especially in the early 1930s, ecumenism was often (not always) linked with nationalism, conservatism, and eventually with National Socialism. The battle lines, therefore, are not where we expect them: the most anti-fascist and "humanist" Catholics were those most allergic to collaborating, politically or theologically, with their Protestant colleagues.

This would not remain the case forever, of course, and in closing I would like to suggest when and why this began to change. In his recent book *Lions and Lambs*, Noah Strote has suggested that the origin point for post-1945 political sensibilities in West Germany should be located in the later 1930s: the moment when previously squabbling conservatives, liberals, and social democrats discovered that they had more to fear from Hitler than from one another.[50] This seems to be true for ecumenism, too—at least as a matter of intellectual history.

The lines separating Gurian and Thieme from Lortz and Grosche softened in the mid-to-late 1930s. While some Catholic Nazis, notably Alois Hudal, continued to push ecumenical themes, in the face of Hitler's war on the Churches ecumenism became increasingly linked with the Resistance (and this was duly recognized by the Nazi security apparatus).[51] Gurian gave up on his intransigent anti-Protestantism and began to make the case that both confessions were under assault and would need to work together (this was the main point of his 1936 *Hitler and the Christians*). Lortz, for his part, left the party just before his landmark history, *The Reformation in Germany*, appeared in 1939. That book did more than any other to popularize the long-gestating Catholic reappropriation of Luther.[52] What is most surprising about it, though, is that it is not remotely political. In the early 1930s, Lortz had (like Grosche and Eschweiler) linked Luther with the German national project. In the later 1930s, he no longer did so. This allowed the book to be picked up by ecumenical thinkers in the actual Resistance, most notably Max Metzger, who had Lortz write a shorter version of the text for use in parish study circles.[53] This rebuilt ecumenism flowered after the war, when the re-founded *Una Sancta* pushed for interconfessional dialogue and when the CDU brought Catholics and Protestants, with some protest, into the same political movement once again (Gurian and Grosche, at least, became proponents of the CDU).[54]

The postwar flowering of ecumenism, and its roots in the resistance circles of the late 1930s, is not a surprise. The analysis in this essay, though, should cause us to reinterpret that moment in two ways. First, we should recognize that it was based upon a forgetting of the history of ecumenism. Political leaders like Adenauer, alongside theological ones like Joseph Lortz and Matthias Laros, claimed that interconfessional collaboration was rooted in shared suffering, ignoring the spurs to unity that had occasioned Hitler's rise to power. Robert Grosche was shameless in this regard, and he gave multiple addresses in the late 1940s about how ecumenism, and *Catholica* specifically, had been nourished by shared anti-fascism.[55]

Second, and to return to the insight that opened this chapter, we should recognize that interconfessional dialogue is usually undertaken in the name of creating new sorts of communities that might be exclusionary in a new way. The ecumenism of the early 1930s was largely designed to create a new national community that would exclude Jews. What of its successor in the late 1940s? What sort of imagined community did it inhabit? There is no space here to pursue this in any detail, and the nature of the West German political community was very much up for debate, even and especially in Christian circles.[56] And yet it seems clear that at least one endpoint of post-1945 ecumenism was the saber-rattling, anti-Communist militarism of the Cold War and the *Abendländische Akademie*.[57] From inside the family, the friendship of estranged brothers is a cause for celebration. But from the outside, brothers-in-arms can be dangerous indeed.

James Chappel is Associate Professor of History at Duke University, where he studies the intellectual and cultural history of modern Europe. His first book was *Catholic Modern: The Challenge of Totalitarianism and the Remaking of the Church* (Harvard University Press, 2018). He has published numerous articles in the fields of religious and intellectual history.

Notes

1. For another attempt to use a relatively small group, over a small period of time, to analyze this period, see Samuel Koehne, "Nazi Germany as a Christian State: The 'Protestant Experience' of 1933 in Württemberg," *Central European History* 46 (2013): 97–123.

2. Margaret Anderson, *Practicing Democracy: Elections and Political Culture in Imperial Germany* (Princeton: Princeton University Press, 2000); Georg May, *Interkonfessionalismus in der deutschen Militärseelsorge von 1933 bis 1945* (Amsterdam: B.R. Grüner, 1978); Till van Rahden, *Jews and Other Germans: Civil Society, Religious Diversity, and Urban Politics in Breslau, 1860–1925*, trans. Marcus Brainard (Madison: University of Wisconsin Press, 2008); Oliver Zimmer, "Beneath the 'Culture War': Corpus Christi Processions and Mutual Accommodation in the Second German Empire," *The Journal of Modern History* 82 (June 2010): 288–334.

3. Jörg Ernesti, *Ökumene im Dritten Reich. Einheit und Erneuerung* (Paderborn: Bornifatius, 2007); Wolfram Kaiser, *Christian Democracy and the Origins of European Union* (New York: Cambridge University Press, 2007); Maria Mitchell, *The Origins of Christian Democracy: Politics and Confession in Modern Germany* (Ann Arbor: University of Michigan Press, 2012); Noah Strote, *Lions and Lambs: Chaos in Weimar and the Creation of Post-Nazi Germany* (New Haven: Yale University Press, 2017).

4. Eric Kohler, "The Successful German Center-Left: Joseph Hess and the Prussian Center Party, 1908–32," *Central European History* 23 (1990): 313–49.

5. The indispensable work here is Ernesti, *Ökumene im Dritten Reich*. My findings do not contradict his, but I pay more attention than he does to the specific valence of the 1932–33 period.

6. For a recent exploration and judgment of this approach, see Peter Fritzsche, "Nazi Modern," *Modernism/Modernity* 3 (1996): 1–22.

7. James Chappel, *Catholic Modern: The Challenge of Totalitarianism and the Remaking of the Church* (Cambridge, MA: Harvard University Press, 2018).

8. Noel Cary, *The Path to Christian Democracy: German Catholics and the Party. System from Windthorst to Adenauer* (Cambridge, MA: Harvard University Press, 1996); part II is very perceptive on this issue.

9. Robert Krieg, *Catholic Theologians in Nazi Germany* (New York: Continuum, 2004), 42 (citing Berning); Ernst-Wolfgang Böckenförde, "German Catholicism in 1933," *Cross Currents* 11, no. 3 (Spring 1961): 283–303.

10. Karl Eschweiler, *Die Zwei Wege der neueren Theologie* (Augsburg: Benno Filter, 1926), 235–36 (among others).

11. Ibid., 48.

12. Max Scheler, *Politisch-Pädogogische Schriften*, ed. Manfred Frings (Munich: Francke, 1982), 432, 465; Franz-Xaver Kiefl, "Martin Luthers religiöse Psyche: Zum 400jährigen Reformationsjubiläum," *Hochland* 15 (1917–18): 7–28; Sebastian Merkle, "Das Lutherbild in der Gegenwart," *Hochland* 20, no. 1 (1922–23): 294–302. For more detail than I can provide here on the interwar rehabilitation of Luther in Catholic circles, see Werner Beyna, *Das moderne katholische Lutherbild* (Essen: Ludgerus-Verlag, 1969), 28–105.

13. Dietrich Eckart, *Der Bolschewismus von Moses bis Lenin* (Munich: Verlag Eher, 1924), 32–33.

14. As reported in Jacques Maritain to Waldemar Gurian, 19 July 1935, Waldemar Gurian Papers, Library of Congress, Box 5, Folder 18.

15. Karl Eschweiler, *Joh. Adam Möhlers Kirchenbegriff: Das Hauptstuck der katholischen Auseinandersetzung mit dem deutschen Idealismus* (Braunsberg: Herder, 1930), 170 for this quotation.

16. Oded Heilbronner, *Catholicism, Political Culture, and the Countryside: A Social History of the Nazi Party in South Germany* (Ann Arbor: University of Michigan Press, 1998).

17. Karl Eschweiler, "Politische Theologie," *Religiöse Besinnung* 4, no. 2 (1931–32): 72–88, 75–77 on Pilate, 78 for this quotation. He spread these ideas widely. For a typescript of a 1929 address on these themes, see Karl Eschweiler, "Die Kirche als Politische Macht (1929)," Nachlass Carl Schmitt, Düsseldorf (1929), RSW 265, document 20239.

18. Karl Eschweiler, "Der nationale Gedanke als reale Vernunft," *Der Ring* 4, no. 31 (31 July 1931): 577–81, here 580.

19. Eschweiler, *Joh. Adam Möhlers Kirchenbegriff*, 95.

20. Karl Eschweiler to Albrecht Erich Günther, 1 August 1933, Nachlass Carl Schmitt, Düsseldorf, RSW 265 3347.

21. Karl Eschweiler, "Erstes Kapitel: *Der politische Katholizismus und sein Ende*," unpublished MS (1933), in Nachlass Carl Schmitt, RSW 265, document 20239, pages 7–8.

22. "Kibitz" quotation in Eschweiler to Günther, op. cit.; on Strauss, Karl Eschweiler to Carl Schmitt, 20 September 1932, Nachlass Carl Schmitt, Düsseldorf, RSW 265 3367.

23. Krieg, *Catholic Theologians*, 69 for Merkle supporting Hitler; Hermann Greive, *Theologie und Ideologie. Katholizismus und Judentum in Deutschland und Österreich, 1918–1935* (Heidelberg: Verlag Lambert Schneider, 1969), 41 on Kiefl's antisemitism.

24. The editor of *Religiöse Besinnung* was worried that two was too many, and that the two should merge under the title *Zeitschrift for interkonfessionelle Aussprache*. This was rebuffed. Karl Thieme to Robert Grosche, 5 February 1933, Nachlass Karl Thieme, Institut für Zeitgeschichte, Munich, Folder 163/12. Prospective article mentioned in Eschweiler to Günther, op. cit.

25. Robert Grosche, "Luther im Urteil von Heute," *Rhein-Mainische Volkszeitung* 10, no. 7 (January 1930): 1–2.

26. Robert Grosche, "Theologie und Politik," *Der deutsche Weg* 4, no. 39 (24 June 1932): 1–2.

27. Reprinted as Robert Grosche, "Die Grundlagen einer christlichen Politik der deutschen Katholiken," *Die Schildgenossen* 13 (1933): 46–52. For his antisemitism and his reliance on Schmitt, see Robert Grosche, "Georg Simmel," *Die Schildgenossen* 5 (1925): 191–99.

28. Robert Grosche, "Wir und der Protestantismus," *Schönere Zukunft* 8, no. 22 (26 February 33): 510–11.

29. Robert Grosche, "Der deutsche Katholik und 'der deutsche Christ,'" *Catholica* 2, no. 4 (October 1933): 160–72, here 166, 164.

30. Oskar Köhler, "Die Freihet des Geistlichen: Martin Luthers Glaube," *Catholica* 4 (1935): 21–32.

31. Grosche, "Der deutsche Katholik und 'der deutsche Christ,'" 166.

32. Franz Taeschner, "Katholisches Nachwort zur Lutherfeier," *Catholica* 3 (January 1934): 40–43, here 41.

33. Damasus Winzen, "Gedanken zu einer 'Theologie des Reiches,'" *Catholica* 2 (1933): 97–116, here 110–11.

34. Discussed in Manfred Dahlheimer, *Carl Schmitt und der Deutsche Katholizismus, 1888–1936* (Paderborn: Ferdinand Schöningh, 1998), 507. Compare to Joseph Lortz, *Geschichte der Kirche in ideengeschichtlicher Betrachtung*, 17th ed. (Münster: Aschendorffsche Verlagsbuchhandlung, 1953), 420–22. Robert Krieg, it should be noted, believes that Lortz's ecumenism turned towards Nazism because, unlike Max Metzger, he rejected "modernity." Robert Krieg, "Joseph Lortz and Max Metzger on Ecumenism and Hitler," in *In God's Hands: Essays on the Church and Ecumenism in Honor of Michael A. Fahey, S.J.*, ed. Jaroslav Skira and Michael Attridge (Leuven: Leuven University Press, 2006), 89–108. This seems to me incorrect, given that Lortz's histories presumed that each event, the Reformation included, was divinely ordained and would have, in the end, positive benefits for the Church. For a sensitive appreciation of Lortz in context, see Wilhelm Damberg, "Kirchengeschichte zwischen Demokratie und Dictator. Georg Schreiber und Joseph Lortz in Munster 1933–1950," in *Theologische*

Fakultäten im Nationalsozialismus, ed. Leonor Siegele-Wenschkewitz and Carsten Nicolaisen (Göttengen: Vandenhoeck & Ruprecht, 1993), 145–64.

35. Joseph Lortz, "Zur Lutherforschung," *Historisches Jahrbuch* 53 (1933): 220–40, here 239.

36. Joseph Lortz, *Katholischer Zugang zum Nationalsozialismus* (Münster: Aschendorffschen Verlag, 1934), 17.

37. James Chappel, "The Catholic Origins of Totalitarianism Theory in Interwar Europe," *Modern Intellectual History* 8, no. 3 (2011): 261–90.

38. Robert Grosche to Waldemar Gurian, 25 October 1926, Gurian Papers, Box 3, Folder 22.

39. Waldemar Gurian, *Die deutsche Jugendbewegung* (Habelschwerdt: Frankes Buchhandlung, 1924), 70–72.

40. Waldemar Gurian, "Drei Reformaten," *Germania* 498 (24 October 1925): 1, 3; Waldemar Gurian, "Von Rosenstock bis Ernst Michel," *Kölnische Volkszeitung* 68, no. 610 (21 August 1927): 1–2; and 68, no. 629 (28 August 1927): 1–2.

41. For a positive review of Grisar's work in this journal, see Hans Rost, "Der deutsche Luther," *Allgemeine Rundschau* 21 (1924): 667–68.

42. Otto Kunze, "Oekumenische Arbeit," *Allgemeine Rundschau* 26 (1929): 675.

43. See my discussion in Chappel, *Catholic Modern*, ch. 1.

44. Walter Dirks, "Primat der Politik: Zur politischen Aufgabe der Zentrumspartei," *Heilige Feuer* 13 (1926): 129–40, here 131; Hermann Platz, "Die Zerspaltung des Abendlands," *Heilige Feuer* 14 (1927): 262–64.

45. Walter Dirks, "Was ist 'Kulturbolschewismus'?" *Zeitschrift für Religion und Sozialismus* 3 (1931): 220–25, here 221, 220.

46. Walter Gerhart [i.e., Gurian], *Um des Reiches Zukunft: Nationale Wiedergeburt oder politische Reaktion?* (Herder: Freiburg, 1932), 169.

47. Karl Thieme, *Deutsche evangelische Christen auf dem Wege zur katholischen Kirche* (Schlieren-Zürich: Verlagsanstalt Neue Brücke, 1934), 11, 50, 61, 63–64.

48. John Connelly, *From Enemy to Brother: The Revolution in Catholic Teaching on the Jews* (Cambridge, MA: Harvard University Press, 2012), 122–23.

49. It wasn't that Gurian thought Eschweiler had written them, but that one of his students had and Eschweiler had not intervened. Waldemar Gurian to Karl Eschweiler, 23 December 1933, Gurian Papers, Box 3, Folder 6.

50. Strote, *Lions and Lambs*.

51. Ernesti, *Ökumene im Dritten Reich*, 220–326.

52. Joseph Lortz, *Die Reformation in Deutschland*, 2nd ed. (Freiburg: Herder, 1941). Compare Lortz, *Die Reformation in Deutschland*, 3rd ed. (Freiburg: Herder, 1949).

53. Joseph Lortz, *Die Reformation: Thesen als Handreichung bei ökumenischen Gesprächen* (Augsburg: Christkönigsverlag, 1940).

54. Robert Grosche to Konrad Adenauer, 4 January 1950, Nachlass Grosche, Historisches Archiv des Erzbistum Köln, 1313.

55. Robert Grosche, "Die Einheit der Christenheit," *Der Katholische Gedanke: Akademikertagung Bonn 1946*, 35–44. He addresses *Catholica* specifically in Robert Grosche, "Die ökumenische Situation in Deutschland," Nachlass Grosche, HAEK-295, page 7.

56. Ronald Granieri, *The Ambivalent Alliance: Konrad Adenauer, the CDU/CSU, and the West, 1949–1966* (New York: Berghahn Books, 2003).

57. Axel Schildt, "Ökumene wider den Liberalismus: Zum politischen Engagement konservativer protestantischer Theologen im Umkreis der Abendländischen Akademie nach dem Zweiten Weltkrieg," in *Katholiken und Protestanten in den Aufbaujahren der Bundesprepublik*, ed. Thomas Sauer (Stuttgart: Kohlhammer, 2000), 187–205. On the relationship of postwar and interwar anti-Communism, see Paul Hanebrink, *A Specter Haunting Europe: The Myth of Judeo-Bolshevism* (Cambridge, MA: Belknap Press, 2018), ch. 6.

Bibliography

Anderson, Margaret. *Practicing Democracy: Elections and Political Culture in Imperial Germany*. Princeton: Princeton University Press, 2000.
Beyna, Werner. *Das moderne katholische Lutherbild*. Essen: Ludgerus-Verlag, 1969.
Böckenförde, Ernst-Wolfgang. "German Catholicism in 1933." *Cross Currents* 11, no. 3 (Spring 1961): 283–303.
Cary, Noel. *The Path to Christian Democracy: German Catholics and the Party System from Windthorst to Adenauer*. Cambridge, MA: Harvard University Press, 1996.
Chappel, James. *Catholic Modern: The Challenge of Totalitarianism and the Remaking of the Church*. Cambridge, MA: Harvard University Press, 2018.
———. "The Catholic Origins of Totalitarianism Theory in Interwar Europe." *Modern Intellectual History* 8, no. 3 (2011): 261–90.
Connelly, John. *From Enemy to Brother: The Revolution in Catholic Teaching on the Jews*. Cambridge, MA: Harvard University Press, 2012.
Dahlheimer, Manfred. *Carl Schmitt und der Deutsche Katholizismus, 1888–1936*. Paderborn: Ferdinand Schöningh, 1998.
Damberg, Wilhelm. "Kirchengeschichte zwischen Demokratie und Dictator. Georg Schreiber und Joseph Lortz in Munster 1933–1950." In *Theologische Fakultäten im Nationalsozialismus*, edited by Leonor Siegele-Wenschkewitz and Carsten Nicolaisen, 145–64. Göttengen: Vandenhoeck & Ruprecht, 1993.
Dirks, Walter. "Primat der Politik: Zur politischen Aufgabe der Zentrumpsartei." *Heilige Feuer* 13 (1926): 129–40.
———. "Was ist 'Kulturbolschewismus'?" *Zeitschrift für Religion und Sozialismus* 3 (1931): 220–25.
Eckart, Dietrich. *Der Bolschewismus von Moses bis Lenin*. Munich: Verlag Eher, 1924.
Ernesti, Jörg. *Ökumene im Dritten Reich. Einheit und Erneuerung*. Paderborn: Bornifatius, 2007.
Eschweiler, Karl. *Die Zwei Wege der neueren Theologie*. Augsburg: Benno Filter, 1926.
———. "Der nationale Gedanke als reale Vernunft." *Der Ring* 4, no. 31 (31 July 1931): 577–81.
———. *Joh. Adam Möhlers Kirchenbegriff: Das Hauptstuck der katholischen Auseinandersetzung mit dem deutschen Idealismus*. Braunsberg: Herder, 1930.
———. "Politische Theologie." *Religiöse Besinnung* 4, no. 2 (1931–32): 72–88.
Fritzsche, Peter. "Nazi Modern." *Modernism/Modernity* 3 (1996): 1–22.
Granieri, Ronald. *The Ambivalent Alliance: Konrad Adenauer, the CDU/CSU, and the West, 1949–1966*. New York: Berghahn Books, 2003.
Greive, Hermann. *Theologie und Ideologie. Katholizismus und Judentum in Deutschland und Österreich, 1918–1935*. Heidelberg: Verlag Lambert Schneider, 1969.
Grosche, Robert. "Die Einheit der Christenheit." *Der Katholische Gedanke: Akademikertagung Bonn* (1946): 35–44.
———. "Die Grundlagen einer christlichen Politik der deutschen Katholiken." *Die Schildgenossen* 13 (1933): 46–52.
———. "Der deutsche Katholik und 'der deutsche Christ.'" *Catholica* 2, no. 4 (October 1933): 160–72.
———. "Georg Simmel." *Die Schildgenossen* 5 (1925): 191–99.
———. "Luther im Urteil von Heute." *Rhein-Mainische Volkszeitung* 10, no. 7 (January 1930): 1–2.
———. "Theologie und Politik." *Der deutsche Weg* 4, no. 39 (24 June 1932): 1–2.
———. "Wir und der Protestantismus." *Schönere Zukunft* 8, no. 22 (26 February 1933): 510–11.
Gurian, Waldemar. *Die deutsche Jugendbewegung*. Habelschwerdt: Frankes Buchhandlung, 1924.

———. "Drei Reformaten." *Germania* 498 (24 October 1925): 1, 3.
——— [under pseudonym Walter Gerhart]. *Um des Reiches Zukunft: Nationale Wiedergeburt oder politische Reaktion?* Herder: Freiburg, 1932.
———. "Von Rosenstock bis Ernst Michel." *Kölnische Volkszeitung* 68, no. 610 (21 August 1927): 1–2.
———. "Von Rosenstock bis Ernst Michel." *Kölnische Volkszeitung* 68, no. 629 (28 August 1927): 1–2.
Hanebrink, Paul. *A Specter Haunting Europe: The Myth of Judeo-Bolshevism*. Cambridge, MA: Belknap Press, 2018.
Heilbronner, Oded. *Catholicism, Political Culture, and the Countryside: A Social History of the Nazi Party in South Germany*. Ann Arbor: University of Michigan Press, 1998.
Kaiser, Wolfram. *Christian Democracy and the Origins of European Union*. New York: Cambridge University Press, 2007.
Kiefl, Franz-Xaver. "Martin Luthers religiöse Psyche: Zum 400jährigen Reformationsjubiläum." *Hochland* 15 (1917–18): 7–28.
Koehne, Samuel. "Nazi Germany as a Christian State: The 'Protestant Experience' of 1933 in Württemberg." *Central European History* 46 (2013): 97–123.
Kohler, Eric. "The Successful German Center-Left: Joseph Hess and the Prussian Center Party, 1908–32." *Central European History* 23 (1990): 313–49.
Köhler, Oskar. "Die Freiheit des Geistlichen: Martin Luthers Glaube." *Catholica* 4 (1935): 21–32.
Krieg, Robert. *Catholic Theologians in Nazi Germany*. New York: Continuum, 2004.
———. "Joseph Lortz and Max Metzger on Ecumenism and Hitler." In *In God's Hands: Essays on the Church and Ecumenism in Honor of Michael A. Fahey, S.J.*, edited by Jaroslav Skira and Michael Attridge, 89–108. Leuven: Leuven University Press, 2006.
Kunze, Otto. "Oekumenische Arbeit." *Allgemeine Rundschau* 26 (1929): 675.
Lortz, Joseph. *Die Reformation in Deutschland*. 2nd ed. Freiburg: Herder, 1941.
———. *Die Reformation: Thesen als Handreichung bei ökumenischen Gesprächen*. Augsburg: Christkönigsverlag, 1940.
———. *Geschichte der Kirche in ideengeschichtlicher Betrachtung*, 17th ed. Münster: Aschendorffsche Verlagsbuchhandlung, 1953.
———. *Katholischer Zugang zum Nationalsozialismus*. Münster: Aschendorffschen Verlag, 1934.
———. "Zur Lutherforschung." *Historisches Jahrbuch* 53 (1933): 220–40.
May, Georg. *Interkonfessionalismus in der deutschen Militärseelsorge von 1933 bis 1945*. Amsterdam: B.R. Grüner, 1978.
Merkle, Sebastian. "Das Lutherbild in der Gegenwart." *Hochland* 20 (1922–23): 294–302.
Mitchell, Maria. *The Origins of Christian Democracy: Politics and Confession in Modern Germany*. Ann Arbor: University of Michigan Press, 2012.
Platz, Hermann. "Die Zerspaltung des Abendlands." *Heilige Feuer* 14 (1927): 262–64.
Rost, Hans. "Der deutsche Luther." *Allgemeine Rundschau* 21 (1924): 667–68.
Scheler, Max. *Politisch-Pädogogische Schriften*. Edited by Manfred Frings. Munich: Francke, 1982.
Schildt, Axel. "Ökumene wider den Liberalismus: Zum politischen Engagement konservativer protestantischer Theologen im Umkreis der Abendländischen Akademie nach dem Zweiten Weltkrieg." In *Katholiken und Protestanten in den Aufbaujahren der Bundesreprublik*, edited by Thomas Sauer, 187–205. Stuttgart: Kohlhammer, 2000.
Strote, Noah. *Lions and Lambs: Chaos in Weimar and the Creation of Post-Nazi Germany*. New Haven: Yale University Press, 2017.
Taeschner, Franz. "Katholisches Nachwort zur Lutherfeier." *Catholica* 3 (January 1934): 40–43.
Thieme, Karl. *Deutsche evangelische Christen auf dem Wege zur katholischen Kirche*. Schlieren-Zürich: Verlagsanstalt Neue Brücke, 1934.

Van Rahden, Till. *Jews and Other Germans: Civil Society, Religious Diversity, and Urban Politics in Breslau, 1860–1925*. Translated by Marcus Brainard. Madison: University of Wisconsin Press, 2008.

Winzen, Damasus. "Gedanken zu einer 'Theologie des Reiches.'" *Catholica* 2 (1933): 97–116.

Zimmer, Oliver. "Beneath the 'Culture War': Corpus Christi Processions and Mutual Accommodation in the Second German Empire." *The Journal of Modern History* 82 (June 2010): 288–334.

Chapter Six

CONVERSION AS A CONFESSIONAL IRRITANT
Examples from the Third Reich

Benjamin Ziemann

For much of the nineteenth and twentieth centuries, the confessional divide between Protestants and Catholics was a defining feature of German history. Even after the *Kulturkampf* had been formally suspended by 1886–87, deep-reaching animosities between the two confessional camps lingered, leading to a continuation of confessional fault-lines until 1918 and beyond. Eying each other with suspicion and holding on to long-established stereotypes, Catholics and Protestants continued to face irritants that destabilized the confessional divide and undermined the collective mentalities that supported it. One irritant was biconfessional marriages, *Mischehen* in German parlance, between a Protestant and a Catholic spouse.[1] These marriages demonstrated that, at least at a personal level, Protestants and Catholics could not only mingle with impunity but also get along well and establish families together. The other—and from the standpoint of confessional partisanship—even more problematic irritant was conversions in which individuals defected from one church and were admitted into another. Technically speaking, these were *Konfessionswechsel*, a change of confession. As contemporary literature on this topic emphasized, this could mean different things: it could mean switching to another church (*Übertritt*), leaving the current church altogether and remaining unaffiliated (*Austritt*), or rejoining the church that one had left earlier (*Rücktritt*). To be valid, the change in confession had to be presented in writing to the local civil courts. This was true for all those religious communities registered as bodies in public law, which included the Protestant territorial churches, or *Landeskirchen* (of which twenty-eight existed at the end of the Weimar Republic), the Roman Catholic Church, and the *Deutsch-Katholische Kirche*.[2]

Yet behind these formal technicalities, there was always an individual story, and especially so in the case of a conversion to another church and its system of belief. Abandoning the inherited faith and adopting a new one was at any rate a radical step, even more so against the backdrop of the deep confessional divide that separated Protestants and Catholics in Germany. Making the leap required courage—as the existing social network of the individual would usually advise against it—and it presupposed a longer process of reflection, if not a deeper crisis of personal identity. Conversions often included a process of narrative framing in which converts were accounting for their motives in order to rationalize their decision-making amidst a highly emotional transformation and to convey the purposeful nature of the change to those in their immediate social environment. As much as we can distinguish between push and pull factors, conversions remain in the end highly contingent. They depend heavily on individual circumstances and have an uncertain outcome in which converts might ultimately shy away from the consequences and not take the final step.[3]

In this chapter, I will focus on conversions in the Third Reich and their significance against the backdrop of religious changes from 1933 to 1945. I will focus on one high-profile case, the ultimately aborted conversion to the Catholic Church of Martin Niemöller, one of the leaders of the Confessing Church and a high-profile critic of Nazi church politics. I will analyze Niemöller's case in the context of his personal circumstances as "Hitler's Personal Prisoner" in the Sachsenhausen Concentration Camp between 1938 and 1941. But I also consider the wider context of the crisis of the Confessing Church and of confessional politics in the Third Reich more generally. A comparison with other conversion cases prior to 1933 will help us to understand these events' significance. From 1933 to 1945, conversions to the Catholic Church mattered more than they did before or after. Not only were they more numerous, but many were motivated by a deep disaffection with the Protestant Churches' stance vis-à-vis the Nazis.

The Nazi seizure of power in early 1933 had crucial implications for both Christian confessions, but in different ways. Protestant Christians experienced "1933" as a moment of fulfilment and of far-reaching historical change to the better. In the tradition of nationalist Protestantism, hopes for national and religious renewal were deeply intertwined. Believing that the Weimar Republic had ushered in an era of political and moral decline, many Protestants initially viewed the Third Reich as a realization of their hopes for national renewal. The Nazi vision of the people's community (*Volksgemeinschaft*), bonds of national solidarity that could overcome materialism as well as class egotism, deeply resonated among Protestant clergy and laity alike and fuelled hopes for a renewal of the honor and power of the German nation. Protestants with a Nazi affiliation obviously greeted the events in 1933 with exuberance. Following an initiative in Thuringia in 1931, Protestant ministers in Berlin around Joachim Hossenfelder founded the *Glaubensbewegung Deutsche Christen* (Faith Movement of German Christians), in short *Deutsche Christen* (German Christians), in June 1932.[4] With guidelines that echoed all key demands of the Nazi Party program, the *Deutsche Christen* campaigned for a *völkisch* reinterpretation of the Gospel and of Christian tradition more generally. This included a rejection of missionary activities among the Jews, and, in a foreshadowing of the 1935 Nuremberg Laws, a proposed ban on mixed marriages between Jewish and Gentile Germans. Accepted as an official church party for the November 1932 church elections, the *Deutsche Christen* quickly gathered the support of dedicated Nazis among both Protestant clergy and laity. In Berlin, for which reliable figures are available, 44 per cent of all Protestant pastors joined the *Deutsche Christen*, and 20 per cent were NSDAP members.[5] But also Protestant ministers who had not joined the *Deutsche Christen* welcomed "1933" as a moment of national renewal. A case in point is Martin Niemöller, son of a Protestant minister and former officer of the Imperial Navy who had served as a decorated U-boat captain in World War I. From 1931 as one of three pastors in the parish of Berlin-Dahlem, an affluent suburb of the German capital, Niemöller interpreted the Nazi seizure of power in his spring 1933 sermons as a moment of "conversion" and of *Volkwerdung*, or "becoming a people." As he welcomed the political changes and denounced the now defunct Weimar Republic, Niemöller also insisted that a religious "awakening" had to take place, as religion was no "private matter" but part and parcel of the substance of the *Volk*.[6] At least initially, hopes for a religious renewal, shared by members of the *Deutsche Christen* and other Protestant clergy alike, were born out by an increase in the number of conversions to the Protestant Churches. The Weimar Republic had seen a steady stream of Protestants leaving their church, most of them choosing to remain religiously unaffiliated. The number of those leaving peaked in 1920 when 314,005 left altogether, 305,148 of them not joining any other church. Yet the first two years of the Third Reich saw a substantial reversal of this trend. In 1933 and 1934, respectively, a total of 323,618 and 149,471 individuals joined the Protestant Churches. Almost 90 percent of these (figure for 1933) had no confessional affiliation, but the large majority of them were in fact re-joiners who had left the Protestant Churches at some earlier point. Entries from the Judaic faith were entirely marginal. By 1935, however, this had dropped to a mere 76,577, with 51,377 departures in the same year producing only a marginal net gain.[7]

The Catholic Church moved from a different position into the Third Reich. Before 1933, clergy and bishops had denounced the NSDAP for its racial ideology—as it negated the equality in the face of God that baptism provided—and some of them had admonished the laity not to join the party. On 28 March 1933, shortly after the Catholic Center Party had voted in favor of the Enabling Law, which gave the Nazi dictatorship a pseudo-legal basis, the bishops rescinded their instructions not to join the NSDAP while sustaining their critique of racial ideology. Yet the demonstration of national loyalty by the Center Party was not rewarded by the regime. Commencing in 1934, a whole raft of different measures targeted the Catholic Church. Erich Klausener, a popular lay Catholic from Berlin, was murdered on 30 June 1934, in the context of the violent crackdown against the SA. Catholic youth organizations were disbanded, and the Catholic press attacked. In 1935, a smear campaign against Catholic religious orders ensued, followed by an even more aggressive campaign in 1936–37 in which 274 Catholic priests were sentenced in courts for made-up charges on so-called vice offences.[8] State measures were complemented by hostility coming from individual formations of the Nazi party. In Stettin in July 1934, for instance, a crowd of one thousand young men, most of whom were probably members of the Hitler Youth, gathered in front of the rectory and chanted anti-Catholic songs after the priest had attacked four members of the Hitler Youth while celebrating mass. In this case, incidentally, the Gestapo dispersed the crowd.[9]

These differences in the attitudes of Protestants and Catholics vis-à-vis National Socialism had already influenced confessional relations prior to 1933. In regions like the Palatinate in the southwest of Germany in which people from both confessions were mixed together, Catholics perceived the NSDAP as a Protestant party, since few Catholics had supported the Nazis. This hostile attitude was reciprocated by the NSDAP, whose functionaries consistently voiced anticlerical stereotypes about Catholic priests. These tensions continued in the years from 1933. For Protestants, the suppression of the Center Party, the collective participation of Nazi Party or SA members and the return of many individuals who had left the church provided positive signs that the Nazis would be able to unite the nation according to their vision of a people's community. In line with these perceptions, Protestant clergy and church publications also approved of the first state measures against the Catholic Church and against what they saw as the undue political influence of Catholic clergy.[10] Hopes that the Third Reich would lead to the increased political and ideological influence of Protestants and scale back the power of the Catholics, who had been a crucial part of governmental policymaking for most of the Weimar Republic, were widespread among Protestant ministers.[11] As Protestants essentially gave the Nazis a free pass to crack down on the Catholic Church, they made the emergence of a joint response—let alone joint resistance—of Christians of both confessions against the new regime virtually impossible.

In the Protestant camp, however, disillusionment and internal strife returned after the initial hopes for a full recognition of all Protestants as linchpins of the regime's crusade for moral renewal had faded by the end of 1933. Church elections in July 1933 had returned a 70 per cent majority for the *Deutsche Christen*, and a national synod in September duly elected the former Imperial Navy chaplain Ludwig Müller, a member of the *Deutsche Christen*, as the Reich Bishop. The Nazi occupation of the church apparatus—with the exception of the "intact" Lutheran churches in Hanover, Bavaria, and Württemberg, which resisted a takeover by the *Deutsche Christen* until 1945—prompted the formation of an oppositional group, the Pastors' Emergency League. Led by the energetic Niemöller, it quickly brought together about a third of all German Protestant pastors. By 1934, the oppositional forces were ready to declare themselves as the only legitimate Protestant Church in the Barmen Synod of May 1934. The synod accepted the six articles of a Theological Declaration, mainly authored by the Swiss Reformed theologian Karl Barth, as the foundational principles of the Confessing Church (*Bekennende Kirche*, BK).[12] The Nazi state responded with a mixture of repression and attempted integration to the challenge of the Confessing Church. Further fragmentation in the Protestant camp facilitated these efforts. While the *Deutsche Christen* splintered into different competing factions, the Lutherans in the three intact churches supported an accommodation with the *Deutsche Christen*-dominated national church leadership around Ludwig Müller. Within the BK, only the more principled, Dahlemite wing around two Dahlem pastors, Friedrich Müller and Martin Niemöller, resisted any compromise. When the BK split over these conflicts in the spring of 1936, the Nazi authorities seized the opportunity with a crackdown against the Dahlemite wing of the BK, arresting key figures, including Niemöller, in the spring and summer of 1937.[13]

While the different factions with the Protestant camp had already fragmented and pluralized the religious field in the Third Reich, the rise of a Germanic, *völkisch* form of religiosity further complicated confessional relations. The 1939 census returned 2.74 million, or 3.5 percent, Germans who, when asked about their religious affiliation, declared themselves as *gottgläubig*—"believing in God." This artificial category, designed by the Reich Ministry of the Interior under Wilhelm Frick, included a wide range of beliefs that went beyond the Christian confessions and their churches. The majority of those "believing in God" were former Protestants, two-thirds of them men, mostly salaried NSDAP functionaries, civil servants, and teachers. They were united by the perception that the Christian tradition had been irreparably tainted by the presence of "oriental" Jewish elements and their preference for a Germanic, Nordic faith in line with the *völkisch* substance of the German people. Attempts to organize those who considered themselves as *gottgläubig* into a separate religious community that could gain recognition as a church body in public law, comparable to the Protestant and Catholic Churches, nonetheless remained marginal. The Working Group of the German Faith Movement (*Arbeitsgemeinschaft Deutsche Glaubensbewegung*) attracted no more than thirty thousand members. Yet already the wider presence of the *Gottgläubigen* as a large group severely disrupted the established pattern of confessional conflict, turning it from a "duel" between Protestants and Catholics into a "religious three-way fight."[14]

It is against this increasingly complicated and volatile backdrop of confessional relations in the Third Reich that conversions from the Protestant to the Catholic Church have to be considered. In the last decades of the nineteenth century, the number of Catholic converts to the Protestant churches had consistently outnumbered those who had converted to the Catholic Church. The overall numbers remained small. In 1890, for instance, a mere 3,102 Catholics joined the Protestant churches, while 553 Protestants traveled in the other direction.[15] Nevertheless, in the "latent *Kulturkampf*" that permeated Wilhelmine Germany, this was reason enough to speed up the process of establishing a statistical apparatus in the Catholic Church that would, alongside data on Holy Communions and church attendance, also record the number of conversions. The Jesuit Hermann Krose, who was instrumental in establishing an official church statistical office of the German dioceses, which after long debate became operational in 1915, advocated the use of statistics precisely because it would allow Catholics to counter the "boasts of the Protestants and their yearly publications showing ever greater numbers of conversions."[16]

Contrary to Krose's expectation, however, the Protestants could continue to "boast." In 1930, 16,302 Catholics joined the Protestant Churches, while only 1,971 Protestants converted to the Catholic Church. The number of Catholic converts to the Protestant Churches peaked in 1933 with 31,201. This was followed by a steady decline until 1940, the last year for which figures are available, when the number sank to 5,675.[17] Yet while the number of Protestant conversions to the Catholic Church remained low before 1933, several high-profile cases demonstrated the potential of these conversions to disrupt the certainties underpinning the confessional divide. Especially irritating was when women converted, as the example of Elisabeth Gnauck-Kühne (1850–1917) shows. She had become a public figure as a key proponent of the Protestant women's movement. After years of living in an unhappy marriage, a visit to an Austrian convent in 1899, and discussions with a Catholic priest that she met on this occasion triggered a swift decision to convert, which Gnauck-Kühne did in 1900. At its core, her conversion was a rejection of "the Lutheran view of marriage as the ultimate female vocation," as epitomized by Luther's own marriage with Katharina von Bora. The fallout was huge; almost every newspaper in Germany covered Gnauck-Kühne's conversion. The consequences of her decision were felt even after her death, as she cofounded the *Katholischer Deutscher Frauenbund* (Catholic German Women's League, KDF) in 1903 after her conversion. Since its foundation, the KDF has remained the most important body of the Catholic women's movement in Germany.[18]

Another high-profile conversion was that of Fritz Gerlich (1883–1934). He started his career as an archivist but became the editor of a newspaper in Munich in 1920. Gerlich's political preferences fluctuated wildly between the liberalism of the DDP and a staunch anti-Bolshevism which briefly brought him into personal contact with Hitler in 1923, whose anti-semitism he rejected. Suffering from exhaustion and health problems in 1927, Fritz Gerlich, who was a Reformed Christian, gave himself the task of exposing the miracles of Therese Neumann as a fraud. This young Catholic woman in the small community of Konnersreuth, near the border to Czechoslovakia, had started in 1926 to display stigmata that resembled the five wounds of Christ. She also had visions that she communicated to a rapidly growing number of admirers. Visiting her several times in 1927 to debunk her, Gerlich was fascinated and ultimately convinced. He quit his job as a newspaper editor and published in 1929 a two-volume account of the miracles of Therese Neumann. When Resl—as her nickname went—told him in 1931 that he was in all but name already a Catholic, he converted in Neumann's presence, receiving confirmation a few weeks later in November 1931 by Cardinal Michael Faulhaber in Munich. As a Catholic, Gerlich returned to journalism as editor of the journal *The Straight Path* (*Der gerade Weg*), which relentlessly exposed the corruption among the leading Nazis and took a resolutely anti-Nazi stance. In 1933, the Nazis almost immediately detained Gerlich. He was shot to death during the "Night of the Long Knives" on 30 June 1934.[19]

After 1933, the number of changes in confessional affiliation within the Catholic Church increased rapidly, which is reflected in Catholic data.[20] Comparable to developments in the Protestant Churches, the number of those who left the Catholic Church decreased in 1933–34, while the number of entrants increased, most of whom were former Catholics returning to the fold. This was followed by a further increase in the number of departures in the wake of the massive propaganda campaign of the Nazi regime against Catholic priests and its attempts to remove Christianity from the public sphere. At the peak in 1937, about 110,000 Catholics left their church. However, in a clear indication of the increasing volatility of confessional relations, and of the religious field more generally, the number of those who joined the Catholic Church increased as well, vis-à-vis the years of the Weimar Republic. From 1933 to 1945, seventy thousand people joined the Catholic Church who previously had been members of other religious communities; slightly less than 90 percent of these were former Protestants. This figure to be sure indicates only the minimum number of conversions to the Catholic Church, as data for the years 1939 and 1943 to 1945 is not available.[21]

There are good reasons to believe that conversions to the Catholic Church in the Third Reich predominantly remained what they had been in the decades before: the result of a mixed marriage, in which one of the spouses converted so that the children could be brought up in a confessionally unified family.[22] Yet there were also other factors at work, and they indicate an increasing disorientation and frustration especially among those Protestants who belonged to the Confessing Church. In spite of the Barmen Declaration and against the backdrop of the continuous infighting not only between the Confessing Church and the *Deutsche Christen* but also among the different wings within the Confessing Church, some Protestants despaired over the apparent inability of their church to formulate a coherent and meaningful stance vis-à-vis the theological and practical challenges that the Nazi dictatorship posed.

One example that indicates an early frustration with developments in the Protestant churches was that of the historian Karl Thieme (1902–1963). Raised in a Protestant family as the son of a theologian, Thieme had caused a stir when he joined the Social Democratic Party (SPD) in 1924. From 1930, he taught at the Pedagogical Academy in Elbing (East Prussia). He was detained briefly in March 1933 by the Gestapo before the Academy was shut down for good. As an SPD member, Thieme had no chances of getting another academic position. By the summer of 1933, he had abandoned all illusions. Having grasped the violent, brutal nature of the Nazi regime, he decided to join the opposition. His political stance was shaped by his deep disappointment about the speed with which the German Christians gained control of the Protestant Churches and then in September 1933 in church synods held up and down the country they managed to usher through the "Aryan paragraph" that prohibited Protestant Christians of Jewish ancestry to continue in the ministry. In despair about these developments, Thieme turned to Rome. In October 1933, he and a circle of like-minded friends addressed Pope Pius XI and asked for admission to the Roman Catholic Church. They were not attracted by Catholic dogma, but driven by the conviction—not unlike Martin Niemöller's in 1939–40, as we shall soon see—that Rome represented the sole remaining true Christian Church. While a larger turnout had been expected, allegedly up to forty Protestant ministers converted jointly with Thieme, who made the leap on 30 January

1934. Fighting antisemitism and for Jewish-Christian reconciliation stood at the heart of Thieme's religious endeavors in the post-1945 period.[23]

These problems also became visible in the Dahlem parish in Berlin, which was situated in an extremely affluent neighborhood in southwestern Berlin. Since both the Catholic and Protestant Churches in Germany, due to their status as bodies in public law, were funded via a levy on the income tax, the Dahlem parish, the wealthiest Protestant parish in the state of Prussia, could afford to pay the salaries of three pastors. Two of them, Friedrich Müller and Martin Niemöller, emerged as leading figures of the Confessing Church. The Dahlem parish community, after 1945 the subject of mythologized and highly exaggerated reverence for its alleged uniform resistance against the Nazis, was deeply divided. The third Dahlem pastor, Eberhard Röhricht—he was the first in terms of seniority—had parted in late 1935 from the radical Dahlemite wing of the Confessing Church led by his two colleagues. He henceforth supported the state's effort to reconcile all groups within the Protestant Church, including the *Deutsche Christen*, via a Reich Church Committee. This had effectively split the Dahlem parish community right down the middle, and the remaining BK supporters organized in a confessing community that was mostly detached from the institutional structures of the parish.[24] Among the BK supporters in Dahlem there was discontent with the almost total silence of Niemöller and his circle regarding the persecution of the Jews. Elisabeth Schmitz, a lay member of the Dahlem BK group, voiced her concerns repeatedly in letters to the Swiss theologian Karl Barth.[25]

While Schmitz remained a faithful member of the BK, another female member of the Dahlem BK group, Elisabeth Krautzberger, had had enough. On 19 November 1935, she returned her "red card," which indicated membership of the Confessing Church, to Martin Niemöller and appended a long letter in which she explained her decision to convert to the Catholic Church. One of her core motives was the search for a "visible" church in line with a distinction between the "visible" and the "invisible" church that the reformed theologian Zwingli had developed in his 1531 *Fidei expositio*. For Krautzberger, the "visible" church was the Catholic one with its hierarchical apparatus and dogma, whereas the Protestant faith remained in an invisible state. Another motivation for her conversion was the feeling of responsibility for any soul that would perish without adequate spiritual support:

> We in Protestantism leave so easily, while not without painfully sensing our own helplessness, human beings to their fate. We rightly emphasize that the salvation of one's soul would be more important than this mundane, earthly life, but in the process, we forget that amidst the desperation of this earthly struggle, quite a few get mad.[26]

At this point, however, only a few Protestants in Berlin converted. Yet even some of those who did not convert expressed a deep appreciation for the Catholic Church. Elly Heuss-Knapp, the wife of the liberal politician Theodor Heuss, who was herself acquainted with the prominent Protestant theologian Friedrich Naumann and had prior to 1914 worked for his journal *Die Hilfe*, noted that key aspects of the Catholic Church "made increasing sense" to her.[27]

In 1935, Martin Niemöller forwarded Krautzberger's letter to Franz Hildebrandt, who worked as an adjunct pastor in the Dahlem parish at this point and as a Protestant of Jewish descent immigrated to the United Kingdom in 1937. Yet only four years later, in 1939, Niemöller was deeply immersed in his own—and ultimately aborted—plan to convert to the Roman Catholic Church.[28] This was a complex and protracted story which consumed most of his energy from the summer of 1938 to the spring of 1941 while detained as "Hitler's Personal Prisoner" in the Sachsenhausen concentration camp in the wake of his trial in front of a Special Court in Berlin. Niemöller's interest in the Catholic Church was certainly triggered by the lack of spiritual engagement and an opportunity to practice his faith. While in solitary confinement, Niemöller had neither access to Protestant Sunday services nor to conversations with other Protestant ministers, nor even the opportunity to receive Holy Communion. Seeking spiritual orientation, Niemöller discovered and engaged elements of Catholic piety that had been unknown to him before, such as the liturgy of the hours that he now practiced with the help of a *Breviarum Romanum* that someone had sent him. In the spring of 1939, Niemöller widened this excursion into unfamiliar forms of piety into a sustained critical reflection on the inconsistencies of the key Reformation principle of *sola scriptura* (by scripture alone). He embarked on an extended dialogue with his wife Else, expressing his doubts about key results of the Reformation. They carried out this dialogue both through letters and also in person during the few visiting hours twice a month that she had been granted. A silent partner and stakeholder in these debates was the prominent Lutheran theologian Hans Asmussen (1898–1968), a leading member of the Confessing Church and close friend of Niemöller and his wife. Increasingly desperate to talk her husband out of his conversion plans, Else Niemöller relied on Asmussen's theological expertise. He provided her with commentary on the biblical and historical arguments that her husband was sending her and suggested ways to refute his arguments.[29]

A dramatic acceleration of Niemöller's plans occurred when the Berlin consistory of the Church of the Old Prussian Union (ApU) announced in June 1939 its decision to place him in non-active service, claiming that he had failed to dispense his duties as a parish priest for more than two years.

Niemöller was aware that this decision followed an intervention by Friedrich Werner, a Nazi jurist with no actual ties to the Protestant faith who served as head of the Supreme Church Council (EOK) of the ApU. And he expected to be formally removed from the Dahlem parish, and his family evicted from their home by 1 January 1940. The upshot of this episode seemed obvious to him: the territorial church of the ApU was characterized by a fundamental lack of ecclesiological legitimacy. Rejecting ministers who defended the Protestant faith, led and administered by a Nazi with no personal faith, and stuck in its own bureaucratic routines, there was nothing defensible left in the ApU. In July 1939, Niemöller stated in a letter to Else that the "Protestant territorial church has never been a Christian church," not even in the sense of its own "confessional documents" such as the *Confessio Augustana* of 1530.[30]

A few months later in December 1939, Niemöller drew practical conclusions from this insight and wrote to the president of the consistory in Berlin, Johannes Heinrich, to inform him that he would now take steps for himself and his family to "resign" from the "Evangelical territorial church" (*evangelischen Kirche*) of the ApU, a term that he consistently placed in quotation marks to ridicule its lack of any attributes of a proper church.[31] His planned exit never materialized. At any rate, Niemöller understood that leaving the Protestant church would not solve the underlying problem: the very basis of the Christian ecclesiological tradition had to be reconsidered amidst the confusion, division, and internal strife that the struggle over hegemony in the Protestant Church since 1933 had produced. Thus, he got to work and produced a manuscript of 215 handwritten pages entitled *Thoughts on the Path of the Christian Church* between late August and early November 1939. The text is partly a personal recollection and justification of his own interest in the very issue of the Church and partly an extended exegesis of the record of the New Testament on the founding of the Christian Church.[32]

The main thrust of Niemöller's argument was to denounce the Lutheran territorial church as a dead end in the long-term evolution of the Christian churches. In his idealistic conception, the Church had to be a living organism that was rooted in the long pedigree of Christian tradition going back to Christ himself and the twelve apostles. The *Landeskirche*, on the other hand, was a failed product of the unholy alliance between Luther and the rulers in the sixteenth century territories who adopted the Reformation to further their own worldly power. As Luther had turned the secular ruler as the *summus episcopus* into the bishop of a church, he had relinquished the autonomy of a spiritual institution and had turned it into a servant of political interests. Five years after the founding of the Confessing Church, one of its leading proponents arrived at a devastating judgement about the

Protestant church. Niemöller acknowledged that the Confessing Church had functioned as an "'emergency roof" (*Notdach*) for all those who, without joining the Roman Catholic Church, wanted to remain Christians on the grounds of the evangelic proclamation (*Verkündigung*)."[33] But beyond the Confessing Church, there was nothing left in the Protestant Churches that would merit defending them.

A particular point of contention for Niemöller was—both in the book-length manuscript and in a shorter text that he wrote in 1939 on the theme of "Evangelical or Catholic?"—the fundamental lack of knowledge about the core identity of their own church among the Protestant laity.[34] Based on his extensive experience as a pastor and managing director in the Inner Mission from 1924 to 1931 and his subsequent work in the Dahlem parish, Niemöller took a rather dim view of the ordinary lay Protestant. If one asked the "Lutheran average Christian" who attended Sunday services on a regular basis, what would be the distinguishing difference "between us and the Catholics," one would get "the strangest responses," as he knew "from experience": "making the sign of the cross, kneeling in Church, the confession, celibacy," and even "regular church attendance" were some of the answers that lay Protestants had mentioned to him as typical examples of "Catholic faith, i.e. superstition." Only the one difference that was "decisive for Luther"—the different understanding of justification—was never mentioned.[35] Based on these experiences, Niemöller concluded that "opposition to Rome" remained the only reliable "marker" of what it meant to be "Protestant" (*evangelisch*).[36] In the view of a leading Protestant church representative, the confessional divide had been stripped of its core meaning among the average Lutheran, and only the negative hostility towards a fantasized image of the Catholic faith propped up the collective identity of the Protestants.

Niemöller knew that defining the Protestant faith primarily by its opposition to Rome and the Catholics was a legacy of the late nineteenth-century *Kulturkampf*. His father, Heinrich Niemöller (1859–1941), had been a long-standing supporter of the Evangelical League (*Evangelischer Bund*), acting as the chair of the local association in Elberfeld, where he served as a pastor since 1901. In his memoirs, father Niemöller took pride in having delivered sermons and speeches on behalf of the Evangelical League in no less than 317 towns in Germany.[37] Founded in 1886, the Evangelical League represented a concerted effort to aggressively defend Protestant culture vis-à-vis the Catholics following the winding down of the *Kulturkampf* by the Prussian state. With a peak membership of five hundred thousand in 1914, it was one of the largest Protestant pressure groups in Germany.[38] Yet unlike his father and long before he contemplated a conversion to the Catholic Church, Martin Niemöller started to see the Evangelical League as the problem and not the solution. In a letter to the Reformed pastor Bruno Violet, a member of the Confessing Church and chair of the regional association of the League in Berlin, Niemöller described the Evangelical League in January 1937 as a "cancer in the body of the Evangelical church" and declared himself in fundamental disagreement with all those who defined their Protestantism as mere "anti-Catholicism."[39] While in solitary confinement in Sachsenhausen, he returned to this theme and bemoaned the fact that the Protestants would have no "ecclesiastical" but only a "confessional awareness." And he attacked the Evangelical League again, stating that only the name "Anti-Catholic League" would fit its real purpose.[40] Niemöller's conversion plans prompted him to express his rejection of traditional Lutheran anti-Catholicism in no uncertain terms. Yet he had voiced his critique of confessional hostility as the core marker of Protestant identity already two years before he discovered Catholic piety as an emotional resource.

Niemöller's conversion plans were clearly motivated by his very own, highly specific situation, which included—although as only one among several factors—his detention in solitary confinement. But Niemöller was certainly not the only German Protestant who was fundamentally disillusioned by the strife, dogmatic inconsistency, and accommodation with the Nazi state that his church had displayed since 1933. As he was a leading member of the Confessing Church, his conversion plans had repercussions well beyond himself as an individual. Until the end of 1940, only a small circle of his family members and closest friends had knowledge of his intention to convert. Yet in early 1941, the news filtered through to a wider circle of lay members of the Confessing Church who were gathered in the circle of helpers in the Dahlem parish, separately from the official parish structure. In this tightly knit community, the news erupted like a bomb and immediately caused a great deal of confusion and soul-searching. In a series of lectures and meetings, the members of this group reconsidered and debated the differences between the Protestant and the Catholic faith. It quickly transpired that some of them wanted to follow Niemöller and convert themselves. More importantly, key members of the parish, including Ludwig Bartning, the long-standing *Kirchmeister*—the lay person in charge of financial matters of the parish—and close personal friend of Else and Martin Niemöller, suggested that this was a moment in which the group should take a joint stance, that is, convert collectively.[41] While the Dahlem-group of the Confessing Church ultimately decided against this radical step, it appears that some parish members indeed converted, among them Ernst Brandenburg, a high-ranking civil servant in the Reich Transport Ministry. Protestants in other parts of Berlin converted once the news about Niemöller had circulated more widely in the city.[42]

By early 1941, the repercussions of Niemöller's plans reached much farther than Berlin and only amplified doubts that other members of the Confessing Church harbored at the time. A letter by Heinz Kloppenburg is illuminating in this respect. Kloppenburg, a Lutheran pastor and theologian, was a leading member of the Confessing Church in the Oldenburg territorial church. In the decades after 1945, he was one of Niemöller's closest political allies in his many pacifist and anti-nuclear crusades. In March 1941, he responded to the rumor that Niemöller had already converted, and continued:

> The beginning and the end of Niemöller's thoughts on this issue are without doubt the question of the church as a community in the Body of Christ in its shape here on earth. . . . The experiences of recent years lead inevitably to the question whether the evangelical church with its consistories, its German-Christian bishops and with its administrations that act entirely in accordance with the law of the secular world rather than in accordance with the Gospel, whether it is possible to believe in this church as the church of Jesus Christ in the sense of the third article of faith. For many earnest Christians, the answer to this question is today: no![43]

Kloppenburg agreed with Niemöller's assessment that the "introduction of the summepiscopate" was the key reason for all these deformations, as it had turned the Protestant churches into a "pawn of the worldly rulers." Whether Niemöller would finally make the leap and convert to the Catholic Church or not was for Kloppenburg ultimately a "very secondary question." But the gist of the conclusions that he was drawing from the example of his friend was clear:

> Personally, I can only rate it positively and can see a true question of the faith in the rumours about Martin Niemöller, as they put to us once again the question of the reality of the church in such an unmistakeable fashion.[44]

Kloppenburg's letter demonstrates that Niemöller's conversion plans were far more than a personal problem. The key issue that drove Niemöller's intention to convert and the extended rationale that he provided in his manuscript *Thoughts on the Path of the Christian Church* was the lack of legitimacy and historical depth of the Protestant *Landeskirchen*. They could not claim to stand in a line of continuity that reached back to Jesus and the Twelve Apostles, the true founders of the Christian Church. That the Lutheran territorial churches had easily relented to the attack of the German Christians since 1933 and had vacillated in their support for the Confessing Church, as the example of the "intact" churches of Württemberg, Hanover, and Bavaria demonstrated, was both proof of their moral bankruptcy and the manifestation of a much deeper problem.

At this point, in early 1941, Niemöller's conversion had already expanded into an international *cause célèbre*. Newspapers in France, Switzerland, the UK, and the USA reported on his plans. The London *Times* claimed in February 1941—falsely—that the formal conversion had already taken place. As with many other newspapers, the *New York Times* struggled to make sense of the news arriving from Berlin. Based on reports from both Catholic circles in the German capital and members of the Dahlem parish, the newspaper denied that Niemöller had converted, emphasizing that he had only studied Catholic doctrine. His real aim was to "to bring about closer collaboration between Catholic and Protestant churches after his release" from the concentration camp.[45] Thus, the *New York Times* chose to explain the news by pointing to Niemöller's interest in ecumenical work, a convenient but entirely misleading rationale. Given the significance of Niemöller for the Protestant churches in Germany and his status as an internationally recognized symbol for resistance against the Third Reich, it is not surprising that the Holy See also got involved. Writing to the Catholic Bishop of Berlin, Konrad von Preysing, in March 1941, Pope Pius XII expressed his satisfaction that Niemöller had embarked on his spiritual journey without any external intervention from the Catholic side, emphasizing that the Catholic Church was open to anybody who accepted its faith and requested to be admitted.[46] Ultimately, though, Niemöller did not make the final step. After three years of reflection and lengthy deliberation with his wife Else, and, through her, Hans Asmussen, Niemöller decided in the spring of 1941 to abandon his plans for converting. The stubborn, protracted resistance of Else against his plans was the most important factor. In July 1941, Niemöller was transferred to Dachau, where he shared a row of cells at the end of the so-called *Bunker*—the prison within the camp for special detainees—with first two and then three Catholic priests. In the company of these priests, Niemöller gradually rediscovered and reclaimed his identity as a Protestant Christian.[47]

Yet the story does not end there, as Niemöller's conversion plans assumed additional significance for Protestant theologians and members of the Confessing Church. A key conduit in this respect was Hans Asmussen. Asmussen hailed from the north of Germany but had been sent into forced retirement as a pastor in Altona—today a part of Hamburg—in 1934. Moving to Berlin and working for the Confessing Church, he had gained a high profile as a co-author of the Barmen Declaration. His commentary attached to the declaration was declared to be an official part of it at the Barmen Synod in May 1934. Niemöller's search for a deeper, reliable foundation of ecclesiology was in many respects the result of an ongoing dialogue with Asmussen, who had harbored similar thoughts even before his friend Martin had begun to discover Catholic piety. In a book published in 1939, *Kirche und Amt* (*Church and Office*), Asmussen developed lines of thought which in core points resembled ideas that Niemöller discussed in his own book-length manuscript finished shortly after the publication of Asmussen's book. Once a copy of the book had reached him in Sachsenhausen in March 1940, Niemöller asked his wife Else to relay to Asmussen that he would "walk in his [Asmussen's] train of thought [*Gedankenspuren*]."[48] Asmussen wanted to understand the history of the Christian Church in all of its complexity. Doing so, however, required shedding centuries-old Lutheran prejudices and recognizing that the years between the First Council of Nicaea in 325 and the start of the Reformation in 1517 were just as much a valid part of Church history as the years afterwards. Asmussen also drew on organic metaphors, describing the Church as a living organism. And while he based any judgment on the troubled question of the potential unity of all Christian Churches on the record of the New Testament alone, Asmussen asserted that the notion of an "invisible church" lacked any basis in the texts of the New Testament and had thus to be rejected. This in turn brought the Catholic Church, as an eminently visible church, back into the debate.[49] Niemöller's considerations regarding conversion were thus anchored in his larger understanding of Church history.[50]

Asmussen, to be sure, did not support Niemöller's conversion plans, and when these plans were debated in wider Protestant circles in Berlin, Asmussen delivered a series of public lectures on the critique of the Catholic Church in the 1530 Augsburg Confessions, the key confessional document of the Lutherans, to reduce the momentum of the "movement" towards conversion.[51] Yet, at the same time, Asmussen's own interest in putting the Holy Communion at the center of liturgical practice and his calls to develop a more hierarchical understanding of the office of the Church raised interest and suspicion in equal measure among the members of the Confessing Church—and not only in Berlin. In November 1940, a sympathetic Lutheran pastor from Flensburg in the far north of Germany wrote to Asmussen that many of his colleagues were talking about the "Catholicizing tendencies" which he seemed to display. However, having read Asmussen's *Kirche und Amt*, this pastor understood the emphasis on liturgy not so much as an attempt to accommodate or emulate the Catholic Church as a confession, but as a call to take the liturgical elements of the church service more seriously.[52] Asmussen's ideas remained controversial in Berlin, but a more general backlash against him and his ideas emerged only once he had left the city and moved to the southwest of Germany in 1943–44.[53]

Asmussen, however, not only tried to convince his fellow Brethren in the Confessing Church of the necessity of developing a deeper, more "Catholic" understanding of ecclesiological and liturgical issues. He was also engaged in a sustained and meaningful ecumenical dialogue with Catholic priests in Berlin. The platform for these contacts was provided by the Una Sancta movement, an ecumenical group that the Catholic priest Max Josef Metzger (1887–1944) had initiated in May 1939.[54] Following his experiences as a military chaplain in World War I, Metzger had become a radical pacifist and acted as a leading member of the *Friedensbund Deutscher Katholiken* (Peace League of German Catholics), the main pacifist platform for Catholics in the Weimar Republic. Following a denunciation by a member of his circle, which relayed Metzger's plans for a democratic Germany and his rejection of the Nazis, to the Gestapo, Metzger was sentenced to death in a sham-trial by Freisler's notorious People's Court and executed in 1944.[55] Another member of the Una Sancta group in Berlin and interlocutor of Asmussen was Georg von Sachsen, SJ, the last Crown Prince of Saxony and member of the House of Wettin. He was yet another convert to the Catholic Church, having taken this step after becoming disillusioned by World War I in 1918, who subsequently joined the Jesuit order.[56]

Members of the Confessing Church provide us insight into some of the meetings that the Una Sancta circle held in the crucial years 1940 and 1941. The Protestant theologian Günther Dehn, who had stirred up controversy in the 1920s as one of the members of a group of religious socialists and was involved in the theological training of BK pastors in Berlin, reported about an "ecumenical dialogue" on 5–6 November 1940.[57] About eighty Catholic priests and Protestant theologians—the latter both active members of Una Sancta, representatives of the High Church movement, and of the *Berneuchen* movement, which emphasized greater emphasis on liturgy—and Protestant laypeople had gathered in a Dominican Cloister in Berlin-Moabit. The Confessing Church was represented by Hans Asmussen, Heinz Kloppenburg, Fritz Schipper and Hans Urner, the pastor of the Paul Gerhardt Stift in Berlin, a deaconess house.[58] Dehn sensed that there was a "strong urge" for a "reconciliation" (*Ausgleich*) with the Catholic Church among the Protestants in the audience. Asmussen delivered a talk about "Office and Church"—based on his book with the same title. At least for the Protestant theologians in the group, the way forward to a closer alignment seemed to be a more pronounced separation between the laity and those holding church offices, the introduction of a "*successio apostolica*" (Apostolic succession) in the ministry, ideally through the laying on of hands and a hierarchical ministerial structure. Here, Asmussen envisaged introducing bishops with a distinctive "spiritual quality." Controversy emerged only over the question of papal authority, which the Protestants were ready to accept "*iure humano*" (by human law), but not as derived from "divine law." Interestingly, one of the Catholics also opined that the authority of the pope was only by human law. A resolute defense of uniquely Protestant positions was offered only by some of the Protestant laypersons. Personally, Dehn took a rather dim view of the proceedings, which he interpreted, as far as the Protestants were concerned, as a "shrinking of the belief in our own cause."[59]

It should come as no surprise that Asmussen left the meeting with a rather different impression. He worked with the premise that currently "many Protestant Christians were looking to Rome," and they did so, he was convinced, because they expected to find something that their own church was not able to provide. Asmussen was adamant that the myths and rumors that the confessional divide had nurtured on the side of the Protestants were no longer sufficient to understand the situation. Anybody who would try to "shoot dead" the "Romans," i.e., Roman Catholics, with the "cartridges" that the Gustav Adolf Association founded in 1832 to support Protestants in the diaspora and that the *Evangelischer Bund* had "delivered," would do so in vain, as he would fire with "blank ammunition." This was an apt and not-so-subtle metaphor for the zeal with which the Protestants had pursued their culture wars against the Catholics in the past. The metaphor made unmistakeably clear that for Asmussen the age of confessional division had come to an end. In the meeting, Asmussen had emphasized that he was neither interested in conversions to the Catholic Church—clearly a disapproving nod in the direction of his close friend Niemöller—nor in the notion of a "union" between the churches. But there were theological and practical issues at stake which were "crying out for a clarification."[60] Niemöller's rationale for his conversion plans—which could be gleaned from his letters to his wife, which were apparently widely circulating in circles of the Confessing Church—provided the reason for another, subsequent meeting among Protestant theologians. However, Asmussen's attempts to find a path for a reconciliation with the Catholic Church were also relevant for this debate, which demonstrates the extent to which the debate on Niemöller's conversion and the work of the Una Sancta movement were closely entwined in the eyes of key members of the Confessing Church.[61]

Did conversion to the Catholic Church and the interest that leading Protestant theologians had shown in its teachings have lasting repercussions in the post-1945 period? The immediate answer to this question is "no." Hans Asmussen initially continued his work in the Confessing Church after being elected as the leader of the Council of Brethren in 1945. He also took a leading role in the EKD, the umbrella body of the German Protestant Churches established in 1945 and which he represented internally and abroad. Yet he became increasingly skeptical of the more critical political role that his old friend Niemöller took vis-à-vis the newly founded Federal Republic and demanded a more prominent role for the Lutherans within the EKD. This led to his break with the EKD in 1948 and a return to low-level ministry in his old home in the north of Germany.[62] While Niemöller's political preferences remained highly controversial within EKD circles, which he joined in 1945 as the deputy chairman of the EKD Council, his position as a leading representative of West Germany in the context of the ecumenical movement was undisputed. He was highly regarded in all of the different currents in the Protestant Churches. He had assumed this position in 1945, using his authority as a former concentration camp prisoner and victim of Nazi persecution to initiate the first contact with the ecumenical representatives of the Western Allies. He continued to serve the ecumenical movement until his death in 1984. Yet Niemöller's ecumenical engagement was not driven by his immersion into Catholicism from 1938 to 1941. On the contrary: he returned to a kneejerk anti-Catholic confessionalism when he interpreted the hegemony of the Christian Democratic Union in the Federal Republic as an indication that the West German state was a puppet of Rome. His ecumenical work was in the first instance an attempt to reintroduce the German Protestant Churches into the community of the Western world. Over the years, this goal lost significance, and Niemöller learned to understand the significance of Christianity—Protestant, Catholic, and Orthodox—in non-Western countries in a globalized world.[63]

What larger conclusions can we draw from the history of conversions to the Catholic Church during the Third Reich and in particular from Niemöller's ultimately aborted conversion? First, the confessional divide became more complex and volatile from 1933 to 1945, when we take both the substantial number of those "believing in God"—and hence operating outside the two Christian confessions—and the increased number of *Übertritte* and *Rücktritte* among both Protestants and Catholics into account. Second, the reflections that Niemöller wrote while he contemplated a conversion demonstrate the deep suspicions that a Protestant minister had about the actual knowledge of the laity about the reasons for and the relevance of the divide between Protestants and Catholics. This should be reason enough to reconsider the actual depth of the confessional divide in the perceptions of Protestant laypeople, something that has not been the subject of sustained historical inquiry. The third and surely most important conclusion is that the conversions especially of members of the Confessing Church show a pattern of discontent with the infighting between the various factions within the Protestant churches. In the eyes of the converts, these conflicts laid bare a fundamental lack of ecclesiological depth and coherence on the side of the Protestants, which resulted in a neglect of the true purpose of Christian religion, communicating the meaning of spirituality and transcendence. Whereas the Protestant Churches were entangled in bitter conflicts over the administrative and judicial implications of the challenge posed by the *Deutsche Christen*, the Catholic Church appeared to the converts as a bastion of Christian unity and as uniquely focused on the promise of salvation. Fourth, it is worth mentioning that neither Niemöller's conversion plans nor those of other Protestants were motivated by an interest in ecumenical reconciliation. However, while the Lutheran theologian Hans Asmussen tried to talk his friend Niemöller out of his plans, he was also engaged in interconfessional conversations with Catholics in Berlin. In many ways, for all their differences, Niemöller's and Asmussen's interest in the Catholic Church fed off each other, indicating an interest in the Catholic faith at the very center of the Confessing Church.

Benjamin Ziemann is Professor of Modern German History at the University of Sheffield. He is the author and editor of numerous books, including *Encounters with Modernity: The Catholic Church in West Germany, 1945–1975* (Berghahn Books, 2014); *Martin Niemöller. Ein Leben in Opposition* (DVA, 2019), and its forthcoming English translation, *Hitler's Personal Prisoner: The Turbulent Life of Martin Niemoeller* (Oxford University Press, 2022); and the coeditor of *The Oxford Handbook of the Weimar Republic* (Oxford University Press, 2021).

Notes

1. Tillmann Bendikowski, "'Eine Fackel der Zwietracht.' Katholisch-protestantische Mischehen im 19. und 20. Jahrhundert," in *Konfessionen im Konflikt. Deutschland zwischen 1800 und 1970: Ein zweites konfessionelles Zeitalter*, ed. Olaf Blaschke (Göttingen: Vandenhoeck & Ruprecht, 2002), 215–41.

2. Hermann Gerlach, *Staatskirchentum und Religionsfreiheit unter besonderer Berücksichtigung der kirchlichen Zustände im Königreich Sachsen am Ende des 19. Jahrhunderts* (Halle/Saale: Strien, 1899), 43–45.

3. Detlef Pollack, "Überlegungen zum Begriff und Phänomen der Konversion aus religionssoziologischer Perspektive," in *Konversion und Konfession in der Frühen Neuzeit*, ed. Ute Lotz-Heumann, Jan-Friedrich Mißfelder, and Matthias Pohlig (Gütersloh: Gütersloher Verlagshaus, 2007), 33–55, esp. 52.

4. The semantic ingenuity of this label has been often noted, since every baptized German was technically a "German Christian." To avoid confusion, I will continue to use the German name.

5. For regional case studies, see Manfred Gailus, "Overwhelmed by Their Own Fascination with the 'Ideas of 1933': Berlin's Protestant Social Milieu in the Third Reich," *German History* 20 (2002), 462–93, figures 483; Samuel Koehne, "Nazi Germany as a Christian State: The 'Protestant Experience' of 1933 in Württemberg," *Central European History* 46 (2013): 97–123. Generally, see Klaus Scholder, *The Churches and the Third Reich, Vol 1. Preliminary History and the Time of Illusions, 1919–33*, trans. John Bowden (Philadelphia: Fortress Press, 1987), 189–236, 280–305. On the German Christians, see Doris Bergen, *Twisted Cross. The German Christian Movement in the Third Reich* (Chapel Hill: University of North Carolina Press, 1996).

6. Benjamin Ziemann, *Martin Niemöller. Ein Leben in Opposition* (Munich: DVA, 2019), 174–179, quotes 175.

7. Lucian Hölscher, ed., *Datenatlas zur religiösen Geographie im protestantischen Deutschland. Von der Mitte des 19. Jahrhunderts bis zum Zweiten Weltkrieg*, Vol. 4 (Berlin: de Gruyter 2001), 703–4.

8. Kevin C. Spicer, "'Tu ich unrecht, ... Ein guter Priester und ein guter Nationalsozialist zu sein?' Zum Verhältnis zwischen Katholizismus und Nationalsozialismus," in *Zerstrittene "Volksgemeinschaft." Glaube, Konfession und Religion im Nationalsozialismus*, ed. Manfred Gailus and Armin Nolzen (Göttingen: Vandenhoeck & Ruprecht, 2011), 68–75; Gerhard Besier, *Die Kirchen und das Dritte Reich*, Vol. 3: *Spaltungen und Abwehrkämpfe 1934–1937* (Munich: Propyläen, 2001), 115–65, 657–731; and the excellent regional case study by Werner K. Blessing, "'Deutschland in Not, wir im Glauben . . .': Kirche und Kirchenvolk in einer katholischen Region 1933–1949," in *Von Stalingrad zur Währungsreform. Zur Sozialgeschichte des Umbruchs in Deutschland*, 3rd ed., ed. Martin Broszat, Klaus-Dietmar Henke and Hans Woller (Munich: R. Oldenbourg, 1990), 21–54.

9. Kevin C. Spicer, *Resisting the Third Reich: The Catholic Clergy in Hitler's Berlin* (DeKalb: Northern Illinois University Press, 2004), 74.

10. Thomas Fandel, "Konfessionalismus und Nationalsozialismus," in *Konfessionen im Konflikt. Deutschland zwischen 1800 und 1970: ein zweites konfessionelles Zeitalter*, ed. Olaf Blaschke (Göttingen: Vandenhoeck & Ruprecht, 2002), 309, 313, 316–17.

11. Björn Mensing, *Pfarrer und Nationalsozialismus. Geschichte einer Verstrickung am Beispiel der evangelisch-lutherischen Kirche in Bayern* (Göttingen: Vandenhoeck & Ruprecht, 1998), 161.

12. Klaus Scholder, *The Churches and the Third Reich*, Vol. 2: *The Year of Disillusionment, 1934 Barmen and Rome*, trans. John Bowden (Philadelphia: Fortress Press, 1988), 1–88, 121–70, 212–43.

13. Besier, *Spaltungen und Abwehrkämpfe 1934–1937*, 19–113, 337–655; through the lens of Niemöller's church politics, see Ziemann, *Martin Niemöller*, 195–298.

14. Manfred Gailus, "'Ein Volk—ein Reich—ein Glaube'? Religiöse Pluralisierungen in der NS-Weltanschauungsdiktatur," in *Europäische Religionsgeschichte im 20. Jahrhundert*, ed. Friedrich Wilhelm Graf and Klaus Große Kracht (Cologne: Böhlau, 2007), 251–62, quote 268; see Richard Steigmann-Gall, *The Holy Reich: Nazi Conceptions of Christianity, 1919–1945* (Cambridge, UK: Cambridge University Press, 2003), 218–52.

15. Hölscher, *Datenatlas*, 703.

16. Benjamin Ziemann, *Encounters with Modernity: The Catholic Church in West Germany, 1945–1975*, trans. Andrew Evans (New York: Berghahn Books, 2014), 30–36, quote 34; see August-Hermann Leugers-Scherzberg, "Latente Kulturkampfstimmung im wilhelminischen Kaiserreich. Konfessionelle Polemik als konfessions- und innenpolitisches Kampfmittel," in *Die Verschränkung von Innen-, Konfessions- und Kolonialpolitik im Deutschen Reich vor 1914*, ed. Johannes Horstmann (Schwerte: Katholische Akademie, 1987), 13–37.

17. Hölscher, *Datenatlas*, 703.

18. Catherine Leota Dollard, *The Surplus Woman: Unmarried in Imperial Germany, 1871–1918* (New York: Berghahn Books, 2009), 176–98, esp. 186–93, quote 188.

19. On his conversion, see Rudolf Morsey, *Fritz Gerlich (1883–1934): Ein früher Gegner Hitlers und des Nationalsozialismus* (Paderborn: Ferdinand Schöningh, 2016), 141–52, 174–76, 192–96. On Neumann, see the fascinating study by Michael E. O'Sullivan, *Disruptive Power: Catholic Women, Miracles, and Politics in Modern Germany, 1918–1965* (Toronto: University of Toronto Press, 2018.)

20. Hans-Günter Hockerts, "Konfessionswechsel im Dritten Reich. Zahlenbilder und Fallbeispiele in typologischer Absicht," in *Konvertiten und Konversionen*, ed. Siegfried Hermle and Hans Maier (Annweiler: Plöger, 2010), 149–65, figures 151. The figures of conversions to the Catholic Church prior to 1933 show a marked discrepancy with the Protestant data compiled

by Hölscher, which consistently return lower figures. In the context of this study, it is not possible to reconcile or explain these discrepancies.

21. Ibid., 151.
22. Ibid., 159.
23. John Connelly, *From Enemy to Brother: The Revolution in Catholic Teaching on the Jews, 1933–1965* (Cambridge, MA: Harvard University Press, 2012), 121–25. The figure of forty conversions by Protestant ministers, mentioned by Connelly, is most likely erroneous. Hockerts, "Konfessionswechsel," 156 suggests that only Thieme himself converted. Both Connelly and Hockerts refer to "Der Weg des Protestantismus nach Rom," an August 1935 special report of the head of the *Sicherheitshauptamt* of the SD: Heinz Boberach, ed., *Berichte des SD und der Gestapo über Kirchen und Kirchenvolk in Deutschland 1934–1944* (Mainz: Matthias Grünewald, 1971), 95. The report does not confirm other conversions apart from Thieme's own. See "Der Weg des Protestantismus nach Rom,".
24. See the groundbreaking study by Manfred Gailus, *Protestantismus und Nationalsozialismus. Studien zur nationalsozialistischen Durchdringung des protestantischen Sozialmilieus in Berlin* (Cologne: Böhlau, 2001), 306–56.
25. Manfred Gailus, *Mir aber zerriss es das Herz. Der stille Widerstand der Elisabeth Schmitz*, 2nd ed. (Göttingen: Vandenhoeck & Ruprecht, 2011).
26. Holger Roggelin, *Franz Hildebrandt. Ein lutherischer Dissenter im Kirchenkampf und Exil* (Göttingen: Vandenhoeck & Ruprecht, 1999), quote 100.
27. Ibid., 99.
28. Existing biographies of Niemöller have mentioned this plan only briefly and not really explored its significance. See James Bentley, *Martin Niemöller* (Oxford, UK: Oxford University Press, 1984), 148; and Matthew Hockenos, *Then They Came for Me: Martin Niemöller, the Pastor Who Defied the Nazis* (New York: Basic Books, 2018), 146–47. Steigmann-Gall, *The Holy Reich*, 235, erroneously implies that Himmler simply invented Niemöller's conversion plans.
29. For a detailed reconstruction of Niemöller's conversion plans, see Alf Christophersen and Benjamin Ziemann, "Einleitung," in *Martin Niemöller, Gedanken über den Weg der christlichen Kirche*, ed. Alf Christophersen and Benjamin Ziemann (Gütersloh: Gütersloher Verlagshaus, 2019), 8–26.
30. See Benjamin Ziemann, "Martin Niemöller und die Wartestandsaffäre 1939/40. Ein Kapitel aus der Geschichte des Kampfes gegen die Bekennende Kirche," *Schweizerische Zeitschrift für Religions- und Kulturgeschichte* 111 (2017): 317–38, quote 330.
31. Ibid., 327.
32. Martin Niemöller, *Gedanken über den Weg der christlichen Kirche*, ed. Alf Christophersen and Benjamin Ziemann (Gütersloh: Gütersloher Verlagshaus, 2019), 62–144.
33. Ibid., 206.
34. See Martin Niemöller, "Gedanken zu dem Thema: Evangelisch oder Katholisch?" *Sinn und Form* 53 (2001): 450–51.
35. Niemöller, *Gedanken über den Weg*, 161.
36. Ibid., 160.
37. Heinrich Niemöller, *Aus 56 Amtsjahren* (Bielefeld: Ludwig Bechauf, 1946), 45.
38. Armin Müller-Dreier, *Konfession in Politik, Gesellschaft und Kultur des Kaiserreichs. Der Evangelische Bund 1886–1914* (Gütersloh: Gütersloher Verlagshaus, 1998).
39. Martin Niemöller, 6 January 1937 to Bruno Violet, cited in Christophersen and Ziemann, "Einleitung," 7–59, 18.
40. Niemöller, *Gedanken über den Weg*, 160.
41. See Gerhard Schäberle-Koenigs, *Und sie waren täglich einmütig beieinander. Der Weg der Bekennenden Gemeinde Berlin/Dahlem in den Jahren 1937–1943 mit Helmut Gollwitzer* (Gütersloh: Gütersloher Verlagshaus, 1998), 261–73.
42. Hans Asmussen, *Zur jüngsten Kirchengeschichte. Anmerkungen und Folgerungen* (Stuttgart: Evangelisches Verlagswerk, 1961), 54; Christophersen and Ziemann, "Einleitung," 20.

43. Letter by Heinz Kloppenburg, 11 March 1941, cited in Christophersen and Ziemann, "Einleitung," 54.
44. Ibid., 55.
45. "Pastor Niemöller. Reported Conversion to Rome," *The Times*, 6 February 1941; "Niemoeller's Friends Deny His Conversion: Say Imprisoned Pastor is Only Studying Catholic Doctrine," *New York Times*, 5 February 1941. Further references in Christophersen and Ziemann, "Einleitung," 8.
46. Pius XII 19 March 1941 to Bishop Konrad von Preysing, in *Die Briefe Pius' XII. an die deutschen Bischöfe 1939–1944*, ed. Burkhart Schneider (Mainz: Matthias Grünewald Verlag, 1966), 134. The Catholic author Reinhold Schneider confirmed that von Preysing had read some of Niemöller's letters from Sachsenhausen, which Hans Asmussen had shown him, and that the Catholic Bishop had provided books by Catholic authors, including the Cardinal John Henry Newman, who was himself a convert, to Niemöller. See Reinhold Schneider, *Verhüllter Tag* (Olten: Hegner, 1954), 171–72.
47. Christophersen and Ziemann, "Einleitung," 13–16, 21–26.
48. Hans Asmussen, *Kirche und Amt* (Munich: Christian Kaiser, 1939); Christophersen and Ziemann, "Einleitung," quote 31.
49. Asmussen, *Kirche und Amt*, 7–9, 15, 18, 28.
50. Christophersen and Ziemann, "Einleitung," 29–30.
51. Asmussen, *Zur jüngsten Kirchengeschichte*, 54. See the text of one of these lectures, "Unser Verhältnis zur Römischen Kirche," delivered 2 February 1941, Evangelisches Zentralarchiv Berlin (hereafter EZA), 50/559, fos. 88–102.
52. Enno Konukiewitz, *Hans Asmussen. Ein lutherischer Theologe im Kirchenkampf* (Gütersloh: Gütersloher Verlagshaus, 1984), 227–30, quote 228 (Johann Schmidt, 15 November 1940 to Asmussen).
53. Besier, *Spaltungen und Abwehrkämpfe 1934–1937*, 990.
54. Christoph Mehl and Jörg Thierfelder, "Ökumene im Krieg: Evangelisch-katholische Kirche und innerprotestantische Vergewisserungen in der Endphase des 'Dritten Reiches,'" *Zeitschrift für Kirchengeschichte* 108 (1997): 344–46.
55. Werner Becker, "Max Josef Metzger," in *Ökumenische Menschen. Hermann Hoffmann als Festgabe zum 90. Geburtstag gewidmet*, ed. Werner Becker and Bruno Radom (Leipzig: St.-Benno-Verlag, 1969), 39–59.
56. Christophersen and Ziemann, "Einleitung," 29.
57. Günther Dehn, November 17, 1940, to Hans Böhm, EZA, 50/559, fo. 62.
58. These details on the participants are according to Hans Asmussen, November 16, 1940, to Wilhelm Pressel, EZA, 50/559, fos. 63–66.
59. Günther Dehn, 17 November 1940, to Hans Böhm, EZA, 50/559, fo. 62.
60. Hans Asmussen, November 16, 1940, to Wihelm Pressel, EZA, 50/559, fos. 63–66. For a critique of these Una Sancta meetings, which he deemed "not harmless" but also "not unimportant," see Pastor Hinz, 12 November 1940, to the Council of Brethren of the Confessing Church of the ApU, EZA, 50/559, fo. 67.
61. See the letter by Martin Albertz, 27 December 1940, to Ernst Wolf, EZA, 50/559, fo. 68.
62. Ziemann, *Martin Niemöller*, 393, 399–400, 404, 425.
63. Ibid., 383–412, 475–96.

Bibliography

Asmussen, Hans. *Kirche und Amt*. Munich: Christian Kaiser, 1939.
———. *Zur jüngsten Kirchengeschichte. Anmerkungen und Folgerungen*. Stuttgart: Evangelisches Verlagswerk, 1961.

Becker, Werner. "Max Josef Metzger." In *Ökumenische Menschen. Hermann Hoffmann als Festgabe zum 90. Geburtstag gewidmet*, edited by Werner Becker and Bruno Radom, 39–59. Leipzig: St.-Benno-Verlag, 1969.
Bendikowski, Tillmann. "'Eine Fackel der Zwietracht.' Katholisch-protestantische Mischehen im 19. und 20. Jahrhundert." In *Konfessionen im Konflikt. Deutschland zwischen 1800 und 1970: Ein zweites konfessionelles Zeitalter*, edited by Olaf Blaschke, 215–41. Göttingen: Vandenhoeck & Ruprecht, 2002.
Bentley, James. *Martin Niemöller*. Oxford, UK: Oxford University Press, 1984.
Bergen, Doris. *Twisted Cross. The German Christian Movement in the Third Reich*. Chapel Hill: University of North Carolina Press, 1996.
Besier, Gerhard. *Die Kirchen und das Dritte Reich*, Vol. 3: *Spaltungen und Abwehrkämpfe 1934–1937*. Munich: Propyläen, 2001.
Blessing, Werner K. "'Deutschland in Not, wir im Glauben . . .': Kirche und Kirchenvolk in einer katholischen Region 1933–1949." In *Von Stalingrad zur Währungsreform. Zur Sozialgeschichte des Umbruchs in Deutschland*, 3rd ed., edited by Martin Broszat, Klaus-Dietmar Henke and Hans Woller, 3–111. Munich: R. Oldenbourg, 1990.
Boberach, Heinz, ed. *Berichte des SD und der Gestapo über Kirchen und Kirchenvolk in Deutschland 1934–1944*. Mainz: Matthias Grünewald, 1971.
Christophersen, Alf, and Benjamin Ziemann. "Einleitung." In *Gedanken über den Weg der christlichen Kirche*, by Martin Niemöller, edited by Alf Christophersen and Benjamin Ziemann, 7–59. Gütersloh: Gütersloher Verlagshaus, 2019.
Connelly, John. *From Enemy to Brother: The Revolution in Catholic Teaching on the Jews, 1933–1965*. Cambridge, MA: Harvard University Press, 2012.
Dollard, Catherine Leota. *The Surplus Woman: Unmarried in Imperial Germany, 1871–1918*. New York: Berghahn Books, 2009.
Fandel, Thomas. "Konfessionalismus und Nationalsozialismus." In *Konfessionen im Konflikt. Deutschland zwischen 1800 und 1970: ein zweites konfessionelles Zeitalter*, edited by Olaf Blaschke, 299–334. Göttingen: Vandenhoeck & Ruprecht, 2002.
Gailus, Manfred. "'Ein Volk—ein Reich—ein Glaube'? Religiöse Pluralisierungen in der NS-Weltanschauungsdiktatur." In *Europäische Religionsgeschichte im 20. Jahrhundert*, edited by Friedrich Wilhelm Graf and Klaus Große Kracht, 247–68. Cologne: Böhlau, 2007.
———. *Mir aber zerriss es das Herz. Der stille Widerstand der Elisabeth Schmitz*, 2nd ed. Göttingen: Vandenhoeck & Ruprecht, 2011.
———. "Overwhelmed by Their Own Fascination with the 'Ideas of 1933': Berlin's Protestant Social Milieu in the Third Reich." *German History* 20 (2002): 462–93.
———. *Protestantismus und Nationalsozialismus. Studien zur nationalsozialistischen Durchdringung des protestantischen Sozialmilieus in Berlin*. Cologne: Böhlau, 2001.
Gerlach, Hermann. *Staatskirchentum und Religionsfreiheit unter besonderer Berücksichtigung der kirchlichen Zustände im Königreich Sachsen am Ende des 19. Jahrhunderts*. Halle/Saale: Strien, 1899.
Hockenos, Matthew. *Then They Came for Me: Martin Niemöller, the Pastor Who Defied the Nazis*. New York: Basic Books, 2018.
Hockerts, Hans-Günter. "Konfessionswechsel im Dritten Reich. Zahlenbilder und Fallbeispiele in typologischer Absicht." In *Konvertiten und Konversionen*, edited by Siegfried Hermle and Hans Maier, 149–65. Annweiler: Plöger, 2010.
Hölscher, Lucian, ed. *Datenatlas zur religiösen Geographie im protestantischen Deutschland. Von der Mitte des 19. Jahrhunderts bis zum Zweiten Weltkrieg*, Vol. 4. Berlin: de Gruyter, 2001.
Koehne, Samuel. "Nazi Germany as a Christian State: The 'Protestant Experience' of 1933 in Württemberg." *Central European History* 46 (2013): 97–123.
Konukiewitz, Enno. *Hans Asmussen. Ein lutherischer Theologe im Kirchenkampf*. Gütersloh: Gütersloher Verlagshaus, 1984.

Leugers-Scherzberg, August-Hermann. "Latente Kulturkampfstimmung im wilhelminischen Kaiserreich. Konfessionelle Polemik als konfessions- und innenpolitisches Kampfmittel." In *Die Verschränkung von Innen-, Konfessions- und Kolonialpolitik im Deutschen Reich vor 1914*, edited by Johannes Horstmann, 13–37. Schwerte: Katholische Akademie, 1987.
Mehl, Christoph, and Jörg Thierfelder. "Ökumene im Krieg: Evangelisch-katholische Kirche und innerprotestantische Vergewisserungen in der Endphase des 'Dritten Reiches.'" *Zeitschrift für Kirchengeschichte* 108 (1997): 342–75.
Mensing, Björn. *Pfarrer und Nationalsozialismus. Geschichte einer Verstrickung am Beispiel der evangelisch-lutherischen Kirche in Bayern*. Göttingen: Vandenhoeck & Ruprecht, 1998.
Morsey, Rudolf. *Fritz Gerlich (1883–1934): Ein früher Gegner Hitlers und des Nationalsozialismus*. Paderborn: Ferdinand Schöningh, 2016.
Müller-Dreier, Armin. *Konfession in Politik, Gesellschaft und Kultur des Kaiserreichs. Der Evangelische Bund 1886–1914*. Gütersloh: Gütersloher Verlagshaus, 1998.
Niemöller, Heinrich. *Aus 56 Amtsjahren*. Bielefeld: Ludwig Bechauf, 1946.
Niemöller, Martin. *Gedanken über den Weg der christlichen Kirche*. Edited by Alf Christophersen and Benjamin Ziemann. Gütersloh: Gütersloher Verlagshaus, 2019.
———. "Gedanken zu dem Thema: Evangelisch oder Katholisch?" *Sinn und Form* 53 (2001): 449–59.
O'Sullivan, Michael E. *Disruptive Power: Catholic Women, Miracles, and Politics in Modern Germany, 1918–1965*. Toronto: University of Toronto Press, 2018.
Pollack, Detlef. "Überlegungen zum Begriff und Phänomen der Konversion aus religionssoziologischer Perspektive." In *Konversion und Konfession in der Frühen Neuzeit*, edited by Ute Lotz-Heumann, Jan-Friedrich Mißfelder, and Matthias Pohlig, 33–55. Gütersloh: Gütersloher Verlagshaus, 2007.
Roggelin, Holger. *Franz Hildebrandt. Ein lutherischer Dissenter im Kirchenkampf und Exil*. Göttingen: Vandenhoeck & Ruprecht, 1999.
Schäberle-Koenigs, Gerhard. *Und sie waren täglich einmütig beieinander. Der Weg der Bekennenden Gemeinde Berlin/Dahlem in den Jahren 1937–1943 mit Helmut Gollwitzer*. Gütersloh: Gütersloher Verlagshaus, 1998.
Schneider, Burkhart, ed. *Die Briefe Pius' XII. an die deutschen Bischöfe 1939–1944*. Mainz: Matthias Grünewald Verlag, 1966.
Schneider, Reinhold. *Verhüllter Tag*. Olten: Hegner, 1954.
Scholder, Klaus. *The Churches and the Third Reich. Vol 1: Preliminary History and the Time of Illusions, 1919–33*. Translated by John Bowden. Philadelphia: Fortress Press, 1987.
———. *The Churches and the Third Reich. Vol. 2: The Year of Disillusionment, 1934: Barmen and Rome*. Translated by John Bowden. Philadelphia: Fortress Press, 1988.
Spicer, Kevin C. *Resisting the Third Reich. The Catholic Clergy in Hitler's Berlin*. DeKalb: Northern Illinois University Press, 2004.
———. "'Tu ich unrecht, . . . Ein guter Priester und ein guter Nationalsozialist zu sein?' Zum Verhältnis zwischen Katholizismus und Nationalsozialismus." In *Zerstrittene "Volksgemeinschaft." Glaube, Konfession und Religion im Nationalsozialismus*, edited by Manfred Gailus and Armin Nolzen, 66–95. Göttingen: Vandenhoeck & Ruprecht, 2011.
Steigmann-Gall, Richard. *The Holy Reich: Nazi Conceptions of Christianity, 1919–1945*. Cambridge, UK: Cambridge University Press, 2003.
Ziemann, Benjamin. *Encounters with Modernity. The Catholic Church in West Germany, 1945–1975*. Translated by Andrew Evans. New York: Berghahn Books, 2014.
———. *Martin Niemöller. Ein Leben in Opposition*. Munich: DVA, 2019.
———. "Martin Niemöller und die Wartestandsaffäre 1939/40. Ein Kapitel aus der Geschichte des Kampfes gegen die Bekennende Kirche." *Schweizerische Zeitschrift für Religions- und Kulturgeschichte* 111 (2017): 317–38.

Chapter Seven

IMPERFECT INTERCONFESSIONALISM

Women, Gender, and Sexuality in Early Christian Democracy

Maria Mitchell

In power for fifty of the Federal Republic's first seventy years, the Christian Democratic Union (CDU) has indisputably dominated German postwar democracy. The realization of a decades-old project of Christian political reconciliation, Germany's first avowedly democratic interconfessional party represented the most significant innovation of the West German political order, one that laid essential groundwork for unprecedented domestic and European stability. Opposed to secularization and its manifestations from the left to the right, devout Christians committed themselves after World War II to the re-Christianization of Germany and the primacy of religion as a value of the state. By drawing upon a history of political cooperation, shared apprehensions about the family, and a rejection of socialism and communism, devout Protestants and Catholics pursued a common vision of patriarchy and religiously endowed motherhood, one that played an important role in securing interconfessional accord in a body riven by inner Christian conflict. This project held special resonance for a party that would long rely on women's votes in a disproportionately female state.[1]

While Christian Democratic social and cultural politics helped bridge the Protestant-Catholic confessional breach, interconfessional alliances on issues of gender and sexuality had long been tactical and incomplete. From its origins, Christian Democracy followed its Weimar antecedents to reveal gendered as well as confessional divisions on cultural issues. In the early postwar years, devout Protestant and Catholic women, informed by a tradition of maternalism, denounced the patriarchy of the Nazi *Männerstaat* to call for a feminization of German politics. During and after the

Parliamentary Council (1948–49), female CDU politicians resisted party sexism while challenging Christian Democratic policy on issues pertaining to women, gender, and sexuality. At the same time, Protestants in and outside the party articulated increasingly liberal views on social issues while the Catholic Church resisted reform. As politics advanced by CDU Catholics increasingly lost favor with party Protestants and women, the effectiveness of cultural and social policies to bridge the inner Christian divide diminished. The consequential narrowing of the gap on cultural and social issues between Christians on one hand, and German liberals and socialists on the other, would have manifold effects, not least on CDU electoral results, underscoring the centrality of intersecting dynamics of confession and gender relations to Christian Democratic and West German politics.

The Origins of Christian Democracy

The CDU's organization across Germany was led by former Center Party members, Christian trade unionists, and priests, many of whom had been involved in anti-Nazi oppositional circles. Inspired by shared resistance experiences with Protestants, wary of Marxist power at home and abroad, and convinced that political Catholicism had lost its political and moral mandate, Center Party veterans seized the initiative in 1945 to found the new Germany's most successful political party. True to the vision of interconfessionalism articulated by Julius Bachem, Heinrich Brauns, and Adam Stegerwald, Catholics sought out devout anti-Marxist Protestants whom they regarded as untainted by collaboration with Nazism. Absent viable political alternatives, religious Protestants ultimately embraced the CDU in substantial numbers, with Protestant support increasing from just over 30 percent of the Protestant electorate in 1953 to 42 percent of all Protestant votes in 1957.[2] Strikingly, while the Confessing Church and Christian Social People's Party (CSVP) incubated many first-hour CDU Protestants, those who remained in the party were largely prewar conservatives linked to the German National People's Party (DNVP); in particular, Lutherans showed a consistent preference for the CDU compared to Reform Protestants.[3]

At its founding, the CDU's legitimacy rested not simply on the public association of Catholics and Protestants, but on the party's ability to establish consensus on the broader meanings of Christian Democracy. That pre-1933 interconfessional initiatives were grounded in bourgeois and religious solidarity underscores the importance of cultural and social policies not only in bridging the Weimar Center Party's internal factions, but in forging a postwar alliance between Catholics and Protestants.[4] Just as they had rallied during the Weimar Republic to resist secularism and materialism by defending confessional schools, Protestants on the right, led by conservative Lutherans in the DNVP, joined Catholics in regarding women as agents of Christian morality with distinctly female and maternal responsibilities.[5]

Foreshadowing the post-1945 consensus that would undergird Christian Democracy, the Center Party joined the DNVP to oppose socialist attempts to codify full gender equality in the Weimar constitution.[6] Rejecting reforms to divorce laws and the 1900 Civil Code's guarantee of patriarchal privilege, the Center Party and DNVP further agreed on banning birth control and abortion, on secondary legal status for children born outside marriage, and on excluding married women from the civil service.[7] Despite its many confessional and gendered tensions, this pact between the political right and the Weimar *Zentrum* was so effective that it has been credited with preventing any revisions to the Civil Code and inspiring a broad-based Christian backlash against progressive Weimar politics on women, gender, and sexuality.[8]

Even as the relatively free practice of Catholicism and Protestantism facilitated an integration of sacred and political life in the Third Reich, Christianity continued to shape understandings of women, gender, and sexuality.[9] Notably, the biconfessional agenda of religiously informed social conservatism forged during the Weimar Republic continued into the Third Reich.[10] That Christian practice gained strength and support in Germany during the late war years enabled religious beliefs to emerge as powerful ideological currents in 1945. Not surprisingly, Christian notions of women as mothers and nurturers surfaced immediately in postwar political rhetoric.

Hour of the Church / Hour of the Woman

The CDU was founded as Europe endured its greatest social and political instability in centuries. Widespread death and destruction were compounded by confessionalized population dislocations, military occupation, and public health crises. As both cause and effect of the tumult, Germans simultaneously experienced the so-called Hour of the Church and the Hour of the Woman. Too often studied in isolation, these contemporary phenomena signaled the degree to which interconfessional politics were forged in an extraordinary atmosphere of Christian fervor and female independence. Significantly, the origins of Christian Democracy rested at their intersection.

In occupied Germany, administrative continuity and an inflated reputation for resistance conferred on especially Catholic leaders' unparalleled authority.[11] As the churches offered a platform for criticizing the Allies, life-saving sources of war relief, and moral direction for former Nazis seeking faith, their hour of power appeared to have arrived.[12] But, as Michael O'Sullivan insightfully reminds us, there can be no discussion of religious revival without close attention to gender. Highlighting the importance of Catholic women in postwar Germany, O'Sullivan describes how the unprecedented postwar upsurge in visions of Mary signaled female "disruptive power," provoking clerical elites to join political forces to contain or commandeer popular religious movements that contested traditional gender ideals.[13]

Catholic women's challenges to church authority represented just one dynamic in a convulsive gender environment. Of the sources of societal instability in defeated Germany, perhaps none was experienced more intimately than the revolution in family and gender relations, as rising divorce and nonmarital birth rates as well as nontraditional households and relationships, including with Allied soldiers, transformed family life.[14] The subject of mythicization and a forge for German popular memory, the Hour of the Woman was above all a function of male absence and weakness.[15] As women perceived unprecedented professional and personal opportunities, private conversations about liberation and equality inspired many to petition for female influence on German public life.[16]

CDU Ideology on Women, Gender, the Family, and Sexuality

It was in this environment of dramatically heightened religious and gender consciousness that Christian Democracy took hold. Party leaders called for a Christian revolution, which resonated among both devout Protestants and Catholics as an antidote for the double scourge of secularism and materialism that Christians believed animated the ideologies of communism, fascism, and Manchester capitalism.[17] Inherent in the program of re-Christianization was a commitment to restoring a traditional familial, gender, and sexual order. Echoing clerical pronouncements, Christian Democrats emphasized the importance of restoring Christian patriarchy, with the woman serving as "guardian of the Christian family" and the man as "head and father of a family."[18] While Catholics dominated Christian Democratic discourse on gender and the family, party Protestants revealed no discernable difference of opinion on these issues.[19] Reclaiming their Weimar-era alliance, religious Protestants and Catholics alike regarded Christianity as the salve for familial integrity and female dignity damaged by Nazism and threatened by military occupation.[20]

Reinforcing early Christian political unity, female Christian Democrats drew upon the ideological tradition of maternalism and the political experiences of the Weimar Republic to echo male CDU rhetoric. Like their liberal and socialist counterparts, Christian women had historically embraced "organized maternalism" to assert that female public engagement should stem from motherly roles at home.[21] This expectation obtained similarly for women without children, who were to fulfill their spiritual motherhood and affirm their femininity through caritative work.[22] Female members of Weimar's religious parties did break with their male colleagues to ally with socialist and liberal feminists, in particular on birth control and prostitution.[23] Overwhelmingly, though, the alliance between Catholic and devout Protestant women was strong and sustained, even as Catholics—male and female—consistently articulated a more traditional moral vision and politics than did Protestants.[24]

The contradictions and complexities of maternalism—creating opportunities for female agency while resting female claims to power on the very characteristics used to undermine gender and sexual equality—colored not only religious women's political activism during the Weimar and early Federal Republic years but also the history of early Christian Democracy.[25] As cultural and social politics served effectively to unite a party fractured by confessional tension, female party members, as they had during the Weimar Republic, exploited the potential of maternalism to assert their own positions. In so doing, they signaled an independent CDU female voice, one that ultimately intersected with Protestant-Catholic tensions to undermine the Christian Democratic consensus on issues of women, gender, and sexuality.

Christian Democracy Contested: The *Männerstaat*

Small in number and typically Catholic, unmarried, and educated, women in early Christian Democracy were products of the Center Party and confessional and caritative organizations.[26] Though influential on a number of policy questions, early CDU women were, like most female German politicians, experienced in cultural and social politics in both associational and party life.[27] If successful recruitment of Protestant women was more easily desired than done, Catholic women undertook varied efforts, including outreach to Protestant church officials, to bridge the CDU's female religious divide.[28] While party rallies for women stressed Christian women's shared values, personnel appointments followed the party's rule of confessional parity, even when the search for a "Protestant woman" left some positions unfilled.[29]

As they did during the Weimar Republic, religious women embodied the paradoxes of maternalism by participating in the Hour of the Woman while remaining committed to conservative policies, placing them at odds with women in other political camps. In particular, CDU women contributed directly to the emergence of a distinctly female public discourse in occupied Germany, one widespread among women of all political persuasions. In speeches and the female press that flourished during the Hour of the Woman, women argued that male responsibility for the Nazi catastrophe justified female intervention in the public sphere.[30] The hallmark of this discourse—the use of the term *Männerstaat*—reclaimed Weimar-era feminist pleas to infuse male politics with maternalist pacifism.[31]

While its form varied—occasionally the word appeared in quotation marks, suggesting that it had been invented or borrowed—references to the *Männerstaat* rarely left doubt about its meaning. In the words of Christine Teusch, member of the British Zone's CDU Executive Committee, a woman's voice was "hardly heeded even in the lower levels of society in such a "pure '*Männerstaat*'"; it certainly "never penetrated to the heads of the political and economic leadership of the *Reich* and *Volk*."[32] The consequences of such male domination, explained Elfriede Nebgen, a cofounder of the Berlin CDU, were clear: German women had been rendered defenseless victims of the Nazi state: "The *Hitlerreich* was a '*Männerstaat*,'" she declared. "The chaotic condition of our *Volk* shows where the state led. War, destruction, hunger, epidemics, that is the result of the politics of the 'strong man' . . ."[33]

As they looked to the future, CDU women touted qualities derived from women's "special nature" to argue that women should "humanize" German public and political life.[34] Extrapolating from reproductive capabilities to assert an essentially feminine proclivity for peace, female Christian Democrats of both confessions joined women across the country to demand an end to German militarism.[35] Beyond enriching politics and ensuring peace, CDU women asserted that female participation made the very establishment of democracy possible. In an October 1946 speech, Protestant Hilde von der Gablentz explained that, "I am convinced that we women bring a great deal that in most cases men lack: an unbiased view uninhibited by rigid principles, flexibility, the art of improvisation, the intimate relationship with nature, a reasonable, practical sense—all qualities that are of great value precisely for self-government."[36] Von der Gablentz was seconded by Catholic Maria Sevenich, who maintained that women's "truly maternal love" would not only ease the suffering of Nazi victims but facilitate the establishment of democracy.[37] In the view of Sevenich, "The spirit of true responsibility and the indispensably necessary understanding for the democratic life of our *Volk*" were created in the "wombs of our mothers."[38]

While female Christian Democrats joined their socialist and liberal sisters in calling on women to redeem the "derailed politics of their husbands," the early postwar years made clear that, despite such attacks on masculinity, CDU women's participation in the Hour of the Woman posed no fundamental threat to party unity.[39] Consistent with religious maternalism, female Christian Democrats constructed female interventions in the new state along essentialist lines, stressing women's unique responsibility for safeguarding Christianity from further assault.[40] As they had during the Weimar Republic, Christian women argued that women were meant to participate in politics by "lead[ing] the men in unshakable faith."[41] Since the woman was "more deeply rooted than the man in things religious," she bore a special responsibility to "uphold in public life the spirit of life-creating and life-preserving maternalism . . ."[42] As Nebgen explained in November 1945, the atmosphere of the nursery as determined by the mother had "the power to shape history." Anyone who did not recognize that, Nebgen concluded, should pay heed to the papal declaration that, "'the new world will be built not on the parquet floor of the diplomats, but on the knees of the mothers.'"[43]

As politically active Christians equated women with religious and heteronormative motherhood, they also supported the reestablishment of the traditional family. While impassioned on the topic of German public life, no woman in the CDU called before 1949 for greater female authority within the family or Church. Instead, female Christian Democrats continued to define the woman as "the recipient and carrier of life" who would "do justice best and most nobly to her calling within the natural order."[44] Though seemingly unforgiving in their condemnation of male values and politics, CDU women nevertheless endorsed patriarchal family structures and the institution of Christian motherhood. Their ideological positions as women and as Christians placed them at a crossroads of gender equality and delimiting religious tradition; that a Christian patriarchal vision of family life remained determinate for CDU women as well as men provided a crucial ideological foundation for early Christian Democracy.[45]

Christian Democratic Consensus: Patriarchal Anti-Communism

Rooted in decades of political cooperation across the confessional divide, Christian Democratic cultural and social policies were necessarily shaped by the larger global context of party organization. As the Cold War dawned, the party's conviction that Germany's reconstruction should rest on a patriarchal family structure was reinforced by the anti-Marxism that bound bourgeois Protestants with Catholics.[46] Like their male colleagues, CDU women condemned Soviet Zone cultural and social policies, particularly the German Social Democratic Party (SPD)'s "degradation of the family and motherhood."[47] Framing Germans' political choice as one between "Christianity and collectivism," CDU women denounced anti-Christian Marxists for denying the "most profound intrinsic value of the woman."[48]

Protestant-Catholic accord on these questions was especially consequential in the late 1940s, when CDU members struggled to translate their vision of interconfessional harmony into politics. Mutual professions of Christian unity notwithstanding, early CDU politicians' constructions of a Christian Democratic ideology would lay bare unresolved confessional divisions. Economic policy in particular pitted party Protestants against Catholic Christian Socialists; although cast in a Christian anti-socialist, anti-materialist mold, the Social Market Economy was, from its debut, the product of confessionalized compromise and controversy. At the same time, confessional schools, a defining issue for the pre-1933 Center Party, tested the CDU's negotiation of the liminal space between political Catholicism and interconfessionalism. CDU efforts to anchor religiously segregated public schools in the Basic Law would fail, though not before exposing sharp disagreements between party Protestants and Catholics. Against a backdrop of deeply sown political and religious animosity, the Christian Democratic consensus on women and the family played an especially valuable role in securing the new interconfessional alliance.

Women and Gender in the Parliamentary Council

As the first national stage for West German legislators and platform for democratic interconfessional politics, the Parliamentary Council showcased the fissures in and solidity of the Christian Democratic alliance on cultural and social policy. At the same time, the Council would highlight the difficulties German women faced in acting on their claims to power. Just one of four women and the only female Christian Democrat appointed to the Council, Helene Weber frequently provided the public face for CDU positions on issues pertaining to the family, especially confessional schools.[49] In so doing, Weber embodied the paradoxes of religious maternalism, suffering from sexism and challenging her male colleagues even as she and other CDU women endorsed and defended party positions on issues of women, gender, and sexuality.

The most controversial of those measures in the Parliamentary Council suggested that German women could exercise palpable political influence. Initially opposed to the SPD motion stipulating that "men and women have the same rights," the CDU was forced to backtrack after an outpouring of grassroots, largely female, pressure.[50] Consistent with her maternalist and patriarchal understanding of gender relations, Weber supported the CDU's unsuccessful proposal to codify female "equal responsibilities" alongside women's "equal rights."[51] Despite CDU complaints about public overreaction, the party ultimately agreed to support the SPD petition, enabling its adoption with the proviso that the *Bundestag* revise the Civil Code by 1953 in order to reconcile family law with gender equality.[52]

In representing CDU positions in the Parliamentary Council, Weber articulated an ideology of religious conservatism consistent with the interconfessional Christian consensus practiced during the Weimar years. By simultaneously contesting party policy, however, she also continued a tradition established by women in the Center Party of demonstrating issue-specific independence. Although Weber would later refer to the codification of male and female equality as "strictly a matter of formulation," she nonetheless forged common cause with socialist and communist deputies in support of equal pay for equal work, attracting public and pointed criticism from her male Christian Democratic colleagues.[53]

Weber's confrontations with CDU men were stylistic as well as substantive, reflecting the dynamics of patriarchy inherent in early Christian Democracy. As evident in her objections to the term *Frauenüberschuß*—she stipulated that "we are no surplus because we haven't married"—Weber infused her ideology of religious maternalism with the spirit of the Hour of the Woman.[54] In December 1949, for example, Weber renewed her calls in the *Bundestag* for equal pay for equal work with special protections for mothers, declaring that "the pure *Männerstaat* is the ruin of nations [*der Völker*]!"[55] In direct response, CDU Protestant Robert Lehr observed that it was not only men who exhibited warlike traits, but certain women could be temperamental and aggressive as well.[56]

Christian Democratic Women in Party Politics

Weber's treatment in the Parliamentary Council and *Bundestag* reified a gendered schism that ran through the CDU, one that would remain largely concealed during early party years but that came increasingly to color Christian Democratic cultural and social policies. To their ongoing dismay, CDU women faced open sexism and disregard from male Christian Democrats.[57] While Catholic CDU men labored mightily to ensure male Protestant representation at early gatherings, they devoted few resources to the recruitment of women of either confession. As they had in the Weimar-era religious parties, female Christian Democrats continually petitioned male colleagues to appoint women to leadership positions, including at the first Christian Democratic inter-zonal gathering and on the Parliamentary Council, the Frankfurt Economic Council, and the CDU Executive Committee.[58] Party women were particularly aggrieved at male officials' insistence that there were no suitable female candidates available in certain electoral districts; arguing that female politicians were given too few opportunities to engage in meaningful party work, some CDU women called for quotas.[59]

Lamenting that German women were less politically engaged than in 1919, Weber noted privately in September 1948 that, "We women are at present accomplishing less in the party and in the press than before 1933."[60] At a meeting of the British Zonal Committee in February 1950, Elisabeth Zillken warned that current internal gender dynamics threatened the CDU's future as a democratic organization.[61] Weber's observation that Adenauer paid little heed to women's political desires within the party appears borne out by his surprise at women's "very vigorous complaints."[62] If Catholic female CDU leaders decried their treatment in the party, Protestant women were especially distressed by their lack of representation.[63] As Weber warned in the spring of 1949, "The relationship between Catholic and Protestant female candidates will be completely destroyed if certain areas do not put up a Protestant woman."[64]

CDU women's repeated protests that the party neglected them and their activities until election time were all the more striking in light of the party's disproportionate reliance on female votes for its electoral strength.[65] Already in the first federal election in 1949, when the CDU and Christian Social Union (CSU) together drew almost twice the level of SPD female support, a pattern took hold that would shape the coming decades of West German politics. Highlighting their electoral power, Catholic women voted not only overwhelmingly for the CDU, but at greater percentages than other women.[66] What Michael O'Sullivan has termed the "uneasy proposition" of a party committed to patriarchy simultaneously dependent on women's votes remained a hallmark of West German politics.[67]

Cultural and Social Politics in the Early Federal Republic

Despite the CDU's internal divisions along confessional and gender lines, female and growing Protestant support in the elections of 1953 and 1957 enabled the party to secure the dominant role in constructing the new West German state. Well positioned to influence public discourse and social and cultural policies, Christian Democrats enjoyed considerable success in legislating their vision of a Christian state resting on a patriarchal family. That their agenda was fundamentally embraced by party Protestants as well as

Catholics both reflected and reaffirmed long-standing patterns of interconfessionalism. But as internal CDU politics would make clear, consensus on issues of women, gender, and sexuality by no means implied unanimity. Ultimately, the power of the Protestant-Catholic union would only mark a moment—if a long one—in time, as the dynamics of dechristianization, feminism, and confessional difference steadily weakened Christian Democratic concord and, with it, political power.

Against the backdrop of the far-reaching postwar reassertion of traditional gender norms, Christian Democratic familial and sexual ideals initially resonated broadly.[68] Even as the chimes of the Hour of the Church grew fainter, religious renewal remained a defining experience for Protestants and especially Catholics, whose rates of weekly religious celebration in the 1950s exceeded those since the aftermath of the *Kulturkampf*.[69] The establishment in 1953 of a new Ministry of the Family empowered devout Catholic Franz-Josef Wuermeling to enshrine conservative Christian values in West German law and amplify the already patent influence of the Catholic Church in West German political life.[70] If alternative visions of Christian morality and democratic fatherhood inspired by French Left Catholics took hold on the discursive margins, they shed more light on the diversity of West German religious intellectual life than on pre-Vatican II theology or policies.[71] Indeed, devout Catholics and Protestants enjoyed unprecedented success realizing their shared ambitions for social and cultural politics in the early Federal Republic, uniting to adopt, among other measures, anti-pornography legislation and film censorship designed to protect motherhood and the family.[72]

And yet, within the party and then publicly, confessional and gendered differences consistently colored CDU cultural and social policy. In the Parliamentary Council, following the CDU/CSU's initial opposition to codifying gender equality, it was Protestant party women who privately pressured Weber to change course.[73] As lawmakers worked to revise the Civil Code following the adoption of the Basic Law, male and female CDU Protestants, backed by the Protestant Church's call for marital (but not parental) equality of decision-making, would dissent from the party's position supporting the husband's authority over wife and children.[74] While many exchanges remained internal, the first public Christian Democratic break came in 1953, when Protestant Christian Democrat and *Bundestag* President Hermann Ehlers opposed codifying husbands' legal ability to overrule their wives. That Ehlers was soon followed by a list of prominent Protestant CDU women, led by Protestant Church official Elisabeth Schwarzhaupt, and Protestant women's organizations signaled that divisions within the house of Christian Democracy were gendered as well as confessional.[75]

A male-female divide soon became evident within the CDU Catholic camp as well. In 1951, much to the consternation of Catholic Church officials, the German Catholic Women's Association (KDFB) rejected patriarchal authority within marriage, asserting decision-making rights for both spouses. Although the KDFB quickly moderated its stance and joined two other leading organizations of Catholic women in expressing official support for patriarchal marriage, a private July 1952 meeting of CDU women revealed ongoing dissension within the party's female ranks.[76]

Following the *Bundestag*'s failure to meet the April 1953 deadline to revise the Civil Code regarding family law, confessional and gendered differences continued to percolate, forcing the CDU/CSU in May 1957 to admit that a minority of party members disagreed with the Union's endorsement of patriarchal authority.[77] Initially, the dissenters appeared contained: when the *Bundestag* passed the Equal Rights Law codifying paternal authority in 1957, it was largely due to Christian Democratic advocacy and votes; indeed, almost all CDU leaders supported the measure, including Weber, who argued consistently for patriarchal marital and familial relations.[78] The CDU/CSU's family law victory would prove illusive, however. Not only did a small number of Christian Democrats cross party lines to defeat the retention of marital patriarchy, but two years later the Federal Constitutional Court overturned the *Bundestag* legislation codifying paternal authority. That a significant number of CDU women sided with Schwarzhaupt in welcoming the decision signaled the diminishing appeal of Weber's conservative Catholicism within the female CDU.[79] In particular, Weber's consistent support for female civil service celibacy put her at increasingly public odds with younger CDU women seeking to reconcile family and work life.[80] In 1961, Schwarzhaupt's appointment as the first female cabinet member would mark the ascendance of her competing vision of Christian Democratic cultural policy.[81]

Economic and Religious Transformations of the Federal Republic

Exploring shifting dynamics within the CDU on issues of women, gender, and sexuality reminds us that, if the political manifestations of the Hour of the Woman appeared ephemeral, the demographic and social impact of the war was deep and long-lasting. In 1950, just 60 percent of West Germans were living in traditional, nuclear families.[82] Despite the widely held belief that female labor was impermanent, women's paid employment rates increased steadily across the 1950s; by decade's end, nearly half of married women were working.[83] As advertisers targeted housewives as feminine and rational managers, West German society negotiated conflicting images of women as dutiful wives and mothers on one hand, and self-indulgent shoppers on the other, the latter eliciting especially sharp criticisms from leading CDU Catholics.[84]

While the economic legacies of the Hour of the Woman continued to shape West German life, the Hour of the Church tolled its final bell, with profound implications for the Christian Democratic project. Although church attendance would not drop precipitously until the late 1960s, its steady decline across the 1950s effected and reflected momentous demographic, generational, and cultural change, not least the ongoing deconfessionalization of West German public and private life.[85] The attenuation of religious discursive hegemony and clerical political authority had immediate implications for ecclesiastical influence on the CDU, particularly on issues of gender and sexuality.[86] While the Protestant Church's institutional disunity, practice of clerical marriage, and early membership losses informed Protestant doctrinal pluralization on cultural and social issues, the Catholic Church demonstrated little accommodation of the postwar revolution in family structure, sexual mores, and gender relations.[87] In a CDU still beset by confessional and gendered tensions, policies pertaining to women and the family became increasingly less effective in bridging the party's religious and especially gender divides. Religious women remained faithful CDU voters, to be sure, but—as education, employment, feminism, and secularism transformed female lives—women's electoral preferences shifted steadily left until Christian Democracy lost its female majority in 1972.[88]

Christian Democracy Confessionalized and Gendered

Testifying to continuities across twentieth-century Germany, the legacies of the Weimar Republic infused Christian Democratic demands for re-Christianization with clearly delineated female roles. As CDU Protestants and Catholics reclaimed their pre-1933 cooperation on cultural and social policies, cross-gender and interconfessional accord on family law helped stabilize their fractious new movement. But if gender and sexuality worked to secure early Protestant-Catholic unity, crevices in the Weimar-era Christian alliance foretold fissures in postwar interconfessionalism, signaling how the interrelated dynamics of religious maternalism and female solidarity consistently colored Christian politics. Even as postwar legislative projects testified to the ongoing potency of Christians' shared moral vision, Protestants in general, and Protestant women in particular, repeatedly demonstrated weaker support for Christian Democratic cultural conservatism. That their reservations were increasingly shared by Catholic women, including those in a party buffeted by male indifference and discrimination, reminds us that, like all political movements, Christian Democracy was intrinsically gendered.[89]

Whereas female dissent within the CDU highlights the value of integrating women, gender, and sexuality into analyses of religion and politics, the confessional line running through the party on social and cultural policies underscores the salience of religious culture and difference. Both determinative and reflective of German Protestant-Catholic relations, Christian Democracy's religious complexion has shifted dramatically over the Federal Republic's decades. Dechristianization may well have weakened female support for CDU policies, but it also facilitated interconfessionalism, inducing practicing Protestants and Catholics to ally in an increasingly secular age.[90] Elections since 1990 in unified Germany demonstrate that Christian churchgoers continue to vote disproportionately for the CDU, suggesting that cultural and social politics, despite challenges from within and without, play an ongoing role in defining German public life.[91] Recognizing the centrality of these issues to the construction of (West) Germany's dominant political movement informs us not only about the history of Christian Democracy; it also reminds us of the consequence of the intersecting dynamics of confessional and gender relations to modern German history.

Maria Mitchell is Professor of History at Franklin & Marshall College in Lancaster, PA. She is the author of *The Origins of Christian Democracy: Politics and Confession in Modern Germany* (University of Michigan Press, 2012) and is currently writing a history of the storied 1982 semi-final World Cup match between France and West Germany.

Notes

1. As a result of war losses, West Germany was still 56 percent female as late as 1960. John Robert Stark, "The Overlooked Majority: German Women in the Four Zones of Occupied Germany, 1945–1949, A Comparative Study" (PhD diss., Ohio State University, 2003), 2.

2. Christof Wolf, "Konfessionelle versus religiöse Konfliktslinie in der deutschen Wählerschaft," *Politische Vierteljahresschrift* 37, no. 4 (1996): 714.

3. Gerhard Besier, "'Christliche Parteipolitik' und Konfession: Zur Entstehung des Evangelischen Arbeitskreises der CDU/CSU," *Kirchliche Zeitgeschichte* 3 (1990): 167; Frank Bösch, *Die Adenauer-CDU: Gründung, Aufstieg, und Krise einer Erfolgspartei, 1945–1969* (Stuttgart: Deutsche Verlags-Anstalt [DVA], 2001), 46; Karl Rohe, *Wahlen und Wählertraditionen in Deutschland: Kulturelle Grundlagen deutscher Parteien und Parteiensysteme im 19. und 20. Jahrhundert* (Frankfurt am Main: Suhrkamp, 1992), 167.

4. Karsten Ruppert, "Die Deutsche Zentrumspartei in der Mitverantwortung für die Weimarer Republik: Selbstverständnis und politische Leitideen einer konfessionellen Mittelpar-

tei," in *Die Minderheit als Mitte: Die Deutsche Zentrumspartei in der Innenpolitik des Reiches, 1871–1933*, ed. Winfried Becker (Paderborn: Ferdinand Schöningh, 1986), 47–69.

5. Sebastian Müller-Rolli, *Evangelische Schulpolitik in Deutschland, 1918–1958: Dokumente und Darstellung* (Göttingen: Vandenhoeck & Ruprecht, 1999), 57–63; Traugott Jähnichen, "Das Ideal eines 'starken Staates' zur Sicherung von Freiheit und sozialem Ausgleich: Beiträge des politischen Protestantismus zur christliche-demokratischen Programmatik," in *Das christliche Menschenbild*, ed. Hanns Jürgen Küsters, Jörg-Dieter Gauger, and Rudolf Uertz (Freiburg: Herder, 2013), 87.

6. Barbara Greven-Aschoff, *Die bürgerliche Frauenbewegung in Deutschland, 1894–1933* (Göttingen: Vandenhoeck & Ruprecht, 1981), 168–79.

7. Atina Grossmann, *Reforming Sex: The German Movement for Birth Control and Abortion Reform, 1920–1950* (New York: Oxford University Press, 1995), 78–87; Greven-Aschoff, *Die bürgerliche Frauenbewegung*, 169–70.

8. Robert G. Moeller, *Protecting Motherhood: Women and the Family in the Politics of Postwar West Germany* (Berkeley: University of California Press, 1993), 47–49; E.R. Dickinson, et al., "A Backlash Against Liberalism? What the Weimar Republic Can Teach Us About Today's Politics," *International Journal for History, Culture and Modernity* 5, no. 1 (2018): 91–107.

9. Thomas Brodie, *German Catholicism at War, 1939–1945* (Oxford, UK: Oxford University Press, 2018); Richard Steigmann-Gall, *The Holy Reich: Nazi Conceptions of Christianity, 1919–1945* (Cambridge, UK: Cambridge University Press, 2003).

10. Dagmar Herzog, *Sex after Fascism: Memory and Morality in Twentieth-Century Germany* (Cambridge, UK: Cambridge University Press, 2005), 33, 55.

11. Wolfgang Zapf, *Wandlungen der deutschen Elite: Ein Zirkulationsmodell deutscher Führungsgruppen, 1919–1961* (Munich: Piper, 1965), 103; Beth A. Griech-Polelle, *Bishop von Galen: German Catholicism and National Socialism* (New Haven: Yale University Press, 2002), 5.

12. Peter Fäßler, *Badisch. Christlich und Sozial: Zur Geschichte der BCSV/CDU im französisch besetzten Land Baden (1945–1952)* (Frankfurt am Main: Peter Lang, 1995), 30, 37; Martin Onnasch, "Die Situation der Kirchen in der sowjetischen Besatzungszone, 1945–1949," *Kirchliche Zeitgeschichte* 2, no. 1 (1989): 210–21; Christoph Kösters, ed., *Caritas in der SBZ/DDR, 1945–1989: Erinnerungen, Berichte, Forschungen* (Paderborn: Ferdinand Schöningh Verlag, 2001), 239; Ernst-Alfred Jauch and Gisela Helwig, "Katholische Kirche," in *Kirchen und Gesellschaft in beiden deutschen Staaten*, ed. Gisela Helwig and Detlef Urban (Cologne: Edition Deutschland Archiv im Verlag Wissenschaft und Politik, 1987), 11; Anthony Kauders, "Catholics, the Jews and Democratization in Post-war Germany, Munich, 1945–65," *German History* 18, no. 4 (2000), 468; Jerry Z. Muller, *The Other God That Failed: Hans Freyer and the Deradicalization of German Conservatism* (Princeton: Princeton University Press, 1987), 336.

13. Michael O'Sullivan, *Disruptive Power: Catholic Women, Miracles, and Politics in Germany, 1918–1965* (Toronto: University of Toronto Press, 2018), 168–69, 206–9.

14. Susanne Fuchs, *Frauen Bewältigen den Neuaufbau: Eine lokalgeschichtliche Analyse der unmittelbaren Nachkriegszeit am Beispiel Bonn* (Pfaffenweiler: Centaurus-Verlagsgesellschaft, 1993), 13; Elizabeth D. Heineman, *What Difference Does a Husband Make? Women and Marital Status in Nazi and Postwar Germany* (Berkeley: University of California Press, 1999), 108–36.

15. Mariatte C. Denman, "Visualizing the Nation: Madonnas and Mourning Mothers in Postwar Germany," in *Gender and Germanness: Cultural Productions of a Nation*, ed. Patricia Herminghouse and Magda Hueller (Providence: Berghahn Books, 1997); Elizabeth D. Heineman, "The Hour of the Woman: Memories of Germany's 'Crisis Years' and West German National Identity," *American Historical Review* 101, no. 2 (1996): 354–95.

16. Elizabeth H. Tobin and Jennifer Gibson, "The Meanings of Labor: East German Women's Work in the Transition from Nazism to Communism," *Central European History* 28, no. 3 (1995): 320; Geno Hartlaub, "Ich war ein Wunderkind und ein Mädchen," in *Der Hunger nach Erfahrung: Frauen nach '45*, ed. Inge Stolten (Berlin: J.H.W. Dietz, 1981), 15.

17. ACDPStA, I-009-005/4, 13. Ulrich Steiner, speech delivered at the *Landesversammlung* of the CDU of Südwürttemberg-Hohenzollern (Biberach, 30 March 1947).

18. Lukas Rölli-Alkemper, *Familie im Wiederaufbau: Katholizismus und bürgerliches Familienideal in der Bundesrepublik Deutschland, 1945–1965* (Paderborn: Ferdinand Schöningh, 2000), 59–65; HAStK, 1187, 41. "An alle Frauen!" (Dortmund, August 1946); Gelnhausen CDU, "An Dich, Deutsche Frau und Mutter" (Gelnhausen, February 1946), in Heinrich Rüschenschmidt, "Die Entstehung der hessischen CDU, 1945/46: Lokale Gründungsvorgänge und Willensbildung im Landesverband" (Staatsexamen, Philipps-Universität Marburg, 1979), 6; StBKAH, 08.54, 393–98. "Ein Ruf zur Sammlung des deutschen Volkes: Vorläufiger Entwurf zu einem Programm der Christlichen Demokraten Deutschlands, Vorgelegt von den Christlichen Demokraten Köln im Juni 1945" (Cologne, June 1945); ACDPStA, I-208-003/2. Mannheim CDU, draft party program (Mannheim, undated); NA, OMGUS (Württemberg-Baden), RG 260, 707; BAK, NL 391, 13. "Grundsätzliches zum Programm der christlich-sozialen Volkspartei (Christliche Union) " (Stuttgart, October 1945); StBKAH, 08.54, 404–10. British Zone CDU, program (Neheim-Hüsten, March 1946); Theodor Scharmitzel, "Christliche Demokratie im neuen Deutschland," *Schriftenreihe der Christlich Demokratischen Union des Rheinlandes* 1 (Cologne, 1945), 492; ACDPStA, I-194-001-009. CDU, "Ein Sinn, ein Weg, ein Ziel" (Düsseldorf, undated); BAK, NL 5, 475, 118–26. "Frankfurter Leitsätze" (Frankfurt am Main, September 1945).

19. Regina Illemann, *Katholische Frauenbewegung in Deutschland 1945–1962: Politik, Geschlecht und Religiosität im Katholischen Deutschen Frauenbund* (Paderborn: Ferdinand Schöningh 2016), 64–65; ACDPStA, I-071-002/5. Theophil Kaufmann, speech (undated).

20. BAK, NL 391, 13. Paul Bausch, speech (Plahingen, December 15, 1945); BAK, NL 5, 475, 120. Hermann Pünder, speech (Frankfurt am Main, 1945); BAK, NL 5, 475, 118–26. "Frankfurter Leitsätze" (Frankfurt am Main, September 1945); Anonymous, "Frauen im Männerstaat," in *Frauen Gestern und Heute: Wege in die Neue Zeit* 3 (Berlin, 1946), 42–44; ACDPStA, I-90-015/1. Elfriede Nebgen, "Christlich-Demokratische Union und Frauenprobleme der Gegenwart" (December 1945); Christine Teusch, "Die christliche Frau im politischen Zeitgeschehen," *Schriftenreihe der Christlich-Demokratischen Union Westfalen-Lippe* 2 (September 1946), 5; ACDPStA, I-009-005/7, 5; NA, OMGUS, Manpower Division, RG 260, 93. Cf. Herzog, *Sex After Fascism*, 10, 43, 62.

21. Ann Taylor Allen, *Feminism and Motherhood in Western Europe, 1800–1914* (New Brunswick: Rutgers University Press, 1991), 13; Birgit Sack, *Zwischen religiöser Bindung und moderner Gesellschaft: Katholische Frauenbewegung und politische Kultur in der Weimarer Republik (1918/19–1933)* (Münster: Waxmann, 1998), 25; Douglas J. Cremer, "The Limits of Maternalism: Gender Ideology and the South German Catholic Workingwomen's Associations, 1904–1918," *The Catholic Historical Review* 87, no. 3 (2001): 428–29.

22. Christine Wittrock, "Das Frauenbild in faschistischen Texten und seine Vorläufer in der bürgerlichen Frauenbewegung der zwanziger Jahre" (PhD diss., Johann-Wolfgang-Goethe-Universität zu Frankfurt am Main, 1981), 12–13, 37.

23. Greven-Aschoff, *Die bürgerliche Frauenbewegung*, 169; O'Sullivan, *Disruptive Power*, 115–16, 137–38; Julia Roos, *Weimar through the Lens of Gender: Prostitution Reform, Woman's Emancipation, and German Democracy, 1919–33* (Ann Arbor: University of Michigan Press, 2010), 13, 205; Sack, *Zwischen religiöser Bindung und moderner Gesellschaft*, 2, 37; Ute Gerhard and Ulla Wischermann, *Unerhört: Die Geschichte der deutschen Frauenbewegung* (Reinbeck bei Hamburg: Rowohlt, 1990), 205, 296; Marion Röwekamp, "Der Kampf um die Ehe: Der Katholische Frauenbund und das Zentrum im Richtungsstreit um eine Reform des Ehescheidungsrechts," in *Die Frauen und der politische Katholizismus: Akteurinnen, Themen, Strategien*, ed. Markus Raasch and Andreas Linsenmann (Leiden: Ferdinand Schöningh, 2018): 209–38; Helen Boak, "Women in Weimar Politics," *European History Quarterly* 20, no. 3 (July 1990): 378; Doris Kaufmann, *Frauen zwischen Aufbruch und Reaktion* (Munich: Piper, 1991), 97–98, 185.

24. Roos, *Weimar through the Lens of Gender*, 9, 13, 100, 135–36, 178, 186–211; Laurie Marhoefer, "Degeneration, Sexual Freedom, and the Politics of the Weimar Republic, 1918–1933," *German Studies Review* 34, no. 3 (October 2011): 533.

25. Roos, *Weimar through the Lens of Gender*, 98–102, 133 ff; Allen, *Feminism and Motherhood in Western Europe*, 1–13; Cremer, "The Limits of Maternalism," 428–52.

26. Gabriele Bremme, *Die politische Rolle der Frau in Deutschland* (Göttingen: Vanderhoeck & Ruprecht, 1956), 157.

27. Helen Boak, "'Our Last Hope': Women's Votes for Hitler—A Reappraisal," *German Studies Review* 12, no. 2 (May 1989): 291–92.

28. Raffael Scheck, "Women on the Weimar Right: The Role of Female Politicians in the Deutschnationale Volkspartei (DNVP)," *Journal of Contemporary History* 36, no. 4 (2001): 560; Manfred Agethen, "Der Widerstand der demokratischen Kräfte in der CDU gegen den Gleichschaltungsdruck von sowjetischer Besatzungsmacht und SED, 1945–1952," in *Die CDU in der sowjetisch besetzten Zone/DDR 1945–1952*, ed. Alexander Fischer and Manfred Agethen, (Sankt Augustin: Konrad-Adenauer-Stiftung, 1994), 23; Winfried Becker, *CDU und CSU: Vorläufer, Gründung und regionale Entwicklung bis zum Entstehen der CDU-Bundespartei* (Mainz: Hasse & Koehler, 1987), 128; IZG, ED 160/31, 77. Letter from Weber to Superintendent Held (20 September 1948).

29. IZG, ED 160/11, 11, 13. C-D U Hessisches Landessekretariat, Frauensekretariat (Frankfurt am Main, 11 August 1947); NA, OMGUS (Hesse), RG 260, 471. Plakat-u. Handzetteltext, "An alle Frauen in Seckbach!" Cf. Bremme, *Politische Rolle*, 158; HAStK, 1187, 43, 21. Letter from Lingens to Teusch (5 August 1946); HAStK, 1187, 36/4. CDU des Rheinlandes. Protokoll über die Sitzung des Landesvorstandes (Cologne, 10 April 1946); IZG, ED 160/9, 103. Niederschrift über die Sitzung des Frauenausschusses der CDU (3 February 1947); IZG, ED 160/9, 109. Frauenausschuss der CDU-Sitzung (7 March 1947).

30. Rebecca Boehling, "Gender Roles in Ruins: German Women and Local Politics under American Occupation, 1945–1955," in *Gender and the Long Postwar: The United States and the Two Germanys, 1945–1989*, ed. Karen Hagemann and Sonya Michel (Baltimore: Johns Hopkins University Press, 2014), 52; Irene Stoehr, "Cold War Communities: Women's Peace Politics in Postwar West Germany, 1945–1952," in *Home/Front: The Military, War and Gender in Twentieth-Century Germany*, ed. Karen Hagemann and Stefanie Schüler-Springorum (Oxford, UK: Berg, 2002), 312.

31. The term *Männerstaat* was used by women during the Third Reich with both positive and negative connotations. Geraldine Theresa Horan, *Mothers, Warriors, Guardians of the Soul: Female Discourse in National Socialism, 1924–1934* (Berlin: De Gruyter, 2003), 101–10; Fuchs, *Frauen Bewältigen den Neuaufbau*, 35–39.

32. Teusch, "Die christliche Frau," 4.

33. ACDPStA, I-90-015/1. Elfriede Nebgen, "Die geistigen Grundlagen der Christlich-Demokratischen Union," Schulungskonferenz für Frauen (presumably Berlin, 10 November 1945). Cf. ACDPStA, I-90-015/1. Elfriede Nebgen, "Christlich-Demokratische Union und Frauenprobleme der Gegenwart" (1945–1946). Few CDU women acknowledged female responsibility for the Third Reich. BAK 278, 139. Frau Dr. Martha Pfad-Laureck, "Frau und Politik," *Niedersächsische Rundschau: Wochenschrift der Christlich-Demokratischen Union*, Landesverband Hanover 1, 3 (Hanover, 1 June 1946); ACDPStA, I-448-002/6. Maria Dietz, "Das christliche Menschenbild und die Frau von heute" (1949).

34. Teusch, "Die christliche Frau," 6–7.

35. ACDPStA, I-448-001/6. Maria Dietz, "Stunde der Frau" (Mainz, 1948); Donna Harsch, "Public Continuity and Private Change? Women's Consciousness and Activity in Frankfurt, 1945–1955," *Journal of Social History* 27, no. 1 (Fall 1993): 29–58.

36. ACDPStA, I-152-001/1. Hilde von der Gablentz, Rede zur Wahl von Berliner Stadtparlament (Berlin, 20 October 1946); ACDPStA, I-152-001/1. Hilde von der Gablentz, Vortrag vor dem Wilmersdorfer Frauenbund (Wilmersforer, 3 August 1946).

37. ACDPStA, I-059-002/6. Maria Sevenich, "Die Christlich-Demokratische Union in der Not der Zeit" (Stuttgart, 23 February 1946).
38. Maria Sevenich, "Unser Gesicht: Abhandlung über Christlichen und Marxistischen Sozialismus," *Politik aus Christlicher Verantwortung*, vol. 1 (Recklinghausen: Verlag Bitter & Co., 1946), 14–15.
39. Anonymous, "'Nur' Hausfrau?" in *Frauen Gestern und Heute: Wege in die Neue Zeit* 3, 21.
40. Teusch, "Die christliche Frau," 5–6.
41. ACDPStA, I-90-015/1. Nebgen, "Die geistigen Grundlagen;" HAStK, 1187, 45. Entwurf von Frau Dr. Pfad, "Für welche Partei entscheidet sich die deutsche Frau?" (no date); StBKAH, 08.54, 065. Christlich-Demokratische Union Deutschlands, Sondermaterial (Berlin, no date), 6/III. "Was wir von der deutschen Frau erwarten": Über die Frage der geistigen und politischen Situation der Frauen nach dem Zusammenbruch des Nazi-Regimes äussert sich programmatisch ein Artikel der "Neuen Zeit" Nr. 44.
42. ACDPStA, I-176-013. Elisabeth Pitz, "Die Mitverantwortung der Frau," *Kölnische Rundschau* (29 August 1947); ACDPStA, I-208-003/2. Der Frauen-Wahlausschuß der CDU, "An alle Frauen!" (Karlsruhe, May 1946).
43. ACDPStA, I-90-015/1. Nebgen, "Die geistigen Grundlagen."
44. Teusch, "Die christliche Frau," 7.
45. ACDPStA, I-152-001/3. Entschliessungsentwurf der Frauenarbeitsgemeinschaft zur 2. Jahrestagung der Union (Berlin, 1947); ACDPStA, I-105-045/2. Maria Sevenich, "Neue Wege in der Politik," *Schriftenreihe "Neue Politik" Stuttgart*, 1 (Württemberg, October 1946), 18.
46. BAK, Z5/34. PRSB, 30 November 1948.
47. HAStK, 1187, 41. Flyer, "An alle Frauen!" (Dortmund, August 1946). In 1947, the Soviet Zone would temporarily decriminalize abortion. Grossmann, *Reforming Sex*, 197.
48. Teusch, "Die christliche Frau," 7.
49. On efforts to appoint Helene Weber to the Parliamentary Council, see Petra Holz, *Zwischen Tradition und Emanzipation: CDU-Politikerinnen in der Zeit von 1946 bis 1960* (Königstein, 2004), 122. Cf. IZG, ED 160/10, 82. Letter from Lang-Brumann to Weber (27 August 1948); IZG, ED 160/7, 66. Stephy Roeger, Frauenarbeitsgemeinschaft der CDU/CSU, Die Geschäftsführung (Stuttgart, 14 July 1948).
50. Ines Reich-Hilweg, *Männer und Frauen sind gleichberechtigt: Der Gleichberechtigungsgrundsatz (Art. 3 Abs. 2 GG) in der parlamentarischen Auseinandersetzung, 1948–1957, und in der Rechtssprechung des Bundesverfassungsgerichts, 1953–1975* (Frankfurt am Main: Europäische Verlagsanstalt, 1979), 18–19; BAK, Z5/65. PRSB, 18 January 1949. For a list of the petitions submitted, see Reich-Hilweg, *Männer*, 21, n26.
51. BAK, Z5/128, 376, 214. Antrag der Fraktion der CDU/CSU, Artikel 4, Abschnitt 2 (14 December 1948); BAK Z5/65. PRSB, January 18, 1949.
52. Michael F. Feldkamp, *Der Parlamentarischer Rat 1948–1949: Die Entstehung des Grundgesetzes* (Göttingen: Vanderhoeck & Ruprecht 2008), 74; Anna Späth, "Vielfältige Forderungen nach Gleichberechtigung und 'nur' ein Ergebnis: Artikel 3 Absatz 2 GG," in *Das Schicksal Deutschlands liegt in der Hand seiner Frauen: Frauen in der deutschen Nachkriegsgeschichte*, ed. Anna-Elisabeth Freier and Annette Kuhn (Düsseldorf: Schwann, 1984), 122–67; Moeller, *Protecting Motherhood*, ch. 2.
53. ACDPStA, VII-004-127/4. Helene Weber, Niederschrift über die Tagung der Frauenarbeitsgemeinschaft der CDU/CSU Deutschlands (Königswinter, 25–26 May 1949); BAK, Z5/65. PRSB, 12 April 1949; PRSB, 4 November 1948; IZG, ED 160/7, 66–68. Letter from Roeger to Weber, 14 July 1948; BAK, Z5/65. PRSB, 18 January 1949. Cf. Reich-Hilweg, *Männer*, 25–29.
54. BAK, Z5/35. PRSB, 4 December 1948; cf. BAK, Z5/35. PRSB, 6 December 1948.
55. Reich-Hilweg, *Männer*, 31–32.

56. *Bundestag Protocol, 20.-21. Sitzungen*, 2 December 1949.

57. Ludger Gruber, *Die CDU-Landtagsfraktion in Nordrhein-Westfalen 1946–1980: Eine parlamentshistorische Untersuchung* (Düsseldorf: Droste, 1998), 306; Holz, *Zwischen Tradition und Emanzipation*, 65; HStAD RWV 26, 544. II. 260. LV Rheinland, 1. Vierteljahresbericht 1946 (11 May 1946); IZG, ED 160/6. Letter from Dietz to Weber (Mainz, 26 July 1948).

58. ACDPStA, I-182-008/03, B. III.2. Letter from Kannengießer to Lensing (7 December 1945); Boak, "Women in Weimar Politics," 384–385; BAK, NL 18, 129, 207. Letter from Nebgen to Hermes (12 December 1945). Cf. ACDPStA, I-182-008/03, B. III.2. Letter from Kannengießer to Lensing (7 December 1945); IZG, ED 160/10, 82. Letter from Lang-Brumann to Weber (27 August 1948); IZG, ED 160/10, 77. Letter from Weber to Lang-Brumann (27 June 1948); cf. BAK 278, 269. Protokoll der Tagung von Frauen der CDU/CSU aller Zonen (Frankfurt am Main, 14 February 1948); IZG, ED 160/9, 191. Letter from Rhabanus to Teusch (13 January 1948); StBKAH, 08.60, 222–225. Protokoll der Tagung von Frauen der CDU/CSU aller Zonen (14 February 1948).

59. BAK 278, 269. Letter from Weber to Andre (14 February 1948); IZG, ED 160/9, 103. Niederschrift über die Sitzung des Frauenausschusses der CDU (3 February 1947); IZG, ED 160/9, 113. Sitzungsbericht des Frauenausschusses der CDU (27 June 1947); IZG, ED 160/9, 246–248. Frauenbesprechung beim 2. Zonen-Parteitag der CDU (Recklinghausen, 29 August 1948); IZG, ED 160/7, 127. Letter from Weber to Roeger (25 March 1949); IZG, ED 160/9, 109. Frauenausschuss der CDU-Sitzung (7 March 1947); Holz, *Zwischen Tradition und Emanzipation*, 75; IZG, ED 160/9, 194–95. Protokoll der Arbeitstagung der Hess. CDU-Frauen (9 May 1949).

60. BAK 278, 269. Protokoll der Tagung der Frauenarbeitsgemeinschaft der CDU/CSU Deutschlands (Frankfurt am Main, 1 May 1948); IZG, ED 160/10, 83. Letter from Weber to Lang-Brumann, 6 September 1948.

61. Horstwalter Heitzer, *Die CDU in der britischen Zone: Gründung, Organisation, Programm und Politik* (Düsseldorf: Droste, 1988), 443.

62. IZG, ED 160/11, 147. Letter from Weber to Zillken (19 December 1949); Letter from Adenauer to Zimmer (24 July 1950), in Konrad Adenauer, *Briefe über Deutschland 1945–1955* (Munich: Seidler, 1999), 107–9.

63. BAK 278, 269. Protokoll der Tagung der Frauenarbeitsgemeinschaft der CDU/CSU Deutschlands (Frankfurt am Main, 1 May 1948).

64. IZG, ED 160/7, 137–138. Letter from Weber to Roeger (28 May 1949).

65. IZG, ED 160/11, 133. Letter from Weber to Pesch (25 March 1949); IZG, ED 160/7, 184. Letter from Roeger to Weber (30 October 1950).

66. Bremme, *Politische Rolle*, 31–32, 36–38, 90–92, 253, Table V.

67. O'Sullivan, *Disruptive Power*, 21.

68. Boehling, "Gender Roles in Ruins," 63–64.

69. Till van Rahden, "Fatherhood, Rechristianization, and the Quest for Democracy in Postwar West Germany," in *Raising Citizens in the "Century of the Child": The United States and German Central Europe in Comparative Perspective*, ed. Dirk Schumann (New York: Berghahn Books, 2010), 143.

70. Erica Carter, *How German Is She? Postwar West German Reconstruction and the Consuming Woman* (Ann Arbor: University of Michigan Press, 1997), 32–36.

71. James Chappel, *Catholic Modern: The Challenge of Totalitarianism and the Remaking of the Catholic Church* (Cambridge, MA: Harvard University Press, 2018), 189–200; Till van Rahden, "Fatherhood, Rechristianization, and the Quest for Democracy in Postwar West Germany." Cf. Dagmar Herzog, *Sexuality in Europe: A Twentieth-Century History* (Cambridge, UK: Cambridge University Press, 2011), 113–14.

72. Herzog, *Sex after Fascism*, 113; Heide Fehrenbach, "The Fight for the 'Christian West': German Film Control, the Churches, and the Reconstruction of Civil Society in the Early Bonn Republic," *German Studies Review* 14, no. 1 (1991): 39–63.

73. IZG, ED 160/10. Letter from Grehm to Weber (7 December 1948). Cf. Holz, *Zwischen Tradition und Emanzipation*, 127.
74. "Der Rat der Evangelischen Kirche in Deutschland (Hannover) an den Bundesminister der Justiz Dehler" (22 March 1952), reprinted in Gabriele Müller-List, ed. *Gleichberechtigung als Verfassungsauftrag: Eine Dokumentation zur Entstehung des Gleichberechtigungsgesetzes vom 18. Juni 1957 (Dokumente und Texte)* (Düsseldorf: Droste, 1996), 194–201.
75. Holz, *Zwischen Tradition und Emanzipation*, 170–76, 212–19; Moeller, *Protecting Motherhood*, 94, 200.
76. Petra Holz, "CDU-Politikerinnen und KDFB: Kontinuitäten und Neuansätze," in *Katholikinnen und Moderne: Katholische Frauenbewegung zwischen Tradition und Emanzipation*, ed. Gisela Muschiol (Münster: Aschendorff, 2003), 322–324; Holz, *Zwischen Tradition und Emanzipation*, 167–68; Moeller, *Protecting Motherhood*, 93.
77. Moeller, *Protecting Motherhood*, 199.
78. Herzog, *Sex after Fascism*, 118–19.
79. Moeller, *Protecting Motherhood*, 206.
80. Holz, *Zwischen Tradition und Emanzipation*, 21–22, 58–64, 272–79.
81. Reich-Hilweg, *Männer*, 34–37.
82. Boehling, "Gender Roles in Ruins," 51.
83. Carter, *How German Is She?* 36–37.
84. Carter, *How German Is She?* 7–8, 42, 65, 97, 102–6, 145, 177, 189, 203–38.
85. Mark Edward Ruff, *Wayward Flock: Catholic Youth in Postwar Germany, 1945–1965* (Chapel Hill: University of North Carolina Press, 2005). For figures on so-called mixed marriages, see Franz Greiner, "Die Katholiken in der technischen Gesellschaft der Nachkriegszeit," in *Deutscher Katholizismus nach 1945: Kirche, Gesellschaft, Geschichte*, ed. Hans Maier (Munich: Kosel Verlag, 1964), 104; Rölli-Alkemper, *Familie*, 190–91; Müller-Rolli, *Evangelische Schulpolitik*, 44; Ellen Lovell Evans, *The Cross and the Ballot: Catholic Political Parties in Germany, Switzerland, Austria, Belgium and the Netherlands, 1785–1985* (Boston: Humanities Press, 1999), 271–72.
86. Herzog, *Sexuality in Europe*, 127–29.
87. Thomas Großbölting, *Losing Heaven: Religion in Germany since 1945*, trans. Alex Skinner (New York: Berghahn Books, 2017).
88. Claus A. Fischer, ed., *Wahlhandbuch für die Bundesrepublik Deutschland: Daten zu Bundestags-, Landtags- und Europawahlen in der Bundesrepublik Deutschland, in den Ländern und in den Kreisen, 1946–1989*, Vol. 1 (Paderborn: F. Schöningh, 1990), 12; Hans Süssmuth, *Kleine Geschichte der CDU-Frauen-Union: Erfolge und Rückschläge, 1948–1990* (Baden-Baden: Nomos Verlagsgesellschaft, 1990), 82, 130; Frank L. Rusciano, "Rethinking the Gender Gap: The Case of West German Elections, 1949–1987," *Comparative Politics* 24, no. 3 (1992): 335–57.
89. On CDU Catholic women's independence from party doctrine on abortion, see Kimba Allie Tichenor, "Protecting Unborn Life in the Secular Age: The Catholic Church and the West German Abortion Debate, 1969–1989," *Central European History* 47 (2014): 612–45.
90. Evans, *The Cross and the Ballot*, 14.
91. Ibid., 277.

Bibliography

Adenauer, Konrad. *Briefe über Deutschland 1945–1955*. Munich: Seidler, 1999.
Agethen, Manfred. "Der Widerstand der demokratischen Kräfte in der CDU gegen den Gleichschaltungsdruck von sowjetischer Besatzungsmacht und SED, 1945–1952." In *Die CDU in der sowjetisch besetzten Zone/DDR 1945–1952*, edited by Alexander Fischer and Manfred Agethen, 21–44. Sankt Augustin: Konrad-Adenauer-Stiftung, 1994.

Allen, Ann Taylor. *Feminism and Motherhood in Western Europe, 1800–1914*. New Brunswick: Rutgers University Press, 1991.

Becker, Winfried. *CDU und CSU: Vorläufer, Gründung und regionale Entwicklung bis zum Entstehen der CDU-Bundespartei*. Mainz: Hasse & Koehler, 1987.

Besier, Gerhard. "'Christliche Parteipolitik' und Konfession: Zur Entstehung des Evangelischen Arbeitskreises der CDU/CSU." *Kirchliche Zeitgeschichte* 3 (1990): 166–87.

Boak, Helen. "'Our Last Hope': Women's Votes for Hitler—A Reappraisal." *German Studies Review* 12, no. 2 (May 1989): 289–310.

———. "Women in Weimar Politics." *European History Quarterly* 20, no. 3 (July 1990): 369–99.

Boehling, Rebecca. "Gender Roles in Ruins: German Women and Local Politics under American Occupation, 1945–1955." In *Gender and the Long Postwar: The United States and the Two Germanys, 1945–1989*, edited by Karen Hagemann and Sonya Michel, 51–72. Baltimore: Johns Hopkins University Press, 2014.

Bösch, Frank. *Die Adenauer-CDU: Gründung, Aufstieg, und Krise einer Erfolgspartei, 1945–1969*. Stuttgart: Deutsche Verlags-Anstalt (DVA), 2001.

Bremme, Gabriele. *Die politische Rolle der Frau in Deutschland*. Göttingen: Vanderhoeck & Ruprecht, 1956.

Brodie, Thomas. *German Catholicism at War, 1939–1945*. Oxford, UK: Oxford University Press, 2018.

Carter, Erica. *How German Is She? Postwar West German Reconstruction and the Consuming Woman*. Ann Arbor: University of Michigan Press, 1997.

Chappel, James. *Catholic Modern: The Challenge of Totalitarianism and the Remaking of the Catholic Church*. Cambridge, MA: Harvard University Press, 2018.

Cremer, Douglas J. "The Limits of Maternalism: Gender Ideology and the South German Catholic Workingwomen's Associations, 1904–1918." *The Catholic Historical Review* 87, no. 3 (2001): 428–52.

Denman, Mariatte C. "Visualizing the Nation: Madonnas and Mourning Mothers in Postwar Germany." In *Gender and Germanness: Cultural Productions of a Nation*, edited by Patricia Herminghouse and Magda Hueller, 189–201. Providence: Berghahn Books, 1997.

Dickinson, E.R., et al. "A Backlash Against Liberalism? What the Weimar Republic Can Teach Us About Today's Politics." *International Journal for History, Culture and Modernity* 5, no. 1 (2018): 91–107.

Evans, Ellen Lovell. *The Cross and the Ballot: Catholic Political Parties in Germany, Switzerland, Austria, Belgium and the Netherlands, 1785–1985*. Boston: Humanities Press, 1999.

Fäßler, Peter. *Badisch. Christlich und Sozial: Zur Geschichte der BCSV/CDU im französisch besetzten Land Baden (1945–1952)*. Frankfurt am Main: Peter Lang, 1995.

Fehrenbach, Heide. "The Fight for the 'Christian West': German Film Control, the Churches, and the Reconstruction of Civil Society in the Early Bonn Republic." *German Studies Review* 14, no. 1 (1991): 39–63.

Feldkamp, Michael F. *Der Parlamentarischer Rat 1948–1949: Die Entstehung des Grundgesetzes*. Göttingen: Vanderhoeck & Ruprecht, 2008.

Fischer, Claus A., ed. *Wahlhandbuch für die Bundesrepublik Deutschland: Daten zu Bundestags-, Landtags- und Europawahlen in der Bundesrepublik Deutschland, in den Ländern und in den Kreisen, 1946–1989*, Vol. 1. Paderborn: F. Schöningh, 1990.

Fuchs, Susanne. *Frauen Bewältigen den Neuaufbau: Eine lokalgeschichtliche Analyse der unmittelbaren Nachkriegszeit am Beispiel Bonn*. Pfaffenweiler: Centaurus-Verlagsgesellschaft, 1993.

Gerhard, Ute, and Ulla Wischermann. *Unerhört: Die Geschichte der deutschen Frauenbewegung*. Reinbeck bei Hamburg: Rowohlt, 1990.

Greiner, Franz. "Die Katholiken in der technischen Gesellschaft der Nachkriegszeit." In *Deutscher Katholizismus nach 1945: Kirche, Gesellschaft, Geschichte*, edited by Hans Maier, 103–35. Munich: Kosel Verlag, 1964.

Greven-Aschoff, Barbara. *Die bürgerliche Frauenbewegung in Deutschland, 1894–1933*. Göttingen: Vandenhoeck & Ruprecht, 1981.
Griech-Polelle, Beth A. *Bishop von Galen: German Catholicism and National Socialism*. New Haven: Yale University Press, 2002.
Großbölting, Thomas. *Losing Heaven: Religion in Germany since 1945*. Translated by Alex Skinner. New York: Berghahn Books, 2017.
Grossmann, Atina. *Reforming Sex: The German Movement for Birth Control and Abortion Reform, 1920–1950*. New York: Oxford University Press, 1995.
Gruber, Ludger. *Die CDU-Landtagsfraktion in Nordrhein-Westfalen 1946–1980: Eine parlamentshistorische Untersuchung*. Düsseldorf: Droste, 1998.
Harsch, Donna. "Public Continuity and Private Change? Women's Consciousness and Activity in Frankfurt, 1945–1955." *Journal of Social History* 27, no. 1 (Fall 1993): 29–58.
Hartlaub, Geno. "Ich war ein Wunderkind und ein Mädchen." In *Der Hunger nach Erfahrung: Frauen nach '45*, edited by Inge Stolten, 9–21. Berlin: J.H.W. Dietz, 1981.
Heineman, Elizabeth D. "The Hour of the Woman: Memories of Germany's 'Crisis Years' and West German National Identity." *American Historical Review* 101, no. 2 (1996): 354–95.
———. *What Difference Does a Husband Make? Women and Marital Status in Nazi and Postwar Germany*. Berkeley: University of California Press, 1999.
Heitzer, Horstwalter. *Die CDU in der britischen Zone: Gründung, Organisation, Programm und Politik*. Düsseldorf: Droste, 1988.
Herzog, Dagmar. *Sex after Fascism: Memory and Morality in Twentieth-Century Germany*. Cambridge, UK: Cambridge University Press, 2005.
———. *Sexuality in Europe: A Twentieth-Century History*. Cambridge, UK: Cambridge University Press, 2011.
Holz, Petra. "CDU-Politikerinnen und KDFB: Kontinuitäten und Neuansätze." In *Katholikinnen und Moderne: Katholische Frauenbewegung zwischen Tradition und Emanzipation*, edited by Gisela Muschiol, 315–31. Münster: Aschendorff, 2003.
———. *Zwischen Tradition und Emanzipation: CDU-Politikerinnen in der Zeit von 1946 bis 1960*. Königstein: Helmer, 2004.
Horan, Geraldine Theresa. *Mothers, Warriors, Guardians of the Soul: Female Discourse in National Socialism, 1924–1934*. Berlin: De Gruyter, 2003.
Illemann, Regina. *Katholische Frauenbewegung in Deutschland 1945–1962: Politik, Geschlecht und Religiosität im Katholischen Deutschen Frauenbund*. Paderborn: Ferdinand Schöningh, 2016.
Jähnichen, Traugott. "Das Ideal eines 'starken Staates' zur Sicherung von Freiheit und sozialem Ausgleich: Beiträge des politischen Protestantismus zur christliche-demokratischen Programmatik." In *Das christliche Menschenbild*, edited by Hanns Jürgen Küsters, Jörg-Dieter Gauger, and Rudolf Uertz, 86–119. Freiburg: Herder, 2013.
Jauch, Ernst-Alfred, and Gisela Helwig. "Katholische Kirche." In *Kirchen und Gesellschaft in beiden deutschen Staaten*, edited by Gisela Helwig and Detlef Urban, 7–43. Cologne: Edition Deutschland Archiv im Verlag Wissenschaft und Politik, 1987.
Kauders, Anthony. "Catholics, the Jews and Democratization in Post-war Germany, Munich, 1945–65." *German History*, 18, no. 4 (2000): 461–84.
Kaufmann, Doris. *Frauen zwischen Aufbruch und Reaktion*. Munich: Piper, 1991.
Kösters, Christoph, ed. *Caritas in der SBZ/DDR, 1945–1989: Erinnerungen, Berichte, Forschungen*. Paderborn: Ferdinand Schöningh Verlag, 2001.
Marhoefer, Laurie. "Degeneration, Sexual Freedom, and the Politics of the Weimar Republic, 1918–1933." *German Studies Review* 34, no. 3 (October 2011): 529–49.
Moeller, Robert G. *Protecting Motherhood: Women and the Family in the Politics of Postwar West Germany*. Berkeley: University of California Press, 1993.
Muller, Jerry Z. *The Other God That Failed: Hans Freyer and the Deradicalization of German Conservatism*. Princeton: Princeton University Press, 1987.

Müller-List, Gabriele, ed. *Gleichberechtigung als Verfassungsauftrag: Eine Dokumentation zur Entstehung des Gleichberechtigungsgesetzes vom 18. Juni 1957 (Dokumente und Texte)*. Düsseldorf: Droste, 1996.

Müller-Rolli, Sebastian. *Evangelische Schulpolitik in Deutschland, 1918–1958: Dokumente und Darstellung*. Göttingen: Vandenhoeck & Ruprecht, 1999.

Onnasch, Martin. "Die Situation der Kirchen in der sowjetischen Besatzungszone, 1945–1949." *Kirchliche Zeitgeschichte* 2, no. 1 (1989): 210–21.

O'Sullivan, Michael. *Disruptive Power: Catholic Women, Miracles, and Politics in Germany, 1918–1965*. Toronto: University of Toronto Press, 2018.

Reich-Hilweg, Ines. *Männer und Frauen sind gleichberechtigt: Der Gleichberechtigungsgrundsatz (Art. 3 Abs. 2 GG) in der parlamentarischen Auseinandersetzung, 1948–1957, und in der Rechtsprechung des Bundesverfassungsgerichts, 1953–1975*. Frankfurt am Main: Europäische Verlagsanstalt, 1979.

Rohe, Karl. *Wahlen und Wählertraditionen in Deutschland: Kulturelle Grundlagen deutscher Parteien und Parteiensysteme im 19. und 20. Jahrhundert*. Frankfurt am Main: Suhrkamp, 1992.

Rölli-Alkemper, Lukas. *Familie im Wiederaufbau: Katholizismus und bürgerliches Familienideal in der Bundesrepublik Deutschland, 1945–1965*. Paderborn: Ferdinand Schöningh, 2000.

Roos, Julia. *Weimar through the Lens of Gender: Prostitution Reform, Woman's Emancipation, and German Democracy, 1919–33*. Ann Arbor: University of Michigan Press, 2010.

Röwekamp, Marion. "Der Kampf um die Ehe: Der Katholische Frauenbund und das Zentrum im Richtungsstreit um eine Reform des Ehescheidungsrechts." In *Die Frauen und der politische Katholizismus: Akteurinnen, Themen, Strategien*, edited by Markus Raasch and Andreas Linsenmann, 209–38. Leiden: Ferdinand Schöningh, 2018.

Ruff, Mark Edward. *Wayward Flock: Catholic Youth in Postwar Germany, 1945–1965*. Chapel Hill: University of North Carolina Press, 2005.

Ruppert, Karsten. "Die Deutsche Zentrumspartei in der Mitverantwortung für die Weimarer Republik: Selbstverständnis und politische Leitideen einer konfessionellen Mittelpartei." In *Die Minderheit als Mitte: Die Deutsche Zentrumspartei in der Innenpolitik des Reiches, 1871–1933*, edited by Winfried Becker, 47–69. Paderborn: Ferdinand Schöningh, 1986.

Rüschenschmidt, Heinrich. "Die Entstehung der hessischen CDU, 1945/46: Lokale Gründungsvorgänge und Willensbildung im Landesverband." Masters thesis, Philipps-Universität Marburg, 1979.

Rusciano, Frank L. "Rethinking the Gender Gap: The Case of West German Elections, 1949–1987." *Comparative Politics* 24, no. 3 (1992): 335–57.

Sack, Birgit. *Zwischen religiöser Bindung und moderner Gesellschaft: Katholische Frauenbewegung und politische Kultur in der Weimarer Republik (1918/19–1933)*. Münster: Waxmann, 1998.

Scheck, Raffael. "Women on the Weimar Right: The Role of Female Politicians in the Deutschnationale Volkspartei (DNVP)." *Journal of Contemporary History* 36, no. 4 (2001): 547–60.

Sevenich, Maria. "Unser Gesicht: Abhandlung über Christlichen und Marxistischen Sozialismus." *Politik aus Christlicher Verantwortung*, vol. 1. Recklinghausen: Verlag Bitter & Co., 1946.

Späth, Anna. "Vielfältige Forderungen nach Gleichberechtigung und 'nur' ein Ergebnis: Artikel 3 Absatz 2 GG." In *Das Schicksal Deutschlands liegt in der Hand seiner Frauen: Frauen in der deutschen Nachkriegsgeschichte*, edited by Anna-Elisabeth Freier and Annette Kuhn, 122–67. Düsseldorf: Schwann, 1984.

Stark, John Robert. "The Overlooked Majority: German Women in the Four Zones of Occupied Germany, 1945–1949, A Comparative Study." PhD diss., Ohio State University, 2003.

Steigmann-Gall, Richard. *The Holy Reich: Nazi Conceptions of Christianity, 1919–1945*. Cambridge, UK: Cambridge University Press, 2003.

Stoehr, Irene. "Cold War Communities: Women's Peace Politics in Postwar West Germany, 1945–1952." In *Home/Front: The Military, War and Gender in Twentieth-Century Germany*, edited by Karen Hagemann and Stefanie Schüler-Springorum, 311–44. Oxford, UK: Berg, 2002.

Süssmuth, Hans. *Kleine Geschichte der CDU-Frauen-Union: Erfolge und Rückschläge, 1948–1990*. Baden-Baden: Nomos Verlagsgesellschaft, 1990.

Teusch, Christine. "Die christliche Frau im politischen Zeitgeschehen." *Schriftenreihe der Christlich-Demokratischen Union Westfalen-Lippe* 2 (September 1946).

Tichenor, Kimba Allie. "Protecting Unborn Life in the Secular Age: The Catholic Church and the West German Abortion Debate, 1969–1989." *Central European History* 47 (2014): 612–45.

Tobin, Elizabeth H., and Jennifer Gibson. "The Meanings of Labor: East German Women's Work in the Transition from Nazism to Communism." *Central European History* 28, no. 3 (1995): 299–342.

Van Rahden, Till. "Fatherhood, Rechristianization, and the Quest for Democracy in Postwar West Germany." In *Raising Citizens in the "Century of the Child": The United States and German Central Europe in Comparative Perspective*, edited by Dirk Schumann, 141–66. New York: Berghahn Books, 2010.

Wittrock, Christine. "Das Frauenbild in faschistischen Texten und seine Vorläufer in der bürgerlichen Frauenbewegung der zwanziger Jahre." PhD diss., Johann-Wolfgang-Goethe-Universität zu Frankfurt am Main, 1981.

Wolf, Christof. "Konfessionelle versus religiöse Konfliktslinie in der deutschen Wählerschaft." *Politische Vierteljahresschrift* 37, no. 4 (1996): 713–34.

Zapf, Wolfgang. *Wandlungen der deutschen Elite: Ein Zirkulationsmodell deutscher Führungsgruppen, 1919–1961*. Munich: Piper, 1965.

Chapter Eight

IMPORTING CONTROVERSY

The Martin Luther Film of 1953 and Confessional Tensions

Mark Edward Ruff

On 4 March 1954, at the Filmstudio Theatre in Hanover, Germany, bishops of the Evangelical Church of Germany, high-ranking representatives of the Lutheran World Federation, West German governmental officials and a team of American filmmakers nervously awaited the premiere of a film about Martin Luther. With good reason, they feared that *Martin Luther* would inflame long-simmering tensions between Catholics and Protestants. For from its moment of inception in late 1949 and early 1950 in New York City and long past its American premiere in early May 1953 in the Lutheran heartland of Minneapolis, *Martin Luther* had been enmeshed in controversy.[1] It was the artistic creation of a newly created American corporation with pronounced anti-Catholic sensitivities, Lutheran Film Productions, Inc. (LFP). Its filming in 1952 in the Federal Republic of Germany had generated enmity. Scattered protests and boycotts had accompanied its American run in rented cinemas and church basements. The Legion of Decency, the American Catholic film ratings organization, had given it a "separate classification," warning that it would be "dangerous" to those "unfamiliar with the historical facts" because it contained "theological and historical references and interpretations which are unacceptable to Catholics."[2] Even worse, the government of Maurice Duplessis in the Canadian province of Québec had prohibited all public showings in theaters, allowing it to be screened only in the basements of Protestant churches until the ban was lifted in 1963.[3]

The whiff of controversy naturally had followed the film to Germany. Swiftly synchronized in 1953 for a German audience, the German version had immediately run afoul of the German film commission (*Die Freiwillige*

Selbstkontrolle der Filmwirtschaft), a committee with representatives from both Catholic and Protestant churches. Commissioning an expert opinion from the prominent Catholic Church historian and Reformation scholar Joseph Lortz, the committee barred its release until certain scenes were cut, citing historical errors. But divisions also opened up where the producers least expected it—within Protestant ranks. Protestant theologians and politicians questioned the wisdom of antagonizing German Catholics at a time of rising confessional tensions. Sharing Catholic reservations about the film's historical accuracy and its tendentious theological simplifications, they excoriated its superficiality and lack of theological complexity.

The producers' fears that *Martin Luther* would prove divisive were prescient. Just weeks after the premiere, the West German Catholic bishops reproached *Martin Luther* at their meeting in Pützchen for "disrupting the confessional peace," its tendentious simplification of historical reality, its historical errors, and above all its "false depiction of the Catholic Church."[4] The question of whether schoolchildren should be allowed to view the film in public schools reached Chancellor Konrad Adenauer. And precisely because of the controversies it was generating, *Martin Luther* went on to become a smash hit in the Federal Republic of Germany, just as it had been in the United States. Nominated for two Oscars, it attracted more than a million viewers across the United States in less than six months. Thanks to the enthusiastic support of many German Lutheran pastors who persuaded churchgoers to attend screenings in parish halls and over the objections of Catholic and Protestant theologians, the film went on to be seen in the next six months by even more. It was viewed by a record four-and-a-half million German filmgoers, mostly Protestants, a number that surpassed all expectations for a black-and-white film which even its champions knew to be extraordinarily slow-paced.[5]

What triggered this welter of responses to this film—enthusiastic promotion from at least two Lutheran bishops, the critical disdain of Protestant and Catholic theologians, hostility from Catholic bishops and millions of viewers? This chapter examines two competing forces. The first was a rise in confessional tensions from the 1940s onward. Incident after incident seemed to summon the ghosts of the *Kulturkampf* of the 1870s and the Catholic Counter-Reformation. Protestant hardliners, mostly confessional Lutherans like the Bishop of Hanover, Hanns Lilje, were troubled by Catholic political assertiveness and the electoral gains of the Catholic-dominated CDU/CSU coalition. As Lilje put it: "We stand in real danger of being pushed back culturally to the margins."[6]

The second was an opposite force—a search for complex reasons among Catholics and Protestants for interconfessional cooperation or at the minimum maintaining what they termed "the confessional peace." These included former "bridge-builders" to National Socialism in the 1930s like Lortz who continued to seek national and confessional unity. But they also included Catholics and Protestants active in the resistance against Hitler who had helped found the interconfessional CDU. The critical players were Protestant CDU leaders, a tiny minority statistically but arguably the engine of its electoral success. Like Chancellor Konrad Adenauer, they recognized that the CDU would have to win over Protestant voters in regions historically hostile to Catholicism and expand beyond its predominantly Catholic base for it to remain dominant in German politics. In part because of the difficulties in maintaining interconfessional peace within the CDU, the controversy over *Martin Luther* rose to the highest rungs of German politics. This chapter examines how and why this happened.

Martin Luther bore the anti-Catholic stamp of both American Lutheranism and the worldwide ecumenical movement. The idea for the film was broached in the late 1940s by the National Lutheran Council (NLC), an assembly of six synods founded in 1918. The Council found a rallying force in the anti-Catholicism gaining traction throughout American Protestantism by the close of World War II.[7] It regularly alleged that the Catholic Church had forsaken biblical truths. "Which will you choose?" one typical pamphlet asked, "The Word of God or The Word of Man?"[8]

It was only natural that the NLC was developing close ties to the World Council of Churches (WCC) created in 1948. Its ecumenism too was profoundly anti-Catholic. Fitting with its domicile in Calvinist Geneva, it sought to provide succor to Protestants struggling under allegedly repressive Catholic regimes in Spain, Portugal, Latin America, and Italy. Its anti-Catholicism was fueled by the victory in April 1948 of Alcide de Gasperi's Italian Christian Democratic Party, which it attributed to Vatican machinations. Angered by Catholic triumphalism and fearful of the Church's political ambitions in the United States, the head of the National Lutheran Council and driving force behind the film, Paul C. Empie, cited in mid-December 1949 the growing "aggressiveness and arrogance of Roman Catholicism" and its "smearing of Martin Luther" as reasons to act.[9] Because of the "strength" of their "confessional position," Lutherans needed to take the lead in combating "both the Catholic totalitarianism on one hand and political atheism on the other" and rallying other Protestant denominations.[10]

The curious trope of "Catholic totalitarianism"—the other two varieties of totalitarianism were Islamic and Communist—came from WCC offices in Geneva.[11] As Henry Endress, the associate producer on the film, put it, *Martin Luther* was to make clear "the relevance of Luther's work for our own day." For the producers, this entailed sounding a call for freedom of conscience and religious liberty against tyranny.[12] "You cannot command our conscience," a Lutheran prince informed Emperor Charles V at the close of the film.[13]

For the scriptwriters, this meant sculpting an avowedly dogmatic and anti-Catholic plot.[14] Though Luther had lived from 1483 to 1546, the writers restricted the plot to the years 1505 through 1530, leaving out Luther's role in the Peasants War and his later anti-Judaic and anti-Catholic excesses. The script portrayed the late medieval Church as a den of theological ignorance. "The church had largely forgotten the mercy of God and instead emphasized God's implacable judgment," the narrator informed viewers at the opening.

Above all, the scriptwriters carefully selected encounters, real and fictional, intended to show why Luther's efforts at reform were warranted theologically. They centered the plot on Luther's insistence that the Church had to be called to account for its jettisoning of the word of God. An early fictional scene showed Staupitz, Luther's superior in his Augustinian order, informing townspeople that venerating all of the holy relics in his possession would lead to forgiveness of "1,920,202 years plus 270 days" in purgatory. An angry Luther, who had just begun discovering the idea of salvation through faith alone, conspicuously walked out of the ceremony. In another fictional scene, Luther encountered a drunkard on a stairwell clutching a bottle, who muttered to Luther: "I don't need confession. My sins are already forgiven forever." The drunkard showed Luther an indulgence which bore the signature of Johannes Teztel, the famous Dominican hawker of indulgences. From there, the movie presented dramatic moments and showdowns long part of Lutheran lore. These included the posting of the 95 Theses in Wittenberg, the Leipzig Disputation (inaccurately portrayed as an unambiguous victory for Luther over his scholastic interlocutor, Johannes Eck), the Diet of Worms and Luther's kidnapping at the behest of his protector, Frederick the Wise. The film subsequently depicted Luther translating the New Testament in the Wartburg Castle, battling with his former colleague and former reformer Andreas Karlstadt in Wittenberg over iconoclasm in a dispute left unexplained to the audience and giving young boys catechism instruction. The film concluded triumphantly by showing a crowd singing the isometric—and historically inaccurate—version of Luther's famous hymn, "A Mighty Fortress is Our God," following the signing of the Augsburg Confession of 1530, an event for which Luther was in reality notably absent.

The tendentious choices made by the scriptwriters alone explain the infuriated Catholic reactions to *Martin Luther* in North America. But German Catholic perceptions were shaped by the fact that this American import had received powerful German assistance. *Martin Luther* was a de facto German-American collaboration. The script committee drew on German language scholarship on the Reformation, including Lortz's monumental two-volume history of the Reformation from 1949.[15] A multilingual cast of directors, actors, singers, and extras and a largely German crew filmed *Martin Luther* on West German soil over three months in the summer and fall of 1952.[16] Its producer was Lothar Wolff, a German editor and director born in Bromberg in 1908 and an exile from Nazi Germany. Even its finances bore a German mark. The film had cost more than $500,000, a sum so vast for a non-profit religious partnership that its leaders had been forced to finance itself by establishing a German corporation, die Luther-Film-Gesellschaft M.B.H., that could pay its expenses not through regular currency but through so-called restricted marks (*Sperrmarken*) that offered a better return on the dollar.[17] This corporation was almost an equal partner to the Lutheran Film Productions; its head, Johannes Stuhlmacher, was given quite a degree of latitude, including by late 1953 the task of bringing the synchronized German version to market.

Launching the film in Germany would have been impossible without the powerful support of high-ranking Protestant officials in the German Evangelical Church who repeatedly provided feedback on the script, filming, and promotional efforts.[18] One champion was the bishop of Bavaria, Hans Meiser, like Lilje an orthodox Lutheran and active member in the Lutheran World Federation. Viewing the film in mid-January 1953 at a private showing in a studio in Geiselgasteig before its American premiere, Meiser encouraged the Lutheran Film Production team to move forward on a German synchronization.[19]

The most influential collaborator was Hanns Lilje, the conservative Hanoverian state bishop who from 1952 through 1957 served as President of the Lutheran World Federation. Lilje's advocacy had its roots in movements for religious revival from the 1920s and 1930s. During the Weimar era, Lilje had served as the General Secretary of the German Student Christian Federation, a branch of the World Student Christian Federation (WSCF). Well versed in English, Lilje traveled abroad no fewer than seventeen times between 1929 and 1939, including three times to the United States and once to Geneva as a seminar leader.[20] Lilje was also a founding member of the *Kronberger Kreis*, a small circle of Protestants with roots in the Christian student movement of the Weimar era.[21] Seeking to orient members toward the political culture of the United States, this circle resolutely opposed fellow Protestants like Martin Niemöller who were decrying West German rearmament and urging neutrality vis-à-vis the Communist East. As much as he supported Adenauer's policy of binding Germany to the West, Lilje believed that confessional parity—Catholics now amounted to 46 percent of the West German population and wielded genuine political power—could doom Protestants politically.

It was only fitting that his state church was headquartered in Lower Saxony, an SPD-controlled and largely Protestant state mounting aggressive opposition to Adenauer's Catholic-dominated government and policies. In mid-1954, Lower Saxony became the first to pass a school law restricting the number of "denominational schools" (*Bekenntnisschulen*), state-funded public schools championed by the Catholic Church and intended to be segregated by confession. Catholic supporters sought to anchor the "parents' right" to these schools in Article 23 of the Reichskonkordat, the treaty signed on 20 July 1933 by the Vatican and Hitler's government.[22] For Lilje, this was cause for extreme concern: the Reichskonkordat was being used for "a strategic major offensive" to overrun the Protestant heartland of Northern Germany—just as in the Counter-Reformation.[23] The birthplaces of the Lutheran Reformation—Thuringia and Saxony—had already been "lost" to atheistic Communism. But even more alarming to him was how German Protestant schoolchildren were being subjected to a wave of Marian films in advance of the 1954 Marian Year declared by Pope Pius XII.[24]

It was thus almost predestined that Lilje would not just promote but actively work on *Martin Luther*. For him, releasing a German-language version of an American import that had played to sold out theaters in Chicago for fourteen weeks was an act of grace; we will "never again for years" have such a PR opportunity with such power and vigor.[25] Consistent with the *Kronberger Kreis*'s goals, he sought to launch an aggressive defense of not just Protestant political and cultural interests, but of the faith itself: "I judge the film as a great tool to say why we have the Reformation in the first place." Lilje repeatedly corresponded and met with officials from Lutheran Film Productions. As early as 1951, he commented in detail on several of the script's nine iterations.[26] He wrote a lengthy circular to the pastors in his state church encouraging them to show the film in their parishes.[27]

In keeping with its purpose of bolstering Lutheran confessional identity worldwide, the National Lutheran Council intended to release *Martin Luther* during the annual conference of the Lutheran World Federation (LWF) in 1952 in Hanover, allowing for nearly simultaneous showings at Lutheran centers across the world.[28] But it experienced delays in scriptwriting: it went through no fewer than nine iterations as its lead writer, Allan Sloane, born Allan Silverman, had been neither raised Lutheran nor was sufficiently versed in Reformation history. The LWF opted to showcase instead a much tamer eighty-two-minute black-and-white documentary more music than text. *The Obedient Rebel*, the work of the German cinematographer Curt Oertel, had been put together by the same two Lutheran film companies responsible for *Martin Luther*. Focusing primarily on

Luther's spiritual struggles, this film was warmly received by Catholics and Protestants alike, belying Lutheran Film Production's claim that any film honestly depicting the career of the great religious reformer would trigger Catholic opposition.[29]

The assembly in Hanover having come and gone, the American filmmakers shot the film between August and October 1952. They were determined to produce a historically accurate film but were stymied by having been denied permission to film on the actual Luther sites in Erfurt, Wittenberg, and Leipzig under the control of the Communist regime in East Germany. As a surrogate for the Augustinian monastery in Erfurt, they used the famed Maulbronn monastery, a Cistercian abbey turned Protestant seminary near Stuttgart; the Eberbach Cloister near Heidelberg and the castle at Eltville near Mainz had to duplicate Wittenberg.[30]

But these southwestern surrogates were more heavily Catholic regions, where filmmaking risked inflaming confessional tensions. The film required hundreds of extras, some Catholics, to play the roles of Augustinian monks and townspeople. Seeking to defuse rising tensions was Peter Heinemann, an Augustinian monk turned Lutheran pastor. He provided assistance from an Augustinian monastery and help from the Catholic priests in all the towns in which the filmmakers worked.[31] He also won over a priest in Eberbach who had earlier informed his parishioners that all Catholics working on the film would be denied the Eucharist, last rites, and a Christian burial. The priest subsequently allowed Heinemann to borrow a Missal and other books for one scene.[32] The filmmakers even turned to a Catholic choir director from Munich, who used his choir and 450 extras, Catholics and Protestants alike, to sing Luther's chorale, "A Mighty Fortress is our God," with which the film closed.[33]

During the filming, a team of reporters from Germany's leading newsmagazine, *Der Spiegel*, had accompanied the cast and crew of sixty caravanning across southern and western Germany.[34] The widespread publicity ensured that German Catholic leaders knew about the film long before work on the German synchronization began in the summer of 1953. But alarms did not sound until criticism from the American Legion of Decency arrived in Germany. Reading the Legion's reports, the German Catholic wire services association, the KNA, proclaimed the film's "theological and historical depiction" to be "unacceptable."[35]

These attacks put the Bishops Conference of the United Lutheran Churches in Germany in an awkward position as it met in Tutzing on 30 September 1953, to screen the just completed German synchronization. The film's leading champion, Lilje, was unable to attend, and some of those assembled agreed with Catholic criticism. They were troubled by the overly heroic portrayal of Luther, which glossed over his spiritual struggle, and the equally overwrought and cartoonish portrayal of the indulgence salesman, Johannes Tetzel.[36] *Martin Luther* conflated Luther's plea for religious conscience with modern liberal notions of freedom of conscience. Not least, the film was too long for a German audience.[37]

Opting for a middle ground, the Lutheran bishops issued a statement endorsing the film and rebutting the Legion of Decency's published criticisms but also recommended minor cuts, mostly to scenes they deemed overwrought.[38] They also assembled a commission of four pastors and academics, including Landesbischof Hugo Hahn from Dresden, to proof and promote the German version of *Martin Luther*. All were German: no member of Lutheran Film Productions, Inc., was included.

But unbeknownst to the theologians and clergymen gathered in Tutzing, a reporter from the *Süddeutsche Zeitung*, one of Munich's leading daily newspapers, had attended the meeting.[39] He wrote a lengthy and mostly positive dispatch, noting that the German version had been put together through the "assistance of Protestant theologians in Berlin."[40] Believing that the film bore the imprimatur of the German Protestant Church, Catholic opponents targeted the FSK (*Freiwillige Selbstkontrolle der Filmwirtschaft*), the state-sponsored German film commission and ratings organization that had to approve all films shown in Germany. It included Catholics and Protestants appointed by their respective denominations; the chairmanship rotated every two years between Catholics and Protestant. In 1953, the chair was Werner Hess, a Protestant pastor who had worked on *The Obedient Rebel*. Though Hess was enthusiastic about *Martin Luther*, he, Johannes Stuhlmacher, and the Protestant representatives on the committee were concerned about its potential to upset Catholics and "endanger the confessional peace."[41] As a precaution, they invited two Catholic Church historians to a screening on 4 December 1953. Both were instructed to assess the film's historical accuracy and determine whether inaccuracies might prove "injurious" to Catholic sentiment.[42]

The best-known and most influential of these scholars was the church historian and Reformation scholar Joseph Lortz.[43] The choice of Lortz was no coincidence. He had a reputation as a maverick and ecumenical advocate eager to build bridges to non-Catholics and—in the 1930s—National Socialists. Critical of portions of the Catholic theological past, his recent scholarship had highlighted corruption in the late medieval era, including the abuse of indulgences.[44] But contrary to Stuhlmacher's and Hess's hopes, Lortz forcefully spoke out against the film. Though lauding the filmmakers for attempting to reconstruct the events of the past as non-tendentiously as possible, he vocally objected to the scene showing the drunkard telling Luther that he no longer needed confession since his sins had already been forgiven forever.[45] As he correctly pointed out, this scene grotesquely distorted Church teachings on indulgences: confession and absolution were preconditions for receiving indulgences. He also criticized a scene in which Staupitz counted aloud indulgences in the Castle Church in Wittenberg. Frederick the Wise no doubt would have allowed such tallies to take place, but to do so would have been completely out of character for Luther's spiritual director, Staupitz, a monk of utmost integrity who had helped guide the young monk out of his spiritual despair. Lortz also noted that Catholics could also take umbrage in the fact that catechism instruction was falsely presented as a Protestant innovation. The film, he concluded, was ultimately "one-sided."[46]

But for Lortz, the film represented something more: a missed ecumenical opportunity. Though it "did not originate from a background of hate," if one measures the film against the facts, "it is a failure."[47] Showing "not a trace of the mentioned corrections which modern historical research has made," the film "might have been made 40 years ago, and then it could have been rightly regarded as restrained."[48] Its failure lay in its inability to promote joint Catholic-Lutheran cooperation and to take into account how self-critical Protestants were now using the Reformation as a call for repentance. "What Catholic-Protestant cooperation might have done with this material. Without softening the explosive material, it could have been a mighty clarion call to both sides." The Reformation's tragedy "for Christianity, for Germany, for Europe and for the world" lay in its inability to promote "cleansing and healing." Lortz concluded by calling for the "unity of the divided" and offering prayers to end division.

But Lortz's criticism was not universally shared. An SPD-representative on the committee went so far as to suggest recommending the film for a national film prize, a sign of its tremendous support from Germany's second largest party.[49] It was clear that the message of the film—freedom of conscience—resonated with its heavily Protestant SPD viewers at a time when questions of "tolerance" were being debated at the highest parliamentary levels in both state and nation.

Facing obvious differences of opinion within its ranks, the committee engineered a compromise: it allowed the German version of *Martin Luther* to be released, but only under the condition that the scene depicting Tetzel and the beggar either be "brought into accordance with the historical reality" or cut altogether. Stuhlmacher gratefully agreed to these conditions, but he did not communicate the news of the cuts either to Lilje, Meiser, or Lutheran Film Productions, no doubt rightly fearing that none would agree to the cuts and thus jeopardize the film's future in Germany.[50] Word nonetheless spread back to the New York headquarters about what had transpired. Henry Endress was furious. The cuts, undertaken with no consultation with LFP, were "disturbing" and threatened to undermine LFP's hardline stance in its battle with censors in Québec who were refusing to release the film at all.⁵¹ They were also imperiling the battle with American Catholic opponents of the film who, learning of the German language cuts, apparently began calling for the same cuts in the English-language original.⁵² Recognizing that LFP did not wish to appear as bowing to Catholic pressure, Stuhlmacher was forced to defend the cuts as "unimportant."⁵³

But it was not only Catholic but Protestant theologians who showed little indulgence towards *Martin Luther*. After Lortz had delivered his critical commentary on the film, the film's German champions invited a group of Protestant theologians, most university professors, to a private screening. Their verdict was scathing.⁵⁴ One Protestant church historian, Hanns Rückert, a Luther and Calvin scholar (as well as a former member of the Nazi party), lamented the decision to release the film as a "lost battle in our confessional situation today." According to his report, the film was "teeming" with "cloddishness, sentimentalities and tastelessness," to say nothing of the "historical monstrosities" in the Reichstag scene, which to him appeared how a "small farmer in the (American) Midwest would have imagined a German parliament" and in which the emperor appeared "like Hitler in the Reichstag in the Kroll Opera House." For Rückert, the film was worthy of scorn only: "I can imagine how Lortz laughed himself to death as he saw this film. He knew exactly why he limited himself to contesting only one scene (the Tetzel scene). Nothing could have been better for him and for active Catholics than this embarrassment for the Protestant church and this discrediting of the Reformation."⁵⁵ Just before the premiere, he wrote to the Protestant political liaison in Bonn, Prelate Hermann Kunst, bemoaning the complicated state of affairs in which the Protestant Church had let itself be maneuvered. This was the result of the "lack of niveau" of American Lutheranism and mistakes made by the German Lutheran Bishops Conference. While he favored using "every means possible" to prevent "this bad film" from being released, he resisted the sole means to accomplish that—bowing to the ecclesiastical and political might of Catholicism.⁵⁶

Martin Luther was thus facing criticism from all sides—from the LFP home office in New York, from American and German Catholics objecting to its pro-Protestant slant and wishing to keep its showings confined to parish halls, and from German Protestant theologians objecting to its superficiality. For its adversaries, it had gone too far in its depiction of the Catholic Church and in injuring Catholic sentiment; for its champions, it had been shorn of power.

Torn between these competing pressures, the Protestant commission of four met with Lilje in late January 1954 to plot a marketing and public relations strategy. They sought to underscore the Great Reformer's relevance for the present day while not openly provoking Catholics.⁵⁷ Lilje unequivocally rejected the criticism of the scornful Protestant theologians who "see things quite incorrectly." The wave of Catholic Marian films "could" have a "confusing" effect on the Protestant brethren: "one cannot deny us a cinematic depiction of the start of the Reformation." Lilje proceeded to sharpen the draft of a letter that Werner Hess was writing to all Protestant parishes in the name of the bishop. Lilje added the lines that it was his duty of conscience to inform them that *Martin Luther* was a first-rate PR piece. Instead of trying to enter into futile ecumenical dialogue, Lutherans needed to return to their roots. If the Catholic Church could use the pulpit to promote its Marian films, why could Protestant churches not do the same with a film about Martin Luther?

However strident Lilje's formulations, the commission actually ended up exercising caution. Though determined to make *Martin Luther* a financial success, it opted to not "provoke the Catholic church" by showing it publicly in nearly exclusively Catholic regions.⁵⁸ In these, it intended to show the film only privately in Lutheran parish halls.⁵⁹ In regions in which Protestants made up at least 25 percent of the population, it planned to show the film in the best of theaters.⁶⁰

Because of the influx of refugees and expellees at the close of World War II, however, there were few regions that were still confessionally homogenous. *Martin Luther*, moreover, was being released when relations between Catholics and Protestants were rapidly deteriorating. As Johannes Stuhlmacher correctly recognized, confessional conflict was riskier in Germany than in the United States.⁶¹ Tensions were rampant between the CDU and its mostly Protestant rivals in the SPD and FDP. Within the interconfessional CDU itself, the founding in May 1952 of a Protestant Working Group (*Evangelischer Arbeitskreis*) had alarmed the largely Catholic CDU leadership. This working group, concerned with the Catholicization of high governmental positions, recognized that there had to be equal opportunity for Protestants within the new party for it to be palatable to Protestant voters: it would be disastrous for the CDU to be perceived as a purely Catholic party.⁶² Because of the precarious confessional dance within the CDU, every confessional disturbance could and would become a political question. As they saw it, the stability of Adenauer's governing coalition at a crucial time of mounting Cold War tensions ultimately hinged on upholding the "confessional peace."

Fearing that *Martin Luther* could easily destabilize this "confessional peace," Stuhlmacher arranged for a private showing and open discussion of the film in Bonn before a circle of Catholic and Protestant luminaries. But he continually postponed the screening until 2 March 1954, a mere two days before the German premiere in Hanover. The delays, he noted, were necessary to ensure that any outraged reactions would be unable to "damage" the premiere.[63] He made a point of inviting those likely to express outrage. These included: Wilhelm Böhler, the Catholic liaison to the federal government in Bonn who was extremely mistrustful of the film; Gerhard Schröder, the CDU Interior Minister; Wilhelm Neuß, a Catholic Church historian and emeritus professor; and Adolf Süsterhenn, a high-ranking CDU politician.[64] Among the Protestants invited were Hermann Kunst, the official Protestant political liaison to the federal government in Bonn; Robert Tillmanns, a high-ranking CSU cabinet member; and Edo Osterloh, a CDU minister in the Department of the Interior.[65]

But the crucial role was played by Dr. Hermann Ehlers, the President of the West German parliament. Ehlers was also the highest-ranking Protestant in the CDU and appropriately the leader of its Protestant Working Group. Ehlers, too, grasped that his party's electoral fortunes hinged on its ability to pull enough Protestants away from the liberal and socialist parties. Ehlers thus assumed a crucial function as a bridge-builder within the CDU between Catholic hardliners calling for confessional segregation, Protestant warriors relishing a fight, and Protestants put off by both.

For Ehlers, keeping the fight contained was not only a political necessity: it was a theological and moral imperative. From formative experiences in his twenties in the Bible Circles of the Protestant Youth Movement during Weimar, he concluded that faith and politics were inseparable. He also emerged as a critic of parliamentary democracy.[66] After beginning work for the Protestant State Church of Prussia in 1931 on church-state relations, however, his attitudes profoundly shifted. Refusing to join the Nazi party, he became active instead in the Confessing Church. Arrested by the Gestapo in 1937, he was removed from his position in 1939. While fighting with the army, he became aware of the necessity for interconfessional cooperation. He joined the CDU in 1946, seeing it as the only truly new political creation in the postwar era and hoping to expand its interconfessionalism by founding two Protestant working circles. This meant a delicate dance—fending off anti-Catholicism within Protestant ranks while ensuring a substantial Protestant presence in Catholic circles.[67] It was not the duty of Catholics and Protestants to overcome the confessional divide, but to understand and respect the theological precepts of the other confession.[68]

But this was easier said than done with a film like *Martin Luther* designed to counter "Catholic totalitarianism." Ehlers's hopes of preventing the open discussion from endangering "the confessional peace" was made more difficult when Catholic representatives began by launching a "declaration of war" against its historical inaccuracies, no doubt hoping to prevent public screenings.[69] They presented Ehlers with an ultimatum: either prevent the film's release or face massive protests and a rift within the CDU. Ehlers and

Kunst opted to sidestep the ultimatum. Kunst asked instead "whether confessional cooperation to maintain Christianity in Germany would be burdened by the film" and proceeded to cast doubt on the film's merits.[70] Ehlers went further. Declaring that he "had no enthusiasm for the film," and with "exaggerated irony," he praised the film for presenting "some quite pretty pictures as one would recognize from films about the Wild West." But the film was "no asset" for the Protestant Church but a relic from twenty-five years earlier, one redolent of the old Evangelical League (*Evangelischer Bund*). Ehlers's position was clear: since the film came from America and was not an official presentation of the German Protestant Church, there was no chance to either delay or limit the film's run.[71] Believing that the film would fall into obscurity because of its "dubious quality," Catholics agreed to hold off on public protests.[72] The German Catholics and Protestants gathered in Bonn were thus able to step back from the brink by agreeing on a more egregious enemy: American superficiality.[73] Doing so had a rich history. Opposition to "materialism" had served as foundational glue for Protestants and Catholics in the CDU, and resistance to American consumer culture held a high place on the conservative agenda.[74]

This stratagem was not lost on the American film team. Arriving for the German debut in Hanover, the American filmmaking team was clearly on the defensive. Its representative, Carl Lundquist, president of Bethel College and Seminary, ruefully noted that even the German Protestants promoting the film at the premiere were apologizing for "these poor benighted Americans who could never be expected to understand the life of Martin Luther and the issues of the Reformation."[75] They were "shadow boxing with the Catholic church, the government, the intellectuals" and had to try "too hard to justify the idea that such a film was being shown at all."[76] Even their remarks at the premiere lauding *Martin Luther*'s technical skill and artistry amounted to damning with faint praise. Lundquist could ultimately reflect on only the cultural divide between the Lutheran brethren on both sides of the Atlantic:

> The Germans seem to me to have the remarkable ability to complicate the simple and to be indirect when straightforwardness is needed. This attempt to try to weigh the philosophical, theological, sociological and historical factors before a movie audience makes me want to walk out of the theatre. I kept asking myself why [they don't] let the film talk to the average man without raising all of these non-essential items.[77]

It took two bravado speeches to break through the diffidence of their German hosts and the sense that the film had become an unwelcome embarrassment. The lead actor, the Irish thespian Niall MacGinnis, in a rare abstention from the bottle, delivered two short rousing speeches in German that went over "like a house fire."[78] The film's leading German champion, the Lutheran Bishop of Hanover Hanns Lilje, who had been intricately involved in its creation, put forward a blockbuster defense. He praised the film's extraordinary objectivity, asserting, falsely as it turns out, that it had been made not for "confessional reasons," but rather in a spirit of "spiritual nobility." As a film designed to educate viewers about life-threatening sixteenth-century political and spiritual realities, it was a lesson in the role of conscience in making decisions. Precisely because of its importance for Protestant identity, Lilje urged his Protestant brethren to view the film.

Ehlers' strategy of deflecting blame to the Americans thus proved only partially successful. The problem was that record numbers of Germans were flocking to the cinema in the 1950s—and *Martin Luther* had appeal on its cinematic merits alone. Even its critics saw this American import as a cinematic masterpiece, one whose elaborate sets and technical expertise compensated for its historical and theological defects. Its Catholic opponents could respond to the throngs of viewers with one thing alone—criticism. Others blamed its success on Lilje's outspoken support.[79] But fearing that overwrought condemnations would only further pique public interest, the West German Catholic bishops decided to keep their criticism muted. They delegated the task of criticizing to the Catholic press instead. It was instructed to "enlighten" its readers about the film's historical errors, distortions, and regrettable support from Protestant church officials.[80] Newspapers, in turn, traded volleys. An SPD newspaper in Hanover praised its potential for pulling people out of their "indifference to confessional conflicts . . . in the ongoing political questions between political Catholicism and Protestantism."[81] A Catholic writer for the *Deutsche Tagespost* argued that the film threatened to poison the confessional atmosphere in the Federal Republic in spite of the fact that a "good and responsible" portion of the Protestant leadership had reacted "cooly and soberly" to the film's launch. Why? The film had provided ammunition to anticlerical forces well represented in German liberalism, like the fiery FDP leader Thomas Dehler, and "its red brother," a clear reference to German socialism.[82] That East Germany banned all screenings of *Martin Luther* on its territory was obviously lost on this writer.

The other problem was that decisions to show *Martin Luther* in public schools became caught up in schoolyard culture wars. The German Film Commission had specifically given the film a designation as "suitable for youth" and "beneficial for youth."[83] For its Protestant champions, the film provided the opportunity to set "the record straight on the facts of the Protestant Reformation" and to provide a counterweight to the Marian films shown to German schoolchildren during the preceding years.[84] All public schools offered regular religious education segregated by confession: Protestant children were to receive instruction from Protestants. But the reality at the grassroots was murkier, particularly when the number of Catholic or Protestant pupils was too small to merit separate instruction. On a number of occasions, Protestant schoolchildren were shown Marian films. Outraged Protestant church committees responded by lobbying for showing *Martin Luther* in the schools.[85] With no time to screen the film and apparently confusing it with Curt Oertel's film about Luther from the preceding year, the director of the State Media Center (*Landesbildstelle*) for the Lower Rhine, a region within the archdiocese of Cologne, bowed to this pressure. He specifically cited the need for confessional parity. Having announced the film *The Vatican* to all schools, he now needed to do the same for the Luther film, even if was to be shown to Protestant schoolchildren only. It was left to the discretion of school leadership whether or not to show or promote the film.[86]

Taking umbrage, the archdiocesan leadership published a short article in the archdiocesan newsletter warning parish leaders and Catholic school leaders about the dangers posed by the film: the "peaceful confessional coexistence" is a "vital question" (*Lebensfrage*) for "our people."[87] Already in the open forum preceding the premiere, Süsterhenn had argued that *Martin Luther* was in no way comparable with Marian films, since the latter did not contain even the slightest attack against "the Protestant side."[88] Not least, the archdiocesan leadership contacted authorities in the Ministry of Culture in North-Rhine Westphalia, which informed it that it could do little. It had only announced (*bekannt geben*) the film to the schools: it had not recommended it. The decision to show the film lay in the hands of the local school leadership.[89] Cardinal Josef Frings could take solace only in the fact that only 9,500 schoolchildren, almost all Protestant, had seen the film in Düsseldorf—in spite of massive Protestant promotion.[90]

Unable to alter the decision of the state authorities, Wilhelm Böhler informed Ehlers that the Church was no longer going to exercise its self-imposed restraint because of what was transpiring in Düsseldorf.[91] Ehlers accordingly commissioned his secretary to investigate the controversy. He learned that Protestants had not responded at all to the classroom showing of the Catholic films *The Song of Bernadette* and *Monsieur Vincent*, even though Protestant schoolchildren had been taken to both.[92] Ehlers too opted to defer to local authorities, having learned that *Martin Luther* was being seen "overwhelmingly" by Protestants in the schools. As he explained to Konrad Adenauer, it was a matter of fairness.[93] He could understand why the Catholic Church would insist on not allowing its pupils to attend *Martin Luther*; but it was unjust that the Church would seek to bar Protestant schoolchildren from viewing it in confessionally closed screenings.

Ehlers also bore the wrath of Protestants convinced that he had been too appeasing of Catholic sentiment. After stating at a church meeting that

"Luther is causing the politician headaches here in Germany," Ehlers was confronted by a visibly angered Lilje. According to Carl Mau, an American Lutheran pastor and member of Lutheran Film Productions, Inc., Lilje had a "conference with him on the subject" and told him some of the "facts of life."[94] Ehlers responded by publishing a more favorable commentary on *Martin Luther* in Lilje's weekly newspaper, the *Sonntagsspiegel*.[95] With obvious satisfaction, Mau reported back to New York, "That's a slight over-simplification—but I thought you'd be happy to hear that Ehlers is now for Luther!"[96] This was an overstatement, if not wishful thinking, for Ehlers did not laud the film. He merely noted that its depictions of the religious situation in the early sixteenth century were more accurate than the film's Catholic critics would have it. Its portrait of Church corruption was, in fact, identical to that of Joseph Lortz's monumental history of the Reformation: it "could have been filmed according to Lortz," he told Adenauer.[97] To underscore the point, Ehlers provided his readers with four extensive quotations from Lortz's twin tomes that highlighted the corruption and primitive forms of popular piety of the late medieval era. The ultimate points of division, Ehlers concluded, were not historical but theological. If the film succeeded in launching a dialogue on these crucial questions, it would have served its purpose. It seems that Lortz agreed. Less than six months after the film premiere, Henry Endress quoted him saying that the film was "accurate," his earlier criticisms notwithstanding.[98]

What was the significance of the controversy over *Martin Luther*? The decision to promote and release this film represented the attempt to resurrect a confessional Protestant identity in a political culture unexpectedly dominated by Catholics. It proved to be a potent short-term confessional irritant because it touched on the hot-button issues that had been at the heart of Catholic-Protestant tensions since the *Kulturkampf*: the role of the state in fostering culture, supervising education, enacting state censorship, and promoting confessional parity. Disputes over screenings in religiously mixed schools thus provided fuel for ongoing controversies over whether German schools could and should be religiously segregated. These disputes erupted just months after *Martin Luther*'s German release with a series of highly publicized school strikes in Lower Saxony that resulted in federal litigation later that year.[99]

Releasing *Martin Luther* thus forced a series of meetings and correspondence between the highest-ranking West German political and religious authorities, including Hermann Ehlers, Konrad Adenauer, Wilhelm Boehler, Cardinal Josef Frings, the chairman of the Fulda Bishops Conference, Lilje, and Meiser. But what distinguished this controversy from other confessional conflicts was the fact that the film did not destroy the "confessional peace." Why did this prove the case? For one, religious leaders ultimately exercised restraint. Catholic protests were few, even though the film enjoyed record numbers of mostly Protestant viewers. But many attended, it turns out, not because of the urgings of the Lutheran clergy but because they were going to the cinema anyway. For another, Catholics and Protestants found a common enemy: American superficiality.

In spite of this common ground, Catholic and Protestant theologians found fault separately. This was because their theologies continued to remain far apart on key questions. It would indeed take many decades before Catholics and Protestants with confessional obligations to uphold would find agreement on the questions of justification, salvation, and Church abuses at the heart of the film. Lilje himself had no illusions about ecumenism: "Don't kid yourself about the difficulty of confessional dialogue in Germany."[100]

But Protestants could also not agree about the film, and this too should not surprise. *Martin Luther*'s champions like Lilje were Lutherans, not Reformed or United Protestants whose theological heritages were not as dependent upon the Wittenberg reformer. Lutherans were a minority among German Protestants, and Lilje's attempt to reassert Lutheran orthodoxy was hardly sustainable. But *Martin Luther*'s opponents also included Protestant Church historians who, independently echoing criticisms of Lortz, were troubled by its theological simplifications and historical distortions. Though not in any way an ecumenical vanguard, they heralded a "Zwischenprotestantismus" determined to move away from a past they deemed a hindrance.

The growing tide of ecumenical engagement, critical self-reflection, theological innovation and secularism rendered the fervent defense of *Martin Luther* and the real Martin Luther anachronistic. As confessional identities faded, tensions abated. By the time of the five hundredth anniversary of the Lutheran Reformation in 2017, many German Protestant leaders saw the events of the 1510s and 1520s as tragic and avoidable. Lortz would have been proud: there was no longer the need for commemorations arising out of confessional animus.

Mark Edward Ruff is Professor of History at Saint Louis University. He is the coeditor of three volumes on Christianity and Catholicism in the nineteenth and twentieth centuries and the author of two monographs, including *The Battle for the Catholic Past in Germany, 1945–1980* (Cambridge University Press, 2017). He has received research fellowships from the American Council of Learned Societies (ACLS), the National Endowment of the Humanities (NEH), and the Alexander-von-Humboldt Stiftung.

Notes

1. For existing scholarly publications on the film, see: Esther Pia Wipfler, *The Image of Martin Luther in Motion Pictures: History of a Metamorphosis* (Göttingen: Vandenhoeck & Ruprecht, 2011), 48–50, 79–112; Dan Chuytin, "'A Remarkable Adventure': Martin Luther and the 1950s Religious Marketplace," *Cinema Journal* 52, no. 3 (2013): 25–48; Esther Pia Wipfler, "Die vielen Gesichter Martin Luther im Kino. Ein Beitrag über das Verhältnis der evangelischen Kirche zum Medium Film," in *Kulturelle Wirkungen der Reformation*, ed. Klaus Fitschen, Marianne Schröter, Christopher Spehr, and Ernst-Joachim Waschke (Leipzig: Evangelische Verlagsanstalt, 2018), 105–15.

2. Catholic University Archives, Records of the Communications Department/Office of Film and Broadcasting, Box 83, Folder 34, Reverend Thomas Little, Executive Secretary, to the Most Reverend Matthew F. Brady, 6 October 1953.

3. Esther Pia Wipfler, *Martin Luther in Motion Pictures*, 118.

4. Historisches Archiv des Erzbistums Köln (HAEK), CR II 2.19,13, Protokoll der Beratungen auf dem Konveniat der westdeutschen Bischöfe in Pützchen vom 15.-17. März 1954.

5. Landeskirchliches Archiv, Hanover (LKA), L3 IIII/1348, Werner Hess, Tätigkeitsbericht des Filmbeauftragten der Evangelischen Kirche in Deutschland für die Jahre 1953 und 1954, 31 December 1954.

6. LKA, D 15, VII, A., No. 30, Vermerk, Betr.: Besprechung mit Landesbischof Dr. H. Lilje über den Start des Lutherfilms in Deutschland, 26 January 1954.

7. Richard O. Johnson, *Changing World, Changeless Christ: The American Lutheran Publicity Bureau, 1914–2014* (Delhi, NY: ALPB Books, 2018), 159–64.

8. Ibid., 160.

9. ELCA Archives, Elk Grove Village, IL (ELCA Archives), LFA 0/8/2, Correspondence, 1950–1962, Box 1, Folder: Introductory and Explanatory, 1950–1954. Paul C. Empie to William G. Fisher, Lutheran Brotherhood, 15 December 1950.

10. Ibid.

11. Bastiaan Bouwman, "From Religious Freedom to Social Justice: The Human Rights Engagement of the Ecumenical Movement from the 1940s to the 1970s," *Journal of Global History* 13 (2018): 252–73.

12. ELCA Archives, LFA 0/8/2, Correspondence, 1950–1962, Box 1, Preface to Reader, Henry Endress, 24 March 1952.

13. *Martin Luther*, directed by Irving Pichel (1953; Minneapolis, MN: De Rochement/Lutheran Film Productions), DVD.

14. ELCA Archives, LFA 0/8/2, Correspondence, 1950–1962, Box 1, Preface to Reader, Henry Endress, 24 March 1952.

15. ELCA Archives, LFA 08/2, Correspondence, 1950–1962, Box 1, Folder: General, 1954, Henry Endress to Johannes Stuhlmacher, 21 April 1954; Joseph Lortz, *Die Reformation in Deutschland*, 2 volumes (Freiburg: Herder Verlag, 1949).

16. ELCA Archives, LFA 08/2, Correspondence, 1950–1962, Box 1, Folder: General, 1954, Henry Endress to Johannes Stuhlmacher, 21 April 1954.

17. ELCA Archives, LFA 08/2, Correspondence, 1950–1962, Folder: Production, 1951–1958, Report of Dr. Oswald Hoffmann and Henry Endress Re: Production of the Luther Film, 27–28 October 1952.

18. For one of many examples: ELCA Archives, LFA 09/2, Correspondence, 1950–1952, Box 1, Folder: LFA Productions, Martin Luther, Correspondence, Introductory and Explanatory, 1950–1954, Henry Endress to Robert Geisendorfer, Evangelischer Presseverband fuer Bayern, Munich, 9 July 1952.

19. LKA, D 15 VII, A. No. 30, Hans Meiser to Oswald Hoffmann, 21 January 1953; Hans Meiser to Paul Empie, 3 February 1953.

20. Thomas Sauer, "Der Kronberger Kreis: Christlic-Konservative Positionen in der Bundesrepublik Deutschland," in *Katholiken und Protestanten in den Aufbaujahren der Bundesrepublik*, ed. Thomas Sauer (Stuttgart: Kohlhammer Verlag, 2000), 121–47 and especially 124–28. See also: Emmet E. Eklund and Marion Lorimer Eklund, *He Touched the Whole World: The Story of Carl E. Lund-Quist* (Bethany: Bethany College Press, 1990), 10–11.

21. Thomas Sauer, *Westorientierung im deutschen Protestantismus? Vorstellungen und Tätigkeit des Kronberger Kreises* (Munich: Oldenbourg, 1999).

22. Mark Edward Ruff, *The Battle for the Catholic Past in Germany, 1945–1980* (Cambridge, UK: Cambridge University Press, 2017), 69–71.

23. Hessisches Hauptstaatsarchiv, Wiesbaden (HHSTA), 502-6279; Lilje as quoted in Matthäus Ziegler, "Gültigkeit und Zweckmäßigkeit des Reichskonkordats," *Stimme der Gemeinde zum kirchlichen Leben, zur Politik, Wirtschaft und Kultur*, Sonderheft, March 1956, 1.

24. LKA, L3 1111/1134, Hans Lillje to Herr Amtsbruder, 3 February 1954; EZAB, Bestand: 87, Nr. 1178, 08.1959—09.1962, Lilje to Herr Amtsbruder, no date, but probably late February 1954.

25. EZAB, Bestand: 87, Nr. 1178, 08.1959—09.1962, Lilje to Herr Amtsbruder, no date, but probably late February 1954.

26. ELCA Archives, LFA 08/2, Lutheran Film Associations, Box 1, Paul Empie to Henry Endress, 30 July 1951; LKA Hanover L3 III/435, Henry Endress to Hanns Lilje, 25 September 1952.

27. EZB, Bestand: 87, Nr. 1178, 08.1959-09.1962, Hanns Lilje to Herr Amtsbruder, no date, but most likely late February or early March 1954.

28. ELCA Archives, ULCA, Office of the President, Franklin Clark Fry Papers, 1945–1962, Box 41, Folder: Luther Film Committee 1951–1952, pt. 2 of 2, Paul Empie to Franklin Clark Fry, 8 November 1950.

29. Esther Pia Wipfler, *Martin Luther in Motion Pictures*, 50–55; Heide Fehrenbach, *Cinema in Democratizing Germany: Reconstructing National Identity after Hitler* (Chapel Hill: University of North Carolina Press, 1995), 293, n25; ELCA Archives, LFA 08/2, Correspondence, 1950–1952, Box 1, Folder: LFA Productions, Martin Luther, Correspondence, Introductory and Explanatory, 1950–1964, Lothar Wolff to Henry Endress, 27 February 1953.

30. ELCA Archives, LFA 08/2, Correspondence, 1950–1962, Box 1, Folder: Introductory and Explanatory, 1950–1954, Production of the Luther Film by Lothar Wolff.

31. Lutheran Hour Archives, Report of Henry Endress and Oswald C.J. Hoffmann, no date.

32. Ibid.

33. Ibid.

34. "Vergessen Sie Hollywood," *Der Spiegel* 39/1952, 24 September 1952.

35. LKA, DI5, VII, A, No. 30, KNA, Pressedienst, Nr. 210 vom 17. September 1953, Lutherfilm abgelehnt: Unannehmbare Theologische und Historische Darstellung.

36. LKA, D15, X, No. 4689, Vermerk, Besprechung über den Film "MARTIN LUTHER" auf der Bischofskonferenz der Vereinigten Lutherischen Kriche in Deutschland am 30. 9. 53 in Tutzing.

37. LKA, D15 XI Nr. A-2442, Johannes Stuhlmacher to Henry Endress, 15 February 1954 (German original).

38. Ibid.

39. LKA, D15X I Nr. A-2442, Hans Ketterfeld to Franklin C. Fry, 15 February 1954.

40. "'Martin Luther' kommt in die deutschen Kinos: Die Lutherische Bischofskonferenz betrachtet kritisch den erfolgreichen amerikanischen Spielfilm," *Süddeutsche Zeitung*, 2 October 1953.

41. Archiv der FSK, Luther-Film-Gesellschaft, Protokoll der Prüfungssitzung des Arbeitsausschusses vom 4.12.1953, 2–3.

42. Ibid., 2; HAEK, Gen II 23.33.11, Kirchliche Hauptstelle für Bild-und Filmarbeit to the H.H.Erzbischöfe und Bischöfe der deutschen Diözesen, 14 December 1953.

43. Lortz was actually the second choice; the first choice, Prof. Karl Schmidt of the Department of Catholic Theology at the University of Mainz, was already a member of the committee. LKA Hanover, D 1 5 VII, A, No. 30, Betr: Prüfung des Films MARTIN LUTHER durch die Freiwillinge Selbstkontrolle der Filmwirtschaft. The other was Prof. Gerber. For more on Lortz, see Chapter 5 by James Chappel in this volume.

44. See Joseph Lortz, *Die Reformation in Deutschland*, 2 vols.

45. Archiv der FSK, Luther-Film-Gesellschaft, Protokoll der Prüfungssitzung des Arbeitsausschusses vom 4.12.1953, 2–3.

46. Ibid.

47. ELCA Archives, LFA 0/8/5, Publicity Program File, 1951–1960, Box 2, Folder: Rebuttal to Catholic Criticisms, n.d. 1951, On the Motion Picture Martin Luther, by Father Joseph Lortz, no date.

48. Ibid.

49. LKA, D 15 VII, A, No. 30, Betr: Prüfung des Films MARTIN LUTHER durch die Freiwillinge Selbstkontrolle der Filmwirtschaft.

50. ELCA Archives, LFA 0/8/6, Foreign Distribution Correspondence, Agreements, 1953–1958, Carl Lundquist to Henry Endress, 5 March 1954.

51. LKA, L 3 IIII/1134, Henry Endress to Johannes Stuhlmacher, 4 February 1954; for an angrier reaction, see D15 VII, A, No. 30 Henry Endress to Hans Katterfeld, 23 February 1954.

52. LKA, D15 VII, A, No. 30, Werner Hess to Johannes Stuhlmacher, 9 February 1954. It was unclear who these American Catholic opponents were, however.

53. LKA, D15 XII, A., 2442, Johannes Stuhlmacher to Henry Endress, 15 February 1954.

54. Evangelisches Zentralarchiv in Berlin (EZAB), Bestand: 87, Nr. 1178, 08.-1959 09.1962, Hanns Rückert to Unnamed (Dr. Johannes Stuhlmacher), no date, but probably late February 1954.

55. Ibid.

56. EZAB, Bestand: 87, Nr. 1178, Hanns Rückert to D. Kunst, 3 March 1954.

57. LKA, D15 VII, A, No. 30, Vermerk: Betr.: Besprechung mit Landesbischof Dr. D. Lilje über den Start des Lutherfilms in Deutschland, 26 January 1954. On the commission were Dr. Hübner, Pfarrer Geisendörfer, Hans Katterfeld, Stuhlmacher, and a secretary.

58. LKA, F15 VII, A. No. 30, Hans Katterfeld to Dekan W. Schwinn, 1 January 1954.

59. LKA, D15, VII, A. No. 30, W. Schwinn to Hans Katterfeld, 29 January 1954.

60. Ibid.

61. LKA, D15, VII, A. No. 30, Johannes Stuhlmacher, Bericht des Geschäftsführers (manager) über die Tätigkeit der Luther-Film-G.m.b.H. vom 1.4.1953—10.3.1954, 12 March 1954, 5.

62. Torsten Oppelland, "Der evangelische Arbeitskreis der CDU/CSU, 1952–1969," *Historisch-Politische Mitteilungen* 5, no. 1 (1998): 105–44 and especially 111–12; Gerhard Besier, "'Christliche Parteipolitik' und Konfession: Zur Entstehung des Evangelischen Arbeitskreises der CDU/CSU, *Kirchliche Zeitgeschichte* 3, no. 1 (1990): 166–87 and especially 171–75.

63. LKA, D15, VII, A. No. 30, Johannes Stuhlmacher, Bericht des Geschäftsführers (manager) über die Tätigkeit der Luther-Film-G.m.b.H. vom 1.4.1953—10.3.1954, March 12, 1954, 5.

64. M.B., "Brüderliches Gespräch der Konfessionen: Eine evangelisch-katholische Diskussion um den Lutherfilm," *Rheinischer Merkur*, 12 March 1954.

65. Ibid.

66. See Rüdiger Wenzel, ed., *Hermann Ehlers: Präsident des Deutschen Bundestages. Ausgewählte Erden, Aufsätze und Briefe, 1950–1954* (Boppard: Harald Boldt Verlag, 1991), 4–6.

67. Ibid., 14.

68. Hermann Ehlers, "6. Oktober 1954: Aufgaben und Grenzen der Zusammenarbeit der Konfessionen in der Politik," in Wenzel, *Hermann Ehlers*, 348–62.
69. LKA, D15, VII, A. No. 30, Johannes Stuhlmacher, Bericht des Geschäftsführers (manager) über die Tätigkeit der Luther-Film-G.m.b.H. vom 1.4.1953—10.3.1954, 12 March 1954, 6.
70. M.B., "Brüderliches Gespräch der Konfessionen."
71. Archiv für Christliche-Demokratische Politik (ACDP), NL Hermann Ehlers, 01-369: 010/3, Hermann Ehlers to Heinrich Höfler, 11 March 1954.
72. M.B., "Brüderliches Gespräch der Konfessionen"; ACDP, NL Ehlers, 01-369: 010/3, Wilhelm Böhler to Hermann Ehlers, 24 April 1954.
73. LKA, D15, VII, A. No. 30, Johannes Stuhlmacher, Bericht des Geschäftsführers (manager) über die Tätigkeit der Luther-Film-G.m.b.H. vom 1.4.1953—10.3.1954, no date.
74. Maria Mitchell, "Materialism and Secularism: CDU Politicians and National Socialism, 1945–1949," *The Journal of Modern History* 67, no. 2 (June 1995): 278–308; Heide Fehrenbach, *Cinema in Democratizing Germany*.
75. ELCA Archives, LFA 0/8/6, Foreign Distribution Correspondence, Agreements, 1953–1958, Carl Lundquist to Henry Endress, 5 March 1954.
76. Ibid.
77. Ibid.
78. Ibid.
79. HAEK, Gen 23.33, 11, Sonderdruck aus "Herder-Korrespondenz" Heft 7, April 1954, Martin Luther, Made in USA.
80. HAEK, CR II 2.19, 13, Protokoll der Beratungen auf dem Konveniat der westdeutschen Bischöfe in Pützchen vom 15.-17. March 1954.
81. M.B. "Brüderliches Gespräch der Konfesesionen."
82. J.O. Zöller, "Lutherfilm lichtet die Fronten," *Deutsche Tagespost*, 17 March 1954.
83. HAEK, Gen II 23.33.11, Kirchliche Hauptstelle für Bild-und Filmarbeit to the H.H.Erzbischöfe und Bischöfe der deutschen Diözesen, 14 December 1953.
84. ELCA Archives, LFA 08/2, Correspondence, 1950–1962, Box 1, Folder: General, Henry Endress to Johannes Stuhlmacher, 21 April 1954; HAEK, Gen II 23.33.11, Stadt Düsseldorf, Der Oberstadtdirektor to the Erzbischöfliches Generalvikariat, Cologne, 12 May 1954.
85. ACDP, NL Hermann Ehlers, 01-369: 010/3, *Leseproben als Steiflichter, Das Evangelische Düsseldorf*, May 1954; HAEK, Gen II 23.33.11, Der Oberstadtdirektor der Stadt Düsseldorf to the Erzbischöfliches Generalvikariat, Cologne, 12 April 1954.
86. HAEK, Gen II 23.33.11, Der Oberstadtdirektor der Stadt Düsseldorf to the Erzbischöfliches Generalvikariat, Cologne, 12 April 1954.
87. HAEK, Dienstakten Böhler (DA), 161, Abschrift, Kirchlcicher Anzeiger der Erzdiözese Köln, Nr. 11, vom 22.4, 1954, Bekanntmachungen des Erzbischöflichen Generalvikariates, Nr. 191, Betr.: Martin-Luther Film.
88. M.B., "Brüderliches Gespräch der Konfessionen."
89. HAEK, Gen II 23.33.11, Der Kultusminister des Landes Nordrhein-Westfalen to das Erzbischöfliches Generalvikariat, Köln, 12 June 1954.
90. HAEK, Gen II 23.33.11, Josef Frings to Aloyisius Muench, 17 April 1954.
91. ACDP, NL Ehlers, 01-369: 010/3, Wilhelm Böhler to Hermann Ehlers, 24 April 1954.
92. ACDP, NL Ehlers, 01-369: 010/3, Vermerk, 28 April 1954; Oberkirchenrat Rößler to Schramm, 10 May 1954.
93. ACDP, NL Ehlers, 01-369: 3/1, Hermann Ehlers to Konrad Adenauer, 1 May 1954.
94. ELCA Archives, LFA 08/2, Correspondence, 1950–1952, Box 2, Folder: Correspondence, Reaction of Catholics to Film, 1953–1959, 1962, Carl Mau to Borden Mace, 20 April 1954.
95. Hermann Ehlers, "Die Debatte um den Lutherfilm," *Sonntagsspiegel*, 11 April 1954.

96. ELCA Archives, LFA 08/2, Correspondence, 1950–1952, Box 2, Folder: Correspondence, Reaction of Catholics to Film, 1953–1959, 1962, Carl Mau to Borden Mace, 20 April 1954.
97. ACDP, NL Ehlers, 01-369: 3/1, Hermann Ehlers to Konrad Adenauer, 1 May 1954.
98. ELCA Archives, LFA 08/2, Productions, Martin Luther, Correspondence, 1950–1962, Box 1, Folder: LFA Productions, Martin Luther, Correspondence, Lutheran Church in America, n.d. 1952–1955, Henry Endress to Robert E.A. Lee, 5 November 1954.
99. Ruff, *The Battle for the Catholic Past in Germany*, 70.
100. LKA, D 15, VII, A., No. 30, Vermerk, Betr.: Besprechung mit Landesbischof Dr. H. Lilje über den Start des Lutherfilms in Deutschland, 26 January 1954.

Bibliography

Besier, Gerhard. "'Christliche Parteipolitik' und Konfession: Zur Entstehung des Evangelischen Arbeitskreises der CDU/CSU." *Kirchliche Zeitgeschichte* 3, no. 1 (1990): 166–87.
Bouwman, Bastiaan. "From Religious Freedom to Social Justice: The Human Rights Engagement of the Ecumenical Movement from the 1940s to the 1970s." *Journal of Global History* 13 (2018): 252–73.
Chuytin, Dan. "'A Remarkable Adventure': Martin Luther and the 1950s Religious Marketplace." *Cinema Journal* 52, no. 3 (2013): 25–48.
Eklund, Emmet E., and Marion Lorimer Eklund. *He Touched the Whole World: The Story of Carl. E. Lund-Quist*. Bethany: Bethany College Press, 1990.
Fehrenbach, Heide. *Cinema in Democratizing Germany: Reconstructing National Identity after Hitler*. Chapel Hill: University of North Carolina Press, 1995.
Johnson, Richard O. *Changing World, Changeless Christ: The American Lutheran Publicity Bureau, 1914–2014*. Delhi, NY: ALPB Books, 2018.
Lortz, Joseph. *Die Reformation in Deutschland*, 2 vols. Freiburg: Herder Verlag, 1949.
Mitchell, Maria. "Materialism and Secularism: CDU Politicians and National Socialism, 1945– 1949." *The Journal of Modern History* 67, no. 2 (1995): 278–308.
Oppelland, Torsten. "Der evangelische Arbeitskreis der CDU/CSU, 1952–1969." *Historisch-Politische Mitteilungen* 5, no. 1 (1998): 105–44.
Pichel, Irving, dir. *Martin Luther*. 1953; Minneapolis, MN: De Rochement/Lutheran Film Productions. DVD.
Ruff, Mark Edward. *The Battle for the Catholic Past in Germany, 1945–1980*. Cambridge, UK: Cambridge University Press, 2017.
Sauer, Thomas. "Der Kronberger Kreis: Christlic-Konservative Positionen in der Bundesrepublik Deutschland." In *Katholiken und Protestanten in den Aufbaujahren der Bundesrepublik*, edited by Thomas Sauer, 121–47. Stuttgart: Kohlhammer Verlag, 2000.
———. *Westorientierung im deutschen Protestantismus? Vorstellungen und Tätigkeit des Kronberger Kreises*. Munich: Oldenbourg, 1999.
Wenzel, Rüdiger, ed. *Hermann Ehlers: Präsident des Deutschen Bundestages. Ausgewählte Erden, Aufsätze und Briefe, 1950–1954*. Boppard: Harald Boldt Verlag, 1991.
Wipfler, Esther Pia. "Die vielen Gesichter Martin Luther im Kino. Ein Beitrag über das Verhältnis der evangelischen Kirche zum Medium Film." In *Kulturelle Wirkungen der Reformation*, edited by Klaus Fitschen, Marianne Schröter, Christopher Spehr, and Ernst-Joachim Waschke, 105–15. Leipzig: Evangelische Verlagsanstalt, 2018.
———. *The Image of Martin Luther in Motion Pictures: History of a Metamorphosis*. Göttingen: Vandenhoeck & Ruprecht, 2011.

Chapter Nine

IN THE PRESENCE OF ABSENCE

Transformations of the Confessional Divide in West Germany after the Holocaust

Brandon Bloch

"Precisely at the moment that there is the greatest interest in Germany for Christian-Jewish dialogue, there are the fewest Jewish dialogue partners."[1] Writing in 1969, the Dominican priest Willehad Paul Eckert captured the tragic irony of West German initiatives toward Christian-Jewish cooperation after the Holocaust. From a German-Jewish population of over five hundred thousand in 1933, the Jewish community in West Germany numbered just 21,499 by the late 1950s, once the Jewish Displaced Persons who poured into Allied-occupied Germany's refugee camps migrated onward to Israel or the United States.[2] Before a new wave of post-Soviet immigration in the 1990s, the Jewish community's membership would reach only 28,000, mostly Jews of East European origin without ties to prewar German Jewry.[3] The postwar Protestant and Catholic churches, by contrast, reconstructed themselves as powerful institutions representing millions of West Germans. Following centuries of adversity, Protestants and Catholics founded Germany's first interdenominational political party, cooperated to shape the West German welfare state and educational system, and by the late 1960s had largely abandoned confessional polemics.

Historians of West Germany have attributed the remarkable process of Catholic-Protestant reconciliation to the churches' common front against new Cold War antagonists—secularism, Communism, or political Islam.[4] Yet as Eckert's remark reminds us, the confessional divide in postwar West Germany was never reduced to a Catholic-Protestant binary. In light of the theological proximity between Judaism and Christianity, as well as the ambiguous—often highly compromised—role of the churches during the Nazi period, Jewish absence hung over Catholic-Protestant encounters as a spectral presence. Examining how West German Catholics and Protestants confronted the question of Christian-Jewish relations after the Holocaust, this chapter contends that efforts toward Christian-Jewish dialogue played a crucial role in the amelioration of intra-Christian tensions. New initiatives toward Christian-Jewish cooperation reshaped interconfessional dynamics despite the fact that—and even because—such initiatives fell short of including Jews as equal partners.[5]

The shifting contours of Christian-Jewish dialogue in West Germany reflected generational and political transformations of the postwar decades. In the first years after 1945, as the official Protestant and Catholic churches competed to whitewash their records under National Socialism, proponents of Christian-Jewish dialogue within each confession, often themselves victims of Nazi persecution, set out to address the legacies of Christian anti-Judaism. It was only in the 1960s, as one-time dissidents gained influence at high ranks of their confessions, that West Germany's Protestant and Catholic churches pressured one another to abandon longstanding antisemitic prejudices and adopt theological reforms. The Arab-Israeli War of 1967 marked a turning point, bringing together Catholics and Protestants in defense of Israel while drawing new lines of conflict between participants in Christian-Jewish dialogue and emergent anti-Zionist currents on the Left. In the following decade, organizers of Christian-Jewish dialogue gained increasing influence in the political mainstream, as generational change, international relations, and media events of the 1970s lent credence to their efforts to promote Christian Zionism and Holocaust memory. By the 1980s, Catholics and Protestants, church leaders and interfaith activists alike, jointly championed reconciliation with Jews, support for Israel, and critical engagement with the Nazi past as pillars of German identity.

Yet across the postwar decades, the transformative impact of Christian-Jewish dialogue remained limited by the relative absence of Jewish participants. Postwar initiatives toward Christian-Jewish cooperation largely succeeded in uprooting antisemitic stereotypes from Christian theology and initiating a culture of Holocaust memory in West Germany. But following the destruction of European Jewry, and before the onset of political debate about rising Muslim immigration, participants could avoid the challenge of creating a multireligious society in practice. The circumscribed embrace of religious pluralism by Germany's Christian churches leaves an ambiguous legacy for an age when religious diversity on the ground far surpasses that of the postwar era.

An Inauspicious Beginning

Traces of the Holocaust permeated Protestant-Catholic interactions in Allied-occupied Germany even before the institutional formation of Christian-Jewish dialogue. Concerned with protecting their own reputations and exercising political influence over Germany's postwar reconstruction, leaders in both confessions jockeyed to exonerate their churches for their role in the Nazi cataclysm. A competitive dynamic emerged already in the statements on guilt released by the Catholic Fulda Bishops Conference and the newly founded Protestant Church in Germany (Evangelische Kirche in Deutschland, EKD) in the months after the war. While the Catholic statement of August 1945 acknowledged only individual, not collective or institutional, guilt for Nazi crimes, the EKD Council issued a statement at its October meeting in Stuttgart announcing the Protestant Church's "solidarity of guilt" with the German people.[6] Yet far from inaugurating a critical examination of the Nazi era, Protestant leaders used the Stuttgart Declaration as an alibi to launch scathing attacks on the Allied denazification and war crimes trials programs.[7] Even as they cooperated to undermine Allied occupation policies, Catholics and Protestants did not refrain from indicting their counterparts for furnishing the ideological foundations of Nazism. Catholic politicians including Konrad Adenauer, the chair of the interconfessional Christian Democratic Union, highlighted the culpability of Protestant-Prussian authoritarianism.[8] Conversely, in correspondence with the EKD Synod, one Protestant pastor castigated Joseph Goebbels's "Jesuit" conviction that "the ends justify the means."[9]

In the shadow of the Holocaust, the work of reckoning with the long legacy of Christian antisemitism instead took place outside the power centers of Germany's Protestant and Catholic hierarchies. The pioneers of Christian-Jewish dialogue were individuals at the margins of their respective churches who often had engaged in wartime resistance, several risking their own lives. Of the Catholics, the Freiburg social worker Gertrud Luckner figured among the most prominent. Under the auspices of the Caritas Association, Luckner had worked as a "courier" smuggling Jews over the Swiss border and transmitting messages about impending deportations, before her 1943 arrest and imprisonment at Ravensbrück.[10] Luckner's postwar colleague, the historian and theologian Karl Thieme, had served as editor of the Catholic oppositional journal *Junge Front* and fled Nazi Germany for Switzerland in 1935, continuing to press the Vatican to speak out against attacks on German Jews.[11] Their Protestant counterparts were frequently veterans of the radical splinter wing of the Nazi-era Confessing Church. Several, including the jurist Adolf Freudenberg and Lutheran pastor

Helmut Gollwitzer, had belonged to the resistance network around Dietrich Bonhoeffer, among the only theologians in Nazi Germany to call for Christian solidarity with Jews.[12] Wartime resistance circles cut across confessional lines, fostering postwar steps toward ecumenical dialogue. Luckner undertook her rescue efforts in cooperation with the Protestant pastor Heinrich Grüber and Berlin's Chief Rabbi Leo Baeck.[13] Thieme and his longtime collaborator, the Austrian émigré priest John Oesterreicher, were converts to Catholicism from Protestantism and Judaism, respectively.[14]

The minority of Catholics and Protestants who sought out a new approach to Jews in the immediate postwar years confronted a set of interlocking challenges: the intransigence of church hierarchies, the paucity of Jewish dialogue partners, and antisemitic preconceptions shared even by advocates of good-faith discussion. Within the EKD, the first pastors to promote outreach to Jews after 1945 were veterans of the prewar Protestant mission to the Jews, which continued to operate—albeit with scant success—in displaced persons camps across Allied-occupied Germany. The first official EKD organization dedicated to dialogue with Jews, the German Protestant Committee for Service to Israel, invited Jewish leaders to speak at its annual conferences but maintained close ties to missionary organizations. The Committee's director, the Lutheran theologian Karl Heinrich Rengstorf, was himself a founder of the reconstituted postwar *Judenmission* alongside Adolf Freudenberg. The EKD Synod's 1950 "Statement on the Jewish Question," on which Rengstorf's Committee exerted a "decisive influence," reflected this ambivalence. The statement recognized the ongoing validity of "God's promise . . . for his Chosen People," while continuing to look toward the ultimate salvation of Jews in the cross.[15]

Catholic proponents of Christian-Jewish dialogue faced an equally daunting task, with the Catholic hierarchy in Germany even more reluctant to address the postwar Christian-Jewish relationship. Frustrated with the limits of official statements, the circle of Freiburg Catholic intellectuals around Gertrud Luckner and Karl Thieme founded the *Newsletter of the Friends of the Old and New People of God* (*Freiburger Rundbrief*) to promote interreligious dialogue.[16] Even as they condemned racial antisemitism and decried the narrow scope of their Church's pronouncements, however, members of the Catholic Freiburg Circle shared missionary assumptions with their Protestant counterparts. A statement submitted by Luckner and Thieme to the 1948 *Katholikentag* in Mainz prayed for "the surely promised homecoming of the entire Jewish people."[17] The very language of the "Old and New People of God" reflected a supersessionist teleology that the journal would later abandon.

Despite these divergent institutional settings, fault lines in the origins of Christian-Jewish dialogue ran less along confession than between proponents of a new approach to Jews and conservative leaders within each church. Authorities in the US occupation zone played a role in linking Catholic and Protestant efforts via the National Conference of Christians and Jews (NCCJ), the American interfaith organization whose representatives helped form the first Societies for Christian-Jewish Cooperation in Munich, Stuttgart, and Wiesbaden during the late 1940s.[18] Nevertheless, the American influence should not be overstated. By 1952, the newly formed West German state had taken over the financing of local Societies for Christian-Jewish Cooperation, now also established in Frankfurt and Berlin, as well as the national-level Coordinating Council.[19] Furthermore, Catholic and Protestant activists themselves forged interconfessional networks. Luckner and Thieme distributed the *Freiburger Rundbrief* to Protestant regional churches, and the journal reported regularly on the German Protestant Committee for Service to Israel.[20] Local Societies for Christian-Jewish Cooperation were each led by one Protestant, one Catholic, and one Jewish director.

The first major statement issued by the Societies for Christian-Jewish Cooperation, concluded at a joint Catholic-Protestant conference held at the Hessian town of Bad Schwalbach in the summer of 1950, reflected both the extent and limitations of postwar Christian reorientation. Distributed to twenty-five thousand religion teachers and clergy members across West Germany, the Schwalbach statement called for wide-ranging reforms in Christian religious education. The drafters, who included Adolf Freudenberg, Karl Thieme, and the Confessing Church pastor Martin Niemöller, opened the document by deploring the "ignominious failure" of the "great majority" of Christians during the "systematic mass murder of European Jewry." Jews did not worship a "different God" from Christians, nor did they bear "collective guilt" for the death of Jesus. Yet the Schwalbach statement also testified to Thieme's belief that conversion remained the ultimate goal of Jewish-Christian encounters. It affirmed the Jewishness of Jesus not to acknowledge the autonomy of the Jewish faith, but to present a Christianized version of Judaism itself. Christians should demonstrate love toward Jews precisely in emulating the love of Jesus for "his own people"; Jews alongside "heathens" were ultimately reconciled in the Church of Jesus Christ. "God," the document concluded, "promises Yes to Jesus as the final word of the Jews' history."[21]

Similar expressions of supersessionism repackaged as philosemitism were commonplace in Christian statements on Jews during the early 1950s. Christian proponents of interconfessional dialogue frequently invoked Jews toward their own purposes, whether as witnesses to Christian salvation or paragons of "German culture." At the annual "Week of Brotherhood," organized by the Societies for Christian-Jewish Cooperation beginning in

1952, complex realities of the Holocaust were reduced to stereotypes: the story of Anne Frank, the eternally suffering Jew, the promise of Christian redemption. By purporting that the problem of antisemitism could be addressed within a single week, or that "brotherhood" represented an adequate response to Nazi genocide, the speeches and ceremonies surrounding the annual event served as much to assuage as to confront German guilt. As the Jewish chair of the Berlin Society for Christian-Jewish Cooperation recognized in 1949, "A lot of speeches were given after 1945, but little has been done along practical lines. There has been little restitution for the moral and material injustices perpetrated against Jews . . . One could say that Jews in general viewed such cooperation skeptically."[22]

For all of their shortcomings, however, networks promoting Christian-Jewish dialogue raised questions of Christian responsibility toward Jews that most West Germans in the 1950s preferred to ignore. Both the *Katholikentag* and the Protestant Committee for Service to Israel petitioned the West German government to recognize the state of Israel, and the economist Franz Böhm, the Protestant chair of the Society for Christian-Jewish Cooperation in Frankfurt, served as the lead negotiator in the reparations treaty concluded between the two countries in 1952.[23] Karl Thieme organized a series of triconfessional conferences during the 1950s that addressed the interdependence of Catholic-Protestant and Christian-Jewish ecumenism. According to one participant, "We cannot even begin to approach the schism in the Church of Jesus Christ if we do not understand the division of Jews and Christians as the foundational schism of the people of God."[24] Such a statement still looked toward the ultimate reunion of Jews and Christians, but the inclusion of Jews among the "people of God" refuted tropes of their divine abandonment.

Most significantly, the Societies for Christian-Jewish Cooperation opened a practical space for Christian dialogue with Jews, who despite their underrepresentation played critical roles in fostering theological reform. The first Jewish participants derived primarily from the tiny group of German rabbis who escaped the Holocaust and returned after the war. These men were doubly outcast: viewed with suspicion in the international Jewish community for their decision to live in Germany, and culturally distant from the East European refugees who made up the majority of postwar West Germany's Jews. Among the most active was Robert Raphael Geis, who fled for Palestine in 1938 but took up a post as *Landesrabbiner* of Baden in 1952 due both to disillusionment with Zionism and his refusal to concede the end of Jewish life in Germany.[25] Although a proponent of dialogue, Geis was a sharp critic of the missionary thinking that continued to mark Christian-Jewish encounters, above all the conceit that the redemption of Jews formed the endpoint of a Christian teleology of salvation. True tolerance, Geis admonished his Christian colleagues at a 1959 conference, required "not merely patience for the other's convictions, but recognition of the reality of their beliefs."[26] Against a long history of Christian supersessionism, Geis's plea entailed a radical demand, one that would continue to provoke controversy in the ensuing decades.

Theology Transformed

By the late 1950s, Christian-Jewish interactions in West Germany had progressed from missions operating in displaced persons camps to a dense network of organizations aimed at confronting deep-rooted prejudices. Although proponents of interconfessional dialogue remained marginalized within their respective churches, the arrival of a new generation of church leaders, less tainted than their predecessors by a legacy of complicity with Nazism, would transform the relationship between the Societies for Christian-Jewish Cooperation and the Catholic and Protestant hierarchies. During the 1960s, as high-ranking clergy in both confessions amplified the work of early activists, the grounds of Catholic-Protestant competition shifted: from establishing Christian blamelessness under Nazism to exemplifying a message of repentance and reform. By the outbreak of the Arab-Israeli War in 1967, proponents of Christian-Jewish cooperation in both confessions sought to defend their views less against intransigent church leaderships than against an emergent New Left.

On the Catholic side, the death of Pope Pius XII in 1958 and the accession of Cardinal Angelo Giuseppe Roncalli, a leader of wartime Catholic rescue efforts, as Pope John XXIII marked a turning point in global Catholic-Jewish relations. Pius XII, whose own record during the Holocaust remains hotly contested, was skeptical of interfaith initiatives. The Vatican Holy Office under his papacy charged the *Freiburger Rundbrief* with "indifferentism," a shallow ecumenism that effaced the strictures of the Catholic faith.[27] The Second Vatican Council, initiated by John XXIII from his first days in office and concluded by his successor Paul VI, wiped away these barriers toward Catholic-Jewish cooperation. Although the Council modernized Catholic doctrine across theological domains, its effects were perhaps nowhere more transformative than in shifting the Church's stance toward Judaism. As the historian John Connelly has demonstrated, the Council's 1965 statement on non-Christian religions, *Nostra Aetate* (*In Our Time*), drew heavily on the work of Christian-Jewish dialogue in Germany. The German Cardinal Augustin Bea, appointed by John XXIII in 1960 to compose an initial statement on the Church's relationship to Jews, had quietly supported the publication of the *Freiburger Rundbrief* when it struggled to fend off charges of "indifferentism."[28] The Catholic theologian who composed the early drafts of *Nostra Aetate*, the Austrian émigré John Oesterreicher, was a close friend of Karl Thieme and contact of the Freiburg Circle. While still holding out the possibility of Jews' salvation in Christ, Oesterreicher's drafts rejected the charge of deicide and the myth of Jews' eternal punishment.[29] The final version of *Nostra Aetate* followed Oesterreicher's framework, invoking "the bond that spiritually ties the people of the New Covenant to Abraham's stock" and imploring that "the Jews should not be presented as rejected or accursed by God."[30]

At the same time that the papacy of John XXIII paved the way for what Connelly has termed a "revolution in Catholic teaching on the Jews," West German Protestants debated yet wider reforms, as the EKD's diffuse structure allowed dissident pastors to gain greater influence. In 1958, the EKD Synod agreed to support the Action Reconciliation Service (*Aktion Sühnezeichen*), an organization founded by the lay church official and Confessing Church veteran Lothar Kreyssig to arrange voluntary service trips of German youth to countries formerly occupied by Nazi Germany.[31] By the early 1960s, some Protestant participants sought to go beyond the supersessionist assumptions of early Christian-Jewish dialogue—that would also mark John Oesterreicher's *Nostra Aetate*—to take seriously Judaism's claim to represent an autonomous faith. A key site for these conflicts was the Working Group on "Jews and Christians" at the Protestant Lay Assembly (*Kirchentag*), founded in 1961 by the Berlin theologian and former Confessing Church pastor Helmut Gollwitzer. Gollwitzer, who had returned from postwar Soviet imprisonment to emerge as a leading critic of the Adenauer government's Cold War foreign policy, advocated for a transformation of Christian-Jewish relations, rooted in a vision of postwar atonement and reconciliation. More than appealing to common bonds, Gollwitzer believed, Christians should expose their own certainties to the standpoint of Judaism. Although *Kirchentag* organizers vetoed Gollwitzer's plan for a Jewish-led Bible study at the 1961 assembly, an address to the Working Group by Rabbi Robert Raphael Geis emphasized the mission of the Jews as God's chosen people.[32]

Ongoing interconfessional tensions as well as generational change in the Protestant churches contributed toward transformations of Christian-Jewish dialogue along the lines Gollwitzer envisioned. The 1963 premier of Rolf Hochhuth's play *The Deputy*, which depicted Pius XII as a craven enabler of Hitler, reignited confessional competition over the Christian response to Nazism. Protestant commentators, including Gollwitzer and Heinrich Grüber, addressed the controversy by criticizing Catholic "mythmaking" and calling on leaders in both confessions to resist the appeal of "self-justification."[33] The 1961 election of the ecumenical activist and former Confessing Church *Präses* Kurt Scharf as chair of the EKD Council, succeeding the unapologetic supersessionist Otto Dibelius, simultaneously fostered a reorientation within German Protestantism. Scharf shared Gollwitzer's commitment to the legitimacy of the Jewish faith, and the place of the Working Group on "Jews and Christians" at the Protestant *Kirchentag* was secured during Scharf's tenure. These trends converged with the appearance of *Nostra Aetate* in October 1965. The *Kirchentag* welcomed the Catholic condemnation of antisemitism, but Scharf regretted that the Vatican Council had stopped short of recognizing the Jewish covenant with God. Underlining the shifting grounds of intra-Christian rivalry by the mid-1960s, Scharf criticized *Nostra Aetate* for its insufficient ambition. Whereas *Nostra Aetate* referred to "the people of Israel as God's people only in the past," Scharf wrote in the *Freiburger Rundbrief*, Protestant theology had moved to acknowledge "the character of the people of God as an enduring divine institution."[34]

Transformations in the Protestant Church of the early 1960s also catalyzed expanded engagement with the state of Israel. Although Israel was not entirely neglected in the first decade of Christian-Jewish dialogue, early discussions remained largely circumscribed within theological frameworks. In his critique of *Nostra Aetate*, however, Kurt Scharf emphasized the importance of moving beyond theological reform to deepen practical cooperation between Christians and Jews.[35] During Scharf's term as EKD Council chair, Protestant pastors and lay activists emerged as prominent advocates for West German recognition of Israel, an effort that stalled due to West German leaders' fears of triggering the recognition of East Germany by Israel's Arab neighbors.[36] The *Aktion Sühnezeichen*, guided by Lothar Kreyssig's belief that forgiveness could not be demanded but only fostered through service, organized trips to Israel for West German youth beginning in 1961.[37] Helmut Gollwitzer first traveled to Israel in 1963, working for West German diplomatic recognition upon his return.[38] Although Chancellor Ludwig Erhard's decision to officially recognize Israel in May 1965 stemmed from political considerations—following the embarrassing exposure of West German armament sales to Egypt—it quickened the pace of Christian, especially Protestant, advocacy. In 1966, the Protestant biblical scholar Rolf Rendtorff founded the German Israel Society (*Deutsch-Israelische Gesellschaft*), which aimed to deepen the connections between the two countries beyond the level of elite politics.[39]

The crisis that broke out in the Middle East during the spring of 1967 brought the political convictions of West German advocates for Christian-Jewish cooperation into sharper focus, serving as a landmark in the recalibration of Catholic-Protestant relations. In the years prior, the predominately left-liberal cohort had framed its engagement with Israel as a matter of post-Nazi reconciliation, rather than partisan politics. Following his return from his 1963 visit, Gollwitzer argued for greater attention to Palestinian grievances, development cooperation between Israel and its Arab neighbors, and West German engagement in securing Middle East peace.[40] With the deployment of Egyptian troops to the Sinai Peninsula, however, the *Deutsch-Israelische Gesellschaft* and *Aktion Sühnezeichen* mobilized rapidly to organize pro-Israel rallies.[41] At the height of the June 1967 war, Kurt Scharf, now bishop of the Protestant Church of Berlin-Brandenburg, arranged a joint Christian-Jewish worship service at West Berlin's magisterial Kaiser Wilhelm Memorial Church. Led by two clergymen each from the Protestant, Catholic, and Jewish communities, congregants prayed for Israel's survival while sermons invoked Germans' responsibility for the Jewish state. The EKD Council arranged similar services throughout West Germany.[42] The significance of such events should not be overlooked. A generation earlier, Catholic participation in a religious service at the symbolic center of Imperial German Protestantism would have been unthinkable.

If the June 1967 war united West German Catholics and Protestants, its conclusion with a resounding Israeli victory generated new lines of tension, both internationally and generationally. Christian leaders in West Germany clashed with their counterparts in other European countries, who sought to avoid the crossfires of Cold War politics and maintain solidarity with Arab Christian minorities. On the Protestant side, the Prague-based Christian Peace Conference issued a statement deeming Israel a secular state of no special significance for Christians. In contrast, the chair of its West German branch, the Confessing Church theologian Heinz Kloppenburg, adopted a line of critique that reflected recent developments in Christian-Jewish dialogue: "When one is dealing with the Jewish people, which has formed a new state in Israel, one is dealing with a people that still is the bearer of a special promise from God."[43] When the Vatican offered a tepid plea for peace that made no reference to the political dimensions of the Arab-Israeli conflict, the Freiburg Catholic journal *Herder-Korrespondenz* criticized institutional churches for their failure to defend Israel's right of existence.[44]

Most significantly, Israel's victory marked the rise of left-wing anti-Zionism in the West German student movement. Locally, the war coincided with the police shooting of the West Berlin student Benno Ohnesorg, which student leaders blamed on the right-wing press magnate and Israel supporter Axel Springer. At a deeper level, the students understood themselves as part of a global anti-imperialist revolution, for which the creation of Israel signified less the post-Holocaust rebirth of Jewish life than the expansion of Western colonialism. For an older generation of left-liberal intellectuals, the student movement's anti-Zionism marked a flight from Germans' historical responsibility. Prominent activists for Christian-Jewish dialogue numbered among the signatories of a "Common Statement of Twenty Representatives of the German Left on the Middle East Conflict," which castigated the student movement's stance as "an outlet for unacknowledged anti-Judaism."[45]

The Ambiguities of Christian Zionism

The Six Day War and its aftermath proved to be a turning point in the history of Christian-Jewish encounters in West Germany. Whereas the postwar generation of dissident Protestants and Catholics clashed with conservatives in their own confessions, proponents of interfaith dialogue now operated with greater backing from their churches but against political headwinds. Beyond the rise of anti-Zionism, the Israeli government's refusal to withdraw from its newly conquered territories, along with the beginning of Jewish settlement in the West Bank, divided West German public opinion. The early 1970s saw a cooling of West German-Israeli relations, as the new Bonn government under Social Democratic Prime Minister Willy Brandt sought to bolster its ties with Arab countries and establish a more evenhanded approach to Cold War hostilities in the Middle East.[46] The unsettling of the West German consensus on Israel prompted a recentering of Christian-Jewish dialogue around questions of Zionism, a shift that cut across confessional lines. At the levels of both theology and politics, organizers framed their support for Israel as an outgrowth of the ongoing Christian reorientation toward Jews, while avoiding thornier issues of power and territory.

Among the activists who rose to prominence in Christian-Jewish dialogue in the wake of the 1967 war, the Protestant theologian Friedrich-Wilhelm Marquardt established himself as the most influential Christian thinker on Zionism. Born in 1928, Marquardt belonged to the first cohort of Germans too young to bear personal responsibility for Nazism, a generation that has been credited with impelling a more forthright reckoning with the Nazi past.[47] Yet, in Marquardt's case, ties to critical members of an older generation proved equally significant. Following studies with Karl Barth, the theological lodestar of the Nazi-era Confessing Church, Marquardt began his career as an assistant to Helmut Gollwitzer. Marquardt embraced Zionism after leading a 1959 student trip to Israel, according to his later recollections his first experience of Judaism as "not at all a religion but a real, living people!"⁴⁸ Assuming the leadership of the *Kirchentag* Working Group on "Jews and Christians" in 1968, Marquardt developed a theological defense of Israel around a concept that had emerged out of two decades of Christian-Jewish dialogue: the ongoing validity of God's covenant with the Jews. Just as Christian revelation became manifest in the incarnation of Jesus Christ, Marquardt argued before the Working Group in 1968, so too did the emergence of "the Jewish people as a people" demonstrate "the objective reality of revelation." Zionism represented not only a political struggle but a theological event, "the historical process by which the Jewish people in Palestine found a Jewish state to become there a blessed state, a witness to the kingdom of God." ⁴⁹

Marquardt's theological Zionism resonated with the new leaders who took over the Coordinating Council of Societies for Christian-Jewish Cooperation in the mid-1960s: the Protestant pastor Martin Stöhr (born 1932), the Catholic priest Willehad Paul Eckert (born 1926), and the returned émigré rabbi Nathan Peter Levinson (born 1921). All three eschewed a fundamentalist Zionism that equated the contemporary state with the biblical Israel, yet invoked Jews' spiritual ties to the land to deflect charges of colonialism. During the 1970s, the three arranged a series of triconfessional conferences and publications that delved deeper into the idea of the "promised land." Following Marquardt, Catholic and Protestant participants underscored the theological basis of the Jewish state in Judaism's understanding of religion, land, and peoplehood as co-constitutive. As the founder of the *Deutsch-Israelische Gesellschaft* Rolf Rendtorff put the point in 1975, "from the perspective of the Jewish people . . . Zionism is in fact nothing fundamentally new, but only the modern form of the deep-rooted connection between the Jewish people and [the] land of Israel."⁵⁰ Frequent exchange fostered consensus around what Martin Stöhr and Willehad Eckert termed "critical solidarity" with Israel, the recognition of the Jewish state's right of existence and fundamental significance for Christians regardless of disagreements over Israeli politics.⁵¹

The concept of "critical solidarity" formed the basis not only for theological agreement between Protestants and Catholics but for shared advocacy. Reflecting the new centrality of Zionism in Christian-Jewish dialogue, the Societies for Christian-Jewish Cooperation moved to elevate support for Israeli statehood to the center of their political activism. The 1972 "Week of Brotherhood" in West Berlin centered on the sharp-edged theme of "Antizionism: A New Form of Antisemitism?," in contrast to the bromides of the years prior. ("Act on the Word!" exhorted the festival's slogan in 1961.)⁵² In 1976, the Göttingen Society critically addressed the recent United Nations resolution characterizing Zionism as a "form of racism," the first time Zionism appeared on the group's calendar.[53] The journal *Emuna/Israel-Forum*, co-sponsored by the national-level Coordinating Council, enjoyed a short-lived but vocal role as a forum for polemics against left-wing anti-Zionism.[54]

What differences remained by the mid-1970s between the positions of the Protestant and Catholic churches pertained largely to their distinct institutional structures, rather than disagreements among West German church leaders. Whereas the Vatican continued to avoid the question of Zionism, establishing diplomatic relations with Israel only in 1993, the EKD's unique status as a West German church—after the East German Protestant churches split off in 1969—meant that it faced little international pressure against advocating for close ties with Israel. In mid-1975, the EKD Council adopted a memorandum on "Christians and Jews," co-authored by Helmut Gollwitzer, Rolf Rendtorff, and Martin Stöhr, that adopted the views of the Societies for Christian-Jewish Cooperation as the official position of the Protestant Church. The state of Israel, the memorandum announced, belonged "in the framework of the history of the chosen people."[55] Later that year, the EKD Synod, but not the Catholic bishops, issued a statement condemning the UN resolution on Zionism.[56] Yet because the Societies for Christian-Jewish Cooperation operated independently of the institutional churches, confessional distinctions proved of little significance for their impact on West German politics. Already in 1968, Rendtorff's *Deutsch-Israelische Gesellschaft* counted seventy-three Christian Democratic and Social Democratic Bundestag deputies among its members; throughout his term of office, Willy Brandt faced criticism from members of both parties for his Middle East policies.[57] In part due to the work of Rendtorff and his colleagues, the mainstream of West Germany's political class remained soundly supportive of a Jewish state in Israel.

If 1970s Christian Zionism facilitated the amelioration of fault lines between Catholics and Protestants, however, the work of the Societies for Christian-Jewish Cooperation continued to fall short of the ideal of equal Jewish participation. This was not only a matter of demographic realities. Many Jewish leaders joined the Societies' activities only during the annual "Week of Brotherhood," Nathan Peter Levinson would later recall, and even then, "their heart wasn't in it."[58] Narratives of the Jewish state promoted through interconfessional initiatives continued to reflect Christian understandings of Judaism and elided the tensions between religious and political conceptions of Jewish identity, not least the long history of intra-Jewish debate over Zionism. Such absences would persist as Christian theologians and the Societies for Christian-Jewish Cooperation began to address the catastrophe that formed the very condition of Christian-Jewish dialogue in West Germany.

Auschwitz and German Memory

Although three decades of interconfessional dialogue fostered consensus on the autonomy of the Jewish faith and the legitimacy of the state of Israel, only in the late 1970s, with the passing of the perpetrator generation, did Nazi genocide emerge as a central theme. Given the ongoing underrepresentation of Jews in West Germany, international contacts helped spur this shift. A 1975 Hamburg conference of the Societies for Christian-Jewish Cooperation on "The Holocaust and its Teachings Today," bringing together longtime West German participants with younger American-Jewish scholars, formed a milestone in the reorientation of Christian-Jewish dialogue.[59] But transformations within West German Christianity proved equally crucial. Inspired by the global rise of liberation theology, a new generation of German theologians, including the Catholics Johann Baptist Metz and Hans Küng and the Protestants Friedrich-Wilhelm Marquardt, Dorothee Sölle, and Jürgen Moltmann, called for a new political theology to liberate humankind from thoughtless obedience to worldly authority. For these thinkers, Auschwitz formed a chasm that compelled a reassessment of Christian notions of justice and a new engagement with Judaism. Metz called for the recovery of the prophetic Jewish core of Christian theology, while Sölle adapted the Jewish concept of the *shekinah*, the worldly presence of God who shares in human suffering.[60]

Although radical theologians in both Christian confessions challenged prevailing assumptions about the Nazi past, they could forge stronger connections to the institutional churches, given the groundwork laid by the Societies for Christian-Jewish Cooperation. The Würzburg Synod of 1971–75, convened by the German Catholic bishops to implement the guidelines of Vatican II, signaled this new cross-pollination. Despite initial disagreements, the synod adopted a statement in 1975 titled "Our Hope," drafted by Johann Baptist Metz, that for the first time acknowledged shared Catholic guilt for Nazi crimes against Jews:

> In the time of National Socialism, despite the exemplary behavior of individual people and groups, we were overall a church community that too often lived with its backs turned on the fate of the persecuted Jewish people, whose view was too strongly fixed on threats to its own institutions, and that remained silent before the crimes perpetrated against Jews and Judaism.[61]

The fortieth anniversary of the *Kristallnacht* pogrom in November 1978 touched off further reflection in both churches, the first such anniversary to receive nationwide commemoration. The EKD Council lamented the "silence" of the Protestant Church in the face of the "murder" of six million Jews; Catholic bishops across West Germany issued statements acknowledging the connection between *Kristallnacht* and the "final solution." The 1978 statements remained vague, foregrounding Christian passivity during *Kristallnacht* rather than the ways in which Christians had authorized the exclusion of Jews from German society and then participated in their annihilation. Still, the forthright acknowledgment of a burden of guilt marked a shift from the evasions of 1945.[62]

With the foundations for a more critical reckoning in place, the 1979 broadcasting of the American miniseries *Holocaust* on West German television, viewed by twenty million West Germans, ignited a wider public discussion.[63] While the West German government feared that the film would revive negative attitudes toward Germans in the United States, leaders in Christian-Jewish dialogue seized on the opportunity to further their work. At the 1979 Nuremberg *Kirchentag*, in response to both the *Holocaust* series and the convention's location in a city indelibly associated with Nazism, organizers elevated "Jews and Christians" to the primary theme.[64] The German-Jewish actress Peggy Parnass, whose parents perished in Theresienstadt after she was brought to Sweden on the *Kindertransport*, highlighted one plenary discussion; the other featured Ella Lingens, an Austrian Catholic physician imprisoned at Auschwitz after she was discovered sheltering Jews.[65] At the same time, local Societies for Christian-Jewish Cooperation moved Holocaust memory to the center of their programming. The Göttingen Society published a handbook on *Prayer after Auschwitz*, while holding film evenings on the Warsaw Ghetto and discussions of the *Holocaust* series.[66] The Darmstadt Society financed the construction of a new synagogue, whose dedication would take place in 1988.[67]

The shifting landscape of memory politics in the late 1970s sparked new theological engagement with the legacies of Christian anti-Judaism as well. A pioneering 1980 statement of the Rhineland Protestant Church, prepared by the committee on "Christians and Jews" at the regional synod, took a decisive stance on the theological problem that had dogged Christian-Jewish dialogue from the outset, affirming "the permanent election of the Jewish people as the people of God." Surpassing any other statement by postwar German churches, the Rhineland Church's "Toward a Renewal of the Relationship of Christians and Jews" acknowledged the intrinsic link between Christian supersessionism and the Holocaust: "This disrespect to the permanent election of the Jewish people ... marked Christian theology, the preaching and work of the church again and again right to the present day. Thereby we have made ourselves guilty also of the physical elimination of the Jewish people."[68] During the following years, Protestant churches across West Germany adopted the statement's tenets, while the Central Committee of German Catholics similarly called for acknowledgement of both individual and collective Christian guilt.[69]

Interfaith initiatives of the 1980s fostered a more forthright discussion of the Nazi past not only within the churches but in the public debates that erupted around the fortieth anniversary of the end of World War II. In the controversy over the visit of US President Ronald Reagan and West German Chancellor Helmut Kohl to the Bitburg military cemetery, where *Waffen-SS* soldiers were interred, activists for Christian-Jewish dialogue emerged at the forefront of opposition to Kohl's call for the "normalization" of German national identity. Johann Baptist Metz allied forcefully with Jürgen Habermas, who led the charge among West German public intellectuals for a critical interrogation of the German past; the *Aktion Sühnezeichen* issued a scathing rebuke to Kohl's relativization of Nazi atrocities.[70] Bundestag President Philipp Jenninger chose the occasion of a speech before the Stuttgart Society for Christian-Jewish Cooperation to remedy the political damage of Bitburg. Invoking an earlier injunction by Helmut Kohl not to forget "the crime against our Jewish fellow citizens," Jenninger acknowledged the passivity, if not the active complicity, of the churches and most non-Jewish Germans in the face of Nazi anti-Jewish attacks.[71]

The successes of the Societies for Christian-Jewish Cooperation during the 1980s, both within the churches and in political debate, catalyzed new discussion surrounding the organizations' scope. By mid-decade, some leaders in Christian-Jewish dialogue sought to move beyond the Societies' traditional focus on antisemitism to reckon more broadly with the history of racism and exclusion in modern Germany. As early as 1980, the Protestant and Catholic churches co-organized a "Day of the Foreign Fellow Citizen" that aimed to educate (Christian) Germans about the traditions of the Turkish minority living in the Federal Republic.[72] At a time when the question of cultural diversity was just coming into the view of West German politicians, the event underscored how outreach toward—and setting the terms of engagement with—non-Christian communities had become a driver of Catholic-Protestant cooperation. The Protestant Academy in Arnoldshain, directed by Martin Stöhr, was especially active in initiatives to widen the scope of interreligious dialogue, convening conferences of Christian, Jewish, and Muslim scholars.[73] A new focus on race and diversity also came to shape Holocaust commemoration. On the fiftieth anniversary of the *Kristallnacht* pogrom in 1988, the Society for Christian-Jewish Cooperation in Cologne launched a public exhibition on "One Hundred Years of German Racism," setting the Holocaust in a German context of antisemitism, imperialism, and eugenics.[74]

Yet efforts to expand ecumenical dialogue to include Muslim participants and address issues of racism did not ultimately transform the scope of Christian-Jewish cooperation. In light of not only the Holocaust but also Christianity's dependence on Jewish scripture, questions of a special relationship remained at the fore: between German perpetrators and Jewish victims, West Germany and Israel, Jewish prophecy and Christian salvation. Moreover, longstanding participants feared that outreach toward new immigrants conflicted with the purpose of the Societies for Christian-Jewish Cooperation. Taking over the editorship of the *Freiburger Rundbrief* in 1985 following Gertrud Luckner's four decades at the helm, the Catholic theologian Clemens Thoma bristled at the prospect that the mainstay of post-Holocaust Christian-Jewish dialogue could be transformed into a wider "Christian-ecumenical magazine." His reasoning was straightforward: "On Christian-Jewish questions, there is no Catholic-Protestant dissent."[75]

To be sure, even by the late 1980s, theological distinctions between Catholics and Protestants were not entirely overcome. The German Catholic bishops never affirmed the ongoing election of the Jewish people with the clarity of their Protestant counterparts. Finer points of theology, however, hardly counteracted the wider shifts in both churches since the end of World War II, especially in attitudes toward guilt for the Holocaust. Calls for reconciliation with Jews had formed a glue of Catholic-Protestant rapprochement in West Germany, taking precedence over outreach to other religious communities. The Holocaust had not dissolved the connection of Christianity and Judaism; instead, reflection on the Nazi past allowed for the reconstruction of this relationship on new grounds. In interconfessional discussions where Protestants and Catholics constituted the overwhelming majority, such reflection prompted long-divided Christian churches to declare their own common origin.

Conclusion

The story of Christian-Jewish dialogue in West Germany is one of fatefully belated achievement. It unfolded in the aftermath of genocide, when West German international diplomacy required the acknowledgement of moral debts for the Nazi past. Nevertheless, this chapter has argued that it was dissident clergy members and lay activists who first grappled with Christian antisemitism, the founding of the state of Israel, and the Holocaust, initially in the face of opposition from church leaders. The Societies for Christian-Jewish Cooperation ultimately fostered new understandings of the Christian-Jewish relationship within both churches, while forging strong links to West German politics. These efforts had an additional, crucial, consequence: helping to break down the confessional barriers between Protestants and Catholics that for centuries had structured German religious life.

The years following the end of the Cold War witnessed the rise of a different interconfessional dynamic in Germany. Both major churches issued updated statements affirming their commitments to Christian-Jewish dialogue and Israel's security, culminating in the EKD's third study on "Christians and Jews" in 2000 and the first papal visit to Israel that same year.[76] The Jewish community responded with the pioneering statement "Dabru Emet" (Speak the Truth), signed by 225 scholars and religious leaders, which recognized a transformation in Christian views on Judaism.[77] At the same time, German initiatives toward Christian-Muslim dialogue proceeded in the opposite direction. Calls in the 1980s for tri-religious discussion scarcely survived the end of the Cold War, as anxieties about terrorism and fundamentalism came to dominate public discourse about Islam. Statements by leaders in both Christian confessions less welcomed Muslim immigrants and their descendants than confirmed popular suspicions about Muslims' dubious commitment to democracy.[78]

The resurgence of interreligious tensions around the question of Muslim immigration gives cause to ask whether the relative absence of Jews constituted not only a sober reality, but a precondition for the very success of Christian-Jewish dialogue in postwar West Germany. For all of the symbolic burdens faced by the self-proclaimed successor state to the Third Reich, the fledgling German-Jewish community, especially before the arrival of post-Soviet Jews, made few visual, cultural, and material demands on West German society. Most synagogues destroyed on *Kristallnacht* were not restored; financial reparations from the West German state went primarily to Jews living abroad.[79] Christian-Jewish dialogue involved revolutions in church doctrine, religious pedagogy, and even public representations of the Nazi past, but hardly the transformation of daily life. Unlike Jews in the postwar era, Muslims constitute a highly visible minority in Germany at more than six percent of the population and rising. Muslim demands for material accommodations—mosque construction, public calls to prayer, acceptance of the *hijab* and other forms of veiling—far outstrip those of the postwar Jewish community.[80] Even more than the Holocaust, which could increasingly be approached from the safe distance of succeeding generations, questions of practical integration and public space have proven difficult to address.

The collapse of the Soviet Union brought a wave of Jewish immigrants to a reunified Germany, raising similar issues of creating interreligious solidarities in practice. Yet rather than engaging the needs of this struggling community, church leaders underscored the threat of "reimporting" antisemitism to Germany through Muslim immigration.[81] While such concerns are not without warrant—Germany's intelligence services have tracked a rise of Islamist antisemitism in recent years—police statistics continue to attribute the overwhelming majority of antisemitic attacks to the far right.[82] A singular focus on Muslim antisemitism, moreover, elides complex questions of opportunity and inequality.

In light of shifting lines of religious conflict in contemporary Germany, postwar Christian-Jewish dialogue offers a model and a warning. After the near total destruction of European Jewry, growing numbers of German Catholics and Protestants, along with surviving remnants of the Jewish community, came together to address historically, theologically, and emotionally fraught questions facing all three groups. Their discussions and activism across cultural divides challenged old prejudices and forged new solidarities. Yet the achievements of Christian-Jewish dialogue often came at the expense of the full inclusion of Jewish participants and proved inadequate to addressing issues of race and xenophobia beyond the Christian-Jewish binary. Forged in the crucible of post-Nazi Europe and matured amidst the upheavals of the 1960s and 1970s, Christian-Jewish dialogue in Germany again faces transformed political stakes.

Brandon Bloch is Assistant Professor of History at the University of Wisconsin-Madison, where his research and teaching center on modern German and European history and the history of human rights. His writings have appeared in *The Journal of Modern History*, *Modern Intellectual History*, and *Boston Review*. He is currently completing a book manuscript, provisionally titled *Reinventing Protestant Germany: Religion, Nation, and Democracy after Nazism*.

Notes

1. Willehad P. Eckert, "Forderungen und Chancen einer christlich-jüdischen Begegnung nach dem Zweiten Vatikanischen Konzil," in *Die geistige Gestalt des heutigen Judentums*, ed. Ernst Ludwig Ehrlich (Munich: Kösel, 1969), 159.

2. Atina Grossmann, "Where Did All 'Our' Jews Go? Germans and Jews in Post-Nazi Germany," in *The Germans and the Holocaust: Popular Responses to the Persecution and Murder of the Jews*, ed. Susanna Schrafstetter and Alan E. Steinweis (New York: Berghahn Books, 2015), 150.

3. Pól Ó. Dochartaigh, *Germans and Jews since the Holocaust* (Basingstoke: Palgrave Macmillan, 2016), 83.

4. Udi Greenberg, "Catholics, Protestants, and the Violent Birth of European Religious Pluralism," *American Historical Review* 124, no. 2 (2019): 511–38; Maria D. Mitchell, *The Origins of Christian Democracy: Politics and Confession in Modern Germany* (Ann Arbor: University of Michigan Press, 2012); Noah Benezra Strote, *Lions and Lambs: Conflict in Weimar and the Creation of Post-Nazi Germany* (New Haven: Yale University Press, 2017), 175–96.

5. For an alternative perspective on Christian-Jewish cooperation that foregrounds its role in West Germany's economic reconstruction, see Noah Benezra Strote, "Sources of Christian-Jewish Cooperation in Early Cold War Germany," in *Is There a Judeo-Christian Tradition? A*

European Perspective, ed. Emmanuel Nathan and Anya Topolski (Berlin: De Gruyter, 2016), 75–100.

6. Michael Phayer, *The Catholic Church and the Holocaust, 1930–1965* (Bloomington: Indiana University Press, 2000), 134–38; Council of the Evangelical Church in Germany, "Stuttgart Declaration of Guilt," in Matthew D. Hockenos, *A Church Divided: German Protestants Confront the Nazi Past* (Bloomington: Indiana University Press, 2004), 187.

7. On the Protestant campaign against denazification, see Clemens Vollnhals, "Die Hypothek des Nationalprotestantismus. Entnazifierung und Strafverfolgung von NS-Verbrechen nach 1945," *Geschichte und Gesellschaft* 18, no. 1 (1992): 51–69.

8. Mitchell, *Origins of Christian Democracy*, 95–99.

9. Pfarrer Dr. Mehlhose to EKD Synod, 22 January 1949, Evangelisches Zentralarchiv, Berlin, 2/2802.

10. Hans-Josef Wollasch, *Gertrud Luckner: "Botschafterin der Menschlichkeit"* (Freiburg: Herder Verlag, 2005), 22–39.

11. John Connelly, *From Enemy to Brother: The Revolution in Catholic Teaching on the Jews, 1933–1965* (Cambridge, MA: Harvard University Press, 2012), 124, 151.

12. Martin Stöhr, "Notwendigkeiten und Schwierigkeiten einer Christlich-Jüdischen Zusammenarbeit—Einige Rückblicke," in *"Wenn nicht ich, wer? Wenn nicht jetzt, wann?" Zur gesellschaftspolitischen Bedeutung des Deutschen Koordinierungsrates der Gesellschaften für Christlich-Jüdische Zusammenarbeit*, ed. Christoph Münz and Rudolf W. Sirsch (Münster: LIT Verlag, 2004), 49–51.

13. Wollasch, *Luckner*, 26, 29.

14. Connelly, *From Enemy to Brother*, 7, 121, 161.

15. Hockenos, *A Church Divided*, 157–70, quoted 167; Synod of the Evangelical Church in Germany, "Statement on the Jewish Question," in Hockenos, *A Church Divided*, 199.

16. Elias H. Füllenbach, "'Freunde des alten und des neuen Gottesvolkes': Theologische Annäherungen an das Judentum nach 1945," *Rottenburger Jahrbuch für Kirchengeschichte* 32 (2013): 236–45.

17. Cited in Füllenbach, "Freunde," 237–38.

18. Josef Foschepoth, *Im Schatten der Vergangenheit: Die Anfänge der Gesellschaften für Christlich-Jüdische Zusammenarbeit* (Göttingen: Vandenhoeck & Ruprecht, 1993), 61–74.

19. Ibid., 139–40.

20. Connelly, *From Enemy to Brother*, 215; "Der neue Staat Israel und die Christenheit: Bericht von der Düsseldorfer Tagung des deutschen evangelischen Ausschusses für Dienst an Israel, 26. Februar bis 2. März 1951," *Freiburger Rundbrief* 3–4, no. 12–15 (December 1951): 16–17.

21. "Thesen christlicher Lehrverkündigung im Hinblick auf umlaufende Irrtümer über das Gottesvolk des Alten Bundes," *Freiburger Rundbrief* 2, no. 8–9 (August 1950): 9–11; "Bemerkungen zur Schwalbacher Fassung der Seelisberger Thesen," *Freiburger Rundbrief* 2, no. 8–9 (August 1950): 11–12. See also Connelly, *From Enemy to Brother*, 216–19.

22. Frank Stern, *The Whitewashing of the Yellow Badge: Antisemitism and Philosemitism in Postwar Germany*, trans. William Templer (Oxford, UK: Pergamon Press, 1992), 322–34, quoted 322, 334.

23. "Der neue Staat Israel und die Christenheit"; Jay Howard Geller, *Jews in Post-Holocaust Germany, 1945–1953* (Cambridge, UK: Cambridge University Press, 2005), 232–39.

24. "Una Sancta mit den Juden? Eine Berliner Tagung des Katholischen Bildungswerkes mit der Evangelischen Akademie," *Freiburger Rundbrief* 10, no. 37–40 (October 1957): 57–58.

25. Andrea Sinn, "The Return of Rabbi Robert Raphael Geis to Germany: One of the Last Witnesses of German Jewry?" *European Judaism: A Journal for the New Europe* 45, no.2 (Autumn 2012): 123–38.

26. Quoted in Willehad Eckert, "Christlich-jüdische Begegnungen in Deutschland nach 1945," *Freiburger Rundbrief* 12, no. 49 (September 1960): 7.

27. Connelly, *From Enemy to Brother*, 213–15; Foschepoth, *Im Schatten der Vergangenheit*, 59–60.
28. Connelly, *From Enemy to Brother*, 66, 191.
29. Ibid., 241–45.
30. "Declaration on the Relation of the Church to Non-Christian Religions: *Nostra Aetate*," *The Holy See*, Retrieved 1 December 2020 from http://www.vatican.va/archive/hist_councils/ii_vatican_council/documents/vat-ii_decl_19651028_nostra-aetate_en.html.
31. Christian Staffa, "Die 'Aktion Sühnezeichen': Eine protestantische Initiative zu einer besonderen Art der Wiedergutmachung," in *Nach der Verfolgung: Widergutmachung national-sozialistischen Unrechts in Deutschland?* ed. Hans Günter Hockerts and Christiane Kuller (Göttingen: Wallstein Verlag, 2003), 140.
32. Gabriele Kammerer, *In die Haare, in die Arme: 40 Jahre Arbeitsgemeinschaft "Juden und Christen" beim Deutschen Evangelischen Kirchentag* (Gütersloh: Gütersloher Verlagshaus, 2001), 34–36. See also Benjamin Pearson, "Faith and Democracy: Political Transformations at the German Protestant Kirchentag, 1949–1969" (PhD diss., University of North Carolina-Chapel Hill, 2007), 269–80.
33. "'Entscheidend ist, was ausgesprochen wird': Propst Grüber stellt sich vor Rolf Hochhuth," *Kölner Stadt-Anzeiger*, 14 March 1963; Helmut Gollwitzer, "Die böse Kunst, sich selbst zu vergeben," *Kölner Stadt-Anzeiger*, 15 March 1963. On the Hochhuth controversy, see Mark Edward Ruff, *The Battle for the Catholic Past in Germany, 1945–1980* (Cambridge, UK: Cambridge University Press, 2017), 153–92.
34. Kurt Scharf, "Das christlich-jüdische Verhältnis und das Zweite Vatikanische Konzil in der evangelischen Sicht," *Freiburger Rundbrief* 18, no. 65–68 (September 1966): 39–42. See also Deutscher Evangelischer Kirchentag, "Zur Konzilserklärung über die Juden," *Freiburger Rundbrief* 16–17, no. 61–64 (July 1965): 176.
35. Scharf, "Das christlich-jüdische Verhältnis."
36. Carole Fink, *West Germany and Israel: Foreign Relations, Domestic Politics, and the Cold War, 1965–1974* (Cambridge, UK: Cambridge University Press, 2019), 5.
37. Staffa, "'Aktion Sühnezeichen,'" 144–52.
38. Helmut Gollwitzer, *Vietnam, Israel und die Christenheit* (Munich: Kaiser, 1967), 5.
39. Fink, *West Germany and Israel*, 15–24, 37.
40. Gollwitzer, "Der Staat Israel und die Araber," in *Vietnam, Israel und die Christenheit*, 55–83.
41. Fink, *West Germany and Israel*, 55.
42. "Der Krieg im Nahen Osten und die Weltchristenheit: Gebete, Aufrufe, praktische Hilfe," *Evangelische Welt*, 16 June 1967; Gollwitzer, "Nach der Nahost-Krise des Sommers 1967," in *Vietnam, Israel und die Christenheit*, 90.
43. "Die Erklärung des Arbeitsausschusses der Christlichen Friedenskonferenz zur Situation im Nahen Osten," *Junge Kirche*, 10 August 1967; Heinz Kloppenburg, "Bemerkungen zum Krieg zwischen Israel und den Arabern," *Junge Kirche*, 10 July 1967.
44. Yona Malachy, "Christliches Nein zum jüdischen Staat? Der Sechs-Tage-Krieg im Spiegel kirchlicher Urteile," *Evangelische Kommentare* 2 (1969): 98; "Der Nahost-Krieg und die christlich-jüdische Beziehungen," *Herder-Korrespondenz* 22, no. 1 (January 1968): 21–23.
45. Jeffrey Herf, *Undeclared Wars with Israel: East Germany and the West German Far Left, 1967–1989* (Cambridge, UK: Cambridge University Press, 2016), 75–88, quoted 88. The signatories included the Protestant theologian Helmut Gollwitzer, sociologist Dietrich Goldschmidt, and pastor Hans-Werner Bartsch, as well as the Catholic publicist Walter Dirks.
46. Fink, *West Germany and Israel*, 124–53.
47. A. Dirk Moses, *German Intellectuals and the Nazi Past* (Cambridge, UK: Cambridge University Press, 2007), 55–73.
48. Quoted in Andreas Pangritz, "Friedrich-Wilhelm Marquardt—A Theological-Biographical Sketch," *European Judaism: A Journal for the New Europe* 38, no. 1 (Spring 2005): 24–25.

49. Friedrich-Wilhelm Marquardt, "Christentum und Zionismus," *Evangelische Theologie* 28, no. 12 (1968): 629–60, quoted 638. Marquardt led the Working Group from 1968–1971: Pangritz, "Marquardt," 29.

50. Rolf Rendtorff, *Israel und sein Land: Theologische Überlegungen zu einem politischen Problem* (Munich: Kaiser, 1975), 42.

51. Willehad P. Eckert, "Streiflichter auf die Geschichte des christlichen Zionismus," in *Zionismus: Beiträge zur Diskussion*, ed. Martin Stöhr (Munich: Kaiser, 1980), 134–37; Martin Stöhr, "Vorwort," in *Jüdisches Volk—gelobtes Land: Die biblischen Landesverheißung als Problem des jüdischen Selbstverständnisses und der christlichen Theologie*, ed. Willehad Paul Eckert, Nathan Peter Levinson, and Martin Stöhr (Munich: Kaiser, 1970), 12.

52. Lorenz Weinrich, ed., *Toleranz und Brüderlichkeit: 30 Jahre Gesellschaft für christlich-jüdische Zusammenarbeit in Berlin* (Berlin: Gesellschaft für Christlich-Jüdische Zusammenarbeit, 1979), 11.

53. Uta Hinze, Martin Steinberg, and Hannah Vogt, eds., *25 Jahre Gesellschaft für christlich-jüdische Zusammenarbeit in Göttingen* (Göttingen: Gesellschaft für Christlich-Jüdische Zusammenarbeit, 1983), 68.

54. For instance, Henryk M. Broder, "Vom Antisemitismus zum Antizionismus—oder: Wie die Linke das Erbe der Rechten übernommen hat," *Emuna/Israel-Forum* 1, no. 4 (1976): 37–42.

55. "Christen und Juden I (1975)," in *Christen und Juden I-III: die Studien der Evangelischen Kirche in Deutschland 1975–2000*, ed. Kirchenamt der Evangelischen Kirche in Deutschland (Gütersloh: Gütersloher Verlagshaus, 2002), 38–39.

56. Rolf Rendtorff and Hans Hermann Henrix, eds., *Die Kirchen und das Judentum, Bd. I: Dokumente von 1945–1985*, 3rd. ed. (Paderborn: Bonifatius, 2001), doc. E.III.20. On the absence of Israel in Catholic statements of the time, see Eckert, "Streiflichter," 138.

57. Fink, *West Germany and Israel*, 85, 295.

58. Nathan Peter Levinson, *Ein Ort ist, mit wem du bist: Lebensstationen eines Rabbiners* (Berlin: Edition Hentrich, 1996), 227.

59. N. Peter Levinson, "Internationale 'Holocaust'-Konferenz in Hamburg: Der Holocaust und seine Lehren heute," *Freiburger Rundbrief* 27, no. 101–4 (December 1975): 24–25.

60. Johann Baptist Metz, "Christians and Jews after Auschwitz," in Johann Baptist Metz, *The Emergent Church: The Future of Christianity in a Postbourgeois World*, trans. Peter Mann (New York: Crossroad, 1981), 17–33; Dorothee Sölle, *Suffering*, trans. Everett R. Kalin (Philadelphia: Fortress Press, 1975), 145–46.

61. Rendtorff and Henrix, *Die Kirchen und das Judentum*, doc. K.III.9. On the composition of the statement, see Michael Schüßler, "Auf dem Sprung in die Gegenwart: 'Unsere Hoffnung' als Inspiration für das Zeugnis vom Gott Jesu in unserer Zeit," in *Die Würzburger Synode: Die Texte neu gelesen*, ed. Reinhart Feiter, Richard Hartmann, and Joachim Schmiedl (Freiburg: Herder, 2013), 11–12.

62. Rendtorff and Henrix, *Die Kirchen und das Judentum*, docs. E.III.27, K.III.10-K.III.13.

63. On the television series and its impact, see Jacob S. Eder, *Holocaust Angst: The Federal Republic of Germany and American Holocaust Memory since the 1970s* (Oxford, UK: Oxford University Press, 2016), 30–37.

64. Kammerer, *In die Haare*, 93–100.

65. "Nach dem Holocaust: Konsequenzen für Zivilisation, Kultur, Politik, Religion," in *Glaube und Hoffnung nach Auschwitz: Jüdisch-christliche Dialoge, Vorträge, Diskussionen*, ed. Peter von der Osten-Sacken (Berlin: Institut Kirche und Judentum, 1980), 90–109.

66. *25 Jahre Gesellschaft für christlich-jüdische Zusammenarbeit in Göttingen*, 32, 72–74.

67. Gabriella Deppurt and Godehard Lehwark, eds., *40 Jahre Gesellschaft für christlich-jüdische Zusammenarbeit in Darmstadt 1954–1994* (Darmstadt: Gesellschaft für Christlich-Jüdische Zusammenarbeit, 1994), 6.

68. Synod of the Evangelical Church of the Rhineland, "Towards Renovation of the Relationship of Christians and Jews," *Boston College*, Retrieved 1 December 2020 from https://

www.bc.edu/content/dam/files/research_sites/cjl/texts/cjrelations/resources/documents/protestant/EvChFRG1980.htm.

69. Birte Petersen, *Theologie nach Auschwitz? Jüdische und christliche Versuche einer Antwort* (Berlin: Institut Kirche und Judentum, 1996), 39–40.

70. Johann Baptist Metz, "Anamnestic Reason: A Theologian's Remarks on the Crisis in the *Geisteswissenschaften*," in *Cultural-Political Interventions in the Unfinished Project of Enlightenment*, ed. Axel Honneth et al., trans. Barbara Fultner (Cambridge, MA: MIT Press, 1992), 189–94; "Aktion Sühnezeichen ruft die Kirche gegen Kohl auf," *Frankfurter Rundschau*, 12 January 1987.

71. Quoted in Jeffrey K. Olick, *The Sins of the Fathers: Germany, Memory, Method* (Chicago: University of Chicago Press, 2016), 376.

72. Rita Chin, *The Guest Worker Question in Postwar Germany* (Cambridge, UK: Cambridge University Press, 2007), 202–5.

73. Doron Kiesel, Şener Sargut, and Rosi Wolf-Almanasreh, eds., *Fremdheit und Angst: Beiträge zum Verhältnis von Christentum und Islam* (Frankfurt: Haag + Herchen, 1988); Ulrich O. Sievering, ed., *Politisches Asyl und Einwanderung* (Frankfurt: Haag + Herchen, 1984); Martin Stöhr, ed., *Abrahams Kinder: Juden—Christen—Moslems* (Frankfurt: Haag + Herchen, 1983).

74. Kölnische Gesellschat für Christich-Jüdische Zusammenarbeit, ed., *100 Jahre deutscher Rassismus: Katalog und Arbeitsbuch* (Cologne: Gesellschaft für Christlich-Jüdische Zusammenarbeit, 1988).

75. Clemens Thoma, "Freiburger Rundbrief—Dokument christlich-jüdischer Begegnung nach 1945," *Freiburger Rundbrief* 37–38 (Summer 1987): 37–39.

76. "Christen und Juden III (2000)," in *Christen und Juden I-III*, 113–214; Jörg Therstappen, "Der Umgang mit den Juden nach dem Holocaust," in *Kirche der Sünder, sündige Kirche? Beispiele für den Umgang mit Schuld nach 1945*, ed. Rainer Bendel (Münster: LIT Verlag, 2002), 88–89.

77. "Dabru Emet: A Jewish Statement on Christians and Christianity," *Institute for Islamic-Christian-Jewish Studies*, Retrieved 1 December 2020 from https://icjs.org/dabru-emet-text.

78. Kirchenamt der Evangelischen Kirche in Deutschland, ed., *Klarheit und gute Nachbarschaft: Christen und Muslime in Deutschland: Eine Handreichung des Rates der EKD* (Hanover: Kirchenamt der EKD, 2007); Andreas Renz, *Die katholische Kirche und der interreligiöse Dialog: 50 Jahre 'Nostra aetate': Vorgeschichte, Kommentar, Rezeption* (Stuttgart: Kohlhammer, 2014), 197.

79. On the example of synagogues in West Berlin, see Michael Meng, *Shattered Spaces: Encountering Jewish Ruins in Postwar Germany and Poland* (Cambridge, MA: Harvard University Press, 2011), 96–108.

80. "The Growth of Germany's Muslim Population," *Pew Research Center*, 29 November 2017, Retrieved 1 December 2020 from https://www.pewforum.org/essay/the-growth-of-germanys-muslim-population/.

81. Kirchenamt der Evangelischen Kirche in Deutschland, *Klarheit und gute Nachbarschaft*, 92. On Jewish immigration from the former Soviet Union and the challenges of integration, see Eliezer Ben-Rafael, "Russian-Speaking Jews in Germany," in *The New Jewish Diaspora: Russian-Speaking Immigrants in the United States, Israel, and Germany*, ed. Zvi Gitelman (New Brunswick: Rutgers University Press, 2016), 173–85.

82. Toby Axelrod, "Germany issues an 'early warning' report about rise of Islamist anti-Semitism," *Jewish Telegraphic Agency*, 8 May 2019, Retrieved 1 December 2020 from https://www.jta.org/2019/05/08/global/germany-issues-an-early-warning-report-about-rise-of-islamist-anti-semitism; "Germany sees 20 percent rise in anti-Semitic crime in 2018, blames far right," *Reuters*, 14 May 2019, Retrieved 1 December 2020 from https://www.reuters.com/article/us-germany-politics-seehofer/germany-sees-20-rise-in-anti-semitic-crime-in-2018-blames-far-right-idUSKCN1SK1QX.

Bibliography

Ben-Rafael, Eliezer. "Russian-Speaking Jews in Germany." In *The New Jewish Diaspora: Russian-Speaking Immigrants in the United States, Israel, and Germany*, edited by Zvi Gitelman, 173–85. New Brunswick: Rutgers University Press, 2016.

Chin, Rita. *The Guest Worker Question in Postwar Germany*. Cambridge, UK: Cambridge University Press, 2007.

Connelly, John. *From Enemy to Brother: The Revolution in Catholic Teaching on the Jews, 1933–1965*. Cambridge, MA: Harvard University Press, 2012.

Deppurt, Gabriella, and Godehard Lehwark, eds. *40 Jahre Gesellschaft für christlich-jüdische Zusammenarbeit in Darmstadt 1954–1994*. Darmstadt: Gesellschaft für Christlich-Jüdische Zusammenarbeit, 1994.

Dochartaigh, Pól Ó. *Germans and Jews since the Holocaust*. Basingstoke: Palgrave Macmillan, 2016.

Eckert, Willehad P. "Forderungen und Chancen einer christlich-jüdischen Begegnung nach dem Zweiten Vatikanischen Konzil." In *Die geistige Gestalt des heutigen Judentums*, edited by Ernst Ludwig Ehrlich, 141–65. Munich: Kösel, 1969.

———. "Streiflichter auf die Geschichte des christlichen Zionismus." In *Zionismus: Beiträge zur Diskussion*, edited by Martin Stöhr, 116–43. Munich: Kaiser, 1980.

Eder, Jacob S. *Holocaust Angst: The Federal Republic of Germany and American Holocaust Memory since the 1970s*. Oxford, UK: Oxford University Press, 2016.

Fink, Carole. *West Germany and Israel: Foreign Relations, Domestic Politics, and the Cold War, 1965–1974*. Cambridge, UK: Cambridge University Press, 2019.

Foschepoth, Josef. *Im Schatten der Vergangenheit: Die Anfänge der Gesellschaften für Christlich-Jüdische Zusammenarbeit*. Göttingen: Vandenhoeck & Ruprecht, 1993.

Füllenbach, Elias H. "'Freunde des alten und des neuen Gottesvolkes': Theologische Annäherungen an das Judentum nach 1945." *Rottenburger Jahrbuch für Kirchengeschichte* 32 (2013): 235–51.

Geller, Jay Howard. *Jews in Post-Holocaust Germany, 1945–1953*. Cambridge, UK: Cambridge University Press, 2005.

Gollwitzer, Helmut. *Vietnam, Israel und die Christenheit*. Munich: Kaiser, 1967.

Greenberg, Udi. "Catholics, Protestants, and the Violent Birth of European Religious Pluralism." *American Historical Review* 124, no. 2 (2019): 511–38.

Grossmann, Atina. "Where Did All 'Our' Jews Go? Germans and Jews in Post-Nazi Germany." In *The Germans and the Holocaust: Popular Responses to the Persecution and Murder of the Jews*, edited by Susanna Schrafstetter and Alan E. Steinweis, 131–54. New York: Berghahn Books, 2015.

Herf, Jeffrey. *Undeclared Wars with Israel: East Germany and the West German Far Left, 1967–1989*. Cambridge, UK: Cambridge University Press, 2016.

Hinze, Uta, Martin Steinberg, and Hannah Vogt, eds. *25 Jahre Gesellschaft für christlich-jüdische Zusammenarbeit in Göttingen*. Göttingen: Gesellschaft für Christlich-Jüdische Zusammenarbeit, 1983.

Hockenos, Matthew D. *A Church Divided: German Protestants Confront the Nazi Past*. Bloomington: Indiana University Press, 2004.

Kammerer, Gabriele. *In die Haare, in die Arme: 40 Jahre Arbeitsgemeinschaft "Juden und Christen" beim Deutschen Evangelischen Kirchentag*. Gütersloh: Gütersloher Verlagshaus, 2001.

Kiesel, Doron, Şener Sargut, and Rosi Wolf-Almanasreh, eds. *Fremdheit und Angst: Beiträge zum Verhältnis von Christentum und Islam*. Frankfurt: Haag + Herchen, 1988.

Kirchenamt der Evangelischen Kirche in Deutschland, ed. *Christen und Juden I-III: die Studien der Evangelischen Kirche in Deutschland 1975-2000*. Gütersloh: Gütersloher Verlagshaus, 2002.

———. *Klarheit und gute Nachbarschaft: Christen und Muslime in Deutschland: Eine Handreichung des Rates der EKD.* Hanover: Kirchenamt der EKD, 2007.
Kölnische Gesellschat für Christich-Jüdische Zusammenarbeit, ed. *100 Jahre deutscher Rassismus: Katalog und Arbeitsbuch.* Cologne: Gesellschaft für Christlich-Jüdische Zusammenarbeit, 1988.
Levinson, Nathan Peter. *Ein Ort ist, mit wem du bist: Lebensstationen eines Rabbiners.* Berlin: Edition Hentrich, 1996.
Marquardt, Friedrich-Wilhelm. "Christentum und Zionismus." *Evangelische Theologie* 28, no. 12 (1968): 629–60.
Meng, Michael. *Shattered Spaces: Encountering Jewish Ruins in Postwar Germany and Poland.* Cambridge, MA: Harvard University Press, 2011.
Metz, Johann Baptist. "Anamnestic Reason: A Theologian's Remarks on the Crisis in the Geisteswissenschaften." In *Cultural-Political Interventions in the Unfinished Project of Enlightenment*, edited by Axel Honneth et al., translated by Barbara Fultner, 189–94. Cambridge, MA: MIT Press, 1992.
———. *The Emergent Church: The Future of Christianity in a Postbourgeois World.* Translated by Peter Mann. New York: Crossroad, 1981.
Mitchell, Maria D. *The Origins of Christian Democracy: Politics and Confession in Modern Germany.* Ann Arbor: University of Michigan Press, 2012.
Moses, A. Dirk. *German Intellectuals and the Nazi Past.* Cambridge, UK: Cambridge University Press, 2007.
Olick, Jeffrey K. *The Sins of the Fathers: Germany, Memory, Method.* Chicago: University of Chicago Press, 2016.
Osten-Sacken, Peter von der, ed. *Glaube und Hoffnung nach Auschwitz: Jüdisch-christliche Dialoge, Vorträge, Diskussionen.* Berlin: Institut Kirche und Judentum, 1980.
Pangritz, Andreas. "Friedrich-Wilhelm Marquardt—A Theological-Biographical Sketch." *European Judaism: A Journal for the New Europe* 38, no. 1 (Spring 2005): 17–47.
Pearson, Benjamin. "Faith and Democracy: Political Transformations at the German Protestant Kirchentag, 1949–1969." PhD diss., University of North Carolina-Chapel Hill, 2007.
Petersen, Birte. *Theologie nach Auschwitz? Jüdische und christliche Versuche einer Antwort.* Berlin: Institut Kirche und Judentum, 1996.
Phayer, Michael. *The Catholic Church and the Holocaust, 1930–1965.* Bloomington: Indiana University Press, 2000.
Rendtorff, Rolf. *Israel und sein Land: Theologische Überlegungen zu einem politischen Problem.* Munich: Kaiser, 1975.
Rendtorff, Rolf, and Hans Hermann Henrix, eds. *Die Kirchen und das Judentum, Bd. I: Dokumente von 1945–1985.* 3rd ed. Paderborn: Bonifatius, 2001.
Renz, Andreas. *Die katholische Kirche und der interreligiöse Dialog: 50 Jahre "Nostra aetate": Vorgeschichte, Kommentar, Rezeption.* Stuttgart: Kohlhammer, 2014.
Ruff, Mark Edward. *The Battle for the Catholic Past in Germany, 1945–1980.* Cambridge, UK: Cambridge University Press, 2017.
Schüßler, Michael. "Auf dem Sprung in die Gegenwart: 'Unsere Hoffnung' als Inspiration für das Zeugnis vom Gott Jesu in unserer Zeit." In *Die Würzburger Synode: Die Texte neu gelesen*, edited by Reinhart Feiter, Richard Hartmann, and Joachim Schmiedl, 11–40. Freiburg: Herder, 2013.
Sievering, Ulrich O., ed. *Politisches Asyl und Einwanderung.* Frankfurt: Haag + Herchen, 1984.
Sinn, Andrea. "The Return of Rabbi Robert Raphael Geis to Germany: One of the Last Witnesses of German Jewry?" *European Judaism: A Journal for the New Europe* 45, no. 2 (Autumn 2012): 123–38.
Sölle, Dorothee. *Suffering.* Translated by Everett R. Kalin. Philadelphia: Fortress Press, 1975.
Staffa, Christian. "Die 'Aktion Sühnezeichen': Eine protestantische Initiative zu einer besonderen Art der Wiedergutmachung." In *Nach der Verfolgung: Widergutmachung nationalsozia-*

listischen Unrechts in Deutschland?, edited by Hans Günter Hockerts and Christiane Kuller, 139–56. Göttingen: Wallstein Verlag, 2003.

Stern, Frank. *The Whitewashing of the Yellow Badge: Antisemitism and Philosemitism in Postwar Germany*. Translated by William Templer. Oxford, UK: Pergamon Press, 1992.

Stöhr, Martin, ed. *Abrahams Kinder: Juden—Christen—Moslems*. Frankfurt: Haag + Herchen, 1983.

———. "Notwendigkeiten und Schwierigkeiten einer Christlich-Jüdischen Zusammenarbeit— Einige Rückblicke." In *"Wenn nicht ich, wer? Wenn nicht jetzt, wann?" Zur gesellschaftspolitischen Bedeutung des Deutschen Koordinierungsrates der Gesellschaften für Christlich-Jüdische Zusammenarbeit*, edited by Christoph Münz and Rudolf W. Sirsch, 30–106. Münster: LIT Verlag, 2004.

———. "Vorwort." In *Jüdisches Volk—gelobtes Land: Die biblischen Landesverheißung als Problem des jüdischen Selbstverständnisses und der christlichen Theologie*, edited by Willehad Paul Eckert, Nathan Peter Levinson, and Martin Stöhr, 9–14. Munich: Kaiser, 1970.

Strote, Noah Benezra. *Lions and Lambs: Conflict in Weimar and the Creation of Post-Nazi Germany*. New Haven: Yale University Press, 2017.

———. "Sources of Christian-Jewish Cooperation in Early Cold War Germany." In *Is There a Judeo-Christian Tradition? A European Perspective*, edited by Emmanuel Nathan and Anya Topolski, 75–100. Berlin: De Gruyter, 2016.

Therstappen, Jörg. "Der Umgang mit den Juden nach dem Holocaust." In *Kirche der Sünder, sündige Kirche? Beispiele für den Umgang mit Schuld nach 1945*, edited by Rainer Bendel, 61–91. Münster: LIT Verlag, 2002.

Vollnhals, Clemens. "Die Hypothek des Nationalprotestantismus. Entnazifizierung und Strafverfolgung von NS-Verbrechen nach 1945." *Geschichte und Gesellschaft* 18, no. 1 (1992): 51–69.

Weinrich, Lorenz, ed. *Toleranz und Brüderlichkeit: 30 Jahre Gesellschaft für christlich-jüdische Zusammenarbeit in Berlin*. Berlin: Gesellschaft für Christlich-Jüdische Zusammenarbeit, 1979.

Wollasch, Hans-Josef. *Gertrud Luckner: "Botschafterin der Menschlichkeit."* Freiburg: Herder Verlag, 2005.

Chapter Ten

A Tense Triangle

The Protestant Church, the Catholic Church, and the SED State

Claudia Lepp
Translated by Jeffrey Verhey

Little attention has been paid to the network of relationships between the two large Christian churches in East Germany and to the relationship of these churches to the East German state.[1] This is unfortunate because the makeup of the Christian population in East Germany was markedly different from that of the Federal Republic of Germany or from other Eastern Bloc states. Only in the German Democratic Republic (GDR) did Protestants enjoy a clear majority (1949: 81.6 percent Protestant, 12.2 percent Catholic).[2] This relative strength had an impact not only on ecumenical relationships but also on each church's relationship to the East German state and on traditions and reorientations of social ethics after 1945. In 1981, speaking in London in front of an international audience, the East German State Secretary for Church Affairs Klaus Gysi labeled the church policy of the SED (*Sozialistische Einheitspartei Deutschlands*) toward the Protestant Church an "important historical experiment," since the Protestant Church, unlike its Catholic and Orthodox counterparts, was willing to accept social responsibility.[3]

In this chapter, I will analyze the relationship between the two Christian denominations against the background of the self-positioning of the Protestant Church in the SED state.[4] Was there cooperation between the two churches over politics and social concerns, and, if so, how did it change over time? How did the government view political cooperation between the churches? How did the two churches perceive the church-state relationship, especially in relationship to each other? To answer these questions, we will need to pay attention to how political, social, and theological developments were interconnected as well as the role played by transnational processes.

Parallel and Common Paths in the First Years after World War II

After World War II, the Allied military administrations in Western Germany were favorably disposed to the churches.[5] In principle, the Soviet Military Administration in Eastern Germany was too, although there was evidence of both goodwill and restrictive practices. Very quickly after the war ended, the churches were up and running again as institutions, and amid the rubble and ruins the churches took on the role of spokespersons for the German people. The Protestant Church did this with a new self-understanding. In response to its political and moral failures during the Nazi period, it embraced the Church's new responsibility for engaging in public affairs. Therefore, the Church often referred to Theses 2 and 5 of the Barmen Declaration of 1934, which proclaimed that Jesus Christ should have an impact on all areas of life and which assigned to the Church the task of reminding everyone of "the kingdom of God, God's commandment and righteousness, and thereby the responsibility both of rulers and the ruled."[6] The willingness of the Protestant Church and especially of the laity to turn away from a purely inward-looking individualistic understanding of salvation to an outward-looking understanding which acknowledged the importance of actively engaging in politics and in society was one of the most fundamental changes in the Protestant self-understanding after 1945.

In the Soviet zone, when the two Christian churches criticized political developments, they addressed the occupying powers both independently and collectively. For example, in an interdenominational initiative in 1948, the Berlin Cardinal Konrad Graf von Preysing and the Protestant bishop of Berlin-Brandenburg Otto Dibelius jointly complained to the Commanding General in Berlin about the new Berlin school law, which had been strongly influenced by the Communist Party. From the outset, the Catholic Church in East Germany pursued the strategy it had used during the Nazi era of presenting a united front to government authorities. Cardinal Preysing decreed on 20 December 1947, and his successor affirmed this decree, that only the collective representation of the German bishops was authorized to comment on the pressing questions of the day.[7] Thus, the Catholic Church regulated—and to a large degree centralized—who was authorized to participate in official conversations. Such a political strategy—a united front and a hierarchy—was hardly possible in the Protestant Church, which was organized into regional churches and run by synods.

Thus, structural conditions had an impact on how the churches interacted with the state.

In its provisions on the church, the GDR constitution of 1949 adhered to the Weimar constitution of 1919; in theory, it guaranteed the churches many privileges and institutional autonomy. The reality looked quite different because of the SED's understanding of the constitution as flexible and dynamic. Increasingly, hopes that legal decisions would be predictable, or that the Church would be able to share some public responsibilities, were disappointed. During these years, the Church concentrated on its own legal rights as a corporation, although the Church was also interested more generally in the rule of law in East Germany. In the early years of the postwar era, the eight East German regional and provincial churches as well as the Catholic Church took decidedly anti-totalitarian, democratic, and liberal positions. The churches' public image as a force for resistance against National Socialism seemed to oblige them to criticize the totalitarian socialist dictatorship being established. Knowing that they commanded popular support, they expressed themselves with confidence on such topics as legal arbitrariness, freedom of expression, religious schools, conditions in internment camps, publicity for the National Front among pastors and church employees, and the ideological orientation of university education. On 28 April 1950, these topics were discussed at the first major "summit meeting" between representatives of the East German government and the Protestant Church. Representatives of the Catholic Church were present as observers. The meeting, however, did not produce any long-term easing of tensions.[8]

When the SED attempted to assert an ideological monopoly for its Marxist-Leninist worldview, the relationship between the state and the Church became more confrontational. In the middle of 1952, in the course of the systematic "building of socialism," the SED started to attack the Church openly, especially the Church's youth work. In a deliberate analogy to the conflicts with the NS-state, the Protestant churches characterized the events of 1952–53 as a *Kirchenkampf*. For them, the struggle was about their institutional autonomy, their spiritual independence, and their public role and ministry. Self-preservation and limiting the extent of the SED dictatorship went hand-in-hand.

After Stalin's death in the summer of 1953, the new leadership of the communist party in the Soviet Union intervened in East Germany, and the churches enjoyed a reprieve. At this time, the SED developed a new strategy vis-à-vis the Church—"differentiation" and "infiltration," trying to break up the still relatively cohesive front of the Protestant churches in the GDR. In spite of the new strategy, the SED's long-term goals remained eliminating the Church as a social and political power and restricting the Church to the realm of religious and ritual practices. Accordingly, between 1954 and 1958 the SED used all means at its disposal to replace confirmation as the coming-of-age ritual with its own atheistic rite of passage, the so-called *Jugendweihe*. The Church resisted. At first the Church proclaimed the incompatibility of *Jugendweihe* and confirmation.[9] Their self-confidence in this ideological confrontation was based on the positive experiences of 1952–53, when young people had been steadfast. However, beginning in the summer of 1958, the united front that Protestant Church leaders had put forward began to crumble. The leaders of the various regional churches reviewed their decision on the incompatibility of confirmation and *Jugendweihe* and came to different conclusions. Church leaders and pastors increasingly found less support among church members for their confrontational course; they had become an officer corps without foot soldiers.[10] Some parents even threatened to leave the Church if their children were not allowed to participate in confirmation because they had participated in the *Jugendweihe*.

For Catholics, the conflict of interests took a somewhat different form. Whereas confirmation and *Jugendweihe* happened at approximately the same time, First Communion took place much earlier—in the second school year—so that it was possible to do both. The state's sanctions for refusing to participate in the *Jugendweihe* were harsh; they included restrictions in employment possibilities and being barred from college entrance examinations, thus effectively being blocked from attending university. These sanctions proved effective. In 1959, 80.4 to 86.7 percent of eligible young people took part in the *Jugendweihe*.[11] Among Catholics, it was only 37.8 percent; the Catholic diaspora proved more resistant.[12] With the implementation of the *Jugendweihe*, the SED thus struck a massive blow against the Protestant Church as a social, cultural, and educational power. Indeed, the traditions surrounding confirmation collapsed.

A further decisive blow against the Protestant *Bildungsbürgertum* took place with the implementation of the "socialist university." The SED saw Protestant theological departments and student communities as "reactionary" centers. There were criminal trials against university pastors in 1957–58; a number of professors active in the Church lost their jobs; and there were numerous exmatriculations of members of both the Catholic and the Protestant student congregations. Through 1961, approximately two thousand university teachers fled East Germany, as did nearly thirty-five thousand university students and high school students who were not allowed to take their university entrance exams.[13] This exodus of the bourgeois elite had a long-term impact on East German Protestantism.

Protestant Difficulties in Finding
New Theological Positions after the 1950s

In 1958, the open confrontation between the state and the church was defused through a series of official state-church dialogues. Representatives from the state and the Protestant Church announced in a communiqué largely dictated by the SED that their blunt ideological struggle was over. The SED promised that it would comply with the constitutional promise of a fundamental right to the freedom of belief and conscience and agreed not to hinder the practice of religion. The Protestant Church retracted its accusation that the SED had breached the constitution when pushing through the *Jugendweihe* and declared its fundamental agreement with the "peace efforts" of the GDR. From now on, Christians would fulfill their civic duties on the basis of legality and would respect the development toward socialism. With this communiqué, the SED leadership had won a partial victory. At least indirectly, East German churches had declared their support for the social developments in the GDR. Within the Church, however, responses to the communiqué ranged from sharp criticism to sympathetic approval; more rejected than approved the development.[14]

This shift in the official attitude of the Protestant churches needs to be seen in its proper historical context. The state insisted on a declaration of loyalty from the largest church, a de facto demand for the Church to acknowledge its policy goals. The prospect of an early end to the SED regime was receding. Because the forced collectivization of agriculture had convinced many educated and propertied farmers to emigrate to the West, Protestantism had lost a significant part of its social base. Accordingly, grassroots support for the Church's confrontation course proved to be too weak for it to be continued. As the process of dechristianization advanced dramatically—the most important foundation for the autonomy of a national church—its support in the population, was crumbling. Membership decline disproportionately affected the Protestant Church, which was evolving from being a majority to a minority church. In contrast, the Catholic Church was and remained a minority church.[15]

This changing reality had consequences for ecclesiological self-understanding. Towards the end of the 1950s, individual Protestant theologians in the GDR began to think about developing new paths and new forms of church work in an atheistic environment. As early as 1956, at the all-German synod of the Protestant Church in Germany (EKD), the Cottbus General Superintendent Günter Jacob, talking about the "End of the Age of Constantine" for the Church in East and West Germany, called on the Church to accept that it was now going to play a much more minor role in society, regardless of the causes for the secularization. He also called on

Christians to accept a stronger separation of church and state. The Church should not be tied to any particular social order, it should concentrate on the gospel and its ministry. An environment in which people were hostile to the concept of faith could be an opportunity for Christianity. Jacob also referred in his lecture to the Church's and to a Christian's right to resist the state in case of conflict, and he even interpreted this as a "form" of loyalty to the SED state.[16]

While Catholic leaders were less willing to engage in theological reflection about the new situation in state socialism, East German Protestants developed a wide spectrum of theological and religious policy positions. These ranged from opportunists loyal to the state, to theologians who tried to maintain a constructive yet critical position, to critical pragmatists oriented to the West, and to real opponents of the state.[17] The whole spectrum of diverging positions vis-à-vis the SED state was found in the "quarrel over the authorities" of 1959–60. Otto Dibelius launched this dispute when he offered a theological justification for parliamentary democracy—which he by no means loved—and a theological rejection of the eastern state system in which, according to him, there was no rule of law and no justice. Dibelius's claim triggered a fierce controversy in East and West Germany.[18] Concerned that the debate could spread to his own church, the Catholic Bishop of Berlin, Julius Döpfner, emphasized to his own clergy that the East German state should be seen as the ultimate authority in all matters concerning law and order.[19] Indeed, noting the differences within the Protestant Church, Döpfner believed that the Catholic bishops would soon be the only ones resisting the ideological claims of the SED state.[20]

Prior to 1961, hopes for German reunification had taken a lot of the pressure off the Church to come to a *modus vivendi* with the GDR and wrestle theologically with what life in a communist state would mean. After the construction of the wall in 1961, such hopes largely disappeared. However, both churches dealt differently with the reality that the SED state was consolidating its power. During his inaugural visit to Willi Stoph, the Deputy Chairman of the Council of Ministers, Alfred Bengsch, the newly appointed bishop of Berlin who was also the chairman of the Berlin Bishops Conference in the GDR, made it clear that the Catholic Church would not comment on everyday political issues. In return for this public abstinence on political issues, Bengsch expected Catholics to be allowed to practice their religion without interference and he himself be allowed to carry out the duties associated with his episcopacy in West Berlin.[21] Although there was no binding agreement, the two sides did develop a *modus vivendi* on the basis of this conversation. In the following years, Bengsch repeatedly called on state authorities to consider his silence and his restraint "as a conscious act of loyalty."[22] In practice, this meant that after 1961, the Berlin Conference of the Leaders of the Catholic Church in the GDR took a public position on very few social developments, such as abortion.[23]

On the Protestant side, East German church leaders came together for the first time in 1963 to discuss and publish a religious-theological statement on the place of the church and Christians in the GDR. In the "Ten Articles of Freedom and Service of the Church," leaders defended their Christian identity and their way of life against the demands of an ideological atheistic state.[24] The articles rejected both conformity and retreat into a religious ghetto. Instead, the articles called upon Christians to differentiate in socialism between "the requirement to work to preserve the quality of life and the requirement to reject any and all engagement with atheism."[25] Demanding the rule of law, human dignity, and religious freedom, the articles held out the possibility of resistance. Representatives of the party and the state in East Germany naturally characterized the text as antisocialist. The Weißenseer working group, a kind of ecclesiastical brotherhood which since 1958 had taken up the fight against *Dibelianismus* and to which Albrecht Schönherr (amongst others) belonged, criticized the text from a theological perspective. In November 1963, the working group published as an alternative theological concept, a seven-sentence statement, "On the Church's Freedom to Serve."[26] In these sentences, the authors expressed a new understanding of the relationship of the Christian faith to the world in a socialist society.[27] Basing their interpretation on a distinct reading of Dietrich Bonhoeffer, they insisted that Christ had given us the unconditional freedom to serve, and that this could be realized in a socialist society in particular; they emphasized solidarity with the godless and the central meaning of social justice and world peace. What ultimately motivated the authors of the seven sentences to develop this theological perspective was that they wanted the Church to emerge from its defensive posture: its theology was to be one of adaptation.

During the 1960s, the SED pursued a policy of divide and conquer. It sought to divide both within and between the two major churches. After the construction of the Berlin wall, for instance, the churches worked hard to help people deal with the consequences of the division. Doing so required working together on a number of activities. Thus, for example, at the end of May 1964, the Protestant and Catholic churches both attempted to move forward with negotiations between the East German and West Berlin governments to allow citizens from West Berlin to visit East Berlin (*Passierscheinverhandlungen*). Günter Jacob, who in the meantime had become the acting director of the bishopric of the eastern region of the Protestant Church in Berlin-Brandenburg, wrote to Willi Stoph, the Chairman of the Council of Ministers. Jacob offered the West Berlin parish halls as offices where the passes could be issued, and he made this offer also on behalf of the Catholic Church.[28] The State Secretary for Religious Affairs in the GDR, Hans Seigewasser, to whom Jacob made the offer verbally, stated with a good deal of displeasure that this was the first time the two churches had agreed on a concrete joint action.[29] In a resolution from 14 January 1964 the Politburo already instructed state officials to effectively counter joint action by the two churches "through a differentiating policy at all levels, taking into account the contrasts and contradictions between the two churches."[30] Accordingly, on 25 June, Seigewasser advised Jacob to stay out of the negotiations to allow West Berliners to travel to East Berlin.[31] On 18 August, during the ongoing negotiations, Walter Ulbricht, the Chairman of the Council of State, and Moritz Mitzenheim, the Thuringian state bishop, met at the Wartburg. Ulbricht blamed the West German government for the stalled negotiations, and Mitzenheim agreed.[32] During this discussion, the two also talked about the possibility of allowing East German pensioners to travel to West Germany, and on 9 September Mitzenheim was allowed to announce the SED government's decision to allow GDR senior citizens to travel to the West to visit their relatives.[33] The Thuringian bishop was thus singled out as one of the state's favorite negotiating partners. At the same time, the state conveyed the message that in the GDR one only had to speak with those in charge in order to obtain some relief for human problems. The SED's policy of differentiation could, however, also be used against the SED. When Seigewasser pointed out to Bengsch that the Protestant churches were giving public political support to the government, Bengsch pointed out that they were also raising criticisms, and that therefore the Catholic course of political abstinence was more favorable for the state.[34]

The SED's most important goal in the 1960s was the legal separation of the East German churches from the all-German organization of the Protestant Churches in Germany (EKD). The SED achieved this goal with the assistance of the new constitution of 1968. In the new constitution, the formal rights of the Church were considerably reduced, and even these rights depended more than before on the state's goodwill. Article 39, paragraph 2 stated: "Churches and other religious communities organize their affairs and carry out their activities in accordance with the constitution and the legal provisions of the German Democratic Republic. Details may be stipulated in agreements."[35] Cardinal Bengsch made it clear in a discussion with State Secretary Seigewasser on 15 July 1968 that the Catholic Church both in East Germany and in the Vatican did not plan to negotiate any such agreements.[36] Instead, they continued to rely on "secret personal diplomacy . . . in order to be able to negotiate and preserve the church's ability to influence affairs through informal agreements."[37]

The East German regional churches interpreted Article 39 (2) as a criminalization of their work in the all-German EKD. Although this certainly influenced their decision, there were ultimately a whole bundle of reasons why in 1969 the East German member churches decided—controversially—to break away from the EKD to found the Federation of the Protestant Churches in the GDR (BEK).[38] They did this because of the paralysis of the all-German EKD. They also wanted to secure the solidarity of the East German regional churches vis-à-vis the state. Not least, they were driven by their conviction that in so doing, they could best carry out their ministry in its societal context. Theological reflections like the last one were mentioned in particular by Albrecht Schönherr, General Superintendent of the Evangelical Church in Berlin-Brandenburg for the eastern part of Berlin and Brandenburg, who was in charge of founding the federation. Not everyone agreed. The Berlin Superintendent Reinhard Steinlein, a harsh critic of the policy of taking the East German churches out of the EKD, considered the behavior of the Catholic Church exemplary.[39] The Catholic Church in East Germany, because it was part of a worldwide organization, had admittedly an institutional protection which the Protestant Church lacked: by stating that only Rome had the authority to make decisions, the bishops in East Germany were able to sidestep some of the state's demands.[40] In contrast, the fact that the East German regional churches were integrated into the all-German EKD was the focus of many state attacks on the Protestant Church through 1969.

The two churches kept each other informed about their responses to the new constitution. Indeed, this exchange of information was institutionalized in a new Protestant-Catholic advisory group (*Konsultativgruppe*), which consisted of three senior representatives of each church. The group was set up after and as a consequence of the Second Vatican Council, which otherwise had little impact on the official line of the Catholic Church in East Germany. Cardinal Bengsch, a defender of the ecclesiastical tradition both in East Germany and abroad, refused to carry out in East Germany the theological impulses of the pastoral constitution, *Gaudium et spes*, which called for the Church to participate in the affairs of the world.[41] He stuck to his defensive strategy of sealing off the Church's internal affairs from outside influences. On the other hand, in the Decree on Ecumenism, *Unitatis redintegratio*, Catholics were called upon to work with Christians of different confessions to find a path to unity and to walk down it together. The decree also mentioned the possibility of the churches cooperating on social issues. After conversations between the joint Chairmen of the Conference of the Church Leaders, the Greifswald bishop Friedrich-Wilhelm Krummacher, and Cardinal Bengsch, the bishops of the East German regional churches agreed in mid-January 1968 to set up an "advisory group between the two bishops conferences responsible for practical tasks in church leadership."[42] The minutes of the first meeting in May 1968 not only contained a description of the current state of affairs among the church leaders in regard to ecumenical relations in the GDR, but also set future goals: both churches desired to "work well together" and for there to be "a genuine growth in community between us, without pandering to ecumenical ecstasy." They welcomed "the already existing solidarity," which "especially within the borders of the GDR, is both a blessing and a necessity."[43] The central task of the commission was to exchange information and experiences.[44] The Catholic side made no provision for any joint action on any political questions. Thus in early October 1968 during a visit, Cardinal Bengsch informed Bishop Niklot Beste, the Chairman of the Conference of the Church Leaders, that joint declarations from the pulpit by the Catholic and Protestant churches in the GDR on political issues were "not to be recommended" because "the state would view such actions as a *casus belli*."[45]

The advisory group was not the only ecumenical body in the GDR. Already in 1966, an ecumenical theology working group had been formed, a venue where theology professors of both denominations could regularly meet and exchange ideas.[46] The Catholic Church participated as observers in the Working Group of Christian Churches (*Arbeitsgemeinschaft Christlicher Kirchen*), founded in 1970. In March 1971, the Berlin Conference of the Leaders of the Catholic Church in the GDR (*Ordinarienkonferenz*) formed an Ecumenical Commission, which beginning in 1976 organized conferences with the Ecumenical Commission of the Church Confederation. Ecumenical contacts also took place at the level of the regional Protestant churches and the Catholic dioceses. And at the grassroots level, the contacts between the confessions in the GDR started earlier. For example, in 1958 a Catholic priest and a Protestant minister founded a "Protestant-Catholic Letter Circular." Up through 1969, the circular published a newsletter—with the approval of the leadership of the Catholic Church—with a circulation of approximately fourteen hundred. This newsletter contained theological essays, reports on ecumenical events, and letters to the editor. In 1970, the Church withdrew its official stamp of approval for the letter circular. The Berlin Conference of Church Leaders in the GDR accused the periodical of bias in their choice of authors and of reprinting contributions critical of the pope and of church teaching. After this, the letter circular continued privately until state authorities prohibited any further publication in 1976.[47]

At the congregational level, the degree of interdenominational contacts varied.[48] They were quite strong in the areas of new housing constructed in the 1970s, where church work had to be built from the ground up.[49] Yet in the 1970s, previously important forms of interdenominational interaction were playing less of a role. After the end of the war, Protestant churches had opened up their doors to neighboring Catholic churches and allowed them to hold their services in their chapels; the Catholic churches needed the space because of the stream of refugees. But even in the 1950s, this did not produce an ecumenical breakthrough.

Opening Up versus Sealing Off: Diverging Strategies in the 1970s

In a meeting of the advisory group on 3 July 1969, "both sides emphasized that the emerging state awareness among the younger generation, as well as [of] modern theological concepts such as were being articulated in a theology of the world, a theology of revolution, etc., force us to ask the question[:] how are we to draw borders between the church and the socialist state[?]"[50] In the 1970s, the two churches followed different paths in their answers. The Protestant churches began to be more engaged with the socialist state; they were slowly becoming a part of the GDR. The protagonists in this process were middle-aged and younger. Especially following the founding of the Church Confederation, they reflected openly about how the Church could actively participate in a socialist society. Many found inspiration for their ideas and thoughts in the writings of Western ecumenism, where many authors campaigned for the church to open up to the modern secular world and to be open to socialist ideas. Many also made reference to the Barmen Declaration and to the Darmstadt Statement and read the theology of Dietrich Bonhoeffer and Karl Barth. In a theological clarification of their situation, the authors affirmed and justified the independence of the Church within a socialist society but, at the same time, argued it was possible for the Church and Christians to work within this socialist society. This theological reorientation is especially clear in the following formulation. According to the Federal Synod of 1970, the Federation of Protestant Churches in East Germany was defined as a "church community of witness and service in the socialist society of the GDR." The Church wanted—according to the Federal Synods of 1971 and 1972—to be a "church for others," thereby bridging the gap between the church and society. Interestingly, the Church saw itself more responsible for this gap than the state and its enforcement of socialist ideology.

The Church never precisely defined the term "socialism" and officially understood it as a mere description. Attempts to reinterpret "socialism" positively and capable of being reformed, however, encountered resistance from the SED. The Erfurt Propst Heino Falcke discovered this in 1972 when he expressed his hopes at the Dresden Federal Synod for an "improvable socialism." His use of this term was naturally understood as criticism of East Germany's "real, existing socialism." In order to safeguard its power and secure its authority, the SED insisted that it alone could define socialism. Of course, reflecting on the "Witness and Ministry of the Protestant Church and Christians in the Socialist Society of the GDR" did not take place entirely without dialogue with Catholic representatives. For example, at a meeting of the advisory group in February 1974 on "The Fundamental Question of the Church and Society," the group discussed the position paper of the committee on "religion and society" of the Federation of Protestant Churches in East Germany and agreed that the statements in the paper—"on the content of the mission of Christ: reconciliation"—should be seen as a "good starting point for further discussion of the topic."[51]

In possession of these theological reflections, the newly founded Federation of Protestant Churches in East Germany maintained a "balancing act" between conformity and opposition. It did so carefully in order to preserve its independence. Already in the first few years, it encountered difficulties. Although the SED government recognized the Federation, this did not mean that the state and the party ceased their policy of excluding and marginalizing the church and Christians. Under Schönherr's guidance, the Church Confederation attempted to avoid confrontation with the state leadership and the party and to maintain a cooperative attitude. Only by the mid-1970s did this seem to have a positive effect. The SED became increasingly willing to talk and acknowledged that the churches could do things that went beyond simply holding services and administering sacraments. This change in church policy was a result of the increasing self-confidence of the state and party leadership, which was partly the result of greater international recognition. Party leaders nonetheless had to pay attention to international public opinion for economic reasons. As a condition for the degree of autonomy and opportunities for independent action which it was willing to grant the churches, the SED government demanded that the churches show their loyalty in order to help stabilize the system. The SED attempted to achieve this attitude of loyalty through private conversations with church officials at all church levels and through a massive infiltration of the churches by the State Security Services that reached all the way to very top of the church hierarchy. Of course, the state never hesitated from using a more confrontational approach and of "differentiating," an approach that had a greater chance of success in the structurally and theologically more heterogeneous Protestant Church.

The self-immolation of the Protestant pastor Oskar Brüsewitz in Zeitz in 1978 occurred during a lessening of the tensions in church policy; his suicide endangered the fragile relationship between the Church and the state. With his public suicide, Brüsewitz wanted to make a statement against the discrimination of Christians in the education sector and to move the Church to a position of stronger opposition. The case became known publicly in East Germany through the West German media, which irritated the SED enormously. At the grassroots level of the Church, the "Zeitz case" caused considerable discontent and produced tensions with church leaders, whose conduct and behavior toward the state continues to be criticized to the present day. All the same, the policy of easing the tension between the state and the Protestant Church continued. Indeed—and this astonished the grassroots both in the party and in the Church—the policy produced a "summit talk" between the Chairman of the Council of State Erich Honecker and the Chairman of the Conference of Church Leaders on 6 March 1978. The summit talk resulted in some relief for the Church, but no legal certainty. Nevertheless, in the following years the meeting on 6 March 1978 was invoked by both the Protestant and the state authorities as evidence of peaceful coexistence.

The summit talk led to unpleasant verbal exchanges between the denominations, which were played out in the media of the Federal Republic. The West German media for years had been serving as a substitute public sphere for the East: it printed articles of concern to Germans in the East that were intended to become the focus of debate there. The West German "Information Service of the Catholic Working Group on Contemporary Issues" thus published a polemical article by its editor-in-chief Michael Albus about the summit. In it, Albus suggested, among other things: "Could it be that the motivation of Bishop Schönherr and his friends to participate in the summit talks was the unspoken aim to secure the material basis of the church, given that the church is losing public support? And that the reason behind this was that they could find it easy enough to imagine that in the long run there were likely to be dangerous attacks by ideological opponents on a church which had been identified as weakened?"[52] The Protestant Church "had only thought of itself[,]" but the Catholic side had received "not as much as a blessed word" about the talks in the run-up to the talks from the Church Confederation, Albus explained, picking up on a statement by Cardinal Bengsch.[53] "From the point of view of the essential community of the Christian churches of different denominations, this fact of non-information must be considered an affront to the Catholic brethren," he added. "Does one go too far when one speaks here of a deliberate omission by the Protestant side?" was Albus's rhetorical question.[54] The church offices of the EKD in Hanover protested strongly, charging that the EKD did not refer to the motives suggested for agreeing to the summit, but rather to the incorrect statement about the absence of information.[55] In fact, on 2 March, the Protestant managing director of the advisory group, the high ranking church official (*Oberkirchenrätin*) Christa Lewek, after trying in vain to make a personal appointment, wrote a letter on behalf of the Chairman of the Conference of the Church Leaders to the secretary of the Berlin Bishops Conference, Prelate Paul Dissemond. In the letter, Lewek did indeed inform Dissemond about the upcoming summit. However, no concrete details were given about what was going to be discussed. The letter said only that the conversation would be on "questions of principle which are of interest to both sides as well as individual issues."[56] On 10 March, Lewek sent Dissemond brief information from the Secretary about the conversation, and on 15 March she talked to him personally about it. On 31 March, during a visit to his official residence, Bishop Schönherr informed Cardinal Bengsch about the conversation.[57] Bengsch, when asked explicitly by Schönherr, stated that he agreed with the content of the summit.[58] At a meeting of the conference of church leaders on July 7, several members reported that in meetings representatives of the Catholic Church had repeatedly accused the Protestant Church of not having informed the Catholic side before 6 March. Even the KNA (*Katholische Nachrichtenagentur*), the Catholic wire services, made this accusation. The conference therefore expected the Catholic side to "clean these things up . . . otherwise relations would deteriorate."[59] As a result, Dissemond wrote to Lewek on July 10, confirming that they had been informed before and after the summit talks.[60] The KNA reported on 27 July that the Bishops Conference had been "informed about the meeting on March 6 in advance."[61] The irritated reactions on both sides suggest that there was considerable tension in their relationship, but, given the SED's policy of differentiating between the two churches, neither side had an interest in escalating conflicts.

In September 1978, the advisory group discussed the relationship between the two churches, describing "respect and trust as constitutive for this relationship." All members of the advisory group believed that the topic, "'the position of the church in society' ('the Church in Socialism') was well-suited to develop mutual understanding of each other's positions in an exemplary way and, if necessary, to discuss openly with each other the differences in each other's basic views."[62] At the meeting in January 1979, thirty years after the founding of the GDR, there was, for the first time, an open discussion, albeit not a public one, between representatives of the Protestant and Catholic churches about their different theology and religious policy strategies in the GDR.[63] The Protestant Bishop of Saxony, Johannes Hempel, first gave a general presentation from the perspective of Protestant theology on the relationship of the Church and society in the GDR.[64] He stated that the path of the churches in the GDR should be such that society should be taken seriously "as a work of the hidden God." The congregations must therefore try to serve this society. This ministry in the name of God must come from one's own motivation and must "be a service to society without surrendering to society." He noted that there was a strong movement within the field of Protestant ethics that argued that individual ethical solutions were no longer sufficient to address contemporary problems, as everyone was integrated into supra-individual structures. Individual ethics, therefore, had to be supplemented with social ethics. In practice, this was a dangerous balancing act, as there was always the danger of "sliding into too little or too much." In positive terms, this meant that the Church would decide as a church in which societal tasks and obligations to participate.

During the discussion, the Catholic side asked with regard to the relationship between the church and the state: "whether a genuine dialogue was possible, if there was a basic level of trust, to what extent there was a basic level of tolerance, and if the preconditions existed such that Christians would not be co-opted, since the Communists had explicitly stated that they rejected any form of ideological coexistence." The answers from the Protestant side documented the different approaches of the two churches to the church-state relationship. The Protestant side stated that although there was no "willingness to discuss ideology," "ideology was only one part of reality." The fact that the state evaluated and analyzed the conversations meant that "to a certain degree there was in fact a dialogue." Furthermore, state representatives "were also aware of the necessity of coexistence as a basis." According to the Protestant participants, tolerance had been practiced. They pointed to some positive results: they were able to clear up some "cases" in the Saxon regional church in the educational field; a pastoral ministry was to be allowed in retirement homes, in nursing homes, and in hospitals; television broadcasts could be used for the Church's public relations; and the Church's affiliation with the state's old-age retirement system was assured. One issue still open was the question of a pastoral ministry in the prison system. Christa Lewek, whose administrative tasks also included serving as secretary for the "Church and Society" in the secretariat of the BEK, summed up the *volkskirchliche* approach of the Church confederation. She pointed out that that the Church was continuing to play a significant societal role in the GDR and that it could not simply abandon these responsibilities or engage in what she called "abstinence." The Protestant Church could and desired to rise to the responsibility for the public welfare. For this purpose, structures had to be found for meetings and conversations with the state's leaders that the Church found acceptable. The "theory of the dialogue" is "unimportant here." With this, the differences were clearly marked. Because of its ideological opposition to the SED, the Catholic Church continued to follow its religious policy strategy of political distance and political abstinence in public, which had characterized the entire Bengsch era (1961–79). Given their ideological opposition to the socialist state, they also did not pursue an independent, contextual theology, that is, a theology that insists that it is necessary to understand the cultural context to fully understand scripture. Bishop Schönherr summed up the different positions with reference to a conversation with Bengsch in 1979 as follows: "The Catholic Church is interested above all in the preservation of its church; we are interested above all in witness and service in this society."[65] Protestants thus suspected that the "different basic conceptions of the mission and of the place of the church in society" also helped explain the Catholic Church's ecumenical restraint.[66] This observation was certainly true for the top Catholic leadership.

Because it wanted to expand its own possibilities and scope for action, during the 1970s the Protestant Church was undoubtedly interested in reducing its confrontation with the state. All the same, it continued to criticize discrimination against Christians in education and the workplace. At the local, county, or district level, pastors spoke with state officials about the lack of freedom and self-determination. From the end of the 1960s onwards and encouraged by developments in international ecumenical Christianity, East German churches came to hold collective values and social rights in high esteem. This did not mean that they abandoned individual civil rights and liberties. However, the Church did not speak publicly for them—with the exception of religious freedom—and they did not do so largely because of tactical religious policy considerations.

Given their membership numbers, the East German Church had not been a *Volkskirche*, a genuine national church, since the 1970s. Yet their future was not altogether dim. They received significant financial assistance from the West German Protestant Church (EKD). Largely out of its foreign policy interests, the East German state, moreover, took an interest in ascribing continued importance to them. The churches thus assumed the character of being *minoritäre Volkskirchen*, that is, national churches that were now numerically a minority. But this was not how the churches saw themselves. In their ecclesiastical self-interpretation, they saw themselves as a minority church shorn of its privileges, but one that in a secularized society was now in fact free from the state. Instead of giving way to resignation, they thus actively searched for new paths and religious models. They reflected theologically on missionary parish work and made changes in church practices, such as visiting parishioners at home, developing home groups and ministries in new housing areas, and introducing congress work at the national church congresses (*Kirchentage*). It was in their public role and ministry, however, that the East German churches still remained attached to the idea that they were indeed *Volkskirchen*.

Beginning in the 1970s, the East German churches, which were held in high esteem internationally for what they had accomplished under especially difficult conditions, became active internationally and ecumenically, especially in areas of anti-racism and peace and disarmament, including at the Conference for Security and Cooperation Process (CSCE). The relationship with the Catholic Church in the GDR, which rejected any cooperation in political questions, took a back seat.[67]

Tentative Rapprochement in the 1980s

The international activities of the Protestant churches had domestic consequences not intended by the SED regime. Through their international activities, the churches were able to demonstrate the social relevance of the Gospel and demonstrate autonomous ecclesiastical action in areas of political ethics. The Protestant churches were especially able to make their mark in their work for peace. When military service was made mandatory in 1962, Protestant church leaders—unlike Catholic Church leaders—asked the state for a provision for conscientious objectors. They continuously campaigned for the freedom of belief and conscience of Christian military service members. And they supported both those who refused military service completely as well as those who performed unarmed military service as "construction soldiers" (*Bausoldaten*). This was acknowledged and commended by those Catholics who worked with the Protestants on the ground.[68] Protestant youth showed a particular enthusiasm for the work of peace and in particular for the "peace decades," large assemblies promoting peace taking place every year in the ten days before the *Buß- und Bettag* in which young Catholics also took part. For the "peace decade" in 1981, the Protestant Church produced a textile print with the biblical slogan "swords to plowshares." The patch, which one could sew on clothes, later became the symbol of the independent peace movement in the GDR. The SED government responded nervously because of the increasingly difficult international situation and the unrest in Poland, and at times cracked down on youths who wore the patch. The church leadership persisted, however, and campaigned that the wearing of the symbol be allowed. However, in the face of government threats it eventually compromised and declared in September 1982 that it would no longer promote wearing the patch. This retreat by the Church did not mean, however, that the Protestant churches gave up their claim to be able to independently provide Christian testimony for peace vis-à-vis the state, which equated its own ideological fundamentals with its understanding of peace. In church leadership circles, in synods and in the Church's working groups, the new peace policy was discussed, and the prevailing doctrine of deterrence rejected.

The Catholic Church in the GDR did not engage publicly on questions of peace in any comparable way. It saw these questions instead as ethical decisions that individuals themselves had to make and merely sought to sustain and uphold an ethics of peace at the individual level.[69] The *Aktionskreis Halle*, which criticized society and the Church, thus complained about the "speechlessness" of the Catholic Church on peace and called for an interdenominational commitment to peace. Between 1975 and 1985, the *Aktionskreis*, which counted priests, Catholic laypeople, and Protestants among its members, published thirteen newsletters on peace, armament, and human rights.[70] In its engagement for a Christian testimony for peace in the GDR, the *Aktionskreis* referred to statements made by Protestant bishops, synods, and theologians and used them in its own writings and reflections.[71] On Pentecost in 1982, the group accused Catholic leaders of being unduly suspicious of Protestant peace work. Catholic leaders assumed that Protestant peace work was driven by political opportunism, even as they criticized it for imposing an unnecessary burden on the state-church relationship at the same time. According to the *Aktionskreis*, the bishops thought that they had to protect the Catholic Church from the "bacillus of 'accommodation'" by setting clear boundaries around it.[72] On 28 October 1982, in an audience, Pope John Paul II, however, encouraged the Berlin Bishops Conference to seek an exchange of views with the Protestant churches about the responsibility for peace.[73] In January 1983, for the first time in a common pastoral letter on the occasion of the Church's World Peace Day, the East German bishops criticized the SED's assessments of peace and the arms race, suggesting that on this issue they agreed with the Protestant churches.[74] However, in the final version of the pastoral letter—in contrast to the first draft—ecumenical action on the peace issue was reduced to common prayer.[75]

Beginning in the 1980s, the two sides made an effort in the advisory group to understand each other's positions on peace initiatives.[76] Both sides also made an effort to understand each other's attitudes towards "grassroots groups," composed mostly of younger people. These groups represented an alternative political culture which had emerged out of the peace groups at the beginning of the 1980s. By mid-decade, they had grown in size and were concentrating on peace, ecology, human rights, women's rights, and the "Third World." Because in the GDR open communication and alternative cultures were possible only under the protective roof of the Church, the groups were formed primarily within the Protestant churches or on their periphery. The Protestant churches offered the groups the opportunity to meet, hold events, and discuss and spread ideas in church rooms. The churches stood up for these groups in talks with state representatives, and in so doing passed on their positions to the state. In Protestant congregations, these groups' use of church facilities and open advocacy was not uncontroversial. These groups were composed of Protestant and Catholic members, as well as those of no religious faith. In a paper in 1984, the BEK Committee for Church and Society addressed how the Church should comport itself vis-à-vis groups who were not a part of a congregation either as formal members or through some other form of integration into a parish. The ecclesiological question of whether the congregation was the only legitimate organizational form of the Church and whether membership in a local congregation was the only way to show one's membership in the Church was taken up by Catholics "with great reluctance," according to the minutes of the meeting of the Protestant-Catholic advisory group from 15 March 1985.[77] As late as January 1988, Cardinal Joachim Meisner believed that the Protestant Church was in danger "of allowing itself to be exploited by groups who are in reality quite distant from the church and its genuine mission."[78]

Catholic leaders responded with restraint not only to "grassroots groups" but to the plans for a conciliar process which had been agreed to at the Assembly of the World Council of Churches in Vancouver in 1983 and put forward by the BEK delegates there. In these conciliar processes, the Christian churches prepared for an ecumenical pan-European "Council of Peace" in 1989 in Basel as well as for a Christian world assembly on "peace, justice and the integrity of creation" to take place in 1991 in Seoul. The initial Protestant minutes of the meeting of the advisory group on 25 November 1985, noted that "Prelate Dissemond reported that there was no great desire on the part of the Berlin Bishops Conference to become engaged in this project."[79] In the final version of the minutes of this meeting, which were revised because the Catholics had requested it, this passage read: "Prelate Dissemond reported on the concerns shared by Orthodoxy about the term 'Council' and on the fact that on the Catholic side the Holy See has the ultimate authority over this concern. Both put a certain reserve on the Berlin Bishops Conference."[80] At the beginning of July 1986, the board of the Conference of the Church Leaders asked the Berlin Bishops Conference to consider the proposal of the *Stadt-Ökumene-Kreis* in Dresden to convene an ecumenical meeting on justice, peace, and the integrity of creation in the GDR.[81] As a result, the question of what the two churches shared ecumenically over political and societal questions became urgent. Participation by the Catholic Church would affect the religious policy status quo and the *modus vivendi* of the Catholic Church in the GDR.[82] At the local church level, since the end of the 1970s there had been approaches toward a "political ecumenism."[83] On the Catholic side, the most important participant at the local level was the *Aktionskreis Halle*.[84]

In other words, Catholicism in the GDR was not completely homogenous in this field of action. This was true even at the highest levels of church leadership. Starting in the early 1980s, several individual bishops began to acknowledge the responsibility of the church and of the faithful to participate in a secular society. Their shift, however hesitant, had both theological and pastoral causes.[85] Traces of it could be found in the Bishops' Conference's pastoral letter from 8 September 1986, "The Catholic Church in the Socialist State."[86] That the steps were hesitant was made clear by the explanation given by the Görlitz Bishop Bernhard Huhn to the Protestant partners in the advisory group. He underscored that the pastoral letter was based on previous statements by the Bishops Conference and was merely a summary of Church positions on East German society. The letter nonetheless alluded to the "positive possibilities of bearing witness to one's faith in a socialist society."[87]

The pastoral letter once again led to a fundamental debate over the differing positions on state and society in the GDR. The Protestants perceived the cautious opening of the Catholic Church to be insufficient, as they made clear in their questions concerning the letter:

> What does it mean: to "sanctify the world"? Are not the boundaries set forth in the pastoral letter too narrow, too cramped, if the sanctification of the world can only be carried out by individual Christians? How is the church to preserve its identity and autonomy? Can this identity and autonomy only be upheld by staying out of things? In these efforts to protect the church's identity, is not too little attention being paid to the public mission of the church? Was it not the case that in all of the examples cited, where Christians had an opportunity to prove themselves, the emphasis was too strongly couched in terms of individual ethics and too little in terms of social ethics? How about the concrete responsibility of the church to intervene in the affairs of this world?[88]

Protestants speculated that what lay behind these statements was a rejection of the GDR and its society because in other countries one did not witness similar restraint from the Catholic Church. Catholic members pointed out that there were no Catholic ancillary organizations (*Verbände*) in the GDR, and that they therefore did not have any institutional way of carrying out the responsibility of the Church to participate in the affairs of this world. The two sides agreed that they both had to accept that the two churches in actuality were going down different paths in their relationship to the GDR and its society. For the Protestant Church, there was the "danger of accommodation"; for the Catholic Church, there was the "danger of total denial." At least both sides could agree that "much would already have been achieved if both sides could acknowledge that the path the other had chosen was a legitimate form of social activity for a church." However, this did not mean that both churches understood their behavior as "complimentary"—in a sort of implicit division of labor—as was suggested years later and long after the fact by Gerhard Lange, the man who was for many years the Catholic Church representative in the GDR in charge of contacts with the government from 1974 through 1990.[89]

After having sent only three observers in December 1986 to the working group preparing for an ecumenical convention in the GDR, the Catholic Bishops decided one year later to participate in the conciliar process through their working group, "Justitia et Pax," with twenty-five delegates. Following a first explanatory meeting on 13 October 1986, Protestants warned the Catholic side in November not to postpone the decision for too long, as there was a danger that "developments could get out of hand because of the impatience of the groups involved."[90] When it became clear that only delegates of the Church would participate, Catholic fears that in the ecumenical convention "all sorts of possible forces would be included who could have an impact on the outcome" dissipated.[91] Catholic congregations and the *Aktionskreis Halle* viewed critically the hesitation long displayed by the Berlin Bishops Conference.[92] At the three events of the conciliar process in East Germany in 1988 and 1989, official representatives of the Christian churches in the GDR discussed in a forum together for the first time socioethical questions concerning the social developments in the GDR, aiming to produce a common statement.[93] The perceived "rapprochement" of the Catholic Church to positions in the Protestant churches in the course of the ecumenical convention greatly interested the Stasi, and with good reason.[94] Indeed, statements made in or by the ecumenical convention were later found not only in synods and in Bishops Conferences, but also in the founding documents and proclamations of opposition groups and political parties. As it turned out, many of the delegates who participated in the ecumenical convention also participated in the peaceful revolution of 1989.

At the end of the 1980s, the Protestant Church publicly expressed its interest in social reforms through intercessory prayers, discussions, official statements, and at synods. At the same time, however, Protestant church leaders continued to try to maintain their precarious balance between loyalty and criticism and did not break off their dialogue with the state. The churches increased their demands step-by-step through the summer of 1989, but only by September 1989 was the federal synod ready to call for the basic elements of a liberal democracy. The Protestant churches nonetheless did help to create the prerequisites for the manner in which the radical change unfolded in the GDR. Their churches and parish rooms were sites where free speech was possible, where people accepted different views and lifestyles, and where people could practice pluralistic patterns of behavior. Because of its structural independence, the Church became both a platform and a shelter for alternative political groups. The Church represented the East German citizens who did not have a political voice in discussions with the state, and the Church had a humanizing influence on the state. With its appeals for nonviolence, the church helped shape the peaceful course of the revolution and worked to de-escalate confrontations. The forms of protest during the October Revolution—peace prayers and solemn vigils—had their origins in Church practices, and indeed these became the focal points of the mass protests. Trained by their work in synods in democratic procedures and thanks to the high moral prestige they enjoyed among the population, representatives of the Protestant Church—often working together with representatives of the Catholic Church—moderated the negotiations at the countless roundtables. The Protestant Church assisted in the democratic transformation of the GDR and negotiated and reconciled until the very end. However, neither it nor the oppositional forces who met under its roofs were "the forces of upheaval."[95] Rather, this transformation was the result of a series of factors which seemingly came together accidentally. Among the most important of these was increased social tensions, the opening of the borders, the loss of Soviet backing, and the failure of the SED machinery of power. The "peaceful revolution" was not a "Protestant Revolution."[96]

The Catholic Bishops Conference refrained from public statements until the beginning of November. On 11 November, it made a public statement which contained a new self-understanding: "We bishops see it as our duty—one which is a part of the tasks of our ministry—to take a position on current political affairs, not only when religious and church affairs are being debated, but also when what is being debated is the dignity and the fundamental rights of man, when what is at stake is the common good and social justice." The laity were called upon as "Christians in the world" to assume their "duty of political responsibility."[97] Of course, lay Catholics and clerics working at the grassroots had been politically active already since October.[98]

Confessional Differences in Interpreting the GDR Past

Most Protestants in East Germany saw their hopes for liberation from a country in which they were not free fulfilled in the months and years after November 1989. However, a minority of East and West German Protestants had hoped for a democratic socialism, and they saw this dream disappear with the end of the GDR in 1990.[99] Although criticisms of the Catholic

Church were not contained to only these Protestant, social-democratic circles, the attacks were concentrated there. When after the elections of 1990 Catholics were overrepresented in parliament and in government, many Protestants made the accusation that "we've made the revolution and now the Catholics are taking power."[100] It was not only the sustained appeals of the bishops to the Catholic laity to take on political responsibility that upset them so greatly; it was also the Catholic interpretation of their public political abstinence in the GDR as having taken a "clear position of rejecting . . . the claim to power of the socialist state"—according to the formulation in the Berlin Bishops' Conference's pastoral letter from 19 December 1989.[101] Ehrhart Neubert, formerly the Secretary for Community Sociology at the Church Confederation and one of the cofounders of the *Demokratische Aufbruch*, sharply criticized this "mythmaking": "in effect this retreat was not a way of expressing any critical inquiry about the SED state. It corresponded to the religious policy of the Communist state."[102] And the Wittenberg minister and civil rights activist Friedrich Schorlemmer angrily commented that the Catholic Church had been silent for forty years and had called on its members to be silent as well until after the *Wende*, when the Catholic Church presented itself as a determined, resolute opponent of the SED state. Those who had remained silent all that time, he continued, should now, too, "be silent."[103] It had not been possible to have such a public debate on the differing strategies for taking action in the GDR before 1989. If one had done so, one would have gone along with the SED's policy of divide and conquer, of differentiation. Now, however, some Protestant representatives were harshly critical of the Catholic Church hierarchy. And yet, the lines in this debate were not exclusively between Protestants and Catholics. Thus, in February 1990, the new chairman of the Berlin Bishops' Conference, Georg Sterzinsky, expressed a good deal of self-criticism in front of the BEK synod in regard to possible mistakes by the Catholic side.[104] And, in a letter at the end of December 1990 to all the members of the Bishops Conference, the Catholic theologian Wolfgang Trilling criticized the "lack of even a trace of admission of errors, omissions, etc.," the absence of a "grateful acknowledgement of our Protestant sister church" as well as "the complete absence of any ecumenical dimension" in the pastoral letter of December 1989.[105]

The confessional disputes over the interpretation of the GDR's history and the history of the revolution petered out in the following years as the churches embraced the ecumenical movement as it had been practiced for decades in the West. In the GDR, however, church leaders mostly acted separately. Their strategies diverged, even if there was hardly any public confessional animosity. Initiatives toward political ecumenism thus had to start at the grassroots. This has decisively changed: in the new, pluralistic Federal Republic, the two large Christian churches are now capable of acting jointly both at the highest levels of church leadership and at the local level.

Claudia Lepp heads the research center of the Protestant Working Group for Contemporary Church History and is an adjunct professor at Ludwig-Maximilian-University in Munich. The recipient of the Wolf-Erich-Kellner Memorial Foundation Prize and the Therese von Bayern Prize, she is the coeditor of the *Kirchliches Jahrbuch für die Evangelische Kirche in Deutschland* and the *Mitteilungen zur Kirchlichen Zeitgeschichte*. She is also the author of numerous books, including: *Protestantisch-liberaler Aufbruch in die Moderne, Die Ost-West-Gemeinschaft der evangelischen Christen und die deutsche Teilung*, and *Wege in die DDR: West-Ost-Übersiedelungen im kirchlichen Bereich vor dem Mauerbau*.

Notes

1. The political scientist Herbert Heinecke undertook the first attempt at a comparison. Heinicke, however, used exclusively secondary literature. See Herbert Heinecke, *Konfession und Politik in der DDR. Das Wechselverhältnis von Kirche und Staat im Vergleich zwischen evangelischer und katholischer Kirche* (Leipzig: Evangelische Verlagsanstalt, 2002).

2. The statistics are from Georg Dietrich, Bernd Schäfer, and Jörg Ohlemacher, *Jugendweihe in der DDR. Geschichte und politische Bedeutung aus christlicher Sicht* (Schwerin: Landeszentrale für politische Bildung Mecklenburg-Vorpommern, 1998), 6.

3. Lecture given at the Royal Institute of International Affairs in London on 13 May 1981. Reprinted in Wolfgang Thumser, *Kirche im Sozialismus. Geschichte, Bedeutung und Funktion einer ekklesiologischen Formel* (Tübingen: Mohr Siebeck, 1996), 433.

4. For an overview of scholarship on the relationship between the churches and the East German state, see Friedemann Stengel, "Kirchen-DDR-Geschichte zwischen Gedächtnispolitik und Erinnern," *epd Dokumentation* 40 (2015): 4–15.

5. On the religious policy of the various occupying powers, see Martin Greschat, *Die evangelische Christenheit und die deutsche Geschichte nach 1945. Weichenstellungen in der Nachkriegszeit* (Stuttgart: Kohlhammer, 2002).

6. Quoted in Evangelische Kirche in Deutschland, "Barmer Theologische Erklärung: Einführung zur Barmer Theologischen Erklärung," Retrieved 31 January 2019 from http://www.ekd.de/glauben/bekenntnisse/barmer_theologische_erklaerung.html. Reprinted in Martin Höllen, *Loyale Distanz? Katholizismus und Kirchenpolitik in SBZ und DDR. Ein historischer Überblick in Dokumenten. Vol. 1: 1945 bis 1955* (Berlin: self-published, 1994), 152.

7. Reprinted in Höllen, *Loyale Distanz? Vol. 1*, 152.

8. On the conversation, see Gerhard Besier, *Der SED-Staat und die Kirche. Der Weg in die Anpassung* (Munich: Bertelsmann, 1993), 74–77.

9. See Detlef Pollack, *Kirche in der Organisationsgesellschaft. Zum Wandel der gesellschaftlichen Lage der evangelischen Kirchen in der DDR* (Stuttgart: Kohlhammer, 1994), 131–33.

10. See Johannes Hamel, *Christ in der DDR* (Berlin [West]: Vogt, 1957), 10.

11. Statistics in Markus Anhalt, *Die Macht der Kirchen brechen. Die Mitwirkung der Staatssicherheit bei der Durchsetzung der Jugendweihe in der DDR* (Göttingen: Vandenhoeck & Ruprecht, 2016), 198.

12. Statistics in Ibid., 199.
13. See Friedemann Stengel, "Bedrängt. Bedrückt. Bearbeitet. Christen unter der DDR-Diktatur," in *Ökumenische Vorträge 2016*, ed. Christian Wagner and Winfried Weinrich (Erfurt), 16.
14. See Pollack, *Kirche*, 151–53.
15. Heinecke refers to this difference in his *Konfession*, 432. The Protestant Church lost between 25–30 percent of their previous members; the Catholic Church about 40–45 percent.
16. The Conference took place in Berlin in 1956. See Kirchenkanzlei der EKD, ed., *Bericht über die außerordentliche Tagung der zweiten Synode der EKD vom 27. bis 29. Juni 1956* (Hanover: Verlag des Amtsblatts der Evangelischen Kirche in Deutschland, 1956), 27.
17. See Pollack, *Kirche*, 166.
18. See Martin Greschat, "Römer 13 und die DDR. Der Streit um das Verständnis der 'Obrigkeit' (1957–1961)," *Zeitschrift für Theologie und Kirche* 105 (2008): 63–93.
19. See Heinecke, *Konfession*, 403.
20. Ibid., 404.
21. See the comments on this conversation in Höllen, *Loyale Distanz? Vol. 1*, 95–310.
22. Report from Seigewasser from 10 October 1966, concerning a conversation with Bengsch quoted in Bernd Schäfer, *Staat und katholische Kirche in der DDR* (Cologne: Böhlau, 1998), 234–36.
23. See Ibid., 236.
24. Reprinted in *Kirchliches Jahrbuch für die Evangelische Kirche in Deutschland* 90 (1963): 181–83.
25. Ibid., 182.
26. Reprinted in Ibid., 194.
27. See Thumser, *Kirche*, 237.
28. See Gerhard Kunze, *Grenzerfahrungen. Kontakte und Verhandlungen zwischen dem Land Berlin und der DDR 1949–1989* (Berlin: Akademie Verlag, 1999), 154.
29. See Besier, *SED-Staat*, 574.
30. Reprinted in Höllen, *Loyale Distanz? Vol. 1*, 396.
31. See Besier, *SED-Staat*, 575.
32. See *Kirchliches Jahrbuch für die Evangelische Kirche in Deutschland* 91 (1964): 134–36.
33. See Besier, *SED-Staat*, 578.
34. See Schäfer, *Staat*, 235.
35. DocumentArchiv.de, "Verfassung der Deutschen Demokratischen Republik vom 6. April 1968," Retrieved 14 January 2019 from http://www.documentarchiv.de/ddr/verfddr1968.html#39.
36. EZA (Evangelisches Zentralarchiv) Berlin, 104/570.
37. Schäfer, *Staat*, 458.
38. See Claudia Lepp, *Tabu der Einheit? Die Ost-West-Gemeinschaft der evangelischen Christen und die deutsche Teilung 1945–1969* (Göttingen: Vandenhoeck & Ruprecht, 2005), 790–921.
39. See Reinhard Steinlein, *Die gottlosen Jahre* (Berlin: Rowohlt, 1993), 80–83.
40. See Heinecke, *Konfession*, 442.
41. Ibid., 435.
42. Compilation of the Protestant-Catholic consultative group by Christa Lewek from 5 November 1969, EZA Berlin, 104/574.
43. Minutes of the meeting of the Protestant-Catholic consultative group on 30 May 1968, EZA Berlin, 104/570.
44. Ibid.
45. Note for the files concerning a visit by Beste to Bengsch on 8 October 1968, EZA Berlin, 104/570.
46. Reinhard Henkys has put together an overview of the ecumenical bodies in the GDR in his "Die DDR-Kirchen als ökumenische Partner," in *Die evangelischen Kirchen in der DDR*.

Beiträge zu einer Bestandsaufnahme, ed. Reinhard Henkys (Munich: Kaiser, 1982), 198–200, 201–3.

47. On the letter circular, see Reinhard Grütz, *Katholizismus in der DDR-Gesellschaft 1960–1990. Kirchliche Leitbilder, theologische Deutungen und lebensweltliche Praxis im Wandel* (Paderborn: Ferdinand Schöningh, 2004), 126–31.

48. See Heinecke, *Konfession*, 395.

49. See Hartmut Nikelski, "Ökumenische Zusammenarbeit im Neubaugebiet Leipzig-Grünau," in *Über Grenzen hinweg zu wachsender Gemeinschaft. Ökumene in der DDR in den achtziger Jahren,* ed. Matthias Sens and Roswitha Bodenstein (Frankfurt am Main: Lembeck, 1991), 63–66.

50. Minutes of the meeting of the consultative group on 3 July 1969, EZA Berlin, 104/573.

51. Minutes of the meeting of 11 February 1974, EZA Berlin, 101/368.

52. Michael Albus, "Ein 'konstruktives Gespräch'—für wen? Fragen, Überlegungen und Meinungen zum Gespräch zwischen Erich Honecker und Bischof Schönherr," *Informationsdienst des Katholischen Arbeitskreises für zeitgeschichtliche Fragen e. V.* 90 (1978): 8.

53. Ibid., 9. See Gerhard Lange, "Politische Gemeinsamkeiten zwischen der katholischen und evangelischen Kirche in der DDR?" in *Christen, Staat und Gesellschaft in der DDR,* ed. Gert Kaiser and Ewald Frie (Frankfurt am Main: Campus, 1996), 86.

54. Albus, *Gespräch*, 9.

55. See Lange, "Politische Gemeinsamkeiten," 86.

56. Letter from Lewek to Dissemond from 2 March 1978, EZA Berlin, 101/371.

57. See EZA Berlin, 101/371.

58. See Albrecht Schönherr, *. . . aber die Zeit war nicht verloren. Erinnerungen eines Altbischofs* (Berlin: Aufbau Verlag, 1993), 402.

59. Minutes of the 56th meeting of the KKL in the GDR on 7/8 July 1978, EZA Berlin, 101/371.

60. Excerpts of the letter are reprinted in Besier, *SED-Staat*, 115.

61. EZA Berlin, 101/371.

62. Minutes of the meeting of 29 September 1978, EZA Berlin, 101/371.

63. See the minutes of the meeting of 31 January 1979, EZA Berlin, 101/371. The following quotes are taken from these minutes.

64. On Hempel, see Sebastian Engelbrecht, *Kirchenleitung in der DDR. Eine Studie zur politischen Kommunikation in der Evangelisch-Lutherischen Landeskirche Sachsens 1971–1989* (Leipzig: Evangelische Verlagsanstalt, 2000).

65. Schönherr, *Zeit*, 313.

66. This at least is suggested in the report of the church leaders at the second session of the IX Synod of the Church Province of Saxony in Halle on 13 November 1980. See the quotes in Sebastian Holzbrecher, *Der Aktionskreis Halle. Postkonziliare Konflikte im Katholizismus der DDR* (Würzburg: Echter, 2014), 231–33.

67. This is also the opinion of Henkys, *DDR-Kirchen*, 172.

68. See Schäfer, *Staat*, 239.

69. See Bishop Schaffran at a meeting of the Consultative Group on 20 January 1981, EZA Berlin, 101/373.

70. See Holzbrecher, *Aktionskreis*, 203.

71. See Ibid., 246.

72. "Stellungnahme des Aktionskreises Halle zum Friedenszeugnis der Kirche in der DDR, Pfingsten 1982," quoted in Ibid., 207, 210.

73. The address to the audience is reprinted in Martin Höllen, *Loyale Distanz? Katholizismus und Kirchenpolitik in SBZ und DDR. Ein historischer Überblick in Dokumenten. Vol. 3/2: 1977 bis 1990* (Berlin: self-published, 2000), 78.

74. Reprinted in Gerhard Lange, et al., eds., *Katholische Kirche—Sozialistischer Staat DDR. Dokumente und öffentliche Äußerungen 1945–1990* (Leipzig: St. Benno Verlag, 1993), 306–11.

See Peter Maser, *Kirchen und Religionsgemeinschaften in der DDR 1949–1989. Ein Rückblick auf vierzig Jahre in Daten, Fakten und Meinungen* (Konstanz: Christliche Verlagsanstalt, 1992), 126.

75. See Jürgen Selke, *Katholische Kirche im Sozialismus? Der Hirtenbrief der katholischen Bischöfe in der DDR zum Weltfriedenstag 1983 und seine Bedeutung für das Verhältnis von Katholischer Kirche und Staat DDR* (Altenberge: Oros-Verlag, 1995), 163–65.

76. Minutes of the meeting on 20 January 1981, EZA Berlin, 101/373.

77. EZA 101/4263.

78. Ulrich Ruh, "DDR: Schwierige Gratwanderung der evangelischen Kirche," *Herderkorrespondenz* 42 (1988): 109.

79. Draft minutes, EZA Berlin, 101/4263.

80. Final version of the minutes, EZA Berlin, 101/4263.

81. See Letter from the director of the secretariat of the BEK Martin Ziegler to Dissemond, 1 July 1986, EZA Berlin,101/4263.

82. See Lange, "Politische Gemeinsamkeiten," 93.

83. On the conceptual history, see Holzbrecher, *Aktionskreis*, 242.

84. Ibid., 250.

85. See Christoph Kösters, "Revolution, Wiedervereinigung und katholische Kirche 1989/90," *Historisch Politische Mitteilungen* 17 (2010): 108.

86. The letter is reprinted in Höllen, *Loyale Distanz? Vol. 3/2*, 155–61.

87. The corrected version of the minutes of the meeting on 24 November 1986, EZA Berlin, 101/4263.

88. These questions were formulated by the Greifswald chief consistorial officer Siegfried Plath and given to the consultative group. Plath, who had the code name of Hiller, worked for the Ministry for State Security (MfS) as an "unofficial collaborator for the political-operative penetration and for protection of responsibility areas (IMS)." From 1984 on, Hiller was an "unofficial collaborator for homeland defense with enemy-connections and for the immediate processing of persons suspected of enemy-connected actions (IMB)."

89. Lange, "Politische Gemeinsamkeiten," 92–94.

90. See Ziegler at a meeting of the Consultative Group on 24 November 1986, EZA Berlin, 101/4264.

91. Minutes of the meeting of the Consultative Group from 8 April 1987, EZA Berlin, 101/4264.

92. Ibid.; Holzbrecher, *Aktionskreis*, 246.

93. On the "ecumenical assemblies," see Katharina Seifert, *Glaube und Politik. Die Ökumenische Versammlung in der DDR 1988/89* (Leipzig: St. Benno-Verlag, 2000).

94. See Schäfer, *Staat*, 423.

95. Pollack, *Kirche*, 454.

96. See on this, and on the discussion surrounding the interpretation, Beatrice Jansen-de Graaf, "Eine protestantische Revolution? Die Rolle der ostdeutschen evangelischen Kirche in der 'Wende' 1989/1990," *Deutschland Archiv* 32, no. 2 (1999): 264–70.

97. Quoted in Höllen, *Loyale Distanz? Vol. 3/2*, 272.

98. See Kösters, "Revolution," 71–73.

99. See Katharina Kunter, *Erfüllte Hoffnungen und zerbrochene Träume. Evangelische Kirchen in Deutschland im Spannungsfeld von Demokratie und Sozialismus (1980–1993)* (Göttingen: Vandenhoeck & Ruprecht, 2006).

100. On the reasons for this, see Kösters, "Revolution," 104. Quoted in Ehrhart Neubert, *Vergebung oder Weißwäscherei? Zur Aufarbeitung des Stasiproblems in den Kirchen* (Freiburg im Breisgau: Herder, 1993), 81.

101. Quoted in Höllen, *Loyale Distanz? Vol. 3/2*, 287.

102. Ehrhart Neubert, "Im Wettkampf bleibt die Ökumene auf der Strecke," *Deutsches Allgemeines Sonntagsblatt*, 6 December 1991, 3.

103. Quoted in *epd* ZA Nr. 130, 10 July 1991.

104. Quoted in Höllen, *Loyale Distanz?* Vol. 3/2, 296.
105. Quoted in Ibid., 289–91.

Bibliography

Albus, Michael. "Ein 'konstruktives Gespräch'—für wen? Fragen, Überlegungen und Meinungen zum Gespräch zwischen Erich Honecker und Bischof Schönherr." *Informationsdienst des Katholischen Arbeitskreises für zeitgeschichtliche Fragen e. V.* 90 (1978): 1–11.

Anhalt, Markus. *Die Macht der Kirchen brechen. Die Mitwirkung der Staatssicherheit bei der Durchsetzung der Jugendweihe in der DDR.* Göttingen: Vandenhoeck & Ruprecht, 2016.

Besier, Gerhard. *Der SED-Staat und die Kirche. Der Weg in die Anpassung.* Munich: Bertelsmann, 1993.

Dietrich, Georg, Bernd Schäfer, and Jörg Ohlemacher. *Jugendweihe in der DDR. Geschichte und politische Bedeutung aus christlicher Sicht.* Schwerin: Landeszentrale für politische Bildung Mecklenburg-Vorpommern, 1998.

Engelbrecht, Sebastian. *Kirchenleitung in der DDR. Eine Studie zur politischen Kommunikation in der Evangelisch-Lutherischen Landeskirche Sachsens 1971–1989.* Leipzig: Evangelische Verlagsanstalt, 2000.

Greschat, Martin. *Die evangelische Christenheit und die deutsche Geschichte nach 1945. Weichenstellungen in der Nachkriegszeit.* Stuttgart: Kohlhammer, 2002.

———. "Römer 13 und die DDR. Der Streit um das Verständnis der 'Obrigkeit' (1957–1961)." *Zeitschrift für Theologie und Kirche* 105 (2008): 63–93.

Grütz, Reinhard. *Katholizismus in der DDR-Gesellschaft 1960–1990. Kirchliche Leitbilder, theologische Deutungen und lebensweltliche Praxis im Wandel.* Paderborn: Ferdinand Schöningh, 2004.

Hamel, Johannes. *Christ in der DDR.* Berlin (West): Vogt, 1957.

Heinecke, Herbert. *Konfession und Politik in der DDR. Das Wechselverhältnis von Kirche und Staat im Vergleich zwischen evangelischer und katholischer Kirche.* Leipzig: Evangelische Verlagsanstalt, 2002.

Henkys, Reinhard. "Die DDR-Kirchen als ökumenische Partner." In *Die evangelischen Kirchen in der DDR. Beiträge zu einer Bestandsaufnahme,* edited by Reinhard Henkys, 172–212. Munich: Kaiser, 1982.

Höllen, Martin, ed. *Loyale Distanz? Katholizismus und Kirchenpolitik in SBZ und DDR. Ein historischer Überblick in Dokumenten. Vol. 1: 1945 bis 1955.* Berlin: self-published, 1994.

———, ed. *Loyale Distanz? Katholizismus und Kirchenpolitik in SBZ und DDR. Ein historischer Überblick in Dokumenten. Vol. 3/2: 1977 bis 1990.* Berlin: self-published, 2000.

Holzbrecher, Sebastian. *Der Aktionskreis Halle. Postkonziliare Konflikte im Katholizismus der DDR.* Würzburg: Echter, 2014.

Jansen-de Graaf, Beatrice. "Eine protestantische Revolution? Die Rolle der ostdeutschen evangelischen Kirche in der 'Wende' 1989/1990." *Deutschland Archiv* 32, no. 2 (1999): 264–70.

Kirchenkanzlei der EKD, ed. *Bericht über die außerordentliche Tagung der zweiten Synode der EKD vom 27. bis 29. Juni 1956.* Hanover: Verlag des Amtsblatts der Evangelischen Kirche in Deutschland, 1956.

Kirchliches Jahrbuch für die Evangelische Kirche in Deutschland 90 (1963).

Kirchliches Jahrbuch für die Evangelische Kirche in Deutschland 91 (1964).

Kösters, Christoph. "Revolution, Wiedervereinigung und katholische Kirche 1989/90." *Historisch Politische Mitteilungen* 17 (2010): 55–112.

Kunter, Katharina. *Erfüllte Hoffnungen und zerbrochene Träume. Evangelische Kirchen in Deutschland im Spannungsfeld von Demokratie und Sozialismus (1980–1993).* Göttingen: Vandenhoeck & Ruprecht, 2006.

Kunze, Gerhard. *Grenzerfahrungen. Kontakte und Verhandlungen zwischen dem Land Berlin und der DDR 1949–1989*. Berlin: Akademie Verlag, 1999.

Lange, Gerhard. "Politische Gemeinsamkeiten zwischen der katholischen und evangelischen Kirche in der DDR?" In *Christen, Staat und Gesellschaft in der DDR*, edited by Gert Kaiser and Ewald Frie, 63–100. Frankfurt am Main: Campus, 1996.

Lange, Gerhard, et al., eds. *Katholische Kirche—Sozialistischer Staat DDR. Dokumente und öffentliche Äußerungen 1945–1990*. Leipzig: St. Benno Verlag, 1993.

Lepp, Claudia. *Tabu der Einheit? Die Ost-West-Gemeinschaft der evangelischen Christen und die deutsche Teilung 1945–1969*. Göttingen: Vandenhoeck & Ruprecht, 2005.

Maser, Peter. *Kirchen und Religionsgemeinschaften in der DDR 1949–1989. Ein Rückblick auf vierzig Jahre in Daten, Fakten und Meinungen*. Konstanz: Christliche Verlagsanstalt, 1992.

Neubert, Ehrhart. "Im Wettkampf bleibt die Ökumene auf der Strecke." *Deutsches Allgemeines Sonntagsblatt*, 6 December 1991.

———. *Vergebung oder Weißwäscherei? Zur Aufarbeitung des Stasiproblems in den Kirchen*. Freiburg im Breisgau: Herder, 1993.

Nikelski, Hartmut. "Ökumenische Zusammenarbeit im Neubaugebiet Leipzig-Grünau." In *Über Grenzen hinweg zu wachsender Gemeinschaft. Ökumene in der DDR in den achtziger Jahren*, edited by Matthias Sens and Roswitha Bodenstein, 63–66. Frankfurt am Main: Lembeck, 1991.

Pollack, Detlef. *Kirche in der Organisationsgesellschaft. Zum Wandel der gesellschaftlichen Lage der evangelischen Kirchen in der DDR*. Stuttgart: Kohlhammer, 1994.

Ruh, Ulrich. "DDR: Schwierige Gratwanderung der evangelischen Kirche." *Herderkorrespondenz* 42 (1988): 108–10.

Schäfer, Bernd. *Staat und katholische Kirche in der DDR*. Cologne: Böhlau, 1998.

Schönherr, Albrecht. *. . . aber die Zeit war nicht verloren. Erinnerungen eines Altbischofs*. Berlin: Aufbau Verlag, 1993.

Seifert, Katharina. *Glaube und Politik. Die Ökumenische Versammlung in der DDR 1988/89*. Leipzig: St. Benno-Verlag, 2000.

Selke, Jürgen. *Katholische Kirche im Sozialismus? Der Hirtenbrief der katholischen Bischöfe in der DDR zum Weltfriedenstag 1983 und seine Bedeutung für das Verhältnis von Katholischer Kirche und Staat DDR*. Altenberge: Oros-Verlag, 1995.

Steinlein, Reinhard. *Die gottlosen Jahre*. Berlin: Rowohlt, 1993.

Stengel, Friedemann. "Bedrängt. Bedrückt. Bearbeitet. Christen unter der DDR-Diktatur." In *Ökumenische Vorträge 2016*, edited by Christian Wagner and Winfried Weinrich, 14–19. Erfurt, 2016.

———. "Kirchen-DDR-Geschichte zwischen Gedächtnispolitik und Erinnern." *epd Dokumentation* 40 (2015): 4–15.

Thumser, Wolfgang. *Kirche im Sozialismus. Geschichte, Bedeutung und Funktion einer ekklesiologischen Formel*. Tübingen: Mohr Siebeck, 1996.

Chapter Eleven

A Minority between Confession and Politics

Catholicism in the Soviet Zone of Occupation and the GDR (1945–90)

Christoph Kösters
Translated by Jeffrey Verhey

On New Year's Eve, 1989, the Catholic bishops in the German Democratic Republic (GDR) jointly addressed their faithful in a pastoral letter. Looking back at the recent days and weeks, they stressed that the principles of the revolution were the same principles "that have determined our past behavior and that determine our present behavior." They asserted that although previously the bishops had been the spokesmen on the "vital questions that affect our lives," such as the education system, peace and disarmament, or the protection of unborn life, now "we all" are called upon "to become spokespeople for our people and for a community based on law and justice." At stake here was "the dignity of the unborn child and of the disabled," the "dignity of the young people in educational institutions and in the barracks, and the dignity of those convicted of criminal offences." In this address the bishops established a direct line of continuity in terms of the "shared responsibility" and the "vital contribution" which "we Christians, we Catholics must bring." They admitted that there was no such thing as "Catholic politics," as Christians could in good conscience come to different positions. Still, it was worth considering whether or not the "groups of socially engaged Catholic lay people should form a single central body at the organizational level of the Berlin Bishops' Conference, one able to work both independently and with us bishops in the public sphere."[1]

The bishops' calls to inject a decidedly Catholic voice into the revolutionary discourse without any self-critical reflection about their previously tepid support for ecumenism and without any explicit statement of gratitude to the much more courageous Protestant Church caused considerable consternation among politically engaged Catholics like the theologian Wolfgang Trilling. Trilling, well-known throughout the GDR as a Church critic, stated that in light of this statement, "the previous ecumenical statements and declarations of intent have become a farce."[2] What was the Catholic Church's self-understanding in the diaspora conditions of the German east after 1945, and how and why did it change after the GDR was founded in 1949? And above all, what effect did Catholic self-understanding have on relations with the Protestant Church and on the political thoughts and activities of bishops, priests, and laity?

Fundamentally, every minority acquires a significant part of its self-understanding and identity by setting a boundary between itself and a "foreign" majority and establishing "closed" rules of behavior for its members.[3] This meant that in the GDR, Catholics were forced to draw back on the centuries-old experiences of belonging to a denominational minority and the lessons gleaned from these experiences. But there was one significant change: the Catholic diaspora suddenly became both denominational *and* ideological. Its relationship to the "foreign" majority—Protestantism—was perceived not only through a religious but also through a political lens. From the end of the 1950s on, Catholics followed a rule of thumb: they were not to seek ecumenical common ground in political questions. They were to streamline and standardize policy guidelines. But the latter inevitably led to tensions. Such conflicts were the result of changing confessional relations, a dramatic decline in church attendance and membership both locally and globally, a worldwide re-evaluation of understandings of the Church at the Second Vatican Council (1962–65) and, last but not least, ecumenical experiences at the grassroots. New possibilities for ecclesiastical and sociopolitical action began to emerge only when, at the beginning of the 1980s, the Catholic Church slowly but surely began to shed its defensive nature, one long shaped by its "double" fixation on the church and the state in the diaspora. It began to depict itself instead as a Christian minority of believers in a "secular, materialistic environment."[4]

I would like to develop this argument in three phases.[5] The first examines the basic conditions facing Catholics in the GDR, which were fundamentally different from those facing Protestants. In the 1940s and 1950s, these differences shaped guiding political and ideological principles—the specifically Catholic lens used to perceive the experiences of the "foreign" Protestant majority Church amid ideological repression. The second shows how Catholic perceptions of Protestants became more inflexible after

Catholic leaders stipulated that the Church had to practice "political abstinence" vis-à-vis the SED regime. The Catholic withdrawal from the public sphere made it possible to draw clear boundaries with the SED regime and Protestant paths of a "church in socialism." It also allowed the unity of the diocese of Berlin, broken in two by a wall and barbed wire, to be preserved. This allowed the Catholic minority to keep open an existentially important link to the majority Catholicism in the west. Internally, however, this practice of a "double" diaspora came to be increasingly experienced more as a Catholic "ghetto" blocking any sort of ecumenical *aggiornamento*, to use the term from the Second Vatican Council. This made it far more difficult to provide effective responses to declines in church membership and the secularization of socialist society. The third examines how pastoral concerns about the sudden loss of longstanding religious traditions led Catholics to provide a new justification for their minority status: they now redefined themselves as committed Christians operating in a secularized society. This not only made it possible to build a bridge to the Protestant Church; it also paved the way for Catholic laity to become more involved in society. I will conclude with a perspective on how this change in the self-understanding of the Catholic Church affected discussions about the GDR past 1990.

Denominational "Heritage," the Socialist State, and the "Double" Diaspora

In the "birthplace of the Reformation," Catholics had always been a minority and accordingly suffered from a lower status in society and culture. Already in the nineteenth century, Catholicism in the areas of central Germany that would become the GDR had depended on support both financially and in personnel from other areas in Germany where Catholics were the majority. This support was provided especially by Catholic Boniface Associations based in Paderborn, which had indeed been founded for this very purpose in 1849.[6] After the Allies' territorial and political reorganization of Germany at the Potsdam Conference in 1945, the area that would become the GDR in 1949 was left with a religious makeup that was largely Protestant, but home to a small Catholic enclave in Eichsfeld and to the Sorbian Catholics of the Oberlausitz[7].

The effects were far-reaching. From the Catholic perspective, the unity between east and west was primarily seen in religious terms, and from the Protestant perspective in national terms. The new boundaries created by the zones of occupation in 1945 cut through six Catholic dioceses—Osnabrück, Paderborn, Fulda, Würzburg, Berlin, and Wrocław (formerly Breslau).

In Berlin, the western sectors of the city were cut off from the rest of the diocese, which contained East Berlin and the surrounding areas. The diocese of Wrocław was reduced by the new Polish-German border to a very small region, which was administered from Görlitz. The Holy See, which only in the 1920s had contractually reorganized the Church's legal relationships with the German state and which in 1933 had safeguarded these relationships with the *Reichskonkordat*, did not believe that it had any room to restructure diocesan boundaries under the given political circumstances.[8]

The large number of refugees and displaced persons flowing into the Soviet zone overwhelmed Catholic parishes, especially those in cities that had been turned into piles of rubble. The number of Catholics in these areas doubled from slightly less than one million in 1939 to over two million by the postwar era. This intensified the "old" rifts between the denominations, while at the same time creating new ones between "native" and "foreign" Catholics. This in turn increased the already-strong pressures on the refugees to leave the Soviet zone and continue further west. For those Christians who remained in the GDR, the construction of a socialist society meant political persecution and the suppression of church life. Already by the end of 1947 initial hopes that the Christian Democratic Union (CDU), which had just started up in many locations, could serve as an intermediary between church and state vanished. As a result, those members of the clergy and the Catholic lay people who were politically engaged broke away from the Christian Democratic Union, which was a "block party," that is, a nominally independent party which in practice had become a puppet of the SED.[9] Contrary to legal assurances in the constitution, after the founding of the state in 1949 the GDR ruthlessly enforced its ideological claim to wield a monopoly over education. The government accordingly cut back religious instructions in the schools and pushed Church youth groups like "Kolping-Families" to the margins. It did so by promoting the state-run Free German Youth (FDJ) and the socialist coming-of-age ceremony and substitute for confirmation, *Jugendweihe*.[10]

It took the Catholic Church until the mid-1950s to respond organizationally and theologically to this upending of the political and social order. The establishment of the first independent Catholic administrative and educational institutions such as the Conference of Catholic Church Leaders (*Berliner Ordinarienkonferenz*) in 1950, the central seminary at Erfurt in 1952, the Church press, and Caritas organizations went hand-in hand with attempts to take stock of how changing conditions in the East German diaspora were altering pastoral work and theological reflection.[11] It was inevitable that the self-understanding of the religious minority was deeply affected by these political experiences. Leading clerics such as Bishop Wilhelm Weskamm of Berlin and Bishop Hugo Aufderbeck of Erfurt came to see these as pastoral challenges and strove to spiritualize them. They urged the faithful to participate in "building up the body of Christ" during this missionary "Hour of the Church" in order "to prove oneself" in the way of the cross.[12] At the same time, these tropes reflected the aggressive and militant legacy of Catholic social teachings—the struggle for the *libertas ecclesiae* ("freedom of the Church") vis-à-vis the all-powerful state and the Church's doctrinal condemnation of socialism and communism.[13] The German bishops' pastoral letters from 1950 and 1956 in both the East and West against materialism were thus unambiguous.[14] In the words of the Meissen bishop Otto Spülbeck at the Cologne *Katholikentag* (Catholic Annual Congress) in 1956, "we are living in a diaspora not only religiously but also politically." This phrase called on Catholics to accept their marginal status as both a political *and* religious minority in a "foreign house."[15] This reality of diaspora shaped above all how the Catholic minority saw the Protestant churches. That in the course of the Church Struggle after 1933 none of the Lutheran or Reformed regional churches within the boundaries of what would become the GDR had remained "intact" did not change the fact that the Protestant churches continued to maintain their dominant position both culturally and religiously. The generous liturgical "hospitality" which the Protestant congregations initially showed to the "foreign" Catholics by allowing them to celebrate their masses in Protestant churches was not free from customary confessional irritations like those over Marian forms of piety. And although originally both Christian churches protested against the functional materialism of the SED regime, in the second half of the 1950s they responded differently to the enormous ideological pressure put on Christian youth. In retrospect, the discussion on general principles which the leaders of the Protestant and Catholic churches had in April 1950 with the Grotewohl government did not mark the beginning but rather the end of common initiatives between the churches for a long time.[16]

A number of developments were responsible for Catholics closing ranks. The building of new Catholic communities as homes for refugees, a program which had been pursued with vigor at the beginning of the 1950s, gave way to disappointment that the program had not been very successful.[17] Toward the end of the decade, the Church became increasingly frightened and horrified that the Ulbricht regime's ideological battle against religion had led to a massive abandonment of a Christian way of life. According to the last GDR-wide survey of religious beliefs there were only 1,370,000 Catholics left in the GDR by 1964. This was a decline of almost one-third from 1950.[18] (Protestants experienced a similar decline.) This decline happened because Catholic displaced persons migrated in large numbers to the Federal Republic of Germany. In addition, many Catholics left the

Church after watching distressing developments in the majority Protestant churches.[19] Between 1956 and 1959, the number of confirmations in the Protestant Regional Churches fell precipitiously from about three-quarters of the population to about one-third. At the same time, the number of youths who participated in the *Jugendweihe* rose from 12 percent to about 80 percent.[20] In November 1958 the bishop of Meissen reported to the pope about "the difficulties of the diaspora, the nihilism among the Protestants, the distress caused by Marxism, the dangers of the *Jugendweihe*, and the pressures on parents. The parents will lose their present positions in their jobs if they do not send their children to the *Jugendweihe*. However, the Catholics are remaining loyal and brave."[21]

Such fearful self-reassurances shaped the Catholic Church's view of the developments in Protestantism. The controversies in Protestantism concerning the legitimacy of the existing authorities (*Obrigkeit*) and the loyalty demanded by the SED regime reinforced the impression that the Protestant churches in the east and the west were taking very different paths.[22] Catholics, in turn, hoped that the unity and solidarity on the Catholic side would be able to counteract similar centrifugal forces. In a report for the pope at the end of 1959, Cardinal Julius Döpfner of Berlin looked critically at the path to reach an understanding with the socialist state taken by the Protestant regional bishop of Thuringia Hartmut Mitzenheim: "Things are moving in the direction that it is to be expected that in the future in the GDR only the bishops of the Catholic Church will put forward a continuous and resolute defense against the ideological pressure on Christians. This increases both our burden and our responsibility."[23] Toward the end of the 1950s, although the churches were fighting a common ideological enemy, they increasingly felt that they were on their own.

By 1947, the participation of Protestant bishops in the *Volkskongress* prompted the Berlin bishop von Preysing to prohibit the clergy of his diocese from making any public political statements. With this, he sent a clear signal to his colleagues in Schwerin, Magdeburg, Erfurt, Meiningen, Bautzen, and Görlitz.[24] In July 1957 the bishops instructed the subordinate clergy to refrain from making not only any political statements on behalf of the Church but also any joint statements with representatives of the Protestant Church at the local or regional level: "Every denomination negotiates for itself. Joint discussions of issues which affect the church and which concern more than one denomination are to be rejected in principle."[25] The search for ecumenical common ground in *political* matters was believed to be of such importance that it was reserved exclusively for the bishops.

Without a doubt, the 1957 provisions, binding in all of the Church's administrative districts, were very effective in protecting the Catholic

Church from the numerous attempts by the SED to coopt the church for its political purposes. In July 1959, the Catholic bishops, including Auxillary and Metropolitan bishops, agreed on "principles for the management of the episcopate in the GDR."[26] These principles called for speaking with one voice; for refraining from all individual agreements with the government, including declarations of loyalty to the regime; and for "introducing to the government our ideas concerning the freedom of religion and the other basic human rights of the faithful." The faithful were to be kept regularly informed through pastoral letters and ultimately through the public sphere. The protests by the bishops were directed above all against those state measures which systematically aimed to remove education and upbringing from the Church's religious nexus in favor of a socialist worldview. These principles noted that the aggressive campaign for the freedom and the rights of the Catholic Church had its roots in the Church's social and political "heritage": the conduct of the Catholic Church in the GDR and its bishops was to make clear to all that the atheistic SED state was suppressing the right to religious freedom.

"Modern" Socialism, the Second Vatican Council, and Tensions in the "Double" Diaspora

Döpfner's successor as the Berlin bishop, Alfred Cardinal Bengsch, revised this course of action into one of "political abstinence." In his first visit in November 1961 to the Deputy Chairman of the Council of Ministers, Willy Stoph, Bengsch suggested that the Church's pastoral work was in the state's interest because it furthered public peace and public order and helped people to accept the importance of conscientiously carrying out their duties to the state authorities. Within the context of a "peaceful cooperation" there was therefore no need for public declarations of loyalty to the SED state, either voluntarily, as had been the case for the Protestant Church in 1958, or through coercion.[27]

With this "course of political abstinence and thus of a minimum of loyalty to the state in the form of foregoing any public statements," a sort of *modus vivendi* was achieved.[28] This would alleviate the difficulties that had resulted, for example, in everyday pastoral work in the diaspora as a result of the bishops' open protest from the pulpit against the regime's anti-religious policies. The Berlin bishop himself felt it was crucial to preserve the unity of his diocese, which had been divided by the construction of the wall. The ability to travel from East to West Berlin (and vice versa) would prove to be essential in the coming decades for the Catholic Church in the GDR and especially for Caritas, which was organized and run by the Church.

This *modus vivendi* with the state did not make the Catholic Church "unpolitical." In accordance with Catholic social teachings, Bengsch emphasized to Stoph that Catholic Christians were dutiful and conscientious in their obedience to the state, but only insofar as this was compatible with their conscience. He criticized unequivocally the ideological state pressure which stood in the way of the "peaceful cooperation" necessary to achieve the common good. In this vein, the bishops did not remain silent when the state intervened in parish pastoral work and put pressure on believers. Whether in regard to the introduction of general conscription (1962), the law on minors (1963, 1973, 1974), the law on families (1965), the termination of pregnancy (1965 and 1972), the draft constitution (1968), the *Jugendweihe* (1972), or the introduction of the *Wehrkunde* instruction (1978)—all of the bishops' statements either to the state or to the clergy included an explicit reference to the state's unfulfilled promise to respect the freedom of conscience and belief.[29] "As far as Christians are concerned," wrote the Catholic bishops in 1963 to Minister President Otto Grotewohl,

> their own conscience requires them to do a good job and so fulfill their duty within the state. However, they cannot give up their faith. Consequently they cannot agree to a prohibition—for all intents and purposes—of expressing their beliefs and of teaching their beliefs. The freedom of religion means not only the freedom to participate in ritual acts; it means objectively and necessarily as well the freedom to educate in a Christian sense and to lead a Christian family life.[30]

The bishops saw themselves as silent guardians of a Christian conscience and of Catholic social teachings. The SED regime could make do with this "loyal distance," to use the phrase of the historian and journalist Martin Höllen, since it was easy to control and gave the GDR the appearance of being a legitimate secular state. Such guardianship and advocacy had considerable consequences for the self-understanding of the "double" diaspora: it had to be implemented consistently *within* the Church as well. From the perspective of the bishops, ecumenical engagement in parish and student communities ran the risk of becoming a conflict-ridden political issue.

Starting in the early 1960s, it was no longer only the openly atheistic and actively anti-religious SED regime that put pressure on the Church. Rather, the Christian churches, even in the GDR, were caught up in the worldwide whirlwind of global social change.[31] By the end of the 1950s, the "cold" *Kulturkrieg* of anti-communism gave way in some circles to the conviction that humanity was on the brink of achieving a new humane, modern, progressive order worldwide—without religion. As political tensions between East and West seemed to be easing, the world-wide project of "socialism" appeared "secular" and even attractively "modern." In the Catholic Church, after the death of Pope Pius XII in 1958, his successors Pope John XXIII (1958–63) and Pope Paul VI (1963–78) stated that Christians had to recognize "the signs of the times" and to participate in shaping global changes. The papal encyclicals *Mater et magistra* (1961), *Pacem in terris* (1963), and *Populorum progressio* (1967) dealt with the major challenges of these years: social justice throughout the world, the universal validity and implementation of human rights, and the emerging north-south conflict. Above all, the Church sought new fundamental orientation. At the end of the Second Vatican Council (1962–65), the worldwide congregation of Catholic bishops professed unanimously that it subscribed to the principle of universal religious freedom. This paved the way for opening up a dialogue with other Christian denominations and even with non-Christian religions. The Church even modified its ecclesiology, its liturgical practice, and its social teachings "in the world of today" in order to adapt them to the rapid societal changes worldwide. It even offered to enter into dialogue with atheists, who saw the Church as their enemy, and with communists whom the Church had once called "hostile to God."[32]

But internal Catholic uniformity and coherence over how to position themselves vis-à-vis a socialist society gradually broke down, particularly when newer self-understandings emerged. Since the 1950s, many important pastors had become increasingly convinced that the GDR as a whole should also be acknowledged as the sphere for pastoral ministry. This new position made sense in light of the Second Vatican Council's call to adapt to larger global changes in church and society, including even those in the GDR.[33]

This was clear to the bishop of Meissen, Otto Spülbeck, when he sought advice on this issue in 1966—the first bishop in his diocese to do so—and when he convened a diocesan synod in 1969.[34] This was also clear to the delegates at this synod who were influenced by the Second Vatican Council and who included laity for the first time. These delegates and their bishop were no longer content with walling themselves off as a diaspora surrounded by Protestantism and the communist SED state. They saw the reality of life in the "socialist society with an atheistic form" as characterized above all by an "ideological" materialism which stood next to a "practical" materialism, which was, in fact, no less challenging.[35] In the words of the synod, "in this situation we are called upon to give testimony of our faith. As Christians we have to embrace this historic hour and our place in this historical location. We try to recognize the will of God in it."[36] The ecumenical testimony of a Christian minority was clearly given priority over dwelling on confessional differences with Protestants.

The Erfurt bishop Hugo Aufderbeck put a greater stress on pastoral theology. Warning of the dangers of a Catholic "ghetto church" which turned its back to the world, he called on Christians to confront the "powerful world views" with courage and to take the "narrow path" of being a vibrant (core) congregation serving Jesus Christ as missionaries.[37] Aufderbeck's pioneering ideas, which shaped generations of Catholic priests in the GDR, remained (unlike Spülbeck's) "chemically pure of the ecumenical idea."[38] According to the author of a pocket-sized paperback, "The Hour of the Church," the undisputed guiding principle of any and all Christian engagement was nonetheless that it must be impossible to misinterpret any efforts to "shape the life lived in the socialist society" of the GDR as participation in the "socialism of the GDR."[39] Aufderbeck had no desire to participate in the conversation about a "church in socialism" being carried out with great intensity in the Protestant Church. In this, he concurred with the Berlin Cardinal Bengsch.

Bengsch also recognized the effects of secularization on GDR society. Already in 1963, he had quite shrewdly characterized as "anachronistic" the search for "unity in our world-views in the modern, diverse, and complex world of today."[40] For Bengsch neither ecumenical *witness* nor letting the flock shrink and ministering to the "little flock" were viable answers in the diaspora to these global and ideological challenges.[41] In a series of theological reflections, he explored how to make salvation relevant for individual Catholics and their Church. It was not "dialogue" with the modern world or the "bourgeois" way of thinking and life that was important spiritually to those following Christ, but rather the "obedient acceptance of an inescapable life in the diaspora."[42] It is obvious that this understanding of diaspora remained shaped by the political realities of an anti-religious socialist state, and that meant continuing the course of "political abstinence."

Although the consensus on the "double" diaspora was beginning to break down among the bishops, the Berlin cardinal left no doubt he would vigorously pursue his course within the Church as well. He directed his efforts above all at the "leftist" campaign groups (*Aktionskreise*) and working groups composed of clerics, academics, and students that emerged after the Second Vatican Council. These groups were calling for a "dialogue" with socialist society, for a democratization of the Church, and for greater participation of Catholic laity in the Church. Bengsch's efforts impeded independent attempts by the grassroots to build bridges to the Protestant Church, as the *Aktionskreis Halle* in particular would painfully learn.[43] Bengsch and his closest colleagues on Church policy believed that a practical "political ecumenism" in areas like peace work endangered not only the *modus vivendi*, but the bishop's authority as well.

Bengsch, it turns out, was worried about the fragile unity of his divided Berlin diocese. His sensitivity on this issue, which was indeed of great significance for the Catholic Church in the GDR, was no doubt even greater because it was the Vatican itself that had launched a new *Ostpolitik* after the Second Vatican Council. The implications of this *Ostpolitik* were unmistakeable: a legal separation of the East German from the West German Church as well as an abrupt change in state-church law.[44] The path of independence taken by the Protestant Church of Berlin-Brandenburg in 1972 with the election of the prominent church official Albrecht Schönherr as the *Bischof der Ostregion der Berlin-Brandenburgischen Kirche* was particularly striking. The unity of the EKD, which had only been achieved with great difficulty in 1948, had already been undone two decades later through the founding of the United Evangelical Lutheran Church in the GDR in 1968 and the Federation of the Protestant Churches in the GDR (BEK) in 1969.[45]

The Catholic bishops in the GDR remained committed to "political abstinence." They were unable and unwilling to go down the path of a "church in socialism," such as had been taken by the Protestant Church.[46] But by the end of the 1970s the understanding of the "double" diaspora started to lose some of its confessional dimensions. An important semantic change was formulated in the doctrinal text "Faith Today" at a GDR-wide pastoral synod in 1974–75.[47] Seeing "the faith as decision," the synod redefined a series of tasks long understood as Catholic as "Christian" for the diaspora in a "non-Christian" socialist society. These tasks included parish pastoral work to its "little flock," social welfare work, ecumenism, and Christian engagement "for reconciliation and peace."[48]

Being a Christian in a Society without God and Ecumenism *In Politicis*

At the beginning of the 1980s, one could clearly see the effects of two decades of a "dramatically worsening situation for the diaspora." To be sure, the Honecker regime's change of course, one motivated by foreign policy considerations, had led to lessen open persecution of the Church and slowed down the migration from the Church. The "modernization of everyday life in the GDR" had nevertheless left a lasting mark on the two Christian churches.[49] It seemed that in small towns and villages and even for whole regions in the GDR, a cultural seachange was taking place.[50] Religious values and traditions were no longer being passed on to the next generation. In the words of the Erfurt bishop Joachim Wanke: "we have . . .

to define our situation as a 'church in a materialistic, secularized environment.'" He added: "secularization means that social and private life is largely free of religion. Materialist means: [the] theoretical, materialistic, and atheistic worldview is actively propagated and is indeed also practiced by the majority of the people . . . The 'absence' of God is drastic and encompasses all aspects of life."[51]

It was no coincidence that in 1982 attentive observers such as Martin Höllen, the West Berlin reporter for the *Katholische Nachrichten-Agentur*, realized that Wanke's words had provided a new self-understanding of the "double" diaspora.[52] Höllen saw this as the start of a new era, the "era *after* Bengsch," who had died in 1979. It was clear to Wanke that the fundamental break in the role of religion in society required the Church to change its self-understanding as a minority in order to make spirituality and the Church's social ministries in the GDR viable in the future. "Will we as pastors be able to convey spiritual experiences to this secular youth? I believe this is the key question facing our ministry."[53] To be able to spell out the "gospel of Jesus Christ in the dialects of central Germany" or "in GDR-German" meant for Wanke to no longer only preserve one's rights and fight against any infringement of these but also to see the "positive possibilities of permeating tangible living spaces with the spirit of Christ."[54] The goal here was a firm commitment to being a Christian and to authentic actions whose testimony would serve to allow the "church in our area" to become visible.[55] Catholic laity in particular were called to this "Christian world service" by participating conscientiously and constructively in building up society and holding it together (*bonum commune*). At the same time, Catholics were to offer resistance "especially where injustice and a disregard of human dignity cast their shadow over the common good."[56]

Because of this "post-Christian generation," Wanke urged representatives of the Protestant Church "to bear witness to God in this time and in this country and so search together for unity in faith."[57] The Erfurt bishop also moved Church policy forward. In September 1986, in a greeting to the Synod of the Federation of the Protestant Churches in East Germany in the GDR meeting in Erfurt, he signaled that the Catholic Church was willing to participate in the planned Ecumenical Assembly of the Evangelical Churches in the GDR.[58] In so doing, he not only helped revive tough discussions within the Catholic Church on this topic; he also risked arousing resentment within the Berlin Bishops Conference, for his statement anticipated the then still unpublished pastoral letter on the "Catholic Church in the socialist state," which turned out to be more reserved in its formulations.[59]

Wanke reported that he had theological reservations about the Protestant mantra of a "church in socialism." This formula expressed a different understanding of the concept of the "church": "We cannot allow ourselves both as a church and as Christians to be defined by our relationship to 'socialism.'"[60] There was neither a "church in socialism" nor a "church in capitalism," but only a Catholic Church, which had to carry out its mission under all sorts of conditions. In his eyes, the idea of a church in socialism or a church in capitalism overlooked the real challenges all religions faced:

> I believe that the church has entered a new epoch in terms of the attitude towards life and the world; it has entered an epoch of secularism, which is, arguably, different from atheism. It is not only that God or rather transcendence is denied, but that, indeed, they do not occur at all, and by this I mean not only officially, but also practically. For the individual these things are no longer natural and unquestioned. There are signs by the way that this will in the future become an even more urgent task for all of the world's great religions given the secularism we have described.[61]

This new understanding of one's position as a religious minority was the result of a generational shift. There were new and younger faces in the Berlin Bishops Conference, including the bishop of Berlin, Joachim Meisner, and of Erfurt, Joachim Wanke. More than anything, Wanke's initiative reflected a keen sense that towards the end of the 1970s in the GDR as elsewhere, a "turning of the tide" was taking place. This stemmed from a waning faith in the major ideologies in the Cold War, and emerging out of this loss of faith were new visions and fears.[62] This change in mood was also facilitated from the very top by Pope John Paul II.[63] As he helped mobilize religious forces in neighboring Poland through events like the World Prayer Meeting in 1986 in Assisi, the Church began to show unexpected political power. Comparable impulses came from the World Council of Churches in Geneva. Such worldwide conciliar processes "for justice, peace, and preserving the integrity of God's creation" led to the formation of numerous dissident and civil rights groups in the GDR, including many which were religiously motivated, and which came together under the roof of the Protestant Church.[64] From the mid-1980s on, the young peace movement was also strongly influenced and motivated by the changes in the Soviet Union. Its demands for "glasnost" and "perestroika" in the GDR provoked the Honecker government into taking a hard domestic political line, even though the government could no longer be sure of political support from the USSR's new General Secretary, Mikhail Gorbachev.

Yet it was by no means clear how these impetuses could be converted into practical action. For starters, the Catholic Church once again became visible in public. The bishops used pastoral letters to address their faithful.[65] Pilgrimages and youth gatherings drew large numbers. In 1981, around fifty thousand Catholics from all parts of the GDR made a pilgrimage to Erfurt to mark the 750th anniversary of the death of St. Elizabeth of Thuringia.[66]

In 1985, one thousand young people came to East Berlin for a Catholic Congress, "Christ—Our Future."[67] At the *Katholikentreffen*, the GDR-wide meeting of Catholics, in Dresden in 1987, up to one hundred thousand believers came together for public events and three thousand delegates for events in closed circles.[68] Not every Catholic bishop supported this aggressive use of the public sphere, one similar to the *Katholikentage* in West Germany in which Catholics discussed pressing social questions.[69] Even though John Paul II encouraged the episcopate in the GDR to embrace it, the bishops retained a deep mistrust of using the media of both East and West Germany, fearing that their efforts might be misused for political purposes.[70]

The peace issue appeared to be even more politically charged. It had been on the Church's agenda at the very latest since 1978, when worldwide protests against growing rearmament led to the formation of a civil rights movement in the GDR. Dissidents had taken umbrage over the introduction in the GDR of compulsory military instruction, but they were not welcome in every Protestant parish.[71] All the same, the Protestant Church began to address "peace," a topic of crucial importance to the younger generation, with much greater resolve than the reluctant Berlin Bishops Conference. Even worse: the bishops used all of the means at their disposal to marginalize the members of the *Aktionskreis Halle* who committed to peace and were then considered *persona non gratae* both by state and church.[72] The "darkest day and the absolute low point in the history of the Berlin Bishops Conference" was reached in January 1982, when Gerhard Schaffran, the bishop of Dresden-Meissen prevented the reading of a pastoral letter on peace.[73] It does not appear that the Stasi had a hand in this; rather, the differences within the Catholic Church hierarchy had become too great. One year later, on 2 January 1983, the pastoral letter was read from all the pulpits in the Catholic Churches of the GDR: "This is our basic belief: peace is possible. War is not our inevitable fate. The church, of course, cannot present a political concept on how to keep the peace. But the church cannot remain silent where it sees undesirable developments which could lead to ruin. Furthermore, the church is committed to promote, with all its authority, those principles and values on which a just peace is based."[74]

In 1987, Catholic Church leaders were faced with a fundamental problem when the Church was invited to participate in an ecumenical assembly, "Justice, Peace and the Preservation of the Creation." This required social activism *outside* of the areas for which the Church had responsibility. Bishop Wanke succinctly summarized the theological and structural challenges the Church faced at a March 1987 meeting with representatives of West German lay Catholicism in East Berlin. According to Wanke, the bishops were still trying to encourage pastors and Church officials to "abstain from politics" so as "to protect themselves from the danger, as can be seen in the Protestant Church, of becoming politically dependent either as an individual or as a church group." Of course, "a Catholic Christian in the GDR must not become a 'sacristy Catholic.'" The individual Christian can and should be a *"homo politicus"* because the Catholic Church as a sacramental community can never be "a *societas politica* in the literal sense."[75] In other words, a Catholic lay movement was also needed in the GDR, which in line with the Second Vatican Council's Pastoral Constitution on the Church in the Modern World, *Gaudium et spes*, would on its own accord express the Catholic voice in civil society. This was inherently not the job of the Church, including its bishops, for the Church was an institution for salvation.

In contrast to the Protestant Church, the specifically Catholic understanding of the Church required the creation of lay organization and action structures. This ecclesiastical challenge was made more difficult because in the East German diaspora lay Catholicism had always been weak. After 1945, the previously independent Caritas and Kolping Associations were incorporated into the governance structures of the Church.[76] Since then, the role of the lay person was understood and defensively put into practice as one of "consistent non-cooperation . . . with the regime."[77] At the very latest since the Döpfner decree of 1957, it was clear that the priest or the bishop alone was allowed to speak "politically" for the Catholic Church. Accordingly, during the "political abstinence" after 1961, with few exceptions only the clerical hierarchy spoke out politically. Of course, after the Second Vatican Council high-level discussions took place with representatives of the Protestant churches. Given the different paths taken in regard to church politics, these discussions could hardly remain free of irritations.[78] This practice of political abstinence nonetheless enabled the Church to draw a simple and clear line between itself, Catholic lay groups close to the state, such as the Berlin Conference of European Catholics and the CDUD, the Christian Democratic *Blockpartei* in the GDR.[79]

The fundamental changes in the GDR by the beginning of the 1980s, however, exposed the Church's theological and structural shortcomings. In the autumn of 1987, tensions crystalized around whether the Church should participate actively as a voting member in the upcoming deliberations in the Ecumenical Assembly. This would have required approval, if not from the Catholic bishops themselves then from the handpicked deputies of the Berlin Bishops Conference. By the end of the 1970s, Prelate Dieter Grande, who was very well connected in the ecumenical community in Dresden, had set up a small working group, *Iustitia et Pax*, which discussed current peace issues. The group developed personal contacts with Joachim

Garstecki, one of the leading figures for peace issues in the "Federation of the Protestant Churches in the GDR" (*Bund der Evangelischen Kirchen in der DDR*). At the end of 1986, the bishops appointed Grande, along with two other clerics, to participate as observers in the preparations for the Ecumenical Assembly. Only at the last minute, in mid-November 1987, did they come up with a way out of this dilemma. Instead of the bishops, *Iustitia et Pax*, composed of nine clerics and sixteen laypersons, participated as an institutional body and served as the voice of the Catholic Church in the Ecumenical Assembly.[80]

For all practical purposes, this punctured the bishops' longstanding strategy of "political abstinence." It was now possible for those like the thirty-three-year-old Caritas welfare worker Eva Storrer from Güstrow to become politically active on behalf of the Church outside narrow church walls. Storrer was elected to the Executive Committee of the Ecumenical Assembly, and she headed the meetings of the working group Education for Peace, which met in 1988 in Dresden and Magdeburg.[81] The Catholic Church had taken a first, albeit still very tentative step, towards a lay Catholicism. That this took place within the framework of an ecumenical movement *in politicis* was admittedly not viewed positively by all bishops. Nonetheless, the Catholic Church participated in the discussions on "justice, peace, and preserving the integrity of God's creation," and this opened up a "space for social articulation which was not subject to the instructions and the control of the SED."[82]

There were only twenty-four months between the decision by the bishops to participate in the Ecumenical Assembly and the Leipzig demonstrations for freedom in October 1989. Four weeks later the Berlin Wall fell. On 3 December 1989, the Politburo and the Central Committee of the SED stepped down; three days later Egon Krenz resigned as Chairman of the State Council. On 7 December 1989, the Central Round Table met for the first time in Berlin. This was a group organized and moderated by Church representatives with the aim of preparing free elections, drafting a democratic constitution, and dissolving the state security apparatus. Amid this revolutionary dynamic, however, the Church found itself unable to speak with one voice, later claims to the contrary notwithstanding. The different groups within the Church and her bishops as well assessed the revolutionary dynamic differently. More than ever, it appeared that the bishops were the ones being driven by events, and not the other way around.

In a pastoral letter from 22 September 1989, which he had authorized but not written himself, the bishop of Magdeburg, Johannes Braun, called for an open dialogue about the shortcomings in the state and society that could no longer be overlooked because of the number of people leaving the country.[83] It was not until the beginning of November and at an extraordinary general meeting on 14 November in Erfurt that the bishops suspended their directives dating back to 1947 regarding conversations between the Church and government agencies. They instead explicitly called on lay Catholics "to participate in the political parties and in the various groups and fractions."[84] But there was no consensus as to how this "Catholicism" was to be organized. On 6 November, Prelate Gerhard Lange, who had been for many years the bishop's representative for negotiations with the GDR government, advised the bishops to set up a Catholic office for the GDR government, similar to that in Bonn.[85] Three days later, with the fall of the wall, this suggestion was not worth the paper it was written on. Hans Joachim Meyer, one of the leading figures in the emerging Catholic lay movement, strove to bring together all the various lay initiatives sprouting up in the churches and the Church communities; he believed it was important for Catholics to bring their own independent positions into the process of social and political democratization. Among the bishops, however, the idea of organizing lay Catholicism along the lines of the West German Central Committee of German Catholics initially found little support. The ideas of the bishops were more along the lines of a lay apostolate modeled after Catholic Action.

Numerous Catholic laity putting forward their own initiatives, however, also mistrusted Meyer's efforts. After having taken part for the first time in the round tables set up to discuss political ecumenism, they were caught up in the revolutionary fervor. They suddenly found themselves able to participate in democratic practices made possible by the revolutionary dynamic. These experiences seemed to speak against the project of building up a nation-wide, centrally organized, and decidedly Catholic lay movement. Meyer was able to move his initiative forward only in the middle of January 1990 when he founded the Common Campaign Committee of Catholic Christians in the GDR (*Gemeinsamer Aktionsausschuss katholischer Christen in der DDR*).[86]

Ideas about "political Catholicism" diverged even more. On the one hand, the East Berlin church newspaper *St. Hedwigsblatt* argued, with an eye to the "nascent" (*werdende*) CDU, that because there were very few Catholics in the GDR, it was impossible to pick up where the Center Party had left off in 1933. On the other hand, collaboration with Protestant Christians had shown that it was possible for there to be responsible cooperation with Protestants not organized along partisan political lines.[87] The bishops agreed. In the statement for the press released by the new Berlin Cardinal Sterzinsky on 21 December 1989, after his meeting in Dresden with Chancellor Helmut Kohl, the Cardinal stated: "We are pleased that Christians are being asked to contribute." However, there would not be a "political Catholicism" in the future GDR, just as there had not been in the past. And in regard to the upcoming elections, the Dresden bishop Joachim Reinelt added that the the lay initiatives that were starting to come together as they crossed regional boundaries were "not about one party, but rather about an umbrella organization for groups with different party affiliations."[88] As a result, the *Aktionskreis Halle*'s call to action in the middle of January 1990 caused a sensation. It called for people to join the CDU in large numbers in order "to turn this party into a genuine party of Christians in the GDR."[89]

It was the representatives of the Protestant churches whose members of the CDU initiated the process of reform in the GDR in mid-September 1989.[90] The "letter from Weimar" to the party leadership was written by the synodalin Martina Huhn, pastor Christine Lieberknecht, and the members of the High Consistory Gottfried Müller and Martin Kirchner.[91] (It would later be discovered that Kirchner was an "unofficial employee of the Stasi"). On 11 November, the CDU, which was in the process of reforming itself, elected Lothar de Maizière, an attorney and Vice President of the Federation of the Protestant Churches in East Germany, as the new chairperson. As the top candidate, and in a coalition with the DSU and the *Demokratischen Aufbruch*, he led the party to a clear victory on 18 March 1990, in the elections for parliament. On 12 April, the first freely elected parliament of the GDR chose him as its Minister President; Hans-Joachim Meyer, an independent, became the Minister for Education and Science. Of the four hundred members of the East German parliament, fifty-eight were Catholic. Of these, forty-three belonged to the CDU and six to the newly-founded DSU. The fact that 15 percent of the members of parliament were Catholic, almost three times the percentage of Catholics in the population, was due in part to the strong electoral victory of the CDU election alliance, Alliance for Germany. This alliance made use of the reservoir of politically untainted personnel found in the Catholic lay movement, which was then only forming. That said, one has to acknowledge that sixteen of the forty-three Catholic members of the East German parliament had been members of the SED since 1969.[92]

The GDR Past and Confessional "Heritage"

On 17 February 1990, the Joint Action Committee of Catholic Christians in the GDR (*Gemeinsame Aktionsausschuss katholischer Christen*) published a declaration on the upcoming free East German election for the *Volkskammer*. It reminded Catholics of the "selfless service" of Protestant Christians on the difficult path to this moment of change. "The Ecumenical Assembly, which brought together sisters and brothers from all Christian churches and which spoke out clearly for peace, for justice, and for preserving the integrity of God's creation, was a signal which could not be overlooked on the path to a turnaround and a new beginning."[93] With this declaration, the Catholic laity consciously made up for what was missing in the bishops' pastoral letters on New Year's Eve, 1989. In hindsight, obviously, how one passed judgment on the significance of political ecumenism depended to a large degree on the way in which one had positioned oneself in the GDR on the "double" diaspora of the Catholic Church—whether as bishop, priest, or lay Catholic.

That political ecumenism had enabled Catholics to participate in the democratic configuration of the revolutionary upheaval ran up against the conviction that the Catholic Church "had at no time recognized the legality of the Communist one-party state."[94] Indeed, from the very outset, the Church had openly criticized injustice and later helped free—in negotiations born of necessity—those who were being politically persecuted. If the one viewpoint emphasized the ecumenical engagement of lay Catholics in civil society, the other emphasized the relationship between church and state, a task reserved to the bishops until the very end. The tensions and disputes that had already shaped Catholic religious life in the German east continued even after the demise of the GDR, because those who had participated in the shaping of religious life back then also participated in and influenced greatly the debate about their own past.

The West German voices made clear the asymmetry of the discussions. West Germans generally emphasized how the Catholic Church had uncomprisingly rejected the GDR's totalitarian system.[95] This corresponded to the understanding of the role the Catholic Church had played in the resistance to the totalitarian dictatorships of the twentieth century. This understanding had taken shape since the 1960s as the Federal Republic examined its National Socialist past, and it reflected the anti-totalitarian founding consensus of the West German state, a consensus which remained intact during the transition from the Cold War to détente.[96] Applying this interpretation to the GDR dictatorship was made easier by contemporary debates about the Stasi. The Stasi had never been able to penetrate the Catholic Church; furthermore, the question concerning the "unofficial informants" (*Inoffiziellen Mitarbeitern*) in the Catholic Church was seen as an East German "problem." It is thus not surprising that the different perspectives on the GDR past continue to find their way into current historical analysis.[97]

As I have shown, even these partly contradictory judgments concerning the past resulted from the church's self-understanding as a minority in a "double" diaspora. This self-understanding was deeply rooted in the confessional history of the German nation, one characterized by Protestant dominance. The history of the Catholic Church in the GDR is the history of a *minority* both in terms of religion and politics. Expanding our perspective this way grants us distance from the often fiercely contested discussions within the Catholic Church itself. It allows us to examine the historic changes in the Church's self-understanding as a religious minority through the lens of its relationship to the Protestant majority Church.

The choice to reject political ecumenism, which had far-reaching implications, was the result of an understanding of the Catholic diaspora which perceived Protestant fragmentation in the larger ideological struggles. It was through this lens, one deeply influenced by the building of the wall, that the Church made "political abstinence" a central part of its own strategy. The pressure for conformity within the Church increased both at the beginning of the 1960s and at the beginning of the 1980s, when global political, social, and religious changes also began to be seen and felt in the GDR. While the dismantling of "old" denominational barriers as a result of the Second Vatican Council still seemed compatible with a rigorous rejection of any Catholic rapprochement with Protestant conceptions of a "church in socialism," the recognition starting in the early 1980s that religious traditions were changing and had to change required a new direction and outlook. This was one that almost by definition had to leave behind the "double diaspora," which had been so obsessed with building walls. The self-understanding of being a Christian church in a "secular, materialistic environment" made it possible ultimately in 1988–89 for Catholic laity to open the door to a political ecumenism outside of the narrow ecclesiastical sphere still under Catholic control.

The new path towards being decisively Christian and of independent lay social activism was quickly rendered irrelevant by the revolutionary upheaval and German reunification. Both churches once again went their own ways. On the Catholic side, the organizational merger between the Bishops Conference and the lay organizations in 1990 went quite smoothly; it concluded in 1994–95 with the establishment of the new dioceses of Erfurt, Görlitz, Magdeburg, and Hamburg. However, the newly achieved institutional unity took place amid other tensions, those generated by secularization. As this process has affected both churches profoundly, more than ever the churches face a common challenge.[98]

Christoph Kösters is a member of the Research Center of the Association for Contemporary History in Bonn (Kommission für Zeitgeschichte). He is the author and coeditor of numerous books and articles about the history of Catholicism in the nineteenth and twentieth centuries, including *Katholische Verbände und Moderne Gesellschaft: Organisationsgeschichte und Vereinskultur im Bistum Münster 1918 bis 1945* and *Staatssicherheit und Caritas: Zur politischen Geschichte der katholischen Kirche in der DDR*.

Notes

1. "Hirtenwort der Berliner Bischofskonferenz, 30./31.12.1989," in Martin Höllen, *Loyale Distanz? Katholizismus und Kirchenpolitik in SBZ und DDR. Ein historischer Überblick in Dokumenten*, Bd. 3, 2: *1977–1990* (Berlin: Höllen, 1997), 287ff.
2. "Trilling an Berliner Bischofskonferenz, 2.1.1990," in Ibid., 290.
3. Christoph Kösters, "Minderheit und Konfession. Einige Überlegungen zur Erforschung der Diaspora in Deutschland im 19. und 20. Jahrhundert," in *Die katholische Diaspora in Deutschland—Stand und Perspektiven der Forschung* (Wichmann Jahrbuch, N.F. 13), ed. Benjamin Gallin, Michael Höhle, and Konstantin Manthey (Heiligenstadt: F. W. Cordier, 2015), 9–39.
4. "Bischof Wanke in seiner Ansprache auf Pastoralkonferenzen in Erfurt und Heiligenstadt im Oktober 1981," in Höllen, *Loyale Distanz?* Bd. 3, 2, 68.
5. Bernd Schäefer, *Staat und katholische Kirche in der DDR* (Cologne: Böhlau, 1998). For an English translation, see Bernd Schäefer, *The East German State and the Catholic Church, 1945–1989* (New York: Berghahn Books, 2010); Wolfgang Tischner, *Katholische Kirche in der SBZ/DDR 1945–1951. Die Formierung einer Subgesellschaft im entstehenden sozialistischen Staat* (Paderborn: Schöningh, 2001); Reinhard Grütz, *Katholizismus in der DDR-Gesellschaft 1960–1990. Kirchliche Leitbilder, theologische Deutungen und lebensweltliche Praxis im Wandel* (Paderborn: Schöningh, 2004); Josef Pilvousek, ed., *Die katholische Kirche in der DDR. Beiträge zur Kirchengeschichte Mitteldeutschlands* (Münster: Aschendorff, 2014). On the Protestant Church, see Claudia Lepp and Kurt Nowak, eds., *Evangelische Kirche im geteilten Deutschland (1945–1989/90)* (Göttingen: Vandenhoeck & Ruprecht, 2001); Rudolf Mau, *Der Protestantismus im Osten Deutschlands (1945–1990)* (Leipzig: Evangelische Verlagsanstalt, 2005); and Veronika Albrecht-Birkner, *Freiheit in Grenzen. Protestantismus in der DDR* (Leipzig: Evangelische Verlagsanstalt 2018).
6. Tilman Bendikowski, "'Damit sie religiös nicht verwildern'—der Bonifatiusverein und die Katholiken in der Diaspora 1849–1918," in *Die katholische Diaspora in Deutschland—Stand und Perspektiven der Forschung* (Wichmann Jahrbuch, N.F. 13), ed. Benjamin Gallin, Michael Höhle, and Konstantin Manthey (Heiligenstadt: F. W. Cordier, 2015), 99–116.
7. See the map "Deutschland. Konfessionelle Gliederung in der Gegenwart," in *Lexikon für Theologie und Kirche III* (Freiburg: Herder, 1959), 289. On Eichsfeld, see Christian Stöber, *Rosenkranzkommunismus. Die SED-Diktatur und das katholische Milieu im Eichsfeld 1945–1989* (Berlin: Christoph Links, 2019).
8. Erwin Gatz, ed., *Die Bistümer der deutschsprachigen Länder. Von der Säkularisation bis zur Gegenwart. Ein historisches Lexikon* (Freiburg: Herder, 2005).
9. Tischner, *Katholische Kirche in der SBZ/DDR*, 203–45.
10. Thorsten Müller, *Neue Heimat Eichsfeld? Flüchtlinge und Vertriebene in der katholischen Ankunftsgesellschaft* (Duderstadt: Mecke, 2010); Christoph Kösters and Wolfgang Tischner, eds., *Katholische Kirche in SBZ und DDR* (Paderborn: Schöningh, 2005). Petra Heinicker, *Kolpingsarbeit in der SBZ und DDR 1945–1990* (Paderborn: Brill, 2020).
11. See Josef Pilvousek, *Theologische Ausbildung und gesellschaftliche Umbrüche. 50 Jahre Katholische Theologische Hochschule und Priesterausbildung in Erfurt* (Leipzig: St. Benno, 2002); Elisabeth Preuß, *Die Kanzel in der DDR. Die ungewöhnliche Geschichte des St.-Benno-Verlages* (Leipzig: St. Benno, 2006); Christoph Kösters, ed., *Caritas in der SBZ/DDR 1945–1989. Erinnerungen, Berichte, Forschungen* (Paderborn: Schöningh, 2001).
12. Thomas Thorak, *Wilhelm Weskamm. Diasporaseelsorger in der SBZ/DDR* (Würzburg: Echter, 2009); Clemens Brodkorb, *Bruder und Gefährte in der Bedrängnis. Hugo Aufderbeck als Seelsorgeamtsleiter in Magdeburg. Zur pastoralen Grundlegung einer "Kirche in der SBZ/DDR"* (Paderborn: Bonifatius, 2002); Thomas Brechenmacher, ed., *"In dieser Stunde der Kirche." Zum 100. Geburtstag von Julius Kardinal Döpfner* (Würzburg: Schöningh, 2013). On the personality and theology of Döpfner, see Stefan Mokry, "Dreimal Diaspora? Kardinal Julius Döpfners

Sicht auf seine bischöflichen Wirkungsstätten Würzburg, Berlin und München in den Jahren 1948–1976 anhand von Predigten und Hirtenbriefen," in *Die katholische Diaspora in Deutschland—Stand und Perspektiven der Forschung* (Wichmann Jahrbuch, N.F. 13), ed. Benjamin Gallin, Michael Höhle, and Konstantin Manthey (Heiligenstadt: F. W. Cordier, 2015), 241–53; Stefan Mokry, *Kardinal Julius Döpfner und das Zweite Vatikanum. Ein Beitrag zur Biografie und Konzilsgeschichte* (Stuttgart: Kohlhammer, 2016), 63–289; Klaus Wittstadt, *Julius Kardinal Döpfner. Anwalt Gottes und der Menschen* (Munich: Don Bosco, 2001).

13. Thomas Brechenmacher, "Katholische Kirche und (Anti-)Kommunismus in der frühen Bundesrepublik," in *"Geistige Gefahr" und "Immunisierung der Gesellschaft." Antikommunismus und politische Kultur in der frühen Bundesrepublik*, ed. Stefan Creuzberger and Dierk Hoffmann (Munich: DeGruyter, 2014), 177–97.

14. Tischner, *Katholische Kirche in der SBZ/DDR*, 141–59; Christoph Kösters, ed., *Akten deutscher Bischöfe seit 1945. Die DDR 1951–1957* (Paderborn: Schöningh, 2012), 646–53.

15. "Predigt Spülbecks auf dem Kölner Katholikentag," in Christoph Kösters, ed., *Akten deutscher Bischöfe seit 1945*, 775. Christian März, *Otto Spülbeck. Ein Leben für die Diaspora* (Leipzig: St. Benno, 2010).

16. Tischner, *Katholische Kirche in der SBZ/DDR*, 160–63.

17. Grütz, *Katholizismus in der DDR-Gesellschaft*, 309–15.

18. Statistisches Bundesamt, *Sonderreihe mit Beiträgen für das Gebiet der ehemaligen DDR, Heft 15: Ausgewählte Zahlen der Volks- und Berufszählungen und Gebäude- und Wohnungszählungen 1950–1981* (Wiesbaden: Statistisches Bundesamt, 1994), 42. The population of the GDR declined between 1950 and 1964 from 18,388,172 to 17,003,631 (a decline of 7.5 percent) and the number of Protestants declined from 14,802,217 to 10,091,907 (a decline of 32 percent). The number of those who had no religious affiliation almost quadrupled, from 1,399,691 (1950) to 5,416,814 (1964); this corresponded to a population share of 32 percent.

19. Thomas Schulte-Umberg, ed., *Akten deutscher Bischöfe seit 1945. Die DDR 1957–1961* (Paderborn: Schöningh, 2006).

20. Detlef Pollack, "Ostdeutschland. Keine Anzeichen einer Trendwende," in *Religion in der Moderne. Ein internationaler Vergleich*, ed. Detlef Pollack and Gergely Rosta (Frankfurt: Campus, 2015), 277.

21. "Aufzeichnungen Spülbecks über die Audienz bei Papst Johannes XXIII., 11.11.1958," in Schulte-Umberg, *Akten deutscher Bischöfe seit 1945. Die DDR 1957–1961*, 445.

22. Martin Greschat, *Protestantismus im Kalten Krieg. Kirche, Politik und Gesellschaft im geteilten Deutschland 1945–1963* (Paderborn: Schöningh, 2010), 193–250.

23. "Aide-mémoire Döpfners, 1.12.1959," in Schulte-Umberg, *Akten deutscher Bischöfe seit 1945. Die DDR 1957–1961*, 669.

24. Tischner, *Katholische Kirche in der SBZ/DDR*, 107–11.

25. "Erklärungen zu Zeitfragen, (vor dem) 2.7.1957," in Schulte-Umberg, *Akten deutscher Bischöfe seit 1945. Die DDR 1957–1961*, 144.

26. Ibid., 590; see Schäfer, *Staat und katholische Kirche*, 162.

27. See the extensive documentation of the conversation in Martin Höllen, *Loyale Distanz? Katholizismus und Kirchenpolitik in SBZ und DDR. Ein historischer Überblick in Dokumenten*, Bd. 2: 1956–1965 (Berlin: Höllen, 1997), 295–310.

28. Schäfer, *Staat und katholische Kirche*, 166.

29. "Stellungnahme an den Klerus zum Wehrpflichtgesetz," 6 February 1962; "Eingabe an Grotewohl zum Entwurf eines neuen Jugendgesetzes," 1 December 1963; "Eingabe an Stoph zum Entwurf des neuen Familiengesetzes," 12 July 1965; "Öffentliche Erklärung zum Schwangerschaftsabbruch," 1 November 1965; "Pastoralbrief zur Festigung des Glaubens," 4 September 1967; "Eingabe an Ulbricht zum Verfassungsentwurf," 5 February 1968; "Stellungnahme zur Jugendweihe," 25 February 1969; "Öffentliche Erklärung zum § 218," 3 January 1972; "Pastoralbrief zur Jugendweihe," 3 March 1972; "Stellungnahme zum Entwurf des neuen Jugendgesetzes," 18 October 1973; "Hirtenwort zur christlichen Erziehung," 17 November

1974; "Eingabe an Seigewasser zum Wehrkundeunterricht," 12 June 1978, in Gerhard Lange, et al., eds., *Katholische Kirche—sozialistischer Staat DDR. Dokumente und öffentliche Äußerungen 1945–1990*, 2. Aufl. (Leipzig: St. Benno, 1993), 193, 203–10, 219–30, 247–62, 294–96.

30. Ibid., 204.

31. Petra Gödde, "Globale Kulturen," in *Geschichte der Welt. 1945 bis heute—Die globalisierte Welt*, ed. Iriye Akira (Bonn: Beck, 2014), 585–641.

32. Peter Hünermann and Bernd Hilberath, eds., *Herders theologischer Kommentar zum Zweiten Vatikanischen Konzil, Bd. 4, Sonderausgabe* (Freiburg: Herder, 2009), 676, 694ff., 734–39.

33. Grütz, *Katholizismus in der DDR-Gesellschaft*, 92–77; Schäfer, *Staat und katholische Kirche*, 365–85.

34. Dieter Grande and Peter-Paul Straube, eds., *Die Synode des Bistums Meißen 1969 bis 1971. Die Antwort einer Ortskirche auf das Zweite Vatikanische Konzil* (Leipzig: St. Benno, 2005); Martin Höllen, *Loyale Distanz? Katholizismus und Kirchenpolitik in SBZ und DDR. Ein historischer Überblick in Dokumenten*, Bd. 3, 1: 1966–1976 (Berlin: Höllen, 1998), 182ff.; März, *Otto Spülbeck*, 326–77; Grütz, *Katholizismus in der DDR-Gesellschaft*, 103–7.

35. "Synode des Bistums Meißen, Synodaldekret I, Nr. 2–3," in Grande and Sraube, *Die Synode des Bistums Meißen 1969 bis 1971*, 75. See "Vorpapier 5 zur Dresdner Pastoralsynode vom 5./6.2.1972," in Höllen, *Loyale Distanz?* Bd. 3, 1, 279ff.

36. "Synode des Bistums Meißen, Synodaldekret I, Nr. 3," in Grande and Sraube, *Die Synode des Bistums Meißen 1969 bis 1971*, 75.

37. "Ansprache Aufderbecks anlässlich der Dresdner Pastoralsynode am 24.3.1973," in Höllen, *Loyale Distanz?* Bd. 3, 1, 322; see Grütz, *Katholizismus in der DDR-Gesellschaft*, 107–19.

38. This was the verdict of the *Dogmatiker* and *Regens* of the Erfurt seminarian Lothar Ullrich, quoted in Grütz, *Katholizismus in der DDR-Gesellschaft*, 113.

39. "Vortrag Aufderbecks beim Studientag für katholische Lehrer, Februar 1972," in Josef Pilvousek, ed., *Kirchliches Leben im totalitären Staat. Seelsorge in der SBZ/DDR 1945–1976. Quellentexte aus den Ordinariaten* (Leipzig: St. Benno, 1994), 329–34.

40. Schäfer, *Staat und katholische Kirche*, 235.

41. This is the poignant picture of the experience of Catholic congregations in the GDR diaspora that Aufderbeck especially helped make a part of the self-understanding of the Catholic Church. See Grütz, *Katholizismus in der DDR-Gesellschaft*, 306, 337, 344.

42. Ibid., 101ff.

43. Sebastian Holzbrecher, *Der Aktionskreis Halle. Postkonziliare Konflikte im Katholizismus der DDR* (Würzburg: Echter, 2014); Grütz, *Katholizismus in der DDR-Gesellschaft*, 123–26.

44. Roland Cerny-Werner, *Vatikanische Ostpolitik und die DDR* (Göttingen: Vandenhoeck & Ruprecht, 2011); Karl-Josef Hummel, ed., *Vatikanische Ostpolitik unter Johannes XXIII und Paul VI 1958–1978* (Paderborn: Schöningh, 1999).

45. Albrecht-Birkner, *Freiheit in Grenzen*, 106ff; Claudia Lepp, *Tabu der Einheit? Die Ost-West-Gemeinschaft der evangelischen Christen und die deutsche Teilung (1945–1969)* (Göttingen: Vandenhoeck & Ruprecht, 2005), 790–927; Gerhard Besier, *Der SED-Staat und die Kirche. Der Weg in die Anpassung* (Munich: Bertelsmann, 1993); Gerhard Besier, "Der SED-Staat und die Kirche 1969–1990. Die Vision vom 'dritten Weg'" in *Der SED-Staat und die Kirche 1983–1991. Höhenflug und Absturz*, ed. Gerhard Besier (Berlin: Propyläen, 1995).

46. Christoph Kähler, "Kirche im Sozialismus," in *Staatslexikon. Recht, Wirtschaft, Gesellschaft*, 8th ed., ed. Görres-Gesellschaft and the Herder-Verlag (Freiburg: Herder, 2019), 711–15; Herbert Heinecke, *Konfession und Politik in der DDR. Das Wechselverhältnis von Kirche und Staat im Vergleich zwischen evangelischer und katholischer Kirche* (Leipzig: Evangelische Verlagsanstalt, 2002), 385–428; Peter Maser, *Glauben im Sozialismus. Kirchen und Religionsgemeinschaften in der DDR* (West Berlin: Holzapfel, 1989), 140–54.

47. Berliner Bischofskonferenz, *Konzil und Diaspora. Beschlüsse der Pastoralsynode der Katholischen Kirche in der DDR* (West Berlin: Benno, 1977), no. 1–81, 9–35.

48. Ibid., 14ff, 31ff ("Glaube heute"), 41–61 ("Diakonie und Gemeinde"), 136–54 ("Ökumene im Bereich der Gemeinde"), 235–52 ("Dienst der Kirche für Versöhnung und Frieden"). See as well Höllen, *Loyale Distanz?* Bd. 3, 1, 379ff.

49. Detlef Pollack, "Renaissance des Religiösen? Veränderungen auf dem religiösen Feld in ausgewählten Ländern Ost- und Ostmitteleuropas," *Archiv für Sozialgeschichte* 51 (2011): 135; See Grütz, *Katholizismus in der DDR-Gesellschaft*, 81, 146. The statistics are based on internal estimates of the Catholic Church.

50. Pollack, "Renaissance des Religiösen," 136.

51. "Vortrag Wankes vom Oktober 1981," in Höllen, *Loyale Distanz?* Bd. 3, 2, 68.

52. Martin Höllen used this term for the first time while lecturing about the "Church between [the] Elbe and [the] Oder" at the *Katholikentag* in Düsseldorf. See also Josef Pilvousek, "Von der 'Gärtnerei im Norden' zur 'doppelten Diaspora.' Überlegungen zum Diasporabegriff in der katholischen Kirche in der DDR," in *Diaspora als Ort der Theologie. Perspektiven aus Tschechien und Ostdeutschland*, ed. Benedikt Kranemann, et al. (Würzburg: Echter, 2016), 114ff.

53. "Vortrag Wankes vom Oktober 1981," in Höllen, *Loyale Distanz?* Bd. 3, 2, 71.

54. Ibid., 68. "Grußwort Wankes an die Teilnehmer des Evangelischen Kirchentags in Erfurt, 15.5.1983," in Josef Pilvousek, ed., *Kirchliches Leben im totalitären Staat. Seelsorge in der SBZ/DDR 1977–1989. Quellentexte aus den Ordinariaten, Teil II* (Leipzig: St. Benno, 1998), 252. "Pastoralschreiben der Bischöfe an den Klerus vom 8.9.1986," in Höllen, *Loyale Distanz?* Bd. 3, 2, 160.

55. "Vortrag Wankes vom Oktober 1981," in Ibid., 68.

56. "Vortrag Wankes beim Diözesan-Akademikertag in Erfurt, 15.10.1988," in Pilvousek, *Kirchliches Leben II*, 338.

57. "Grußwort Wankes an die Teilnehmer des Evangelischen Kirchentags in Erfurt, 15.5.1983," in Ibid., 251.

58. "Grußwort Wankes vom 19.9.1986 vor der BEK-Synode," in Ibid., 280–84.

59. "Pastoralschreiben der Bischöfe an den Klerus vom 8.9.1986," in Höllen, *Loyale Distanz?* Bd. 3, 2, 154–61, with the reference to the publication on 25 September 1986 (155, n177); "Wankes Nachbetrachtung zum Pastoralschreiben vom Oktober 1987," in Pilvousek, *Kirchliches Leben II*, 302–307.

60. "Vortrag Wankes beim Diözesan-Akademikertag in Erfurt, 15.10.1988," in Ibid., 335.

61. "Vortrag Wankes vom Oktober 1981," in Höllen, *Loyale Distanz?* Bd. 3, 2, 69.

62. Frank Bösch and Jens Gieseke, "Der Wandel des Politischen in Ost und West," in *Geteilte Geschichte. Ost- und Westdeutschland 1970–2000*, ed. Frank Bösch (Göttingen: Vandenhoeck & Ruprecht, 2015), 59; Frank Bösch, *Zeitenwende 1979. Als die Welt von heute begann*, 4. Aufl. (Munich: Beck, 2019), 80–94.

63. Johannes Paul II (John Paul II [Karol Józef Wojtyła, 1920–2005]): 1946 Priesterweihe (Priest); 1948 Dr. phil., Rom (Doctor of Philosophy, Rome); 1953 Professor für Moraltheologie (Professor of Moral Theology); 1964–1978 Erzbischof von Krakau (Archbishop of Kraków); 1967 Kardinal (Cardinal); 1978–2005 Papst (Pope).

64. Katharina Kunter, *Erfüllte Hoffnungen und zerbrochene Träume. Evangelische Kirchen in Deutschland im Spannungsfeld von Demokratie und Sozialismus (1980–1993)* (Göttingen: Vandenhoeck & Ruprecht, 2006); Katharina Seifert, *Glaube und Politik. Die Ökumenische Versammlung in der DDR 1988/89* (Leipzig: St. Benno, 2000), 56ff.

65. "Hirtenbrief zum Weltfriedenstag, 1.1.1983"; "Pastoralschreiben 'Kirche im sozialistischen Staat' an die Priester und Diakone, 8.9.1986"; "Aufruf der Berliner Bischofskonferenz an die Kirchengemeinden, an der Vorbereitung der Ökumenischen Versammlung mitzuwirken, 1.12.1987"; and "Hirtenbrief über die Sendung der Kirche, 14.9.1988," in Lange, et al., *Katholische Kirche*, 306–11, 320–31, 339ff., 352–57.

66. Höllen, *Loyale Distanz?* Bd. 3, 2, 66.

67. "Hirtenwort der Berliner Bischofskonferenz, 4.12.1984," in Ibid., 131ff.; 140ff.

68. Schäfer, *Staat und katholische Kirche*, 411; Höllen, *Loyale Distanz?* Bd. 3, 2, 176f. (wie Anm. 1).

69. Dieter Grande and Bernd Schäfer, *Zur Kirchenpolitik der SED. Auseinandersetzungen um das Katholikentreffen 1983–1987* (Leipzig: St. Benno, 1994); Sebastian Holzbrecher, "Katholikentage in der DDR? Zur Bedeutung einer katholischen Institution für den ostdeutschen Diasporakatholizismus," in *Profil und Prägung. Historische Perspektiven auf 100 deutsche Katholikentage*, ed. Christoph Kösters, Hans Maier, and Frank Kleinehagenbrock (Paderborn: Schöningh, 2017), 98–101.

70. Christoph Kösters, "Revolution, Wiedervereinigung und katholische Kirche," *Historisch Politische Mitteilungen* 17 (2010): 55–112, and in particular 63; "Interview Meisners, 10.5.1984," in Höllen, *Loyale Distanz?* Bd. 3, 2, 106.

71. Maser, *Glauben im Sozialismus*, 117.

72. Holzbrecher, *Der Aktionskreis Halle*, 341–412.

73. Notes of Theissing quoted in Georg M. Diederich, *Chronik der katholischen Kirche in Mecklenburg. 1961 bis 1990 (Kirche unter Diktaturen, 3)* (Schwerin: Heinrich-Theissing-Institut, 2018), 675; see Jürgen Selke, *Katholische Kirche im Sozialismus? Der Hirtenbrief der katholischen Bischöfe in der DDR zum Weltfriedenstag 1983 und seine Bedeutung für das Verhältnis von Katholischer Kirche und Staat DDR* (Altenberge: Oros, 1995), 124–229.

74. "Hirtenbrief zum Weltfriedenstag, 1.1.1983," in Höllen, *Loyale Distanz?* Bd. 3, 2, 81.

75. Notes from Wanke from October 1987, in Pilvousek, *Kirchliches Leben II*, 306.

76. Christoph Kösters, *Staatssicherheit und Caritas 1950–1989. Zur politischen Geschichte der katholischen Kirche in der DDR, 2., korr. Aufl.* (Paderborn: Schöningh, 2002); Heinicker, *Kolpingsarbeit in der SBZ und DDR*, 253–323.

77. Antonius Liedhegener, Christoph Kösters, and Thomas Brechenmacher, "Katholizismus. Zur Geschichte, Gegenwart und Zukunft seines modernen Begriffs," *Historisches Jahrbuch* 139 (2019): 613.

78. Albrecht-Birkner, *Freiheit in Grenzen*, 111; Gerhard Lange, "Politische Gemeinsamkeiten zwischen der katholischen und den evangelischen Kirchen in der DDR?" in *Christen, Staat und Gesellschaft in der DDR*, ed. Gert Kaiser and Ewald Frie (Frankfurt: Campus, 1996), 80–86.

79. Bernd Schäfer, "Um 'anzukommen' muß man sich 'ankömmlich' artikulieren. Zur 'Berliner Konferenz' (BK) zwischen 1964 und 1993," in *Die Ost-CDU. Beiträge zu ihrer Entstehung und Entwicklung*, ed. Michael Richter and Martin Rißmann (Cologne: Böhlau, 1995), 111–25.

80. Dieter Grande, *Dem Frieden eine Chance. Die Arbeit von Justitia et Pax in der ehemaligen Deutschen Demokratischen Republik (DDR)* (Bonn: Schriftenreihe Gerechtigkeit and Frieden, 2003), 7–22; Erik Gieseking, *Justitia et Pax 1967–2007. 40 Jahre Einsatz für Gerechtigkeit und Frieden. Eine Dokumentation* (Paderborn: Schöningh, 2007), 31–36; Gerhard Lange, "Die Ökumenische Versammlung in der DDR. Zu einigen Aspekten der 'Theologischen Grundlegung,'" in *Der konziliare Prozess in der DDR in den 1980er Jahren*, ed. Gesellschaft zur Förderung vergleichender Staat-Kirche-Forschung e.V. (Berlin: 2009), 35–52.

81. Schäfer, *Staat und katholische Kirche*, 422–36.

82. Hans Joachim Meyer, *In keiner Schublade. Erfahrungen im geteilten und vereinten Deutschland* (Freiburg: Herder, 2015), 30; Kunter, *Erfüllte Hoffnungen*, 116–19.

83. Höllen, *Loyale Distanz?* Bd. 3, 2, 256–58; Holzbrecher, *Der Aktionskreis Halle*, 249.

84. "Protokoll der Berliner Bischofskonferenz, 14.11.1989," in Höllen, *Loyale Distanz?* Bd. 3, 2, 274.

85. "Vorlage Langes für die Berliner Bischofskonferenz, 6.11.1989," in Ibid., 268.

86. Kösters, "Revolution," 93–97; Meyer, *In keiner Schublade*, 32–61.

87. Kösters, "Revolution," 82, 98.

88. Ibid., 82.

89. Höllen, *Loyale Distanz?* Bd. 3, 2, 290ff.

90. Manfred Agethen, "Unruhepotentiale und Reformbestrebungen an der Basis der Ost-CDU im Vorfeld der Wende," *Historisch-politische Mitteilungen* 1 (1994): 89–114; Bertram Triebel, *Die Thüringer CDU in der SBZ/DDR. Blockpartei mit Eigeninteresse* (Sankt Augustin: Konrad-Adenauer-Stiftung e.V., 2019), 146–63.
91. Ehrhart Neubert, *Der Brief aus Weimar. Zur Selbstbefreiung der CDU im Herbst 1989* (Sankt Augustin: Konrad-Adenauer-Stiftung e.V., 2014), 16.
92. Kösters, "Revolution," 105.
93. Höllen, *Loyale Distanz?* Bd. 3, 2, 292.
94. "Erklärung Langes, 5.12.1989," in Ibid., 282; Kösters, "Revolution," 107; Lange, "Politische Gemeinsamkeiten."
95. See Kösters, "Revolution," 87.
96. Brechenmacher, "Katholische Kirche und (Anti-)Kommunismus."
97. Josef Pilvousek, "Die katholische Kirche und die Anfänge einer historischen Aufarbeitung 1990 bis 1996. Überlegungen zu einem fortwährenden Prozeß," in *Die katholische Kirche in der DDR. Beiträge zur Kirchengeschichte Mitteldeutschlands*, ed. Josef Pilvousek (Münster: Aschendorff, 2014), 375–390; Christoph Kösters, "Katholische Kirche und Katholizismus in der SBZ/DDR. Eine Bilanz neuerer Forschungen," *Historisches Jahrbuch* 121 (2001): 534–39; Albrecht-Birkner, *Freiheit in Grenzen*, 10–25.
98. Thomas Großbölting, *Der verlorene Himmel, Glaube in Deutschland seit 1945* (Göttingen: Vandenhoeck & Ruprecht, 2013).

Bibliography

Agethen, Manfred. "Unruhepotentiale und Reformbestrebungen an der Basis der Ost-CDU im Vorfeld der Wende." *Historisch-politische Mitteilungen* 1 (1994): 89–114.
Albrecht-Birkner, Veronika. *Freiheit in Grenzen. Protestantismus in der DDR.* Leipzig: Evangelische Verlagsanstalt, 2018.
Bendikowski, Tilman. "'Damit sie religiös nicht verwildern'—der Bonifatiusverein und die Katholiken in der Diaspora 1849–1918." In *Die katholische Diaspora in Deutschland—Stand und Perspektiven der Forschung* (Wichmann Jahrbuch, N.F. 13), edited by Benjamin Gallin, Michael Höhle, and Konstantin Manthey, 99–116. Heiligenstadt: F. W. Cordier, 2015.
Berliner Bischofskonferenz. *Konzil und Diaspora. Beschlüsse der Pastoralsynode der Katholischen Kirche in der DDR.* West Berlin: Benno, 1977.
Besier, Gerhard. *Der SED-Staat und die Kirche. Der Weg in die Anpassung.* Munich: Bertelsmann, 1993.
———, ed. *Der SED-Staat und die Kirche 1983–1991. Höhenflug und Absturz.* Berlin: Propyläen, 1995.
Bösch, Frank. *Zeitenwende 1979. Als die Welt von heute begann*, 4. Aufl. Munich: Beck, 2019.
Bösch, Frank, and Jens Gieseke. "Der Wandel des Politischen in Ost und West." In *Geteilte Geschichte. Ost- und Westdeutschland 1970–2000*, edited by Frank Bösch, 39–78. Göttingen: Vandenhoeck & Ruprecht, 2015.
Brechenmacher, Thomas, ed. *"In dieser Stunde der Kirche." Zum 100. Geburtstag von Julius Kardinal Döpfner.* Würzburg: Schöningh, 2013.
———. "Katholische Kirche und (Anti-)Kommunismus in der frühen Bundesrepublik." In *"Geistige Gefahr" und "Immunisierung der Gesellschaft." Antikommunismus und politische Kultur in der frühen Bundesrepublik*, edited by Stefan Creuzberger and Dierk Hoffmann, 177–97. Munich: De Gruyter, 2014.
Brodkorb, Clemens. *Bruder und Gefährte in der Bedrängnis. Hugo Aufderbeck als Seelsorgeamtsleiter in Magdeburg. Zur pastoralen Grundlegung einer "Kirche in der SBZ/DDR."* Paderborn: Bonifatius, 2002.

Cerny-Werner, Roland. *Vatikanische Ostpolitik und die DDR*. Göttingen: Vandenhoeck & Ruprecht, 2011.
Diederich, Georg M. *Chronik der katholischen Kirche in Mecklenburg. 1961 bis 1990 (Kirche unter Diktaturen, 3)*. Schwerin: Heinrich-Theissing-Institut, 2018.
Gatz, Erwin, ed. *Die Bistümer der deutschsprachigen Länder. Von der Säkularisation bis zur Gegenwart. Ein historisches Lexikon*. Freiburg: Herder, 2005.
Gieseking, Erik. *Justitia et Pax 1967–2007. 40 Jahre Einsatz für Gerechtigkeit und Frieden. Eine Dokumentation*. Paderborn: Schöningh, 2007.
Gödde, Petra. "Globale Kulturen." In *Geschichte der Welt. 1945 bis heute—Die globalisierte Welt*, edited by Iriye Akira, 535–669. Bonn: Beck, 2014.
Grande, Dieter. *Dem Frieden eine Chance. Die Arbeit von Justitia et Pax in der ehemaligen Deutschen Demokratischen Republik (DDR)*. Bonn: Schriftenreihe Gerechtigkeit and Frieden, 2003.
Grande, Dieter, and Bernd Schäfer. *Zur Kirchenpolitik der SED. Auseinandersetzungen um das Katholikentreffen 1983–1987*. Leipzig: St. Benno, 1994.
Grande, Dieter, and Peter-Paul Straube, eds. *Die Synode des Bistums Meißen 1969 bis 1971. Die Antwort einer Ortskirche auf das Zweite Vatikanische Konzil*. Leipzig: St. Benno, 2005.
Greschat, Martin. *Protestantismus im Kalten Krieg. Kirche, Politik und Gesellschaft im geteilten Deutschland 1945–1963*. Paderborn: Schöningh, 2010.
Großbölting, Thomas. *Der verlorene Himmel, Glaube in Deutschland seit 1945*. Göttingen: Vandenhoeck & Ruprecht, 2013.
Grütz, Reinhard. *Katholizismus in der DDR-Gesellschaft 1960–1990. Kirchliche Leitbilder, theologische Deutungen und lebensweltliche Praxis im Wandel*. Paderborn: Schöningh, 2004.
Heinecke, Herbert. *Konfession und Politik in der DDR. Das Wechselverhältnis von Kirche und Staat im Vergleich zwischen evangelischer und katholischer Kirche*. Leipzig: Evangelische Verlagsanstalt, 2002.
Heinicker, Petra. *Kolpingsarbeit in der SBZ und DDR 1945–1990*. Paderborn: Brill, 2020.
Höllen, Martin. *Loyale Distanz? Katholizismus und Kirchenpolitik in SBZ und DDR. Ein historischer Überblick in Dokumenten*, Bd. 2: 1956–1965, Bd. 3, 1: 1966–1976, Bd. 3, 2: 1977–1990. Berlin: Höllen, 1997–2000.
Holzbrecher, Sebastian. *Der Aktionskreis Halle. Postkonziliare Konflikte im Katholizismus der DDR*. Würzburg: Echter, 2014.
———. "Katholikentage in der DDR? Zur Bedeutung einer katholischen Institution für den ostdeutschen Diasporakatholizismus." In *Profil und Prägung. Historische Perspektiven auf 100 deutsche Katholikentage*, edited by Christoph Kösters, Hans Maier, and Frank Kleinehagenbrock, 89–102. Paderborn: Schöningh, 2017.
Hummel, Karl-Josef, ed. *Vatikanische Ostpolitik unter Johannes XXIII und Paul VI, 1958–1978*. Paderborn: Schöningh, 1999.
Hünermann, Peter, and Bernd Hilberath, eds. *Herders theologischer Kommentar zum Zweiten Vatikanischen Konzil*, Bd. 4: Sonderausgabe. Freiburg: Herder, 2009.
Kähler, Christoph. "Kirche im Sozialismus." In *Staatslexikon. Recht, Wirtschaft, Gesellschaft*, 8th ed, edited by Görres-Gesellschaft and the Herder-Verlag. Freiburg: Herder, 2019.
Kösters, Christoph, ed. *Akten deutscher Bischöfe seit 1945. Die DDR 1951–1957*. Paderborn: Schöningh, 2012.
———, ed. *Caritas in der SBZ/DDR 1945–1989. Erinnerungen, Berichte, Forschungen*. Paderborn: Schöningh, 2001.
———. "Katholische Kirche und Katholizismus in der SBZ/DDR. Eine Bilanz neuerer Forschungen." *Historisches Jahrbuch* 121 (2001): 532–80.
———. "Minderheit und Konfession. Einige Überlegungen zur Erforschung der Diaspora in Deutschland im 19. und 20. Jahrhundert." In *Die katholische Diaspora in Deutschland—Stand und Perspektiven der Forschung* (Wichmann Jahrbuch, N.F. 13), edited by Benjamin Gallin, Michael Höhle, and Konstantin Manthey, 9–39. Heiligenstadt: F.W. Cordier, 2015.

———. "Revolution, Wiedervereinigung und katholische Kirche." *Historisch Politische Mitteilungen* 17 (2010): 55–112.
———. *Staatssicherheit und Caritas 1950–1989. Zur politischen Geschichte der katholischen Kirche in der DDR*, 2., korr. Aufl. Paderborn: Schöningh, 2002.
Kösters, Christoph, and Wolfgang Tischner, eds. *Katholische Kirche in SBZ und DDR*. Paderborn: Schöningh, 2005.
Kunter, Katharina. *Erfüllte Hoffnungen und zerbrochene Träume. Evangelische Kirchen in Deutschland im Spannungsfeld von Demokratie und Sozialismus (1980–1993)*. Göttingen: Vandenhoeck & Ruprecht, 2006.
Lange, Gerhard. "Die Ökumenische Versammlung in der DDR. Zu einigen Aspekten der 'Theologischen Grundlegung.'" In *Der konziliare Prozess in der DDR in den 1980er Jahren*, edited by Gesellschaft zur Förderung vergleichender Staat-Kirche-Forschung e.V., 35–52. Berlin: 2009.
———. "Politische Gemeinsamkeiten zwischen der katholischen und den evangelischen Kirchen in der DDR?" In *Christen, Staat und Gesellschaft in der DDR*, edited by Gert Kaiser and Ewald Frie, 63–120. Frankfurt: Campus, 1996.
Lange, Gerhard, et al., eds. *Katholische Kirche—sozialistischer Staat DDR. Dokumente und öffentliche Äußerungen 1945–1990*, 2. Aufl. Leipzig: St. Benno, 1993.
Lepp, Claudia. *Tabu der Einheit? Die Ost-West-Gemeinschaft der evangelischen Christen und die deutsche Teilung (1945–1969)*. Göttingen: Vandenhoeck & Ruprecht, 2005.
Lepp, Claudia, and Kurt Nowak, eds. *Evangelische Kirche im geteilten Deutschland (1945–1989/90)*. Göttingen: Vandenhoeck & Ruprecht, 2001.
Lexikon für Theologie und Kirche III. Freiburg: Herder, 1959.
Liedhegener, Antonius, Christoph Kösters, and Thomas Brechenmacher. "Katholizismus. Zur Geschichte, Gegenwart und Zukunft seines modernen Begriffs." *Historisches Jahrbuch* 139 (2019): 609–26.
März, Christian. *Otto Spülbeck. Ein Leben für die Diaspora*. Leipzig: St. Benno, 2010.
Maser, Peter. *Glauben im Sozialismus. Kirchen und Religionsgemeinschaften in der DDR*. West Berlin: Holzapfel, 1989.
Mau, Rudolf. *Der Protestantismus im Osten Deutschlands (1945–1990)*. Leipzig: Evangelische Verlagsanstalt, 2005.
Meyer, Hans Joachim. *In keiner Schublade. Erfahrungen im geteilten und vereinten Deutschland*. Freiburg: Herder, 2015.
Mokry, Stefan. "Dreimal Diaspora? Kardinal Julius Döpfners Sicht auf seine bischöflichen Wirkungsstätten Würzburg, Berlin und München in den Jahren 1948–1976 anhand von Predigten und Hirtenbriefen." In *Die katholische Diaspora in Deutschland—Stand und Perspektiven der Forschung* (Wichmann Jahrbuch, N.F. 13), edited by Benjamin Gallin, Michael Höhle, and Konstantin Manthey, 241–53. Heiligenstadt: F. W. Cordier, 2015.
———. *Kardinal Julius Döpfner und das Zweite Vatikanum. Ein Beitrag zur Biografie und Konzilsgeschichte*. Stuttgart: Kohlhammer, 2016.
Müller, Thorsten. *Neue Heimat Eichsfeld? Flüchtlinge und Vertriebene in der katholischen Ankunftsgesellschaft*. Duderstadt: Mecke, 2010.
Neubert, Ehrhart. *Der Brief aus Weimar. Zur Selbstbefreiung der CDU im Herbst 1989*. Sankt Augustin: Konrad-Adenauer-Stiftung e.V., 2014.
Pilvousek, Josef, ed. *Die katholische Kirche in der DDR. Beiträge zur Kirchengeschichte Mitteldeutschlands*. Münster: Aschendorff, 2014.
———. "Die katholische Kirche und die Anfänge einer historischen Aufarbeitung 1990 bis 1996. Überlegungen zu einem fortwährenden Prozeß." In *Die katholische Kirche in der DDR. Beiträge zur Kirchengeschichte Mitteldeutschlands*, edited by Josef Pilvousek, 375–90. Münster: Aschendorff, 2014.
———, ed. *Kirchliches Leben im totalitären Staat. Seelsorge in der SBZ/DDR 1945–1976. Quellentexte aus den Ordinariaten*. Leipzig: St. Benno, 1994.

———, ed. *Kirchliches Leben im totalitären Staat. Seelsorge in der SBZ/DDR 1977–1989. Quellentexte aus den Ordinariaten, Teil II.* Leipzig: St. Benno, 1998.

———. *Theologische Ausbildung und gesellschaftliche Umbrüche. 50 Jahre Katholische Theologische Hochschule und Priesterausbildung in Erfurt.* Leipzig: St. Benno, 2002.

———. "Von der 'Gärtnerei im Norden' zur 'doppelten Diaspora.' Überlegungen zum Diasporabegriff in der katholischen Kirche in der DDR." In *Diaspora als Ort der Theologie. Perspektiven aus Tschechien und Ostdeutschland,* edited by Benedikt Kranemann, et al., 101–16. Würzburg: Echter, 2016.

Pollack, Detlef. "Ostdeutschland. Keine Anzeichen einer Trendwende." In *Religion in der Moderne. Ein internationaler Vergleich,* edited by Detlef Pollack and Gergely Rosta, 274–88. Frankfurt: Campus Verlag, 2015.

———. "Renaissance des Religiösen? Veränderungen auf dem religiösen Feld in ausgewählten Ländern Ost- und Ostmitteleuropas." *Archiv für Sozialgeschichte* 51 (2011): 109–40.

Preuß, Elisabeth. *Die Kanzel in der DDR. Die ungewöhnliche Geschichte des St.-Benno-Verlages.* Leipzig: St. Benno, 2006.

Schäfer, Bernd. *The East German State and the Catholic Church, 1945–1989.* New York: Berghahn Books, 2010.

———. *Staat und katholische Kirche in der DDR.* Cologne: Böhlau, 1998.

———. "Um 'anzukommen' muß man sich 'ankömmlich' artikulieren. Zur 'Berliner Konferenz' (BK) zwischen 1964 und 1993." In *Die Ost-CDU. Beiträge zu ihrer Entstehung und Entwicklung,* edited by Michael Richter and Martin Rißmann, 111–25. Cologne: Böhlau, 1995.

Schulte-Umberg, Thomas, ed. *Akten deutscher Bischöfe seit 1945. Die DDR 1957–1961.* Paderborn: Schöningh, 2006.

Seifert, Katharina. *Glaube und Politik. Die Ökumenische Versammlung in der DDR 1988/89.* Leipzig: St. Benno, 2000.

Selke, Jürgen. *Katholische Kirche im Sozialismus? Der Hirtenbrief der katholischen Bischöfe in der DDR zum Weltfriedenstag 1983 und seine Bedeutung für das Verhältnis von Katholischer Kirche und Staat DDR.* Altenberge: Oros, 1995.

Statistisches Bundesamt. *Sonderreihe mit Beiträgen für das Gebiet der ehemaligen DDR, Heft 15: Ausgewählte Zahlen der Volks- und Berufszählungen und Gebäude- und Wohnungszählungen 1950–1981.* Wiesbaden: Statistisches Bundesamt, 1994.

Stöber, Christian. *Rosenkranzkommunismus. Die SED-Diktatur und das katholische Milieu im Eichsfeld 1945–1989.* Berlin: Christoph Links, 2019.

Thorak, Thomas. *Wilhelm Weskamm. Diasporaseelsorger in der SBZ/DDR.* Würzburg: Echter, 2009.

Tischner, Wolfgang. *Katholische Kirche in der SBZ/DDR 1945–1951. Die Formierung einer Subgesellschaft im entstehenden sozialistischen Staat.* Paderborn: Schöningh, 2001.

Triebel, Bertram. *Die Thüringer CDU in der SBZ/DDR. Blockpartei mit Eigeninteresse.* Sankt Augustin: Konrad-Adenauer-Stiftung, e.V., 2019.

Wittstadt, Klaus. *Julius Kardinal Döpfner. Anwalt Gottes und der Menschen.* Munich: Don Bosco, 2001.

Chapter Twelve

THE CHURCHES AND CHANGES IN MISSIONARY WORK

Biconfessionalism and Developmental Aid
to the "Third World" since the 1960s

Florian Bock
Translated by Jeffrey Verhey

For some time now, there has been a strong scholarly interest in Christian aid to the developing world.[1] Consistent with his birth in Argentina, Pope Francis has to some extent made his biography the agenda of his pontificate. Since his election in 2013, he has repeatedly stated his interest in the "edges" of the globalized world, and this has increased the media's interest in this topic.[2] Pope Francis wants to make visible the West's power structures, which have manifested themselves in a specific form of Christian aid to developing countries.

Both the Catholic and the Protestant churches began to change how they thought about Christian aid to developing countries in "1968," whereby what is meant with "1968" is not so much the year 1968 itself as the 1960s.[3] The Christian churches shifted from campaigning for donations to cultivating a "genuine" solidarity with the Christians of Africa, Asia, and Latin America in the face of worldwide hunger catastrophes widely covered by the media like that in Biafra.[4] This chapter focuses on this shift which affected both confessions, the reasons for it, including the theological and the political mindsets, and not least the so-called agents of change.

New Beginnings in the 1950s

When in the 1950s the churches in the Federal Republic of Germany and the German Democratic Republic began to collect money for Africa and

Asia, their model was the British "miss-a-meal movement."[5] This campaign, started in 1957, was a nondenominational initiative by Jews and Christians for the countries of the "Third World." The idea behind the "miss-a-meal movement" was to donate the equivalent of a daily meal. The campaign was very effective; even in divided postwar Germany, donations for underdeveloped countries quickly became popular. For example, the Protestant churches of Berlin-Brandenburg, Westphalia, and Saxony dedicated their Thanksgiving service (*Erntedank*) collection to the hungry. Catholic associations such as the League of German Catholic Youth (*Bund der Katholischen Jugend* or BDKJ) or Pax Christi also organized several campaigns with the same objective and transferred the donations they received to the poorer nations.[6]

The large church collections for the "Third World" which started at the end of the 1950s—carried out by Bread for the World on the Protestant side and by Misereor on the Catholic side—shattered previous financial records.[7] On the basis of a resolution from the Fulda Bishops' Conference in which the minor Catholic aid campaigns of the 1950s were bundled in 1959 into a single campaign, the Catholic Church collected 35.5 million DM for a fasting effort.[8] Although this had been planned as a one-time endeavor, Misereor, the German Catholic Bishops' Organization for Development Cooperation created to eliminate "hunger and leprosy," was born out of this venture.[9] A second Catholic Bishops' Organization for Development Cooperation, Adveniat, was founded in 1961 to look after the interests of the churches in Latin America.[10] It was no accident that both relief organizations were founded at roughly the same time. After the horrors of the Nazi terror and in the middle of the nationwide "economic miracle," German households were starting to learn more about the hunger disasters in the "Third World."

Scholars have pointed out that what lay behind the West German Catholics' charity campaign was a theological approach to confronting the past, a broad framework of understanding which went far beyond simple Christian charity. For one thing, these campaigns can be understood within the context of "German victim theology." Through their donations, Germans were able to thank others for the aid they had received after the war and, at the same time, atone for what they had done during National Socialism as well as during the colonial period.[11] The fundraising campaigns were organized by the churches, organizations that because they were supposedly not contaminated by National Socialism were thereby credible agents in any campaign to improve Germany's reputation. The widespread hunger which Germans had experienced in the postwar period allowed Germans to feel empathy for those suffering famine and food deprivation in developing countries. Those making financial donations also remembered how acute hunger had allegedly led to moral decline in the immediate postwar years in Germany: they feared that this could also prove to be the case in the developing world.[12] And, of course, fears of the spread of communism in the underdeveloped countries were also a driving force behind the German willingness to donate.[13]

On top of this, one can still recognize in the large-scale appeals for donations the last traces of a missionary impetus to proclaim the good news to the "ends of the earth," as called for in Acts 1:8. Finally, researchers have pointed out that the Catholic Bishops' Organization for Development Cooperation was also motivated by simple power-political calculations. Misereor and Adveniat fit in quite well with the ecclesiastical tenor of the time, which was characterized by a concentration of power within the hierarchy and at the expense of lay ancillary institutions. The influence of the bishops over these lay associations, which themselves would also be appealing for donations, thus became stronger, not least because the bishops demonstrated to the Vatican that they were capable of building up and sustaining bilateral contacts to other national churches.[14] It was the age of forceful preachers and missionaries such as Pater Johannes Leppich, SJ (1915–1992), who still relied entirely on financial or material donations.[15] In raising funds, such celebrity clerics and fundraisers could still make use of the "Nickneger," a small figure that bowed when you put a coin into the slot. This figure could still be found in churches well into the 1970s.[16] Centralizing operations and authority in the hands of the bishops (*Verkirchlichung*), it turns out, went hand-in-hand with deploying increasingly professional methods of raising money.

As if synchronized with Catholicism, Protestantism was undergoing a similar process of professionalization. The Protestant churches founded Bread for the World in 1959, the same year Misereor was launched. For both Bread for the World and Misereor, the motivation for providing aid was the assistance one had personally experienced after 1945. God's compassion and mercy was to be passed on—and not in the form of a one-time collection that pacified one's conscience like a narcotic, but rather as a firmly established program of assistance and aid for the worldwide body of Christ.[17] Although there were many similarities with the Catholic programs, it would be a mistake to conclude that what was involved here was simply appropriating the argumentation from the Catholic context.[18] Though Protestants paid close attention to the discussions on this topic in the Catholic church, as indeed they did to discussions on other topics, what emerged instead was a sort of productive "competition" in the field of neighborly love.[19]

It is important to note that because of their experiences in missionary work, the churches were far more sensitive—and had been for much longer—to the precarious situation in the developing countries than the state or German political parties. It took the Cold War for the general population to learn about Asia, Africa, and Latin America.[20] In the 1950s, only a few politicians such as the West German President Heinrich Lübke (1894–1972) addressed this problem in their speeches, a marked contrast with the political parties and the state, which did not.[21] Only in the 1960s did the Federal Republic define aid to underdeveloped countries as part of its agenda.[22] By then, as will be shown, within the churches religious developmental aid was already in the process of being transformed. Interestingly enough, the church's development aid services were financed in part by the state, although the state stated explicitly that it would do nothing to influence the content of the aid work. The initiative for this state financing came from the first Chancellor of West Germany, Konrad Adenauer (1876–1967).[23] Because Adenauer was a practicing Catholic, the Catholic Church probably found it much easier than the Protestant Church to accept this offer. In contrast, Protestants feared that their aid campaign could be politically appropriated in a manner incompatible with Bread for the World, which was intended to be a joint action of Protestants in both East and West Germany.[24]

But the Protestant Church in Germany eventually also agreed.[25] Protestant champions of accepting state funds successfully argued that acute problems of hunger throughout the world required as much aid as possible.[26] In the middle of 1962, a Protestant Central Agency for Development Aid (*Evangelische Zentralstelle für Entwicklungshilfe e.V.* [EZE]) was founded. This was, however, a West German institution, one that accepted state funds for aid projects to developing countries as long as no conditions had been placed on their use.[27] For its part, the West German state anticipated that such indirect subsidies of church aid to developing countries would help it to find ways to influence development in countries in which direct aid was not possible for political reasons. However, the state was also hoping to use this aid to win over the Christian churches as partners: by demonstrating the state's loyalty to the churches, the churches would hopefully respond in kind.[28]

On the other side of the Iron Curtain, the GDR branch of Bread for the World was used to provide special development aid to socialist brother states.[29] This could be done in a roundabout way. In the 1960s, the East German government used money collected by Bread for the World to strengthen the East German Red Cross, even though the East German government was at the same time criticizing the Church's collections.[30] The East German state could not afford to diverge from its anticlerical course, even though it was de facto financing its developmental aid programs through church moneys and gaining international recognition and prestige in the process.

In 1968, Misereor and Bread for the World founded the interconfessional working group *Brüderlich Teilen*, together with World Hunger Relief (*Welthungerhilfe*).[31] These two groups were representative of nondenominational aid campaigns, even though there continued to be independent denominational aid organizations.[32] In spite of these successful examples of cooperation, well into the 1970s Bread for the World continued to reject calls for an amalgamation of the two relief organizations, referring "to the important 450-year history of two denominations, to the interest of the donors, and the local partner organizations on the ground which collect charitable contributions and which are attached to a certain denomination and to the ineffectiveness of a merger . . . in practice."[33]

Turning Away from the Earlier Forms of Missionary Work in the 1960s

Already in the decades before the Second Vatican Council, Catholicism had developed into an increasingly "polycentric" denomination, to use the term of the Catholic theologian Johann Baptist Metz (1928–2019).[34] The Catholic Church was confronted with newer pluralist theological and cultural understandings in the wake of the Second Vatican Council (1962–65) and movements for decolonization. Traditional forms of mission work were accordingly called into question, and this criticism in turn shaped how developmental aid, which was being created in the late 1950s and early 1960s, would take further shape. How did this unfold? After 1945, Catholic missionaries were accused of participating in a paternalistic way in colonialism, of imposing a European version of Christianity, and of racial discrimination.[35] Clearly, reforms of mission work were necessary. Even theologians in orders that carried out missionary work, such as the advocates of *Nouvelle Théologie*, a school of thought in Catholic theology, supported these reforms.[36] But as the Church's so-called devil's advocates on theological questions, they questioned traditional theological positions from within and stressed that non-Christian religions also possessed paths to salvation.[37]

At the same time, the ranks of the hierarchy were beginning to reflect these global changes. The "Negro bishops"—so called by the Mainz bishop Hermann Volk (1903–1988) and others—were still new to many Council fathers at the Second Vatican Council. At the council, the sixty-one Africans presented themselves as a unanimous and united front, wanting to be heard and to have an equal say in the theological debates with their North Atlantic brethren.[38] As a result, the Church was having to position itself as a "global player" in a completely new manner. This was reflected not only in the Church's Decree on Missionary Activity, *Ad gentes*, but also in one of the most prominent texts of the council, the pastoral constitution *Gaudium et spes*. Section 44 of *Gaudium et spes* represented a quantum leap. In order to be able to act, according to this document, the Church needed to understand the context in which it lived and worked. Understanding the local situation was not a part of the *depositum fidei*, that is, of the findings and insights that are part of the Church's doctrine of faith.[39] In terms of pastoral theology, genuine Christian faith can be found only when renewed from an external source.[40] In his 1967 encyclical *Populorum progressio*, Pope Paul VI thus gave development aid a well-founded theological underpinning. In doing so, he opened a new chapter in Catholic development aid: development had to become the new word for peace (PP 76), according to the conclusion of this pastoral "pop encyclical."[41] "Conservative" circles were publicly outraged by the statements on revolution found in section 30–1. Though speaking out against any and every form of violence, the encyclical in the context of just war teachings defined certain limited conditions under which domestic action against an unjust regime could be legitimate.[42] According to its article 31, such uprisings could take place only where there had been a "manifest, longstanding tyranny which would do great damage to fundamental personal rights and dangerous harm to the common good of the country."

Portions of this document read from today's vantage point as though they could have been written by contemporary globalization critics—and certainly not by the Catholic Church.[43] Those working in the field of moral theology, on the other hand, noted back in 1999 that "from a greater temporal distance," much of what was written there appears today "to be very optimistic and characterized by a belief in progress."[44] At any rate, the conciliar documents in connection with the encyclical *Populorum progressio* triggered a flood of conferences and publications. Admittedly, in Rome one first had to get used to the idea of receiving accolades from the SPD.[45] But such approval was short-lived. By the summer of 1968, a mere year after the publication of *Populorum progressio*, Pope Paul VI's positive public image in terms of development policy was abruptly upended. In the controversial encyclical *Humanae vitae*, Paul VI spoke out against artificial contraception. As a result, many people throughout the world accused him of negligence in his development policy: how could one justify a policy promoting overpopulation in the face of the growing scarcity of natural resources?

As a result of all these developments, the orders carrying out missionary work felt that their work was being radically called into question. This sentiment grew at the same time that the number of people called to the missionary vocation began to decline. Between 1962 and 1977, the large missionary orders lost an average of 20 percent of their members; in many European countries, after the Second Vatican Council the number of missionaries declined by half.[46] A transformation process began. The orders shed their European forms and character and transformed themselves into genuinely international organizations; people from areas that had previously been the focus of the missionaries' efforts now comprised the majority of the new members. To stabilize Church structures, missionaries were no longer sent just to Africa or to Asia: they were also sent to Europe. It was no longer a question of converting people living in distant colonies, but of a selfless service to the Mother Church by stabilizing local churches.[47]

In Protestantism, one could perhaps describe the 1966 worldwide conference of the World Council of Churches (WCC) in Geneva or the 1968 general meeting of the World Council of Churches in Uppsala, Sweden, as the counterpart to developments in Catholicism. Here, too, participants called for a "renewal of the world" and saw the "call of people throughout the world for social justice" as one of the greatest challenges of the present.[48] As a result, the WCC increasingly became a global organization with a global agenda.[49] As many within this organization began to prioritize incorporating "Third World" perspectives into their work, battles broke out within the EKD between the Church leadership on one side and the wing of Protestantism and the evangelical movement engaged in development aid on the other. These battles were waged primarily over the politics of racism in the south of Africa. Fights over development thus became proxy wars for the programmatic and political reorientation of the WCC (ÖRK) that churches in the developing world had steadfastly advocated for since the 1960s.[50]

The central theme of the disputes between the two wings was repeatedly the relationship between "horizontal," that is, social, and "vertical," that is, theological, work. What should the relationship between development aid and missionary work be?[51] How much orientation toward "left-wing" politics for church development workers would be permissible at national church conferences? In order to avert an imminent one-sided "politicization," the German Protestant Alliance (DEA) created counter structures to Bread for the World. The ensuing conflicts would continue through the 1990s.[52] Similar internal conflicts within Catholicism do not appear to have taken place, even though there was a massive intra-Catholic criticism of Misereor at the 1970 congress on development policy, "Give each Person a Chance" (Jedem Menschen eine Chance). The criticism arose over how money and aid were awarded, as well as over the fact that Misereor was organized and controlled by the bishops, and finally not least over the fact that Misereor, which had been established to collect donations, was suddenly claiming to be able to solve all of the political problems associated with development aid.[53]

Starting in the 1960s, then, parallel to these developments, many African, Latin American, or Asian students came to Europe and educated their West German peers about the development policy situation in their own countries. It would thus be a misnomer to claim like the historian Quinn Slobodian that it was the West that discovered the "Third World."[54]

To sum up, since the 1960s at the latest, missionary work underwent a fundamental change.[55] For one, it took on a decidedly interconfessional character, a departure from the past when Catholics and Protestants competed against each other in the mission field. For another, it underwent a transition from a model which saw missionary work as responding to a deficiency in those whom it sought to convert. Models that saw mission work as indoctrination, as therapy, as instruction or even as judgment all presupposed some deficiency in its subjects. This shifted to a model based on alterity, which put missionaries and those they encountered on a more equal footing. Mission was seen as dialog or as an experience of plurality, a presupposition which allowed missionaries to emerge just as transformed as those with whom they were in contact.[56] Those Protestant institutions which created a link between the various Protestant churches such as Council for World Mission were largely responsible for this development.[57]

New Concepts for Missionary Work: The Klausenhof Example

Today, it is clear that the history of the Christian missions and the churches' development aid is one of interdependence.[58] A restructuring of the spaces in which these cultural contacts took place, such as we can see in the churches from the 1960s on, led to the production of new knowledge about developing countries.[59] This was to a large degree because these countries had a strong presence in the media: in the press, in TV, or in radio. This was accompanied by new approaches within Europe to the "Third World." Of particular importance here on the Catholic side was the Working Group for Developmental Aid (*Arbeitsgemeinschaft für Entwicklungshilfe*, or AGEH), founded in 1959 as a kind of placement agency for development workers working for Catholic organizations such as Misereor who planned to go overseas.[60] The Protestant counterpart to AGEH, the Service Abroad (*Dienste in Übersee e.V.*, or DÜ), was established in 1961. Because of internal quarrels with the EKD and Protestant mission societies, it remained significantly smaller than its Catholic counterpart, although it was more independent and more homogenous in its structure.[61] The training courses for development work, which provided instruction in the local languages and their tasks abroad, were quite similar in both confessions and in their respective developmental aid organizations, AGEH and DÜ, although the programs remained independent of each other. Both sought to train and send over specialists, manual workers, and skilled craftsmen who could bring their technical abilities to the developing world.[62] In the following section, I would like to focus on the generational and mental shifts of the 1960s and in particular on the phase immediately after the Second Vatican Council.

The Catholic Academy Klausenhof provides an ideal case study of these transformations. The Catholic Academy Klausenhof was founded before the Second Vatican Council in 1959 in Dingden in the Lower Rhine, a "heart of the rural and farming world," as it was called in the Catholic periodical *Mann in der Zeit*.[63] The Klausenhof became the first Catholic vocational training center for Misereor and, specifically, for the occupational profile of a "social assistant for development aid." Those who applied for these positions would be given placements in Africa, Asia, and Latin America if they were male, over twenty-one, and had completed a vocational training program in agriculture.[64] The vocational training itself was organized into several stages. At the beginning of the training, there were courses in farming and the social issues related to farming. There were also courses in ethnology, sociology, development policy, and theology. The theology courses had a particular focus on "Caritas as a way of life," in which students discussed socioethical principles of subsidiarity and solidarity and—in the first few years—the encyclical *Mater et magistra*.[65] Compared to other training centers, which had a teaching style based on direct instruction or lecturing, the Klausenhof's approach was different: it was characterized from the very beginning by the principle of "healthy self-control and self-criticism." Course participants mostly created their weekly work plans themselves, coming up with their own assignments and electing their own leadership democratically.[66] This nine-month training course in the Klausenhof was intended to ensure independent thinking, planning, and action in the developing countries: it aimed to prepare the participants for their first contacts with counterparts of the same level. This was followed by language training lasting two to three months in either England, Spain, or France before one was sent to the specific deployment location.[67]

At a "sending-off ceremony" that closed the training period, the speakers emphasized what was to be the true task of all development aid workers: in the words of the Essen auxiliary bishop (*Weihbischof*) Julius Angerhausen (1911–1990), they implemented the Council only when they engaged with their fellow human beings in order to recognize the presence of God within.[68] The academy director Jochen Schmauch, who served from 1961 to 1966, warned in 1964: "Your pulpit is the farmlands, the workshop, the office. Your sermon is the silent activity of your hands. The most sophisticated technique is of no use if the soul is missing . . . He who has the star of the wise men in front of him comes home."[69] At the same time, one can find in the press releases of the time the first indications of a new generational self-understanding among young Catholics. No longer was the desire to evangelize the primary motivation to become involved in development work in developing countries. Rather, the primary reason was now the desire to develop one's own personality. One wanted to find out "what sort of person one actually is."[70] This Vatican Council generation was less motivated by an idealistic conviction in one's mission than by the desire "to do something which was right" and to "fully use" one's skills and knowledge. And this was true regardless of the activity of international aid organizations, including Church aid organizations, which had swelled up into "pity industries."[71] A pragmatic approach clearly won out here. "We simply want to help improve the living conditions of people."[72]

According to a letter from its first chairman, Karl Osner (1927–2014), who served as managing director from 1959 to 1961, the target group of the AGEH were lay Catholics in a middle-class occupation who were available for a temporary period (about two to four years) for the development and the implementation of Church institutions overseas.[73] The AGEH had arisen out of the Kolping Vereine and the Catholic Rural Youth Movement (*Katholische Landjugendbewegung*). In the late 1950s, Osner sketched a picture of the ideal development worker: he (or less often she) was someone who acted out of apostolic responsibility and sought to be a witness to Christian life. His professional knowledge and ability was coupled with a Christian work ethic; he or she was also an advocate outside of his or her job for Catholic Action.[74] As time progressed, this image was to change decisively, as can be seen by examining the archival material of the organization's twenty-fifth and fiftieth anniversaries in 1984 and 2009, respectively. In the 1980s, the organization posited that it was time to turn one's back on the "man of action" idea as the prototype of a development worker and to orient oneself instead on the model of a patient advisor: "We have to make ourselves superfluous."[75]

The contrast to the initial phase of the AGEH is striking; for the earlier period, the focus was still on "God's employees," with a dual goal of personal sanctification and the salvation of souls.[76] This "secular" transformation of the Christian development aid program, associated with a younger generation, largely leveled out confessional differences. For example, starting in March 1967, the DÜ accepted Catholic applicants.[77] The AGEH had begun already in 1962 to accept Protestant applicants, male and female alike, although this institution maintained its association with Catholicism much longer than the DÜ did with Protestantism.[78] Not only Misereor and Bread for the World but also the Church's aid services, maintained a confessional identity on the outside which was in fact no longer lived on the inside.

The history of how the understanding of developmental aid changed within these groups thus calls into question or at least forces us to modify the arguments made by Udi Greenberg. Greenberg argued that the ecumenical movement embraced decolonization, seeing it potentially as a spiritual asset for the rebuilding of European Christianity. These groups, in contrast, never claimed that restricting developmental aid would renew Christianity at home and fundamentally alter longstanding theologies.[79] Because Catholics and Protestants tended to be stronger in certain regions of the developing world than others, Catholics were more likely to concentrate more on the hunger catastrophe in Biafra, Protestants on the fight against South African apartheid.[80] By the end of the 1970s, an additional—and fundamental—change in perspective had become clear. The developing countries were constructing a new self-image, one in which the ideal development assistance was believed to be the influx of capital from abroad. Less valued was help from foreign experts, which they saw as paternalistic and a relic of colonialism.[81]

Change of Values and New Theologies after 1968

At the very latest, since the beginning of the 1970s, newer theologies were emerging that were critical of religious development aid as it had been practiced by church institutions. Countless groups and initiatives found aid campaigns such as those envisaged by Misereor no longer sufficient. For example, in July 1968, the Catholic *Studententag* in Tübingen passed the following "resolution on the task of the student community":

> At a time when in Vietnam people are being murdered in the name of freedom, when millions in Biafra are at risk of starvation, and when the Third World is being plundered by highly industrialized countries for their own consumption, Christians can no longer live in their bourgeois closet.
>
> These global problems have been most keenly perceived at the universities, and here people are searching for ways to tackle these issues. In such a situation, the Christian student community cannot continue to live in the idyll of "brotherly" congregations, removed from society; rather, the student community must accept it has a responsibility which goes beyond the efforts to reform the church internally; it has a responsibility for social and political conditions. . . .
>
> Parish congregations in their previous form understood salvation as something independent of one's relationship to society; salvation was something in which the world had largely no bearing.
>
> Confronted with a church which had kept all too little critical distance to the affluent, prosperous society of the Federal Republic of Germany, indeed, which

all too often had accommodated itself to this society, student religious communities must play a leading role in criticizing the church in order to uphold the church's credibility. The church must also strip away those church structures that encourage the dependency and immaturity of parishes and replace them with alternative models of a democratized parish.[82]

According to critics of the earlier forms of development assistance, which merely called on parishioners to donate money, the main cause of the problems of the developing countries was the economic power gap between the "First" and the "Third World." This criticism, of course, was embedded in a larger social and theological framework, which included the student protests against the Vietnam War and against the visit by the Persian Shah to West Berlin in 1967—and the death during these protests of Benno Ohnesorg, a student of German literature.[83] Ohnesorg's death was the initial impetus behind the 1968 movement in the Federal Republic.

A "change of values" (*Wertewandel*) played a decisive role in the developments around 1968. To some extent, this transformation had its origins in the 1950s and ended only toward the middle of the 1970s, so that one can say that social processes which had been in progress for a long time were only radicalized by the events of "1968."[84] Responsible for this revolution in values, at least in part, was a revolution in lifestyles and morays.[85] It led to a decline in the importance of the values of duty and of accepting one's fate and place in society, and to an increase in the importance of the values of freedom and self-fulfillment.[86]

The change in values was reflected in changes in theology. Numerous campaign and grassroots groups were founded in which the participants intensively discussed interdenominationally the "God is dead" theology of Dorothee Sölle (1929–2003), as well as the new political theology of Johann Baptist Metz or Jürgen Moltmann (b. 1926).[87] One forum for this discussion was the so-called political evening prayer, first presented at the Essen *Katholikentag* in 1968 but essentially ecumenical in its orientation. This was a controversial prayer form in which political information, campaign proclamations, and even discussions within the congregation were matched with biblical texts.[88]

Such politicization had ramifications for the image of God. The focus of faith was no longer a God waiting in the hereafter, an Old Testament God who punished, but a human God who was active in this world, who was interested, without conditions, in people's individual problems as long as people opened themselves up to God.[89] This new image of God was reflected clearly in missionary work and development aid. As has been shown, missionary work characterized by thetic, that is, dogmatic, preaching was replaced by a dialogical pattern of communication in which one wanted to teach and to persuade.[90]

Ultimately, one version of the political theology was liberation theology.[91] The enthusiasm for this Latin American theology, especially among younger Christians in the Federal Republic, can be explained in part by the contrast offered by personalities such as Leonardo Boff (b. 1938), Dom Hélder Câmara (1909–1999), and Oscar Romero (1917–1980). In contrast to Church leaders in Germany, their appearance was very modest, and they practiced an ascetic lifestyle.[92] Only recently have blind spots in the first generation of liberation theologians been pointed out. For one, they were initially almost exclusively men. For another, even allowing for all their harsh criticism of colonial dependency, they had little understanding of and sympathy for the basic Western skepticism toward modernity and its mode of thought. That, for example, power relationships could be expressed not only in economic terms but also in language or through thinking in categories that excluded, only became apparent to subsequent generations of liberation theologians.[93] Nonetheless, in their initial period, the South American "grassroots congregations" were increasingly idealized, especially in the modern Western countries, as people were enthusiastic for what was perceived as a vibrant effort organized "from below" to fight oppression.[94]

It was ultimately against this background that Catholic and Protestant youth groups began in May 1970 to carry out their first joint hunger marches.[95] Christian youth groups can be described as the avant-garde of development policy, as here the various strands of the criticism by students and by members of the churches came together.[96] But for older people engaged in these activities as well, the rule for the most part remained: "confessional borders play no role in our joint work."[97] As a result of the cooperation between Catholics and Protestants, the concept of fair trade with the "Third World" found a home in Germany and has remained an important focus of the Church's development aid programs until the present day.[98] At least through the late 2010s, most of those leading development work think in global categories, as the widespread use of the moniker "one world" makes clear. The end of the Cold War reduced the need to think in strong ideological polarities such as the "East versus West" or "capitalism versus communism." The continued threat from nuclear armaments also strengthened tendencies to think globally rather than confessionally.[99]

Closing Reflections

Since the end of World War II, development aid itself underwent a decolonization process which—bolstered by programmatic theological changes brought on by the Second Vatican Council, the WCC assembly in Uppsala in 1968, and liberation theology—led to a pluralization of the possible courses of Christian action toward hunger and the "Third World." No longer were denominational fundraising campaigns insulated from each other; church development aid instead became more ecumenical, as is shown by the joint hunger marches of Catholic and Protestant youth.[100] Since the 1960s at the latest, moreover, new challenges such as globalization and religious fundamentalism increasingly made people overlook and even forget altogether confessional differences when working together for international causes. That said, both Catholics and Protestants held on to their own organizations for international development. Both deemed it necessary to keep them separate in order to hold on to their own confessional identities and structures: interconfessional mergers were not going to happen.

The pluralization of Christian action in the field of development aid led, however, to problems.[101] Because Catholics and Protestants, state and non-state groups alike, had their hand in administering development aid, competition and conflicts arose both within and between these individual groups. This was true even for the churches, in spite of the fact that developmental aid was a field in which church groups were supposedly working together.[102] The Catholic Workers Movement (*Katholische Arbeitnehmer-Bewegung*, KAB) with its *Weltnotwerk*, for instance, retained the classic model of social work that emphasized charity and compassion (following the example of the Good Samaritan), rather than striving toward justice and equality. The BDKJ, in contrast, found a way to have a stronger presence in the public sphere and to help raise public awareness in the Federal Republic through action-oriented campaigns such as the interconfessional hunger marches discussed earlier.[103] At the beginning of the 1980s, the controversial Protestant campaign, "Hunger through abundance?" which compared the overabundance of food in the West with the lack of food in underdeveloped countries, was similarly effective in gaining public attention. Because of the fixation on global exports in the commodities market in the development world, producing foodstuffs for the local population was neglected.[104]

Tensions also arose within the Catholic youth organizations. On the one hand, organizations like the BDKJ criticized the traditional forms of aid work for the "Third World." However, they also provided a platform for young Christians to work within the Church and remain within the Church fold, even where they criticized and even rejected the approaches taken by large fundraising organizations such as Misereor.[105] The BDKJ leadership argued that to show solidarity, one had to expand the communal understanding of what it meant to be a Christian. It went from being one rooted in passivity to one that entailed being actively engaged globally, one that required dialog and empathy instead of supercilious teaching.[106] In this vein, the charitable gift of putting money into a "Nickneger" was replaced by erecting miniature "slum cities" and shantytowns in parish community centers. In assuming such an explicit ethical responsibility for the world, which could very easily take on an elitist habitus, young Christians in Germany were governed by a process of self-discovery. But this often took the form of moral superiority, particularly in terms of how they perceived those who were not taking part in their actions.

As large as this movement was, it quickly spread to embrace far more causes, including human rights and environmentalism. It is not surprising, then, that researchers have noted that the "Third World" movement proved to be structurally anything but homogeneous and diffuse in its membership.[107] For German Christians—regardless of whether they were Catholic or Protestant, male or female—the strong interest in development aid may have been due to the guilt feelings produced by the crimes of National Socialism and even by the crimes Germany had committed during its relatively short colonial past. Indeed, this feeling of guilt may have been more pronounced in Germany than in countries with longer colonial histories.[108]

But there is one final point to consider. Those mostly younger activists seeking to redress the National Socialist atrocities also believed—erroneously—that Germany's colonial past was less tainted than those of its neighbors like Great Britain and France. Germany's colonial ventures lay in the distant past, while the often-bloody experiences of decolonization in the 1950s and 1960s had exposed the corruption and crimes of the major colonial powers. This juxtaposition generated among the German faithful an additional, special motivation to become engaged in Africa, Asia, and Latin America. The belief that Germany lay untainted by colonial sins—scholarly publications detailing the genocide in German Southwest Africa had either yet to be produced or had been ignored—produced a feeling of moral superiority amongst the younger generation of Church activists, particularly vis-a-vis their European neighbors.[109] The result was a seismic shift. Those concerned about the developing world went from simply passing the offering plate and asking for donations to training activists and waging developmental campaigns in which both Catholics and Protestants took part.

Florian Bock is Assistant Professor of Church History of the Middle Ages and Modern Times at the Ruhr-Universität Bochum. He has studied Catholic Theology and German Studies in Bochum, Padua (Italy), and Tübingen. In 2015, he published his first monograph *Der Fall "Publik:" Katholische Presse in der Bundesrepublik um 1968*. In 2021, he completed his habilitation on Catholic sermons in the seventeenth and eighteenth centuries. He is one of the subproject leaders of the research group "Katholischsein in der Bundesrepublik," funded by the Deutsche Forschungsgemeinschaft.

Notes

1. This chapter is a revised version of Florian Bock, "'Wir wollen einfach die Lebensbedingungen der Menschen verbessern.' Zum Paradigmenwechsel der katholischen Entwicklungshilfe in der Bundesrepublik um 1968," in *Wenn Hunger droht. Bewältigung und religiöse Deutung (1400–1980)*, ed. Andreas Holzem (Tübingen: Mohr Siebeck, 2017), 275–94. I have learned many things about the "Third World" from the works of my former Bochum colleague Sebastian Tripp, especially from his doctoral dissertation: *Fromm und politisch. Christliche Anti-Apartheid-Gruppen und die Transformation des westdeutschen Protestantismus 1970–1990* (Göttingen: Wallstein, 2015), as well as his article, "Die Weltkirche vor Ort. Die Globalisierung der Kirchen und die Entstehung christlicher 'Dritte Welt'-Gruppen," in *Soziale Strukturen und Semantiken des Religiösen im Wandel. Transformationen in der Bundesrepublik Deutschland 1949–1989*, ed. Wilhelm Damberg, Frank Bösch, Lucian Hölscher, et al. (Essen: Klartext-Verlag, 2011), 123–36. I have also profited from Daniel Gerster, *Friedensdialoge im Kalten Krieg. Eine Geschichte der Katholiken in der Bundesrepublik 1957–1983* (Frankfurt am Main: Campus-Verlag, 2012).
2. Sebastian Pittl, "Für eine 'Globalisierung der Hoffnung.' Zur Relevanz postkolonialen Denkens für Theologie und Missionswissenschaft—Einleitung," in *Theologie und Postkolonialismus. Ansätze—Herausforderungen—Perspektiven*, ed. Sebastian Pittl (Regensburg: Friedrich Pustet, 2018), 19ff.
3. Clemens Pfeffer, "Missionshistoriographie post 1968. Postkoloniale Perspektive avant la lettre," in *Theologie und Postkolonialismus. Ansätze—Herausforderungen—Perspektiven*, ed. Sebastian Pittl (Regensburg: Friedrich Pustet, 2018), 191–218.
4. See on this Johannes Stollhof, "'Ein Millionen-Volk wird ausgehungert!' Die Wahrnehmung der Hungerkatastrophe in Biafra zwischen 1967 und 1970 im deutschen Katholizismus," in *Wenn Hunger droht. Bewältigung und religiöse Deutung (1400–1980)*, ed. Andreas Holzem (Tübingen: Mohr Siebeck, 2017), 295–315.
5. Uwe Kaminsky, "Nothilfe über die Grenzen hinaus. Die Entstehung von 'Brot für die Welt' in der DDR," in *Diakonie im geteilten Deutschland. Zur diakonischen Arbeit unter den Bedingungen der DDR und der Teilung Deutschlands*, ed. Ingolf Hübner and Jochen-Christoph Kaiser (Stuttgart: Kohlhammer, 1999), 181.
6. Ibid.
7. Konstanze Evangelia Kemnitzer, *Der ferne Nächste. Zum Selbstverständnis der Aktion "Brot für die Welt"* (Stuttgart: Kohlhammer, 2008). The online version of Kemnitzer's book is more comprehensive and can be found at: https://augustana.de/fileadmin/user_upload/dokumente/promotionen/Kemnitzer_2007.pdf, Retrieved 6 January 2020. See Tripp, "Weltkirche," 128; and Gabriele Lingelbach, *Spenden und Sammeln. Der westdeutsche Spendenmarkt bis in die 1980er Jahre* (Göttingen: Wallstein, 2009), 288 and 466 (statistic 1).
8. Kaminsky, "Nothilfe," 181ff.
9. Norbert Trippen, *Josef Kardinal Frings (1887–1978), Vol. 2: Sein Wirken für die Weltkirche und seine letzten Bischofsjahre* (Paderborn: Schöningh, 2005), 115 and 132.
10. On the two aid agencies, see Sylvie Toscer, "Das bischöfliche Hilfswerk Misereor und die Rolle von Kardinal Frings auf dem Konzil," in *Die deutschsprachigen Länder und das II. Vatikanum*, ed. Hubert Wolf and Claus Arnold (Paderborn: Schöningh, 2000), 53–60; Stefan Voges, "Hilfe in der Not: Nachkriegserfahrungen in der Begründung von Entwicklungshilfe," in *Zwischen Kriegs- und Diktaturerfahrung. Katholizismus und Protestantismus in der Nachkriegs-*

zeit, ed. Christoph Holzapfel and Andreas Holzem (Stuttgart: Kohlhammer, 2005), 91–108; and Stefan Voges, "Solidarität in der Weltkirche. Die Gründung der bischöflichen Aktion 'Adveniat,'" *Historisches Jahrbuch* 125 (2005): 327–47.

11. Gerster, *Friedensdialoge*, 174ff. Gerster himself makes reference to Herman H. Schwedt, as cited in Hubert Wolf and Claus Arnold, "Einleitung," in *Die deutschsprachigen Länder und das II. Vatikanum*, ed. Hubert Wolf and Claus Arnold (Paderborn: Schöningh, 2000), 13. See also Kaminsky, "Nothilfe," 183.

12. Voges, "Hilfe," 93–101 and 107ff.

13. Johannes Stollhof, *Zwischen Biafra und Bonn. Hungerkatastrophen und Konsumkritik im deutschen Katholizismus 1958–1979* (Paderborn: Schöningh, 2019), 367.

14. Gerster, *Friedensdialoge*, 175; and Voges, "Solidarität," 332 and 344–46.

15. On Leppich, see also Tripp, "Weltkirche," 132.

16. Joachim Schmiedl, "Weltkirchliche Verantwortung und Partnerschaft: Zum Wandel des Missionsverständnisses in der katholischen Kirche Deutschlands von Heinrich Hahn bis zur Würzburger Synode," *Schweizerische Zeitschrift für Religions- und Kulturgeschichte* 105 (2011): 221.

17. Kemnitzer, *Der ferne Nächste*, 54.

18. Voges, "Hilfe," 100–3.

19. Kemnitzer, *Der ferne Nächste*, 46, n205; Martin Üffing, "Die pilgernde Kirche ist ihrem Wesen nach 'missionarisch' . . . Zur Mission und Missionswissenschaft nach 'Ad Gentes,'" *Zeitschrift für Missionswissenschaft und Religionswissenschaft* 89 (2005): 266.

20. Martin Greschat, *Der Protestantismus in der Bundesrepublik Deutschland (1945–2005)* (Leipzig: Evangelische Verlagsanstalt, 2010), 115.

21. Kemnitzer, *Der ferne Nächste*, 62.

22. Bastian Hein, *Die Westdeutschen und die Dritte Welt. Entwicklungspolitik und Entwicklungsdienste zwischen Reform und Revolte 1959–1974* (Munich: Oldenbourg, 2006), 37.

23. Ibid., 61ff.

24. Kaminsky, "Nothilfe," 192.

25. Hein, *Die Westdeutschen und die Dritte Welt*, 62.

26. Kemnitzer, *Der ferne Nächste*, 67.

27. Kaminsky, "Nothilfe," 192.

28. Ulrich Willems, *Entwicklung, Interesse und Moral. Die Entwicklungspolitik der Evangelischen Kirche in Deutschland* (Wiesbaden: Springer VS, 1998), 244ff.

29. Kaminsky, "Nothilfe," 189 ff.; and Roland Spliesgart, "Theologie und 'Dritte Welt,'" in *Umbrüche. Der deutsche Protestantismus und die sozialen Bewegungen in den 1960er und 70er Jahren*, ed. Siegfried Hermle, Claudia Lepp, and Harry Oelke (Göttingen: Vandenhoeck & Ruprecht, 2007), 193ff.

30. Kaminsky, "Nothilfe," 188ff. and 190ff.

31. Kemnitzer, *Der ferne Nächste*, 72.

32. Ibid., 147, n869.

33. Ibid., 166ff., n970.

34. Üffing states that Johann Baptist Metz came up with the concept of "polyzentrisch," and that H. J. Margull came up with the term "tertiaterran." See Üffing, "Die pilgernde Kirche," 265 and 272.

35. Joachim Schmiedl, "Weltmission und religiöse Orden im 19. und 20. Jahrhundert. Trends und Deutungen im Spiegel der Forschung," *Historisches Jahrbuch* 129 (2009): 496.

36. Rudolf Voderholzer, "Nouvelle Théologie," *Religion in Geschichte und Gegenwart* 6 (2003): 414–15.

37. Schmiedl, "Weltmission," 496ff.

38. Tripp, "Weltkirche," 125ff.; and Eva-Maria Jung, "Afrika auf dem Konzil," in *Echo der Zeit*, 6 January 1963, quoted in Walter Kampe, ed., *Das Konzil im Spiegel der Presse, Vol. 1* (Würzburg: Echter, 1963), 259ff.

39. Karl Rahner, "Zur theologischen Problematik einer 'Pastoralkonstitution,'" in *Schriften zur Theologie*, Vol. VIII (Einsiedeln: Benziger, 1967), 628; and Matthias Sellmann, *Zuhören, Austauschen, Vorschlagen. Entdeckungen pastoraltheologischer Milieuforschung* (Würzburg: Echter, 2012), 42.

40. Sellmann, *Zuhören, Austauschen, Vorschlagen*, 31.

41. Luitpold A. Dorn, *Paul VI. Der einsame Reformer* (Graz: Styria, 1989), 221.

42. Konrad Hilpert, "Populorum progressio," *Lexikon für Theologie und Kirche* 8 (1999), 426.

43. Wilhelm Damberg, "Einführung in die Studientage," in *Paul VI und Deutschland. Studientage Bochum, 24.–25. Oktober 2003*, ed. Hermann Josef Pottmeyer (Brescia: Istituto Paulo VI, 2006), 12.

44. Hilpert, "Populorum progressio," 426.

45. Werner Höfer, "Bonner Echo auf den Ruf aus Rom. Bundesentwicklungsminister Hans-Jürgen Wischnewski zur päpstlichen Enzyklika," in *Die Zeit*, 7 April 1967, 10.

46. Schmiedl, "Weltmission," 498.

47. Ibid.

48. Reinhard Frieling, "Die Aufbrüche von Uppsala 1968," in *Umbrüche. Der deutsche Protestantismus und die sozialen Bewegungen in den 1960er und 70er Jahren*, ed. Siegfried Hermle, Claudia Lepp, and Harry Oelke (Göttingen: Vandenhoeck & Ruprecht, 2007), 177–79.

49. Katharina Kunter and Annegreth Schilling, "'Der Christ fürchtet den Umbruch nicht.' Der Ökumenische Rat der Kirchen im Spannungsfeld von Dekolonisierung, Entwestlichung und Politisierung," in *Globalisierung der Kirchen. Der Ökumenische Rat der Kirche und die Entdeckung der Dritten Welt in den 1960er und 70er Jahren*, ed. Katharina Kunter and Annegreth Schilling (Göttingen: Vandenhoeck & Ruprecht, 2014), 60ff.

50. Willems, *Entwicklung*, 260.

51. Kemnitzer, *Der ferne Nächste*, 75ff.

52. Ibid., 92ff.

53. Stollhof, *Zwischen Biafra und Bonn*, 168.

54. Quinn Slobodian, *Foreign Front. Third World Politics in Sixties West Germany* (Dur-ham, NC: Duke University Press, 2012).

55. Bernhard Dinkelaker, "Weltmission zwischen Ökumene und Entwicklungszusammenarbeit—Gemeinsames Zeugnis und interkulturelles Lernen in ökumenischer Partnerschaft," *Amt und Gemeinde* 57 (2006), 152ff.

56. Markus-Liborius Hermann, "Glaube, Ökumene und Mission in säkularer Gesellschaft. Wer von Mission reden will, muss die Ökumene immer im Blick haben," *Ökumenische Rundschau* 4 (2016), 529.

57. Desmond van der Water, "Council for World Mission: A Case Study and Critical Appraisal of the Journey of Partnership in Mission," *International Review of Mission* 97 (2008): 305–22.

58. For an example, see Rebekka Habermas and Richard Hölzl, eds., *Mission global. Eine Verflechtungsgeschichte seit dem 19. Jahrhundert* (Cologne: Böhlau, 2014).

59. See, for the relatively early period, Richard Hölzl, "'Mitleid' über große Distanz. Zur Fabrikation globaler Gefühle in Medien der katholischen Mission, 1890–1940," in *Mission global. Eine Verflechtungsgeschichte seit dem 19. Jahrhundert*, ed. Rebekka Habermas and Richard Hölzl (Cologne: Böhlau, 2014), 265–94. The development shown by Hölzl toward the production of empathy, for example, was intensified by further developments in the media in the second half of the twentieth century. See Rebekka Habermas and Richard Hölzl, "Mission global—Religiöse Akteure und globale Verflechtung seit dem 19. Jahrhundert," in *Mission global. Eine Verflechtungsgeschichte seit dem 19. Jahrhundert*, ed. Rebekka Habermas and Richard Hölzl (Cologne: Böhlau, 2014), 22.

60. Hein, *Die Westdeutschen und die Dritte Welt*, 62–70.

61. Ibid., 70–77, especially 72 and 75.

62. Ibid., 67 and 161.
63. "Der Klausenhof: Herzmitte bäuerlicher Welt," *Mann in der Zeit*, November 1960.
64. Hein, *Die Westdeutschen und die Dritte Welt*, 66ff.
65. Deutsche Landjugendakademie Klausenhof, *Vorbereitungskurs Entwicklungshilfe für landwirtschaftliche Fachkräfte* (Dingden, 1961) and Deutsche Landjugendakademie Klausenhof, *Vorbereitung von landwirtschaftlichen Mitarbeitern an sozialökonomischen Projekten in Übersee* (Dingden, 1961).
66. Hein, *Die Westdeutschen und die Dritte Welt*, 68ff.
67. "Entwicklungshelfer—Sendung und Aufgabe," *Kirchenbote für Tirol und Voralberg*, 11 August 1963, 2–3; and Hein, *Die Westdeutschen und die Dritte Welt*, 67.
68. "19 Entwicklungshelfer aus drei Nationen ausgesandt," *KNA—Inland*, 23 April 1966.
69. "Eure Kanzel: Feld, Werkstatt und Büro!" *Bocholter-Borkener Volksblatt*, 27 January 1964.
70. "Jugend will helfen," *Deutsche Tagespost, Beilage "Völker im Aufbruch,"* February 1966.
71. Linda Polman, *Die Mitleidsindustrie. Hinter den Kulissen internationaler Hilfsorganisationen* (Frankfurt am Main: Campus-Verlag, 2010).
72. Hansjosef Theyßen, "Eine Schulungsstätte für Entwicklungshelfer," *CR-Illustrierte*, March–April 1968.
73. Karl Osner, "Erinnerungen des ersten Geschäftsführers zur Gründung der AGEH, 23. Juli 1984, 2," in Ordner "25 Jahre AGEH/30 Jahre AGEH," /1.5 K, Archiv der AGEH, Köln. See also Karl Osner, "Assessor, Entwurf, 10. August 1959," in Ordner "Vorgeschichte der AGEH 54-59" /0.5, Archiv der AGEH, Köln.
74. Klaus Große Kracht, *Die Stunde der Laien? Katholische Aktion in Deutschland im europäischen Kontext 1920–1960* (Paderborn: Schöningh, 2016).
75. "Georg Sticker an Westdeutsche Zeitung, 5. November 1984, Artikelvorschläge," in Ordner "25 Jahre AGEH" /7.1, Archiv der AGEH, Köln.
76. "Laienmissionshelfer. Merkblatt des Vikariates von Alexishafen. New Guinea—Bischof Noser (4 Oktober 1958)," in Ordner "50 Jahre AGEH," 1. Ordner, Archiv der AGEH, Köln.
77. Hein, *Die Westdeutschen und die Dritte Welt*, 161.
78. Ibid., 66.
79. Udi Greenberg, "Protestants, Decolonization, and European Integration, 1885–1961," *The Journal of Modern History* 89 (2017): 353ff.
80. Stollhof, *Zwischen Biafra und Bonn* and Tripp, *Fromm und politisch*.
81. Josef Bennemann, *Entwicklungspolitische Bildungsarbeit. Unsere Erfahrungen. Ein Protokoll* (Dingden, 1979), 3.
82. "Resolution zur Aufgabe der Studentengemeinde. Erarbeitet von einer Arbeitsgruppe des Arbeitskreises 8, vom Plenum mit großer Mehrheit verabschiedet am 20. Juli 1968," *Zukunft des Christentums. Zukunft der Kirche. 16. Katholischer Studententag vom 17. bis 21. Juli 1968 in Tübingen* (Bonn, 1968), 76ff. Text cited from Christian Schmidtmann, *Katholische Studierende 1945–1973. Ein Beitrag zur Kultur- und Sozialgeschichte der Bundesrepublik Deutschland* (Paderborn: Schöningh, 2006), 345.
83. Dorothee Weitbrecht, *Aufbruch in die Dritte Welt. Der Internationalismus der Studentenbewegung von 1968 in der Bundesrepublik Deutschland* (Göttingen: Vandenhoeck & Ruprecht, 2012). On the protest potential of Catholic students, see Gerster, *Friedensdialoge*, 150–72.
84. Wolfgang Kraushaar, *1968 als Mythos, Chiffre und Zäsur* (Hamburg: Hamburger Edition, 2000); and Pascal Eitler, "Gott ist tot—Gott ist rot." *Max Horkheimer und die Politisierung der Religion um 1968* (Frankfurt am Main: Campus-Verlag, 2009), 341–47.
85. Thomas Großbölting, "Zwischen Kontestation und Beharrung. Katholische Studierende und die Studentenbewegung," *Westfälische Forschungen* 48 (1998): 184. For a better understanding of the term "lifestyle revolution," Großbölting refers us to Rainer Bieling, *Die Tränen der Revolution. Die 68er zwanzig Jahre danach* (Berlin: Siedler, 1988), 24.

86. See on this the works by the research group organized by Andreas Rödder, for example Bernhard Dietz, Christopher Neumaier, and Andreas Rödder, eds., *Gab es den Wertewandel? Neue Forschungen zum gesellschaftlich-kulturellen Wandel seit den 1960er Jahren* (Munich: Oldenbourg, 2014). I owe important insights to these works.

87. Thomas Großbölting, *Der verlorene Himmel. Glaube in Deutschland seit 1945* (Göttingen: Vandenhoeck & Ruprecht, 2013), 172–73.

88. See Dorothee Sölle, *Gegenwind. Erinnerungen* (Hamburg: Hoffmann and Campe, 1995), 71ff.

89. Großbölting, *Der verlorene Himmel*, 169, with reference to Michael N. Ebertz, "'Tote Menschen haben keine Probleme?'—oder: Der Zwang zum Vergessen und Erinnern. Die Beschneidung eschatologischer Codes im 20. Jahrhundert," in *Normieren, Tradieren, Inszenieren. Das Christentum als Buchreligion*, ed. Andreas Holzem (Darmstadt: Wissenschaftliche Buchgesellschaft, 2004), 294.

90. Thomas Mittmann, "Moderne Formen der Kommunikation zwischen 'Kirche' und 'Welt.' Der Wandel kirchlicher Selbstentwürfe in der Bundesrepublik in evangelischen und katholischen Akademien," in *Kirche—Medien—Öffentlichkeit. Transformationen kirchlicher Selbst- und Fremddeutungen seit 1945*, ed. Frank Bösch and Lucian Hölscher (Göttingen: Wallstein, 2009), 218ff.

91. Gustavo Gutiérrez, *Teología de la liberación. Perspectivas* (Lima: CEP, 1996).

92. Großbölting, *Der verlorene Himmel*, 175.

93. See on this Gerhard Kruip, "Entkolonialisierung des Christentums und der Vernunft? Zur notwendigen Kritik postkolonialer Diskurse," in *Transformationen der Missionswissenschaft. Festschrift zum 100. Jahrgang der ZMR*, ed. Mariano Delgado, Michael Sievernich, and Klaus Vellguth (St. Ottilien: EOS, 2016), 301.

94. Großbölting, *Der verlorene Himmel*, 175.

95. Tripp, "Weltkirche," 133ff.; and Markus Raschke, *Fairer Handel. Engagement für eine gerechte Weltwirtschaft* (Ostfildern: Matthias-Grünewald-Verlag, 2009), 46.

96. Hein, *Die Westdeutschen und die Dritte Welt*, 144.

97. Tripp, *Fromm und politisch*, 170.

98. Tripp, "Weltkirche," 134; and Franz Nuscheler, et al., *Christliche Dritte-Welt-Gruppen. Praxis und Selbstverständnis* (Mainz: Matthias-Grünewald-Verlag, 1995), 83.

99. See, for example, Berthold Unfried and Eva Himmelstoss, eds., *Die eine Welt schaffen. Praktiken von "Internationaler Solidarität" und "Internationaler Entwicklung." Create One World. Practices of "International Solidarity" and "International Development"* (Leipzig: Akademische Verlagsanstalt, 2012).

100. Cornelia Füllkrug-Weitzel, "Reformation, Würde und Entwicklung—reformatorische Essentials und der Beitrag der Kirchen zum entwicklungspolitischen Diskurs," in *Impulse der Reformation. Der zivilgesellschaftliche Diskurs*, ed. Ansgar Klein and Olaf Zimmermann (Wiesbaden: Springer VS, 2017), 282.

101. Benjamin Ziemann, *Katholische Kirche und Sozialwissenschaften 1945–1975* (Göttingen: Vandenhoeck & Ruprecht, 2007).

102. Stollhof, *Zwischen Biafra und Bonn*, 370.

103. Ibid., 218ff. and 184.

104. Kemnitzer, *Der ferne Nächste*, 88–91.

105. Tripp, "Weltkirche," 135ff.

106. Ibid., 136.

107. Claudia Lepp, "Zwischen Konfrontation und Kooperation: Kirchen und soziale Bewegungen in der Bundesrepublik (1950–1983)," *Zeithistorische Forschungen/Studies in Contemporary History* 7 (2010): 379.

108. Greenberg, "Protestants, Decolonization, and European Integration" on the relationship between Christianity, decolonization, and integration.

109. See, for example, Udo Kaulich, *Geschichte der ehemaligen Kolonie Deutsch-Südwestafrika (1884–1914). Eine Gesamtdarstellung* (Frankfurt am Main: Lang, 2003).

Bibliography

"19 Entwicklungshelfer aus drei Nationen ausgesandt." *KNA—Inland*, 23 April 1966.
Bennemann, Josef. *Entwicklungspolitische Bildungsarbeit. Unsere Erfahrungen. Ein Protokoll*. Dingden, 1979.
Bieling, Rainer. *Die Tränen der Revolution. Die 68er zwanzig Jahre danach*. Berlin: Siedler, 1988.
Bock, Florian. "'Wir wollen einfach die Lebensbedingungen der Menschen verbessern.' Zum Paradigmenwechsel der katholischen Entwicklungshilfe in der Bundesrepublik um 1968." In *Wenn Hunger droht. Bewältigung und religiöse Deutung (1400–1980)*, edited by Andreas Holzem, 275–94. Tübingen: Mohr Siebeck, 2017.
Damberg, Wilhelm. "Einführung in die Studientage." In *Paul VI und Deutschland. Studientage Bochum, 24.–25. Oktober 2003*, edited by Hermann Josef Pottmeyer, 7–15. Brescia: Istituto Paulo VI, 2006.
"Der Klausenhof: Herzmitte bäuerlicher Welt." *Mann in der Zeit*, November 1960.
Deutsche Landjugendakademie Klausenhof. *Vorbereitung von landwirtschaftlichen Mitarbeitern an sozialökonomischen Projekten in Übersee*. Dingden, 1961.
———. *Vorbereitungskurs Entwicklungshilfe für landwirtschaftliche Fachkräfte*. Dingden, 1961.
Dietz, Bernhard, Christopher Neumaier, and Andreas Rödder, eds. *Gab es den Wertewandel? Neue Forschungen zum gesellschaftlich-kulturellen Wandel seit den 1960er Jahren*. Munich: Oldenbourg, 2014.
Dinkelaker, Bernhard. "Weltmission zwischen Ökumene und Entwicklungszusammenarbeit—Gemeinsames Zeugnis und interkulturelles Lernen in ökumenischer Partnerschaft." *Amt und Gemeinde* 57 (2006): 147–55.
Dorn, Luitpold A. *Paul VI. Der einsame Reformer*. Graz: Styria, 1989.
Ebertz, Michael N. "'Tote Menschen haben keine Probleme?'—oder: Der Zwang zum Vergessen und Erinnern. Die Beschneidung eschatologischer Codes im 20. Jahrhundert." In *Normieren, Tradieren, Inszenieren. Das Christentum als Buchreligion*, edited by Andreas Holzem, 279–300. Darmstadt: Wissenschaftliche Buchgesellschaft, 2004.
Eitler, Pascal. *"Gott ist tot—Gott ist rot." Max Horkheimer und die Politisierung der Religion um 1968*. Frankfurt am Main: Campus-Verlag, 2009.
"Entwicklungshelfer—Sendung und Aufgabe." *Kirchenbote für Tirol und Voralberg*, 11 August 1963, 2–3.
"Eure Kanzel: Feld, Werkstatt und Büro!" *Bocholter-Borkener Volksblatt*, 27 January 1964.
Frieling, Reinhard. "Die Aufbrüche von Uppsala 1968." In *Umbrüche. Der deutsche Protestantismus und die sozialen Bewegungen in den 1960er und 70er Jahren*, edited by Siegfried Hermle, Claudia Lepp, and Harry Oelke, 176–88. Göttingen: Vandenhoeck & Ruprecht, 2007.
Füllkrug-Weitzel, Cornelia. "Reformation, Würde und Entwicklung—reformatorische Essentials und der Beitrag der Kirchen zum entwicklungspolitischen Diskurs." *Impulse der Reformation. Der zivilgesellschaftliche Diskurs*, edited by Ansgar Klein and Olaf Zimmermann, 273–84. Wiesbaden: Springer VS, 2017.
"Georg Sticker an Westdeutsche Zeitung, 5. November 1984, Artikelvorschläge." Ordner "25 Jahre AGEH" /7.1, Archiv der AGEH, Köln.
Gerster, Daniel. *Friedensdialoge im Kalten Krieg. Eine Geschichte der Katholiken in der Bundesrepublik 1957–1983*. Frankfurt am Main: Campus-Verlag, 2012.
Greenberg, Udi. "Protestants, Decolonization, and European Integration, 1885–1961." *The Journal of Modern History* 89 (2017): 314–54.

Greschat, Martin. *Der Protestantismus in der Bundesrepublik Deutschland (1945–2005)*. Leipzig: Evangelische Verlagsanstalt, 2010.
Großbölting, Thomas. *Der verlorene Himmel. Glaube in Deutschland seit 1945*. Göttingen: Vandenhoeck & Ruprecht, 2013.
———. "Zwischen Kontestation und Beharrung. Katholische Studierende und die Studentenbewegung." *Westfälische Forschungen* 48 (1998): 157–89.
Große Kracht, Klaus. *Die Stunde der Laien? Katholische Aktion in Deutschland im europäischen Kontext 1920–1960*. Paderborn: Schöningh, 2016.
Gutiérrez, Gustavo. *Teología de la liberación. Perspectivas*. Lima: CEP, 1996.
Habermas, Rebekka, and Richard Hölzl, eds. *Mission global. Eine Verflechtungsgeschichte seit dem 19. Jahrhundert*. Cologne: Böhlau, 2014.
———. "Mission global—Religiöse Akteure und globale Verflechtung seit dem 19. Jahrhundert." In *Mission global. Eine Verflechtungsgeschichte seit dem 19. Jahrhundert*, edited by Rebekka Habermas and Richard Hölzl, 9–28. Cologne: Böhlau, 2014.
Hein, Bastian. *Die Westdeutschen und die Dritte Welt. Entwicklungspolitik und Entwicklungsdienste zwischen Reform und Revolte 1959–1974*. Munich: Oldenbourg, 2006.
Hermann, Markus-Liborius. "Glaube, Ökumene und Mission in säkularer Gesellschaft. Wer von Mission reden will, muss die Ökumene immer im Blick haben." *Ökumenische Rundschau* 4 (2016): 520–33.
Hilpert, Konrad. "Populorum progressio." *Lexikon für Theologie und Kirche* 8 (1999): 425–26.
Höfer, Werner. "Bonner Echo auf den Ruf aus Rom. Bundesentwicklungsminister Hans-Jürgen Wischnewski zur päpstlichen Enzyklika." *Die Zeit*, 7 April 1967, 10.
Hölzl, Richard. "'Mitleid' über große Distanz. Zur Fabrikation globaler Gefühle in Medien der katholischen Mission, 1890–1940." In *Mission global. Eine Verflechtungsgeschichte seit dem 19. Jahrhundert*, edited by Rebekka Habermas and Richard Hölzl, 265–94. Cologne: Böhlau, 2014.
"Jugend will helfen." *Deutsche Tagespost, Beilage "Völker im Aufbruch,"* February 1966.
Jung, Eva-Maria. "Afrika auf dem Konzil." *Echo der Zeit*, 6 January 1963.
Kaminsky, Uwe. "Nothilfe über die Grenzen hinaus. Die Entstehung von 'Brot für die Welt' in der DDR." In *Diakonie im geteilten Deutschland. Zur diakonischen Arbeit unter den Bedingungen der DDR und der Teilung Deutschlands*, edited by Ingolf Hübner and Jochen-Christoph Kaiser, 180–95. Stuttgart: Kohlhammer, 1999.
Kampe, Walter, ed. *Das Konzil im Spiegel der Presse, Vol. 1*. Würzburg: Echter, 1963.
Kaulich, Udo. *Geschichte der ehemaligen Kolonie Deutsch-Südwestafrika (1884–1914). Eine Gesamtdarstellung*. Frankfurt am Main: Lang, 2003.
Kemnitzer, Konstanze Evangelia. *Der ferne Nächste. Zum Selbstverständnis der Aktion "Brot für die Welt."* Stuttgart: Kohlhammer, 2008.
Kraushaar, Wolfgang. *1968 als Mythos, Chiffre und Zäsur*. Hamburg: Hamburger Edition, 2000.
Kruip, Gerhard. "Entkolonialisierung des Christentums und der Vernunft? Zur notwendigen Kritik postkolonialer Diskurse." In *Transformationen der Missionswissenschaft. Festschrift zum 100. Jahrgang der ZMR*, edited by Mariano Delgado, Michael Sievernich, and Klaus Vellguth, 297–305. St. Ottilien: EOS, 2016.
Kunter, Katharina, and Annegreth Schilling. "'Der Christ fürchtet den Umbruch nicht.' Der Ökumenische Rat der Kirchen im Spannungsfeld von Dekolonisierung, Entwestlichung und Politisierung." In *Globalisierung der Kirchen. Der Ökumenische Rat der Kirche und die Entdeckung der Dritten Welt in den 1960er und 70er Jahren*, edited by Katharina Kunter and Annegreth Schilling, 21–74. Göttingen: Vandenhoeck & Ruprecht, 2014.
"Laienmissionshelfer. Merkblatt des Vikariates von Alexishafen. New Guinea—Bischof Noser (4 Oktober 1958)." Ordner "50 Jahre AGEH," 1. Ordner, Archiv der AGEH, Köln.
Lepp, Claudia. "Zwischen Konfrontation und Kooperation: Kirchen und soziale Bewegungen in der Bundesrepublik (1950–1983)." *Zeithistorische Forschungen/Studies in Contemporary History* 7 (2010): 364–85.

Lingelbach, Gabriele. *Spenden und Sammeln. Der westdeutsche Spendenmarkt bis in die 1980er Jahre*. Göttingen: Wallstein, 2009.
Mittmann, Thomas. "Moderne Formen der Kommunikation zwischen 'Kirche' und 'Welt.' Der Wandel kirchlicher Selbstentwürfe in der Bundesrepublik in evangelischen und katholischen Akademien." In *Kirche—Medien—Öffentlichkeit. Transformationen kirchlicher Selbst- und Fremddeutungen seit 1945*, edited by Frank Bösch and Lucian Hölscher, 216–46. Göttingen: Wallstein, 2009.
Nuscheler, Franz, et al. *Christliche Dritte-Welt-Gruppen. Praxis und Selbstverständnis*. Mainz: Matthias-Grünewald-Verlag, 1995.
Osner, Karl. "Assessor, Entwurf, 10. August 1959." Ordner "Vorgeschichte der AGEH 54-59" /0.5, Archiv der AGEH, Köln.
———. "Erinnerungen des ersten Geschäftsführers zur Gründung der AGEH, 23. Juli 1984, 2." Ordner "25 Jahre AGEH/30 Jahre AGEH," /1.5 K, Archiv der AGEH, Köln.
Pfeffer, Clemens. "Missionshistoriographie post 1968. Postkoloniale Perspektive avant la lettre." In *Theologie und Postkolonialismus. Ansätze—Herausforderungen—Perspektiven*, edited by Sebastian Pittl, 191–218. Regensburg: Friedrich Pustet, 2018.
Pittl, Sebastian. "Für eine 'Globalisierung der Hoffnung.' Zur Relevanz postkolonialen Denkens für Theologie und Missionswissenschaft—Einleitung." In *Theologie und Postkolonialismus. Ansätze—Herausforderungen—Perspektiven*, edited by Sebastian Pittl, 9–23. Regensburg: Friedrich Pustet, 2018.
Polman, Linda. *Die Mitleidsindustrie. Hinter den Kulissen internationaler Hilfsorganisationen*. Frankfurt am Main: Campus-Verlag, 2010.
Rahner, Karl. "Zur theologischen Problematik einer 'Pastoralkonstitution.'" In *Schriften zur Theologie, Vol. VIII*, 613–36. Einsiedeln: Benziger, 1967.
Raschke, Markus. *Fairer Handel. Engagement für eine gerechte Weltwirtschaft*. Ostfildern: Matthias-Grünewald-Verlag, 2009.
"Resolution zur Aufgabe der Studentengemeinde. Erarbeitet von einer Arbeitsgruppe des Arbeitskreises 8, vom Plenum mit großer Mehrheit verabschiedet am 20. Juli 1968." *Zukunft des Christentums. Zukunft der Kirche. 16. Katholischer Studententag vom 17. bis 21. Juli 1968 in Tübingen*. Bonn: 1968.
Schmidtmann, Christian. *Katholische Studierende 1945–1973. Ein Beitrag zur Kultur- und Sozialgeschichte der Bundesrepublik Deutschland*. Paderborn: Schöningh, 2006.
Schmiedl, Joachim. "Weltkirchliche Verantwortung und Partnerschaft: Zum Wandel des Missionsverständnisses in der katholischen Kirche Deutschlands von Heinrich Hahn bis zur Würzburger Synode." *Schweizerische Zeitschrift für Religions- und Kulturgeschichte* 105 (2011): 221–46.
———. "Weltmission und religiöse Orden im 19. und 20. Jahrhundert. Trends und Deutungen im Spiegel der Forschung." *Historisches Jahrbuch* 129 (2009): 479–500.
Sellmann, Matthias. *Zuhören, Austauschen, Vorschlagen. Entdeckungen pastoraltheologischer Milieuforschung*. Würzburg: Echter, 2012.
Slobodian, Quinn. *Foreign Front. Third World Politics in Sixties West Germany*. Durham, NC: Duke University Press, 2012.
Sölle, Dorothee. *Gegenwind. Erinnerungen*. Hamburg: Hoffmann and Campe, 1995.
Spliesgart, Roland. "Theologie und 'Dritte Welt.'" In *Umbrüche. Der deutsche Protestantismus und die sozialen Bewegungen in den 1960er und 70er Jahren*, edited by Siegfried Hermle, Claudia Lepp, and Harry Oelke, 189–209. Göttingen: Vandenhoeck & Ruprecht, 2007.
Stollhof, Johannes. "'Ein Millionen-Volk wird ausgehungert!' Die Wahrnehmung der Hungerkatastrophe in Biafra zwischen 1967 und 1970 im deutschen Katholizismus." In *Wenn Hunger droht. Bewältigung und religiöse Deutung (1400–1980)*, edited by Andreas Holzem, 295–315. Tübingen: Mohr Siebeck, 2017.
———. *Zwischen Biafra und Bonn. Hungerkatastrophen und Konsumkritik im deutschen Katholizismus 1958–1979*. Paderborn: Schöningh, 2019.

Theyßen, Hansjosef. "Eine Schulungsstätte für Entwicklungshelfer." *CR-Illustrierte*, March–April 1968.
Toscer, Sylvie. "Das bischöfliche Hilfswerk Misereor und die Rolle von Kardinal Frings auf dem Konzil." In *Die deutschsprachigen Länder und das II. Vatikanum*, edited by Hubert Wolf and Claus Arnold, 53–60. Paderborn: Schöningh, 2000.
Tripp, Sebastian. "Die Weltkirche vor Ort. Die Globalisierung der Kirchen und die Entstehung christlicher 'Dritte Welt'-Gruppen." In *Soziale Strukturen und Semantiken des Religiösen im Wandel. Transformationen in der Bundesrepublik Deutschland 1949–1989*, edited by Wilhelm Damberg, Frank Bösch, Lucian Hölscher, et al., 123–36. Essen: Klartext-Verlag, 2011.
———. *Fromm und politisch. Christliche Anti-Apartheid-Gruppen und die Transformation des westdeutschen Protestantismus 1970–1990.* Göttingen: Wallstein, 2015.
Trippen, Norbert. *Josef Kardinal Frings (1887–1978), Vol. 2: Sein Wirken für die Weltkirche und seine letzten Bischofsjahre.* Paderborn: Schöningh, 2005.
Üffing, Martin. "Die pilgernde Kirche ist ihrem Wesen nach 'missionarisch' . . . Zur Mission und Missionswissenschaft nach 'Ad Gentes.'" *Zeitschrift für Missionswissenschaft und Religionswissenschaft* 89 (2005): 263–79.
Unfried, Berthold, and Eva Himmelstoss, eds. *Die eine Welt schaffen. Praktiken von "Internationaler Solidarität" und "Internationaler Entwicklung." Create One World: Practices of "International Solidarity" and "International Development."* Leipzig: Akademische Verlagsanstalt, 2012.
Van der Water, Desmond. "Council for World Mission: A Case Study and Critical Appraisal of the Journey of Partnership in Mission." *International Review of Mission* 97 (2008): 305–22.
Voderholzer, Rudolf. "Nouvelle Théologie." *Religion in Geschichte und Gegenwart* 6 (2003): 414–15.
Voges, Stefan. "Hilfe in der Not: Nachkriegserfahrungen in der Begründung von Entwicklungshilfe." In *Zwischen Kriegs- und Diktaturerfahrung. Katholizismus und Protestantismus in der Nachkriegszeit*, edited by Christoph Holzapfel and Andreas Holzem, 91–108. Stuttgart: Kohlhammer, 2005.
———. "Solidarität in der Weltkirche. Die Gründung der bischöflichen Aktion 'Adveniat.'" *Historisches Jahrbuch* 125 (2005): 327–47.
Weitbrecht, Dorothee. *Aufbruch in die Dritte Welt. Der Internationalismus der Studentenbewegung von 1968 in der Bundesrepublik Deutschland.* Göttingen: Vandenhoeck & Ruprecht, 2012.
Willems, Ulrich. *Entwicklung, Interesse und Moral. Die Entwicklungspolitik der Evangelischen Kirche in Deutschland.* Wiesbaden: Springer VS, 1998.
Wolf, Hubert, and Claus Arnold. "Einleitung." In *Die deutschsprachigen Länder und das II. Vatikanum*, edited by Hubert Wolf and Claus Arnold, 9–16. Paderborn: Schöningh, 2000.
Ziemann, Benjamin. *Katholische Kirche und Sozialwissenschaften 1945–1975.* Göttingen: Vandenhoeck & Ruprecht, 2007.

Chapter Thirteen

DECONFESSIONALIZATION AFTER 1945

Protestants and Catholics, Jews and Muslims as Actors within the Religious Sphere of the Federal Republic of Germany

Thomas Großbölting
Translated by Alex Skinner

As a Protestant, would it bother you if your neighbor were Catholic? Or, flip it around—as a Catholic, are you disturbed by the thought of a Protestant family moving in next door? If the answer is no, your feelings are in line with those of the vast majority of Germans. In 2017, on the 500th anniversary of the Reformation, the North American Pew Research Center, a combination of polling institute and think tank, surveyed twenty-four thousand individuals in Europe and five thousand in the United States. The most pleasing though not terribly surprising finding was that European Catholics and Protestants are entirely undisturbed by the thought of a member of the other major Christian confession as their neighbor or even as a member of their family (97 percent of Catholics and 98 percent of Protestants).

Members of the two major Christian groups share very similar perceptions both of their own and of the other confession. Even when it comes to the core religious beliefs that divided the two groups from one another for centuries, the respondents' convictions turn out to be virtually identical: not only are both groups indifferent to the question of whether salvation can be achieved *sola scriptura*, *sola fide*, *sola gratia*, or whether "good deeds" also play into the picture; they also articulate a syncretic belief system combining a plethora of elements. For example, half of American Protestants assume that you have to combine faith and good deeds to get to heaven. Not only have respondents forgotten the earlier conflict between these two branches of Christianity, but in both confessions many individuals take inspiration from well beyond the horizon of Christian belief. For example, they embrace the idea of reincarnation following the death of the individual.[1] Overall, these findings for the United States would almost certainly pertain to Germany as well, with at most minor differences.

If we look at immediate postwar and later divided Germany, it is apparent just how much this picture is bound up with a shift in attitudes and mentalities. In the first two decades after World War II, confessional differences that are now largely irrelevant were still highly present. The so-called Ochsenfurt Incident, a scandal widely noted at the time that made a significant political impact, is representative of many other events. On 28 June 1953, a row broke out over the consecration of the country's largest sugar factory in Ochsenfurt, Lower Franconia. Catholics and Protestants had first held separate services. The plan was for Catholic bishop Julius Döpfner and Protestant regional dean Wilhelm Schwinn to then jointly consecrate the factory. The organizers of this program of events had failed to grasp just what a hot potato this shared act of consecration was; in any case, they had done nothing to mitigate the potential risks. On site, the bishop declared that he could not carry out an act of consecration if a Protestant clergyman were present in his cassock, intending to consecrate the factory. This prompted the indignant dean to call off his planned participation. The incident could not be concealed from the celebrants, as the Protestant clergyman's blessing had been announced in the program. There was an uproar within the mounted escort from the nearby small town of Gnostadt, which was supposed to accompany the Protestant dean, with calmer heads struggling to dampen their ire. The bishop's entrance triggered vociferous expressions of discontent, with one Protestant CDU Bundestag deputy in attendance loudly warning that there would be consequences.[2] This was an unmitigated scandal, and much more than just a provincial farce in which the conceits of clerical dignitaries ran riot. The press attention garnered by this incident is itself testimony to the fact that it touched on a more profound tension with deep roots in West German political culture.[3]

The confessional factor was palpable in many other spheres of politics and society as well. The debate on the best way of organizing children's education long focused on the establishment of denominational schools for the two confessions. Meanwhile, discussions regarding the founding of the *Bundeswehr*—and the concomitant re-arming of West Germany—were charged with religious arguments, as was the question of the military use of nuclear weapons. Even the debate on West German policies relating to the country's divided status had a strong confessional element. A variety of Protestant groups advocated rapid reunification and, therefore, possible concessions to the GDR or the Soviet Union. The West German government did not embrace these ambitions. Meanwhile, the chancellor's policy of integration with the West was always accompanied by suspicions that, for confessional reasons, the Catholic Adenauer was less concerned about the fate of Protestant brothers and sisters in East Germany.

In addition to fundamental disagreements over German reunification, the political field was pervaded by religious and especially confessional tensions. Liberals, Social Democrats, and Protestants repeatedly complained that Catholics had gained too much power. As early as 1950, Kurt Schumacher had referred to the Catholic Church as the "fifth occupying power" in West Germany, while also describing Europe as a confederation of states of a "conservative, clerical, capitalist, and cartelistic" character.[4] Liberal Thomas Dehler seconded this with his reference to a "Vatican Europe"; and in a position paper produced for the EKD (the Federation of Protestant Churches in Germany), Protestant theologian and church official Heinrich Bornkamm warned of Catholicism's advance in both Germany and across the globe, a process, he asserted, that was occurring in four different ways at once, namely territorially, politically, spiritually, and biologically. The CDU, Bornkamm remarked, was also "under evident or tacit Catholic leadership," and many of its Catholic members regarded it as the "contemporary iteration of the old Centre Party." The All-German People's Party (*Gesamtdeutsche Volkspartei*), which was founded in 1952 and whose central figure was former Minister of the Interior Gustav Heinemann, was largely inspired by "pan-German-Protestant resentment" towards Catholic West Germany.[5]

In the 1950s, West German politics and society, and even everyday life, were strongly shaped by religious motives, attitudes, and, above all, the fundamental tension between the confessions. With clergy of both confessions labeling "mixed marriages" between Catholics and Protestants as undesirable, West Germans generally opted to marry within their confession, they sent their children to the appropriate denominational school, and at times they even joined sports associations in light of their institutional roots in a particular confession. According to historian Michael Maurer, confessional thinking played a crucial role in West Germans' mentality and was "perhaps even more important than national or social" attitudes.[6]

At present and just fifty or sixty years later, these differences have been almost entirely forgotten. When quipping about differences between German regions and cities, historians often are still quick to make confessional differences the butt of their jokes. The crucial point about this practice, however, is that they no longer do so in a mean-spirited way or to discriminate. They use it self-deprecatingly as well as to distinguish themselves from the ever-growing number of those unfamiliar with these distinctions.

According to Maurer: "Today there are two groups of people who are informed about confessional matters: those who are themselves active Catholics or Protestants and those who have acquired knowledge of such things through education."[7] In a remarkable development, what had for centuries been a defining element of political culture has become little more than a posture of the educated upper middle classes.

In this chapter, I seek to trace and offer a preliminary explanation for this profound change. I begin by putting forward a number of conceptual definitions to provide greater purchase on these phenomena, before going on to discuss a number of explanatory factors and, finally, exploring changes in the religious field with a view to whether, and if so how, we might observe new confessional formations and matching tensions.

Confessionalization, Confessionalism, and Confessional Consciousness

To analyze confessional consciousness and confessionalism in the twentieth century is to move far away from the concept of confessionalization in early modern history introduced into the historiographical debate around 1980 by Heinz Schilling and Wolfgang Reinhard. These scholars' and their students' key objective was to analyze the relationships between two major religious confessions and their organizations, as well as those between state and society from the perspective of social and political history.[8] As representatives of a new generation of researchers interested in the paradigm of confessionalization, Schilling and Reinhard were concerned neither with the development of special confessional worlds nor with the conflict between Catholics, Lutherans, and Calvinists or members of the Reformed churches. They had something else in mind when they "took their lead chiefly from the sociology of religion and social history and [dedicated their research] above all to the relationship between state, society and religion or the church."[9] Their ideas and research centered on the processes occurring within the confessions, largely in parallel, of the formalization, centralization, and bureaucratization of the religious sphere, as well as the disciplining of the faithful associated with these developments. Hence, what they were chiefly interested in were the social consequences flowing from the various ways in which people sought salvation and redemption from sin.

They were soon to put forward their core thesis of a close connection between nascent statehood and confessionalization, interpreting theological reflections and religious articulations of faith essentially as a product of political and societal competition. The idea here was that through uniform religious convictions formulated in opposition to the other Christian confession and through forms of organization that fit with this doctrinal tendency, the general population was socially disciplined and thus integrated into the emerging early modern state system. This side effect, in many ways brought about unwittingly by religious actors, was not limited to Protestantism in its Lutheran and Reformed guises—as described especially by Max Weber and Ernst Troeltsch—but could also be seen within Catholicism.[10] As functional equivalents, all three processes of confessionalization constituted the bedrock and key engines of fundamental processes of social and political modernization.

Focusing on the differences between these developments and phenomena of the nineteenth and twentieth centuries, Olaf Blaschke revisited these ideas and developed them further. His trenchant remarks characterized confessionalization in the aforementioned sense as "external confessionalization." In systems theory terms, the factor of confession was exported and integrated into the subsystems of society and dealt with within them, though the subsystems themselves were not part of the sphere of religion. There was no separation, or at least no more than an incipient one: if the guiding principle of *cuius regio eius religio* meant that the faith of a given ruler must be reflected in the faith of the subjects within his territory, then this amounts to a palpable absence of differentiation: secular power and the religious belief system were inextricably linked.[11] And it was this mechanism of keeping the confessions geographically separate that ensured that confessional differences did not automatically end in conflict: the different branches of Christianity could simply avoid one another. Only in those cases in which the confessions collided and in which "confessionalization was too rigorous did a latent 'confessionalism' become a manifest one."[12]

The fundamental premise of this kind of research is that in premodern times religion and the church were not functionally differentiated parts of society, but rather its central pillars, and this is why they played such a fundamental and transformational role. If we turn to the twentieth century, this was no longer the case. Not only did religion become less important (in a quantitative sense), but it also became one functional system among others (to adopt a qualitative perspective). It was the self-rationalization of religion, particularly in the case of Protestantism, that repressed the magical and enchanted elements. As a result, economy and society could shine forth as social realms in their own right. Thus religion could no longer function as a generally binding representation of the unity of society—and could no longer claim to do so.

If we take this account as our basis, then we can write the history of religion above all as an interplay between a number of variables: between de-sacralization and re-sacralization, between differentiation and de-differentiation, along with many other factors. But in seeking to describe modernity, one thing no longer seems appropriate, and that is to refer to confessionalization as envisaged by Reinhard or Schilling, or to the contrasting notion of deconfessionalization. Instead, I believe it makes sense to refer to a special confessional consciousness, one that has shaped and continues to shape people's circumstances and the political culture in a quite different way than in premodern times. In some respects, we are returning to the older concept of confessionalism or confession formation, as introduced as early as the 1950s by Ernst Walter Zeeden. For him, this referred chiefly to intra-church developments and processes occurring after the Reformation. He regarded confession formation as "the spiritual and organizational consolidation of the Christian confessions, which had been diverging since the religious schism, towards a reasonably stable churchdom in terms of dogma, constitution and a religiously ethical way of life."[13]

With the modern age in mind, Blaschke took up and developed these ideas, distinguishing confessionalism from confessionalization and identifying three different levels. Within a confession, the accusation of confessionalism reflected a division between the orthodox and those who espoused reform and/or liberalism. "In Protestantism, these intra-confessional wings were called 'confessionalists,' in Catholicism integralists or ultramontanists."[14] The internal diversity of Protestantism, its division into a number of confessional strands, created a need for a negative ideology of integration, and anti-Catholicism fit the bill: "Because you were born a Protestant, you were anti-Catholic, and because you were anti-Catholic, you felt 'Protestant.'"[15] The Catholic milieu was born out of Catholics' desire to assert and defend themselves from Protestant anti-Catholicism, but it was also the result of ultramontanization within Catholicism itself. The need to maintain boundaries and a corresponding form of conduct persisted even when this threat—at times very real, at other times more imagined than real—had largely ceased to exist. "For the most part, what people mean by the term confessionalism is a dynamic centered on confessional polemics and the polarization of confessional lifeworlds."[16]

Confessionalism understood in this sense differed from its early modern counterpart: in the wake of modernity the territorial division between the confessional groups increasingly dissolved and, concomitant with this, individuals of Protestant and Catholic faith increasingly found themselves living and working together. For more than two hundred years, due to the terms of the Peace of Augsburg of 1555, the German territories were constituted as confessionally homogenous regions. This culture began to break down in the early nineteenth century, the key contributory factors here being industrialization, urbanization, and a policy of tolerating those of different faiths that gained traction from the eighteenth century onwards.

Among merchants trading across regional borders, businesspeople, and artisans outside the guilds, and later among administrative staff and members of the armed forces, the closed confessional worlds began to dissolve. By the late eighteenth century, the state had responded to the confessional division by pursuing "confessional mixing": particularly in the core Prussian territories, and later in the Rhineland as well, a relocation policy funneled Protestant elites into Catholic regions and vice versa.[17]

The position of the religious communities had thus changed quite fundamentally, even if this found little reflection in their self-understanding. But in contrast to the religious conflicts of the early modern period, neither major confession could continue to conduct itself as a monopoly within its "own" territory. As at least theoretically equal forces, they competed to solicit the attention of the faithful and to exert an influence within society and the power system. Both Protestant religious life and Catholic piety were heavily influenced by these modernizing impulses.

Lucian Hölscher has highlighted the fact that, in both major Christian confessions and well beyond them, the German religious field was molded by biconfessional rivalry: myriad religious and political groups such as the Freemasons, various free churches, and revivalist and fellowship movements were motivated, among other things, by a desire to overcome Germany's confessional division by means of a religious belief that was sometimes regarded as more original, but at least as superior, and these groups made their offer to the people on that basis. The life reform movements, as well as communities of political conviction anchored in the socialist and labor movements, were influenced, at least to some extent, by the basic tension of biconfessionalism.[18] Even National Socialism, which deftly mobilized its base by espousing anticlericalism, tried to increase its appeal by marketing itself as a Christian-Germanic coalition movement standing above the different confessions, the key slogan here being "positive Christianity."[19] Furthermore, from an intra-church perspective, in principle both confessions increasingly ceased to see themselves as an alternative to the state—the Protestant movements earlier than their Catholic counterparts. Instead, "'society' [was] described as the temporal realm in which church and religion had to prove themselves as spiritual and social powers."[20]

Confessionalism and Deconfessionalism after 1945

Today, confession has ceased to be a political factor in Germany and instead functions as a vehicle for small talk. This transformation of confession and confessional consciousness demands explanation, above all because it occurred rapidly and within two or three generations. An initial explanation for the precipitous decline in the importance of confession is rather obvious. It works with quantitative arguments asserting that deconfessionalism has much to do with the decline in religion as a whole. For now let us think of secularization as a process in which religion becomes far less important; its capacity to shape the organization of society decreases; it ceases to be a major source for interpreting the world, both figuratively and literally; and no longer guides individuals in their everyday lives. In accordance with this premise, it makes sense for the loss of knowledge about religion and its decreasing relevance to go hand-in-hand with a decline in the distinctiveness of the religious communities.

If we take church membership as one key indicator, the changes that have occurred are only too apparent. Immediately after the end of World War II, more than 95 percent of Germans in both the Soviet and Western occupation zones were members of one of the two major Christian confessions. At present the figure is less than 60 percent, and the trend is downward. The East German dictatorship under the SED, with its antireligious and anti-church policy, is partly responsible for this process.[21] Nonetheless, this break with tradition was and is just as conspicuous in the old West Germany as in its reunited iteration. The majority of statisticians agree that even if, from today, no one else left the two major Christian confessions, in significantly less than two generations only half the German population would be a member of either of them: the older age cohorts, the majority of whom were baptized, are dying off. In the context of a generally decreasing population, ever fewer young people are offsetting these losses due to a marked decline in the willingness to be baptized. The notion of a Christian Germany, which has always been highly problematic, thus makes less and less sense. Ever fewer church members mean that knowledge of religion is also decreasing. In the United States, despite the churches' public presence, knowledge of Christianity is restricted to a small number of key elements, mainly love for one's neighbor and Jesus, while even the cross, as a fundamental and today highly problematic symbol, is rarely mentioned in surveys as a characteristic feature of Christianity. Pastoral theologians now refer to a widespread religious illiteracy.[22]

Amid this fog of religious ignorance, knowledge of unique confessional traits and forms is also disappearing. Confessional consciousness is declining along with religion—an obvious point that is easily grasped. But we can gain a deeper understanding of the causes of deconfessionalism by using the distinction introduced earlier: in the modern age, secularization is not just a quantitative decline in the importance of religion, but it also represents a qualitative shift. In a functionally differentiated modernity, a number of functional systems with their own logic and significance coexist. This means we need to focus our attention on ambivalences, on cases in which we can discern a shift in the scope of functional systems and in the boundaries between them, and on instances of differentiation and de-differentiation.

To demonstrate and explain the loss of confessional consciousness, I would like to raise several points. Our starting point is the relationship between religion and politics as it existed in the 1940s and 1950s in the western occupation zones and early years of the Federal Republic. At the end of the war, confessionalism was in full bloom. It was underpinned by a strong sense of euphoria surrounding re-Christianization, a sentiment that extended far beyond church circles. The armed forces defeated, the nation rent asunder: on what foundation could the German polity now stand? Leaving to one side the "Goethe communities" brought into play by Friedrich Meinecke, it was above all Christianity that many in Germany understood to be this foundation. The churches were only too happy to take on this challenge while simultaneously entering into lively competition with one another.

The notion of maintaining a confessional balance was firmly anchored in the political mindset of the Bonn Republic at all levels. In the first instance this pertained to the state's top two figures: whatever the chancellor's confession, the other high representative of the state, namely the president, had to be a member of the other main religious community. That both would be male was still taken for granted at the time. This proportionalism based on confession was not limited to the upper and uppermost echelons of politics, but extended deep into society and its functional systems. On 9 October 1955, regional Bishop Hanns Lilje of Hanover complained publicly that Catholic members of staff in the armed forces, and in particular at the Federal Ministry of Defense, were surely receiving preferential treatment. This prompted the defense ministry itself to survey the confessional affiliation of senior officers and publish a corresponding statistical analysis.[23]

While *Der Spiegel* milked this controversy for all it was worth, circles that were not particularly close to the churches felt provoked. Liberal political scientist Thomas Ellwein published a polemical text entitled "Clericalism in German Politics," which marked both the high point and the turning point of this debate. There was a growing sensitivity to the significant extent to which the "halting separation of church and state" affected the political sphere. While a Catholic bishop could blithely issue advice on how to vote in a pastoral letter until the early 1960s, to do so subsequently would be to risk severe public criticism.[24]

But the break with the confessional consciousness was not only propelled from outside but also actively advanced from inside. A prime example is the CDU, which started life after the war as a cross-confessional coalition movement that consciously sought to distance itself from the confession-bound Center Party. As a practitioner of power politics, from the outset it was clear to Adenauer that if the CDU were to have a chance of power, it was crucial to attract the support not just of Catholic but of Protestant voters as well. In any case, the CDU leadership was determined to get beyond the Center Fortress (*Zentrumsturm*) so roundly criticized by Catholic politician Julius Bachem. But this form of inter-confessionalism was not a self-propelling process; it required an active approach. Many observers of political affairs and many Protestants in particular read the acronym CDU backwards, with UDC standing for *Und Doch Zentrum*, or "Center After All." What they were seeking to convey here was that in many of its local and regional associations, the CDU, which was supposed to bridge the confessional divide, was nonetheless Catholic-dominated. Many Protestants within the CDU harbored such suspicions until well into the 1970s.[25]

As party chairman, Konrad Adenauer had recognized with great perspicacity how problematic this was, and he systematically sought to reverse the party's excessively pro-Catholic tendencies. Signal left and turn right—this is how American crime shows teach us to shake off a pursuer. Signal Catholic and act Protestant, while highlighting proportionality, would be a fair characterization of Adenauer's policy when it came to the confessional problem.[26]

A prime example was education policy, a field in which the Catholic bishops went out of their way to make their mark. The battle over denominational schools was the most important one fought by Catholicism in early West Germany. The CDU leadership pursued a wavering course vis-à-vis the senior Catholic clergy and expressed verbal support for things they were actually prepared to sacrifice in political practice. In January 1949, when signs emerged during deliberations on the Basic Law, the constitution of West Germany, that parental rights would not be enshrined, believing Catholics mobilized to campaign on this crucial issue. On the Parliamentary Council, however, parents' rights had already been sacrificed to a compromise: "While Catholics demanded parental rights at meetings, in submissions, and so on, and while organizations and associations in Cologne gathered for a rally on January 30, 1949, the Christian Democrats had already abandoned this position without consulting the church authorities."[27] To the extent that the party continued to cultivate close political ties to Catholicism, Adenauer and the rest of the CDU leadership sought to make systematic structural alterations. Highlighting confessional proportionality, in cases in which Catholic candidates had managed to be directly elected at constituency level, Protestant party members were placed on the regional lists. In particular, the party systematically appointed Protestants to roles in the state-level ministries of education and cultural affairs in order to weaken the Catholic influence on education policy.[28] Later, the Sputnik crisis and the education reforms caused the original political conflicts over the schools to fade away rapidly and with little ado.

Within both major churches, religious consciousness was eroding in the 1960s. This was at least in part the result of the fact that the churches themselves were changing both their orientations and structures to place a greater emphasis on the immanent. If we read pastoral texts, in other words all the gray literature with which the churches sought to maintain the chain of tradition, such as letters to parents and families and guides for First Communion catechists, the shift is palpable. "The Fires Have Gone out in Hell"—to quote the pithy headline capturing this new approach on the cover of *Der Spiegel* magazine in the early 1970s. Over the centuries, in both theology and pastoral care, Christianity had sought to come to grips with guilt, sin, and salvation, but in the postwar period pastoral activities underwent a radical transformation. Today, it is terms such as love, healing, and redemption that predominate. As transcendence became more diffuse and, in particular, as the threat of punishment in the hereafter receded, attempts were made to reconstruct the religious code in small-scale contexts and on a collaborative basis. If we look for evidence of these profound shifts, we will find a large number of relevant texts. My favorite quote is as follows: Through the "immanence of the small group," according to a book featuring outline sermons produced by the regional church of Westphalia in 1976, the goal was to cultivate love between *Ich und Du*, that is, between I and thou, *Du* being the informal term for "you." This approach coexisted with the great transcendence of a deeply human God who, "through creative love," puts right all those things "that do not completely refuse to be put right."[29] The shift, palpable within popular religious literature, away from "damnation and salvation" and toward "love" or "hurting and healing," corresponded with a new social figure of the Christian: the seeker who undergoes experiences and somehow finds his or her way. Just fifteen years earlier, the ideal Catholic, for example, looked completely different: being a good Catholic meant fitting oneself into the "well-ordered phalanx," the *acies bene ordinata*, and thus demonstrating the Church's unity and strength.[30] This change had major consequences for the confessional consciousness. The clear boundaries and semantics of exclusion that previously dominated were gradually supplanted by inclusive patterns of speech and thought. Differentiation on the basis of confession thus also became less credible because the inclusionary mentality increasingly pushed the pronounced differences at the level of theology into the background. If the fires have gone out in hell, there is no longer any need for disputes over the best route to salvation.

To this observation concerning the internal relationship between Catholics and Protestants, we may add a third element that relates to the religious field as a whole. This is summed up in the question: Would it bother you if a Jewish or Muslim family moved in next door?

At the start of this chapter, I alluded to the Catholic-Protestant variant of this question; in the shape of Judaism and Islam, other faiths now come into play. In a narrow sense, neither Judaism nor Islam are "confessions," but rather world religions that are in turn subdivided into various traditions and strands. And yet, within the religious field in Germany they have made an impact, and continue to do so, in much the same way as the two Christian confessions in relation to one another: they challenge the other players within the religious sphere, which at best prompts innovations on all sides and at worst triggers hostility and discrimination. But the developments associated with these two religious communities are quite different.

To this day, the fraught background to Jewish life in Germany is the presence of Judaism as a religious community in the land of the Holocaust. Immediately after the war it seemed highly doubtful that Jewish life would ever resume in the Western occupation zones or in the Federal Republic. Jewish theologian Leo Baeck, who had survived persecution by the National Socialists, stated apodictically that the "era of the Jews in Germany [is] over once and for all."[31] In 1948, the World Jewish Congress declared that no Jew would ever set foot on German soil again.[32]

Yet a new and vibrant Jewish life took off in the occupation zones and early West Germany. It was flanked both by an enduring antisemitism that still exists today and by a gradually more pronounced philosemitism. These two tendencies do not contradict one another but are, in fact, part of a larger, consistent whole. Surveys carried out by the Official Military Government of the United States and various polling institutes revealed the still-strong presence of a latent antisemitism. As late as 1952, 37 percent of respondents stated that it would be better if there were no Jews in the country. The number of those supporting this view then fell to 26 percent in 1956 and hovered at just under 20 percent during the 1960s.[33] Neither the West German government nor any of its subdivisions called for or invited émigré Jews to move back to the country. Hans Mayer, a Jewish literary scholar who returned to Germany in 1946, highlighted the "absence of a gesture that was expected but that never came" as a major failing. "No attempt was made to bring back [those who had been driven out]. No one [within the German state] even considered doing so."[34]

This was not contradicted by a philosemitism enacted chiefly on the official stage. The Adenauer administration in particular utilized the commitment to making amends primarily as a means of rapidly reintegrating Germany into the West. And throughout West German society more generally, "the public avowal of a pro-Jewish stance generally [followed] stereotypical patterns and had a highly symbolic character."[35] Yet it is also true that the widespread renaissance of Jewish centers, educational institutions and cultural sites, such as the Center for Jewish Studies Heidelberg and the Abraham Geiger College in Potsdam, have attracted a great deal of public interest. Many of their students and many of those visiting Jewish cultural institutions or attending relevant events and exhibitions are not themselves Jewish. They come out of curiosity, to learn something or to enjoy a form of cultural entertainment. While we must be careful not to confuse this cultural appeal with lived religiosity, these trends do open up a wide range of opportunities for exchange with the non-Jewish environment. This tendency cannot disguise the fact that there are a number of serious and growing forms of antisemitism. But it is also apparent that antisemitism has had its day as a form of discrimination with broad social acceptance. The largely ritualized, sometimes even sclerotic philosemitism found in the old Federal Republic has been supplanted by an open interest in exchange that is sensitive both to history and religion.

Changed attitudes on the part of the Christian churches have contributed to this more relaxed relationship between the Jewish communities and the non-Jewish population. For centuries, both the Catholic and Protestant Church were bearers of a pronounced anti-Judaism that was justified in religious terms and that—within political and social practice—could, and often did, easily tip over into a form of race-based antisemitism. While some Christian theologians struck a more thoughtful note before and particularly after the Shoah, even after 1945 both of the major Christian confessions cleaved to various anti-Jewish stereotypes.

One of the common argumentative constructs here was rooted in the idea of substitution, as alluded to, for example, in the Darmstadt Declaration (*Darmstädter Wort*) of 1948, which was adopted by the Councils of Brethren of the Confessing Church. On this view, the Jews had forfeited their status as the "chosen people" by crucifying Christ. God's "old covenant" with the people of Israel had supposedly been supplanted by a "new covenant" with Christendom. While the Councils of Brethren recognized the Jews as the errant brother "whom [the Church] loves and calls to," they nonetheless interpreted the recent past through traditional substitutionist theology, declaring "Israel under judgement" to be "God's perpetual warning to his community." "That God permits no one to scorn him is the tacit preaching of the Jewish fate, a warning to us and admonition to the Jews to consider whether they ought not to convert to that which, despite everything, offers them the prospect of salvation."[36]

In the Catholic Church, anti-Jewish beliefs found expression, for example, in the Good Friday liturgy, in one of which Catholics offered "intercessory prayers" annually for the "perfidious Jews." God was asked to remove the "veil from their hearts," help them to know Jesus Christ and thus wrest them from the "blindness of their people" and from "darkness," to quote the 1884 German translation of the Latin Mass text.[37]

Nonetheless, there were soon signs of a shift, with certain actors at least setting a quite different tone. Within the Protestant Church, the "Schuld an Israel" declaration published in 1950 by the EKD synod in Berlin-Weißensee articulated a quite different vision, distancing the Church from condemnations of Israel: "We confess our faith in a Church that is a fusion into one body of Jewish Christians and heathen Christians and whose peace is Jesus Christ. We believe that God's promise regarding the people of Israel, whom he had chosen, remained in force even after the crucifixion of Jesus Christ," to quote the second and third of a total of eight key principles set out in the declaration. The synod members admitted their own guilt with respect to the Holocaust, calling on believers to treat Jews in a "brotherly" fashion and to actively oppose antisemitism.[38] Many bodies within civil society and to some extent even cross-confessional coalitions such as *Aktion Sühnezeichen*, as well as the societies for Christian-Jewish cooperation, sought to improve Christian-Jewish dialogue, though their influence was limited. Representatives of both Christian theologies in Germany such as Johann Baptist Metz, Jürgen Moltmann, and Elisabeth Schuessler-Fiorenza also regarded it as a special challenge to develop a model of Christian faith "after Auschwitz." The much-discussed "Synodal Resolution on the Renewal of the Relationship between Christians and Jews," published by the regional synod of the Protestant Church in the Rhineland on 11 January 1980, made a particular impact. The resolution consciously turned away from the notion of a "mission to the Jews" and instead underlined the enduring election of Israel by God.[39]

Two decades after the Shoah, according to Cardinal Karl Lehmann, the Catholic Church made an "almost complete about-turn." Certainly, there had already been initiatives aimed at redefining the relationship with Jews, but they had failed to make much impact.[40] In the *Nostra aetate* declaration, the Council Fathers of the Second Vatican Council argued against the charge of "deicide," which had been the basis for discrimination and persecution for centuries. "True, the Jewish authorities and those who followed their lead pressed for the death of Christ; still, what happened in His passion cannot be charged against all the Jews, without distinction, then alive, nor against the Jews of today." Further, "the Jews should not be presented as rejected or accursed by God, as if this followed from the Holy Scriptures." Finally, "in her rejection of every persecution against any man, the Church, mindful of the patrimony she shares with the Jews and moved not by political reasons but by the Gospel's spiritual love, decries hatred, persecutions, displays of anti-Semitism, directed against Jews at any time and by anyone."[41] The Church changed both its liturgy and doctrine, which has led to a significant easing of the tensions between the Catholic Church and Judaism. Nonetheless, certain demonstrative actions have brought the centuries-old conflicts back to the fore, as in 2008 when Pope Benedict XVI gave permission to use once again the 1962 Roman Missal in the Tridentine Good Friday liturgy, which included a petition for the Jews and reinvigorated the notion of a Christian mission to them. The lifting of the excommunication against Richard Williamson, bishop, member of the Society of Saint Pius X, and Holocaust denier, also provoked heated debates.

In order to understand these shifts and perhaps also the decreased tensions in the relationship between Jews and the non-Jewish environment, it is worth taking a look at changes in the religious field as a whole. The religious minority that the majority society uses in order to assert and shore up its own identity is no longer Judaism, but Islam. A simple example reveals the present state of the debate. While every mayor regards the local synagogue as an important symbol of lived tolerance and pluralism, every mosque-building project is virtually predestined to be a source of contention.

Opinion polls and statistics paint a very clear picture of how Germans would feel about having a Muslim neighbor: more of them have reservations about this prospect than in neighboring European countries such as the Netherlands, the United Kingdom, or France.[42] The distance is greater, and the intensity of contact is lower, than in the nearby parts of Europe, even in cases in which the supposed "guest workers," to use the dated term, have long since become citizens who see their future not in Turkey but in Germany. Islam is not a new religion in Germany; quite the opposite: people of Muslim faith made their home in the country in its early centuries. But it was only from the mid 1960s onward, as a result of the recruitment agreement with Turkey, that large numbers of Muslims came to West Germany, to the point that they were recognized and acknowledged as a politically relevant group.

It is from the world of business and economics that we have the idea that competition is good for business. On occasion scholars have also analyzed religious fields as markets of transcendence in which a variety of actors tout their particular religious interpretation of the world and compete with one another. In many cases, the confessional rivalry between Catholics and Protestants has in fact operated in this manner: the development of the structures of a *Volkskirche* in accordance with the Principal Decree of the Imperial Deputation (*Reichsdeputationshauptschluss*) occurred while the key actors were closely observing their confessional other. Mutual confessional polemics acted to stimulate innovation because those involved had to make the effort to deflect their opponent's verbal attacks, and perhaps even trump their critique.

By the late 1960s, that which had functioned for more than a century in the dispute between Catholics and Protestants no longer applied. When it comes to the new "confession" of Muslims, this invigorating effect seems to have been, and still appears to be, entirely absent. The stronger presence of Muslim communities has had no mobilizing effect within the religious field. First and foremost, this is bound up with the fact that, with the exception of a small number of phenomena on the Islamist periphery, Muslim communities are not engaged in missionary work, limiting themselves to their members' religious affairs. But it is also linked with the Christian communities' specific reaction to Muslim immigrants. It is interesting to note that few commentators have contrasted Muslims with an emphatically religious opposite number. Even the churches did not emphasize "Christians" as the contrasting other in an attempt to highlight their religious core. Instead, both Catholics and Protestants underlined how superbly their own religion had fitted into the social and political structures of the Federal Republic. The Protestant Church in particular emphasized its modernity as a "'secular church' and thus as an instance of communitization appropriate to 'modern' Western society."[43] This was embodied above all in its commitment to the basic liberal-democratic order and the modern constitutional state. The Catholic Church was initially more reticent about the postulate of its own secularism. In the mid-1960s, the Second Vatican Council had smoothed the way for attempts to identify common ground between Islam and Christianity. But in the Catholic sphere, too, it was ultimately the demand that Islam adapt to European traditions and interests that predominated. Against this background of "modern Christian" religion, Islam then provided the counter-image: there was "still a long way to go" before "Islam undergoes a process of secularization comparable to that of European Christianity," stated the *Evangelische Kommentare* journal in 1987, and only "when Islamic society has created its own rationalist culture will it be possible to banish the mediaeval instincts and religious excesses from the faith of the Prophet."[44] In the first instance, these observations say a great deal more about those making them than about those being observed. They are indirect evidence of just how much the two major Christian churches had lost their own special character, and, not least, a clear confessional profile—and were now seeking to regain these clear contours by emphasizing their distance from religious groups that were less established in Germany.[45]

The churches' strategy of exclusion in the early 1970s is an element of the glass ceiling that presently makes it more difficult for Muslim communities to integrate in Germany than in other European societies. Going by the findings of the Bertelsmann Religion Monitor, Muslim men and women in Germany are nonetheless closely incorporated into state and society. They reflect deeply upon their religious beliefs and, in international comparison, have liberal views.[46] Meanwhile, their religious convictions have not seen the same kind of intergenerational weakening observable, for example, in Christianity. Though the individual strands of the Islamic faith are following their own paths of modernization, there remains a high degree of individual religiosity, though Muslims frame this in religiously inclusive terms, generally trusting members of other religions more than nonreligious people.[47] But the openness of this religious group stands in contrast to the general population's widespread rejection of it. Certainly, Germans describe democracy and diversity as desirable, but here Islam is "not included."[48] While a frequently articulated skepticism about Islam does not equate with rejection of the religion, it does provide a basis for it. Because direct contact and acquaintance with individuals of the Islamic faith are less common in Germany than in other European societies, it is often the small minority of radical Islamists that molds the general perception of Muslims.[49]

Conclusions

To conclude, I would like to emphasize three key points. First, confessional prejudices diminished, even those that had been deeply rooted. As late as 1976, they were still not far from the surface. To quote one German Protestant in a survey carried out by sociologist Gerhard Schmidtchen on religious prejudices in that year, the others, "we were quite clear about this, have dark hair and brown eyes, the girls wear earrings and they all lie through their teeth."[50] This woman respondent, however, did not have those of Muslim faith in mind, as one might have thought in light of the date. In fact, she was recalling the prejudices she had learned as a child about men and women of Catholic faith: alien, uneducated, mostly from the countryside, impossible to integrate and themselves unwilling to do so, beholden to a religious rite in a foreign language, and perhaps even taking instruction from a state outside Germany. If we look at the other side of the coin, in many respects we see a congruent structure of prejudice in the past among Catholics with regard to Protestants. The feelings of disgust and revulsion that built walls between the members of the confessions that developed from the seventeenth century onward, with a degree of intensification beginning in the late eighteenth century, have essentially ceased to exist. Anyone today expressing opposition to a "mixed marriage," in other words, a union between a Protestant and Catholic, would be more likely to be laughed at than anything else.

Second, and conversely, it is evident that confessional boundaries not only changed within specific religious movements and in relation to one another, but also lost distinctiveness and thus credibility within society as a whole: most social movements such as environmental initiatives, human rights campaigns, and work in support of refugees have seen the emergence of forums in which nonbelievers and believers of both the main confessions work together. In contrast to the situation in the United States, home to an emphatically politico-religious movement in the form of the New Christian Right, outside of the shrinking sphere of engagement in clubs and associations, in Germany today there are no major examples of movements closely tied to the churches or other religious communities.[51]

The third and major point refers to the religious field as a whole: what it means to be Catholic or Protestant, and how this molds individual lives, has changed greatly in the seven decades since World War II, and this transformation has shaped the religious field as a whole. However, the dissolution of confessional boundaries in the major Christian churches has not engendered greater acceptance in Germany for relatively new religions such as Islam. The traditional religious patterns remain firmly established: while most people still know very little about religious or theological matters, reservations about other world religions and their adherents persist.

We can sum this up by stating that the religious field as a whole has been, and remains, subject to profound change. Not only are the relations between the religious communities changing, but the major Christian churches have been in a transitional phase at least since the final third of the twentieth century. Old certainties are being re-negotiated. And it seems far from clear whether, and if so in what form, a renewed collective form of religious conviction embraced by a large membership within a religious organization might get off the ground. One thing appears certain, however: if anything of this kind does emerge, the factor of confession will play no significant part in it.

Thomas Großbölting is Director of the Forschungsstelle für Zeitgeschichte in Hamburg and Professor of Contemporary History at the University of Hamburg. From 2009 to 2020 he was Principal Investigator at the Cluster of Excellence "Religion and Politics," University of Münster. His recent books include *Wiedervereinigungsgesellschaft. Aufbruch und Entgrenzung in Germany since 1989/90* (2020), *Was glaubten die Deutschen 1933–1945?* (coedited with Olaf Blaschke, 2020), and *Losing Heaven: Religion in Germany since 1945* (2016).

Notes

1. "Katholiken und Protestanten sind ähnlicher, als sie denken." *Süddeutsche.de*, 31 August 2017, Retrieved 27 November 2019 from https://www.sueddeutsche.de/panorama/jahre-reformation-katholiken-und-protestanten-sind-aehnlicher-als-sie-denken-1.3647303.
2. See *Materialdienst des konfessionskundlichen Instituts. Evangelischer Bund* no. 3/4 (1953): 48–53.
3. See Nicolai Hannig, *Die Religion der Öffentlichkeit. Kirche, Religion und Medien in der Bundesrepublik 1945–1989* (Göttingen: Wallstein-Verlag, 2010), 197.
4. Quoted in Ulrich Hehl, "Konfessionelle Irritationen in der frühen Bundesrepublik," *Historisch-politische Mitteilungen* 6 (1999): 167–87, 178ff.
5. Martin Greschat, "Konfessionelle Spannung in der Ära Adenauer," in *Katholiken und Protestanten in den Aufbaujahren der Bundesrepublik*, ed. Thomas Sauer (Stuttgart: Kohlhammer, 2000), 19–34, 19.
6. Michael Maurer, *Konfessionskulturen. Die Europäer als Protestanten und Katholiken* (Paderborn: Schöningh, 2019), 7.
7. Ibid., 7.
8. Wolfgang Reinhard, "Zwang zur Konfessionalisierung: Prolegomena zu einer Theorie des konfessionellen Zeitalters," *Zeitschrift für Historische Forschung* 10 (1983): 257–77; Wolfgang Reinhard, "Gegenreformation als Modernisierung? Prolegomena zu einer Theorie des konfessionellen Zeitalters," *Archiv für Reformationsgeschichte* 68 (1977): 226–51; Wolfgang Reinhard and Heinz Schilling, eds., *Die katholische Konfessionalisierung* (Münster: Aschendorf, 1993).
9. Thomas Kaufmann, "Konfessionalisierung," *Enzyklopädie der Neuzeit Online*, 2019, Retrieved 27 November 2019 from http://dx.doi.org/10.1163/2352-0248_edn_a2193000.
10. See Ernst Troeltsch, *Die Soziallehren der christlichen Kirchen und Gruppen* (Tübingen: Mohr, 1912), 967.
11. For this line of reasoning in its entirety, see Olaf Blaschke, "Der 'Dämon' des Konfessionalismus. Einführende Überlegungen," in *Konfessionen im Konflikt. Deutschland zwischen 1800 und 1970. Ein zweites konfessionelles Zeitalter*, ed. Olaf Blaschke (Göttingen: Vandenhoeck & Ruprecht, 2002), 13–69, 21.
12. Blaschke, "Der 'Dämon,'" 22.
13. Ernst Walter Zeeden, "Grundlagen und Wege der Konfessionsbildung im Zeitalter der Glaubenskämpfe," *Historische Zeitschrift* 185 (1958): 249–99, 251ff.
14. Blaschke, "Der 'Dämon,'" 24.
15. Thomas Nipperdey, *Religion im Umbruch. Deutschland 1870–1918* (Munich: Beck, 1986), 155.
16. Blaschke, "Der 'Dämon,'" 24.
17. For a comprehensive account, see Lucian Hölscher, *Geschichte der protestantischen Frömmigkeit in Deutschland* (Munich: Beck, 2005), 333–37.
18. See Ibid., 369–77.
19. Olaf Blaschke, *Die Kirchen und der Nationalsozialismus* (Stuttgart: Reclam, 2014), 55, 58, 69ff.
20. Hölscher, *Frömmigkeit*, 407.
21. See Thomas Großbölting, *Der verlorene Himmel. Glaube in Deutschland seit 1945* (Göttingen: Vandenhoeck & Ruprecht, 2013), 22–34.
22. For a lucid overview of this topic, see Christine Brinck, "Wo wohnt Gott? Und wozu müssen wir das wissen? Über den religiösen Analphabetismus der westlichen Gesellschaften. Eine Polemik," *Zeit.de*, 23 August 2012, Retrieved 27 November 2019 from https://www.zeit.de/2012/35/Glaube-Bibel-Religion/komplettansicht.
23. Quoted in "Wohin die Reise geht," *Der Spiegel*, 16 November 1955: 13–14.
24. See Thomas Ellwein, *Klerikalismus in der deutschen Politik* (Munich: Isar Verlag, 1955), 252.

25. Frank Bösch, "'Zu katholisch.' Die Durchsetzung der CDU und das schwierige Zusammengehen der Konfessionen in der Bundesrepublik Deutschland," in *Solidargemeinschaft und fragmentierte Gesellschaft. Parteien, Milieus und Verbände im Vergleich. Festschrift zum 60. Geburtstag von Peter Lösche*, ed. Tobias Dürr and Franz Walter (Opladen: Leske and Budrich, 1999), 295–418, 396.

26. See Anselm Doering-Manteuffel, "Strukturmerkmale der Kanzlerdemokratie," *Der Staat* 30 (1991): 1–18.

27. Burkhard Schewick, *Die katholische Kirche und die Entstehung der Verfassungen in Westdeutschland 1945–1950* (Mainz: Matthias-Gruenewald-Verlag 1980), 113.

28. See Frank Bösch, *Die Adenauer-CDU. Gründung, Aufstieg und Krise einer Erfolgspartei 1945–1969* (Stuttgart: Deutsche Verlags-Anstalt 2001), 427.

29. Michael Ebertz, "'Tote Menschen haben keine Probleme?' oder: Der Zwang zum Vergessen und Erinnerung. Die Bescheidung des eschatologischen Codes im 20. Jahrhundert," in *Normieren, Tradieren, Inszenieren. Das Christentum als Buchreligion*, ed. Andreas Holzem (Darmstadt: Wissenschaftliche Buchgesellschaft, 2004), 279–300, 294.

30. See Wilhelm Damberg, *Abschied vom Milieu? Katholizismus im Bistum Münster und in den Niederlanden 1945–1980* (Paderborn: Schöningh, 1997) 506; Mark Edward Ruff, "Catholics Elites, Gender, and Unintended Consequences in the 1950s: Towards a Reinterpretation of the Role of Religious Conservatives in the Federal Republic," in *Conflict, Catastrophe and Continuity. Essays on Modern German History*, ed. Frank Biess, Mark Roseman and Hanna Schissler (New York: Berghahn Books, 2007), 252–72.

31. Quoted in Wolfgang Benz and Werner Bergmann, *Vorurteil und Völkermord. Entwicklungslinien des Antisemitismus* (Freiburg im Breisgau: Herder, 1997), 402.

32. Quoted in Julius H. Schoeps, *Mein Weg als deutscher Jude. Autobiographische Notizen* (Zürich: Pendo-Verlag, 2003), 237.

33. See Monika Richarz, "Juden in der Bundesrepublik Deutschland und in der Deutschen Demokratischen Republik seit 1945," in *Jüdisches Leben in Deutschland nach 1945*, ed. Micha Brumlik, Doron Kiesel, Cilly Kugelmann and Julius H. Schoeps (Frankfurt am Main: Jüdischer Verlag bei Athenäum, 1986), 13–30, 14.

34. Hans Mayer, "Als der Krieg zu Ende war. Wir haben uns zu rasch mit der Vergangenheit eingerichtet," *Die Zeit*, 1 February 1982.

35. Frank Stern, "'Ein freundlich aufgenähter Davidstern.' Antisemitismus und Philosemitismus in der politischen Kultur der 50er Jahre," in *Modernisierung im Wiederaufbau. Die westdeutsche Gesellschaft der 50er Jahre*, ed. Axel Schildt and Arnold Sywottek (Bonn: Dietz, 1998), 717–34, 732.

36. Rolf Rendtorff and Hans Hermann Henrix, eds., *Die Kirchen und das Judentum. Dokumente von 1945–1985* (Paderborn: Gütersloher Verlagshaus, 2001), 540–44.

37. Quoted in Hubert Wolf, *Papst und Teufel. Die Archive des Vatikans und das Dritte Reich* (Munich: Beck, 2008), 108.

38. Evangelische Kirche in Deutschland, *Kirchliches Jahrbuch für die Evangelische Kirche in Deutschland 1950* (Gütersloh, 1951), 5ff.

39. Rendtorff and Henrix, eds., *Kirchen*, 605ff. On developments in this field, see: Paul Gerhard Aring, *Christen und Juden heute—und die "Judenmission"? Geschichte und Theologie protestantischer Judenmission in Deutschland, dargestellt und untersucht am Beispiel des Protestantismus im mittleren Deutschland* (Frankfurt am Main: Haag + Herchen, 1987).

40. See Wilhelm Damberg, "Die Katholiken und die Juden. Zur Vorgeschichte eines fundamentalen Paradigmenwechsels in der ersten Hälfte des 20. Jahrhunderts," *Internationale katholische Zeitschrift Communio* 39 (2010): 357–70.

41. Peter Hünermann, ed., *Die Dokumente des Zweiten Vatikanischen Konzils. Konstitutionen, Dekrete, Erklärungen* (Freiburg: Herder, 2009), 355–62.

42. Detlef Pollack, "Studie, 'Wahrnehmung und Akzeptanz religiöser Vielfalt.' Bevölkerungsumfrage des Exzellenzclusters 'Religion und Politik' unter Leitung des Religionssozio-

logen Prof. Dr. Detlef Pollack," Retrieved 27 November 2019 from http://www.uni-muenster .de/imperia/md/content/religion_und_politik/aktuelles/2010/12_2010/studie_wahrneh mung_und_akzeptanz_religioeser_vielfalt.pdf, 3.

43. Michael Mildenberger, *Dialog der Religionen und Weltanschauungen. Zur Begegnung der Christen mit Menschen anderen Glaubens* (Stuttgart: Evangelische Zentralstelle für Weltanschauungsfragen, 1975), 2; quoted in Thomas Mittmann, "Säkularisierungsvorstellungen und religiöse Identitätsstiftung im Migrationsdiskurs. Die kirchliche Wahrnehmung 'des Islams' in der Bundesrepublik Deutschland seit den 1960er Jahren," *Archiv für Sozialgeschichte* 51 (2011): 267–89, 274.

44. "Islamisches Glaubensfeuer," *Evangelische Kommentare* 20, no. 9 (1987): 491ff.

45. Cf. Großbölting, *Himmel*, 203–13.

46. See Stephan Vopel and Yasemin El-Menouar, *Sonderauswertung Islam 2015. Die wichtigsten Ergebnisse im Überblick* (Gütersloh: Bertelsmann Stiftung, 2015).

47. Dirk Halm and Martina Sauer, *Lebenswelten deutscher Muslime* (Gütersloh: Verlag Bertelsmann-Stiftung, 2015), 49.

48. Yasemin El-Menouar, "Religiöse Toleranz weit verbreitet—aber der Islam wird nicht einbezogen," *Bertelsmann-Stiftung.de*, 11 July 2019, Retrieved 12 June 2020 from bertelsmannstiftung.de/de/themen/aktuelle-meldungen/2019/juli/religioese-toleranz-weit-verbreitet-aberder-islam-wird-nicht-einbezogen.

49. See Vopel and El-Menouar, *Sonderauswertung Islam*, 3.

50. See Gerhard Schmidtchen, *Zwischen Kirche und Gesellschaft. Forschungsbericht über die Umfrage zur Gemeinsamen Synode der Bistümer in der Bundesrepublik Deutschland* (Freiburg: Herder), 1972.

51. See Thomas Großbölting, "Why is There No Christian Right in Germany? German Conservative Christians and the Invention of a Silent Majority in the 1970s," in *Inventing the Silent Majority in Western Europe and the United States: Conservatism in the 1960s and 1970s*, ed. Anna von der Goltz and Britta Waldschmidt-Nelson (Cambridge, UK: Cambridge University Press, 2017), 210–26.

Bibliography

Aring, Paul Gerhard. *Christen und Juden heute—und die "Judenmission"? Geschichte und Theologie protestantischer Judenmission in Deutschland, dargestellt und untersucht am Beispiel des Protestantismus im mittleren Deutschland*. Frankfurt am Main: Haag + Herchen, 1987.

Benz, Wolfgang, and Werner Bergmann. *Vorurteil und Völkermord. Entwicklungslinien des Antisemitismus*. Freiburg im Breisgau: Herder, 1997.

Blaschke, Olaf. *Die Kirchen und der Nationalsozialismus*. Stuttgart: Reclam, 2014.

———. "Der 'Dämon' des Konfessionalismus. Einführende Überlegungen." In *Konfessionen im Konflikt. Deutschland zwischen 1800 und 1970. Ein zweites konfessionelles Zeitalter*, edited by Olaf Blaschke, 13–69. Göttingen: Vandenhoeck & Ruprecht, 2002.

Bösch, Frank. *Die Adenauer-CDU. Gründung, Aufstieg und Krise einer Erfolgspartei 1945–1969*. Stuttgart: Deutsche Verlags-Anstalt, 2001.

———. "'Zu katholisch.' Die Durchsetzung der CDU und das schwierige Zusammengehen der Konfessionen in der Bundesrepublik Deutschland." In *Solidargemeinschaft und fragmentierte Gesellschaft. Parteien, Milieus und Verbände im Vergleich. Festschrift zum 60. Geburtstag von Peter Lösche*, edited by Tobias Dürr and Franz Walter, 295–418. Opladen: Leske and Budrich, 1999.

Brinck, Christine. "Wo wohnt Gott? Und wozu müssen wir das wissen? Über den religiösen Analphabetismus der westlichen Gesellschaften. Eine Polemik." *Zeit.de*, 23 August 2012.

Retrieved 27 November 2019 from https://www.zeit.de/2012/35/Glaube-Bibel-Religion/komplettansicht.

Damberg, Wilhelm. *Abschied vom Milieu? Katholizismus im Bistum Münster und in den Niederlanden 1945–1980*. Paderborn: Schöningh, 1997.

———. "Die Katholiken und die Juden. Zur Vorgeschichte eines fundamentalen Paradigmenwechsels in der ersten Hälfte des 20. Jahrhunderts." *Internationale katholische Zeitschrift Communio* 39 (2010): 357–70.

Doering-Manteuffel, Anselm. "Strukturmerkmale der Kanzlerdemokratie." *Der Staat* 30 (1991): 1–18.

Ebertz, Michael. "'Tote Menschen haben keine Probleme?' oder: Der Zwang zum Vergessen und Erinnerung. Die Bescheidung des eschatologischen Codes im 20. Jahrhundert." In *Normieren, Tradieren, Inszenieren. Das Christentum als Buchreligion*, edited by Andreas Holzem, 279–300. Darmstadt: Wissenschaftliche Buchgesellschaft, 2004.

Ellwein, Thomas. *Klerikalismus in der deutschen Politik*. Munich: Isar Verlag, 1955.

El-Menouar, Yasemin. "Religiöse Toleranz weit verbreitet—aber der Islam wird nicht eingezogen." *Bertelsmann-Stiftung.de*, 11 July 2019. Retrieved 12 June 2020 from https://www.bertelsmann-stiftung.de/de/themen/aktuelle-meldungen/2019/juli/religioese-toleranz-weit-verbreitet-aber-der-islam-wird-nicht-einbezogen.

Evangelische Kirche in Deutschland. *Kirchliches Jahrbuch für die Evangelische Kirche in Deutschland 1950*. Gütersloh, 1951.

Greschat, Martin. "Konfessionelle Spannung in der Ära Adenauer." In *Katholiken und Protestanten in den Aufbaujahren der Bundesrepublik*, edited by Thomas Sauer, 19–34. Stuttgart: Kohlhammer, 2000.

Großbölting, Thomas. *Der verlorene Himmel. Glaube in Deutschland seit 1945*. Göttingen: Vandenhoeck & Ruprecht, 2013.

———. "Why is There No Christian Right in Germany? German Conservative Christians and the Invention of a Silent Majority in den 1970s." In *Inventing the Silent Majority in Western Europe and the United States: Conservatism in the 1960s and 1970s*, edited by Anna von der Goltz and Britta Waldschmidt-Nelson, 210–26. Cambridge, UK: Cambridge University Press, 2017.

Halm, Dirk, and Martina Sauer. *Lebenswelten deutscher Muslime*. Gütersloh: Verlag Bertelsmann-Stiftung, 2015.

Hannig, Nicolai. *Die Religion der Öffentlichkeit. Kirche, Religion und Medien in der Bundesrepublik 1945–1989*. Göttingen: Wallstein-Verlag, 2010.

Hehl, Ulrich. "Konfessionelle Irritationen in der frühen Bundesrepublik." *Historisch-politische Mitteilungen* 6 (1999): 167–87.

Hölscher, Lucian. *Geschichte der protestantischen Frömmigkeit in Deutschland*. Munich: Beck, 2005.

Hünermann, Peter, ed. *Die Dokumente des Zweiten Vatikanischen Konzils. Konstitutionen, Dekrete, Erklärungen*. Freiburg: Herder, 2009.

"Islamisches Glaubensfeuer." *Evangelische Kommentare* 20, no. 9 (1987): 491–92.

"Katholiken und Protestanten sind ähnlicher, als sie denken." *Süddeutsche.de*, 31 August 2017. Retrieved 27 November 2019 from https://www.sueddeutsche.de/panorama/jahre-reformation-katholiken-und-protestanten-sind-aehnlicher-als-sie-denken-1.3647303.

Kaufmann, Thomas. "Konfessionalisierung." *Enzyklopädie der Neuzeit Online*, 2019. Retrieved 27 November 2019 from http://dx.doi.org/10.1163/2352-0248_edn_a2193000.

Materialdienst des konfessionskundlichen Instituts. Evangelischer Bund no. 3/4 (1953): 48–53.

Maurer, Michael. *Konfessionskulturen. Die Europäer als Protestanten und Katholiken*. Paderborn: Schöningh, 2019.

Mayer, Hans. "Als der Krieg zu Ende war. Wir haben uns zu rasch mit der Vergangenheit eingerichtet." *Die Zeit*, 1 February 1982: 12.

Mildenberger, Michael. *Dialog der Religionen und Weltanschauungen. Zur Begegnung der Christen mit Menschen anderen Glaubens.* Stuttgart: Evangelische Zentralstelle für Weltanschauungsfragen, 1975.

Mittmann, Thomas. "Säkularisierungsvorstellungen und religiöse Identitätsstiftung im Migrationsdiskurs. Die kirchliche Wahrnehmung 'des Islams' in der Bundesrepublik Deutschland seit den 1960er Jahren." *Archiv für Sozialgeschichte* 51 (2011): 267–89.

Nipperdey, Thomas. *Religion im Umbruch. Deutschland 1870–1918.* Munich: Beck, 1986.

Pollack, Detlef. "Studie,'Wahrnehmung und Akzeptanz religiöser Vielfalt.' Bevölkerungsumfrage des Exzellenzclusters, 'Religion und Politik' unter Leitung des Religionssoziologen Prof. Dr. Detlef Pollack." Retrieved 27 November 2019 from http://www.uni-muenster.de/imperia/md/content/religion_und_politik/aktuelles/2010/12_2010/studie_wahrnehmung_und_akzeptanz_religioeser_vielfalt.pdf.

Reinhard, Wolfgang. "Gegenreformation als Modernisierung? Prolegomena zu einer Theorie des konfessionellen Zeitalters." *Archiv für Reformationsgeschichte* 68 (1977): 226–51.

———. "Zwang zur Konfessionalisierung: Prolegomena zu einer Theorie des konfessionellen Zeitalters." *Zeitschrift für Historische Forschung* 10 (1983): 257–77.

Reinhard, Wolfgang, and Heinz Schilling, eds. *Die katholische Konfessionalisierung.* Münster: Aschendorf, 1993.

Rendtorff, Rolf, and Hans Hermann Henrix, eds. *Die Kirchen und das Judentum. Dokumente von 1945–1985.* Paderborn: Gütersloher Verlagshaus, 2001.

Richarz, Monika. "Juden in der Bundesrepublik Deutschland und in der Deutschen Demokratischen Republik seit 1945." In *Jüdisches Leben in Deutschland nach 1945*, edited by Micha Brumlik, Doron Kiesel, Cilly Kugelmann, and Julius H. Schoeps, 13–30. Frankfurt am Main: Jüdischer Verlag bei Athenäum, 1986.

Ruff, Mark Edward. "Catholic Elites, Gender, and Unintended Consequences in the 1950s: Towards a Reinterpretation of the Role of Religious Conservatives in the Federal Republic." In *Conflict, Catastrophe and Continuity. Essays on Modern German History*, edited by Frank Biess, Mark Roseman, and Hanna Schissler, 252–72. New York: Berghahn Books, 2007.

Schewick, Burkhard. *Die katholische Kirche und die Entstehung der Verfassungen in Westdeutschland 1945–1950.* Mainz: Matthias-Gruenewald-Verlag, 1980.

Schmidtchen, Gerhard. *Zwischen Kirche und Gesellschaft. Forschungsbericht über die Umfrage zur Gemeinsamen Synode der Bistümer in der Bundesrepublik Deutschland.* Freiburg: Herder, 1972.

Schoeps, Julius H. *Mein Weg als deutscher Jude. Autobiographische Notizen.* Zürich: Pendo-Verlag, 2003.

Stern, Frank. "'Ein freundlich aufgenähter Davidstern.' Antisemitismus und Philosemitismus in der politischen Kultur der 50er Jahre." In *Modernisierung im Wiederaufbau. Die westdeutsche Gesellschaft der 50er Jahre*, edited by Axel Schildt and Arnold Sywottek, 717–34. Bonn: Dietz, 1998.

Troeltsch, Ernst. *Die Soziallehren der christlichen Kirchen und Gruppen.* Tübingen: Mohr, 1912.

Vopel, Stephan, and Yasemin El-Menouar. *Sonderauswertung Islam 2015. Die wichtigsten Ergebnisse im Überblick.* Gütersloh: Bertelsmann Stiftung, 2015.

"Wohin die Reise geht." *Der Spiegel*, 16 November 1955, 13–14.

Wolf, Hubert. *Papst und Teufel. Die Archive des Vatikans und das Dritte Reich.* Munich: Beck, 2008.

Zeeden, Ernst Walter. "Grundlagen und Wege der Konfessionsbildung im Zeitalter der Glaubenskämpfe." *Historische Zeitschrift* 185 (1958): 249–99.

Conclusion

Closing Reflections

Mark Edward Ruff and Thomas Großbölting

On 20 June 1991, an unprecedented 104 speakers in the *Bundeshaus*, the parliament building in Bonn, took to the podium to voice their opinions about whether the federal capital should be moved to Berlin. While some raised the legal question of whether Bonn merely has been designated a "provisional capital" since 1949, the majority of speakers took to the floor with emotion-laden questions about the cultural identity of the unexpectedly reunified republic. Was the nation to be tied more tightly to the West or to the East? Were the identities of the individual states to be preserved in this larger union of peoples? How were the needs and values of the states formerly part of the German Democratic Republic to be balanced with those that had been part of the Federal Republic since 1949?[1]

What stood out notably in these frequently tense exchanges was the diminished role of confessional tensions between Catholics and Protestants. A smattering of Catholic delegates did speak of the need to defend the "Christian West," noting that the once mighty Protestant fortress in Central Germany had now become a bastion of secularism. But clearly fears of a centralized "Prussian" state had receded, replaced with practical concerns of how to engineer an equitable transfer of ministries and offices to Berlin.

Why did the confessional tensions that had played such a central role in the German national state from its founding in 1871 and that had lingered into the early decades of the Federal Republic dissipate? Why were they no longer able to rouse passions in the reunified Germany of the 1990s and 2000s? What allowed the confessional divide to be overcome, since previous efforts such as those building bridges to National Socialism's Positive Christianity of the 1930s had enjoyed only limited success?

This volume has suggested answers. For starters, the German political parties saw significant changes in their confessional structure. As much as the Rhenish Catholic author Heinrich Böll excoriated the moral hypocrisy and confessional insularity of the CDU and its Catholic base in the early to mid-1960s, its interconfessionalism proved enduring. Gone were the days when a Catholic priest like Ludwig Kaas could be at the helm of a party like the Center Party, one of Germany's major political parties from 1870 through the immediate postwar era, one Catholic to the core. By the turn of the century, the CDU's confessional identity had undergone such a transformation that the daughter of a Berlin Protestant pastor raised in the Communist East could begin serving as Chancellor in 2005 and go on to set a record as the Federal Republic's longest serving Chancellor.

Nor was the CDU's interconfessionalism unique. The Greens, though often seen as a party of lax and lapsed Protestants as well as the religiously disinclined, counted many devout Catholics as founders, including Petra Kelly, who even carried out an extensive correspondence with Raymond Hunthausen, the Archbishop of Seattle, in the early 1980s about Catholic opposition to nuclear armaments.[2] The confessional composition of the Greens underscored the changing political structures of the later Federal Republic: liberal Catholics and progressive Protestants came to work together under the same political umbrella, even if they never abjured their confessional loyalties. In this regard, they were following a path charted by highly regarded Catholic "bridge-builders" to the SPD in the 1960s like the constitutional theorist and future Constitutional Court justice Ernst-Wolfgang Böckenförde, who famously joined the SPD in 1967 not just because he agreed with much of its platform, but because he believed that the political parties needed to be decoupled from their confessional bases.[3] This larger shift reflected something even more fundamental: German Catholics, once seen as second-class citizens and frequently confined to a political ghetto, were being integrated into the political mainstream—and not just in a safe fortress like the CDU-CSU but in parties from political traditions long hostile to Catholicism, like socialism and liberalism.

These observations, however, raise the question of the chicken and the egg. Did the parties themselves alter confessional identities and affiliations by opening their doors to those from once rival confessions? Or did changes in the confessional composition of the political parties merely mirror shifting religious allegiances and affiliations? The decline in church attendance and membership was unmistakable, even in West Germany. Adding fifteen million East German citizens with one of the largest percentages of avowed atheists and nonbelievers in the world so accelerated these trends that by the early 2000s, five centuries after the Reformation, Germany finally attained confessional parity: 40 percent Catholics and 40 percent Protestants. Call it what you like—secularization, dechristianization, pluralization, dechurching—but the effect was ultimately the same: confessional tensions diminished as even conservative Catholics and Protestants began to recognize that they had more in common with each other than with their progressive co-religionists, let alone nonbelievers or those of other faiths.

Clearly tensions between Catholics and Protestants eased in part because of the arrival of large numbers of non-Christians in the Federal Republic, a significant number of whom were Muslims from North Africa, Bosnia, and, above all, Turkey. As Muslims came to comprise over five percent of the German population (in June 1933, by contrast, German Jews amounted to less than .75 percent of the German population), upholding the confessional divide between Protestants and Catholics made less and less sense. Yet confessional walls were torn down both by inclusion and exclusion. For religious progressives, interfaith and ecumenical dialogue meant embracing Muslims—and all Christians—as brothers. Yet for some religious conservatives, Catholic-Protestant partnership was achieved only by finding a new common enemy—Islam. In this vein, the trope of the "Christian West" which had been deployed to great effect in the later war years and immediate postwar era to bring together Catholics and Protestants became one of exclusion. Already in 1955, the newly appointed German Foreign Minister Heinrich von Brentano delivered a speech likening the defense of the Christian West against Soviet Communism to the nearly thousand year Catholic defense of medieval Europe against Islamic intrusions and invasions.[4] Unleashing a firestorm, von Brentano's speech relegated the rhetoric of the Christian West to the political right, or at the least confirmed its right-wing shift and association with the Socialist Reich Party and "neo-fascist" First Legion. But such rhetoric resurfaced decades later in debates over whether Turkey should be admitted as a member of the European Union. Cardinal Joseph Ratzinger, soon-to-be Pope Benedict XVI, worked behind the scenes to torpedo Turkey's admission, citing the need to preserve Europe's "Christian roots." Indeed, Ratzinger had promoted a campaign to insert a clause into the constitution for the European Union that would have referred explicitly to Europe's "Christian roots."[5]

Tellingly, Ratzinger, as Prefect of the Congregation for the Doctrine of the Faith, had served just years earlier as one of the major architects of the Joint Declaration on the Doctrine of Justification, which was signed by representatives of the Vatican and the Lutheran World Federation on 31 October 1999, in Augsburg.[6] Without him, an agreement might not have come to fruition. The Bishop of the Evangelical Lutheran Church of America, George Anderson, described him as the one who "untied the knots" in helping the churches overcome one of the major stumbling blocks between Lutherans and Catholics—"a common understanding of our justification by God's grace through faith in Christ."[7] It was no accident that Lutheran-Catholic rapprochement coincided with increased efforts to exclude Islam, a wariness that only intensified following the attacks of 11 September 2001.

In contrast: until the arrival of larger number of Jews from the former Soviet Union after its collapse in 1991, it was the absence—and not the presence—of Jews that brought together Protestants and Catholics in ways few would have expected. Beginning already in the first years of military occupation, the Catholic and Protestant churches set out to document the history of the churches and National Socialist persecution. Written against the backdrop of criticism for their sins of omission during the Third Reich, these early accounts whitewashed both churches' past, arguing that they had borne the brunt of Nazi ideological fury. Persecution of Jews—or of Jewish converts to Christianity—found little to no place in these early accounts. In the coming decades, skeptics began questioning the veracity of these early chronicles. The Catholic Church in particular became the renewed focus of criticism, often for reasons that had little to do with a disinterested curiosity about its past under National Socialism but instead with resentment at the seemingly undue role of the Catholic Church in the politics of the early Federal Republic.[8] Those troubled by the Church's desire to maintain "denominational schools" (*Bekenntnisschulen*) segregated by confession took umbrage at the Church's recourse to Article 23 of the *Reichskonkordat* that guaranteed the right to these schools. The *Reichskonkordat*, though signed by a criminal regime, remained legally binding, the Church insisted. Critics duly argued that Church leaders not only had done too little to oppose Nazi crimes but had actively collaborated with the regime. After signing the *Reichskonkordat* on 20 July 1933, Church leaders had repeatedly sought to accommodate themselves to the National Socialist state.

Criticism came to a forte in February 1963, when the thirty-two-year-old German playwright, Rolf Hochhuth, premiered his play *The Deputy*, which accused the wartime pontiff Pope Pius XII of willfully remaining silent as Roman Jews were being deported to Auschwitz.[9] The play, which was staged in dozens of countries, generated an international firestorm: it led to scores of protests, some violent, denunciations, lawsuits, and even bombings. A native of Eschwege, a Protestant city of twenty thousand in eastern Hesse, Hochhuth was by his own admission a lapsed Protestant. As much as his incendiary play rekindled confessional animosities and even fears of a renewed *Kulturkampf* by Catholics, his play also led to intense soul-searching within Christian communities around the world. This reflection of the pope's wartime role and what he should have done differently and better ultimately made for strange bedfellows. Left-wing Catholics like Carl Amery and Ernst-Wolfgang Böckenförde came to the defense of Hochhuth and his many Protestant champions, like the Confessing Church pastor Heinrich Grüber and the Alsatian missionary Albert Schweitzer. But other high-ranking Protestant clergymen like Otto Dibelius rose to support the deceased pontiff, and their chorus was eventually joined by the Israeli diplomat Pinchas Lapide, who claimed that Pius XII had rescued between 700,000 and 860,000 Jews, a figure that almost all today regard as utterly exaggerated.[10]

The reaction to *The Deputy* was starting to reveal a phenomenon that would become much more pronounced after the turn of the century: progressive Catholics were discovering that they held much more in common with their progressive Protestant brethren than with conservatives in their own church. Future religious fault lines were to be found within—rather than between—the confessions themselves. As a result, church leaders were forced to devote their energies into internecine fighting—over how to deal with the National Socialist past, over how to implement the resolutions over the Second Vatican Council, over the rise of radicals, often younger, lay activists committed to Marxism, over how to provide development aid to the so-called Third World. These struggles took priority over fighting external confessional enemies—and frequently led to interdenominational cooperation. In this vein, how to reflect on the Nazis' annihilation of European Jews frequently became a litmus test for how one envisioned the churches' ministries and even very purpose: what did it truly mean to be Christian? Was the church to be one of ritual and sacrament or one of sacrifice and service to others, including outsiders. Ironically, these were discussions that took place and were in fact facilitated by the absence of Jews in Germany. Because the numbers of Jews were so few, even fewer than in 1933, fears of the "Jewish cultural threat" within Germany could no longer dominate discussions of Jewish-Christian relations as they did before 1945.[11]

Finally, Hochhuth's play could trigger such an array of emotions from anguish to fury because the memories of Nazi persecution were still raw. It forced those in their fifties and sixties in the 1960s to reflect on their own experiences as adults during the Third Reich. It led the "younger generation"—what the historian Dirk Moses has labeled the "generation of 1945"—to have flashbacks of their traumatic experiences as children or teenagers during the Third Reich.[12] Those who were reflecting remembered events not just differently, but different events themselves. Some recalled how churches had assisted victims of persecution or were victims themselves. Others looked back aghast at the churches' own sins of commission and omission—at what they had done to others and failed to do for those most in need. As Catholics and Protestants reflected on their own histories, a distinct confessional asymmetry became apparent, particularly when professional historians and journalists began writing histories of the church struggles. Protestant histories of the so-called *Kirchenkampf* were almost always written by professional Protestant church historians—with their own pasts to conceal and their own agendas to wage. Accounts of the Catholic Church under Nazi persecution, in contrast, were written not just by Catholics but by Protestant as well as Jewish scholars. Since the Catholic Church was being disproportionately singled out for its errors of judgment and instances of collusion, it is not surprising that confessional animosities shaped how the histories of both the Protestant and Catholic churches during the Third Reich were compiled well through the end of the century and even longer. That Protestants continued to be vastly over-represented in the academy well into the 1970s meant that confessional biases could continue to shape how scholars sculpted their accounts.

But by the 2010s, even these animosities were beginning to fade. Why? Trauma can indeed have a shelf-life. Both the wartime generation and the "generation of 1945"—those who experienced their formative years in the Third Reich but not as adults—were passing from the scene. With their departure, memories of trauma faded as well. In the liberal West, there were no compelling contemporary examples of confessional trauma with which to renew fears of persecution. Though its birth pangs were difficult, pitting members of the Confessing Church against its adversaries and Lutherans against Reformed Christians, the creation of a unified Protestant Church body in 1945, the EKD, helped put an end to Protestant traumas born out of the Revolution of 1918. The loss of Protestantism's once privileged legal and confessional status no longer smarted as it once had done in the Weimar Republic. Just as crucial by the mid-to-late 1950s in easing confessional traumas was the undeniable success of the Federal Republic based in Bonn—and not Berlin. Protestant conservatives actively participated in it through new political parties like the FDP and the CDU formally committed to a liberal democratic republic and no longer through those corrosive to democracy like the DNVP. To be sure, non-socialist Protestants had few viable alternatives. But constructive engagement in politics nonetheless undoubtedly helped quell conservative nostalgia for a monarchical Wilhelmine golden age. Catholic dominance in the CDU put a lid on fears of a renewed *Kulturkampf*, even if such rhetoric resurfaced in debates over the validity of the *Reichskonkordat* in the 1950s and again following the premiere of *The Deputy* in 1963.

The situation in the Communist East was of course utterly different. There, both churches were forced to endure waves of persecution. Though each responding in distinctive ways, neither could legitimately claim to have been singled out by the SED for purely confessional reasons: the SED's atheism did not discriminate. This marked a sharp contrast from Nazi persecution, even where many of the Nazis evinced a powerful hostility towards Christianity as a whole. Catholics could legitimately claim to have been targeted because its institutional structures and alleged ultramontanism posed a political and ideological threat to Nazi nationalist overlords. Protestants could similarly claim to have been singled out because of Nazi desires to unify the fragmented world of Protestantism and create a single unified and Nazified *Reichskirche* under the aegis of the state.

Confessional identity frequently resides in written chronicles of martyrdom as well as vibrant memories of victimization and persecution. All are bolstered by the belief that one's suffering was not just unique but also divinely ordained. When not directed by the malevolent will of state authorities, an onslaught of dechristianization or secularization is unable to sustain a sense of victimization unique to one particular group. Like the SPD's atheism, the temptations of material culture—of television, film, vacations, or luxury spas—do not typically discriminate between Catholics and Protestants. For this reason, Catholic and Protestant conservatives alike could make common cause in their crusades against "materialism," "atheism," "liberalism," and "secularism" from the late 1920s through the early decades of the Federal Republic. But these efforts could be sustained only so long as these could be convincingly personified in the form of an international socialist movement, a godless Communist state like that of the SED and on occasion the Nazi party. The collapse of both the East German state and the Soviet Union between 1989 and 1991 proved the death-knell for fears of renewed victimization. There was no longer an external enemy capable of wielding the sword against one or the other church. But when the erosion came from within, it became increasingly difficult to identify an enemy with a face. As the memory of trauma faded, confessional identities themselves became relics, and animosities vanished.

What then, finally, does it mean to be Catholic and Protestant in Germany today? The commemorations of the 500th anniversary of the Lutheran Reformation in 2017 provided few compelling answers.[13] For the first time, a major Reformation commemoration unfolded in a unified and genuinely liberal, democratic Germany. Flash points for critical commentators were no longer over whether Luther had been lionized and his Catholic opponents demonized, but whether celebrations had been excessively commercialized. Was the Luther Playmobile figure kitsch?[14] Had state governments like Thuringia done too much or too little to generate tourist revenue? Even the historical commentary was no longer digging in old confessional wounds. In agreement that the Lutheran Reformation had torn Western Christianity apart, few even bothered to ask whether Luther was justified in having done so or pointed fingers at who was responsible for having done so. Instead, it was Luther's notoriously anti-Judaic writings—and not his anti-papal and anti-Catholic invective—that took center stage. Others questioned why other reformers—the Swiss Reformers, radical reformers like Thomas Müntzer, to say nothing of the later Calvinist reformers—had been left out of the commemorative stories.[15] As once bitter animosities between Catholics and Lutherans were relegated to the past, questions of Luther's relevancy for contemporary theology and spiritual practice were left to the sidelines. Mostly elder theologians, many conservative Lutherans from the United States, fumed. In so doing, they brought into sharp relief the difficulties in upholding theological orthodoxy in a religiously pluralistic world, one where in Germany the percentage of "official" Christians at some point in the coming decades will dip below fifty percent.

Being Protestant and being Catholic was thus, for many Germans, little more than a set of nonbinding rituals and customs handed down by the accident of birth. For earlier generations, these had been foundational. But by 2017 they no longer provided a common source of cultural and personal identity. For some, being Catholic and being Protestant meant little more than paying a 7.5 percent church tax. In the best case, this tax generated satisfaction from seeing such tax money used for noble causes and charitable purposes; in the worst, it instilled outrage when used, for instance, to install luxury bathtubs in a bishop's palace. As we have seen, Bishop Franz-Peter Tebartz-van Elst's lavish spending prompted both Catholics and Protestants to leave their respective churches instead of triggering a wave of Protestant *Schadenfreude* toward "Catholic" corruption. After all: How could one hold on to confessional prejudices when one was no longer sure of what it meant to be Protestant or Catholic?

Mark Edward Ruff is Professor of History at Saint Louis University. He is the coeditor of three volumes on Christianity and Catholicism in the nineteenth and twentieth centuries and the author of two monographs, including *The Battle for the Catholic Past in Germany, 1945–1980* (Cambridge University Press, 2017). He has received research fellowships from the American Council of Learned Societies (ACLS), the National Endowment of the Humanities (NEH), and the Alexander-von-Humboldt Stiftung.

Thomas Großbölting is Director of the Forschungsstelle für Zeitgeschichte in Hamburg and Professor of Contemporary History at the University of Hamburg. From 2009 to 2020 he was Principal Investigator at the Cluster of Excellence "Religion and Politics," University of Münster. His recent books include *Wiedervereinigungsgesellschaft. Aufbruch und Entgrenzung in Germany since 1989/90* (2020), *Was glaubten die Deutschen 1933–1945?* (coedited with Olaf Blaschke, 2020), and *Losing Heaven: Religion in Germany since 1945* (2016).

Notes

1. See Helmut Herles, ed., *Die Hauptstadtdebatte: Der stenographische Bericht des Bundestages* (Bonn: Bouvier, 1991); Andreas Salz: *Bonn-Berlin: Die Debatte um Parlaments- und Regierungssitz im Deutschen Bundestag und die Folgen* (Münster: Monsenstein and Vannerdat, 2006).
2. This example drawn from research in progress from Florian Bock.
3. Mark Edward Ruff, "Building Bridges between Catholicism and Socialism: Ernst-Wolfgang Böckenförde and the SPD," *Contemporary European History* 29, no. 2 (2020): 1–16.
4. Maria Mitchell, *The Origin of Christian Democracy: Politics and Confession in Modern Germany* (Ann Arbor: University of Michigan Press, 2012), 198–200.
5. Retrieved 5 February 2021 from https://www.theguardian.com/world/2010/dec/10/wikileaks-pope-turkey-eu-muslim.
6. For the full text, see: https://www.lutheranworld.org/sites/default/files/Joint percent20 Declaration percent20on percent20the percent20Doctrine percent20of percent20Justification.pdf. Retrieved 5 February 2021.
7. John Allen, *Pope Benedict XVI: A Biography of Joseph Ratzinger* (New York: Continuum International Publishing Group, 2005), 234.
8. Mark Edward Ruff, *The Battle for the Catholic Past in Germany, 1945–1980* (Cambridge, UK: Cambridge University Press, 2017), especially 48–85.
9. Ibid., 153–92; Rolf Hochhuth, *Der Stellvertreter* (Reinbek: Rowohlt, 1963).
10. Pinchas Lapide, *Three Popes and the Jews* (New York: Hawthorn Books, 1967), 214–15.
11. A contrary example is Poland, where antisemitism continued to appear in spite of the near complete absence of Jews.
12. A. Dirk Moses, *German Intellectuals and the Nazi Past* (Cambridge, UK: Cambridge University Press, 2007).
13. See Thomas Albert Howard, *Remembering the Reformation: An Inquiry into the Meanings of Protestantism* (Oxford, UK: Oxford University Press, 2016), especially, 147–59.
14. "Zwischen Kitsch und Kunst: Das Geschäft mit Martin-Luther-Produkten," *Frankfurter Neue Presse*, Online Ausgabe, 30 October 2017, Retrieved 23 June 2020 from https://www.fnp.de/wirtschaft/zwischen-kitsch-kunst-geschaeft-mit-martin-luther-produkten-10441363.html.
15. Thomas Zimmerman and Theo Geißler, eds., *Disputationen: Reflexionen zum Reformationsjubiläum 2017* (Berlin. Deutscher Kulturrat e.V., 2015), 186.

Bibliography

Allen, John. *Pope Benedict XVI: A Biography of Joseph Ratzinger.* New York: Continuum International Publishing Group, 2005.
Herles, Helmut, ed. *Die Hauptstadtdebatte: Der stenographische Bericht des Bundestages.* Bonn: Bouvier, 1991.
Hochhuth, Rolf. *Der Stellvertreter.* Reinbek: Rowohlt, 1963.
Howard, Thomas Albert. *Remembering the Reformation: An Inquiry into the Meanings of Protestantism.* Oxford, UK: Oxford University Press, 2016.
Lapide, Pinchas. *Three Popes and the Jews.* New York: Hawthorn Books, 1967.

Mitchell, Maria. *The Origin of Christian Democracy: Politics and Confession in Modern Germany.* Ann Arbor: University of Michigan Press, 2012.

Moses, A. Dirk. *German Intellectuals and the Nazi Past.* Cambridge, UK: Cambridge University Press, 2007.

Ruff, Mark Edward. *The Battle for the Catholic Past in Germany, 1945–1980.* Cambridge, UK: Cambridge University Press, 2017.

———. "Building Bridges between Catholicism and Socialism: Ernst-Wolfgang Böckenförde and the SPD." *Contemporary European History* 29, no. 2 (2020): 1–16.

Salz, Andreas. *Bonn-Berlin: Die Debatte um Parlaments- und Regierungssitz im Deutschen Bundestag und die Folgen.* Münster: Monsenstein and Vannerdat, 2006.

Zimmerman, Thomas, and Theo Geißler, eds. *Disputationen: Reflexionen zum Reformationsjubiläum 2017.* Berlin: Deutscher Kulturrat e.V., 2015.

Index

Adam, Karl, 57, 62, 68
Adenauer, Konrad, 17, 65, 138, 179, 195, 196, 198, 204, 208, 209, 218, 303, 326, 333, 335
Ad gentes, 305
Adveniat, 301–302
aggiornamento, 19
Aktionskreise, 280
Aktionskreis Halle, 259, 260, 262, 280, 288
Aktion Sühnezeichen, 223, 225, 337
Albert the Great, 35
Albus, Michael, 254
All-German People's Party (*Gesamtdeutsche Volkspartei*), 326
Altona, 159
Amery, Carl, 8, 351
Anderson, George, 349–350
Angerhausen, Julius, 308
anti-Judaism, 230, 336, 354
antisemitism, 12, 120, 152, 227, 232, 233, 335, 336–337
anti-Zionism, 217, 225–226, 227–228
Aquinas, Thomas, 36
Arab-Israeli War of 1967, 217, 222, 225, 226
Arbeitsgemeinschaft für Entwicklungshilfe. See Working Group for Developmental Aid
Argentina, 300
Aryan paragraph, 152
Asmussen, Hans, 16, 154, 159–164, 167
Aufderbeck, Hugo, 274, 279
Augsburg, 329, 349
Augsburg Confession, 197
Augustine of Hippo, 36, 132
Auschwitz, 337, 350
Austria, 112
Austro-Prussian War of 1866, 26

Bachem, Julius, 171, 333
Baden, 101, 102, 109
Bad Schwalbach, 220
Baeck, Leo, 219, 335

Ball, Hugo, 58–59
Bar, Carl Ludwig von, 34
Barmen, Synod, and Theological Declaration, 149, 152, 159, 243, 252
Barth, Karl, 149, 153, 226, 252
Bartning, Ludwig, 157
Basel, 260
Basic Law (*Grundgesetz*), 180, 333
Bausoldaten, 258
Bautzen, 276
Bavaria, 101–102, 112, 158
Bea, Augustin, 222
Bekennende Kirche. *See* Confessing Church
Bekenntnisschulen (denominational schools), 199, 350
Benedict XVI, Pope, 338
Bengsch, Alfred, 18, 247, 249, 250, 251, 254, 255, 256, 266, 277–278, 280–281, 282
Berlin, 78, 79, 147, 148, 153, 158, 159, 160, 161, 175, 220, 221, 225, 227, 247, 248, 249, 273, 274, 277, 283, 311, 352
Berlin Bishops Conference in the GDR (Berlin Conference on Bishops), 247, 248, 251, 255, 259, 260, 261, 262, 263, 264, 271, 283, 284, 285
Berlin Wall, 248, 286
Berlin-Weißensee, 337
Bernard of Clairvaux, 38
Berneuchen movement, 161
Beste, Niklot, 251, 266
Biafra, 310
Bismarck, Otto von, 31
Bitburg military cemetery, 231
Blackbourn, David, 9
Blaschke, Olaf, 8, 10–11, 328–329
Böckenförde, Ernst-Wolfgang, 127–128, 348, 351
Böhler, Wilhelm, 205, 208, 209
Böhm, Franz, 221
Böll, Heinrich, 2, 348
Boff, Leonardo, 312
Bonhoeffer, Dietrich, 219, 248, 252

Boniface Associations (*Bonifatius-Vereine*), 273
Boniface, Saint, 43
Bonn, 332, 347, 352
Bora, Katharina von, 151
Bornkamm, Heinrich, 326
Brandenburg, Ernst, 157
Brandt, Willy, 226
Braun, Johannes, 286
Brauns, Heinrich, 171
Bread for the World, 301–304, 306, 309
Brentano, Heinrich von, 349
Breslau, 86, 273
Brüning, Heinrich, 104
Brüsewitz, Oskar, 253
Bund der Deutschen Katholischen Jugend (BDKJ). *See* League of German Catholic Youth
Bund der Evangelischen Kirchen in der DDR (BEK). *See* Protestantism in Germany: Federation of the Protestant Churches in the GDR
Bundeshaus, 347
Bundeswehr, 325
Burnham, Walter Dean, 121–122
BVP (*Bayerische Volkspartei*, Bavarian People's Party), 102–103, 105

Calvin, John, 203
Calvinism, 82
Câmara, Dom Hélder, 312
Caritas, 285, 286, 308
Catholica, 131
Catholic Academy Klausenhof, 308–309
Catholic Action, 14, 287
Catholic Bishops' Organization for Development Cooperation, 302
Catholic German Women's League, 151
Catholic milieu, 8, 15, 22, 103, 118, 126, 329
Catholic Rural Youth Movement (*Katholische Landjugendbewegung*), 309
Catholic Workers Movement (*Katholische Arbeitnehmerbewegung*, KAB), 313
Catholics and the Catholic Church, 1–20, 26–44, 51–65, 87–89, 101–122, 125–138, 147–148, 150–154, 156, 159–164, 170–183, 194–210, 242–252, 254–265, 271–290, 300–315, 324–330, 332–341, 347–354; *Bildungsdefizit*, 29, 42; lay Catholicism, 55, 56, 148; nationalization of the Mass, 32; voting patterns, 101–109, 119–122
CDU (*Christliche Demokratische Union*, Christian Democratic Union), 2, 4, 11, 17, 126, 129, 138, 163, 170–183, 195–196, 204–207, 218, 228, 274, 287, 288, 325, 326, 333, 348, 352; Executive Committee, 179; Protestant Working Group (*Evangelischer Arbeitskreis*), 204, 205
CDUD (Christian Democratic bloc party in the GDR, 285)
Center Party, 4, 5, 17, 31, 40, 102–106, 120, 126, 127, 131, 135, 148, 171–172, 177, 178, 333, 348
Central Committee of German Catholics, 230, 287
Charles V, Emperor, 197
Christian Socialists, 171

Christian Social People's Party (CSVD), 171
Christian Social Union (CSU), 179
Christliche Welt, 80–81
Civil Code, German, 172, 178
Cold War, 138, 225, 226, 233, 312
Cologne, 333
Cologne, Archdiocese of, 32, 208
Common Campaign Committee of Catholic Christians in the GDR (*Gemeinsamer Aktionsausschuss katholischer Christen in der DDR*), 287
communism (and Communists), 39
Communist Party, Germany. *See* KPD
Conciliar Process for Justice, Peace and the Integrity of Creation, 260, 262
Conference for Security and Cooperation Process (CSCE), 258
Conference of the Catholic Church Leaders in the GDR (*Berliner Ordinarienkonferenz*), 250, 251, 254, 255, 260, 274
Confessing Church (*Bekennende Kirche*), 16, 90, 146, 149, 152–162, 171, 205, 223, 224, 225, 226, 336, 352; Councils of Brethren of the Confessing Church, 336
Confessio Augustana, 155
confessionalism and confessionalization, 327–330
confessional peace, the, 195, 201, 209–210
confirmation, 245
Congar, Yves, 126
conversion (converts, and change of confession), 16, 133, 136, 145–147, 150–164, 165–166
Copernicus, Nicolaus, 35
Council for World Mission, 307
Council of Brethren, 162
Counter-Reformation, 15, 195, 199

Dabru Emet, 233
Dachau, 159
Dahlem, 147, 149, 153, 154, 155, 156, 157, 159
Dante, 132
Darmstadt, 336
Darmstadt Statement (*Darmstädter Wort*), 252
Darwin, Charles, 35
DDP (*Deutsche Demokratische Partei*, German Democratic Party), 102
dechristianization, 183, 349, 353
decolonization, 19, 310
deconfessionalism, 330–334
Dehler, Thomas, 207, 326
Dehn, Günter, 161–162
Demokratischer Aufbruch, 264, 288
Denifle, Heinrich, 128, 132
Deputy, The (*Der Stellvertreter*), 350–351, 352
Der gerade Weg, 151
Der Spiegel, 200, 332, 334
Deutsche Evangelische Allianz (DEA). *See* German Protestant Alliance
Deutsche Tagespost, 207
Deutsch-Israelische Gesellschaft. *See* German Israel Society

Dibelius, Otto, 79–80, 86–87, 224, 243, 247, 248, 351
Die Freiwillige Selbstkontrolle der Filmwirtschaft (FSK, German Film Commission). See FSK
Die Hilfe, 154
Dienste in Übersee e.V. (DÜ). See Service Abroad
Dingden, 308
Dirks, Walter, 135, 136
Dissemond, Paul, 255, 267, 268
DNVP (*Deutschnationale Volkspartei,* Conservative Party), 89, 135, 171, 172, 352
Döpfner, Julius, 247, 276, 277, 325
Dresden, 252, 260, 284, 285, 286, 287
Duplessis, Maurice, 194
Düsseldorf, 208
DVP (*Deutsche Volkspartei,* German People's Party), 85, 102

East Prussia, 101, 152
Eberle, Joseph, 55
Eck, Johannes, 197
Eckart, Dietrich, 128
Eckert, Willehad Paul, 216, 227
ecological regression, 109
ecumenism (and ecumenical movement), 15, 125, 127, 129, 130–133, 137–138, 196, 210, 220–221, 289–290, 310; ecumenical convention, 262
Egypt, 224, 225
Ehlers, Hermann, 17, 180, 205–209
Eichsfeld, 273
EKD (*Evangelische Kirche in Deutschland,* Protestant Church in Germany), 5, 16, 162, 218–219, 223, 225, 228, 229, 233, 246, 249, 250, 254, 257, 281, 307, 337, 352
Elbing, Pedagogical Academy, 152
elections, Reichstag, 104–109
elections, presidential, 103–104
Ellwein, Thomas, 332
Eltville, 200
Empie, Paul C., 196
Emuna/Israel Forum, 228
Enabling Law, 148
Endress, Henry, 196, 202–203, 209
Erfurt, 274, 276, 279, 283, 290
Erhard, Ludwig, 224
Ermland, 101
Equal Rights Law (1957), 181
Eschwege, 350
Eschweiler, Karl, 127–131, 133, 136, 137, 138
Evangelical Lutheran Church in America (ELCA), 349
Evangelischer Bund. See Evangelical League
Evangelical League, 14, 16, 156–157, 162, 206
Evangelische Kirche Deutschland. See EKD
Evangelische Kommentare, 339
Evangelische Zentralstelle für Entwicklungshilfe e.V. (EZEJ). See Protestant Central Agency for Development

Falcke, Heino, 252

Faulhaber, Michael Cardinal von, 60–61, 151
FDJ (*Freie Deutsche Jugend,* Free German Youth), 274
FDP (*Freie Demokratische Partei,* Free Democratic Party), 5, 204, 207, 352
Federation of the Protestant Churches in the GDR (BEK), 250, 252, 253, 254, 256, 257, 260, 264
Fischer, Antonius, archbishop of Cologne, 32, 33
Flensburg, 160
Foerster, Erich, 81
Foerster, Friedrich Wilhelm, 134
France, 19, 159, 308, 338
Francis, Pope, 300
Franco-Prussian War, 27
Frank, Anne, 221
Frankfurt, 220
Frankfurt Economic Council, 179
Frederick the Wise, 197, 202
Freiburger Rundbrief, 219–220, 222–223, 224, 232
Freikirchen, 81–82, 86
Freisler, Roland, 161
Freudenberg, Adolf, 218–220
Frick, Wilhelm, 149
Friedensbund Deutscher Katholiken (German Catholic Peace League, 161
Frings, Josef, 208, 209
FSK (*Freiwillige Selbstkontrolle der Filmwirtschaft,* German Film Commission), 194–195, 201–202
Fulda, 273
Fulda Conference of Bishops, 209, 218

Gablentz, Hilde von der, 175
Galilei, Galileo, 35
Garstecki, Joachim, 286
Gasperi, Alcide de, 196
Gaudium et spes, 285, 305
Geiger, Abraham, 336
Geis, Robert Raphael, 221, 223
Geiselgasteig, 198
Gemeinsamer Aktionsausschuss katholischer Christen. See Joint Action Committee of Catholic Christians in the GDR
Gemeinsamer Aktionsausschuss katholischer Christen in der DDR. See Common Campaign Committee of Catholic Christians in the GDR
General Incentives Theory, 118
generation of 1945, the, 352
Geneva, 196, 306
Gerlich, Fritz, 151
German Catholic Women's Association (*Katholischer Deutscher Frauenbund*, KDFB), 181
German Christians (*Deutsche Christen, Glaubensbewegung Deutsche Christen*), 16, 90, 131, 136, 147, 149, 150, 152, 164
German Israel Society (*Deutsch-Israelische Gesellschaft*), 224–225, 227, 228
German Protestant Alliance (*Deutsche Evangelische Allianz*), 306
German Southwest Africa, 32, 314
German Student Christian Federation, 198

Gesamtdeutsche Volkspartei. See All-German People's Party
Gestapo, 148, 152, 205
glasnost, 283
Gnauck-Kühne, Elisabeth, 150–151
Gnostadt, 325
Goebbels, Joseph, 218
Gogarten, Friedrich, 131, 136
Gollwitzer, Helmut, 219, 223, 224, 225, 228
Gorbachev, Mikhail, 283
Görlitz, 261, 276, 290
Göttingen, University of, 34
gottgläubig (believing in God), 150, 163
Greenberg, Udi, 19, 310
Greens, the (*die Grünen*), 348
Greifswald, 250, 268
Grande, Dieter, 285–286
Grisar, Hartmann, 128, 132
Grosche, Robert, 63, 64, 70, 131–132, 133–137, 138
Grotewohl, Otto, 275, 278
Grüber, Heinrich, 219, 223, 351
Gurian, Waldemar, 127, 133–138
Gustav Adolf Association, 162
Gysi, Klaus, 242

Habermas, Jürgen, 231
Haenisch, Konrad, 84
Hahn, Hugo, 201
Hamburg, 159, 229, 290
Hanover, 158, 194, 195, 198, 332
Hartmann, Felix von, 32
Heidelberg, 336
Hein, Arnold, 87–88
Heinecke, Herbert, 265, 266
Heinemann, Gustav, 326
Heinemann, Peter, 200
Heinrich, Johannes, 155
Hempel, Johannes, 255
Henkys, Reinhard, 266
Herder Korrespondenz, 225
Herwegen, Ildefons, 63, 64
Hess, Werner, 201, 204
Hesse, 101, 102, 109
Heuss-Knapp, Elly, 154
Heuss, Theodor, 154
Hildebrandt, Franz, 154
Hindenburg, Paul von, 103–104
Hitler, Adolf, 5, 62, 104, 113, 130, 131, 133, 146, 154, 199, 203
Hitler Youth, 148
Hobbes, Thomas, 136
Hochhuth, Rolf, 223, 350–351
Höllen, Martin, 278, 282
Hölscher, Lucian, 330
Hoffmann, Adolph, 51, 84
Hohenzollern monarchy, 4, 14, 352
Holl, Karl, 87
Holocaust and Holocaust memory, 216–221, 229, 231–233, 335, 336, 337, 350–351

Holocaust (miniseries), 230
Honecker, Erich, 254
Horst, Stephan
Hossenfelder, Joachim, 147
Hour of the Church, 172–173, 180, 275
Hour of the Woman, 172–173, 175, 176, 178, 181–182
Hugh of St. Victor, 36
Huhn, Gerhard, 261
Huhn, Martina, 288
Humanae vitae, 305
Hunthausen, Raymond, 348

Islam, 335, 338–339, 349, 350. See also Muslims
Israel, 18, 224, 225, 337

Jacob, Günter, 246, 247, 248, 249
Jenninger, Philipp, 231
Jesuit order (Society of Jesus), 10, 28, 150, 161
Jewish-Christian reconciliation and dialogue, 153, 216–234
Jews, Jewish communities in Germany, and Judaism, 2, 3, 10, 13, 17–18, 130, 138, 147, 216–234, 335–337, 338, 351
Joint Action Committee of Catholic Christians in the GDR (*Gemeinsame Aktionsausschuss katholischer Christen*), 288
Joint Declaration on the Doctrine of Justification, 13, 349–350
John Paul II, Pope, 259, 283, 284
John XXIII, Pope, 222, 223, 279
Joos, Josef, 135
Jugendweihe, 18, 245, 246, 276, 278
Junge Front, 218

Kaas, Ludwig, 348
Kaftan, Julius, 78–79
Kaftan, Theodor, 78–79, 82–83
Kahl, Wilhelm, 85
Katholikentag(e), 221, 275, 284, 311; in Essen (1968), 311
Karlstadt, Andreas, 197
Katholische Arbeitnehmer Bewegung (KAB). See Catholic Workers Movement
Katholische Landjugendbewegung. See Catholic Rural Youth Movement
Katholischer Deutscher Frauenbund. See German Catholic Women's Association
Kelly, Petra, 348
Kiefl, Franz Xaver, 128, 131
Kirchenkampf (Church Struggle of the 1930s), 5, 16, 155, 275, 352
Kirchentag, 223, 224, 230, 257; Working Group on "Jews and Christians," 223, 227
Kirchner, Martin, 288
Kladderatasch, 44
Klausener, Erich, 148
Klausenhof. See Catholic Academy Klausenhof
Kliefoth, Theodor, 76
Kloppenburg, Heinz, 158, 161, 225

Index

KNA (*Katholische Nachrichten-Agentur*, Catholic News Agency), 200, 282
Koch, Friedrich, 88
Kohl, Helmut, 231, 287
Kolping, 274, 285, 309
Konnersreuth, 151
KPD (*Kommunistische Partei Deutschlands*, Communist Party of Germany), 102
Krabbe, Otto Karsten, 76
Kralik, Richard, 55
Krautzberger, Elisabeth, 153, 154
Krenz, Egon, 286
Kreuz und Adler, 63
Kreyssig, Lothar, 223, 224
Kristallnacht, 229–230, 231, 233
Kronberger Kreis, 198, 199
Krose, Hermann, 150
Krummacher, Friedrich-Wilhelm, 250
Kulturfront, 53, 61, 65
Kulturkampf, 2, 4, 7–8, 13, 14, 27–30, 33, 42, 43, 51, 52, 53, 57, 63, 66, 89, 102, 103, 120, 145, 150, 156, 180, 195, 209, 350, 352
Kulturprotestantismus, 12, 14
Kunst, Hermann, 203, 205, 206

Landesherrliches Kirchenregiment, 75
Lange, Gerhard, 262, 287
Lapide, Pinchas, 351
Laros, Matthias, 138
League of German Catholic Youth (*Bund der Deutschen Katholischen Jugend*, BDKJ), 301, 313–314
Legion of Decency, 194, 200, 201
Lehmann, Karl, 337
Lehr, Robert, 178
Leipzig, 286
Leipzig Disputation, 197
Leppich, Johannes, SJ, 302
Lepsius, M. Rainer, 8, 102
Levinson, Nathan Peter, 227, 228
Lewek, Christa, 254, 255, 256, 266, 267
liberalism and liberals, 26–28, 37, 54, 61, 84, 326, 353
liberation theology, 312, 313
Lieberknecht, Christine, 288
Lilje, Hanns, 195, 198–200, 203–204, 207, 209, 210, 332
Lingens, Ella, 230
Liturgical Movement, 55, 58, 63, 67
Leo XIII, Pope, 53
Lortz, Joseph, 15, 17, 132–133, 137–138, 140–141, 195, 198, 201–202, 203, 209, 210
Lower Franconia, 325
Lower Saxony, 199, 209
Lübke, Heinrich, 303
Luckner, Gertrud, 218–220, 232
Lundquist, Carl, 206
Luther, Martin, 1, 3, 9, 128, 130, 131, 133, 134–135, 136, 137–138, 196–197, 203, 204, 206, 210, 353–354

Lutheran-Film-Gesellschaft M.B.H., 198
Lutheran Film Productions, Inc. (LFP), 194, 198, 199–203
Lutheranism (as an ideology), 76, 157
Lutheran World Federation, 194, 199, 349

MacGinnis, Niall, 206
Männerstaat, 170, 175
Magdeburg, 276, 286, 290
Mahling, Friedrich, 76, 77
Maizière, Lothar de, 288
Maria Laach, 63
Marian films, 199, 204, 208
Marian, Year of 1954, 199
Maritain, Jacques, 128, 134, 135
Martin Luther (1953 film), 17, 194–210
Marquardt, Wilhelm, 226–227, 229
Marx, Wilhelm, 103–104
Massis, Henri, 135
Mater et magistra, 279, 308
materialism, 61, 206, 279
maternalism, 175–176, 178
Mau, Carl, 209
Maulbronn, 200
Maurer, Michael, 326–327
Mayer, Hans, 335
Meinecke, Friedrich, 332
Meiningen, 276
Meiser, Hans, 198, 202, 209
Meisner, Joachim, 260
Meissen, 276, 279
Merkel, Angela, 348
Merkle, Sebastian, 128, 131, 132
Metz, Johann Baptist, 229, 304, 311, 337
Metzger, Max Josef, 126, 138, 161
Meyer, Hans Joachim, 287, 288
Michel, Ernst, 134
Minneapolis, 194
Misereor, 301, 302, 304, 306, 308, 309, 310
miss-a-meal movement, 301
missionaries and missionary work, 35, 304–310
Mitzenheim, Hartmut, 276
Mitzenheim, Moritz, 249
mixed marriages (*Mischehen*, biconfessional marriages), 1–2, 52, 145, 152, 340–341
modernism, 54
Moenius, Georg, 134
Möhler, Johann Adam, 128–129, 132
Moltmann, Jürgen, 229, 337
Monsieur Vincent (film), 208
Mortalium animos, 52
Muckermann, Friedrich, 56, 59–60, 61, 62
Müller, Friedrich, 149, 153
Müller, Gottfried, 288
Müller, Ludwig, 149
Münch, Franz-Xaver, 55
Munich, 220
Münster, 56
Müntzer, Thomas, 354
Murray, John Courtney, 126

Muslims, 6, 18, 20, 217, 233–234, 335–336, 338–341. *See also* Islam

nationalism, 26–27
National Lutheran Council, 196, 199
National Socialism, 64, 65, 103, 120–121, 330, 335
National Conference of Christians and Jews (NCCJ), 220
Natur und Offenbarung, 34–35, 37–38
Naumann, Friedrich, 154
Nazi Germany, 63, 65
Nazi party. *See* NSDAP
Nazi state, 64
Nebgen, Elfriede, 175, 176
Nell-Breuning, Oswald von, 54
Netherlands, the, 4, 338
Neubert, Erhart, 264
Neumann, Therese, 151
Neuß, Wilhelm, 205
Newman, John Henry, 167
New York Times, The, 159
Nicaea, Council of, 160
"Nickneger," 302, 314
Niemöller, Else, 16, 154, 155, 157, 159, 160
Niemöller, Heinrich, 156
Niemöller, Martin, 16, 146, 147, 153, 154–160, 162–163, 164, 166, 198, 220
Nipperdey, Thomas, 7
North America, 324
Nostra Aetate, 222, 223, 224
Nouvelle Théologie, 304
Nowak, Kurt, 76
NSDAP, 25, 104–122, 126, 129, 147, 148, 149, 353; members who left, 117–119
Nuremberg Laws, 147

Oberlausitz, 273
Ochsenfurt, 325
Oertel, Curt, 199, 208
Oesterreicher, John, 219, 223
Ohnesorg, Benno, 225, 311
Osnabrück, 273
Osner, Karl, 309
Osterloh, 205

Pacelli, Eugenio, 56. *See also* Pius XII, Pope
Pacem in terris, 279
Paderborn, diocese of, 31, 273
Palatinate, 148
Pan-German League, 9
Papal Magesterium, 53
Papen, Franz von, 63
Parliamentary Council (*Parlamentarischer Rat*), 170–171, 177–179, 180
Parnass, Peggy, 230
Pascendi dominici gregis, 53
Pastors' Emergency League (*Pfarrernotbund*), 90
Paul VI, Pope, 222, 279, 305
Pax Christi, 301

peaceful revolution, 262, 263, 264
Peace of Westphalia, 13
perestroika, 283
Pew Research Center, 324
philosemitism, 12, 335
Pilgrimages, 39
Pius X, Pope, 53, 54, 55, 57, 60, 338
Pius XI, Pope, 52, 55, 60–61, 67, 152
Pius XII, Pope, 56, 159, 199, 222, 279, 350–351
Plath, Siegfried, 268
Plettenberg, 64
Poland, 258, 283
Politburo, 249, 286
Populorum progressio, 279, 305
Positive Christianity, 5, 136
Potsdam, 336
Potsdam Conference, 273
Potestas directa, 54
Preysing, Konrad von, 159, 167, 243, 276
Protestant Central Agency for Development Aid (EZE), 303
Protestantism in Germany, 146–164, 182; in the CDU, 170–175, 177, 179–180, 182–183, 196; Federation of the Protestant Churches in the GDR (*Bund der Evangelischen Kirchen in der DDR*, BEK), 250, 252, 253, 254, 256, 257, 260, 264, 281, 282, 288; Lutherans and Lutheran churches, 5, 13, 58, 172, 210, 275, 327; Protestant Church in Berlin-Brandenburg, 243, 248, 250, 281, 301; Protestant Church in Saxony, 301; Protestant Church in Westphalia, 301, 334; Reformed Churches, 5, 13, 82, 171, 210, 275, 327; regional/state churches (*Landeskirchen*), 84, 85, 88–89, 145, 155, 158; Rhineland Church, 230, 337; United Churches, 5, 13, 16, 200, 210; United Evangelical Lutheran Church, 281; voting patterns, 104–110. *See also* EKD
Prussia and Prussian territories, 330
Prussian Regional Church, 76, 84, 205; Prussian Union (Church of the Old Prussian Union, APU), 16, 154, 155, 205
Pützchen, West German Catholic bishops' meeting, 195

Québec, 194, 203

Rade, Martin, 80–81
Ratzinger, Joseph, 349–350. *See also* Benedict XVI, Pope
Ravensbrück, 218
Reagan, Ronald, 231
re-Christianization, 170, 182, 332
Red Army, 59
Red Cross, East German, 303
Reformation, 1, 15, 54, 57, 58, 130, 135, 154, 160, 202, 207, 273, 348, 353–354; Swiss Reformation, 354
Reich Minister of the Interior, 149
Reich Transport Ministry, 157

Reichsidee, 63
Reichskirche, 353
Reichskonkordat, 63, 64, 113, 199, 274, 350, 352
Reichsmythos, 64
Reichstheologie, 62–63, 69, 131
Reinelt, Joachim, 288
Reinhard, Wolfgang, 327, 329
Religiöse Besinnung, 131
Rendtorff, Rolf, 224, 228
Rengstorf, Heinrich, 219
Repgen, Konrad, 7
Revolution of 1918, 4–5, 14, 75, 77–78, 79–80
Revolution of 1989, 18–19
Rhineland, 127, 330, 337
Röhricht, Eberhard, 153
Rome, 305
Romero, Oscar, 312
Roncalli, Angelo Giuseppe, 222. *See also* John XXIII, Pope
Rosenstock-Huessy, Eugen, 134
Rückert, Hanns, 203
Ruhr, 106

Sachsen, Georg von, 161
Sachsenhausen, 146, 154, 156, 160, 167
Saxony, 199
Schaffran, Gerhard, 267, 284
Scharf, Kurt, 224, 225
Scheler, Max, 128, 131, 134, 135
Schilling, Heinz, 327, 329
Schipper, Fritz, 161
Schmauch, Jochen, 308
Schmidtchen, Gerhard, 7, 340
Schmitt, Carl, 58, 62, 63, 64–65, 130, 134, 135, 136
Schmitz, Elisabeth, 153
Schmitz, Maria, 41
Schneider, Reinhard, 167
Schönherr, Albrecht, 248, 250, 253, 254, 255, 257, 281
Schorlemmer, Friedrich, 264
Schröder, Gerhard, 205
Schuessler-Fiorenza, Elisabeth, 337
Schumacher, Kurt, 326
Schwarzhaupt, Elisabeth, 180, 181
Schweitzer, Albert, 351
Schwerin, 276
Schwinn, Wilhelm, 325
Seattle, 348
Second Vatican Council. *See* Vatican Council, Second
secularism, 60, 61, 182, 353
secularization, 12, 15, 57, 353
SED (*Sozialistische Einheitspartei Deutschlands*, Socialist Union Party of Germany, East German Communist Party), 6, 19, 242, 244–249, 252–254, 256, 258–259, 273, 274–279, 286, 288, 331, 353
Seigewasser, Hans, 249, 266
Seoul, 260

Service Abroad (*Dienste in Übersee e.V.*, DÜ), 307, 309
Sevenich, Maria, 175
Siegkatholizismus, 53, 58, 59
Silesia, Upper, 101, 106
Silverman, Allan. *See* Sloane, Allan
Sloane, Allan, 199
"slum cities," 314
Social Democratic Party. *See* SPD
Social Market Economy, 177
Socialist Reich Party (*Sozialistische Reichpartei Deutschlands*), 349
Societies for Christian-Jewish Cooperation, 220–221, 222, 227, 228, 229, 230, 231, 232; Cologne Society, 231; Darmstadt Society, 230; Göttingen Society, 227–228, 230; Stuttgart Society, 231
Society of Saint Pius X, 338
Sölle, Dorothee, 229, 311
Sonderkirche. *See* Freikirchen
The Song of Bernadette (film), 208
Sonntagsspiegel, 209
South Africa, 310
Soviet Union, 326
Sozialistische Reichpartei Deutschlands. *See* Socialist Reich Party
Spain, 308
Spartacus uprising, 79
SPD (*Sozialdemokratische Partei Deutschlands*, Social Democratic Party of Germany), and Social Democrats, 5, 39, 83, 84, 102, 152, 177, 199, 202, 204, 207, 226, 228, 305, 326, 348
Sperber, Jonathan, 7
Springer, Axel, 225
Spülbeck, Otto, 275, 279, 280
Stalin, Josef, 244
Stasi, 284, 289
Staupitz, Johann von, 197, 202
Stegerwald, Adam, 52, 127, 171
Stephan, Horst, 81–82
Sterzinsky, Georg, 264, 287
Stettin, 148
Stimmen der Zeit, 58, 59
St. Hedwigsblatt, 287
Stöcker, Adolf, 86
Stöhr, Martin, 227, 228, 231
Stoph, Willi, 247, 248, 277–278
Storrer, Eva, 286
Stuhlmacher, Johannes, 198, 201, 202, 204–205
Stuttgart, 220
Stuttgart Declaration of Guilt, 218
Strauss, Leo, 130
Süddeutsche Zeitung, 201
Sudetenland, 112
Süsterhenn, Adolf, 205, 208
summus episcopus, 76, 155
Switzerland, 4, 159

Taeschner, Franz, 132
Tebartz-van-Elst, Franz-Peter, 1, 354
Tertullian, 36

Tetzel, Johannes, 197, 200
Teusch, Christine, 175
Thieme, Karl, 131, 136–137, 152–153, 166, 218, 220, 221, 223
Third Reich. *See* Nazi Germany
Thirty Years War, 9
Thoma, Clemens, 232
throne and altar, marriage of, 76
Thuringia, 101, 199, 276, 353
Tillmanns, Robert, 205
Trier, Diocese of, 33
Trilling, Wolfgang, 264, 272
Troeltsch, Ernst, 59, 328
Tübingen, 67, 310
Turkey, 338, 349
Turks (in Germany), 231, 349
Tutzing, 200

Ulbricht, Walter, 249, 275
Una Sancta, 129, 138
Una Sancta Movement, 161, 167
United Kingdom, 4, 19, 308, 338
United States, 4, 324–326, 331, 335, 341
Uppsala, 306, 312–313
Urner, Hans, 161

Vancouver, 260
Vatican, 55, 113, 196, 199, 225, 228, 339, 349
The Vatican (film), 208
Vatican Council, Second (Vatican II), 19, 180, 222, 229, 250, 272, 279, 285, 304, 306, 312, 351
Venerable Brethren, 61
victorious Catholicism. *See Siegkatholizismus*
Vilnius, 59
Violet, Bruno, 157
Volk, Hermann, 304
völkisch religiosity, 147, 149
Volkskirche, 76–77, 79–83, 85, 86, 88, 89–90, 257, 338
Volkskirchenräte (Volkskirche Councils), 80–81
Volkskirchliche Evangelische Vereinigung, 87
voting patterns (by confession), 101–122

Wanke, Joachim, 281–283, 284–285
Wartburg, 197, 249
Weber, Helene, 177–179, 181
Weber, Max, 328
Wehler, Hans-Ulrich, 7

Weimar National Assembly, 89
Weimar Republic, 59, 61, 62, 66, 75, 84–85, 86, 89, 101–122, 145, 147, 172, 174–175, 178, 182, 352
Weinel, Heinrich, 85–86
Weißensee working group, 248
Weltfrage, 59
Welthungerhilfe. *See* World Hunger Relief
Weltnotwerk, 313
Werner, Friedrich, 155
Weskamm, Wilhelm, 274
Western civilization, 60
Wiesbaden, 220
Wilhelm II, Emperor, 31–32, 79
Williamson, Richard, 338
Winfriedbund, 52, 66
Winzen, Damasus, 132
Wirth, Joseph, 135
Wittenberg, 197, 200, 202
Wolff, Lothar, 198
Working Group for Developmental Aid (*Arbeitsgemeinschaft für Entwicklungshilfe*, AGEH), 307, 309
Working Group of Christian Churches (*Arbeitsgemeinschaft Christlicher Kirchen*), 251
World Council of Churches (WCC), 196, 260, 283, 306, 312
World Hunger Relief (*Welthungerhilfe*), 304
World Jewish Congress, 335
World Prayer Meeting in Assisi, 283
World Student Christian Federation (WSCF), 198
Worms, Diet of, 197
Wrocław, 273–274
Wuermeling, Franz-Josef, 180
Württemberg, 101, 102, 158
Würzburg, 273
Würzburg Synod, 229
Wust, Peter, 57–58, 63

Xanten, 27

Zeeden, Ernst Walter, 329
Zeitz, 253, 254
Ziegler, Martin, 268
Zillken, Elisabeth, 179
Zionism, 217, 221, 226, 227–228; UN Resolution on, 228
Zscharnack, Leopold, 86
Zwingli, Huldrych, 9, 153

Lightning Source UK Ltd.
Milton Keynes UK
UKHW032121100222
398518UK00003B/43